THE INDISPENSABLE PILL BOOK

The Pill Book gives you the answers to the questions millions of Americans are asking about the pills their physicians are prescribing for them and their families.

This newly revised, updated 4th edition of the 3,500,000-copy bestseller gives you the essentials about all the revolutionary new drugs and drug types.

Now, thanks to *The Pill Book*, the general public can easily understand and accurately identify the medicines their doctors prescribe. *The Pill Book* describes practically everything you should know about more than 1600 prescription drugs, including generic and brand names, usual doses, side effects, adverse effects, cautions and warnings, overdose potential, interactions with other drugs, and much more.

It is based on the same information your physician and pharmacist rely on—information seldom available to patients. *The Pill Book* synthesizes the most important facts about each drug in a concise, readable entry. Warnings about drug use are given special prominence.

THE PILL BOOK
4th Edition

NO HOME SHOULD BE WITHOUT IT!

THE PILL BOOK

4th EDITION

BERT STERN

Producer

LAWRENCE D. CHILNICK

Editor-in-Chief

Text by

GILBERT I. SIMON,

Sc.D.

HAROLD M. SILVERMAN,

Pharm. D.

Additional Text
LAWRENCE D. CHILNICK

Consultant
RAYMOND J. GIZIENSKI, R.Ph., M.S.

Photography
BENN MITCHELL

Production
MICHAEL HARKAVY
LISA JENIO

BANTAM BOOKS
NEW YORK • TORONTO • LONDON • SYDNEY • AUCKLAND

THE PILL BOOK

A Bantam Nonfiction Book / June 1979
Bantam Revised edition / October 1982
Bantam 3rd Revised edition / March 1986
Bantam 4th Revised edition / February 1990

This revised edition was published simultaneously in trade paperback and mass market paperback.

BANTAM NONFICTION and the portrayal of a boxed "b" are trademarks of Bantam Books, a division of Bantam Doubleday Dell Publishing Group, Inc.

Library of Congress Cataloging-in-Publication Data
Simon, Gilbert I.
    The pill book / Gilbert I. Simon, Harold M. Silverman; photography, Benn Mitchell.—4th ed.
        p.   cm.
    Includes indexes.
                        ISBN 0-553-27934-3
    1. Drugs—Dictionaries.   2. Drugs—Identification—Pictorial works.
I. Silverman, Harold M.   II. Title.
RS51.S55   1990
615'.1—dc20
                                                            89-34555
                                                            CIP

Published simultaneously in the United States and Canada

Bantam Books are published by Bantam Books, a division of Bantam Double-day Dell Publishing Group, Inc. Its trademark, consisting of the words "Bantam Books" and the trademark of a rooster, is Registered in U.S. Patent and Trademark Office and in other countries. Marca Registrada. Bantam Books, 666 Fifth Avenue, New York, New York 10103.

PRINTED IN THE UNITED STATES OF AMERICA

OPM   18   17   16   15   14   13

Contents

Acknowledgments

The staff of *The Pill Book* wishes to acknowledge the following people, whose professional assistance and dedication have contributed to the value of the fourth edition of this book: Ian Ginsberg, C.O. Bigelow Chemists, New York City; Al Mitrione, Mike Kowgios, and Maria Capone, St. John's Pharmacy, Yonkers, New York; and Henry Resnick, B.S., M.S.

The purpose of this book is to provide educational information to the public concerning the majority of various types of prescription drugs which are presently utilized by physicians. It is not intended to be complete or exhaustive or in any respect a substitute for personal medical care. *Only a physician may prescribe these drugs and the exact dosage which should be taken.*

While every effort has been made to reproduce products on the cover and insert of this book in an exact fashion, certain variations of size or color may be expected as a result of the photographic process. Furthermore, pictures identified as brand name drugs should not be confused with their generic counterparts, and vice versa. *In any event, the reader should not rely upon the photographic image to identify any pills depicted herein, but should rely solely upon the physician's prescription as dispensed by the pharmacist.*

THE
PILL BOOK

How to Use This Book

The Pill Book, like pills themselves, should be used with caution. Used properly, this book can save you money and perhaps your life.

Our book contains a section of life-size pictures of the drugs most often prescribed in the United States. *The Pill Book*'s product identification system is designed to help you check that the drug you're about to take is the right drug. Included are the most prescribed brand name drugs and some of the more frequently prescribed generic versions of those drugs. Although many dosage forms are included, not all dosage forms and available strengths of every drug have been shown.

Each drug has been as faithfully reproduced as possible. While every effort has been made to depict the products accurately, some variations of size or color may be expected as a result of the photographic process. Readers should not rely solely upon the photographic image to identify any pills, but should check with their pharmacist if they have any questions about identification.

Most, although not all, drugs in the color section can be matched with the pill you have by checking to see if:

- The imprinted company logos (e.g., "Lilly," "Roche") are the same.
- The product strengths (e.g., "250 mg.," "10 mg.") which are frequently printed on the pills are the same.
- Any product code numbers which may be imprinted directly on the pill are the same.

To find out more about the drugs depicted, check the descriptive material in the text (page numbers are given). The pill profiles provide a complete description of over 1,600 generic and brand name drugs. These are the drugs most often prescribed to Americans. The descriptions will give you a detailed explanation of everything you need to know about your prescription. Most drugs are listed alphabetically under their generic classification; however, when a drug is a combination of two or more active ingredients, the listing is by major brand name. Every brand and generic name is cross-referenced in the Index.

Each drug profile contains the following information:

Generic or **Brand Name:** The generic name, the common name or chemical description of the drug approved by the Food and Drug Administration, is listed along with the current brand names available for each generic drug.

Most prescription drugs are sold in more than one strength. Some, such as the oral contraceptive drugs, come in packages containing different numbers of pills. A few manufacturers reflect this fact by adding letters and/or numbers to the basic drug name; others do not. An example: Norlestrin 21 1/50, Norlestrin 21 2.5/50, Norlestrin 28 1/50, Norlestrin 28 2.5/50. (The numbers here refer to the number of tablets in each monthly supply—28 or 21—and the strength of medication found in the tablets.) Other drugs come in different strengths: this is often indicated by a notation such as "DS" (double strength) or "Forte" (stronger).

The Pill Book lists only generic or brand names (e.g., Norlestrin) where there are no differences in the basic ingredients. The amount of ingredient (strength) varies from product to product.

Type of Drug: Describes the general pharmacologic class of each drug: "antidepressant," "tranquilizer," "decongestant," "expectorant," and so on.

Prescribed for: The reasons for which a drug is most often prescribed. Most drugs are given for certain symptoms or conditions but a drug may also be prescribed in combination with another for a quite different reason. Check with your doctor if you are not sure why you have been given a certain pill.

General Information: Information on how the drug works,

how long it takes for you to feel its effects, or a description of how this drug is similar to (or differs from) other drugs.

Cautions and Warnings: Any drug can be harmful if the patient is sensitive to any of its actions. The information given alerts you to possible allergic reactions and to certain physical conditions such as heart disease which should be taken into consideration if the drug is prescribed for you.

Pregnancy/Breast-feeding: Women who are pregnant or nursing newborn infants need the latest information on how their medicines can affect their babies. This section will help guide you on how to use medicines if you are or might be pregnant, and what to do if you must take a medicine during the time you are nursing your baby.

Seniors: Our bodies change as we grow older. As an older adult, you want information about how each drug affects you and what kind of reactions to expect. This section presents the special facts you need to know about every drug and how your reactions will differ from those of a younger person. It describes the symptoms you are more likely to develop just because you are older and how your doctor might adjust your drug dosage to take into account the changes in your body.

Possible Side Effects: Side effects are divided into two categories: those that are more common, and those that are less common (or rare), to help you better understand what to expect from your pills. If you are not sure whether you are experiencing an adverse reaction, ALWAYS call your doctor.

Drug Interactions: This section tells you what other drugs should not be taken at the same time as the drug under discussion. Drug interactions with other pills, alcohol, or other substances can cause death. Interactions are more common than overdoses. Obviously, it is important to be careful when taking alcohol with any medication or when taking several medications at the same time. Be sure to inform your doctor of any medication that you have been taking. Your pharmacist should also keep a record of all your prescription and nonprescription medicines. This listing, generally called a Patient Drug Profile, is used to review your record for any potential problems. You may want to keep your own drug profile and bring it to your pharmacist for review whenever a new medicine is added to it.

Food Interactions: This section includes information on foods to avoid while taking a medication, whether or not to take your medicine with meals, and other important facts.

Usual Dose: The maximum and minimum amounts of a drug usually prescribed; however, you may be given different dosage instructions by your doctor. It is important to check with your doctor if you are confused about how often to take a pill and when, or why a different dosage than indicated in the book has been prescribed. You should not change the prescribed dosages for a drug you are taking without first calling your doctor. Dosages differ for different age groups, and this information is also given.

Overdosage: Symptoms of an overdose of drugs and the immediate steps to take in that event.

Special Information: Facts to help you take your medicine more safely, symptoms to watch for, what to do if you forget a dose of your medicine, and special instructions.

The Pill Book also suggests some questions you may want to ask your doctor or pharmacist about your medicine.

This book is a unique visual reference tool. Its use, however, is only intended to amplify the information given by your doctor and pharmacist.

If you read something in *The Pill Book* which does not jibe with your instructions, call your doctor. Any drug can have serious side effects if abused or used improperly.

In an Emergency!

Each year some 1.5 million people are poisoned in the United States; about 70,000 of the poisonings are drug related. In fact, drug overdose is a leading cause of fatal poisoning in this country, with about 7,000 deaths recorded each year. Sedatives, barbiturates, benzodiazepine tranquilizers, and topically applied medicines are responsible for the bulk of the drug-related poisonings or overdoses.

Although each of the product information descriptions in the 4th revised edition of *The Pill Book* has specific information on overdose management, there are also some general rules to remember if you are confronted with someone who has been poisoned.

Do the following:

1. Make sure the victim is breathing—call for medical help immediately.
2. When calling for help, the place to call is your local poison control center. The telephone number can be obtained from information; just ask for "poison control." When you call, be prepared to tell the person who answers:

   • What was taken and how much.
   • What the victim is doing (conscious or sleeping, vomiting, having convulsions, etc.).
   • The approximate age and weight of the victim.
   • Any chronic medical problems of the victim (such as diabetes, epilepsy, or high blood pressure), if you know them.
   • What medicines, if any, the victim takes regularly.

5

3. Remove anything that could interfere with breathing. A person who has poor oxygen supply will turn blue (the fingernails or tongue change color first). If this happens, lay the victim on his back, open the collar, place one hand under the neck, and lift, pull, or push the victim's jaw so that it juts outward. This will open the airway between the mouth and lungs as wide as possible. If the victim is not breathing, begin mouth-to-mouth resuscitation.
4. If the victim is unconscious or having convulsions, call for medical help immediately. While waiting for the ambulance, lay the victim on the stomach and turn the head to one side. This will prevent inhalation of vomit should the victim throw up. Do not give an unconscious victim anything by mouth. Keep the victim warm.
5. If the victim is conscious, call for medical help and give the victim an 8-ounce glass of water to drink. This will dilute the poison.

Only a small percent of poisoning victims require hospitalization. Most can be treated with simple actions or need no treatment at all.

Depending on what was taken, you may be instructed to make the patient vomit. The best way to do this is to use Syrup of Ipecac, which can be purchased without a prescription at any pharmacy. Specific instructions on how much to give infants, children, or adults are printed on the label and will also be given by your poison control center. Remember, *do not* make the victim vomit unless you have been instructed to do so. Never make the victim vomit if the victim is unconscious, is having a convulsion, has a painful, burning feeling in the mouth or throat, or has swallowed a corrosive poison. (Corrosive poisons include bleach—liquid or powder—washing soda, drain cleaner, lye, oven cleaner, toilet bowl cleaner, and dishwasher detergent.) If a corrosive poison has been taken and the victim can still swallow, give milk or water to dilute the poison. The poison control center will give you further instructions.

If the victim has swallowed a petroleum derivative such as gasoline, kerosene, machine oil, lighter fluid, furniture polish, or cleaning fluids, do not do anything. Call the poison control center for instructions.

If the poison or chemical has spilled onto the skin, remove

any clothing or jewelry that has been contaminated and wash the area with plenty of warm water for at least 15 minutes. Then wash the area thoroughly with soap and water. The poison control center will give you more instructions.

Be Prepared

The best way to deal with a poisoning is to be ready for it. Do the following *now:*

1. Get the telephone number of your local poison control center and write it down with your other emergency phone numbers.
2. Decide which hospital you will go to, if necessary, and how you will get there.
3. Buy 1 ounce of Syrup of Ipecac from your pharmacy. The pharmacist will explain how to use it, if needed. Remember, this is a potent drug to be used only if directed.
4. Learn to give mouth-to-mouth resuscitation. You may have to use this on a victim of poisoning.

In order to reduce the possibility of poisoning, do the following:

1. Keep all medicine, household cleaners, disinfectants, insecticides, gardening products, and similar products out of the reach of young children, in a locked place.
2. Do not store poisonous materials in containers that have contained food.
3. Do not remove the labels from bottles so that the contents cannot be read.
4. Discard all medicines after you no longer need them.
5. Do not operate a car engine or other gasoline engine in an unventilated space. Do not use a propane heater indoors.
6. If you smell gas, call the gas company immediately.

Poison prevention is best achieved by common sense. If you follow the simple advice given in this chapter, you will have taken a giant step toward assuring household safety for you and your family members.

The Most Commonly Prescribed Drugs in the United States, Generic and Brand Names, with Complete Descriptions of Drugs and Their Effects

Generic Name

Acebutolol

Brand Name

Sectral

Type of Drug

Beta-adrenergic blocker.

Prescribed for

High blood pressure and abnormal heart rhythms. It may also be prescribed by your doctor to treat angina pectoris, anxiety, tremors, overactive thyroid, and mitral valve prolapse and to prevent second heart attacks in people who have already had one.

General Information

Acebutolol is a relatively weak beta blocker and is given in larger doses than other beta-blocking drugs available in the United States. Otherwise, Acebutolol is remarkably similar to other beta blockers in its ability to lower blood pressure and treat abnormal heart rhythms and other conditions.

Cautions and Warnings

You should be cautious about taking Acebutolol if you have asthma, severe heart failure, very slow heart rate, or heart block because the drug can aggravate these conditions. Compared with the other beta blockers, Acebutolol has less of an effect on your pulse and bronchial muscles, and less of a rebound effect when the drug is discontinued, and it produces less tiredness, depression, and intolerance to exercise than other beta-blocking drugs.

People with angina who take Acebutolol for high blood pressure should have their drug dosage reduced gradually over 1 to 2 weeks rather than suddenly discontinued. This will avoid possible aggravation of the angina.

Acebutolol should be used with caution if you have liver disease, because your ability to eliminate the drug from your body will be impaired.

Pregnancy/Breast-feeding

Animal studies in which rats and rabbits were given amount
of medicine greater than normal human doses revealed n
adverse effects of Acebutolol on the developing baby. How
ever, Acebutolol should be avoided by pregnant women, o
women who might become pregnant while taking it. Whe
the drug is considered essential by your doctor, the potentia
risk of taking the medicine must be carefully weighed agains
the benefit it might produce. Small amounts of Acebutolo
may pass into your breast milk. Nursing mothers taking thi
drug must observe their infants for possible drug-relate
side effects.

Seniors

Senior citizens may absorb more Acebutolol and may re
quire only half as much medicine as younger adults to achiev
the same effect. Your dosage of this drug must be adjuste
to your individual needs by your doctor. Seniors may be
more likely to suffer from cold hands and feet and reduce
body temperature, chest pains, a general feeling of ill health
sudden difficulty breathing, sweating, or changes in heart
beat because of this medicine.

Possible Side Effects

Acebutolol side effects are relatively uncommon, usually develop early in the course of treatment, are relatively mild,
and are rarely a reason to stop taking the medication. Side
effects increase with increasing dosage and include dizziness, tingling of the scalp, nausea, vomiting, upset stomach,
taste distortion, fatigue, sweating, male impotence, urinary
difficulty, diarrhea, bile duct blockage, breathing difficulty,
bronchial spasms, muscle weakness, cramps, dry eyes, blurred
vision, skin rash, hair loss, and facial swelling. Like other
beta blockers, Acebutolol can cause mental depression, confusion, disorientation, short-term memory loss, and emotional instability.

Rare side effects include aggravation of lupus erythematosus (a disease of the body's connective tissues), stuffy nose,
chest pains, back or joint pains, colitis, drug allergy (fever,
sore throat), and unusual bleeding or bruising.

Drug Interactions

Beta-blocking drugs may interact with surgical anesthetics to increase the risk of heart problems during surgery. Some anesthesiologists recommend stopping your beta blocker gradually 2 days before surgery.

Acebutolol may interfere with the normal signs of low blood sugar and can interfere with the action of oral antidiabetes medicines.

Taking Acebutolol together with Aspirin-containing drugs, Indomethacin, or Sulfinpyrazone can interfere with its blood-pressure-lowering effect.

The effects of Acebutolol may be increased by Molindone, Phenothiazine antipsychotic medicines with other antihypertensives like Clonidine, Diazoxide, Nifedipine, or Reserpine, or with other drugs that can reduce blood pressure, like Nitroglycerin.

Cimetidine increases the amount of Acebutolol absorbed into the bloodstream from oral tablets.

Acebutolol may interfere with the effectiveness of some anti-asthma drugs, especially Ephedrine and Isoproterenol and with Theophylline or Aminophylline.

The combination of Acebutolol and Phenytoin or digitalis drugs can result in excessive slowing of the heart and possible heart block.

Estrogen drugs can interfere with the blood-pressure-lowering effect of Acebutolol.

Food Interactions

Take this medicine with food if it upsets your stomach.

Usual Dose

Starting dose, 400 milligrams per day, taken all at once or in 2 divided doses. The daily dose may be gradually increased. Maintenance dose, 400 to 1200 milligrams per day.

Senior: older adults may respond to lower doses of this drug than younger adults and should be treated more cautiously, beginning with 200 milligrams per day and increasing gradually up to a maximum of 800 milligrams per day.

Overdosage

Symptoms are changes in heartbeat (unusually slow, unusually fast, or irregular), severe dizziness or fainting, difficulty breathing, bluish-colored fingernails or palms of the hands, and seizures.

Special Information

Acebutolol is meant to be taken on a continuing basis. Do not stop taking it unless directed to do so by your doctor. Possible side effects of abrupt withdrawal of Acebutolol are: chest pain, difficulty breathing, sweating, and unusually fast or irregular heartbeat.

Call your doctor at once if any of the following symptoms develop: back or joint pains, difficulty breathing, cold hands or feet, depression, skin rash, changes in heartbeat.

Call your doctor only if the following side effects persist or are bothersome: anxiety, diarrhea, constipation, sexual impotence, mild dizziness, headache, itching, nausea or vomiting, nightmares or vivid dreams, upset stomach, trouble sleeping, stuffed nose, frequent urination, unusual tiredness or weakness.

If you forget a dose of Acebutolol, take it as soon as you remember. If it is almost time for your next dose, skip the forgotten tablet. Do not double the dose.

Generic Name

Acetaminophen

Brand Names

A'Cenol	Myapap
Acephen	Neopap Supprettes
Aceta	Oraphen-PD
Actamin	Panadol, Children's Panadol
Amphenol	Panex
Anacin-3, Children's Anacin-3	Pedric Wafers
Anuphen	Peedee
APAP	Phenaphen
APF Arthritis Pain Formula	St. Joseph Aspirin-Free for
Banesin	Children
Bromo Seltzer	Suppap
Conacetol	Tapanol
Dapa	Tapar
Datril	Tempra
Dolanex	Tenol
Genapap, Children's	Tylenol, Children's Tylenol
Genapap	Tylenol Extra Strength
Genebs	Ty-Pap
Halenol	Ty-Tabs, Children's Ty-Tabs
Liquiprin	Valadol
Meda Tab	Valorin

(Also available in generic form)

Type of Drug

Antipyretic analgesic.

Prescribed for

Symptomatic relief of pain and fever for people who cannot take Aspirin.

General Information

Acetaminophen is generally used to provide symptomatic relief from pain and fever associated with the common cold, flu, viral infections, or other disorders where pain or fever may be a problem. It is also used to relieve pain in people who are allergic to Aspirin, or those who cannot take Aspirin because of potential interactions with other drugs such as oral anticoagulants. It can be used to relieve pain from a variety of sources including arthritis, headache, and tooth and periodontic pain, although it does not reduce inflammation.

Cautions and Warnings

Do not take Acetaminophen if you are allergic or sensitive to it. Do not take Acetaminophen for more than 10 consecutive days unless directed by your doctor. Do not take more than is prescribed for you or recommended on the package.

Use with caution if you have kidney or liver disease or virus infections of the liver.

Pregnancy/Breast-feeding

This drug appears safe for use during pregnancy when taken in usual doses. Taking continuous high doses of the drug may cause birth defects or interfere with your baby's development. Check with your doctor before taking it if you are, or might be, pregnant. Small amounts of Acetaminophen may pass into breast milk.

Seniors

Seniors may take Acetaminophen according to package directions or as directed by their doctor.

Possible Side Effects

This drug is relatively free from side effects. For this reason it has become extremely popular, especially among those who cannot take Aspirin. Rarely, large doses or long-term use of Acetaminophen can cause rash, itching, fever, lowered blood sugar, stimulation, and/or yellowing of the skin or whites of the eyes. Other effects of overuse may include a change in the composition of your blood.

Usual Dose

Adult: 300 to 650 milligrams 4 to 6 times per day or 1000 milligrams 3 or 4 times per day. Avoid taking doses greater than 2.6 grams (8 of the 325-milligram tablets) per day for long periods of time.

Child (age 9 to 11): 400 to 480 milligrams 4 to 5 times per day.

Child (age 6 to 8): 320 milligrams 4 to 5 times per day.
Child (age 4 to 5): 240 milligrams 4 to 5 times per day.
Child (age 1 to 3): 120 to 160 milligrams 4 to 5 times per day.
Child (less than 1 year): 40 to 80 milligrams 4 to 5 times per day.

Overdosage

Symptoms are development of bluish color of the lips, fingertips, etc., rash, fever, stimulation, excitement, delirium, depression, nausea and vomiting, abdominal pain, diarrhea, yellowing of the skin and/or eyes, convulsions, and coma. Victims of Acetaminophen overdose should be made to vomit with Syrup of Ipecac and taken to a hospital emergency room. ALWAYS bring the medicine bottle.

Special Information

Unless abused, Acetaminophen is a beneficial, effective, and relatively nontoxic drug.

Generic Name

Acetaminophen with Codeine

Ingredients

Acetaminophen
Codeine Phosphate

Brand Names

Bayapap with Codeine	Papadeine
Capital with Codeine	Phenaphen with Codeine
Codap	Proval No. 3
Empracet with Codeine	Tylenol with Codeine
Myapap with Codeine	Ty-Pap with Codeine
Panadol with Codeine	Ty-Tab

(Also available in generic form)

Type of Drug

Narcotic analgesic combination.

Prescribed for

Relief of mild to moderate pain.

General Information

Acetaminophen with Codeine is generally prescribed for the patient who requires a greater analgesic effect than Acetaminophen alone can deliver, and/or is allergic to Aspirin.

Acetaminophen with Codeine is probably not effective for arthritis or other pain caused by inflammation because the ingredient Acetaminophen does not reduce inflammation. Aspirin with Codeine will produce an anti-inflammatory effect, and this is the major difference between these two products.

Cautions and Warnings

Do not take Acetaminophen with Codeine if you know you are allergic or sensitive to it. Use this drug with extreme caution if you suffer from asthma or other breathing problems, or if you have kidney or liver disease or virus infections of the liver. Long-term use of Acetaminophen with Codeine may cause drug dependence or addiction. Codeine is a respiratory depressant and affects the central nervous system, producing sleepiness, tiredness, and/or inability to concentrate. Be careful if you are driving, operating machinery, or performing other functions requiring concentration.

Pregnancy/Breast-feeding

High doses of Acetaminophen have caused some problems when used during pregnancy or breast-feeding. The regular use of Codeine may cause the unborn child to become addicted. If used during labor, it may cause breathing problems in the infant. If you are pregnant or suspect that you are pregnant, do not take this drug.

Both Acetaminophen and Codeine may pass into breast milk. Wait 4 to 6 hours after taking the medication before breast-feeding.

Seniors

Seniors may be sensitive to the depressant effects of Codeine in this combination. Take this drug product only according to your doctor's prescription.

Possible Side Effects

Most frequent: light-headedness, dizziness, sleepiness, nausea, vomiting, loss of appetite, sweating. If these effects occur, consider calling your doctor and asking him about lowering the dose of Codeine you are taking. Usually the side effects disappear if you simply lie down.

More serious side effects of Acetaminophen with Codeine are shallow breathing or difficulty in breathing.

Rarely, Acetaminophen with Codeine may cause euphoria (feeling high), weakness, sleepiness, headache, agitation, uncoordinated muscle movement, minor hallucinations, disorientation and visual disturbances, dry mouth, loss of appetite, constipation, flushing of the face, rapid heartbeat, palpitations, faintness, urinary difficulties or hesitancy, reduced sex drive and/or potency, itching, rashes, anemia, lowered blood sugar, yellowing of the skin and/or whites of the eyes. Narcotic analgesics may aggravate convulsions in those who have had convulsions in the past.

Drug Interactions

Because of its depressant effect and potential effect on breathing, Acetaminophen with Codeine should be taken with extreme care in combination with alcohol, sleeping medicine, tranquilizers, antihistamines, or other drugs producing sedation.

Food Interactions

Acetaminophen with Codeine is best taken with food or at least ½ glass of water to prevent stomach upset.

Usual Dose

Adult: 1 to 2 tablets every 4 hours.

Child (6 to 12 years): 5 to 10 milligrams every 4 to 6 hours. Not to exceed 60 milligrams in 24 hours.

Child (2 to 6 years): 2.5 milligrams to 5 milligrams every 4 to 6 hours. Not to exceed 30 milligrams in 24 hours.

Overdosage

Symptoms are depression of respiration (breathing), extreme tiredness progressing to stupor and then coma, pinpointed pupils of the eyes, no response to stimulation such as a pin stick, cold and clammy skin, slowing down of the heart rate, lowering of blood pressure, yellowing of the skin and/or whites of the eyes, bluish color in skin of hands and feet, fever, excitement, delirium, convulsions, cardiac arrest, and liver toxicity (shown by nausea, vomiting, pain in the abdomen, and diarrhea). The patient should be made to vomit with Syrup of Ipecac and taken to a hospital emergency room immediately. ALWAYS bring the medicine bottle.

Special Information

If you forget to take a dose of Acetaminophen with Codeine, take it as soon as you remember. If it is almost time for your next dose, skip the forgotten dose and continue with your regular medication schedule. Do not take a double dose of this medication.

Generic Name

Acetazolamide

Brand Names

AK-Zol
Dazamide
Diamox

(Also available in generic form)

Type of Drug

Carbonic anhydrase inhibitor.

Prescribed for

Heart failure, glaucoma, prophylactic treatment of mountain sickness at high altitudes. This drug has also been used in treating some convulsive disorders such as petit mal epilepsy and other unlocalized seizures. How Acetazolamide works for these disorders is not fully known.

General Information

Acetazolamide inhibits an enzyme in the body called carbonic anhydrase. This effect allows the drug to be used as a weak diuretic, and as part of the treatment of glaucoma by helping to reduce pressure inside the eye. The same effect on carbonic anhydrase is thought to make Acetazolamide a useful drug in treating certain epileptic seizure disorders. The exact way in which the effect is produced is not understood.

Cautions and Warnings

Do not take Acetazolamide if you have serious kidney, liver, or Addison's disease. This drug should not be used by people with low blood sodium or potassium.

Pregnancy/Breast-feeding

High doses of this drug may cause birth defects or interfere with your baby's development. Check with your doctor before taking it if you are, or might be, pregnant. Acetazolamide has not caused problems among breast-feeding mothers, but check with your doctor about this.

Seniors

Take this medication according to your doctor's prescription.

Possible Side Effects

Side effects of short-term Acetazolamide therapy are usually minimal. Those which have been noted include tingling feeling in the arms or legs or at lips, mouth, or anus, loss of appetite, increased frequency in urination (to be expected, since this drug has a weak diuretic effect), occasional drowsiness and/or convulsion. Transient myopia has been reported.

Since this drug is chemically considered to be a sulfa drug it can cause all of the side effects of the sulfa drugs: fever, rash, the formation of drug crystals in the urine, and adverse effects of the drug.

Rare side effects of Acetazolamide are: itching, rash, blood in stool or urine, increased blood sugar, convulsions, diarrhea, loss of weight, nausea, vomiting, constipation, weakness, nervousness, depression, dizziness, dry mouth, disorientation, muscle spasms, ringing in the ears, loss of taste or smell, not feeling well.

Drug Interactions

Avoid over-the-counter drug products which contain stimulants or anticholinergics, which tend to aggravate glaucoma or cardiac disease. Ask your pharmacist about ingredients contained in the over-the-counter drugs.

Acetazolamide may increase the effect of Quinidine and predispose patients to Digitalis toxicity by increasing potassium losses.

Acetazolamide may inhibit or delay the absorption of Primidone (for seizures) into the bloodstream. Avoid Aspirin while taking Acetazolamide, since Aspirin side effects can be enhanced by this combination.

Food Interactions

May be taken with food to minimize stomach upset. Acetazolamide may increase potassium loss. Take this drug with foods that are rich in potassium, like apricots, bananas, orange juice, or raisins.

Usual Dose

250 milligrams to 1 gram per day, according to disease and patient's condition.

Special Information

Acetazolamide may cause minor drowsiness and confusion, particularly during the first 2 weeks of therapy. Take care while performing tasks which require concentration, such as driving or operating appliances or machinery.

Call your doctor if you develop sore throat, fever, unusual bleeding or bruises, tingling in the hands or feet, rash, or unusual pains. These can be signs of important drug side effects.

If you forget a dose of Acetazolamide, take it as soon as you remember. If it is almost time for your next dose, skip the forgotten pill. Do not double the dosage.

Generic Name

Acyclovir

Brand Name

Zovirax

Type of Drug

Antiviral; antiherpes.

Prescribed for

Herpes simplex infections of the genitalia (sex organs) and of mucous membrane tissues.

General Information

Acyclovir is the only drug that can reduce the rate of growth of the herpes virus and its relatives, Epstein-Barr virus, cytomegalovirus, and varicella-zoster. It does not cure herpes, but does reduce pain associated with herpes and may help herpes sores heal faster. It does not affect viruses that cause the common cold.

The ointment works only on the viral blisters of an initial infection by interfering with viral DNA. It has little effect on recurrent infection and will not prevent the infection from coming back once it has healed. The drug must be given by mouth or by intravenous injection in a hospital to treat both local and systemic symptoms. The capsules can be taken every day to reduce the number and severity of herpes attacks in people who usually suffer 10 or more a year and may be used to treat intermittent attacks as they occur, but the drug must be started as soon as possible to have the greatest effect.

Cautions and Warnings

Acyclovir ointment should not be applied to your skin if you have an allergic reaction to it or to the major component of the ointment base, Polyethylene Glycol. Acyclovir ointment should not be used to treat a herpes infection of the eye because it is not specifically made for that purpose. Some people develop tenderness, swelling, or bleeding of the gums while taking Acyclovir. Regular brushing, flossing, and gum massage may help prevent this.

High doses of Acyclovir taken over long periods of time have caused reduced sperm count in lab animals, but this effect has not yet been reported in men.

The ointment should not be applied inside the vagina because the Polyethylene Glycol base can irritate and cause swelling of those sensitive tissues.

Pregnancy/Breast-feeding

Very small amounts of the drug are absorbed into the blood after application in the ointment form. While there is no information to indicate that Acyclovir affects a developing baby, you should not use this medication during pregnancy unless it is specifically prescribed by your doctor. Acyclovir capsules and injections have been given to lab animals and found to cause no birth defects. However, Acyclovir has not been studied in pregnant women and should not be used unless the possible benefits clearly outweigh any possible adverse effects. It is not known if Acyclovir passes into breast milk. Mothers who must take this medicine should not breast-feed.

Seniors

Seniors with reduced kidney function should be given a lower oral dose than that described below.

Possible Side Effects

The ointment has few side effects, the most common of which are mild burning, irritation, rash, and itching. Women are 4 times more likely to experience burning than men, and it is more likely to occur when applied during an initial herpes attack than during a recurrent attack.

The most common side effects of Acyclovir capsules are dizziness, nausea, vomiting, and headache. Additional side effects that may be experienced by people taking the drug continuously are diarrhea and aching joints.

Acyclovir capsules may occasionally cause loss of appetite, fatigue, swelling and fluid retention, rash, leg pains, swollen lymph glands in the groin and elsewhere, sore throat, a bad taste in your mouth, sleeplessness, heart palpitations, menstrual abnormalities, superficial blood clots, hair loss, depression, fever, muscle cramps, and acne.

Drug Interactions

Do not apply Acyclovir with any other ointment or topical medicine.

Oral Probenecid may decrease the elimination of Acyclovir from your body and increase drug blood levels, when the Acyclovir is taken by mouth or by injection.

Food Interactions

Acyclovir capsules may be taken with food.

Usual Dose

Capsules: for treatment of an initial herpes attack or an occasional herpes attack, 1 capsule every 4 hours, 5 times per day for 10 days. For maximum benefit, start treatment as soon as possible.

Ointment: apply the ointment every 3 hours, 6 times per day for 7 days, in sufficient quantity to cover all visible lesions. About ½ inch of Acyclovir ointment should cover about 4 square inches of skin lesions. Your doctor may prescribe a longer course of treatment to prevent the delayed formation of new lesions during the duration of an attack.

As suppressive therapy, for people who suffer from chronic herpes infection: 1 capsule 3 to 5 times per day, every day.

Overdosage

The chance of toxic side effects from swallowing Acyclovir ointment is quite small because of the limited amount of drug contained in the ointment (only 50 milligrams per gram). There is no information on Acyclovir overdose, but doses of up to 4.8 grams per day for 5 days have been taken without serious adverse effects. Observe the overdose victim for side effects and call your local poison control center for more detailed information and advice.

Special Information

Use a finger cot or rubber glove when applying the ointment to protect against inadvertently spreading the virus, and be sure to apply the medicine exactly as directed and to completely cover all lesions. If you skip several doses or a day or more of treatment, the therapy will not exert its maximum effect.

Call your doctor if the drug does not relieve your condition, if side effects become severe or intolerable, or if you become pregnant or want to begin breast-feeding.

To avoid transmitting the condition, do not have intercourse while visible herpes lesions are present.

Check with your dentist or doctor about how to take care of your teeth if you notice swelling or tenderness of the gums.

Generic Name

Albuterol

Brand Names

Proventil
Proventil Repetab
Ventolin

Type of Drug

Bronchodilator.

Prescribed for

Asthma and bronchial spasms.

General Information

Albuterol is similar to other bronchodilator drugs like Metaproterenol and Isoetharine but it has a weaker effect on nerve receptors in the heart and blood vessels, and for this reason it is somewhat safer for people with heart conditions.

Albuterol tablets begin to work within 30 minutes and continue working for about 4 hours. There is also a long-acting tablet preparation that continues to work for up to 12 hours. Albuterol inhalation begins working within 15 minutes, and continues for 3 to 4 hours.

Cautions and Warnings

Albuterol should be used with caution by people with a history of angina, heart disease, high blood pressure, stroke or seizure, diabetes, thyroid disease, prostate disease, or glaucoma. Excessive use of Albuterol inhalants can lead to worsening of your asthmatic or other respiratory condition.

Pregnancy/Breast-feeding

This drug should be avoided by pregnant women or those who become pregnant while using it. It is not known if Albuterol causes birth defects in humans, but it has caused defects in pregnant-animal studies. When it is deemed essential, the potential risk of taking Albuterol must be carefully weighed against any benefit it might produce. It is not known if Albuterol passes into breast milk. Nursing mothers must observe for any possible drug effect on their infants while taking Albuterol. You may want to consider using an alternate feeding method.

Seniors

Older adults are more sensitive to the effects of Albuterol. They should closely follow their doctor's directions and report any side effects at once.

Possible Side Effects

Albuterol's side effects are similar to those of other bronchodilators, except that its effects on the heart and blood vessels are not as pronounced. Most common: restlessness, weakness, anxiety, fear, tension, sleeplessness, tremors, convulsions, dizziness, headache, flushing, loss of appetite, pallor, sweating, nausea, vomiting, and muscle cramps.

Less common side effects are: angina, abnormal heart rhythms, heart palpitations, high blood pressure, and urinary difficulty.

Drug Interactions

Albuterol's effects may be increased by monoamine oxidase (MAO) inhibitor drugs, antidepressants, thyroid drugs, other bronchodilator drugs, and some antihlstamines. It is antagonized by the beta-blocking drugs (Propranolol and others.)

Albuterol may antagonize the effects of blood-pressure-lowering drugs, especially Reserpine, Methyldopa, and Guanethidine.

Food Interactions

Albuterol tablets are more effective taken on an empty stomach, 1 hour before or 2 hours after meals, but can be taken with food or meals if they upset your stomach. Do not inhale Albuterol if you have food or anything else in your mouth.

Usual Dose

Inhalation:
Adult and child (age 12 and over): 2 puffs every 4 to 6 hours (each puff delivers 90 milligrams of Albuterol). Asthma brought on by exercise may be prevented by taking 2 puffs 15 minutes before the exercise is to begin.
Tablets:
Adult: 6 to 16 milligrams per day in divided doses to start; the dosage may be slowly increased until it controls patient's asthma, to a maximum of 32 milligrams per day.
Senior: 6 to 8 milligrams per day to start, but increase to the maximum daily adult dosage, if tolerated.
Child (age 6 to 14 years): 2 to 6 milligrams 3 to 4 times per day.
Child (age 2 to 5 years): up to 4 milligrams 3 times a day.

Overdosage

Overdose of Albuterol inhalation usually results in exaggerated side effects, including heart pains and high blood pressure, although the pressure may drop to a low level after a short period of elevation. People who inhale too much Albuterol should see a doctor, who may prescribe a beta-blocking drug, such as Atenolol or Metoprolol.

Overdose of Albuterol tablets is more likely to lead to side effects of changes in heart rate, palpitations, unusual heart rhythms, heart pains, high blood pressure, fever, chills, cold sweats, nausea, vomiting, and dilation of the pupils. Convulsions, sleeplessness, anxiety, and tremors may also develop and the victim may collapse.

If the overdose was taken within the past half hour, give the victim Syrup of Ipecac to induce vomiting and remove any remaining medicine from the stomach. DO NOT GIVE SYRUP OF IPECAC IF THE VICTIM IS UNCONSCIOUS OR CONVULSING. If symptoms have already begun to develop, the victim may have to be taken to a hospital emergency room for treatment. ALWAYS bring the prescription bottle with you.

Special Information

If you are inhaling Albuterol, be sure to follow patient instructions that come with the product. The drug should be inhaled during the second half of your breath, since this will allow it to reach deeper down into your lungs. Wait about 5 minutes between puffs, if you use more than 1 puff per dose.

Do not take more Albuterol than prescribed by your doctor. Taking more than you need could actually result in worsening of your symptoms.

Call your doctor immediately if you develop chest pains, palpitations, rapid heart beat, muscle tremors, dizziness, headache, facial flushing, or urinary difficulty, of if you continue to experience difficulty in breathing after using the medicine.

If a dose of Albuterol is forgotten, take it as soon as you remember. If it is almost time for your next dose, skip the forgotten one. Do not double up.

Brand Name

Aldactazide

Ingredients

Hydrochlorothiazide
Spironolactone

Other Brand Names

Alazide
Spironazide
Spironolactone with Hydrochlorothiazide
Spirozide

(Also available in generic form)

Type of Drug

Diuretic.

Prescribed for

High blood pressure or any condition where it is desirable to eliminate excess water from the body.

General Information

Aldactazide is a combination of two diuretics and is a convenient, effective approach for the treatment of diseases where the elimination of excess water is required. One of the ingredients in Aldactazide has the ability to hold potassium in the body while producing a diuretic effect. This balances off the other ingredient, Hydrochlorothiazide, which normally causes a loss of body potassium.

Combination drugs like Aldactazide should only be used when you need the exact amount of ingredients contained in the product and when your doctor feels you would benefit from taking fewer pills per day.

Cautions and Warnings

Do not use Aldactazide if you have nonfunctioning kidneys, if you may be allergic to this drug or any sulfa drug, or if you have a history of allergy or bronchial asthma.

Do not take any potassium supplements together with Aldactazide unless specifically directed to do so by your doctor.

Pregnancy/Breast-feeding

Aldactazide may be used to treat specific conditions in pregnant women, but the decision to use this medication by pregnant women should be weighed carefully because the drug may cross the placental barrier into the blood of the unborn child. This drug may cause birth defects or interfere with your baby's development. Check with your doctor before taking it if you are, or might be, pregnant.

Both ingredients in Aldactazide can pass into breast milk. No problems have been found in nursing mothers taking Aldactazide, but be sure your baby doctor knows you are taking this medicine.

Seniors

Older adults are more sensitive to the effects of this drug, especially dizziness because of potassium loss. They should closely follow their doctor's directions and report any side effects at once.

Possible Side Effects

Loss of appetite, drowsiness, lethargy, headache, gastrointestinal upset, cramping and diarrhea. Less common side effects are: rash, mental confusion, fever, feeling of ill health, enlargement of the breasts, inability to achieve or maintain erection in males, irregular menstrual cycles or deepening of the voice in females, headache, tingling in the toes and fingers, restlessness, anemias or other effects on components of the blood, unusual sensitivity to sunlight, dizziness when rising quickly from a sitting position. Aldactazide can also produce muscle spasms, gout, weakness, and blurred vision.

Drug Interactions

Aldactazide will increase the effect of other blood-pressure-lowering drugs. This is good and is the reason why many people with high blood pressure take more than one medicine.

The possibility of developing imbalances in body fluids (electrolytes) is increased if you take other medications such as Digitalis and adrenal corticosteroids while you are taking Aldactazide.

If you are taking an oral antidiabetic drug and begin taking Aldactazide, the antidiabetic dose may have to be altered.

Lithium Carbonate taken with Aldactazide should be monitored carefully as there may be an increased risk of Lithium toxicity.

Avoid over-the-counter cough, cold, or allergy remedies containing stimulant drugs which can aggravate your condition.

Aldactazide may interfere with the oral blood-thinning drugs (like Warfarin) by making the blood more concentrated (thicker).

Food Interactions

Take Aldactazide with food if it upsets your stomach.

Usual Dose

2 to 4 tablets per day, adjusted by your doctor until the desired therapeutic effect is achieved.

Overdosage

Signs can be tingling in the arms or legs, weakness, fatigue, changes in your heartbeat, a sickly feeling, dry mouth, restlessness, muscle pains or cramps, urinary difficulty, nausea, or vomiting. Take the overdose victim to a hospital emergency room for treatment at once. ALWAYS bring the prescription bottle and any remaining medicine.

Special Information

This drug may cause drowsiness or sleepiness. Be careful if you drive or operate machinery. Call your doctor if you develop muscle or stomach cramps, nausea, diarrhea, unusual thirst, headache, rash, voice changes, breast enlargement, or unusual menstrual period.

If you forget a dose of Aldactazide, take it as soon as you remember. If it is almost time for your next dose, skip the forgotten dose and continue with your regular schedule. Do not take a double dose of Aldactazide, but call your doctor if you forget to take 2 or more doses in a row.

Brand Name

Aldoril

Ingredients

Hydrochlorothiazide
Methyldopa

(Also available in generic form)

Type of Drug

Antihypertensive combination.

Prescribed for

High blood pressure.

General Information

Be sure to take this medicine exactly as prescribed: if you don't, it cannot exert its maximum effect.

The ingredient Hydrochlorothiazide in this drug can cause loss of body potassium. Potassium loss leads to a condition known as hypokalemia. Warning signs of hypokalemia or other electrolyte imbalances that can be due to Aldoril are dryness of the mouth, excessive thirst, weakness, drowsiness, restlessness, muscle pains or cramps, muscular fatigue, lack of urination, abnormal heart rhythms, and upset stomach. If this happens, call your doctor. You may have to take extra potassium to supplement loss due to Aldoril. This may be taken as a potassium supplement (tablet, powder, liquid) or by increasing certain foods in your diet such as bananas, citrus fruits, melons, and tomatoes.

Cautions and Warnings

Do not take Aldoril if you are allergic to either of its ingredients, if you have any liver diseases such as hepatitis or active cirrhosis (liver disease), or if previous therapy with Methyldopa has been associated with signs of liver reaction (jaundice or unexplained fever).

Pregnancy/Breast-feeding

This drug will pass into the unborn child and can be found in mother's milk. Pregnant women should use this drug only if it is absolutely necessary. Women taking Aldoril should not breast-feed their infants.

Seniors

Older adults are more sensitive to the effects of this drug, especially dizziness. They should closely follow their doctor's directions and report any side effects at once.

Possible Side Effects

Loss of appetite, stomach upset, nausea, vomiting, cramps, diarrhea, constipation, dizziness, headache, tingling in the extremities, restlessness, chest pains, abnormal heart rhythms, drowsiness during the first few days of therapy.

A less common side effect is abnormal liver function in the first 2 to 3 months of therapy. Watch for jaundice (yellowing of the skin or whites of the eyes), with or without fever. If you are taking Aldoril for the first time, be sure the doctor checks your liver function, particularly during the first 6 to 12 weeks of therapy. If fever or jaundice appears, notify your doctor immediately and discontinue therapy. Other adverse effects: stuffy nose, breast enlargement, lactation (in females), impotence or decreased sex drive, mild arthritis, skin reactions such as mild eczema, stomach gas, dry mouth, a sore tongue, fever.

Drug Interactions

Interaction with Digitalis or Quinidine can result in the development of abnormal heart rhythms.

Interaction with Lithium products can lead to Lithium toxicity unless appropriate dose adjustments are made.

Aldoril increases the blood-pressure-lowering effects of other medicines.

Aldoril may increase the sedative effect of Haloperidol.

The effect of antidiabetes drugs may be increased by this medication.

Do not self-medicate with over-the-counter cough, cold, or allergy remedies containing stimulant drugs which may raise your blood pressure. If you are not sure which over-the-counter drugs are safe for you, ask your pharmacist.

Food Interactions

You may take this drug with food to reduce upset stomach.

Usual Dose

Individualized to suit the patient. The usual starting dose, 1 tablet 2 to 3 times per day for the first 2 days, is adjusted up or down as needed. Aldoril is available in different strength combinations to allow your physician to tailor the dose to your specific needs.

Overdosage

Signs can be tingling in the arms or legs, sedation, coma, weakness, dizziness when rising from a sitting or lying position, fatigue, changes in your heartbeat, a sickly feeling, dry mouth, restlessness, muscle pains or cramps, urinary difficulty, nausea, or vomiting. Take the overdose victim to a hospital emergency room for treatment at once. ALWAYS bring the prescription bottle and any remaining medicine.

Special Information

Aldoril may cause temporary mild sedation. Contact your doctor if your normal urine output is dropping or you are less hungry or nauseated.

Be aware that Aldoril can cause orthostatic hypotension (dizziness when rising from a sitting or lying position). Alcohol will worsen this effect, so avoid alcohol at the beginning of Aldoril therapy.

Call your doctor if you develop muscle weakness, cramps, nausea, dizziness, fever, or tiredness.

If you forget to take a dose of Aldoril, take it as soon as you remember. If it is almost time for your next dose, skip the forgotten dose and continue with your regular schedule. Do not take a double dose of Aldoril.

Generic Name

Allopurinol

Brand Names

Lopurin
Zurinol
Zyloprim

(Also available in generic form)

Type of Drug

Anti-gout medication.

Prescribed for

Gout or gouty arthritis. Allopurinol is also useful to help manage other conditions that may occur if too much uric acid is present in the body.

General Information

Unlike other anti-gout drugs which affect the elimination of uric acid from the body, Allopurinol acts on the system that manufactures uric acid in your body. A high level of uric acid can mean that you have gout or that you have one of many other diseases, including various cancers and malignancies, or psoriasis. High uric acid levels can be caused by taking some drugs, including diuretic medicines. The fact that you have a high blood level of uric acid does not point to a specific disease.

Cautions and Warnings

Do not take this medication if you have ever developed a severe reaction to it. If you develop a rash or any other adverse effects while taking Allopurinol, stop taking the medication immediately and contact your doctor.

Allopurinol should be used by children only if they have high uric acid levels due to neoplastic disease.

Pregnancy/Breast-feeding

This drug may cause birth defects or interfere with your baby's development. Check with your doctor before taking it if you are, or might be, pregnant. A nursing mother should not take this medication, since it will pass through the mother's milk into the child.

Seniors

No special precautions are required. Be sure to follow your doctor's directions and report any side effects at once.

Possible Side Effects

You may develop rash. Such rashes have been associated with severe, allergic, or sensitivity reactions to Allopurinol. If you develop an unusual rash or other sign of drug toxicity, stop taking this medication and contact your doctor. Less common side effects: nausea, vomiting, diarrhea, intermittent stomach pains, effects on blood components, drowsiness or lack of ability to concentrate, and, rarely, effects on the eyes.

Other uncommon side effects are: loss of hair, fever, chills, arthritis-like symptoms, itching, loosening of the fingernails, pain in the lower back, unexplained nosebleeds; numbness, tingling, or pain in the hands or feet.

Drug Interactions

Avoid taking Allopurinol with iron tablets or vitamins with iron: Allopurinol can cause iron to concentrate in your liver.

Megadoses of Vitamin C may increase the possibility of kidney stone formation.

Interaction with drugs used to treat cancer is important and should be taken into account by your physician.

Allopurinol may interact with anticoagulant (blood-thinning) medication such as Dicoumarol. The importance of this interaction is not yet known.

Food Interactions

Take each dose with a full glass of water and drink 10 to 12 glasses of water, juices, soda, or other liquids each day to avoid the formation of crystals in your urine and/or kidneys.

This drug may be taken with food to reduce upset stomach.

Usual Dose

Adult: 200 to 800 milligrams per day, depending on disease and patient's response.

Child (age 6 to 10): 300 milligrams per day.

Child (under age 6): 150 milligrams per day.

The dose should be reviewed periodically by your doctor to be sure that it is producing the desired therapeutic effect.

Special Information

Allopurinol can make you sleepy or make it difficult for you to concentrate: take care while driving a car or using other equipment or machinery. Call your doctor at once if you develop rash, hives, itching, chills, fever, nausea, muscle aches, unusual tiredness, fever, or yellowing of the eyes or skin.

If you forget to take your regular dose of Allopurinol, take the missed dose as soon as possible. If it is time for your next regular dose, double this dose. For example, if your regular dose is 100 milligrams and you forget to take it, take 200 milligrams at the next usual dose time.

Generic Name

Alprazolam

Brand Name

Xanax

Type of Drug

Tranquilizer.

Prescribed for

Relief of symptoms of anxiety, tension, fatigue, and agitation.

General Information

Alprazolam is a member of the group of drugs known as benzodiazepines. These drugs are used either as antianxiety agents, anticonvulsants, or sedatives (sleeping pills). They exert their effects by relaxing the large skeletal muscles and by a direct effect on the brain. In doing so, they can relax you and make you either more tranquil or sleepier, depending upon which drug you use and how much you take. Many doctors prefer the benzodiazepines to other drugs that can be used for the same effects because benzodiazepines tend to be safer, have fewer side effects, and are usually as, if not more, effective. The benzodiazepines are generally prescribed in any situation where they can be a useful adjunct.

The benzodiazepines, including Alprazolam, can be abused if taken for long periods of time, and it is possible to experience withdrawal symptoms if you stop taking the drug abruptly. Withdrawal symptoms include tremor, muscle cramp, stomach cramps, vomiting, insomnia, and convulsions.

Cautions and Warnings

Do not take Alprazolam if you know you are sensitive or allergic to this drug or other benzodiazepines such as Diazepam, Oxazepam, Chlorazepate, Temazepam, Halazepam, Lorazepam, Prazepam, Flurazepam, and Clonazepam. Alprazolam and other members of this group can aggravate narrow-angle glaucoma, but if you have open-angle glaucoma you may take the drug. In any case, check with your doctor.

Alprazolam can cause tiredness, drowsiness, inability to concentrate, or similar symptoms. Be careful if you are driving, operating machinery, or performing other activities which require concentration.

Pregnancy/Breast-feeding

This drug, like all members of the benzodiazepine family, crosses into your developing baby's circulation and may cause birth defects if taken during the first 3 months of pregnancy. You should avoid taking this medication while pregnant.

Benzodiazepines pass into breast milk. Since infants break the drug down more slowly than adults, it is possible for the medicine to accumulate and have an undesired effect on the baby. Tell your doctor if you become pregnant or are nursing an infant.

Seniors

Older adults are more sensitive to the effects of the drug. They will require less of the drug. Follow your doctor's directions and report any side effects at once.

Possible Side Effects

Most common: mild drowsiness during the first few days of therapy. If drowsiness persists, contact your doctor.

Less common side effects are: confusion, depression, lethargy, disorientation, headache, inactivity, slurred speech, stupor, dizziness, tremor, constipation, dry mouth, nausea, inability to control urination, sexual difficulties, irregular menstrual cycle, changes in heart rhythm, lowered blood pressure, fluid retention, blurred or double vision, itching, rash, hiccups, nervousness, inability to fall asleep, and occasional liver dysfunction. If you experience any of these symptoms, stop taking the medicine and contact your doctor immediately.

Drug Interactions

Alprazolam is a central nervous system depressant. Avoid alcohol, other tranquilizers, narcotics, barbiturates, monoamine oxidase (MAO) inhibitors, antihistamines, and medicine used to relieve depression. Taking Alprazolam with these drugs may result in excessive depression, tiredness, sleepiness, difficulty breathing, or similar symptoms. Smoking may reduce the effectiveness of Alprazolam by increasing the rate at which it is broken down by the body. The effects of Alprazolam may be prolonged when taken together with Cimetidine.

Food Interactions

Alprazolam is best taken on an empty stomach but may be taken with food if it upsets your stomach.

Usual Dose

Adult: 0.75 to 4 milligrams per day.

The dose must be tailored to the individual needs of the patient. Debilitated patients will require less of the drug to control anxiety or tension.

Child: This drug should not be used.

Overdosage

Symptoms are confusion, sleepiness, lack of response to pain such as a pin stick, shallow breathing, lowered blood pressure, and coma. The patient should be taken to a hospital emergency room for treatment. ALWAYS bring the medicine bottle with you.

Special Information

Do not drink alcoholic beverages while taking Alprazolam. Sleeping pills, narcotics, barbiturates, other tranquilizers, or any other drug which produces central nervous depression should be used with caution while taking Alprazolam.

If you forget a dose of Alprazolam, take it as soon as you remember. If it is almost time for your next dose, skip the forgotten pill and continue with your regular schedule. Do not take a double dose of Alprazolam.

Generic Name

Aminophylline

Brand Names

Amoline	Somophyllin-DF
Phyllocontin	Truphylline Suppositories
Somophyllin	

(Also available in generic form)

Type of Drug

Xanthine bronchodilator.

Prescribed for

Relief of bronchial asthma and breathing difficulties associated with emphysema, bronchitis, and other diseases.

General Information

Aminophylline is one of several drugs known as xanthine derivatives which are the mainstay of therapy for bronchial asthma and similar diseases. Other members of this group include Dyphilline, Oxtriphylline, and Theophylline. Although the dosage for each of these drugs is different, they all work by relaxing bronchial muscles and helping reverse spasms in these muscles.

Timed-release products allow Aminophylline to act continuously throughout the day. This permits you to decrease the total number of doses to be taken every day.

Cautions and Warnings

Do not take this medicine if you are allergic or sensitive to it or any other xanthine drug. Aminophylline can aggravate stomach ulcers or heart disease.

Pregnancy/Breast-feeding

Aminophylline passes into the circulation of the developing baby. It does not cause birth defects but may result in dangerous drug levels in the infant's bloodstream. Babies born of mothers taking this medication may be nervous, jittery, and irritable and may gag and vomit when fed. If you must use this medication to control asthma or other conditions, talk with your doctor about the relative risks of using this medication and the benefits it will produce for you.

Aminophylline passes into breast milk and may cause a nursing infant to have difficulty sleeping and be nervous or irritable.

Seniors

Older adults may take longer to clear this drug from their bodies than younger adults. Older adults with heart failure or other cardiac conditions, chronic lung disease, a virus infection with fever, or reduced liver function may require a lower dosage of this medication to account for the clearance effect.

Possible Side Effects

Nausea, vomiting, stomach pain, diarrhea, irritability, restlessness, difficulty sleeping, excitability, muscle twitching or spasms, palpitations, abnormal heart rhythms, changes in heart rate, low blood pressure, rapid breathing, and local irritation (if the suppository is used).

Infrequent: vomiting blood, fever, headache, dehydration.

Drug Interactions

Taking this drug together with another xanthine drug can increase side effects. Don't do it unless your doctor has directed you to.

Theophylline is often taken together with a stimulant like Ephedrine to treat asthma. Such combinations may result in excessive stimulation and should only be used if directed by your doctor.

Erythromycin, flu vaccine, Allopurinol, and Cimetidine will increase the amount of Aminophylline in your blood and increase the chances for drug side effects. Cigarette or marijuana smoking decreases the effectiveness of Aminophylline.

Food Interactions

This drug is best taken on an empty stomach, 1 hour before or 2 hours after meals. It may be taken with food or meals if it upsets your stomach.

Diet can influence the way this drug works in your body. For example, charcoal-broiled beef may increase the amount of Theophylline eliminated from your body through the urine. Low carbohydrate/high protein diets also produce this effect and may reduce Aminophylline's effectiveness.

Caffeine (another xanthine derivative) may add to drug side effects. Avoid large quantities of caffeine-containing foods including coffee, cola beverages, tea, cocoa, and chocolate.

Usual Dose

Aminophylline dosage must be tailored to your specific needs and the severity of your disease. The best dose for you is the lowest dose that will control your symptoms.

Adult: 100 to 200 milligrams every 6 hours.

Child: 50 to 100 milligrams every 6 hours; or 1 to 2.5 milligrams per pound of body weight every 6 hours.

Timed-release products: 1 to 3 times a day, based on your symptoms and response to treatment. Usual dose is 200 to 500 milligrams per day.

Overdosage

The first symptoms are loss of appetite, nausea, vomiting, difficulty sleeping, and restlessness, followed by unusual behavior patterns, frequent vomiting and extreme thirst with delirium, convulsions, and very high temperature. Some overdose victims collapse.

Overdoses of oral tablets or liquid rarely produce serious symptoms. Most often the overdose victim loses his/her appetite and experiences nausea, vomiting, and stimulation. Take the victim to a hospital emergency room at once for treatment. ALWAYS bring the medicine bottle with you.

Special Information

Even though it is necessary to keep a certain amount of Aminophylline in your blood, do not double the dose if you forget to take one. Skip the missed dose and go back to your regular schedule.

Generic Name

Amiodarone

Brand Name

Cordarone

Type of Drug

Antiarrhythmic.

Prescribed for

Abnormal heart rhythms.

General Information

Amiodarone should be prescribed only in situations where the abnormal rhythm is so severe as to be life threatening and does not respond to other drug treatments. Amiodarone works by affecting the movement of nervous impulses within the heart.

Amiodarone may exert its effects 3 to 5 days after you start taking it and often takes 1 to 3 weeks to affect your heart. Since Amiodarone therapy is often started while you are in the hospital, especially if you are being switched from another antiarrhythmic drug to Amiodarone, your doctor will be able to closely monitor how well the drug is working for you. Amiodarone's antiarrhythmic effects can persist for weeks after you stop taking the drug.

Cautions and Warnings

Do not take Amiodarone if you are allergic or sensitive to it or if you have heart block.

Amiodarone can cause potentially fatal drug side effects. At high doses, 10 to 15 percent of people can develop lung and respiratory effects which have the potential of being fatal. Liver damage caused by Amiodarone can also be fatal.

Amiodarone can cause a heart block, a drastic slowing of electrical impulse movement between major areas of the heart, or extreme slowing of the heart rate. Amiodarone heart block occurs about as often as heart block caused by some other Antiarrhythmic drugs, but its effects may last longer than those of the other drugs.

The majority of adults who take Amiodarone develop tiny deposits in the corneas of their eyes. These deposits may cause halos or blurred vision in up to 10 percent of people taking Amiodarone.

Amiodarone can cause a reduction in thyroid activity or worsen an already sluggish thyroid gland in 2 to 10 percent of people taking the drug.

Antiarrhythmic drugs are less effective and cause abnormal rhythms if blood potassium is low. Check with your doctor to see if you need extra potassium.

One-tenth of people taking Amiodarone can experience unusual sensitivity to the sun. Protect yourself by using an appropriate sunscreen product and reapplying it frequently.

Pregnancy/Breast-feeding

Amiodarone has been found to be toxic to a developing fetus in animal studies when given at a dose 18 times the maximum adult dose. Pregnant women should carefully review the benefits to be obtained by taking this drug, and the potential dangers, with their doctors.

Amiodarone passes into mother's milk. Nursing mothers who must take this drug should use bottle-feeding to avoid any possible complications in their babies.

Seniors

Amiodarone must be used with caution, regardless of your age. This drug is broken down in the liver and a reduced dosage may be needed if you have poor liver function. Kidney function is not a factor in determining how much Amiodarone you need.

Possible Side Effects

About 75 percent of people taking 400 milligrams or more of Amiodarone every day develop drug side effects. As many as 10 percent of people have to stop taking the drug because of a side effect.

Common side effects include fatigue, a feeling of ill health, tremors, unusual involuntary movements, loss of coordination, an unusual walk, muscle weakness, dizziness, tingling in the hands or feet, reduced sex drive, sleeplessness or difficulty sleeping, headache, nervous system problems, nausea, vomiting, constipation, loss of appetite, abdominal pains, unusual sensitivity to bright light, dry eyes, halos.

Unusual sensitivity to the sun is the most common skin reaction to Amiodarone, but people taking this drug may develop a blue skin discoloration that may not go away completely when the drug is stopped. Other skin reactions are sun rashes, hair loss, and black-and-blue spots.

Amiodarone can cause heart failure, slowing of the heart rate, and abnormal rhythms. Up to 9 percent of people taking Amiodarone develop abnormalities in liver function.

Other side effects include inflammation of the lung or fibrous deposits in the lungs, changes in thyroid function, changes in taste or smell, bloating, unusual salivation, changes in blood clotting.

Drug Interactions

Amiodarone increases the effects of Procainamide, Quinidine, Phenytoin, and Warfarin. These interactions can take from 3 days to several weeks to develop, but the dosage of these drugs must be reduced drastically to take the interaction into account.

Amiodarone can interact with beta blockers and calcium channel blockers to cause unusual slowing of the heart.

Food Interactions

Amiodarone is poorly absorbed into the blood and should be taken on an empty stomach. It can be taken with food or meals if it upsets your stomach. Food delays the absorption of Amiodarone into your bloodstream.

Usual Dose

The usual starting dose is 800 to 1,600 milligrams per day, taken in 1 or 2 doses. Your dosage should be reduced to the lowest effective dose to minimize side effects. The usual maintenance dose is 400 milligrams per day.

Overdosage

Three people have been reported as having taken an Amiodarone overdose. None died because the drug usually takes several days or weeks to exert an effect on the body. All were effectively treated at a hospital emergency room.

Anyone who has taken an overdose of Amiodarone should be taken to a hospital emergency room for treatment. ALWAYS remember to take the medicine bottle with you.

Special Information

Side effects are very common with Amiodarone. Three-fourths of people taking the drug will experience some drug-related problem. Call your doctor if you develop chest pains, difficulty breathing, or any other sign of changes in lung function, an abnormal heartbeat, bloating in your feet or legs, tremors, fever, chills, sore throat, unusual bleeding or bruising, changes in skin color, unusual sunburn, or any other unusual side effect.

Amiodarone can make you dizzy or light-headed. Take care while driving a car or performing any complex tasks.

If you take Amiodarone once a day and forget to take a dose, but remember within 12 hours, take it as soon as possible. If you don't remember until later, skip the forgotten dose and continue with your regular schedule. If you take Amiodarone twice a day and remember within 6 hours of your regular dose, take it as soon as you remember. Call your doctor if you forget 2 or more doses in a row. Do not take a double dose of Amiodarone.

Generic Name

Amitriptyline

Brand Names

Amitril	Emitrip
Elavil	Endep

(Also available in generic form)

Type of Drug

Antidepressant.

Prescribed for

Depression with or without symptoms of anxiety.

General Information

Amitriptyline and other members of this group are effective in treating symptoms of depression. They can elevate mood, increase physical activity and mental alertness, improve appetite and sleep patterns in a depressed patient. These drugs are mild sedatives and therefore useful in treating mild forms of depression associated with anxiety. You should not expect instant results with this medicine: results are usually seen after 2 to 4 weeks. If symptoms are not affected after 6 to 8 weeks, contact your doctor. Occasionally this drug and other members of the group of drugs have been used in treating nighttime bed-wetting in young children, but they do not produce long-lasting relief and therapy with one of them for nighttime bed-wetting is of questionable value.

Cautions and Warnings

Do not take Amitriptyline if you are allergic or sensitive to this or other members of this class of drug: Doxepin, Nortriptyline, Imipramine, Desipramine, and Protriptyline. The drugs should not be used if you are recovering from a heart attack. Amitriptyline may be taken with caution if you have a history of epilepsy or other convulsive disorders, difficulty in urination, glaucoma, heart disease, or thyroid disease. Amitriptyline can interfere with your ability to perform tasks which require concentration, such as driving or operating machinery. Do not stop taking this medicine without first discussing it with your doctor, since stopping may cause you to become nauseated, weak, and headachy.

Pregnancy/Breast-feeding

This drug, like other antidepressants, crosses into your developing baby's circulation and may cause birth defects if taken during the first 3 months of pregnancy. There have been reports of newborn infants suffering from heart, breathing, and urinary problems after their mothers had taken an antidepressant of this type immediately before delivery. You should avoid taking this medication while pregnant.

Antidepressants of this type are known to pass into breast milk and may affect a breast-feeding infant, although this has not been proven. Nursing mothers should consider alternate feeding methods if taking this medicine.

Seniors

Older adults are more sensitive to the effects of this drug and often require a lower dose than a younger adult to do the same job. Follow your doctor's directions and report any side effects at once.

Possible Side Effects

Changes in blood pressure (both high and low), abnormal heart rates, heart attack, confusion, especially in elderly patients, hallucinations, disorientation, delusions, anxiety, restlessness, excitement, numbness and tingling in the extremities, lack of coordination, muscle spasms or tremors, seizures and/or convulsions, dry mouth, blurred vision, constipation, inability to urinate, rash, itching, sensitivity to bright light or sunlight, retention of fluids, fever, allergy, changes in composition of blood, nausea, vomiting, loss of appetite, stomach upset, diarrhea, enlargement of the breasts in males and females, increased or decreased sex drive, increased or decreased blood sugar.

Less common side effects: agitation, inability to sleep, nightmares, feeling of panic, a peculiar taste in the mouth, stomach cramps, black coloration of the tongue, yellowing eyes and/or skin, changes in liver function, increased or decreased weight, excessive perspiration, flushing, frequent urination, drowsiness, dizziness, weakness, headache, loss of hair, nausea, not feeling well.

Drug Interactions

Interaction with monoamine oxidase (MAO) inhibitors can cause high fevers, convulsions, and occasionally death. Don't take MAO inhibitors until at least 2 weeks after Amitriptyline has been discontinued.

In patients who require concomitant use of Amitriptyline and an MAO inhibitor, close medical observation is warranted.

Amitriptyline interacts with Guanethidine and Clonidine, drugs used to treat high blood pressure: if your doctor prescribes Amitriptyline and you are taking medicine for high blood pressure, be sure to discuss this with him.

Amitriptyline increases the effects of barbiturates, tranquil-izers, other sedative drugs, and alcohol. Don't drink alcoholic beverages if you take this medicine.

Taking Amitriptyline and thyroid medicine will enhance the effects of the thyroid medicine. The combination can cause abnormal heart rhythms. The combination of Amitrip-tyline and Reserpine may cause overstimulation.

Large doses of Vitamin C (Ascorbic Acid), oral contracep-tives, or smoking can reduce the effect of Amitriptyline. Drugs such as Bicarbonate of Soda, Acetazolamide, Quini-dine, or Procainamide will increase the effect of Amitripty-line. Ritalin and phenothiazine drugs such as Thorazine and Compazine block the metabolism of Amitriptyline, causing it to stay in the body longer. This can cause possible overdose.

The combination of Amitriptyline with large doses of the sleeping pill Etchlorvynol has caused patients to experi-ence passing delirium.

Food Interactions

Take this drug on an empty stomach. If it upsets your stom-ach you may take it with food.

Usual Dose

Adult: 25 milligrams 3 times per day, which may be in-creased to 150 milligrams per day if necessary. The medica-tion must be tailored to the needs of the patient.

Adolescent and senior: lower doses are recommended—generally, 30 to 50 milligrams per day.

Overdosage

Symptoms are confusion, inability to concentrate, hallucina-tions, drowsiness, lowered body temperature, abnormal heart rate, heart failure, enlarged pupils of the eyes, convulsions, severely lowered blood pressure, stupor, and coma (as well as agitation, stiffening of body muscles, vomiting, and high fever). The patient should be taken to a hospital emergency room immediately. ALWAYS bring the medicine bottle.

Special Information

Avoid alcohol and other drugs that depress the nervous system while taking this antidepressant. Do not stop taking this medicine unless your doctor has specifically told you to do so. Abruptly stopping this medicine may cause nausea, headache, and a sickly feeling. This medicine can cause drowsiness, dizziness, and blurred vision. Be careful when driving or operating complicated machinery. Avoid exposure to the sun or sun lamps for long periods of time. Call your doctor if dry mouth, difficulty urinating, or excessive sedation develops.

Do not double the dose if you forget to take one. Skip it and go back to you regular schedule.

Generic Name

Amoxapine

Brand Name

Asendin

Type of Drug

Antidepressant.

Prescribed for

Depression with or without symptoms of anxiety.

General Information

Amoxapine and other members of this group are effective in treating symptoms of depression. They can elevate mood, increase physical activity and mental alertness, improve appetite and sleep patterns in a depressed patient. These drugs are mild sedatives and therefore useful in treating mild forms of depression associated with anxiety. You should not expect instant results with this medicine: results are usually seen after 1 to 4 weeks. If symptoms are not affected after 6 to 8 weeks, contact your doctor. Occasionally this drug and other members of the group of drugs have been used in treating nighttime bed-wetting in young children, but they do not produce long-lasting relief, and therapy with one of them for nighttime bed-wetting is of questionable value.

Cautions and Warnings

Do not take Amoxapine if you are allergic or sensitive to this or other members of this class of drug: Doxepin, Nortriptyline, Imipramine, Desipramine, and Amitriptyline. The drugs should not be used if you are recovering from a heart attack. Amoxapine may be taken with caution if you have a history of epilepsy or other convulsive disorders, difficulty in urination, glaucoma, heart disease, or thyroid disease. Amoxapine can interfere with your ability to perform tasks which require concentration, such as driving or operating machinery.

Pregnancy/Breast-feeding

This drug, like other antidepressants, crosses into your developing baby's circulation and may cause birth defects if taken during the first 3 months of pregnancy. There have been reports of newborn infants suffering from heart, breathing, and urinary problems after their mothers had taken an antidepressant of this type immediately before delivery. You should avoid taking this medication while pregnant.

Antidepressants of this type are known to pass into breast milk and may affect a breast-feeding infant, although this has not been proven. Nursing mothers should consider alternate feeding methods if taking this medicine.

Seniors

Older adults are more sensitive to the effects of this drug and often require a lower dose than a younger adult to do the same job. Follow your doctor's directions and report any side effects at once.

Possible Side Effects

Changes in blood pressure (both high and low), abnormal heart rates, heart attack, confusion (especially in elderly patients), hallucinations, disorientation, delusions, anxiety, restlessness, excitement, numbness and tingling in the extremities, lack of coordination, muscle spasms or tremors, seizures and/or convulsions, dry mouth, blurred vision, constipation, inability to urinate, rash, itching, sensitivity to bright light or sunlight, retention of fluids, fever, allergy, changes in composition of blood, nausea, vomiting, loss of appetite, stomach upset, diarrhea, enlargement of the breasts in males and females, increased or decreased sex drive, increased or decreased blood sugar.

Less common side effects: agitation, inability to sleep, nightmares, feeling of panic, a peculiar taste in the mouth,

stomach cramps, black coloration of the tongue, yellowing
eyes and/or skin, changes in liver function, increased or
decreased weight, perspiration, flushing, frequent urination,
drowsiness, dizziness, weakness, headache, loss of hair, nausea, not feeling well.

Drug Interactions

Interaction with monoamine oxidase (MAO) inhibitors can
cause high fevers, convulsions, and occasionally death. Don't
take MAO inhibitors until at least 2 weeks after Amoxapine
has been discontinued.

Certain patients may require concomitant use of Amoxapine
and an MAO inhibitor, and in these situations close medical
observation is warranted.

Amoxapine interacts with Guanethidine, a drug used to
treat high blood pressure: if your doctor prescribes Amoxapine
and you are taking medicine for high blood pressure, be
sure to discuss this with him.

Amoxapine increases the effects of barbiturates, tranquilizers, other depressive drugs, and alcohol. Don't drink alcoholic beverages if you take this medicine.

Taking Amoxapine and thyroid medicine will enhance the
effects of the thyroid medicine. The combination can cause
abnormal heart rhythms.

Large doses of Vitamin C (Ascorbic Acid) can reduce the
effect of Amoxapine. Drugs such as Bicarbonate of Soda or
Acetazolamide will increase the effect of Amoxapine.

Food Interactions

This drug is best taken on an empty stomach, but can be
taken with food if it upsets your stomach.

Usual Dose

Adult: 100 to 400 milligrams per day. Hospitalized patients
may need up to 600 milligrams per day. The dose of this
drug must be tailored to patient's need.

Senior: lower doses are recommended; for people over
60 years of age, usually 50 to 300 milligrams per day.

Child (under age 16): this drug should not be used.

Overdosage

Symptoms are confusion, inability to concentrate, hallucinations, drowsiness, lowered body temperature, abnormal heart rate, heart failure, large pupils of the eyes, convulsions, severely lowered blood pressure, stupor, and coma (as well as agitation, stiffening of body muscles, vomiting, and high fever). The patient should be taken to a hospital emergency room immediately. ALWAYS bring the medicine bottle.

Special Information

Avoid alcohol and other drugs that depress the nervous system while taking this antidepressant.

Do not stop taking this medicine unless your doctor has specifically told you to do so. Abruptly stopping this medicine may cause nausea, headache, and a sickly feeling.

This medicine can cause drowsiness, dizziness, and blurred vision. Be careful when driving or operating complicated machinery.

Avoid exposure to the sun or sun lamps for long periods of time. Call your doctor if dry mouth, difficulty urinating, or excessive sedation develops.

If you forget to take a dose of Amoxapine, take it as soon as you remember. If it is almost time for your next dose, skip the forgotten dose and continue with your regular schedule. Do not take a double dose of Amoxapine.

Generic Name

Amoxicillin

Brand Names

Amoxil	Trimox
Larotid	Utimox
Polymox	Wymox

(Also available in generic form)

Type of Drug

Penicillin-type antibiotic.

Prescribed for

Gram-positive bacterial infections. Gram-positive bacteria (pneumococci, streptococci, and staphylococci) are organisms which usually cause diseases such as pneumonia, infections of the tonsils and throat, venereal disease, meningitis (infection of the spinal column), and septicemia (general infection of the bloodstream).

Infections of the urinary tract and some infections of the gastrointestinal tract can also be treated with Amoxicillin.

General Information

Penicillin-type antibiotics fight infection by killing bacteria. They do this by destroying the cell wall of invading bacteria. Other antibiotics simply prevent bacteria from reproducing. Many infections can be treated by almost any member of this family, but some infections can only be treated by certain penicillin-type antibiotics.

Penicillins cannot treat against a cold, flu, or any virus infection and should never be taken unless prescribed by a doctor for a specific illness. Always take your antibiotic exactly according to your doctor's directions for use, including the number of pills to take every day and the number of days to take the medicine. If you do not follow directions, you may not get the antibiotic's full benefit.

Cautions and Warnings

Do not take Amoxicillin if you have a known history of allergy to penicillin. The drugs are very similar. The most common allergic reaction to Amoxicillin and the other penicillins is a hive-like rash over the body with itching and redness. It is important to tell your doctor if you have ever taken this drug or penicillins before and if you have experienced any adverse reaction to the drug such as rash, itching, or difficulty in breathing.

Pregnancy/Breast-feeding

This drug has not caused birth defects. Nevertheless, you should be sure your doctor knows you are, or might be, pregnant.

Amoxicillin passes into breast milk and may cause problems in breast-fed infants, such as allergy reactions, fungal infections, skin rashes, or diarrhea. Therefore, it is not recommended for nursing mothers.

Seniors

Seniors may take this medicine without special concern.

Possible Side Effects

Common: stomach upset, nausea, vomiting, diarrhea, and possible rash. Less common: hairy tongue, itching or irritation around the anus and/or vagina. If these symptoms occur, you should contact your doctor immediately.

Drug Interactions

The effect of Amoxicillin can be significantly reduced when it is taken with other antibiotics. Consult your doctor if you are taking both. Otherwise, Amoxicillin is generally free of interaction with other medications.

Food Interactions

Amoxicillin may be taken with food or meals if it upsets your stomach.

Usual Dose

Tablet and capsule:
Adult: 250 milligrams every 8 hours.
Child: 9 to 18 milligrams per pound of body weight per day in 3 divided doses (every 8 hours).
Pediatric drops:
Child (under 3 pounds): 1 milliliter every 8 hours. Dose may be halved for less serious infections or doubled for severe infections.

Overdosage

Overdosage with this drug is unlikely but may result in diarrhea or upset stomach.

Special Information

Do not take this medicine after the expiration date on the label. Be sure to take this medicine exactly according to your doctor's directions.

Stop taking the medicine and call your doctor if any of the following side effects develop: skin rash, hives, itching, wheezing. Other side effects that demand your doctor's attention are: blood in the urine, passage of large amounts of light-colored urine, swelling of the face or ankles, trouble breathing, unusual weakness or tiredness.

Amoxicillin tablets or capsules can be stored at room temperature. The liquid should be refrigerated and shaken well before each use.

If you miss a dose of Amoxicillin, space the dose you forgot and your next regular dose 4 hours apart or take a double dose at your next regular time. Then go back to your regular schedule.

Generic Name

Ampicillin

Brand Names

Amcill	Polycillin
D-Amp	Principen
Omnipen	Totacillin

(Also available in generic form)

Type of Drug

Penicillin-type antibiotic.

Prescribed for

Gram-positive bacterial infections. Gram-positive bacteria (pneumococci, streptococci, and staphylococci) are organisms which usually cause diseases such as pneumonia, infections of the tonsils and throat, venereal disease, meningitis (infection of the spinal column), and septicemia (general infection of the bloodstream).

Infections of the urinary tract and some infections of the gastrointestinal tract can also be treated with Ampicillin.

General Information

Penicillin-type antibiotics fight infection by killing bacteria. They do this by destroying the cell wall of invading bacteria. Other antibiotics simply prevent bacteria from reproducing. Many infections can be treated by almost any member of this family, but some infections can only be treated by certain penicillin-type antibiotics.

Penicillins cannot treat against a cold, flu, or any virus infection and should never be taken unless prescribed by a doctor for a specific illness. Always take your antibiotic exactly according to your doctor's directions for use, including the number of pills to take every day and the number of days to take the medicine. If you do not follow directions, you may not get the antibiotic's full benefit.

Cautions and Warnings

Do not take Ampicillin if you have a known history of allergy to penicillin. The drugs are very similar. The most common allergic reaction to Ampicillin, as well as to the other penicillins, is a hivelike rash over the body with itching and redness. It is important to tell your doctor if you have ever taken this drug or penicillins before and if you have experienced any adverse reaction to the drug such as skin rash, itching, or difficulty in breathing.

Pregnancy/Breast-feeding

This drug has not caused birth defects. Nevertheless, you should be sure your doctor knows you are, or might be, pregnant.

Ampicillin passes into breast milk and may cause problems in breast-fed infants, such as allergy reactions, fungal infections, skin rashes, or diarrhea. Therefore the drug is not recommended for nursing mothers.

Seniors

Seniors may take this medicine without special concern.

Possible Side Effects

Common: stomach upset, nausea, vomiting, diarrhea, and possible rash. Less common: itching or irritation around the anus and/or vagina. If these symptoms occur, you should contact your doctor immediately.

Drug Interactions

The effect of Ampicillin can be significantly reduced when taken with other antibiotics. Consult your doctor if you are

taking both. Otherwise, Ampicillin is generally free of interaction with other medications.

Food Interactions

To ensure the maximum effect of this drug, you should take
the medication on an empty stomach, either 1 hour before
or 2 hours after meals. However, it may be taken with small
amounts of food if it upsets your stomach.

Usual Dose

Adult and child (44 pounds and over): 250 to 500 milligrams every 6 hours.

Child (under 44 pounds): 25 to 50 milligrams per pound per
day.

Overdosage

Ampicillin overdosage is unlikely but can result in diarrhea
or upset stomach.

Special Information

Do not take this medicine after the expiration date on the
label. Be sure to take this medicine exactly according to your
doctor's directions.

Stop taking the medicine and call your doctor if any of the
following side effects develop: skin rash, hives, itching, wheezing. Other side effects that demand your doctor's attention
are: blood in the urine, passage of large amounts of light-
colored urine, swelling of the face or ankles, trouble breathing, unusual weakness or tiredness.

Ampicillin capsules can be stored at room temperature.
The liquid should be refrigerated and shaken well before
each use.

If you forget a dose of Ampicillin, space the dose you
forgot and your next dose 2 to 4 hours apart or take a double
dose at your next regular time. Then go back to your regular
schedule.

Type of Drug

Antacids

Brand Names

Aluminum Antacids

AlternaGel	Basaljel
Aluminum Hydroxide Gel	Dialume
Alu-Cap	Nephrox
Alu-Tab	Phosphaljel
Amphojel	Rolaids

Calcium Antacids

Alka-Mints	Genalac
Amitone	Glycate
Calcilac	Mallamint
Calcium Carbonate	Pama
Calglycine	Titracid
Chooz	Titralac
Dicarbosil	Tums
Equilet	Tums Extra Strength

Magnesium Antacids

Magnesium Carbonate	Maox
Magnesium Oxide	Milk of Magnesia
Magnesium Trisilicate	Par-Mag
Mag-Ox 400	Uro-Mag

Sodium Bicarbonate Antacids

Bell/ans
Soda Mint
Sodium Bicarbonate

Aluminum + Magnesium Antacids

Alamag	Maalox TC
Algemol	Magmalin
Algenic Alka	Magnagel
Algicon	Magnatril
Aludrox	Mintox
Alumid	Neutracomp
Creamalin	Noralac
Delcid	Remegel Squares
Escot	Riopan
Estomul-M	Rolox
Gelamal	Rulox
Kolantyl	TC Suspension
Kudrox	Tralmag
Lowsium	Triconsil
Maalox	WinGel

Aluminum + Magnesium + Sodium Antacids

Algenic Alka	Parviscon
Gaviscon	Triconsil

Calcium + Magnesium Antacids

Alkets	Marblen
Bisodol	Ratio
Lo-Sol	Spastosed

Calcium + Magnesium + Simethicone Antacids

Advanced Formula Di-Gel

Aluminum + Calcium + Magnesium Antacids

Camalox
Duracid

Aluminum + Magnesium + Simethicone (an antigas ingredient) Antacids

Almacone	Maalox Plus
Alma-Mag	Mintox Plus
Alumid Plus	Mi-Acid
Antagel	Mygel
Di-Gel	Mylanta
Gelusil	Mylanta II
Gelusil II	Riopan Plus
Gelusil-M	Silain Gel
Improved Alma-Mag	Simaal
Losotron Plus Liquid	Simeco
Lowsium Plus	

Aluminum + Magnesium + Calcium + Simethicone Antacid

Tempo

Effervescent Powder or Tablet Antacids

Alka-Seltzer	Citrocarbonate
Alka-Seltzer with Aspirin	ENO
Bisodol Powder	Flavored Alka-Seltzer
Bromo Seltzer	

(Also available in generic form)

Type of Drug

Gastrointestinal acid antagonist.

Prescribed for

Relief of heartburn, acid indigestion, sour stomach, or other conditions related to an upset stomach. These drugs are also prescribed for excess acid in the stomach or intestine associated with ulcer, gastritis, esophagitis, and hiatal hernia. Antacid therapy will help these conditions to heal more quickly. Aluminum antacids are prescribed for kidney failure patients to prevent phosphate from being absorbed into the body. Only Aluminum Hydroxide Gel (any brand) and Basaljel have been shown to be useful as phosphate binders.

General Information

In spite of the large number of antacid products available on the market, there are basically only a few different kinds. All antacids work against stomach acid in the same way—by neutralizing the acid through a chemical reaction. The choice of an antacid is based upon its "neutralizing capacity," that is, how much acid is neutralized by a given amount of antacid. Sodium and calcium have the greatest capacity but should not be used for long-term or ulcer therapy because of the effects large amounts of sodium and calcium can have on your body. Of the other products, Magnesium Hydroxide has the greatest capacity. Next come mixtures of magnesium and aluminum compounds, Magnesium Trisilicate, Aluminum Hydroxide, and Aluminum Phosphates, in that order. The neutralizing capacity of an antacid product also depends upon how it is formulated, how much antacid is put in the mixture, and what the form of the mixture is. Antacid suspensions have greater neutralizing capacity than powders or tablets. Antacid tablets should be thoroughly chewed before they are swallowed.

In most cases, the choice of an antacid product is based purely upon advertising, packaging, convenience, taste, or price. The similarity among so many products accounts for the vast amounts of advertising and promotion put behind antacid products.

Calcium antacids have been recommended as a source of supplemental calcium to prevent osteoporosis. Four to six tablets a day are needed to provide the proper amount of calcium. Although Tums has been widely recommended, any product listed in the section **Calcium Antacids** will do the job.

Cautions and Warnings

People with high blood pressure or heart failure, and those on low-sodium diets, must avoid antacids with a high sodium content. Many antacids are considered to be low in sodium, with Riopan having the lowest sodium content of all antacids. Your pharmacist can advise you which of these drugs are considered low-sodium antacids.

Sodium Bicarbonate is easily absorbed and may result in a condition called systemic alkalosis if it is taken for a long period of time. Magnesium antacids must be used with caution by patients with kidney disease.

Pregnancy/Breast-feeding

Antacids can be safely taken in moderation during pregnancy. Be sure your doctor knows you are taking antacids.
Antacids may be taken during breast-feeding.

Seniors

Seniors can safely use antacids without concern. Do not use excessive amounts of antacid unless so directed by your doctor.

Possible Side Effects

Diarrhea (magnesium products); constipation (aluminum and calcium products). Aluminum/magnesium combinations are usually used to avoid affecting the bowel.
Kidney failure patients who take magnesium antacids may develop magnesium toxicity.
Calcium and sodium antacids may cause a rebound effect, with no more acid produced after the antacid is stopped than before it was started.
Magnesium Trisilicate antacids used over long periods may result in the development of silicate renal stones.

Drug Interactions

Antacids can interfere with the absorption of most drugs into the body. Intake of antacids should be separated from that of other oral drugs by 1 to 2 hours. Those drugs with which antacids are known to interfere are anticholinergic drugs, phenothiazines, Digoxin, Phenytoin, Isoniazid, Quinidine, Warfarin, iron-containing products, and tetracycline-type antibiotics.

Food Interactions

Antacids are best taken on an empty stomach but may be taken with food.

Usual Dose

The dose of antacids must be individualized to your requirement. For ulcers, antacids are given every hour for the first 2

weeks (during waking hours) and 1 to 3 hours after meals
and at bedtime thereafter.

Special Information

If you are using antacid tablets, be sure they are completely
chewed. Swallow with milk or water.

Aluminum antacids may cause speckling or add a whitish
coloration to the stool.

Severe stomach or abdominal pain, cramps, and nausea
may be a sign of appendicitis, and cannot be treated with an
antacid.

Type of Drug

Antihistamine–Decongestant Combination Products

Brand Names

Ingredients: Azatadine + Pseudoephedrine

Trinalin

Ingredients: Brompheniramine + Phenylpropanolamine

Bromatapp
Dimetapp Extentabs

Ingredients: Chlorpheniramine + Pseudoephedrine

Anafed	Isoclor
Anamine TD	Klerist D
Brexin LA	Kronofed A
Chlorafed	Napril
Chlor-Trimeton Decongestant	ND Clear
Co-Pyronil 2	Novafed A
Dallergy-D	Pseudo-Chlor
Deconamine SR	Pseudo-Hist
Duralex	Pseudo-Hist Timed Release
Dura-Tap/PD	Sudafed Plus
Fedahist	

Ingredients: Chlorpheniramine + Phenylephrine

Alersole	Histaspan Plus
Demazin	Neotapp Granucaps
Dristan 12 Hour	Sto-Caps Plus

Ingredients: Chlorpheniramine + Phenylpropanolamine

Allerest 12 Hour	Gencold
Condrin L.A.	Histabid
Conex D.A.	Oragest
Contac 12 Hour Caplets	Orahist
Contac Perma Seal	Oraminic
Deconade	Resaid S.R.
Dehist	Rhinolar-EX 12
Demazin Repetabs	Ru-Tuss II
Drize	Supes Capsules
Dura Vent/A	Triaminic-12

Ingredients: Clemastine + Phenylpropanolamine

Tavist-D

Ingredients: Pseudoephedrine + Triprolidine

Actacin	Genac
Actagen	Myfed
Actifed	Norafed
Actihist	Trifed
Allerfrin OTC	Triphed
Aprodine	Tripodrine
Cenafed Plus	Triposed

(Also available in generic form)

Prescribed for

These products are prescribed to relieve symptoms of the common cold, allergy, or other upper respiratory condition, including sneezing, watery eyes, runny nose, itching or scratchy throat, and nasal congestion.

General Information

These products are among the hundreds of different cold and allergy remedies available on both a prescription-only and non-prescription basis. The basic formula that appears in each of these is always the same: an antihistamine to relieve allergy symptoms and a decongestant to treat the symptoms of either a cold or allergy.

Most of these products are taken several times a day, while others are taken once or twice a day because of their natural long-acting effect or the fact that they have been put into a special long-acting dosage form. Since nothing can cure a cold or allergy, the best you can hope to achieve from this or any other cold and allergy remedy is simply symptom relief.

Cautions and Warnings

The antihistamines (listed first in each formula) in these products can cause drowsiness. Clemastine, the antihistamine ingredient in Tavist-D, is distinguishable from other products because it causes less drowsiness. The decongestant ingredient (listed second in each formula) can cause you to become overly anxious and nervous and may interfere with sleep.

Pregnancy/Breast-feeding

The ingredients in these products have not been proven to be a cause of birth defects or other problems in pregnant women, although studies in animals have shown that some antihistamines, used mainly against nausea and vomiting, may cause birth defects. Do not take any of these products without your doctor's knowledge.

Small amounts of antihistamine or decongestant medicines pass into breast milk and may affect a nursing infant. Nursing mothers should either not take this medicine or use alternative feeding methods while taking it.

Seniors

Seniors are more sensitive to the side effects of these medications. Confusion, difficult or painful urination, dizziness, drowsiness, a faint feeling, dry mouth, nose, or throat, nightmares or excitement, nervousness, restlessness, or irritability are more likely to occur among older adults.

Possible Side Effects

Restlessness, sleeplessness, excitation, nervousness, drowsiness, sedation, dizziness, poor coordination, upset stomach.

Less common: low blood pressure, heart palpitations, chest pain, rapid heart beat and abnormal heart rhythm, anemia, fatigue, confusion, tremors, headache, irritability, a "high" feeling, tingling or heaviness in the hands, tingling in the feet or legs, blurred or double vision, convulsions, hysterical reactions, ringing or buzzing in the ears, fainting, changes in appetite (increase or decrease), nausea, vomiting, diarrhea or constipation, frequent urination, difficulty urinating, early periods, loss of sex drive, difficulty breathing, wheezing with chest tightness, stuffed nose, dry mouth, nose, or throat, itching, rashes, unusual sensitivity to the sun, chills, excessive perspiration.

Drug Interactions

Interaction with alcoholic beverages, tranquilizers, antianxiety drugs, and narcotic-type pain relievers may lead to excessive drowsiness or difficulty concentrating.

These products should be avoided if you are taking a monoamine oxidase (MAO) inhibitor for depression or high blood pressure, because the MAO inhibitor may cause a very rapid rise in blood pressure or increase some side effects (dry mouth and nose, blurred vision, abnormal heart rhythms).

The decongestant portion of these products may interfere with the normal effects of blood-pressure-lowering medicines and can aggravate diabetes, heart disease, hyperthyroid disease, high blood pressure, a prostate condition, stomach ulcers, and urinary blockage.

Food Interactions

These drugs are best taken on an empty stomach but may be taken with food if they upset your stomach.

Usual Dose

One tablet or capsule every 4 to 12 hours, depending on the product.

Overdosage

The main symptoms of overdose are drowsiness, chills, dry mouth, fever, nausea, nervousness, irritability, rapid or irregular heartbeat, heart pains, and urinary difficulty. Most cases of overdose are not severe, but should be treated by inducing vomiting and then taking the victim to a hospital emergency room. ALWAYS bring the medicine container with you. Call your local Poison Control Center for more information.

Special Information

Since the antihistamine component of these medicines can slow your central nervous system, you must take extra caution while doing anything that requires concentration, such as driving a car.

Call your doctor if your side effects are severe or gradually become intolerable. There are so many different cold and allergy products available to choose from that one is sure to be the right combination for you.

If you forget to take a dose of your medicine, take it as soon as you remember. If it is almost time for your next dose, skip the one you forgot and go back to your regular schedule. Do not take a double dose.

Brand Name

Apresazide

Ingredients

Hydralazine
Hydrochlorothiazide

Other Brand Names

Apresodex	Hydralazide
Apresoline-Esidrix	Hydra-Zide
Hydral	Hydrazide

(Also available in generic form)

Type of Drug

Antihypertensive combination.

Prescribed for

High blood pressure.

General Information

This is a combination of two drugs used for the treatment of
high blood pressure. Together, they are more effective than
either drug taken alone. Since many people take the individual ingredients for high blood pressure, the combination
may be a more convenient way to take their medicine.

This is a good example of a drug that takes advantage of a
drug interaction. Both of the drugs work by different mechanisms to lower blood pressure. Hydrochlorothiazide is a diuretic which works through its effects on muscles in the
walls of the blood vessels and its effect on lowering fluid
levels in the body. Hydralazine works by affecting the muscles in the walls of the arteries and lowers blood pressure by
dilating, or widening, these blood vessels.

Cautions and Warnings

Do not take Apresazide if you are allergic to either of the
ingredients or to sulfa drugs. It should not be used if you
have certain kinds of heart disease, including rheumatic heart,
or severe kidney disease. It must be used with care in patients who have severe liver disease.

This drug, in a few patients, may produce symptoms of a
serious disease called lupus erythematosus. The symptoms
are aching muscles and joints, skin rash and other complications, fever, anemia, and spleen enlargement. If these occur,
the drug must be stopped immediately. Sudden changes in
position can result in dizziness.

Pregnancy/Breast-feeding

Apresazide must be used with caution by women who
are pregnant or breast-feeding, and only when absolutely
necessary.

This drug may cause birth defects or interfere with your
baby's development. Check with your doctor before taking it
if you are, or might be, pregnant.

Seniors

Be sure to follow your doctor's directions while taking this
product and report anything unusual, especially during the
first few months of treatment.

Possible Side Effects

One of the ingredients in this drug can cause the lowering of potassium levels in the body. Signs of this are dryness of the mouth, thirst, weakness, lethargy, drowsiness, restlessness, muscle pains or cramps, muscle tiredness, low blood pressure, decreased frequency of urination, abnormal heart rate, and stomach upset, including nausea and vomiting. To prevent this, potassium supplements are given in the form of tablets, liquid, or powders, or by increasing consumption of high-potassium foods such as bananas, citrus fruits, melons, and tomatoes. This drug can also cause loss of appetite, diarrhea, rapid heartbeat, and chest pain.

Less common side effects are: stuffy nose, flushing, tearing, itching, and redness of the eyes, numbness and tingling in the hands or feet, dizziness, tremors, muscle cramps, depression, disorientation, anxiety. The drug can also cause nausea, vomiting, cramps and diarrhea, constipation, dizziness, headache, tingling in the arms, hands, legs, or toes, changes in blood composition, sensitivity to the sun, rash, itching, fever, drug allergy, difficulty in breathing, blurred vision, weakness, and dizziness when rising from a sitting or lying position.

Drug Interactions

This combination should be used with caution by people taking a monoamine oxidase (MAO) inhibitor drug.

The possibility of developing imbalances in body fluids is increased if you take medicines like the digitalis drugs or adrenal corticosteroids with Apresazide. This problem can be avoided by periodic laboratory monitoring of the blood.

One of the ingredients in Apresazide will affect oral antidiabetic drugs. If you are already taking an oral drug for diabetes and start taking Apresazide, your dose of diabetes medicine may have to be changed.

Lithium drugs should be monitored closely if given together with Apresazide because of the increased possibility of Lithium toxicity.

Food Interactions

Apresazide may antagonize Vitamin B_6, pyridoxine, which can result in peripheral neuropathy including tremors and tingling and numbness of the fingers, toes, or other extremities. If these occur, your doctor may advise you to take a vitamin containing Vitamin B_6.

This drug may be taken with meals if it causes upset stomach; in fact, food increases the amount of Hydralazine absorbed into the bloodstream.

Usual Dose

1 to 2 tablets per day. The exact dose must be tailored to your needs. This drug comes in several different combinations of dosage strengths.

Overdosage

Symptoms: very low blood pressure, rapid heartbeat, headache, flushing of the skin, chest pain, abnormal heart rhythms, fatigue, and coma may develop. In case of an overdose take the patient to a hospital emergency room immediately. ALWAYS bring the medicine bottle.

Special Information

Always take your medicine exactly as directed.

Avoid over-the-counter stimulants; most of these are for colds and allergies. If you are in doubt, ask your pharmacist.

You may develop headache or heart palpitations, especially during the first few days of therapy with Apresazide.

If you develop weakness, muscle cramps, nausea, dizziness, or other signs of potassium loss, or if you develop fever or muscle aches or chest pains, call your doctor.

Do not stop taking this medication unless told to do so by your physician.

If you forget to take a dose of Apresazide, take it as soon as you remember. If it is almost time for your next dose, skip the one you forgot and continue with your regular schedule. Do not take a double dose of Apresazide.

Generic Name

Aspirin, Buffered Aspirin

Brand Names

A.S.A.	Arthritis Bayer
Aspergum	Arthritis Pain Formula
Bayer	Alka-Seltzer
Bayer Children's Aspirin	Ascriptin
Bayer 8 Hour	Ascriptin A/D
Cosprin	Ascriptin Extra Strength
Easprin	Asperbuf
Ecotrin	Buffaprin
Ecotrin Maximum Strength	Bufferin
Empirin	Bufferin Arthritis Strength
Encaprin	Bufferin Extra Strength
Hipirin	Buffex
Maximum Bayer Aspirin	Buffinol
Measurin	Buf-Tabs
Norwich Extra-Strength	Cama Arthritis Strength
St. Joseph Children's	Magnaprin Arthritis Strength
Aspirin	Maprin-IB
ZORprin	Wesprin Buffered

(Also available in generic form)

Type of Drug

Analgesic, anti-inflammatory.

Prescribed for

Mild to moderate pain; fever, inflammation of bones, joints, or other body tissues; reducing the probability that men who have had a stroke or TIA (oxygen shortage to the brain) because of a problem with blood coagulation will have another such attack. Aspirin may also be prescribed as an anticoagulant (blood-thinning) drug in people with unstable angina, and to protect against heart attack, although it has not been approved by the government for this purpose.

General Information

Aspirin is probably the closest thing we have to a wonder

drug. It has been used for more than a century as a pain and fever remedy but is now used for its effect on the blood as well.

Aspirin is the standard against which all other drugs are compared for pain relief and for reduction of inflammation. Chemically, Aspirin is a member of the group called Salicylates. Other Salicylates include Sodium Salicylate, Sodium Thiosalicylate, Choline Salicylate, and Magnesium Salicylate (Trilisate). These drugs are no more effective than regular Aspirin, although two of them (Choline Salicylate and Magnesium Salicylate) may be a little less irritating to the stomach. They are all more expensive than Aspirin.

Scientists have discovered how Aspirin works. It reduces fever by causing the blood vessels in the skin to open, thereby allowing heat from our body to leave more rapidly. Its effects on pain and inflammation are thought to be related to its ability to prevent the manufacture of complex body hormones called prostaglandins. Of all the Salicylates, Aspirin has the greatest effect on prostaglandin production.

Many people find that they can take Buffered Aspirin but not regular Aspirin. The addition of antacids to Aspirin can be important to patients who must take large doses of Aspirin for chronic arthritis or other conditions. In many cases, Aspirin is the only effective drug and it can be tolerated only with the antacids present.

Cautions and Warnings

People with liver damage should avoid Aspirin. People who are allergic to Aspirin may also be allergic to drugs such as Indomethacin, Sulindac, Ibuprofen, Fenoprofen, Naproxen, Tolmetin, and Meclofenamate Sodium, or to products containing tartrazine (a commonly used orange dye and food coloring). People with asthma and/or nasal polyps are more likely to be allergic to Aspirin.

Reye's syndrome is a life-threatening condition characterized by vomiting and stupor or dullness and may develop in children with influenza (flu) or chicken pox if treated with Aspirin or other Salicylates. Because of this, the U.S. Surgeon General, Centers for Disease Control, and pediatric physicians' associations advise against the use of Aspirin or other Salicylates in children under age 17. Acetaminophen-containing products are suggested instead.

Aspirin can interfere with normal blood coagulation and should be avoided for 1 week before surgery for this reason. It would be wise to ask your surgeon or dentist their recommendation before taking Aspirin for pain after surgery.

Pregnancy/Breast-feeding

Check with your doctor before taking any Aspirin-containing product during pregnancy. Aspirin can cause bleeding problems in the developing fetus during the last 2 weeks of pregnancy. Taking Aspirin during the last 3 months of pregnancy may lead to a low-birth-weight infant, prolong labor, and extend the length of pregnancy; it can also cause bleeding in the mother before, during, or after delivery.

Aspirin has not caused any problems among nursing mothers or their infants.

Seniors

Aspirin, especially in the larger doses that an older adult may take to treat arthritis and rheumatic conditions, may be irritating to the stomach.

Possible Side Effects

Nausea, upset stomach, heartburn, loss of appetite, and loss of small amounts of blood in the stool. Aspirin may contribute to the formation of a stomach ulcer and bleeding.

Drug Interactions

People taking anticoagulants (blood-thinning drugs) should avoid Aspirin. The effect of the anticoagulant will be increased.

Aspirin may increase the possibility of stomach ulcer when taken together with adrenal corticosteroids, Phenylbutazone, or alcoholic beverages. Aspirin will counteract the uric-acid-eliminating effect of Probenecid and Sulfinpyrazone.

Food Interactions

Since Aspirin can cause upset stomach, or bleeding, take each dose with food, milk, or a glass of water.

Usual Dose

Adult: aches, pains, and fever, 325 to 650 milligrams every 4 hours; arthritis and rheumatic conditions, up to 5200 milligrams (16 325-milligram tablets) per day; rheumatic fever, up to 7800 milligrams (24 325-milligram tablets) per day; to prevent heart attack, stroke, or TIA in men, 325 milligrams 2 to 4 times per day.

Child: Not recommended for children age 16 or younger. Consult your doctor for more information.

Overdosage

Symptoms of mild overdosage are rapid and deep breathing, nausea, vomiting, dizziness, ringing or buzzing in the ears, flushing, sweating, thirst, headache, drowsiness, diarrhea, and rapid heartbeat.

Severe overdosage may cause fever, excitement, confusion, convulsions, coma, or bleeding.

The initial treatment of Aspirin overdose involves making the patient vomit to remove any Aspirin remaining in the stomach. Further therapy depends on how the situation develops and what must be done to maintain the patient. DO NOT INDUCE VOMITING UNTIL YOU HAVE SPOKEN WITH YOUR DOCTOR OR POISON CONTROL CENTER. If in doubt, go to a hospital emergency room.

Special Information

Contact your doctor if you develop a continuous stomach pain or a ringing or buzzing in the ears.

Generic Name

Aspirin with Codeine

Brand Names

Anexsia with Codeine   Emcodeine
Aspirin with Codeine   Empirin with Codeine

(Also available in generic form)

ngredients

Aspirin
Codeine Sulfate

Type of Drug

Narcotic analgesic.

Prescribed for

Relief of mild to moderate pain.

General Information

Aspirin with Codeine is one of many combination products containing narcotics and analgesics. These products often contain barbiturates or tranquilizers, and Acetaminophen may be substituted for Aspirin and/or Caffeine may be omitted.

Cautions and Warnings

Do not take Codeine if you know you are allergic or sensitive to it. Use this drug with extreme caution if you suffer from asthma or other breathing problems. Long-term use of this drug may cause drug dependence or addiction. Codeine is a respiratory depressant and affects the central nervous system, producing sleepiness, tiredness, and/or inability to concentrate.

Do not take this product if you are allergic to Aspirin, any Salicylate, or a non-steroidal anti-inflammatory drug (NSAID). Check with your doctor or pharmacist if you are not sure. This and all other aspirin-containing products should not be taken by children under age 17.

Pregnancy/Breast-feeding

Check with your doctor before taking any Aspirin-containing product during pregnancy. Aspirin can cause bleeding problems in the developing fetus during the last 2 weeks of pregnancy. Taking Aspirin during the last 3 months of pregnancy may lead to a low-birth-weight infant, prolong labor, and extend the length of pregnancy; it can also cause bleeding in the mother before, during, or after delivery.

Codeine has not been associated with birth defects. But, taking too much Codeine, or any other narcotic, during pregnancy can lead to the birth of a drug-dependent infant and can lead to drug withdrawal symptoms in the baby. All narcotics, including Codeine, can cause breathing problems in the newborn if taken just before delivery.

Aspirin with Codeine has not caused any problems among nursing mothers or their infants.

Seniors

The Codeine in this combination product may have more of a depressant effect on seniors than on younger adults. Other effects that may be more prominent are dizziness, light-headedness, or fainting when rising suddenly from a sitting or lying position.

Possible Side Effects

Most frequent: light-headedness, dizziness, sleepiness, nausea, vomiting, loss of appetite, sweating. If these occur, consider calling your doctor and asking him about lowering the dose of Codeine you are taking. Usually the side effects disappear if you simply lie down.

More serious side effects of Aspirin with Codeine are shallow breathing or difficulty in breathing.

Less common side effects include euphoria (feeling "high"), weakness, sleepiness, headache, agitation, uncoordinated muscle movement, minor hallucinations, disorientation and visual disturbances, dry mouth, loss of appetite, constipation, flushing of the face, rapid heartbeat, palpitations, faintness, urinary difficulties or hesitancy, reduced sex drive and/or potency, itching, rashes, anemia, lowered blood sugar, yellowing of the skin and/or whites of the eyes. Narcotic analgesics may aggravate convulsions in those who have had convulsions in the past.

Drug Interactions

Interaction with alcohol, tranquilizers, barbiturates, or sleeping pills produces tiredness, sleepiness, or inability to concentrate, and seriously increases the depressive effect of Aspirin with Codeine.

The Aspirin component of Aspirin with Codeine can affect anticoagulant (blood-thinning) therapy. Be sure to discuss this with your doctor so that the proper dosage adjustment can be made.

Interaction with adrenal corticosteroids, Phenylbutazone, or alcohol can cause severe stomach irritation with possible bleeding.

Food Interactions

Take with food or ½ glass of water to prevent stomach upset.

Usual Dose

1 to 2 tablets 3 to 4 times per day.

Overdosage

Symptoms are depression of respiration (breathing), extreme tiredness progressing to stupor and then coma, pinpointed pupils of the eyes, no response to stimulation such as a pin stick, cold and clammy skin, slowing down of the heartbeat, lowering of blood pressure, convulsions, and cardiac arrest. The patient should be taken to a hospital emergency room immediately. ALWAYS bring the medicine bottle.

Special Information

Drowsiness may occur: be careful when driving or operating hazardous machinery.

If you forget a dose of Aspirin with Codeine, take it as soon as you remember. If it is almost time for your next dose, skip the one you forgot and continue with your regular schedule. Do not take a double dose of Aspirin with Codeine.

Generic Name

Astemizole

Brand Name

Hismanal

Type of Drug

Antihistamine.

Prescribed for

Seasonal allergy, stuffed and runny nose, itching of the eyes, scratchy throat caused by allergies, and other symptoms of allergy, such as rash, itching, or hives.

General Information

Astemizole, which has been available in Europe and Canada for several years, is a non-sedating antihistamine. It may be used by people who find other antihistamines unacceptable because of the drowsiness and tiredness they cause. Astemizole appears to work in exactly the same way as Chlorpheniramine and other widely used antihistamines.

Cautions and Warnings

Astemizole should not be taken by people who have had an allergic reaction to it in the past. People with asthma or other deep-breathing problems, glaucoma (pressure in the eye), or stomach ulcer or other stomach problems should avoid Astemizole because it may aggravate these problems.

Pregnancy/Breast-feeding

Astemizole has been studied in lab animals and found to cause no damage to a developing fetus. Nevertheless, this drug should be used by a pregnant woman only if it is absolutely necessary. Nursing mothers should avoid using this drug. Temporarily suspend breast-feeding if you must use Astemizole.

Seniors

Older adults may be more sensitive to the side effects of Astemizole and should be treated with the minimum effective dose, 10 milligrams per day.

Possible Side Effects

Occasional: headache, nervousness, weakness, upset stomach, nausea, vomiting, dry mouth, nose, or throat, cough, stuffed nose, nervousness, weakness, change in bowel habits, sore throat, nosebleeds. In scientific studies, Astemizole was found to cause the same amount of drowsiness as a placebo (inactive pill) and about half of the other antihistamines sold in the U.S. Most commonly used antihistamines cause more sedation than Astemizole.

Less common side effects of Astemizole include hair loss,

allergic reactions, depression, sleeplessness, menstrual ir-regularities, muscle aches, sweating, tingling in the hands or feet, frequent urination, visual disturbances. A few people taking this drug have developed liver damage.

Drug Interactions

Antihistamines may decrease the effects of oral blood-thinning drugs (anticoagulants).

Food Interactions

Astemizole should be taken 1 hour before or 2 hours after food or meals.

Usual Dose

Adult and child (over age 12): 10 milligrams once a day. Your doctor may prescribe 30 milligrams on the first day, 20 milligrams on the second day, and 10 milligrams a day thereafter to increase the speed with which the drug takes effect.

Child (under 12): Not recommended.

Overdosage

Astemizole overdose is likely to cause exaggerated side ef-fects. People who have taken an Astemizole overdose should be given Syrup of Ipecac to cause vomiting and taken to a hospital emergency room for treatment. ALWAYS remember to bring the prescription bottle with you.

Special Information

You should report any unusual side effects to your doctor. Astemizole's only disadvantage is its cost. Equally effective antihistamines are sold without a prescription and can be purchased for relatively little money. This drug is sold by prescription only and is rather costly when compared to over-the-counter products.

If you forget to take a dose of Astemizole, take it as soon as you remember. If it is almost time for your next dose, skip the forgotten dose and continue with your regular schedule. Do not take a double dose of Astemizole.

Generic Name

Atenolol

Brand Name

Tenormin

Type of Drug

Beta-adrenergic blocker.

Prescribed for

High blood pressure and angina. It may also be prescribed by your doctor to treat severe headaches, abnormal heart rhythms, overactive thyroid, mitral valve prolapse and to prevent second heart attacks in people who have already had one.

General Information

Atenolol is much like Metoprolol, another beta blocker with specific effects on the heart and less specific effects on the blood vessels and respiratory tract than Propranolol, the first beta blocker available in America. It is thought that beta blockers lower blood pressure by affecting body hormone systems and the heart, but the exact mechanism is not known. Atenolol and Metoprolol cause fewer side effects than Propranolol because of the specific nature of their effect on the heart.

Cautions and Warnings

You should be cautious about taking Atenolol if you have asthma, severe heart failure, very slow heart rate, or heart block because the drug can aggravate these conditions. Compared with the other beta blockers, Atenolol has less of an effect on your pulse and bronchial muscles, and less of a rebound effect when the drug is discontinued, and it produces less tiredness, depression, and intolerance to exercise than other beta-blocking drugs.

People with angina who take Atenolol for high blood pressure should have their drug dosage reduced gradually over 1 to 2 weeks rather than suddenly discontinued. This will avoid possible aggravation of the angina.

Atenolol should be used with caution if you have liver disease because your ability to eliminate the drug from your body will be impaired.

Pregnancy/Breast-feeding

Animal studies in which rats were given 150 times the human dose of Atenolol revealed no adverse effects of Atenolol on the developing baby. However, Atenolol should be avoided by pregnant women or women who might become pregnant while taking it. When the drug is considered essential by your doctor, the potential risk of taking the medicine must be carefully weighed against the benefit it might produce. Small amounts of Atenolol may pass into your breast milk. Nursing mothers taking this drug must observe their infants for possible drug-related side effects.

Seniors

Senior citizens may be more or less sensitive to the effects of Atenolol than young adults and require a different dose to achieve the same effect. Your dosage of this drug must be adjusted to your individual needs by your doctor. Seniors may be more likely to suffer from cold hands and feet and reduced body temperature, chest pains, a general feeling of ill health, sudden difficulty breathing, sweating, or changes in heartbeat because of this medicine.

Possible Side Effects

Atenolol side effects are relatively uncommon, usually develop early in the course of treatment, are relatively mild, and are rarely a reason to stop taking the medication. Side effects increase with increasing dosage and include dizziness, tingling of the scalp, nausea, vomiting, upset stomach, taste distortion, fatigue, sweating, male impotence, urinary difficulty, diarrhea, bile duct blockage, breathing difficulty, bronchial spasms, muscle weakness, cramps, dry eyes, blurred vision, skin rash, hair loss, and facial swelling. Like other beta blockers, Atenolol can cause mental depression, disorientation, short-term memory loss, and emotional instability.

Rare side effects include aggravation of lupus erythematosus (a disease of the body's connective tissues), stuffy nose, chest pains, colitis, drug allergy (fever, sore throat), and unusual bleeding or bruising.

Drug Interactions

Beta-blocking drugs may interact with surgical anesthetics to increase the risk of heart problems during surgery. Some anesthesiologists recommend stopping your beta blocker gradually 2 days before surgery.

Atenolol may interfere with the normal signs of low blood sugar and can interfere with the action of insulin or oral antidiabetes medicines.

Taking Atenolol together with Aspirin-containing drugs, Indomethacin, or Sulfinpyrazone can interfere with its blood-pressure-lowering effect.

The effects of Atenolol may be increased by Phenothiazine antipsychotic medicines with other antihypertensives like Clonidine, Diazoxide, Nifedipine, Reserpine, or with other drugs that can reduce blood pressure, like Nitroglycerin.

Atenolol may interfere with the effectiveness of some anti-asthma drugs, especially Ephedrine and Isoproterenol, and with Theophylline or Aminophylline.

The combination of Atenolol and Phenytoin or digitalis drugs can result in excessive slowing of the heart and possible heart block.

Estrogen drugs can interfere with the blood-pressure-lowering effect of Atenolol.

Food Interactions

Take this medicine with food if it upsets your stomach.

Usual Dose

Starting dose, 50 milligrams per day, taken all at once. The daily dose may be gradually increased up to 200 milligrams. Maintenance dose, 50 to 200 milligrams given once a day. People with kidney disease may need only 50 milligrams every other day.

Senior: Older adults may respond to lower doses of this drug than younger adults and should be treated more cautiously.

Overdosage

Symptoms are changes in heartbeat (unusually slow, unusually fast, or irregular), severe dizziness or fainting, difficulty breathing, bluish-colored fingernails or palms of the hands, and seizures.

Special Information

Atenolol is meant to be taken on a continuing basis. Do not stop taking it unless directed to do so by your doctor. Possible side effects of abrupt withdrawal of Atenolol are: chest pain, difficulty breathing, sweating, and unusually fast or irregular heartbeat.

Call your doctor at once if any of the following symptoms develop: back or joint pains, difficulty breathing, cold hands or feet, depression, skin rash, changes in heartbeat.

Call your doctor only if the following side effects persist or are bothersome: anxiety, diarrhea, constipation, sexual impotence, mild dizziness, headache, itching, nausea or vomiting, nightmares or vivid dreams, upset stomach, trouble sleeping, stuffed nose, frequent urination, unusual tiredness or weakness.

If you forget to take a dose of Atenolol, take it as soon as possible. If it is within 8 hours of your next dose, go back to your regular dose schedule and skip the missed dose.

Brand Name

Augmentin

Ingredients

Amoxicillin
Clavulanic Acid

Type of Drug

Antibiotic.

Prescribed for

Treatment of infections of the lungs, middle ear, skin and soft tissue, and urinary tract. It can also be used for sinusitis caused by organisms usually sensitive to Amoxicillin or Ampicillin.

General Information

This medicine represents a novel approach to the treatment of resistant infections by adding an "augmentor" to the antibiotic. Clavulanic Acid is a weak antibiotic that is chemically similar to Ampicillin and other penicillin-type antibiotics. However, at low concentrations it has the unique ability to inactivate enzymes produced by bacteria that can neutralize Amoxicillin or Ampicillin before it can kill the bacteria. Clavulanic Acid combined with Amoxicillin or another penicillin-type antibiotic will increase the antibiotic's effectiveness against organisms that may have developed some degree of resistance to it over the years.

Penicillin-type antibiotics fight infection by killing bacteria. They do this by destroying the cell wall of invading bacteria. Other antibiotics simply prevent bacteria from reproducing. Many infections can be treated by almost any member of this family, but some infections can only be treated by certain penicillin-type antibiotics.

Penicillins cannot treat a cold, flu, or any virus infection and should never be taken unless prescribed by a doctor for a specific illness. Always take your antibiotic exactly according to your doctor's directions for use, including the number of pills to take every day and the number of days to take the medicine. If you do not follow directions, you may not get the antibiotic's full benefit.

Cautions and Warnings

The product cannot be taken by anyone who is sensitive or allergic to Amoxicillin, Ampicillin, Hetacillin, Bacampicillin, or to any member of the penicillin group.

Pregnancy/Breast-feeding

This drug should not be taken by women who are or may become pregnant while using it. In situations where it is deemed essential, the drug's potential risk must be carefully weighed against any benefit it might produce. Nursing mothers should watch for any possible drug effect on their infants while taking this medicine.

Seniors

Seniors may take this medicine without special concern.

Possible Side Effects

The side effects of this combination are essentially the same as those associated with Amoxicillin. Most common are upset stomach and diarrhea, more frequent than with plain Amoxicillin. Skin rash may also develop but is not necessarily a sign of drug allergy. More definite signs of drug allergy include wheezing, sneezing, itching, and severe difficulty breathing.

Less frequent side effects of this product include those associated with the other penicillins. The vast majority of people taking this product will tolerate it without any problems. Detailed information can be found in the Amoxicillin monograph on page 56.

Drug Interactions

The effect of this combination will be reduced if it is taken together with Tetracycline or another bacteriostatic antibiotic, one which works by slowing the growth of an organism rather than killing it, as Amoxicillin and other penicillin-type antibiotics do.

Probenecid (Benemid) will reduce the rate at which Amoxicillin is eliminated from your body, extending its effect.

Augmentin can cause false positive test results for urine sugar if Clinitest or similar products are used. It will not interfere with the enzyme method used by Tes-Tape or Clinistix.

Food Interactions

Augmentin may be taken with food if it upsets your stomach because it is unaffected by food in the stomach.

Usual Dose

Adult: 250 to 500 milligrams every 8 hours. Each tablet, regardless of the amount of Amoxicillin it contains, also has 125 milligrams of Clavulanic Acid in it.

Child: 9 to 18 milligrams per pound each day, in divided doses. The dose is based on Amoxicillin content.

Overdosage

The most frequent effects of overdose are nausea, vomiting, and stomach pain. For most people, the symptoms can be treated simply by taking milk or an antacid. Severe and allergic reactions must be treated in a hospital emergency room. ALWAYS bring the medicine bottle with you.

Special Information

Take the full course of treatment prescribed by your doctor, even if you feel better within a day or two of beginning therapy.

Call your doctor if you begin to itch or if hives, skin rash, or breathing difficulty develop.

All antibiotics, including Augmentin, are best taken at even intervals around the clock.

If you forget to take a dose of Augmentin, take it as soon as possible. If it is within 2 to 4 hours of your next dose, double it and go back to your regular schedule.

Brand Name

Auralgan

Ingredients

Antipyrine   Glycerin
Benzocaine   Oxyquinoline Sulfate

The following products contain the same ingredients in different concentrations:

Allergan Ear Drops   Earocol
Auromid   Oto
Auroto

(Also available in generic form)

Type of Drug

Analgesic.

Prescribed for

Earache.

General Information

This drug is a combination product containing a local anesthetic to deaden nerves inside the ear which transmit painful impulses, an analgesic to provide additional pain relief, and Glycerin to remove any water present in the ear.

This drug is often used to treat painful conditions where water is present in the ear canal, such as "swimmer's ear." This drug does not contain any antibiotics and should not be used to treat any infection.

Cautions and Warnings

Do not use Auralgan if you are allergic to any of its ingredients.

Pregnancy/Breast-feeding

Pregnant and breast-feeding women may use this product with no restriction.

Seniors

Older adults may use this product with no restriction.

Possible Side Effects

Local irritation.

Usual Dose

Place drops of Auralgan in the ear canal until it is filled. Saturate a piece of cotton with Auralgan and put it in the ear canal to keep the drug from leaking out. Leave the drug in the ear for several minutes. Repeat 3 to 4 times per day.

Special Information

Before using, warm the bottle of eardrops to body temperature by holding it in your hand for several minutes. Do not warm the bottle to a temperature above normal body temperature. Protect the bottle from light.

Call your doctor if you develop a burning or itching feeling or if the pain does not go away.

Generic Name

Auranofin

Brand Name

Ridaura

Type of Drug

Antiarthritic.

Prescribed for

Rheumatoid arthritis in adults, juvenile arthritis.

General Information

Gold compounds like Auranofin are among the few drugs that can actually be shown to halt the progress of rheumatoid arthritis and may even reverse some of the damage caused to inflamed joints. In 1985 a new gold compound, Auranofin, was released for use in the United States. It is unique because it can be taken by mouth. Some experts in the field believed that the release of Auranofin would be a godsend to a relatively small number of arthritics who can benefit from gold therapy but could not tolerate the series of injections. Preliminary studies have shown Auranofin to be as effective as the injectable gold compounds. If successful, gold treatments may be continued for several months. It may take as long as 6 months before you realize any effect of Auranofin treatments, although you can get results in 3 months.

Cautions and Warnings

Gold cannot be used to treat people with diabetes, kidney disease, liver damage, very high blood pressure, heart disease, bleeding disorders, or those who have recently had radiation treatments. It can cause severe toxic reactions, and people on gold therapy should be given periodic blood and urine tests to check for these reactions.

Pregnancy/Breast-feeding

Gold may cause birth defects and should not be used by women who are, or might become, pregnant. If your arthritis is severe, talk to your doctor about the potential risk of taking Auranofin and the benefits it might provide. Auranofin may pass into breast milk and should be avoided by nursing mothers. Use an alternate feeding method if you must take Auranofin.

Seniors

Generally, seniors become less able to tolerate gold therapy as they get older and may develop more side effects than a younger person would. Your doctor should be available to discuss side effects. Be sure you report anything unusual at once.

Possible Side Effects

People receiving gold treatments can develop side effects at any time during treatment or for months after treatment has been completed. Side effects are most common when the total dose of gold given has reached 400 to 800 milligrams. The most common reactions are skin rashes and itching. Hair and fingernail loss and gray-blue discoloration of the skin may also occur.

The second most common side effect is the formation of small sores on the tongue or mouth. Stomach upset, colitis, respiratory and vaginal inflammation have also occurred. A metallic taste in your mouth should be considered a warning sign that you are about to develop one of these reactions.

Gold therapy can cause fever, rashes, cough, and lung damage. It can cause kidney damage and may cause some abnormalities among various blood components.

Drug Interactions

Auranofin increases the side effects of other drugs, especially those used to suppress bone marrow function, those that are toxic to the kidney or liver, and those that cause severe rashes.

Food Interactions

This drug is best taken on an empty stomach, but you may take it with food if it upsets your stomach.

Usual Dose

6 milligrams per day in one or two doses. Larger doses increase the chance for diarrhea and generally don't improve the results.

Overdosage

Auranofin overdose must be treated in a hospital. Take the victim to an emergency room as quickly as possible. ALWAYS remember to bring the medicine bottle with you.

Special Information

Auranofin can increase your sensitivity to the sun. See your doctor regularly and expect frequent urine and blood tests to screen for drug side effects.

Call your doctor at once if you develop a puffy face, hands, or feet, red marks on the skin, coughing, wheezing, or difficulty breathing.

See your doctor if you develop any persistent symptoms or if you develop severe diarrhea or your diarrhea lasts more than 3 days. See your doctor if you experience a rash, itching, hives, sores or white spots in your mouth or throat, bloody or cloudy urine, vomiting blood or a "coffee ground" material, trouble swallowing, headache, dizziness, fever, irritated tongue or gums, a metallic taste, severe stomach pains, blood in your stool or black stools, yellow eyes or skin, numbness, tingling pain or weakness in your hands or feet, tiredness, or sore throat.

If you forget a dose of Auranofin, take it as soon as you remember. If it is almost time for your next dose (or the next day, if you take Auranofin once a day), skip the forgotten dose and continue with your regular schedule. Do not take a double dose of Auranofin.

Generic Name

Azatadine Maleate

Brand Name

Optimine

Type of Drug

Antihistamine.

Prescribed for

Seasonal allergy, stuffed and runny nose, itching of the eyes, scratching of the throat caused by allergy, and other allergic symptoms such as itching, rash, or hives.

General Information

Antihistamines generally, including Azatadine, act by blocking the release of histamine from the cell at the H_1 histamine receptor site. Antihistamines work by drying up the secretions of the nose, throat, and eyes.

Cautions and Warnings

Azatadine Maleate should not be used if you are allergic to this drug. It should be avoided or used with extreme care if you have narrow-angle glaucoma (pressure in the eye), stomach ulcer or other stomach problems, enlarged prostate, or problems passing urine. It should not be used by people who have deep-breathing problems such as asthma.

Use with care if you have a history of asthma, glaucoma, thyroid disease, heart disease, high blood pressure, or diabetes.

Pregnancy/Breast-feeding

Azatadine has not been proven to be a cause of birth defects or other problems in pregnant women, although studies in animals have shown that some other antihistamines (Meclizine and Cyclizine), used mainly against nausea and vomiting, may cause birth defects. Do not take any antihistamine without your doctor's knowledge.

Small amounts of antihistamine medicines pass into breast milk and may affect a nursing infant. Nursing mothers should avoid antihistamines or use alternate feeding methods while taking the medicine.

Seniors

Seniors are more sensitive to antihistamine side effects. Confusion, difficult or painful urination, dizziness, drowsiness, a faint feeling, dry mouth, nose, or throat, nightmares or excitement, nervousness, restlessness, or irritability are more likely to occur among older adults.

Possible Side Effects

Occasionally seen: itching, rash, sensitivity to light, excessive perspiration, chills, dryness of the mouth, nose, and throat, lowering of blood pressure, headache, rapid heartbeat, sleeplessness, dizziness, disturbed coordination, confusion, restlessness, nervousness, irritability, euphoria (feeling high), tingling of the hands and feet, blurred vision, double vision, ringing in the ears, stomach upset, loss of appetite, nausea, vomiting, constipation, diarrhea, difficulty in urination, tightness of the chest, wheezing, nasal stuffiness.

Drug Interactions

Azatadine Maleate should not be taken with the monoamine oxidase (MAO) inhibitors.

Interactions with tranquilizers, sedatives, and sleeping medication will increase the effect of these drugs; it is extremely important that you discuss this with your doctor so that doses of these drugs can be properly adjusted.

Be extremely cautious when drinking alcohol while taking Azatadine Maleate, which will enhance the intoxicating effect of alcohol. Alcohol also has a sedative effect.

Usual Dose

1 to 2 milligrams twice per day.

Overdosage

Symptoms are depression or stimulation (especially in children), dry mouth, fixed or dilated pupils, flushing of the skin, and stomach upset. Take the patient to a hospital emergency room immediately, if you cannot make him vomit. ALWAYS bring the medicine bottle.

Special Information

Antihistamines produce a depressing effect: be extremely cautious when driving or operating heavy equipment.

If you forget a dose of Azatadine, take it as soon as you remember. If it is almost time for your next dose, skip the forgotten dose and continue with your regular schedule. Do not take a double dose of Azatadine.

Brand Name

Azo Gantrisin

Ingredients

Phenazopyridine
Sulfisoxazole

Other Brand Names

Azo-Sulfisoxazole
Suldiazo

(Also available in generic form)

Type of Drug

Urinary anti-infective.

Prescribed for

Urinary tract infections.

General Information

Azo Gantrisin is one of many combination products used to treat urinary tract infections. The primary active ingredient is Sulfisoxazole. The other ingredient, Phenazopyridine, is added as a pain reliever.

Cautions and Warnings

Do not take Azo Gantrisin if you know you are allergic to sulfa drugs, Salicylates, or similar agents or if you have the disease porphyria. Azo Gantrisin should not be considered if you have advanced kidney disease.

Pregnancy/Breast-feeding

This drug may cause birth defects or interfere with your baby's development. Check with your doctor before taking it if you are, or might be, pregnant.

The sulfa ingredient in this combination may pass into breast milk and can cause problems in infants with an unusual disorder called G6PD deficiency. Normal infants are not affected.

Seniors

Older adults may take this product without special precautions.

Possible Side Effects

Headache, itching, rash, sensitivity to strong sunlight, nausea, vomiting, abdominal pains, feeling of tiredness or lassitude, hallucinations, dizziness, ringing in the ears, chills, feeling of ill health.

Other, less common, side effects are: blood diseases or alterations of normal blood components, itching of the eyes, arthritis-type pain, diarrhea, loss of appetite, stomach cramps or pains, hearing loss, drowsiness, fever, chills, hair loss, yellowing of the skin and/or eyes, reduction of sperm count.

Drug Interactions

When Azo Gantrisin is taken with an anticoagulant (blood-thinning) drug, any drug used to treat diabetes, Methotrexate, Phenylbutazone, Salicylates (Aspirin-like drugs), Phenytoin, or Probenecid, it will cause unusually large amounts of these drugs to be released into the bloodstream, possibly producing symptoms of overdosage. If you are going to take Azo Gantrisin for an extended period, your physician should reduce the dosage of these interactive drugs. Also, avoid large doses of Vitamin C.

Food Interactions

Sulfa drugs should be taken with a full glass of water on an empty stomach, but they can be taken after eating if they upset your stomach.

Usual Dose

First dose, 4 to 6 tablets, then 2 tablets every 4 hours. Take each dose with a full glass of water.

Overdosage

Induce vomiting and give a rectal enema; then take the patient to a hospital emergency room. ALWAYS bring the medicine bottle.

Special Information

Azo Gantrisin can cause photosensitivity—a severe reaction to strong sunlight. Avoid prolonged exposure to strong sunlight while taking it.

Sore throat, fever, unusual bleeding or bruising, rash, and feeling tired are early signs of serious blood disorders and should be reported to your doctor immediately.

The Phenazopyridine ingredient in Azo Gantrisin is an orange-red dye and will color the urine. Do not be worried since this is a normal effect of the drug; but note that if you are diabetic, the dye may interfere with testing your urine for sugar. This dye may also appear in your sweat and tears. Note that this dye may discolor certain types of contact lenses.

If you miss a dose of Azo Gantrisin, take it as soon as possible. If it is almost time for your next dose, take it and skip the missed dose. Do not double up to make up for the missed dose.

Generic Name

Bacampicillin Hydrochloride

Brand Name

Spectrobid

Type of Drug

Penicillin-type antibiotic.

Prescribed for

Gram-positive bacterial infections. Gram-positive bacteria (pneumococci, streptococci, and staphylococci) are organisms that usually cause diseases like pneumonia, infections of the tonsils and throat, venereal diseases, meningitis (spinal infection), and septicemia (blood infection). Bacampicillin Hydrochloride (HCl)is best used to treat infections that are resistant to Penicillin, although it can be used as initial treatment for some people.

General Information

Bacampicillin turns into Ampicillin in the stomach. Its only advantage is that it can be taken every 12 hours while other antibiotics have to be taken every 6 hours. It and other penicillin-type antibiotics fight infection by killing bacteria. They do this by destroying the cell wall of invading bacteria. Other antibiotics simply prevent bacteria from reproducing. Many infections can be treated by almost any member of this family, but some infections can only be treated by certain penicillin-type antibiotics.

Penicillins cannot treat a cold, flu, or any virus infection and should never be taken unless prescribed by a doctor for a specific illness. Always take your antibiotic exactly according to your doctor's directions for use, including the number of pills to take every day and the number of days to take the medicine. If you do not follow directions, you may not get the antibiotic's full benefit.

Cautions and Warnings

Do not take Bacampicillin if you have a history of penicillin allergy. The drugs are similar. The most common allergic reaction to Bacampicillin HCl and other penicillins is a hivelike rash over the body with itching and redness. It is important to tell your doctor if you have ever taken this or any other penicillin before and had an allergic reaction to it such as rash, itching, or trouble breathing.

Pregnancy/Breast-feeding

Bacampicillin has not caused birth defects but you should be sure your doctor knows you are taking it. Bacampicillin passes into breast milk and may affect a nursing infant.

Seniors

Seniors may take Bacampicillin HCl without special precautions.

Possible Side Effects

Common side effects include upset stomach, nausea, vomiting, diarrhea, and rash. Less common side effects include hairy tongue, itching, or irritation around the anus or vagina, stomach pains with or without bleeding.

Drug Interactions

The effect of Bacampicillin HCl can be affected by taking other antibiotics at the same time. Otherwise, Bacampicillin HCl is remarkably free of interactions.

Food Interactions

Bacampicillin liquid is best taken with a full glass of water on an empty stomach, 1 hour before or 2 hours after meals. Bacampicillin tablets can be taken either on an empty stomach or with food.

Usual Dose

Adult and child (55 pounds and over): 400 to 800 milligrams every 12 hours.

Child (under 55 pounds): 1 to 2.5 milligrams per pound of body weight a day, divided into 2 doses.

Overdosage

Bacampicillin overdose is unlikely but may result in diarrhea or upset stomach.

Special Information

Do not take this medicine after the expiration date on the label. Be sure to take this medicine exactly according to your doctor's directions.

Stop taking the medicine and call your doctor if any of the following side effects develop: skin rash, hives, itching, wheezing. Other side effects that demand your doctor's attention are: blood in the urine, passage of large amounts of light-colored urine, swelling of the face or ankles, trouble breathing, unusual weakness or tiredness.

If you forget to take a dose of Bacampicillin, take it as soon as possible. Take the next regular dose at least 5 to 6 hours after the missed dose and begin a new 12-hour schedule.

Generic Name

Beclomethasone

Brand Names

Beclovent
Beconase Nasal Inhaler

Vancenase Nasal Inhaler
Vanceril

Type of Drug

Adrenal corticosteroid.

Prescribed for

Treatment of chronic asthma.

General Information

Beclomethasone is used as an inhaler by mouth and as an intranasal product to relieve symptoms associated with seasonal allergy. It works by reducing inflammation of the mucosal lining within the bronchi, thereby making it easier to breathe. This drug should not be used more than 3 weeks if it has not worked within that time. Beclomethasone will not work immediately, as a decongestant would; it may take several days to exert its effect.

Cautions and Warnings

Do not use this drug if you are allergic to Beclomethasone. This drug cannot be used as the primary treatment of severe asthma. It is only for people who usually take Prednisone, or another adrenal corticosteroid, by mouth and those who are taking other asthma drugs but are still having asthmatic attacks.

Even though this drug is taken by inhaling directly into the lungs, it should be considered a potent adrenal corticosteroid drug. During periods of severe stress, you may have to go back to taking steroid drugs by mouth if Beclomethasone does not control your asthma.

Pregnancy/Breast-feeding

Large amounts of Beclomethasone used during pregnancy or breast-feeding may slow the growth of newborn babies. This drug may cause birth defects or interfere with your baby's development. Check with your doctor before taking it if you are, or might be, pregnant.

This medicine may pass into breast milk and cause unwanted effects in nursing infants.

Seniors

Older adults may use this medication without special precautions. Be sure your doctor knows if you suffer from bone disease, colitis, diabetes, bowel disease, glaucoma, fungus infection, heart disease, herpes infection, high blood pressure, high blood cholesterol, kidney disease, liver disease, or underactive thyroid.

Possible Side Effects

Dry mouth, hoarseness.

Rarely, deaths have occurred in patients taking adrenal corticosteroid tablets or syrup and being switched to Beclomethasone by inhalation due to failure of the adrenal gland. This is a rare complication and usually results from stopping the liquid or tablets too quickly. They must be stopped gradually over a long period of time.

This drug can also cause rash or spasm of the bronchial muscles.

Usual Dose

Intranasal inhalation:
Adult and child (over age 12): 1 inhalation in each nostril 2 to 4 times per day.
Child (under age 12): not recommended.
Oral inhalation:
Adult and child (over age 12): 6 to 20 inhalations per day.
Child (age 6 to 12): 3 to 10 inhalations per day.

Special Information

People using both Beclomethasone and a bronchodilator by inhalation should use the bronchodilator first, wait a few minutes, then use the Beclomethasone. This will allow more Beclomethasone to be absorbed.

This drug is for preventive therapy only and will not affect an asthma attack. Beclomethasone must be inhaled regularly, as directed. Wait at least 1 minute between inhalations.

Dry mouth or hoarseness may be reduced by rinsing your mouth after each use of the inhaler.

Shake well before each use.

If you forget a dose of Beclomethasone, take it as soon as you remember. If it is almost time for your next dose, skip the forgotten dose and continue with your regular schedule. Do not take a double dose of Beclomethasone.

Brand Name

Benylin Cough Syrup

Ingredients

Diphenhydramine Hydrochloride

Other Brand Names

Beldin	Noradryl Cough Syrup
Bydramine	Tusstat
Diphen Cough Syrup	Valdrene

(Also available in generic form)

Type of Drug

Cough syrup.

Prescribed for

Coughs associated with the common cold and other upper respiratory infections.

General Information

Benylin Cough Syrup is one of many products marketed for the relief of coughs. Its major active ingredient is an antihistamine; therefore, the drug is more effective in relieving the symptoms of excess histamine, but it has a cough suppressant effect. Basically, Benylin Cough Syrup can only help you feel well. It cannot help you recover more quickly, only more comfortably.

Cautions and Warnings

Do not use Benylin Cough Syrup if you have narrow-angle glaucoma.

Pregnancy/Breast-feeding

Antihistamines have not been proven to be a cause of birth defects or other problems in pregnant women, although studies in animals have shown that some drugs (Meclizine and Cyclizine), used mainly against nausea and vomiting, may cause birth defects. Do not take any antihistamine without your doctor's knowledge.

Small amounts of antihistamine medicines pass into breast milk and may affect a nursing infant. Nursing mothers should avoid antihistamines or use alternate feeding methods while taking the medicine.

Seniors

Seniors are more sensitive to antihistamine side effects. Con-

usion, difficult or painful urination, dizziness, drowsiness, a
aint feeling, dry mouth, nose, or throat, nightmares or ex-
itement, nervousness, restlessness, or irritability are more
ikely to occur among older adults.

Possible Side Effects

Tiredness, inability to concentrate, blurred vision, dry mouth,
difficulty in urination, constipation.

Drug Interactions

Benylin Cough Syrup contains an antihistamine and may
produce some depression, drowsiness, or inability to concentrate. Don't drink large quantities of alcoholic beverages,
which can increase this depressant effect.

Usual Dose

1 to 2 teaspoons 4 times per day.

Special Information

Take with a full glass of water to reduce stomach upset and
help loosen mucus that may be present in the breathing
passages.

Generic Name

Benztropine Mesylate

Brand Name

Cogentin

(Also available in generic form)

Type of Drug

Anticholinergic.

Prescribed for

Treatment of Parkinson's disease or prevention or control of
muscle spasms caused by other drugs, particularly phenothiazine drugs.

General Information

Benztropine Mesylate has an action on the body similar to that of Atropine Sulfate but side effects are less frequent and less severe. It is an anticholinergic and has the ability to reduce muscle spasms. This property makes the drug useful in treating Parkinson's disease and other diseases associated with spasms of skeletal muscles.

Cautions and Warnings

Benztropine Mesylate should be used with caution if you have narrow-angle glaucoma, stomach ulcers, heart disease, obstructions in the gastrointestinal tract, prostatitis, or myasthenia gravis.

Pregnancy/Breast-feeding

Drugs of this type have not been proven to be a cause of birth defects or of other problems in pregnant women. However, women who are, or may become, pregnant while taking this medication should discuss the possibility of birth defects with their doctor and other therapies that may be substituted for this medicine.

This medication may reduce the amount of breast milk produced by a nursing mother. Infants are also particularly sensitive to Benztropine. Alternative feeding methods should be used.

Seniors

Seniors taking this medication on a regular basis may be more sensitive to drug side effects, including a predisposition to developing glaucoma and confusion, disorientation, agitation, and hallucinations with normal drug doses.

Possible Side Effects

Difficulty in urination, constipation, blurred vision, and increased sensitivity to strong light. The effects may increase if Benztropine Mesylate is taken with antihistamines, phenothiazines, antidepressants, or other anticholinergic drugs.

Drug Interactions

Interaction with other anticholinergic drugs, including tricyclic antidepressants or phenothiazine drugs, may cause severe stomach upset or unusual abdominal pain. If this happens, contact your doctor. Avoid over-the-counter remedies which contain Atropine or similar drugs. Your pharmacist can tell you the ingredients of over-the-counter drugs.

This drug should be used with caution by people taking barbiturates. Use alcoholic beverages with care while taking this drug.

This drug may reduce the absorption and therefore the effect of some drugs, including Levodopa, Haloperidol, and Phenothiazines.

Food Interactions

This medicine is best taken on an empty stomach but may be taken with food if it upsets your stomach.

Usual Dose

0.5 to 6 milligrams per day, depending upon the disease being treated and patient's response.

Overdosage

Signs of drug overdose include clumsiness or unsteadiness, severe drowsiness, severely dry mouth, nose, or throat, hallucinations, mood changes, difficulty breathing, rapid heartbeat, and unusually warm and dry skin. Overdose victims should be taken to a hospital emergency room at once. ALWAYS bring the medicine bottle.

Special Information

Side effects of dry mouth, constipation, and sensitivity to bright lights can be easily relieved with candy or gum, a stool softener like Docusate, and sunglasses.

This medicine will reduce your tolerance to hot weather because it makes you sweat less than normal. Be careful not to become overheated in hot weather because of the chance of developing heat stroke.

If you forget to take a dose of Benztropine, take it as soon as you remember. If it is within 2 hours of your next regular dose, go back to the regular schedule and skip the missed dose.

Generic Name

Betamethasone Topical Ointment/ Cream/Lotion/Gel/Aerosol

Brand Names

Alphatrex Ointment/Cream/Lotion
Benisone Cream/Gel/Ointment/Lotion
Beta-Val Cream/Ointment/Lotion
Betatrex Cream/Ointment/Lotion
Diprolene Ointment/Cream
Diprosone Ointment/Cream/Lotion/Aerosol
Uticort Cream/Gel/Lotion
Valisone Ointment/Cream/Lotion
Valnac Ointment/Cream

Type of Drug

Corticosteroid.

Prescribed for

Relief of skin inflammation, itching, or other skin problems in a localized area.

General Information

Betamethasone is one of many adrenal corticosteroids used today. The major differences between Betamethasone and other adrenal corticosteroids are potency of medication and variation in some secondary effects. In most cases the choice of adrenal corticosteroids to be used in a specific disease is a matter of doctor preference and past experience. Other topical adrenal corticosteroids include Hydrocortisone, Triamcinolone, Methylprednisolone, Dexamethasone, Clobetasol, Amcinonide, Desoximetasone, Diflorasone, Fluocinolone, Fluocinonide, Halcinonide, Alclometasone, and Desonide.

Cautions and Warnings

Betamethasone should not be used if you have viral diseases of the skin (herpes), fungal infections of the skin (athlete's foot), or tuberculosis of the skin, nor should it be used in the ear if the eardrum is perforated. People with a history of allergies to any of the components of the ointment, cream, or gel should not use this drug.

Pregnancy/Breast-feeding

Studies have shown that corticosteroids applied to the skin in large amounts or over long periods of time can be the cause of birth defects. Pregnant women or those who might become pregnant while using this medicine should not do so unless they are under a doctor's care.

Corticosteroid drugs taken by mouth pass into breast milk and large drug doses may interfere with the growth of a nursing infant. Steroids applied to the skin are not likely to cause problems but you should not use the medicine unless under a doctor's care.

Seniors

Older adults are more likely to develop high blood pressure while taking this medicine (by mouth). Also, older women have a greater chance of being susceptible to bone degeneration (osteoporosis) associated with large doses of this class of medicines.

Possible Side Effects

Burning sensations, itching, irritation, dryness and redness of the skin, secondary infection.

Special Information

Clean the skin before applying Betamethasone, to prevent secondary infection. Apply in a very thin film (effectiveness is based on contact area and not on the thickness of the layer applied). If Betamethasone or any other topical steroid is being used on an infant's buttocks or diaper area, do not use tight-fitting diapers. This can cause absorption of the steroid through the skin and increase the likelihood of side effects.

Generic Name

Betaxolol

Brand Name
Betoptic

Type of Drug
Beta-adrenergic blocking agent.

Prescribed for
Glaucoma.

General Information
When applied to the eye, Betaxolol eyedrops work in the same way as the other beta-blocker eyedrops, Timolol and Levobunolol. It reduces fluid pressure inside the eye by reducing the production of eye fluids and slightly increasing the rate at which fluids flow through and leave the eye. Beta-blocking eyedrops produce a greater drop in eye pressure than either Pilocarpine or Epinephrine but may be combined with these or other drugs to produce a more pronounced drop in eye pressure.

Betaxolol differs from Timolol eyedrops in that it does not have an important effect on lung function or heart rate and may be able to be used by people who cannot use Timolol or Levobunolol because of the possible effect of those drugs on heart or lung function.

Cautions and Warnings
Betaxolol should not be used if you have heart failure, heart block, a very slow heart rate. Your doctor should give careful consideration to the use of Betaxolol if you have diabetes or overactive thyroid because Betaxolol may mask important signs of low blood sugar or overactive thyroid. Poor pulmonary (lung) function should be considered as a possible reason to avoid this drug, even though its effect on your lung function is minimal, when compared to the other beta blockers.

Pregnancy/Breast-feeding

This drug may cross into the blood circulation of a developing baby. It has not been found to cause birth defects. Pregnant women, or those who might become pregnant while using these eyedrops, should not take it without their doctor's approval. When the drug is considered essential by your doctor, the potential risk of taking the medicine must be carefully weighed against the benefit it might produce.

It is not known if Betaxolol passes into breast milk. Betaxolol has caused no problems among breast-fed infants. You must consider the potential effect on the nursing infant if breast-feeding while taking this medicine.

Seniors

Senior citizens may be more or less sensitive to the effects of this medication. Your dosage of Betaxolol must be adjusted to your individual need by your doctor. Seniors may be more likely to suffer from drug side effects.

Possible Side Effects

The more common side effects of Betaxolol include tearing, stinging of the eye, and redness or inflammation of the eye.

Rare side effects include sleeplessness, confusion, depression, very slow heartbeat, and increased sensitivity to bright lights.

Drug Interactions

This drug should be used with caution if you are taking a beta-blocking drug by mouth. If Betaxolol is absorbed into your bloodstream, it can increase the effects of that oral drug on your body and also increase the chance for drug side effects.

If Betaxolol is absorbed into the blood, it can mask the effects of antidiabetes medicine and can enhance the effects of Reserpine, producing very low blood pressure, dizziness, and possible fainting.

Food Interactions

Betaxolol eyedrops may be used without regard to meals.

Usual Dose

1 drop in the affected eye 2 times a day.

Overdosage

Possible symptoms are very slow heartbeat, heart failure, low blood pressure, and spasms of the bronchial muscles making it hard to breathe. Take the victim to a hospital emergency room for treatment. ALWAYS bring the medicine container with you.

Special Information

To administer the eyedrops, lie down or tilt your head backward and look at the ceiling. Hold the dropper above your eye and drop the medicine inside your lower lid while looking up. To prevent possible infection, don't allow the dropper to touch your fingers, eyelids, or any surface. Release the lower lid and keep your eye open. Don't blink for about 30 seconds. Press gently on the bridge of your nose at the inside corner of your eye for about a minute. This will help circulate the medicine around your eye. Wait at least 5 minutes before using any other eyedrops.

Generic Name

Bitolterol Mesylate

Brand Name

Tornalate

Type of Drug

Bronchodilator.

Prescribed for

Asthma and bronchospasm.

General Information

Bitolterol is currently available only as an inhalation. It may be taken in combination with other medicines to control your asthma. The drug starts working 3 to 4 minutes after it is taken and continues to work for 5 to 8 hours. It can be used only when needed to treat an asthmatic attack or on a regular basis to prevent an attack.

utions and Warnings

itolterol should be used with caution if you have had angina, heart disease, high blood pressure, a history of stroke r seizures, diabetes, prostate disease, or glaucoma.

Pregnancy/Breast-feeding

Bitolterol should only be used by a pregnant or breast-feeding woman when it is absolutely necessary. The potential benefit of using this medicine must be weighed against the potential, but unknown, hazard it can pose to your baby.

Seniors

Older adults are more sensitive to the effects of this drug. They should closely follow their doctor's directions and report any side effects at once.

Possible Side Effects

Bitolterol's side effects are similar to those associated with other bronchodilator drugs. The most common side effects are restlessness, weakness, anxiety, fear, tension, sleeplessness, tremors, convulsions, dizziness, headache, flushing, loss of appetite, pallor, sweating, nausea, vomiting, and muscle cramps.

Less common side effects include angina, abnormal heart rhythms, heart palpitations, high blood pressure, and urinary difficulty. Bitolterol has been associated with abnormalities in blood tests for the liver and white blood cells, and with tests for urine protein, but the true importance of this reaction is not known.

Drug Interactions

Bitolterol's effects may be enhanced by monoamine oxidase (MAO) inhibitor drugs, antidepressants, thyroid drugs, other bronchodilators, and some antihistamines. It is antagonized by the beta-blocking drugs (Propranolol and others).

Bitolterol may antagonize the effects of blood-pressure-lowering drugs, especially Reserpine, Methyldopa, and Guanethidine.

Food Interactions

Bitolterol does not interact with food, since it is only taken by inhalation into the lungs.

Usual Dose

To treat an attack: 2 inhalations at an interval of at least to 3 minutes, followed by a third inhalation, if needed.

To prevent an attack: 2 inhalations every 8 hours.

Overdosage

Bitolterol overdosage can result in exaggerated side effects including heart pains and high blood pressure, although the pressure can drop to a low level after a short period of elevation. People who inhale too much Bitolterol should see a doctor, who may prescribe a beta-blocking drug like Atenolol or Metoprolol to counter the bronchodilator's effects.

Special Information

Be sure to follow your doctor's directions for using Bitolterol and do not take more than 4 inhalations of Bitolterol over an 8-hour period. Using more than is prescribed can lead to drug tolerance and actually cause your condition to worsen.

The drug should be inhaled during the second half of your breath. This allows the medicine to reach more deeply into your lungs.

Call your doctor at once if you develop chest pains, rapid heartbeat, palpitations, muscle tremors, dizziness, headache, facial flushing, or urinary difficulty, or if you still have trouble breathing after using the medicine.

Generic Name

Brompheniramine Maleate

Brand Names

Bromphen
Diamine T. D.
Dimetane

Dimetane Extentabs
Veltane

(Also available in generic form)

Type of Drug

Antihistamine.

escribed for

easonal allergy, stuffed and runny nose, itching of the eyes,
cratchy throat caused by allergy, and other allergic symp-
oms such as itching, rash, or hives.

eneral Information

ntihistamines, including Brompheniramine, generally act
y antagonizing histamine at the site where histamine works.
his site is often called the H_1 histamine receptor. Antihista-
ines work by drying up the secretions of the nose, throat,
nd eyes.

autions and Warnings

Brompheniramine Maleate should not be used if you are
llergic to this drug. It should be avoided or used with
xtreme care if you have narrow-angle glaucoma (pressure
n the eye), stomach ulcer or other stomach problems, en-
arged prostate, or problems passing urine. It should not be
used by people who have deep-breathing problems such as
asthma.

Use with care if you have a history of glaucoma, thyroid
disease, heart disease, high blood pressure, or diabetes.

regnancy/Breast-feeding

Brompheniramine has not been proven to be a cause of
birth defects or other problems in pregnant women, although
studies in animals have shown that some antihistamines
(Meclizine and Cyclizine), used mainly against nausea and
vomiting, may cause birth defects. Do not take any antihistamine without your doctor's knowledge.

Small amounts of antihistamine medicines pass into breast
milk and may affect a nursing infant. Nursing mothers should
avoid antihistamines or use alternate feeding methods while
taking the medicine.

Seniors

Seniors are more sensitive to antihistamine side effects. Confusion, difficult or painful urination, dizziness, drowsiness, a
faint feeling, dry mouth, nose, or throat, nightmares or excitement, nervousness, restlessness, or irritability are more
likely to occur among older adults.

Possible Side Effects

Occasionally seen: itching, rash, sensitivity to light, perspir
tion, chills, dryness of the mouth, nose, and throat, lowerin
of blood pressure, headache, rapid heartbeat, sleeplessnes
dizziness, disturbed coordination, confusion, restlessness, ne
vousness, irritability, euphoria (feeling "high"), tingling
the hands and feet, blurred vision, double vision, ringing
the ears, stomach upset, loss of appetite, nausea, vomitin
constipation, diarrhea, difficulty in urination, tightness of th
chest, wheezing, nasal stuffiness.

Drug Interactions

Brompheniramine Maleate should not be taken with monc
amine oxidase (MAO) inhibitors.

Interaction with tranquilizers, sedatives, and sleeping medi
cation will increase the effects of these drugs; it is extremel
important that you discuss this with your doctor so tha
doses of these drugs can be properly adjusted.

Be extremely cautious when drinking while taking Brom
pheniramine Maleate, which will enhance the intoxicatin
effect of the alcohol. Alcohol also has a sedative effect.

Usual Dose

Adult: 4 milligrams 3 to 4 times per day.

Child: (age 6 to 12): 2 to 4 milligrams 3 to 4 times per day.
Do not exceed 12 milligrams per day.

Child: (under age 6): ¼ milligram per pound per day in
divided doses.

Time-release doses:

Adult: 8 to 12 milligrams at bedtime or every 8 to 12 hours
during the day.

Child (age 6 to 12): 8 milligrams during the day or at
bedtime.

Overdosage

Symptoms are depression or stimulation (especially in children), dry mouth, fixed or dilated pupils, flushing of the skin,
and stomach upset. Take the patient to a hospital emergency
room immediately, if you cannot make him vomit. ALWAYS
bring the medicine bottle.

Special Information

Antihistamines produce a depressing effect: be extremely cautious when driving or operating heavy equipment.

If you forget a dose of Brompheniramine, take it as soon as you remember. If it is almost time for your next dose, skip the forgotten dose and continue with your regular schedule. Do not take a double dose of Brompheniramine.

Generic Name

Bumetanide

Brand Name

Bumex

Type of Drug

Diuretic.

Prescribed for

Congestive heart failure, cirrhosis of the liver, kidney dysfunction, high blood pressure, and other conditions where it may be desirable to rid the body of excess fluid.

General Information

Bumetanide is a potent diuretic that works in the same way as Furosemide and Ethacrynic Acid. Not only do these drugs affect the same part of the kidney as the more commonly used thiazide diuretics, they also affect the portion of the kidney known as the Loop of Henle. This double action makes Bumetanide and the other "loop" diuretics extremely powerful drugs. All three loop diuretics can be used for the same purposes, but their doses are quite different. One milligram of Bumetanide is equivalent to about 40 milligrams of Furosemide and about 50 milligrams of Ethacrynic Acid.

Cautions and Warnings

Excessive amounts of Bumetanide can lead to dehydration and severe imbalances in your body levels of potassium, sodium, and chloride. Warning signs of dehydration are dry

mouth, excessive thirst, loss of appetite, weakness, lethargy
drowsiness, restlessness, tingling in the hands or feet, mus
cle weakness, pain or cramps, low blood pressure, reduced
urinary volume, rapid heartbeat, abnormal heart rhythms
nausea, and vomiting.

Do not use Bumetanide if you have had an allergic reac
tion to it in the past. People who are allergic to or cannot
tolerate Furosemide may receive a prescription for Bumetanide
as an alternative diuretic.

People with severe kidney or liver disease who take this
medicine should maintain close contact with their doctor
because the drug can accentuate some conditions affecting
these organs.

Pregnancy/Breast-feeding

Animals given doses between 3.4 and 3400 times the maximum human dose showed some effect on developing
embryos. Bumetanide has not caused adverse effects on
developing infants and may even be prescribed to treat severe pregnancy-induced high blood pressure when other
treatments fail. In general, though, this drug should be avoided
by pregnant women or women who may become pregnant
while using it. In those situations where it is deemed essential, the potential risk of taking Bumetanide must be carefully
weighed against any benefit it might produce. It is not known
if Bumetanide passes into breast milk. It is recommended
that women taking Bumetanide use alternative feeding
methods.

Seniors

Elderly patients may be more sensitive to Bumetanide side
effects than younger adults and should be treated with doses
at the low end of the recommended range.

Possible Side Effects

Loss of appetite, nausea, vomiting, diarrhea, inflammation
of the pancreas, yellowing of the skin or whites of the eyes,
dizziness, headache, blurred vision, ringing or buzzing in the
ears, and reduction of blood-platelet and white-blood-cell
levels.

Other side effects: Bumetanide may worsen liver or kidney
disease, cause abdominal pains, dry mouth, impotence, mus-

e weakness or cramps, arthritislike pains in the joints, low
ood pressure, changes in heart rhythm, and chest pains.
he loop diuretics (Bumetanide, Ethacrynic Acid, and Furo-
emide) have been associated with mild ear congestion,
minished hearing, and hearing loss. But these are rare and
sually only follow rapid intravenous injection of these drugs.

rug Interactions

ecause Bumetanide may enhance the effects of drugs that
ower blood pressure, this interaction is beneficial and is
ften used to treat high blood pressure. Bumetanide in-
reases the side effects of Lithium by interfering with the
limination of that drug from the body.

Alcohol, barbiturate-type sleeping pills, and narcotic pain
elievers can cause excessive low blood pressure when taken
vith potent diuretics like Bumetanide.

The possibility of losing body potassium with Bumetanide
s increased by combining it with Digoxin (for the heart) and
adrenal corticosteroids (for inflammation). Potassium loss
also increases the chances of Digoxin side effects.

Probenecid reduces the effectiveness of Bumetanide by
interfering with its action on the kidneys. Indomethacin and
other nonsteroidal anti-inflammatory drugs such as Naproxen,
Sulindac, and Ibuprofen may also reduce Bumetanide effectiveness.

People taking Bumetanide for high blood pressure or heart
failure should take care to avoid nonprescription medicines
that might aggravate those conditions, such as decongestants, cold and allergy treatments, and diet pills, all of which
can contain stimulants. If you are unsure about which medicine to choose, ask your pharmacist.

Food Interactions

Bumetanide may cause loss of body potassium (hypokalemia),
a complication that can be avoided by adding foods high in
potassium to your diet. Some potassium-rich foods are tomatoes, citrus fruits, melons, and bananas. Hypokalemia can
also be prevented by taking a potassium supplement in pill,
powder, or liquid form.

Bumetanide may be taken with food if it upsets your
stomach.

Usual Dose

0.5 to 2 milligrams per day. It may also be taken every other
day for 3 to 4 consecutive days followed by 1 to 2 medicine
free days.

Overdosage

The major symptoms of overdose are related to the potent
diuretic effect of Bumetanide: lethargy, weakness, dizziness,
confusion, cramps, loss of appetite, and vomiting. Victims of
Bumetanide overdose should be taken to a hospital emergency room for treatment. ALWAYS bring the medicine bottle with you.

Special Information

Take your daily dose no later than 10:00 A.M. If taken later in
the day, this potent diuretic could interfere with your sleep
by keeping you up to go to the bathroom.

Call your doctor if any warning signs of dehydration develop while you are taking Bumetanide. The warning signs
are dry mouth, excessive thirst, loss of appetite, weakness,
lethargy, drowsiness, restlessness, tingling in the hands or
feet, muscle weakness, pain or cramps, low blood pressure,
reduced urinary volume, rapid heartbeat, abnormal heart
rhythms, nausea, and vomiting.

Take a missed dose as soon as you remember, but don't
double the dose of Bumetanide.

Generic Name

Buspirone

Brand Name

BuSpar

Type of Drug

Minor tranquilizer, antianxiety drug.

Prescribed for

Anxiety.

General Information

This drug is chemically different from the benzodiazepines, the most widely prescribed antianxiety drugs, but it has a potent antianxiety effect. Although it is approved by the United States Food and Drug Administration for short-term relief of anxiety, it appears that the drug can be safely used for longer periods (more than 4 weeks) of time. Buspirone's exact effect on the body is not known, but it seems to lack the danger of drug addiction associated with other antianxiety drugs, including the benzodiazepines, and does not severely depress the nervous system or act as an anticonvulsant or muscle relaxant, as other antianxiety drugs do. Minor improvement will show after only 7 to 10 days of drug treatment, but the maximum effect does not occur until 3 to 4 weeks after starting treatment.

Cautions and Warnings

Although Buspirone has not shown any potential for drug dependence, you should be aware of the possibility that this might still happen.

This drug causes less sedation than other antianxiety medicines, but it may produce some depression of nervous system activity. Therefore, you should take care when driving or operating complex equipment while taking Buspirone.

Pregnancy/Breast-feeding

Buspirone has not been found to cause birth defects. Pregnant women, or those who might become pregnant while taking this drug, should not take it without their doctor's approval. When the drug is considered essential by your doctor, the potential risk of taking the medicine must be carefully weighed against the benefit it might produce.

This drug passes into breast milk, but has caused no problems among breast-fed infants. You must consider the potential effect on the nursing infant if breast-feeding while taking this medicine.

Seniors

Several hundred older adults participated in drug evaluation studies without any unusual problems. However, the effect of this drug in older adults is not well known and special problems may surface as time passes and the use of Buspirone becomes more widespread.

Possible Side Effects

Most common: dizziness, nausea, headache, fatigue, nervousness, light-headedness, and excitement.

Other common side effects: heart palpitations, muscle aches and pains, tremors, skin rash, sweating, and clamminess.

Less common side effects: sleeplessness, chest pain, rapid heartbeat, low blood pressure, fainting, stroke, heart attack, heart failure, dream disturbances, difficulty concentrating, a drug "high," anger, hostility, depression, depersonalization and disassociation, intolerance to noise, intolerance to cold temperatures, fearfulness, loss of interest, hallucinations, suicidal tendencies, claustrophobia, stupor, and slurred speech.

Other side effects: ringing or buzzing in the ears, a "roaring" sensation in the head, sore throat, red and itchy eyes, changes in taste and smell, inner ear problems, eye pain, intolerance to bright lights, dry mouth, stomach or intestinal upset or cramps, diarrhea, constipation, stomach gas, changes in appetite, excess salivation, urinary difficulty, menstrual irregularity, pelvic inflammatory disease, bed-wetting, muscle cramps and spasms, numbness, tingling in the hands and feet, poor coordination, involuntary movements, slowed reaction time, rapid breathing, shortness of breath, chest congestion, changes in sex drive, itching, facial swelling, flushing, easy bruising, hair loss, dry skin, blisters, fever, a feeling of ill health, bleeding disturbance, and voice loss.

Rare side effects: very slow heartbeat, high blood pressure, seizures and psychotic reactions, blurred vision, stuffed nose, pressure on the eyes, thyroid abnormalities, irritable colon, bleeding from the rectum, burning of the tongue, periodic spotting, painful urination, muscle weakness, nosebleeds, delayed ejaculation and impotence (men), thinning of the nails, and hiccups.

Drug Interactions

The combination of Buspirone with monoamine oxidase (MAO) inhibitor drugs may produce very high blood pressure and can be dangerous.

The effects of Buspirone together with other drugs that

work in the central nervous system are not known. Do not take other tranquilizers, antianxiety, or psychoactive drugs with Buspirone unless prescribed by a doctor who knows your complete medication history.

The combination of Buspirone and Trazodone may cause liver inflammation.

Food Interactions

Food can affect the amount of drug absorbed into the bloodstream and the rate at which it is absorbed. This drug can be taken either with or without food. For the most consistent results, always take your dose at the same time of day in the same way, i.e., with or without food.

Usual Dose

15 to 60 milligrams per day in 3 divided doses.

Overdosage

Symptoms: nausea, vomiting, dizziness, drowsiness, pinpoint pupils, and upset stomach. To date, no deaths have been caused by Buspirone overdose. There is no specific antidote for Buspirone overdose. Take the victim to a hospital emergency room for treatment. ALWAYS bring the medicine bottle with you.

Special Information

Buspirone can cause nervous system depression. Be careful while driving or operating complex equipment.

Studies have shown that Buspirone does not increase the depressant effect of alcohol. Nevertheless, it would be wise for you to avoid alcoholic beverages while taking this, or any other, central nervous system drug product.

Contact your doctor if you develop any intolerable side effects. About 1 out of 10 people who were included in drug studies had to stop taking Buspirone because of drug side effects. Especially important are uncontrolled or repeated movements of the head, face, neck, or other body parts.

If you miss a dose of Buspirone, take it as soon as you remember. If it is almost time for your next dose, skip the missed dose and go back to your regular dose schedule. Do not take a double dose of Buspirone.

Generic Name

Butoconazole Nitrate

Brand Name
Femstat

Type of Drug
Antifungal.

Prescribed for
Fungus infections of the skin or vaginal tract.

General Information
Butoconazole Nitrate is one of several antifungal products available in the United States. This drug may be effective against organisms that are not affected by other drugs. Up to 5 percent of the drug may be absorbed into the bloodstream after vaginal administration.

Cautions and Warnings
Do not use this product if you are allergic or sensitive to it. Stop using it if it causes irritation or itching.

Pregnancy/Breast-feeding
No problems have been reported among infants born of pregnant women who have used Butoconazole Nitrate, but the drug should never be used during the first 3 months of pregnancy. The use of a vaginal applicator may not be advised during pregnancy: another product that comes as a vaginal tablet may be preferred. Pregnant women should not use this drug without their doctor's consent.

It is not known if Butoconazole Nitrate passes into breast milk.

Seniors
Seniors may use this drug without special precautions.

Possible Side Effects
The most common side effects are vaginal burning and itch-

ing. Other side effects include vaginal discharge, irritation, soreness, swelling, and itchy fingers.

Usual Dose

Pregnant women (4th through 9th months only): 1 applicatorful at bedtime for 6 nights.

Nonpregnant women: 1 applicatorful at bedtime for 3 to 6 nights.

Special Information

The effectiveness of this drug is not affected by menstruation. Insert each dose of this medication high into the vagina. For maximum effect, you must complete the full course of treatment, even if you begin to feel better. Refrain from intercourse while using this drug or advise your partner to wear a condom to prevent reinfection. Use a sanitary napkin to prevent your clothes from being stained.

If you forget a dose of Butoconazole Nitrate, apply it as soon as you remember. If it is almost time for your next dose, skip the forgotten dose and continue with your regular schedule. Do not take a double dose.

Brand Name

Capozide

Ingredients

Captopril
Hydrochlorothiazide

Prescribed for

High blood pressure.

Type of Drug

Antihypertensive combination.

General Information

This medicine is a combination of a thiazide diuretic and a member of a relatively new class of blood-pressure-lowering drugs, ACE inhibitors, which work by preventing the conversion of a potent hormone called Angiotensin I. This directly affects the production of other hormones and enzymes which participate in the regulation of blood pressure. The blood-pressure-lowering effects of the two drugs add to each other to produce a result greater than could be expected from either ingredient.

Cautions and Warnings

This drug can cause kidney problems, especially loss of protein in the urine. Patients taking Capozide should have the amount of protein in the urine measured during the first month of treatment and monthly for the next few months. The drug can also cause a reduction in white-blood-cell count, leading to a potential for increased susceptibility to infection. Capozide should be used with caution by people who have kidney disease or diseases of the immune/collagen system (particularly lupus erythematosus) or who have taken other drugs that affect the white-blood-cell count.

Do not take this combination if you are allergic to either ingredient or to sulfa drugs. You may be sensitive to Hydrochlorothiazide if you have a history of allergy or bronchial asthma.

Pregnancy/Breast-feeding

Animal studies show that Captopril may cause birth defects. Hydrochlorothiazide crosses into the developing baby's blood system and can cause jaundice, blood problems, and low potassium. Women who are, or might become, pregnant while taking this drug should discuss the matter with their doctor.

It is not known if Captopril passes into breast milk and if it will affect a nursing infant. Hydrochlorothiazide passes into breast milk, but no problems have been reported in nursing infants.

Seniors

Older adults may be *less* sensitive to the blood-pressure-lowering effects of this drug combination than younger adults. But, they may be *more* sensitive to its side effects. Dosage must be individualized to your needs.

Possible Side Effects

Dizziness, tiredness, headache, diarrhea, rash (usually mild), and cough are the most common side effects.

Less common drug side effects are itching, fever, temporary loss of taste perception, stomach irritation, chest pain, low blood pressure, heart palpitations, difficulty sleeping, tingling in the hands or feet, nausea, vomiting, jaundice and liver damage, excessive sweating, muscle cramps, (male) impotence, and muscle weakness. Some people experience unusual reactions after taking the first dose of the drug, which can include facial flushing and swelling, swelling of the arms and legs, and closing of the throat.

The Hydrochlorothiazide ingredient can cause a loss of body potassium. Signs of low potassium are dry mouth, thirst, weakness, lethargy, drowsiness, restlessness, muscle pains or cramps, muscle tiredness, low blood pressure, low urine production, abnormal heart rate, and upset stomach. Your doctor may prescribe a potassium-rich diet or a potassium supplement to counteract this problem, although Captopril can counteract the Hydrochlorothiazide (see "Food Interactions" below).

Drug Interactions

The blood-pressure-lowering effect of Capozide is additive with diuretic drugs and the beta blockers. Other drugs that cause rapid drops in blood pressure should be used with extreme caution because of a possible severe drop when taken together with Capozide.

The Captopril portion of this combination may increase potassium levels in your blood, especially when given with potassium-sparing diuretics and/or potassium supplements.

People taking oral antidiabetic drugs who start taking Capozide may have to have their antidiabetic dosage adjusted. The chance of Lithium toxicity may be increased by Hydrochlorothiazide.

Food Interactions

This drug is best taken on an empty stomach, usually 1 hour before or 2 hours after meals.

Usual Dose

Adult: 1 tablet 2 or 3 times a day. People with poor kidney function have to take less of the medicine to achieve reduced blood pressure.

Child: as determined by body weight and individual response.

Overdosage

The primary effect of Capozide overdosage is a rapid drop in blood pressure, as evidenced by dizziness or fainting. Take the overdose victim to a hospital emergency room immediately. ALWAYS remember to bring the medicine bottle.

Special Information

Call your doctor if you develop fever, sore throat, mouth sores, abnormal heartbeat, chest pain, or if you have persistent rash or loss of taste perception.

Capozide may cause dizziness when quickly rising from a lying or sitting position.

Avoid strenuous exercise and/or very hot weather as heavy sweating and/or dehydration can cause a rapid drop in blood pressure.

Do not stop taking this medicine without your doctor's knowledge.

Avoid nonprescription medicines such a diet pills, decongestants, and stimulants that can raise your blood pressure.

If you forget a dose of Capozide, take it as soon as you remember. If it is almost time for your next dose, skip the one you forgot and continue with your regular schedule. Do not take a double dose.

Generic Name

Captopril

Brand Name

Capoten

Type of Drug

Antihypertensive; ACE inhibitor.

Prescribed for

High blood pressure. Low doses may be used to treat mild to moderate high blood pressure. Captopril may be taken alone or together with a diuretic drug.

Captopril is also used in the treatment of congestive heart failure.

Captopril has been studied as a treatment for rheumatoid arthritis.

General Information

This drug was the first member of a new class of drugs which work by preventing the conversion of a potent hormone called Angiotensin I. This directly affects the production of other hormones and enzymes which participate in the regulation of blood pressure. The effect is to lower blood pressure relatively quickly, within 1 to 1½ hours after taking the medicine.

Cautions and Warnings

This drug can cause kidney disease, especially loss of protein in the urine. Patients should have the amount of protein in their urine measured during the first month and monthly for a few months afterward. The drug can also cause reduction in the white-blood-cell count, and this can result in increased susceptibility to infection. Captopril should be used with caution by people who have kidney disease or diseases of the immune/collagen system (particularly lupus erythematosus), or who have taken other drugs which affect the white-blood-cell count.

Pregnancy/Breast-feeding

Animal studies show that Captopril may cause birth defects. Women who are, or might become, pregnant while taking Captopril should discuss the matter thoroughly with their doctor.

Captopril passes into breast milk in concentrations about 1 percent of those found in blood. The effect of this drug on nursing infants is not known.

Seniors

Older adults may be *less* sensitive to the blood-pressure-lowering effects of Captopril than younger adults. But, they may be *more* sensitive to drug side effects. Dosage must be individualized to your needs.

Possible Side Effects

Rash (usually mild), itching, fever, loss of taste perception (which usually returns in 2 to 3 months), and gastric irritation.

Less common side effects are those on the kidney including protein in the urine, kidney failure, excessive or frequent urination, reduction in the amount of urine produced; adverse effect on the blood system, especially white blood cells; swelling of the face, mucous membranes of the mouth, or arms and legs, flushing or pale color of skin. Captopril may also cause low blood pressure, adverse effects on the heart (chest pain, abnormal heartbeats, spasms of blood vessels, heart failure).

Drug Interactions

The blood pressure effect of Captopril is additive with diuretic drugs. Some other hypertensive drugs can cause severe blood pressure drops when used with large amounts of Captopril. They should be used with extreme caution. Beta-adrenergic blocking drugs may add some blood-pressure-lowering effect to Captopril.

Captopril may increase serum potassium, especially if given with potassium-sparing diuretics and/or potassium supplements. Avoid over-the-counter cough, cold, and allergy remedies containing drugs which may aggravate your condition. Aspirin or Indomethacin may decrease or completely abolish the blood-pressure-lowering effect of Captopril.

Food Interactions

Do not take this medicine with food or meals. It must be taken at least 1 hour before or 2 hours after meals.

Usual Dose

Adult: 75 milligrams per day to start. Dose may be increased up to 450 milligrams per day, if needed. The dose of this medicine must be tailored to your needs.

Child: about 0.15 milligrams per pound of body weight 3 times a day.

People with poor kidney function have to take less medicine.

Overdosage

The primary effect of Captopril overdosage is very low blood pressure. A person who has taken a Captopril overdose must be taken to a hospital emergency room for treatment. ALWAYS bring the medicine bottle with you.

Special Information

Call your doctor if you develop fever, sore throat, mouth sores, abnormal heartbeat, or chest pain, or if you have persistent rash, or loss of taste perception.

This drug may cause dizziness when you rise quickly from sitting or lying down.

Avoid strenuous exercise and/or very hot weather as heavy sweating and/or dehydration can cause a rapid drop in blood pressure.

If you are taking this medicine for high blood pressure, be certain to avoid nonprescription drugs such as diet pills, decongestants, and stimulants that can raise blood pressure.

Do not abruptly stop taking this medication. If you forget to take a dose, do not double your next dose. Skip the forgotten dose and go back to your regular dose schedule.

Generic Name

Carbamazepine

Brand Name

Tegretol

(Also available in generic form)

Type of Drug

Anticonvulsant.

Prescribed for

Seizure disorders and trigeminal neuralgia. It is also prescribed for diabetes insipidus (a hormonal disease leading to severe water retention), some psychiatric disorders, and alcoholism.

General Information

Carbamazepine was first approved for the relief of severe
pain associated with trigeminal neuralgia. Over the years,
though, it has gained much greater acceptance for seizure
control, especially for people who are not controlled by
Phenytoin, Phenobarbital, or Primidone, or who have suffered severe side effects from these medicines.

This drug is not a simple pain reliever and should not be
taken for everyday aches and pains. It has some potentially
fatal side effects.

Cautions and Warnings

This drug should not be used if you have a history of bone
marrow depression, are sensitive or allergic to this drug or
to the tricyclic antidepressants. Monoamine oxidase (MAO)
inhibitors should be discontinued 2 weeks before Carbamazepine treatment is begun.

Carbamazepine can cause severe, life-threatening blood
reactions. Your doctor should have a complete blood count
done before you start taking this medicine, and repeat that
examination weekly during the first 3 months of treatment
and then every month for the next 2 or 3 years.

Carbamazepine may aggravate glaucoma and should be
used with caution by people with this condition.

Pregnancy/Breast-feeding

This drug causes birth defects in animals studied. However, the exact effect of Carbamazepine on a developing
fetus is not known. Women taking this drug for a seizure
problem should continue taking the drug because of the
possibility of causing a seizure by stopping the drug and
the danger of that seizure to an unborn child. If possible,
anticonvulsant drugs should be stopped before the pregnancy
begins.

Carbamazepine passes into breast milk in concentrations
of about 60 percent of those in the mother's bloodstream
and can affect a nursing infant. Do not nurse your baby if
you must take this drug. You can ask your doctor if it will be
safe to discontinue the medication during the time you will
be nursing your newborn baby.

Seniors

Older adults are more likely to develop Carbamazepine-induced heart problems, psychosis, confusion, or agitation.

Possible Side Effects

The most frequent side effects of Carbamazepine are dizziness, drowsiness, unsteadiness, nausea, and vomiting. Other common side effects are blurred or double vision, confusion or hostility, headache, and severe water retention.

Less common side effects are mood and behavior changes (especially in children), confusion, hives, itching or skin rash, allergic reaction.

Rare side effects are chest pain, fainting, trouble breathing, continuous back-and-forth eye movements, slurred speech, depression, restlessness, nervousness, muscle rigidity, ringing or buzzing in the ears, trembling, uncontrolled body movement, hallucinations, darkening of the stool or urine, yellowing of the eyes or skin, mouth sores, unusual bleeding or bruising, unusual tiredness or weakness, changes in your pattern of urination (frequent, or a sudden decrease of urine production), swelling of the feet or lower legs, numbness, tingling, pain or weakness in the hands or feet, pain, tenderness, and a bluish color of the leg or foot, swollen glands.

Drug Interactions

Carbamazepine blood levels may be increased by Cimetidine, Diltiazem, Isoniazid, Propoxyphene, Erythromycin, Mexilitene, Troleandomycin, or Verapamil, leading to drug toxicity.

Women taking oral contraceptives may experience breakthrough bleeding with Carbamazepine.

Phenobarbital, Phenytoin or Primidone can reduce the amount of Carbamazepine in the blood. Charcoal tablets or powder decrease the amount of Carbamazepine absorbed into the blood.

Carbamazepine decreases the effect of Warfarin, an anticoagulant drug, and Theophylline, for asthma. People taking this combination may need more of these medicines to retain the desired effects. Other drugs counteracted by Carbamazepine are Cyclosporine, Dacarbazine, digitalis drugs, Disopyramide, Doxycycline, Levothyroxine, and Quinidine.

Taking Carbamazepine together with antidepressants or antipsychotic drugs can increase the depressant effects of Carbamazepine.

Food Interactions

Carbamazepine may be taken with food if it causes upset stomach.

Usual Dose

Adult and child (over age 12): 200 to 1200 milligrams per day, depending on the condition being treated. Usual maintenance dose is 400 to 800 milligrams per day in 2 divided doses.

Child (age 6 to 12): 200 to 1000 milligrams per day. Or, 10 to 15 milligrams per pound of body weight per day, divided into 3 or 4 equal doses.

Overdosage

Carbamazepine is a potentially lethal drug. The lowest known single lethal dose was 60 grams. Adults have survived single doses of 30 grams and children have survived single doses of 5 to 10 grams.

Overdose symptoms appear 1 to 3 hours after the drug is taken. The most prominent effects are irregularity or difficulty in breathing, rapid heartbeat, changes in blood pressure, shock, loss of consciousness or coma, convulsions, muscle twitching, restlessness, uncontrolled body movements, drooping eyelids, psychotic mood changes, nausea, vomiting, reduced urination.

The overdose victim must be taken to a hospital emergency room immediately. Successful treatment depends on prompt elimination of the drug from the body. ALWAYS bring the medicine bottle with you.

Special Information

Carbamazepine can cause dizziness and drowsiness. Take care while driving or operating any mechanical equipment.

Call your doctor at once if you develop a yellow coloration of the eyes or skin, unusual bleeding or bruising, abdominal pain, pale stools, dark urine, impotence (men), mood changes, nervous system symptoms, swelling, fever, chills, sore throat, or mouth sores. These may be signs of a potentially fatal drug side effect.

Do not abruptly stop taking Carbamazepine without your physician's advice. If you forget to take a dose, however, skip the missed dose and go back to your regular dose schedule. If you miss more than 1 dose in a day, check with your doctor.

Generic Name

Carbenicillin

Brand Name

Geocillin

Type of Drug

Penicillin-type antibiotic.

Prescribed for

Gram-positive bacterial infections of the urinary tract and prostate.

General Information

The oral form of Carbenicillin is limited in usefulness because it is not well absorbed into the blood. It can be used for urinary infections because the drug is highly concentrated in urine. Oral Carbenicillin may also be used as follow-up treatment for people who had received the drug by intravenous Injection. It and other penicillin-type antibiotics fight infection by killing bacteria. They do this by destroying the cell wall of invading bacteria. Other antibiotics simply prevent bacteria from reproducing. Many infections can be treated by almost any member of this family, but some infections can only be treated by certain penicillin-type antibiotics.

Penicillins cannot treat a cold, flu, or any virus infection and should never be taken unless prescribed by a doctor for a specific illness. Always take your antibiotic exactly according to your doctor's directions for use, including the number of pills to take every day and the number of days to take the medicine. If you do not follow directions, you may not get the antibiotic's full benefit.

Cautions and Warnings

Do not take Carbenicillin if you have a history of penicillin allergy. The drugs are similar. The most common allergic reaction to Carbenicillin and other penicillins is a hivelike rash over the body with itching and redness. It is important to tell your doctor if you have ever taken this or any other penicillin before and had an allergic reaction to it such as rash, itching, or trouble breathing.

Pregnancy/Breast-feeding

Carbenicillin has not caused birth defects but you should be sure your doctor knows you are taking it. Carbenicillin passes into breast milk and may affect a nursing infant.

Seniors

Seniors may take Carbenicillin without special precautions.

Possible Side Effects

Common side effects include upset stomach, nausea, vomiting, diarrhea, and rash. Less common side effects include hairy tongue, itching or irritation around the anus or vagina, stomach pains with or without bleeding.

High doses of the intravenous form of Carbenicillin can cause bleeding problems.

Drug Interactions

The effect of Carbenicillin can be affected by taking other antibiotics at the same time. Otherwise, Carbenicillin is remarkably free of interaction.

Food Interactions

Carbenicillin is best taken with a full glass of water on an empty stomach, 1 hour before or 2 hours after meals.

Usual Dose

1 or 2 tablets 4 times a day.

Overdosage

Carbenicillin overdose is unlikely but may result in diarrhea or upset stomach.

Special Information

Do not take this medicine after the expiration date on the label. Be sure to take this medicine exactly according to your doctor's directions.

Stop taking the medicine and call your doctor if any of the following side effects develop: skin rash, hives, itching, wheezing. Other side effects that demand your doctor's attention are: blood in the urine, passage of large amounts of light-colored urine, swelling of the face or ankles, trouble breathing, unusual weakness or tiredness.

It is important to keep a constant amount of Carbenicillin in your urine or blood. If you miss a dose take it as soon as you remember. If it is almost time for your next dose, take the missed dose, then take the next dose 2 to 4 hours later and begin a new dose schedule. Alternatively, you may double the next dose and continue with your regular dose schedule.

Generic Name

Carprofen

Brand Name

Rimadyl

Type of Drug

Nonsteroidal anti-inflammatory.

Prescribed for

Rheumatoid and gouty arthritis, osteoarthritis.

General Information

Carprofen is one of many nonsteroidal anti-inflammatory drugs sold in the United States to reduce inflammation, relieve pain and fever, and relieve menstrual cramps and discomfort. The choice of one member of this group over another often depends on your individual response to a specific drug. Because of this, it is common to try several of these drugs before you find the one that is right for you. Carprofen should be reserved for people who cannot tolerate, or do not respond to, other nonsteroidal anti-inflammatory drugs. Carprofen starts working in about 1 hour and will last for about 6 hours.

Cautions and Warnings

Do not take this product if you are allergic to Aspirin or to any other nonsteroidal anti-inflammatory drug. This drug can worsen stomach ulcers or cause a new ulcer to develop. It should be used with caution if you have kidney disease.

Pregnancy/Breast-feeding

This drug may cross into the blood circulation of a developing baby. It has not been found to cause birth defects. Pregnant women, or those who might become pregnant while taking this drug, should not take it without their doctor's approval. When the drug is considered essential by your doctor, the potential risk of taking the medicine must be carefully weighed against the benefit it might produce.

This drug may pass into breast milk, but has caused no problems among breast-fed infants. You must consider the potential effect on the nursing infant if breast-feeding while taking this medicine.

Seniors

Older adults are more sensitive to the stomach, kidney, and liver effects of this drug. Some doctors recommend that persons 70 years of age and older take ½ the usual dose. Follow your doctor's directions and report any side effects at once.

Possible Side Effects

Most frequent: upset stomach, dizziness, headache, drowsiness, ringing in the ears, rash.

Other side effects include heartburn, nausea, vomiting, bloating, stomach gas or pain, diarrhea, constipation, dark stools, nervousness, sleeplessness, depression, confusion, tremor, loss of appetite, fatigue, itching, double or blurred vision, dry or irritated eyes, heart failure, palpitations, abnormal heart rhythms, anemia or other changes in the composition of your blood, changes in liver function, hair loss, tingling in the hands or feet, fever, enlarged breasts, blood in the urine, urinary irritation, thirst, frequent urination, kidney damage, low blood sugar, asthma, difficulty breathing, skin rash, itching, swelling, black-and-blue marks.

Drug Interactions

Aspirin causes this drug to be eliminated from the body more rapidly than it usually is.

This drug may increase the effectiveness of Lithium and anticoagulant (blood-thinning), antidiabetes, and antiseizure drugs.

People taking Methotrexate should not take Carprofen or any other nonsteroidal anti-inflammatory drug (NSAID). Four people have died from taking Methotrexate and an NSAID.

Carprofen may reduce the effects of beta-blocking drugs like Propranolol, Atenolol, and others.

Carprofen may increase the effects of sulfa drugs, antidiabetes drugs, and Phenytoin or other drugs for seizure disorders.

Food Interactions

You may take this drug with food if it upsets your stomach.

Usual Dose

300 to 600 milligrams per day. Senior citizens and people with kidney problems should start with a lower dosage.

Overdosage

Symptoms may include drowsiness, dizziness, confusion, disorientation, lethargy, tingling in the hands or feet, numbness, nausea, vomiting, upset stomach, stomach pains, headache, ringing or buzzing in the ears, sweating, and blurred vision. Take the victim to a hospital emergency room at once for treatment. ALWAYS bring the medicine bottle with you.

Special Information

Avoid Aspirin and alcoholic beverages while taking this medication. You may become dizzy or drowsy while taking this medicine; be careful while driving or operating complex equipment.

Call your doctor if you develop a skin rash, itching, swelling, visual disturbances, black stools, or a persistent headache while taking this medication.

If you forget to take a dose of Carprofen, take it as soon as you remember. If it is almost time for your next dose, skip the forgotten dose and continue with your regular schedule.

Type of Drug

Cephalosporin Antibiotics

Brand Names

Generic Name: Cefaclor

Ceclor

Generic Name: Cefadroxil

Duricef
Ultracef

Generic Name: Cefixime

Suprax

Generic Name: Cefuroxime

Ceftin

Generic Name: Cephalexin

Keflet
Keflex
Keftab

(Also available in generic form)

Generic Name: Cephradine

Anspor
Velosef

Prescribed for

Infections caused by organisms sensitive to the antibiotic.

General Information

All of these antibiotics are related to the first member of the family, cephalosporin A. Cephalosporin A was isolated from a microorganism discovered in the sea near Sardinia in 1948. Over the years, researchers have manipulated the basic cephalosporin chemical structure, which is similar to penicillin, to produce more than 20 different antibiotic drugs. These drugs are differentiated from one another by the range of bacteria they can kill and how they can be taken. The cephalosporin antibiotics included in *The Pill Book* are those which can be taken orally, either as a liquid, tablet, or capsule.

Cautions and Warnings

A small number of people with an allergy to penicillin may also be allergic to a cephalosporin. Be sure your doctor knows about your penicillin allergy. The most common allergic reaction to a cephalosporin is a hivelike condition with redness over large areas of the body.

Several of the injectable cephalosporins can interfere with blood coagulation after very high doses. This problem has not occurred with any of the oral products.

The dosage of some cephalosporins must be adjusted for people with poor kidney function.

Pregnancy/Breast-feeding

These drugs are considered to be relatively safe for pregnant women, but there are few reports of pregnant women who have actually taken a cephalosporin antibiotic. These drugs should only be taken if the potential benefit outweighs any harm they could cause.

Small amounts of all of the cephalosporin antibiotics will pass into breast milk. Nursing mothers should temporarily discontinue breast-feeding while taking a cephalosporin antibiotic.

Seniors

Seniors may take any of the oral cephalosporin antibiotics without special precautions. Be sure to report any unusual side effects to your doctor.

Possible Side Effects

Most cephalosporin side effects are quite mild. The most common are nausea, vomiting, diarrhea, itching, and rashes.

Less common: headache, dizziness, tiredness, tingling in the hands or feet, seizures, confusion, drug allergy, fever, joint pains, chest tightness, redness, muscle aches and swelling, loss of appetite, changes in taste perception, abdominal pains and gas, upset stomach. Colitis may develop during treatment because of changes in the normal microorganisms found in the gastrointestinal tract.

Cefaclor may cause serum sickness (a combination of fever, joint pains, and rash).

Cephalosporins may cause changes in some blood cells, but this problem is not generally seen with those drugs that can be taken orally. Some cephalosporins have caused kidney problems, liver inflammation, and jaundice, but these are also rarely a problem with oral cephalosporins.

Drug Interactions

The cephalosporins should not be taken together with Erythromycin or Tetracycline because of conflicting antibacterial action.

Probenecid may increase blood levels of the cephalosporins by preventing their elimination through the kidney.

Food Interactions

Food interferes with the absorption of Cephalexin and Cefaclor into the blood. These drugs should be taken on an empty stomach, 1 hour before or 2 hours after meals, but may be taken with food if they upset your stomach.

Cefadroxil, Cefixime, Cefuroxime, and Cephradine may be taken without regard to food or meals.

Usual Dose

Cefaclor:
Adult: 250 to 500 milligrams every 8 hours.
Child: 3 to 6 milligrams per pound of body weight every 8 hours.

Cefadroxil:
Adult: 1 to 2 grams a day in 1 or 2 doses.

Child: 13 milligrams per pound of body weight per day in 1 or 2 doses.

Cefixime:
Adult: 400 milligrams per day in 1 or 2 doses.
Child: 3½ milligrams per pound of body weight per day given in 1 or 2 doses.

Cefuroxime:
Adult and child (over age 12): 125 to 500 milligrams every 12 hours.
Child (under age 12) *and infant:* 125 to 250 milligrams every 12 hours.

Cephalexin:
Adult: 250 to 1000 milligrams every 6 hours. Some urinary infections may be treated with 500 milligrams every 12 hours.
Child: 11 to 23 milligrams per pound of body weight per day. The dose may be increased to 46 milligrams per pound of body weight to treat middle ear infections.

Cephradine:
Adult: 250 to 500 milligrams every 6 to 12 hours.
Child (over 9 months of age): 11 to 45 milligrams per pound of body weight per day divided into 2 or 4 doses a day.

Overdosage

The most common symptoms of a cephalosporin overdose are nausea, vomiting, and upset stomach. These symptoms can be treated with milk or an antacid. Cephalosporin overdoses are generally not serious, but you may contact a hospital emergency room or local Poison Information Center to learn more about this problem.

Special Information

The cephalosporins, like all antibiotics, will make you feel better within 2 or 3 days after you begin taking them. However, to obtain the maximum benefit from any antibiotic, you must take the full daily dose of antibiotic prescribed by your doctor for the 7 to 10 days of your prescription.

If you miss a dose of a cephalosporin antibiotic and it is almost time for your next dose, and you take the medicine once a day, take the dose you forgot right away and your

next one 10 to 12 hours later. Then go back to your regular
schedule.

If you take the medicine 2 times a day, take the dose you
forgot right away and the next dose 5 to 6 hours later. Then
go back to your regular schedule.

If you take the medicine 3 or more times a day, take the
dose you missed right away and your next dose 2 to 4 hours
later. Then go back to your regular schedule.

Most of the liquid forms of these antibiotics must be kept
in the refrigerator to maintain their strength. Only Cefixime
liquid does not require refrigeration and may be kept at
room temperature.

The cephalosporins may interfere with the "Clinitest" test
for sugar in the urine. They do not interfere with enzyme-
based tests like Tes-Tape and Clinistix.

Generic Name

Chenodiol

Brand Name

Chenix

Type of Drug

Gallstone dissolver.

Prescribed for

People with cholesterol gallstones that are readily identifi-
able by x-ray examination and in whom surgery might be
risky.

General Information

Chenodiol is a natural bile acid found in our bodies. It
suppresses the production of cholesterol and cholic acid in
the liver, leading to the gradual withdrawal of cholesterol
from gallstones, which causes them to dissolve. The success
of this therapy varies according to the characteristics of
individual gallstones, but is most successful in people whose
stones are small and float. Overall, about one-third of all people who take this medicine will achieve complete dissolution

of their gallstones. But the drug is most successful in small, thin women whose cholesterol level is about 227, and who have a small number of floatable gallstones and can tolerate 24 months of drug therapy.

Cautions and Warnings

Before taking this drug, it is important that your doctor perform a complete gallbladder examination, including X-ray tests to be sure that your bile duct is functioning normally and that your condition is not amenable to surgery.

Chenodiol can be toxic to people with liver conditions such as hepatitis or cirrhosis. Also, it can cause liver damage on its own. Some people may be more susceptible to Chenodiol-induced liver damage than others. Your doctor should perform liver-function tests while you are taking this medication to determine your susceptibility and should discontinue the drug at the first negative signs.

Chenodiol may contribute to the development of colon and liver cancer in some people.

Pregnancy/Breast-feeding

Chenodiol should not be used by women who are pregnant or who might become pregnant while using it because it may harm the developing baby. Animal studies in monkeys and baboons have revealed serious effects on fetal liver, kidneys, and adrenal glands. Although such damage has not occurred in humans, the potential risks of taking Chenodiol while pregnant must be weighed heavily against the possible benefits it will produce. It is not known if Chenodiol passes into breast milk. Therefore, nursing mothers must observe for any possible drug effect on their infants while taking this medication.

Seniors

Older adults may take this medicine without restriction.

Possible Side Effects

Liver inflammation, as indicated by an increase in the levels of some liver enzymes, develops in almost one-third of all people who take this medication. Most inflammation is minor and resolves on its own after about 6 months, but 2 to 3 percent of people who take this drug experience more severe inflammation. In virtually all people, the test results return to normal after the medicine is stopped. Other side effects are diarrhea that worsens as the dosage increases and subsides as the dosage is reduced, increase in blood cholesterol levels, and reduction in blood triglyceride levels.

Less common side effects include: cramps, heartburn, constipation, nausea, vomiting, loss of appetite, abdominal discomfort and pain, upset stomach, stomach and intestinal gas, and reductions in the white-blood-cell count.

Drug Interactions

Cholestyramine or Cholestipol, two products used to remove bile acids from the stomach, will interfere with the action of Chenodiol by preventing it from being absorbed into the system. Antacids containing aluminum may also have this effect.

Estrogens, oral contraceptive pills, and Clofibrate increase the amount of cholesterol that passes through the bile ducts into the intestines and all three are associated with an increased risk of cholesterol gallstones. These medicines should not be taken while you are on Chenodiol therapy because they can counteract its effectiveness.

Food Interactions

Follow your doctor's instructions for dietary limitations while under treatment for gallstones. A low-cholesterol diet is often prescribed. Chenodiol is best taken on an empty stomach.

Usual Dose

250 milligrams, morning and night to start. This dose is gradually increased in weekly steps of 250 milligrams until the maximum recommended dose of 6 to 7.25 milligrams per pound of body weight per day is reached, or until side effects develop.

Total daily doses of less than 4.5 milligrams per pound of body weight per day are ineffective and are actually associated with an increased need for gallstone surgery.

Overdosage

There are no reports of accidental or intentional overdose with

Chenodiol. Call your local poison control center for specific advice on what to do in the event of a Chenodiol overdose.

Special Information

You must take this drug exactly as prescribed to get the maximum benefit from it.

Report any side effects to your doctor. Especially important are abdominal pains, severe and sudden pain in the right upper abdominal area that travels to your shoulder, nausea, and vomiting. Minor side effects such as diarrhea may be controlled by reducing your total daily dose, but you must not adjust the dose on your own.

It is essential that you return to your doctor for periodic tests of liver function and tests (ultrasonogram or oral cholecystogram) that allow your doctor to verify that your stones are being dissolved.

It is important for you to realize that this treatment is not a permanent cure. About half of all people whose original stones are completely dissolved by Chenodiol therapy will have another gallstone attack within 5 years.

If you forget a dose of Chenodiol, take it as soon as you remember. If it is almost time for your next dose, do not double your dose, but skip the missed dose and go back to your usual dose schedule.

Generic Names

Chloral Hydrate

Brand Name

Aquachloral Supprettes
Noctec

(Also available in generic form)

Type of Drug

Sedative-hypnotic.

Prescribed for

Insomnia, or as a daytime sedative.

General Information

Chloral Hydrate is very effective in producing sleep. Most people will fall asleep within an hour after taking this medicine. This drug usually does not cause the morning "hangover" seen with other sleeping pills.

Cautions and Warnings

Do not take Chloral Hydrate if you have liver or kidney disease, severe heart disease, or stomach problems, or if you are sensitive or allergic to this or similar drugs.

Chloral Hydrate may be habit-forming or addictive. It should only be taken when absolutely necessary and only in the amounts prescribed.

Pregnancy/Breast-feeding

This drug is known to cause birth defects or interfere with your baby's development. It is not considered safe for use during pregnancy.

Chloral Hydrate passes into breast milk and can sedate a nursing infant. Do not use this medicine while nursing an infant.

Seniors

Older adults are more sensitive to the effects of Chloral Hydrate and usually require less medicine to achieve the desired effect.

Possible Side Effects

Most common: reduction in alertness. If you plan to drive a car or operate other machinery, do so with extreme caution.

Less common side effects are: headache, hangover, hallucinations, drowsiness, stomach upset, nausea, vomiting, difficulty in walking, bad taste in the mouth, feeling of excitement, itching, light-headedness, dizziness, nightmares, feeling unwell, changes in composition of the blood.

Drug Interactions

Taking Chloral Hydrate with blood-thinning drugs may require a change of dosage of the latter: consult your doctor. Chloral Hydrate is a potent depressant, so avoid drinking alcohol or taking other drugs with depressant properties such as tranquilizers, barbiturates, or sleeping pills.

Food Interactions

Stomach upset can be minimized if you take Chloral Hydrate with a full glass of water, juice, or other liquid and never chew or break the capsule.

Usual Dose

Adult: sleeping medicine, 500 milligrams to 1 gram ½ hour before sleep. Daytime sedative, 250 milligrams 3 times per day after meals. Daily dose should not exceed 2 grams.

Child: sleeping medicine, 20 milligrams per pound of body weight (maximum of 1 gram). Daytime sedative, half the dose for sleeping, divided into 3 equal doses.

Overdosage

Symptoms are listed in "Possible Side Effects" above. The patient should be taken to a hospital emergency room immediately. ALWAYS bring the medicine bottle.

Special Information

The combination of Chloral Hydrate and alcohol is as notorious as the Mickey Finn. Avoid it.

Store at room temperature in a night-table drawer, not in an area that is hot and/or humid, such as a bathroom.

Generic Name

Chlordiazepoxide

Brand Names

A-poxide	Mitran
Libritabs	Murcil
Librium	Reposans-10
Lipoxide	

(Also available in generic form)

Type of Drug

Minor tranquilizer.

Prescribed for

Relief of symptoms of anxiety, tension, fatigue, or agitation.

General Information

Chlordiazepoxide is a member of the group of drugs known as benzodiazepines. These drugs are used as either antianxiety agents, anticonvulsants, or sedatives (sleeping pills). They exert their effect by relaxing the large skeletal muscles and by a direct effect on the brain. In doing so, they can relax you and make you either more tranquil or sleepier, depending on the drug and how much you use. Many doctors prefer Chlordiazepoxide and the other members of this class to other drugs that can be used for the same effect. Their reason is that the benzodiazepines tend to be safer, have fewer side effects, and are usually as, if not more, effective.

These drugs are generally used in any situation where they can be a useful adjunct.

Benzodiazepine tranquilizing drugs can be abused if taken for long periods of time and it is possible to develop withdrawal symptoms if you discontinue the therapy abruptly. Withdrawal symptoms include tremor, muscle cramps, stomach cramps, vomiting, insomnia, agitation, sweating, and even convulsions.

Cautions and Warnings

Do not take Chlordiazepoxide if you know you are sensitive or allergic to this drug or to other benzodiazepines such as Diazepam, Oxazepam, Clorazepate, Lorazepam, Prazepam, Flurazepam, Clonazepam, and Temazepam.

Chlordiazepoxide and other members of this drug group may aggravate narrow-angle glaucoma, but if you have open-angle glaucoma you may take the drugs. In this case, check this information with your doctor. Chlordiazepoxide can cause tiredness, drowsiness, inability to concentrate, or similar symptoms. Be careful if you are driving, operating machinery, or performing other activities which require concentration.

Pregnancy/Breast-feeding

This drug, like all members of the benzodiazepine family, crosses into your developing baby's circulation and may cause birth defects if taken during the first 3 months of pregnancy. You should avoid taking this medication while pregnant.

Members of the benzodiazepine family pass into breast milk. Since infants break the drug down more slowly than adults, it is possible for the medicine to accumulate and have an undesired effect on the baby.

Seniors

Older adults are more sensitive to the effects of this drug, especially dizziness and drowsiness. Closely follow your doctor's directions and report any side effects at once.

Possible Side Effects

Most common: mild drowsiness during the first few days of therapy. If drowsiness persists, contact your doctor.

Less common side effects are: confusion, depression, lethargy, disorientation, headache, inactivity, slurred speech, stupor, dizziness, tremor, constipation, dry mouth, nausea, inability to control urination, changes in sex drive, irregular menstrual cycle, changes in heart rhythm, lowered blood pressure, retention of fluids, blurred or double vision, itching, rash, hiccups, nervousness, inability to fall asleep, (occasional) liver dysfunction. If you experience any of these reactions stop taking the medicine and contact your doctor immediately.

Drug Interactions

Chlordiazepoxide is a central nervous system depressant. Avoid alcohol, tranquilizers, narcotics, barbiturates, monoamine oxidase (MAO) inhibitors, antihistamines, and other medicines used to relieve depression. Smoking may reduce the effectiveness of Chlordiazepoxide. The effects of Chlordiazepoxide may be prolonged when taken together with Cimetidine.

Food Interactions

This drug is best taken on an empty stomach, but may be taken with food if it upsets your stomach.

Usual Dose

Adult: 5 to 100 milligrams per day. This tremendous range in dosage exists because of varying response of individuals, related to age, weight, severity of disease, and other characteristics.

Child (over age 6): may be given this drug if it is deemed appropriate by the physician. Initial dose, lowest available (5 milligrams 2 to 4 times per day). Later, may increase in some children to 30 to 40 milligrams per day. The dose must be individualized to obtain maximum benefit.

Overdosage

Symptoms are confusion, sleep or sleepiness, lack of response to pain such as a pin stick, shallow breathing, lowered blood pressure, and coma. The patient should be taken to a hospital emergency room immediately. ALWAYS bring the medicine bottle.

Special Information

Avoid alcoholic beverages while taking Chlordiazepoxide. Sleeping pills, narcotics, barbiturates, other tranquilizers, or other drugs causing nervous system depression should be taken with caution while using Chlordiazepoxide. Tell your doctor if you become pregnant or are breast-feeding.

If you forget to take a dose of Chlordiazepoxide, take it as soon as you remember. If it is almost time for your next dose do not double up, but skip the missed dose and go back to your usual dose schedule. Do not take a double dose of Chlordiazepoxide.

Generic Name

Chlorothiazide

Brand Names

Diachlor
Diuril

(Also available in generic form)

Type of Drug

Diuretic.

Prescribed for

Congestive heart failure, cirrhosis of the liver, kidney malfunction, high blood pressure, and other conditions where it is necessary to rid the body of excess water.

General Information

This drug is a member of the class known as thiazide diuretics. Thiazides act on the kidneys to stimulate the production of large amounts of urine. They also cause you to lose bicarbonate, sodium chloride, and potassium ions from the body. They are used as part of the treatment of any disease where it is desirable to eliminate large quantities of body water. These diseases include heart failure, some kidney diseases, and liver disease. Thiazide drugs are often taken together with other medicines to treat high blood pressure.

Cautions and Warnings

Do not take Chlorothiazide if you are allergic or sensitive to this drug, similar drugs of this group, or sulfa drugs. If you have a history of allergy or bronchial asthma, you may also have a sensitivity or allergy to Chlorothiazide.

Pregnancy/Breast-feeding

Although the drug has been used to treat specific conditions in pregnancy, unsupervised use by pregnant women should be avoided. This drug may cause birth defects or interfere with your baby's development. Check with your doctor before taking it if you are, or might be, pregnant.

Chlorothiazide may pass into breast milk. This has not caused any problems, but your baby doctor should know if you are taking this medicine.

Seniors

Older adults are more sensitive to the effects of this drug, especially dizziness. They should closely follow their doctor's directions and report any side effects at once.

Possible Side Effects

Chlorothiazide will cause a loss of body potassium. Signs of low potassium levels are dryness of the mouth, thirst, weakness, lethargy, drowsiness, restlessness, muscle pains or cramps, gout, muscular tiredness, low blood pressure, decreased frequency of urination and decreased amount of urine produced, abnormal heart rate, and stomach upset including nausea and vomiting.

To treat this, potassium supplements are given in the form of tablets, liquids, or powders, or by increased consumption of foods such as bananas, citrus fruits, melons, and tomatoes.

Less common side effects are: loss of appetite, stomach upset, nausea, vomiting, cramping, diarrhea, constipation, dizziness, headache, tingling of the toes and fingers, restlessness, changes in blood composition, sensitivity to sunlight, rash, itching, fever, difficulty in breathing, allergic reactions, dizziness when rising quickly from a sitting or lying position, muscle spasms, weakness, blurred vision.

Drug Interactions

Chlorothiazide will increase the action of other blood-pressure-lowering drugs. This is good and is the reason why people with high blood pressure often take more than one medicine.

The possibility of developing imbalances in body fluids (electrolytes) is increased if you take medication such as Digitalis and adrenal corticosteroids while you take Chlorothiazide.

If you are taking an oral antidiabetic drug and begin taking Chlorothiazide, the antidiabetic dose may have to be altered.

Lithium Carbonate should not be taken with Chlorothiazide because the combination may increase the risk of Lithium toxicity.

If you are taking Chlorothiazide for the treatment of high blood pressure or congestive heart failure, avoid over-the-counter medicines for the treatment of coughs, colds, and allergies: such medicines may contain stimulants. If you are unsure about them, ask your pharmacist.

Usual Dose

Adult: 0.5 to 1 gram 1 to 2 times per day. Often people respond to intermittent therapy; that is, taking the drug on alternate days or 3 to 5 days per week. This reduces side effects.

Child: 10 milligrams per pound of body weight each day in 2 equal doses.

Infant (under age 6 months): up to 15 milligrams per pound per day in 2 equal doses.

Overdosage

Signs can be tingling in the arms or legs, weakness, fatigue, changes in your heartbeat, a sickly feeling, dry mouth, restlessness, muscle pains or cramps, urinary difficulty, nausea, or vomiting. Take the overdose victim to a hospital emergency room for treatment at once. ALWAYS bring the prescription bottle and any remaining medicine.

Special Information

If you forget a dose of Chlorothiazide, take it as soon as you remember. If it is almost time for your next dose, skip the one you forgot and continue with your regular schedule. Do not take a double dose of Chlorothiazide.

Generic Name

Chlorpheniramine Maleate

Brand Names

Aller-Chlor	Chlor-Trimeton Repetabs
Chlo-Amine	Pfeiffer's Allergy
Chlorate	Phenetron
Chlor-Pro	Telachlor
Chlorspan	Teldrin
Chlortab	Trymegen
Chlor-Trimeton	

(Also available in generic form)

Type of Drug

Antihistamine.

Prescribed for

Seasonal allergy, stuffed and runny nose, itching of the eyes, scratching of the throat caused by allergy, and other allergic symptoms such as itching, rash, or hives.

General Information

Antihistamines, including Chlorpheniramine, generally act by antagonizing histamine at the site where histamine works. This site is often called the H_1 histamine receptor. Antihistamines work by drying up the secretions of the nose, throat, and eyes.

Cautions and Warnings

Chlorpheniramine Maleate should not be used if you are allergic to this drug. It should be avoided or used with extreme care if you have narrow-angle glaucoma (pressure in the eye), stomach ulcer or other stomach problems, enlarged prostate, or problems passing urine. It should not be used by people who have deep-breathing problems such as asthma.

Use with care if you have a history of thyroid disease, heart disease, high blood pressure, or diabetes.

Pregnancy/Breast-feeding

Chlorpheniramine Maleate has not been proven to be a cause of birth defects or other problems in pregnant women, although studies in animals have shown that some antihistamines (Meclizine and Cyclizine), used mainly against nausea and vomiting, may cause birth defects. Do not take any antihistamine without your doctor's knowledge.

Small amounts of antihistamine medicines pass into breast milk and may affect a nursing infant. Nursing mothers should avoid antihistamines or use alternate feeding methods while taking the medicine.

Seniors

Seniors are more sensitive to antihistamine side effects. Confusion, difficult or painful urination, dizziness, drowsiness, a faint feeling, dry mouth, nose, or throat, nightmares or excitement, nervousness, restlessness, or irritability are more likely to occur among older adults.

Possible Side Effects

Occasionally seen: itching, rash, sensitivity to light, perspiration, chills, dryness of the mouth, nose, and throat, lowering of blood pressure, headache, rapid heartbeat, sleeplessness, dizziness, disturbed coordination, confusion, restlessness, nervousness, irritability, euphoria (feeling high), tingling of the hands and feet, blurred vision, double vision, ringing in the ears, stomach upset, loss of appetite, nausea, vomiting, constipation, diarrhea, difficulty in urination, tightness of the chest, wheezing, nasal stuffiness. Young children develop nervousness, irritability, tension and anxiety.

Drug Interactions

Chlorpheniramine Maleate should not be taken with monoamine oxidase (MAO) inhibitors.

Interaction with tranquilizers, benzodiazepines, sedatives, and sleeping medication will increase the effect of these drugs; it is extremely important that you discuss this with your doctor so that doses of these drugs can be properly adjusted.

Be extremely cautious when drinking alcohol while taking Chlorpheniramine Maleate, which will enhance the intoxicating effect of alcohol. Alcohol also has a sedative effect.

Usual Dose

Adult: 4-milligram tablet 3 to 4 times per day.

Child (age 6 to 12): 2-milligram tablet 3 to 4 times per day.

Time-release doses (capsules or tablets):

Adult: 8 to 12 milligrams at bedtime or every 8 to 10 hours during the day.

Child (age 6 to 12): 8 milligrams during the day or at bedtime.

Overdosage

Symptoms are depression or stimulation (especially in children), dry mouth, fixed or dilated pupils, flushing of the skin, and stomach upset. Take the patient to a hospital emergency room immediately, if you cannot make him vomit. ALWAYS bring the medicine bottle.

Special Information

Antihistamines produce a depressing effect: be extremely cautious when driving or operating heavy equipment.

If you forget a dose of Chlorpheniramine, take it as soon

as you remember. If it is almost time for your next dose, skip the one you forgot and continue with your regular schedule. Don't take a double dose.

Generic Name

Chlorpromazine

Brand Names

Promapar   Thorazine
Sonazine   Thor-Prom

(Also available in generic form)

Type of Drug

Phenothiazine antipsychotic.

Prescribed for

Psychotic disorders, moderate to severe depression with anxiety, control of agitation or aggressiveness of disturbed children, alcohol withdrawal symptoms, intractable pain, and senility. Chlorpromazine may also be used to relieve nausea, vomiting, hiccups, and restlessness, and/or apprehension before surgery or other special therapy.

General Information

Chlorpromazine and other members of the phenothiazine group act on a portion of the brain called the hypothalamus. They affect parts of the hypothalamus that control metabolism, body temperature, alertness, muscle tone, hormone balance, and vomiting, and may be used to treat problems related to any of these functions. Chlorpromazine is available in suppositories and liquid forms for those who have trouble swallowing tablets.

Cautions and Warnings

Chlorpromazine should not be taken if you are allergic to one of the drugs in the broad classification known as phenothiazine drugs. Do not take Chlorpromazine if you have any blood, liver, kidney, or heart disease, very low blood pressure, or Parkinson's disease. This medication is a tranquilizer and can have a sedative effect, especially during the first few days of therapy. Care should be taken when performing activities requiring a high degree of concentration, such as driving.

This drug should be used with caution and under strict supervision of your doctor if you have glaucoma, epilepsy, ulcers, or difficulty passing urine.

Pregnancy/Breast-feeding

Infants born to women taking this medication have experienced drug side effects (liver jaundice, nervous system effects) immediately after birth. Check with your doctor about taking this medicine if you are, or might become, pregnant.

This drug may pass into breast milk and affect a nursing infant. Consider alternate feeding methods if you must take this medicine.

Seniors

Older adults are more sensitive to the effects of this medication than younger adults and usually require a lower dosage to achieve a desired effect. Also, older adults are more likely to develop drug side effects. Some experts feel that elderly people should be treated with ½ to ¼ the usual adult dose.

Possible Side Effects

Most common: drowsiness, especially during the first or second week of therapy. If the drowsiness becomes troublesome, contact your doctor. Do not allow the liquid forms of this medicine to come in contact with your skin. This can cause contact reactions.

Chlorpromazine can cause jaundice (yellowing of the whites of the eyes or skin), usually in 2 to 4 weeks. The jaundice usually goes away when the drug is discontinued, but there have been cases when it did not. If you notice this effect or if you develop symptoms such as fever and generally not feeling well, contact your doctor immediately. Less frequent: changes in components of the blood including anemias, raised or lowered blood pressure, abnormal heart rates, heart attack, feeling faint or dizzy.

Phenothiazines can produce "extrapyramidal effects," such as spasm of the neck muscles, rolling back of the eyes, convulsions, difficulty in swallowing, and symptoms associated with Parkinson's disease. These effects look very serious but disappear after the drug has been withdrawn; however, symptoms of the face, tongue, and jaw may persist for as long as several years, especially in the elderly with a history of brain damage. If you experience extrapyramidal effects contact your doctor immediately.

Chlorpromazine may cause an unusual increase in psychotic symptoms or may cause paranoid reactions, tiredness, lethargy, restlessness, hyperactivity, confusion at night, bizarre dreams, inability to sleep, depression, and euphoria. Other reactions are itching, swelling, unusual sensitivity to bright lights, red skin, and rash. There have been cases of breast enlargement, false positive pregnancy tests, changes in menstrual flow in females, and impotence and changes in sex drive in males, as well as stuffy nose, headache, nausea, vomiting, loss of appetite, change in body temperature, loss of facial color, excessive salivation, excessive perspiration, constipation, diarrhea, changes in urine and stool habits, worsening of glaucoma, blurred vision, weakening of eyelid muscles, spasms in bronchial and other muscles, increased appetite, excessive thirst, and changes in the coloration of skin, particularly in exposed areas.

Drug Interactions

Chlorpromazine should be taken with caution in combination with barbiturates, sleeping pills, narcotics, other tranquilizers, or any other medication which may produce a sedative effect. Avoid alcohol.

Usual Dose

Adult: 30 to 1000 milligrams or more per day, individualized according to disease and patient's response.

Child: 0.25 milligram per pound of body weight every 4 to 6 hours up to 200 milligrams or more per day (by various routes including rectal suppositories), depending on disease, age, and response to therapy.

Overdosage

Symptoms are depression, extreme weakness, tiredness, desire to go to sleep, coma, lowered blood pressure, uncontrolled muscle spasms, agitation, restlessness, convulsions, fever, dry mouth, and abnormal heart rhythms. The patient should be taken to a hospital emergency room immediately. ALWAYS bring the medicine bottle.

Special Information

This medication may cause drowsiness. Use caution when driving or operating complex equipment and avoid alcoholic beverages while taking the medicine.

The drug may also cause unusual sensitivity to the sun and can turn your urine reddish-brown to pink.

If dizziness occurs, avoid sudden changes in posture and avoid climbing stairs.

Use caution in hot weather. This medicine may make you more prone to heat stroke.

If you are using the sustained release capsules, do not chew them or break them: swallow them whole.

If you forget to take a dose of Chlorpromazine, take it as soon as you remember. If you are taking 1 dose per day and forget to take the dose, skip the missed dose and continue your regular dose schedule the next day. If you take more than 1 dose per day, do not double your dose, but skip the missed dose and continue with your regular schedule.

Generic Name

Chlorpropamide

Brand Name

Diabinese

(Also available in generic form)

Type of Drug

Oral antidiabetic.

Prescribed for

Diabetes mellitus (sugar in the urine).

General Information

Chlorpropamide is one of several oral antidiabetic drugs that work by stimulating the production and release of Insulin from the pancreas. The action of these agents is also related to improved Insulin sensitivity of peripheral tissues. The primary difference between these drugs lies in the duration of action. Because they do not lower blood sugar directly, they require some function of pancreas cells.

Cautions and Warnings

Mild stress such as infection, minor surgery, or emotional upset reduces the effectiveness of Chlorpropamide. Remember that while you are taking this drug you should be under your doctor's continuous care.

Chlorpropamide is an aid to, not a substitute for, a diet. Diet remains of primary importance in the treatment of your diabetes. Follow the diet plan your doctor has prescribed for you.

Chlorpropamide and similar drugs are not oral Insulin, nor are they a substitute for Insulin. They do not lower blood sugar by themselves.

This drug should not be used if you have serious liver, kidney, or endocrine disease.

Pregnancy/Breast-feeding

This drug may cause birth defects or interfere with your baby's development. Check with your doctor before taking it if you are, or might be, pregnant. For control of diabetes in pregnant women, the use of Insulin and diet is recommended. Nursing women who must take this drug should find an alternative method of feeding their children.

Seniors

Older adults with reduced kidney function may be more sensitive to drug side effects because of a reduced ability to eliminate it from the body. Low blood sugar, the major sign of drug overdose, may be more difficult to identify in older adults than in younger adults. Also, low blood sugar is more likely to be a cause of nervous system side effects in older adults.

Older adults taking antidiabetes drugs must keep in close touch with their doctor and closely follow his/her directions.

Possible Side Effects

Common: loss of appetite, nausea, vomiting, stomach upset. At times, you may experience weakness or tingling in the hands and feet. These effects can be eliminated by reducing the daily dose of Chlorpropamide or, if necessary, by switching to a different oral antidiabetic drug. This decision must be made by your doctor.

Chlorpropamide may produce abnormally low levels of blood sugar when too much is taken for your immediate requirements. (Other factors which may cause lowering of blood sugar are liver or kidney disease, malnutrition, age, drinking alcohol, and disease of the glands.)

Less commonly, Chlorpropamide may cause a yellowing of the whites of the eyes or skin, itching, rash, or changes in the results of laboratory tests made by your doctor. Usually these reactions will disappear in time. If they persist you should contact your doctor.

Drug Interactions

Thiazide diuretics may lessen the effect of Chlorpropamide, while Insulin, sulfa drugs, Oxyphenbutazone, Phenylbutazone, and monoamine oxidase (MAO) inhibitor drugs prolong and enhance the action of Chlorpropamide.

Interaction with alcoholic beverages may cause flushing of the face and body, throbbing pain in the head and neck, difficult breathing, nausea, vomiting, sweating, thirst, chest pains, palpitations, lowered blood pressure, weakness, dizziness, blurred vision, and confusion. If you experience these reactions, contact your doctor immediately.

Because of the stimulant ingredients in many over-the-counter drug products for the relief of coughs, colds, and allergies, avoid them unless your doctor advises otherwise.

Response to Chlorpropamide may be reduced if beta-blocking agents such as Propranolol (Inderal) are given to the same patient.

Food Interactions

This medicine is best taken on an empty stomach, but may be taken with food. Dietary management is an important part of the treatment of diabetes. Be sure to follow your doctor's directions about the foods you should avoid.

Usual Dosage

Adult: 250 milligrams daily.
Senior: 100 to 250 milligrams daily.
For severe cases: 500 milligrams daily.

Overdosage

A mild overdose of Chlorpropamide lowers the blood sugar, which can be treated by consuming sugar in such forms as candy and orange juice. A patient with a more serious overdose should be taken to a hospital emergency room immediately. ALWAYS bring the medicine bottle.

Special Information

The treatment of diabetes is your responsibility. You should follow all instructions about diet, body weight, exercise, personal hygiene, and take all measures to avoid infection. If you are not feeling well, or if you have symptoms such as itching, rash, yellowing of the skin or eyes, abnormally light-colored stools, a low-grade fever, sore throat, or diarrhea—contact your doctor immediately.

Do not discontinue taking this medication unless advised by your physician.

If you forget a dose of Chlorpropamide, take it as soon as you remember. If you don't remember until the next day, skip the forgotten dose and continue with your regular schedule.

Generic Name

Chlorthalidone

Brand Names

Hygroton
Hylidone
Thalitone

(Also available in generic form)

Type of Drug

Diuretic.

Prescribed for

Congestive heart failure, cirrhosis of the liver, kidney malfunction, high blood pressure, and other conditions where it is necessary to rid the body of excess water.

General Information

This drug is a member of the class known as thiazide diuretics. Thiazides act on the kidneys to stimulate the production of large amounts of urine. They also cause you to lose bicarbonate, sodium chloride, and potassium ions from the body. They are used as a part of the treatment of any disease where it is desirable to eliminate large quantities of body water. These diseases include heart failure, some kidney diseases, and liver diseases. Diuretics are often taken together with other medicines to treat high blood pressure.

Cautions and Warnings

Do not take Chlorthalidone if you are allergic or sensitive to this drug, similar drugs of this group, or sulfa drugs. If you have a history of allergy or bronchial asthma, you may also have a sensitivity or allergy to Chlorthalidone.

Pregnancy/Breast-feeding

This drug may cause birth defects or interfere with your baby's development. Check with your doctor before taking it if you are, or might be, pregnant. Chlorthalidone will cross the placenta and pass into the unborn child, possibly causing side effects such as blood problems (jaundice) and low potassium. Chlorthalidone passes into breast milk. Nursing mothers may use an alternative feeding method, but the drug has not caused any problems in nursing infants.

Seniors

Older adults are more sensitive to the effects of this drug, especially dizziness. They should closely follow their doctor's directions and report any side effects at once.

Possible Side Effects

Chlorthalidone will cause a loss of body potassium. Signs of low potassium are dryness of the mouth, thirst, weakness, lethargy, drowsiness, restlessness, muscle pains or cramps, muscular tiredness, low blood pressure, gout, decreased frequency of urination and decreased amount of urine produced, abnormal heart rate, and stomach upset including nausea and vomiting.

To treat this, potassium supplements are given in the form of tablets, liquids, or powders, or by increased consumption of foods such as bananas, citrus fruits, melons, and tomatoes.

Less common side effects are: loss of appetite, stomach upset, nausea, vomiting, cramping, diarrhea, constipation, dizziness, headache, tingling of the toes and fingers, restlessness, changes in blood composition, sensitivity to sunlight, rash, itching, fever, difficulty in breathing, allergic reactions, dizziness when rising quickly from a sitting or lying position, muscle spasms, weakness, blurred vision.

Drug Interactions

Chlorthalidone will add to the action of other blood-pressure-lowering drugs. This is good and is the reason why people with high blood pressure often take more than one medicine.

The possibility of developing imbalances in body fluids (electrolytes) is increased if you take medications such as Digitalis and adrenal corticosteroids while you take Chlorthalidone.

If you are taking an oral antidiabetic drug and begin taking Chlorthalidone, the antidiabetic dose may have to be altered.

Lithium Carbonate should not be taken with Chlorthalidone because the combination may increase the risk of Lithium toxicity.

If you are taking this drug for the treatment of high blood pressure or congestive heart failure, avoid over-the-counter medicines for the treatment of coughs, colds, and allergies: such medicines may contain stimulants. If you are unsure about them, ask your pharmacist.

Usual Dose

50 to 100 milligrams per day; or 100 milligrams on alternate days or 3 days per week.

Some patients may require 150 or 200 milligrams per day; doses of more than 200 milligrams per day generally do not produce greater response. A single dose is taken with food in the morning. Dose often declines from the initial dose, according to patient's need.

Overdosage

Signs can be tingling in your arms or legs, weakness, fatigue, changes in your heartbeat, a sickly feeling, dry mouth, restlessness, muscle pains or cramps, urinary difficulty, nausea, or vomiting. Take the overdose victim to a hospital emergency room for treatment at once. ALWAYS bring the prescription bottle and any remaining medicine.

Special Information

If you forget a dose of Chlorthalidone and take it every day, take the dose as soon as you remember, unless it is time for your next dose. Then, skip the dose you forgot and continue with your regular schedule.

If you take it only a few days a week, take the dose as soon as you remember, unless it is time for your next dose. If so, skip the forgotten dose and continue with your regular schedule. Do not take a double dose of Chlorthalidone.

Generic Name

Cholestyramine

Brand Name

Questran

Type of Drug

Antihyperlipidemic (blood fat reducer).

Prescribed for

High blood cholesterol, itching associated with bile duct obstruction, some forms of colitis, pesticide poisoning.

General Information

This medication reduces blood cholesterol by removing bile acids from the biliary system. Since cholesterol is used by the body to make bile acids and bile acids are necessary for the digestion of dietary fats, the only way the body can continue to digest fats is to make more bile acids from cholesterol, resulting in a lowering of blood cholesterol levels. The medicine works entirely within the bowel and is never absorbed into the bloodstream.

Cautions and Warnings

Do not use Cholestyramine if you are sensitive to it or to Colestipol, another, similar drug product.

Pregnancy/Breast-feeding

The safety of using this medication during pregnancy is not known. If you are pregnant and must use this medication, talk to your doctor about the potential benefit to be gained versus other treatments for your condition.

The medicine is not absorbed into your blood and will not affect a nursing infant. However, it can affect the amounts of vitamins and other nutrients absorbed, possibly making your milk less nutritious. You may want to consider alternate methods or supplemental feedings for your infant.

Seniors

Older adults are more likely to suffer side effects from this medication, especially those relating to the bowel.

Possible Side Effects

The most common side effect is constipation, which may be severe and result in a bowel impaction. Hemorrhoids may be worsened.

Less frequent side effects are abdominal pain and bloating, bleeding in the stomach or intestine, gas, nausea, vomiting, diarrhea, heartburn, and appetite loss. Your stool may have an unusual appearance because of high fat level.

Other side effects include vitamin A and D deficiency, rashes, irritation of the tongue and anus, osteoporosis, black stools, stomach ulcers, dental bleeding, hiccups, a sour taste, pancreas inflammation, ulcer attack, gallbladder attack, bleeding, black-and-blue marks, itching and rash, backache, muscle and joint pains, arthritis, headache, anxiety, dizziness, fatigue, ringing or buzzing in the ears, fainting, tingling in the hands or feet, blood in the urine, frequent or painful urination, an unusual urine odor, eye irritation, weight changes, increased sex drive, swollen glands, swelling of the arms or legs, shortness of breath.

Drug Interactions

This medication interferes with the absorption of virtually all other medicines taken by mouth. Take other medicines at least 1 hour before or 4 to 6 hours after Cholestyramine. Some drugs for which this effect has been proven are: Cephalexin, Chenodiol, Clindamycin, corticosteroids, digitalis drugs, iron, Penicillins, Phenobarbital, Phenylbutazone, Tetracycline, thiazide diuretics, thyroid drugs, Trimethoprim, Vitamins A, D, E, and K, Warfarin.

Food Interactions

Take this medication before meals. It should be mixed with water, juice, applesauce, or crushed pineapple.

Usual Dose

1 packet taken 1 to 6 times a day.

Overdosage

The most severe effect of Cholestyramine overdose is bowel impaction. Take the overdose victim to a hospital emergency room for evaluation and treatment. ALWAYS bring the medicine container with you.

Special Information

Do not swallow the powder in its dry form; mix the contents of each packet with 2 to 6 ounces of water or a noncarbonated beverage and drink as a liquid. The powder may also be mixed with soups or fruit sources like applesauce or crushed pineapple.

Constipation, stomach gas, nausea, and heartburn may occur and then disappear with continued use of this medication. Call your doctor if these side effects continue or if you develop unusual problems such as bleeding from the gums or rectum.

If you forget to take a dose, take it as soon as possible. Do not double any doses. If it is almost time for your next dose, skip the missed dose and go back to your regular dose schedule.

Generic Name

Ciclopirox Olamine

Brand Name

Loprox

Type of Drug

Antifungal.

Prescribed for

Fungus and yeast infections of the skin, including those responsible for athlete's foot, candida, and other fungus infections.

General Information

This drug slows the growth of a wide variety of fungus organisms and yeasts and kills many others. Ciclopirox Olamine penetrates the skin very well and is present in levels sufficient to kill or inhibit most fungus organisms. In addition, it penetrates the hair, hair follicles, and skin sweat glands.

Cautions and Warnings

Do not use if you are allergic to this product.

Pregnancy/Breast-feeding

Ciclopirox may pass into the developing fetus in very small amounts. There is no proof that Ciclopirox causes damage to a developing fetus. When the drug was given by mouth to animals in doses 10 times the amount normally applied to the skin, it was found to be nontoxic to the developing fetus. Ciclopirox is not known to pass into breast milk. As with all drugs, caution should be exercised when using Ciclopirox Olamine during pregnancy.

Seniors

Older adults may use this medication without restriction.

Possible Side Effects

Burning, itching, and stinging in the areas to which the cream has been applied.

Usual Dose

Apply enough of the cream to cover affected areas twice a day and massage it into the skin.

Overdosage

This cream should not be swallowed. If it is swallowed, the victim may be nauseated and have an upset stomach. Little is known about Ciclopirox Olamine overdose, and you should call your local poison control center for more information.

Special Information

Clean the affected areas before applying Ciclopirox Olamine cream, unless otherwise directed by your doctor.

Call your doctor if the affected area burns, stings, or becomes red after using this product. Also, notify your doctor if your symptoms don't clear up after 4 weeks of treatment, since it is unlikely that, after that length of treatment, the cream will be effective at all.

This product is quite effective and can be expected to relieve symptoms within the first week of use. Follow your doctor's directions for the complete 2-to-4-week course of treatment to gain maximum benefit from this product. Stopping it too soon may not completely eliminate the fungus and can lead to a relapse.

Generic Name

Cimetidine

Brand Name

Tagamet

Type of Drug

Antiulcer, histamine H_2 antagonist.

Prescribed for

Ulcers of the stomach and upper intestine (duodenum). Also prescribed for other conditions characterized by the production of large amounts of gastric fluids. Surgeons may prescribe Cimetidine during a surgical procedure when it is desirable for the production of stomach acid to be stopped completely.

General Information

Cimetidine was the first histamine H_2 antagonist to be released in the United States. It works against ulcers and other gastrointestinal conditions by actually turning off the system that produces stomach acid.

Cautions and Warnings

Do not take Cimetidine if you have had an allergic reaction to it in the past. Cimetidine has a mild antiandrogen effect. This is probably the reason why some people experience painful, swollen breasts after taking this medicine for a month or more.

Pregnancy/Breast-feeding

Studies with laboratory animals have revealed no damage to a developing fetus, although Cimetidine does pass into the developing baby's circulation. It is recommended that Cimetidine be avoided by pregnant women, or women who might become pregnant while using it. In those situations where it is deemed essential, Cimetidine's potential risk must be carefully weighed against any benefit it might produce.

Cimetidine is known to pass into breast milk. No problems among nursing infants have been reported, but nursing mothers must consider the possibility of a drug effect while nursing their infants.

Seniors

Older adults respond well to Cimetidine but may need less medication than a younger adult to achieve the desired response, since the drug is eliminated through the kidneys and kidney function tends to decline with age. Older adults may be more susceptible to some side effects of this drug, especially confusion.

Possible Side Effects

Most people taking Cimetidine do not experience serious drug side effects. However, the most common side effects of

Cimetidine are mild diarrhea, muscle pains and cramps, dizziness, skin rash, nausea and vomiting, headache, confusion, and drowsiness. Rarely, the medicine has an effect on white blood cells or blood platelets. Some symptoms of these effects are unusual bleeding or bruising, unusual tiredness or weakness. Other rare side effects are impotence (men), painful swollen breasts.

Drug Interactions

The effects of Cimetidine may be reduced if the drug is taken together with antacids. This minor interaction may be avoided by separating Cimetidine from doses of antacid by about 3 hours.

Cimetidine may increase the effects of a variety of drugs, possibly leading to drug toxicity. Cimetidine exerts this effect by preventing the drugs' breakdown or elimination from the body. The drugs so affected by Cimetidine include alcohol, antidepressants, antidiabetes drugs, Aminophylline, bone marrow depressants used in cancer treatment, Alprazolam, caffeine, Carbamazepine, Chlordiazepoxide, Diazepam and other similar minor tranquilizers, Cyclosporine, Flurazepam, Labetalol, Lidocaine, Mexilitene, Metoprolol, Metronidazole, Phenytoin and Procainamide, Propranolol, Nifedipine, Quinidine, Theophylline, Triazolam, Warfarin (a blood-thinning drug), and these can lead to toxic drug effects.

Enteric-coated tablets should not be taken with Cimetidine. The change in stomach acidity will cause the tablets to disintegrate prematurely in the stomach.

Cimetidine may inhibit the absorption of Ketoconazole into the bloodstream.

Food Interactions

Cimetidine should be taken with food or meals and at bedtime to achieve maximum effect from the drug.

Usual Dose

The usual adult dosage is 400 to 800 milligrams at bedtime, 300 milligrams 4 times a day with meals and at bedtime, or 400 milligrams twice a day. You should not exceed 2400 milligrams per day. However, smaller doses may be as effective for seniors or patients with impaired kidney function.

Overdosage

There is little information on Cimetidine overdosage. Overdose victims might be expected to show exaggerated side effect symptoms, but little else is known. Your local poison center may advise giving the victim Syrup of Ipecac to cause vomiting and remove any remaining drug from the stomach. Victims who have definite symptoms should be taken to a hospital emergency room for observation and possible treatment. ALWAYS remember to bring the prescription bottle with you.

Special Information

You must take this medicine exactly as directed and follow your doctor's instructions for diet and other treatments in order to get the maximum benefit from it. Cigarettes are known to be associated with stomach ulcers and will reverse the effect of Cimetidine on stomach acid.

Call your doctor at once if any unusual side effects develop. Especially important are unusual bleeding or bruising, unusual tiredness, diarrhea, dizziness, rash, or hallucinations. Black, tarry stools or vomiting "coffee-ground" material may indicate your ulcer is bleeding.

If you miss a dose of Cimetidine, take it as soon as possible. If it is almost time for your next dose, skip the missed dose and go back to your usual dose schedule. Do not double the dose.

Generic Name

Clemastine

Brand Names

Tavist
Tavist-1

Type of Drug

Antihistamine.

Prescribed for

Seasonal allergy, stuffed and runny nose, itching of the eyes, scratchy throat caused by allergies, and other allergic symptoms such as rash, itching, or hives.

General Information

Clemastine is distinguished from most other antihistamines in that it is somewhat less sedating than other products. It works in exactly the same way as Chlorpheniramine and other widely used antihistamines.

Cautions and Warnings

Clemastine should not be taken if you have had an allergic reaction to it in the past. People with asthma or other deep-breathing problems, glaucoma (pressure in the eye), stomach ulcer, or other stomach problems should avoid this drug because its side effects may aggravate these problems.

Pregnancy/Breast-feeding

Antihistamines have not been proven to be a cause of birth defects or other problems in pregnant women, although studies in animals have shown that some drugs (Meclizine and Cyclizine) used mainly against nausea and vomiting may cause birth defects. Do not take any antihistamine without your doctor's knowledge.

Small amounts of antihistamine medicines pass into breast milk and may affect a nursing infant. Nursing mothers should avoid Antihistamines or use alternate feeding methods while taking the medicine.

Seniors

Seniors are more sensitive to antihistamine side effects. Confusion, difficult or painful urination, dizziness, drowsiness, a faint feeling, dry mouth, nose, or throat, nightmares or excitement, nervousness, restlessness, or irritability are more likely to occur among older adults.

Possible Side Effects

Most common: headache, nervousness, weakness, upset stomach, nausea, vomiting, dry mouth, nose, or throat, cough, stuffed nose, change in bowel habits, sore throat, nosebleeds.

Less common side effects include drowsiness, hair loss, allergic reactions, depression, sleeplessness, menstrual irregularities, muscle aches, sweating, tingling in the hands or feet, frequent urination, visual disturbances.

Drug Interactions

Taking Clemastine with alcohol, tranquilizers, sleeping pills, or other nervous system depressants can increase the depressant effects of Clemastine.

The effects of oral anticoagulant (blood-thinning) drugs may be decreased by antihistamines. Do not take this combination without your doctor's knowledge.

Monoamine oxidase (MAO) inhibitor drugs (for depression or high blood pressure) may increase the drying and other effects of Clemastine. The combination may also increase urinary difficulty.

Food Interactions

Clemastine should be taken 1 hour before or 2 hours after food or meals, but may be taken with food if it upsets your stomach.

Usual Dose

Adult and child (over age 12): 1.34 milligrams 2 times a day to 2.68 milligrams 3 times a day. Do not take more than 8.04 milligrams (7 tablets of Tavist-1 or 3½ tablets of Tavist).

Child (under age 12): not recommended.

Overdosage

Clemastine overdose is likely to cause exaggerated side effects. A person who has taken a Clemastine overdose should be given Syrup of Ipecac to induce vomiting and taken to a hospital emergency room for treatment. Remember to bring the prescription bottle with you.

Special Information

Clemastine can make it difficult for you to concentrate and perform complex tasks like driving a car. Be sure to report any unusual side effects to your doctor.

If you forget to take a dose of Clemastine, take it as soon as you remember. If it is almost time for your next dose, skip the forgotten dose and continue with your regular schedule. Do not take a double dose of Clemastine.

Generic Name

Clindamycin

Brand Names

Cleocin Hydrochloride
Cleocin T Topical Solution

Type of Drug

Antibiotic.

Prescribed for

Serious infections caused by bacteria which are generally found to be susceptible to this drug.

General Information

This is one of the few drugs, given by mouth, which is effective against anaerobic organisms: bacteria which grow only in the absence of oxygen and are frequently found in infected wounds, lung abscesses, abdominal infections, and infections of the female genital tract. It is also effective against the organisms usually treated by Penicillin or Erythromycin.

Clindamycin may be useful for treating certain skin or soft tissue infections where susceptible organisms are present.

Cautions and Warnings

Do not take Clindamycin if you are allergic to it or to Lincomycin, another antibiotic drug. It may cause a severe intestinal irritation called colitis, which may be fatal. Because of this, Clindamycin should be reserved for serious infections due to organisms known to be affected by it. It should not be taken for the casual treatment of colds or other moderate infections, or for infections which can be successfully treated with other drugs. If you develop severe diarrhea or stomach pains, call your doctor at once.

Pregnancy/Breast-feeding

This drug crosses into the blood circulation of a developing baby. It has not been found to cause birth defects. Pregnant women or those who might become pregnant while taking

this drug should not take it without their doctor's approval.
When the drug is considered essential by your doctor, the
potential risk of taking the medicine must be carefully weighed
against the benefit it might produce.

This drug passes into breast milk, but has caused no problems among breast-fed infants. You must consider the potential effect on the nursing infant if breast-feeding while
taking this medicine.

Seniors

Older adults may take this medication without special
consideration.

Possible Side Effects

Stomach pain, nausea, vomiting, diarrhea, pain when
swallowing.

Less common side effects are: itching and rash or more
serious signs of drug sensitivity, such as difficulty in breathing; also yellowing of the skin or whites of the eyes, occasional effects on components of the blood, and joint pain.

Drug Interactions

Clindamycin may antagonize Erythromycin; these drugs
should not be taken together.

Food Interactions

Take this medication with a full glass of water or food to
prevent irritation of the stomach or intestine.

Usual Dose

Adult: 150 to 450 milligrams every 6 hours.

Child: 4 to 11 milligrams per pound of body weight per
day in divided doses. No child should be given less than 37.5
milligrams 3 times per day, regardless of weight.

Topical lotion: Apply enough to cover the affected area(s)
lightly.

Special Information

Unsupervised use of this drug or other antibiotics can cause
secondary infections from susceptible organisms such as

fungi. Like any antibiotic treatment, take for the full course of therapy as indicated by your physician.

If you miss an oral dose of Clindamycin, take it as soon as possible. If it is almost time for your next dose, double that dose and go back to your regular dose schedule.

Generic Name

Clofibrate

Brand Name

Atromid-S

(Also available in generic form)

Type of Drug

Antihyperlipidemic.

Prescribed for

Reduction of high blood levels of cholesterol and/or triglycerides, in patients not responding to diet, weight control, and exercise measures to control their diabetes.

General Information

Although we don't know exactly how Clofibrate works, we know that it works on blood cholesterol and triglycerides. The lowering of blood levels of these fatty materials may be beneficial, and may have an effect on the development of heart disease. No one knows for sure. However, it is generally considered better to have low levels of cholesterol and triglycerides in the blood. Clofibrate is only part of the therapy for high blood levels of cholesterol and/or triglycerides. Diet and weight control are also very important. You must remember that taking this medicine is not a substitute for other activities or dietary restrictions which have been prescribed for you by your doctor.

Cautions and Warnings

Clofibrate causes liver cancer in rats and may do the same to human patients. Its use has not been definitely associated with reductions in death from heart disease; therefore, this drug should be used only by patients whose diets and other activities have not solved their triglyceride or cholesterol problems. Some studies have reported a large increase in death rates and drug side effects when people have taken Clofibrate over a long term. Clofibrate should not be used if you have severe liver or kidney disease.

Pregnancy/Breast-feeding

Clofibrate should not be used if you are pregnant, or are a nursing mother. There is the possibility that this medication may pass from you into your baby and build up in the unborn child to cause an adverse effect.

Seniors

Older adults may take this medicine without restriction.

Possible Side Effects

The most frequent side effect of Clofibrate is nausea. Other gastrointestinal reactions may be experienced: loose stools, stomach upset, stomach gas, abdominal pain. Less frequent: headache, dizziness, tiredness, cramped muscles, aching and weakness, rash, itching, brittle hair, loss of hair, abnormal heart rhythms, blood clots in the lungs or veins, enlargement of the liver, gallstones (especially in patients who have taken Clofibrate for a long time), decreased sex drive, and sexual impotence. If you suffer from angina pectoris, a specific type of chest pain, Clofibrate may either increase or decrease this pain. It may cause you to produce smaller amounts of urine than usual, and has been associated with blood in the urine, tiredness, weakness, drowsiness, dizziness, headache, and increased appetite. Clofibrate has been accused of causing stomach ulcers, stomach bleeding, arthritislike symptoms, uncontrollable muscle spasms, increased perspiration, blurred vision, breast enlargement, and some effects on the blood.

Drug Interactions

If you are taking an anticoagulant and get a new prescription for Clofibrate, your anticoagulant dose will have to be reduced by as much as ⅓ to ½. It is absolutely essential that your doctor knows you are taking these drugs in combination so that the proper dose adjustments can be made. The effect of Chenodiol may be decreased when it is taken together with Clofibrate. Antidiabetic drug effect may also be increased by Clofibrate.

Food Interactions

This drug may be taken with food or milk if it causes upset stomach.

Usual Dose

4 capsules per day in divided doses.

Special Information

Call your doctor if you develop chest pains, difficulty in breathing, abnormal heart rates, severe stomach pains with nausea and vomiting, fever and chills, sore throat, blood in the urine, swelling of the legs, weight gain, or change in urine habits.

Follow your diet and limit your intake of alcoholic beverages.

Clofibrate capsules are covered with soft gelatin that must be protected from heat and moisture. They should not be stored in the refrigerator, or in a bathroom medicine chest where there may be a lot of heat or moisture in the air, but in a dresser or night table where room temperature is normal.

If you miss a dose, take it as soon as possible. If it is almost time for your next dose, skip the missed dose and go back to your regular dose schedule. Do not double any doses.

Generic Name

Clonazepam

Brand Name

Clonopin

Type of Drug

Anticonvulsant.

Prescribed for

Control of petit mal and other seizures. Clonazepam has also been used to treat panic attacks.

General Information

Clonazepam is a member of the family of drugs known as benzodiazepines. Other members of the family include Diazepam, Chlordiazepoxide, Flurazepam, and Triazolam. Clonazepam is used only to control petit mal seizures in people who have not responded to other drug treatments, such as Ethosuximide. Clonazepam is generally considered a safe and effective treatment for such seizures and shares many of the same side effects, precautions, and interactions as its benzodiazepine cousins.

Cautions and Warnings

When stopping Clonazepam treatments, it is essential that the drug be discontinued gradually over a period of time to allow for safe withdrawal. Abrupt discontinuation of any benzodiazepine, including Clonazepam, may lead to drug withdrawal symptoms. In the case of Clonazepam, the withdrawal symptoms can include severe seizures. Other symptoms include tremors, abdominal cramps, muscle cramps, vomiting, and sweating.

Clonazepam should be used with caution if you have a chronic respiratory illness because the drug tends to increase salivation and other respiratory secretions and can make breathing more labored.

Pregnancy/Breast-feeding

This drug should be avoided by women who may become pregnant while using it and by pregnant and nursing mothers. It will cross into the developing infant, and the possible adverse effects are not known. In those situations where it is deemed essential, the potential risk of the drug must be carefully weighed against any benefit it might produce.

Recent reports suggest a strong association between the use of anticonvulsant drugs and birth defects. Although most of the information pertains to Phenytoin and Phenobarbital, not Clonazepam, other reports indicate a general association between all anticonvulsant drug treatments and birth defects. It is possible that the epileptic condition itself or genetic factors common to people with seizure disorders may also figure in the higher incidence of birth defects. Mothers taking Clonazepam should not breast-feed because of the possibility that the drug will pass into their breast milk and affect the baby. Use an alternative feeding method.

Seniors

Older adults are more sensitive to the effects of this drug, especially dizziness and drowsiness. Follow your doctor's directions and report any side effects at once.

Possible Side Effects

Drowsiness, poor muscle control, and behavior changes.

Less common side effects: abnormal eye movements, loss of voice and/or the ability to express a thought, double vision, coma, a glassy-eyed appearance, headache, temporary paralysis, labored breathing, shortness of breath, slurred speech, tremors, dizziness, fainting, confusion, depression, forgetfulness, hallucination, increased sex drive, hysteria, sleeplessness, psychosis, suicidal acts, chest congestion, stuffy nose, heart palpitations, hair loss, hairiness, rash, swelling of the face or ankles, changes in appetite and body weight (increased or decreased), coated tongue, constipation, diarrhea, involuntary passing of feces, dry mouth, stomach irritation, nausea, sore gums, difficulty urinating, pain on urination, bed-wetting, getting up at night to urinate, muscle weakness or pain, reduced red- and white-blood-cell and platelet levels, enlarged liver, liver inflammation, dehydration, a deterioration in general health, fever, and swollen lymph glands.

Drug Interactions

The depressant effects of Clonazepam are increased by tranquilizers, sleeping pills, narcotic pain relievers, antihistamines, alcohol, monoamine oxidase (MAO) inhibitors, antidepressants, and other anticonvulsants.

The combination of Valproic Acid and Clonazepam may produce severe petit mal seizures.

Phenobarbital or Phenytoin may reduce Clonazepam effectiveness by increasing the rate at which it is eliminated from the body.

Clonazepam treatment may increase the requirement for other anticonvulsant drugs, because of its effects on people who suffer from multiple types of seizures.

Avoid alcoholic beverages, which increase the depressant effects of this medicine.

Smoking may reduce Clonazepam's effectiveness.

Food Interactions

Clonazepam is best taken on an empty stomach but may be taken with food if it upsets your stomach.

Usual Dose

Adult and child (over age 10): 0.5 milligram 3 times per day to start. The dose is increased in steps of 0.5 to 1 milligram every 3 days until seizures are controlled or side effects develop. The maximum daily dose is 20 milligrams.

Infant and child (up to age 10, or 66 pounds): 0.004 to 0.013 milligram per pound of body weight per day to start. The dosage can be gradually increased to a maximum of 0.045 to 0.09 milligram per pound of body weight.

The dosage of Clonazepam must be reduced in people with impaired kidney function since this drug is primarily released from the body via the kidneys.

Overdosage

Clonazepam overdose will cause confusion, coma, poor reflexes, sleepiness, low blood pressure, labored breathing, and other depressive effects. If the overdose is discovered immediately, it may be helpful to make the victim vomit with Syrup of Ipecac to remove any remaining medicine from the stomach. All victims of Clonazepam overdose *must* be taken to a hospital emergency room for treatment. ALWAYS bring the prescription bottle with you.

Special Information

Clonazepam may interfere with your ability to drive a car or perform other complex tasks because it can cause drowsiness and difficulty concentrating.

Your doctor should perform periodic blood counts and liver-function tests while you are taking this drug to check for possible adverse drug effects.

Do not suddenly stop taking the medicine, since to do so could result in severe seizures. The dosage must be discontinued gradually by your doctor.

If you miss a dose and it is within an hour or so of that dose time, take it right away. Otherwise skip the missed dose and go back to your regular dose schedule. Do not double any dose.

Carry identification or wear a bracelet indicating that you suffer from a seizure disorder for which you take Clonazepam.

Generic Name

Clonidine

Brand Name

Catapres
Catapres TTS Transdermal Patch

(Tablets also available in generic form)

Type of Drug

Antihypertensive.

Prescribed for

High blood pressure. Clonidine has also been used in the treatment of nicotine dependence, tourette syndrome, migraine headaches, Methadone/opiate detoxification, and withdrawal from alcohol and benzodiazepines (like Valium).

General Information

Clonidine acts in the brain by causing the dilation of certain blood vessels, thereby decreasing blood pressure. The drug produces its effect very quickly, causing a decline in blood pressure within 1 hour. If you abruptly stop taking Clonidine you may experience an unusual increase in blood pressure with symptoms of agitation, headache, and nervousness. These effects can be reversed by simply resuming therapy or by taking another drug to lower the blood pressure. Under no circumstances should you stop taking Clonidine without your doctor's knowledge. People who abruptly stop taking this medication may suffer severe reactions and even die. Be sure you always have an adequate supply on hand.

Cautions and Warnings

Some people develop a tolerance to their usual dose of Clonidine. If this happens to you, your blood pressure may increase, and you will require a change in the Clonidine dose.

Pregnancy/Breast-feeding

Animal studies have shown this drug to be potentially damaging to a developing fetus in doses as low as ⅓ the maximum human dose. Pregnant women, and those who might become pregnant, should avoid this drug.

Clonidine passes into breast milk, but no effects on nursing infants have been noted. Nursing mothers should avoid this drug or use an alternate feeding method.

Seniors

Older adults are more susceptible to the effects of this drug and should be given lower than normal doses.

Possible Side Effects

Most common: dry mouth, drowsiness, sedation, constipation, dizziness, headache, fatigue. These effects tend to diminish as you continue taking the drug.

Infrequent: loss of appetite, not feeling well, nausea, vomiting, weight gain, breast enlargement, various effects on the heart, changes in dream patterns, nightmares, difficulty sleeping, nervousness, restlessness, anxiety, mental depression, rash, hives, itching, thinning or loss of scalp hair, difficulty urinating, impotence, dryness and burning of the eyes.

Drug Interactions

Clonidine has a depressive effect and will increase the depressive effects of alcohol, barbiturates, sedatives, and tranquilizers. Avoid them.

Antidepressants, appetite suppressants, estrogens, stimulants, Indocin, and other NSAIDs (nonsteroidal antiinflammatory drugs) may counteract the effects of Clonidine.

Food Interactions

Clonidine is best taken on an empty stomach but may be taken with food if it upsets your stomach.

Usual Dose

Starting dose of 0.1 milligram twice per day may be raised by 0.1 to 0.2 milligram per day until maximum control is achieved. The dose must be tailored to your individual needs. It is recommended that no one should take more than 2.4 milligrams per day.

Opiate detoxification: up to 0.008 milligram per pound of body weight in divided doses.

Transdermal patch: 0.1-milligram patch applied every 7 days. Two 0.3-milligram patches have not been shown to increase effectiveness.

Overdosage

Symptoms are severe lowering of blood pressure, weakness, and vomiting. The patient should be taken to a hospital emergency room immediately. ALWAYS bring the medicine bottle.

Special Information

Clonidine causes drowsiness in about 35 percent of those who take it: be extremely careful while driving or operating any sort of appliance or machinery. The effect is prominent during the first few weeks of therapy, then tends to decrease.

Avoid taking nonprescription cough and cold medicines unless so directed by your doctor.

Apply the patch to a hairless area of skin like the upper arm or torso. Use a different skin site each time. If the patch becomes loose during the 7 days, apply the specially supplied adhesive directly over the patch. If the patch falls off apply a new one. The patch should not be removed for bathing.

If you miss a dose of the oral medication, take it as soon as possible and go back to your regular dose schedule. If you miss 2 or more doses in a row, consult your doctor. Missing 2 or more doses could cause your blood pressure to go up and severe unpleasant effects to occur.

Generic Name

Clorazepate

Brand Names

Tranxene
Tranxene-SD

Type of Drug

Tranquilizer.

Prescribed for

Relief of symptoms of anxiety, tension, fatigue, or agitation. Clorazepate is also utilized to treat seizures and alcohol withdrawal.

General Information

Clorazepate is a member of the chemical group of drugs known as benzodiazepines. These drugs are used as either antianxiety agents, anticonvulsants, or sedatives (sleeping pills). They exert their effects by relaxing the large skeletal muscles and by a direct effect on the brain. In doing so, they can relax you and make you either more tranquil or sleepier, depending on the drug and how much you use. Many doctors prefer Clorazepate and the other members of this class to other drugs that can be used for the same effect. Their reason is that the benzodiazepines tend to be safer, have fewer side effects, and are usually as, if not more, effective.

These drugs are generally used in any situation where they can be a useful adjunct.

Benzodiazepine tranquilizing drugs can be abused if taken for long periods of time, and it is possible to develop withdrawal symptoms if you discontinue the therapy abruptly. Withdrawal symptoms include tremor, muscle cramps, stomach cramps, vomiting, insomnia, agitation, sweating, and even convulsions.

Cautions and Warnings

Do not take Clorazepate if you know you are sensitive or allergic to this drug or other benzodiazepines such as Diazepam, Chlordiazepoxide, Oxazepam, Lorazepam, Prazepam,

Flurazepam, Clonazepam, and Temazepam. Chlorazepate and other members of this drug group may aggravate narrow-angle glaucoma, but if you have open-angle glaucoma you may take the drugs. In any case, check this information with your doctor. Clorazepate can cause tiredness, drowsiness, inability to concentrate, or similar symptoms. Be careful if you are driving, operating machinery, or performing other activities which require concentration.

Pregnancy/Breast-feeding

Avoid taking this drug during the first 3 months of pregnancy except under strict supervision of your doctor. Although an increased chance of birth defects has not been seen, there is a risk factor to be considered. Other drugs similar to Clorazepate have been shown to cause birth defects.

The baby may become dependent on Clorazepate if it is used continually during pregnancy. If used during the last weeks of pregnancy or during breast-feeding, the baby may be overly tired, short of breath, or have a low heartbeat.

Use during labor may cause weakness in the newborn.

Seniors

Older adults are more sensitive to the effects of this drug. Follow your doctor's directions and report any side effects at once.

Possible Side Effects

Most common: mild drowsiness during the first few days of therapy, especially in the elderly or debilitated. If drowsiness persists, contact your doctor.

Less common side effects: confusion, depression, lethargy, disorientation, headache, inactivity, slurred speech, stupor, dizziness, tremor, constipation, dry mouth, nausea, inability to control urination, changes in sex drive, irregular menstrual cycle, changes in heart rhythm, lowered blood pressure, retention of fluids, blurred or double vision, itching, rash, hiccups, nervousness, inability to fall asleep, (occasional) liver dysfunction. If you experience any of these reactions stop taking the medicine and contact your doctor immediately.

Drug Interactions

Clorazepate is a central nervous system depressant. Avoid alcohol, tranquilizers, narcotics, barbiturates, monoamine oxidase (MAO) inhibitors, antihistamines, and other medicines used to relieve depression. Smoking may reduce the effectiveness of Clorazepate. The effects of Clorazepate may be prolonged when taken together with Cimetidine.

Food Interactions

This drug is best taken on an empty stomach but may be taken with food if it upsets your stomach.

Usual Dose

15 to 60 milligrams daily; average dose, 30 milligrams in divided quantities. Must be adjusted to individual response for patient to receive maximum effect.

Tranxene-SD, a long-acting form of Clorazepate, may be given as a single dose, either 11.25 or 22.5 milligrams once every 24 hours.

Overdosage

Symptoms are confusion, sleep or sleepiness, lack of response to pain such as a pin stick, shallow breathing, lowered blood pressure, and coma. The patient should be taken to a hospital emergency room immediately. ALWAYS bring the medicine bottle.

Special Information

Avoid alcoholic beverages while you are taking this medicine. Sleeping pills, narcotics, barbiturates, other tranquilizers, or other drugs causing nervous system depression should be used with caution while you are taking the medication. Tell your doctor if you become pregnant or are breast-feeding.

If you miss a dose, take it as soon as you remember. If it is almost time for your next dose, skip the missed dose and go back to your regular dose schedule. Do not double any doses.

Generic Name

Clotrimazole

Brand Names

Gyne-Lotrimin
Lotrimin
Mycelex

Mycelex-G
Mycelex Troches

(Also available in generic form)

Type of Drug

Antifungal.

Prescribed for

Fungus infections of the mouth, skin, and vaginal tract.

General Information

Clotrimazole is one of a group of the newer antifungal drugs available in the United States, although it has been available in other parts of the world for some time. This drug is especially useful against a wide variety of fungus organisms which other drugs do not affect.

Cautions and Warnings

If Clotrimazole causes local itching and/or irritation, stop using it. Do not use in the eyes. Women who are in the first three months of pregnancy should use this drug only if directed to do so by their doctors.

Pregnancy/Breast-feeding

No studies of this medication have been done in pregnant women and no reports of human birth defects exist, but animal studies show that high doses of the drug can cause problems in a developing fetus. Pregnant women, or women who might become pregnant while using this drug, should talk to their doctor about the risk of taking this medicine versus the benefits it can provide.

This drug is poorly absorbed into the bloodstream and not likely to pass into breast milk. Nursing mothers need not worry about adverse effects on their infants while taking Clotrimazole.

Seniors

Seniors may use this medication without restriction.

Possible Side Effects

Side effects do not occur very often and are usually mild. Cream or solution: redness, stinging, blistering, peeling, itching and swelling of local areas. Vaginal tablets: mild burning, skin rash, mild cramps, frequent urination, and burning or itching in a sexual partner. Oral tablets: stomach cramps or pain, diarrhea, nausea, or vomiting.

Food Interactions

The oral form of Clotrimazole is best taken on an empty stomach, but you may take it with food, just as long as you allow the tablet to dissolve in your mouth like a lozenge.

Usual Dose

Cream or solution: apply to affected areas, morning and night.

Vaginal cream: one applicatorful at bedtime for 7 to 14 days.

Vaginal tablets: 1 tablet inserted into the vagina at bedtime for 7 days, or 2 tablets a day for 3 days.

Lozenges: 1 lozenge 5 times a day for 2 weeks or more.

Special Information

If treating a vaginal infection, you should refrain from sexual activity or be sure that your partner wears a condom until the treatment is finished. Call your doctor if burning or itching develops, or if the condition does not show improvement in 7 days.

Dissolve the oral troche slowly in the mouth. This medicine must be taken on consecutive days. If you forget to take a dose of oral Clotrimazole, take it as soon as you remember. Do not double any doses.

Generic Name

Cloxacillin Sodium

Brand Names

Cloxapen
Tegopen

(Also available in generic form)

Type of Drug

Penicillin-type antibiotic.

Prescribed for

Gram-positive bacterial infections. Gram-positive bacteria (pneumococci, streptococci and staphylococci) are organisms that usually cause diseases like pneumonia, infections of the tonsils and throat, venereal diseases, meningitis (spinal infection), and septicemia (blood infection). Cloxacillin is best used to treat infections that are resistant to penicillin, although it can be used as initial treatment for some people.

General Information

Penicillin-type antibiotics fight infection by killing bacteria. They do this by destroying the cell wall of invading bacteria. Other antibiotics simply prevent bacteria from reproducing. Many infections can be treated by almost any member of this family, but some infections can only be treated by certain penicillin-type antibiotics.

Penicillins cannot treat a cold, flu, or any virus infection and should never be taken unless prescribed by a doctor for a specific illness. Always take your antibiotic exactly according to your doctor's directions for use, including the number of pills to take every day and the number of days to take the medicine. If you do not follow directions, you may not get the antibiotic's full benefit.

Cautions and Warnings

Do not take Cloxacillin if you have a history of penicillin allergy. The drugs are similar. The most common allergic reaction to Cloxacillin Sodium and other penicillins is a hivelike rash over the body with itching and redness. It is important to tell your doctor if you have ever taken this or any other Penicillin before and had an allergic reaction to it such as rash, itching, or trouble breathing.

Pregnancy/Breast-feeding

Cloxacillin has not caused birth defects, but you should be sure your doctor knows you are taking it. Cloxacillin passes into breast milk and may affect a nursing infant.

Seniors

Seniors may take Cloxacillin Sodium without special precautions.

Possible Side Effects

Common side effects include upset stomach, nausea, vomiting, diarrhea, and rash. Less common side effects include hairy tongue, itching or irritation around the anus or vagina, stomach pains with or without bleeding.

Drug Interactions

The effect of Cloxacillin Sodium can be affected by taking other antibiotics at the same time. Otherwise, Cloxacillin Sodium is remarkably free of interaction.

Food Interactions

Cloxacillin Sodium is best taken with a full glass of water on an empty stomach, 1 hour before or 2 hours after meals.

Usual Dose

Adult and child (over 44 pounds): 250 to 1000 milligrams every 6 hours.

Child (under 44 pounds): 2 to 4 milligrams per pound of body weight a day, divided into 4 doses.

Overdosage

Cloxacillin overdose is unlikely but may result in diarrhea or upset stomach.

Special Information

Do not take this medicine after the expiration date on the

label. Be sure to take this medicine exactly according to your doctor's directions.

Stop taking the medicine and call your doctor if any of the following side effects develop: skin rash, hives, itching, wheezing. Other side effects that demand your doctor's attention are: blood in the urine, passage of large amounts of light-colored urine, swelling of the face or ankles, trouble breathing, unusual weakness or tiredness.

If you forget to take a dose of Cloxacillin, take it as soon as you remember. If it is almost time for your regular dose, space the dose you forgot and your next regular dose 4 hours apart or double the next dose and continue your regular schedule.

Generic Name

Codeine

(Available only in generic form)

Type of Drug

Narcotic analgesic/cough suppressant combination.

Prescribed for

Relief of moderate to moderately severe pain, and as a cough suppressant.

General Information

Codeine is a narcotic drug with some pain-relieving and cough-suppressing activity. As an analgesic it is useful for mild to moderate pain. 30 to 60 milligrams of Codeine is approximately equal in pain-relieving effect to 2 Aspirin tablets (650 milligrams). Codeine may be less active than Aspirin for types of pain associated with inflammation, since Aspirin reduces inflammation and Codeine does not. Codeine suppresses the cough reflex but does not cure the underlying cause of the cough. In fact, sometimes it may not be desirable to overly suppress a cough, because cough suppression reduces your ability to naturally eliminate excess mucus produced during a cold or allergy attack. Other narcotic cough suppressants are stronger than Codeine, but Codeine remains the best cough medicine available today.

Cautions and Warnings

Do not take Codeine if you know you are allergic or sensitive to it. Use this drug with extreme caution if you suffer from asthma or other breathing problems. Long-term use of this drug may cause drug dependence or addiction. Codeine is a respiratory depressant and affects the central nervous system, producing sleepiness, tiredness, and/or inability to concentrate. Be careful if you are driving, operating machinery, or performing other functions requiring concentration.

Pregnancy/Breast-feeding

No studies of this medication have been done in women and no reports of human birth defects exist, but animal studies show that high doses of the drug can cause problems in a developing fetus. Pregnant women, or women who might become pregnant while using this drug, should talk to their doctor about the risk of taking this medicine versus the benefits it can provide.

This drug passes into breast milk, but no problems in nursing infants have been seen. Breast-feeding women should consider the possibility of adverse effects on their nursing infant. Choose another feeding method if you must take this medicine.

Seniors

Seniors are more likely to be sensitive to side effects of this drug and should be treated with smaller dosages than younger adults.

Possible Side Effects

Most frequent: light-headedness, dizziness, sleepiness, nausea, vomiting, loss of appetite, sweating. If these occur, consider calling your doctor and asking him about lowering the dose of Codeine you are taking. Usually the side effects disappear if you simply lie down.

More serious side effects of Codeine are shallow breathing or difficulty in breathing.

Less common side effects: euphoria (feeling high), sleepiness, headache, agitation, uncoordinated muscle movement, minor hallucinations, disorientation and visual disturbances, dry mouth, loss of appetite, constipation, flushing of the face, rapid heartbeat, palpitations, faintness, urinary difficulties or hesitancy, reduced sex drive and/or potency, itching, rashes, anemia, lowered blood sugar, yellowing of the skin and/or whites of the eyes. Narcotic analgesics may aggravate convulsions in those who have had convulsions in the past.

Drug Interactions

Because of its depressant effect and potential effect on breathing, Codeine should be taken with extreme care in combination with alcohol, sleeping medicine, tranquilizers, or other depressant drugs.

Food Interactions

Codeine may be taken with food to reduce stomach upset.

Usual Dose

Adult: 15 to 60 milligrams 4 times per day for relief of pain; 10 to 20 milligrams every few hours as needed to suppress cough.

Child: 1 to 2 milligrams per pound of body weight in divided doses for relief of pain; 0.5 to 0.75 milligram per pound of body weight in divided doses to suppress cough.

Overdosage

Symptoms are depression of respiration (breathing), extreme tiredness progressing to stupor and then coma, pinpointed pupils of the eyes, no response to stimulation such as a pin stick, cold and clammy skin, slowing down of the heartbeat, lowering of blood pressure, convulsions, and cardiac arrest. The patient should be taken to a hospital emergency room immediately. ALWAYS bring the medicine bottle.

Special Information

Avoid alcohol while taking Codeine. Call your doctor if you develop constipation or dry mouth.

If you forget a dose of Codeine, take it as soon as you remember. If it is almost time for your next dose, skip the one you forgot and continue with your regular schedule. Do not take a double dose of Codeine.

Generic Name

Colchicine

(Available only in generic form)

Type of Drug

Reduces the inflammatory response to gout.

Prescribed for

Gouty arthritis. May also be prescribed for Mediterranean Fever, calcium deposits, amyloidosis, Paget's disease of bone, and nerve problems associated with multiple sclerosis.

General Information

While no one knows exactly how Colchicine works, it appears to affect gout by reducing the body's inflammatory response to gout. Unlike drugs that affect uric-acid levels, Colchicine will not block the progression of gout to chronic gouty arthritis, but it will relieve the pain of acute attacks and lessen the frequency and severity of attacks.

Cautions and Warnings

Do not use Colchicine if you suffer from a serious kidney, liver, stomach, or cardiac disorder.

Safety and effectiveness for use by children has not been established.

Periodic blood counts should be done when you are taking Colchicine for long periods of time.

Pregnancy/Breast-feeding

Colchicine can harm the fetus; use by pregnant women should be considered only when the benefits clearly outweigh the potential hazards to the fetus.

Colchicine may pass into breast milk. No problems with nursing infants are known to exist, but you should consider the possibility of a reaction while taking this medicine.

Seniors

Older adults are more likely to develop drug side effects and should use this drug with caution.

Possible Side Effects

Vomiting, diarrhea, stomach pain, nausea, hair loss, skin rash, loss of appetite.

Less commonly, disorders of the blood may occur in patients undergoing long-term Colchicine therapy.

Drug Interactions

Colchicine has been shown to cause poor absorption of Vitamin B_{12}, a condition that is reversible.

Colchicine may increase sensitivity to central-nervous-system depressants such as tranquilizers and alcohol.

The following drugs can reduce Colchicine's effectiveness: anticancer drugs, Bumetanide, Diazoxide, thiazide diuretics, Ethacrynic Acid, Furosemide, Mecamylamine, Pyrazinamide, Triamterene.

Taking Phenylbutazone together with Colchicine increases the chance of drug side effects.

Food Interactions

This drug may be taken without regard to food or meals.

Usual Dose

To relieve an acute attack of gout: 1 to 1.2 milligrams. This dose may be followed by 0.5 to 1.2 milligrams every 1 to 2 hours until pain is relieved or nausea, vomiting, or diarrhea occurs. The total amount usually needed to control pain and inflammation during an attack varies from 4 to 8 milligrams.

To prevent gout attacks: 0.3 to 1.8 milligrams daily.

Overdosage

Symptoms may include nausea, vomiting, stomach pain, burning sensations in the throat, stomach, and skin, diarrhea (which may be severe and bloody). If you think you are experiencing an overdose, contact your doctor immediately, or go to a hospital emergency room. ALWAYS bring the medicine bottle with you.

Special Information

Notify your doctor if you experience skin rash, sore throat, fever, unusual bleeding or bruising, tiredness, numbness or tingling.

Stop taking Colchicine as soon as gout pain is relieved or at the first sign of nausea, vomiting, stomach pain, or diarrhea. If you experience these side effects, contact your doctor.

If you are regularly taking Colchicine and you forget to take a dose, take it as soon as possible. Do not double any doses.

Generic Name

Colestipol

Brand Name

Colestid

Type of Drug

Antihyperlipidemic (blood fat reducer).

Prescribed for

High blood cholesterol, itching associated with bile duct obstruction, some forms of colitis, pesticide poisoning.

General Information

This medication reduces blood cholesterol by removing bile acids from the biliary system. Since cholesterol is used by the body to make bile acids and bile acids are necessary for the digestion of dietary fats, the only way the body can continue to digest fats is to make more bile acids from cholesterol, resulting in a lowering of blood cholesterol levels. The medicine works entirely within the bowel and is never absorbed into the bloodstream.

In some kinds of hyperlipidemia, Colestipol may be more effective in lowering total blood cholesterol than Clofibrate. There are 6 different types of hyperlipidemia. Check with your doctor as to the kind you have and the proper drug treatment for your condition.

Cautions and Warnings

Do not use Colestipol if you are sensitive to it or to Chole-styramine, another similar drug product.

Pregnancy/Breast-feeding

The safety of using this medication during pregnancy is not known. If you are pregnant and must use this medication, talk to your doctor about the potential benefit to be gained versus other treatments for your condition.

The medicine is not absorbed into your blood and will not affect a nursing infant. However, it can affect the amounts of vitamins and other nutrients absorbed, possibly making your milk less nutritious. You may want to consider alternate methods or supplemental feedings for your infant.

Seniors

Older adults are more likely to suffer side effects from this medication, especially those relating to the bowel.

Possible Side Effects

The most common side effect is constipation, which may be severe and result in a bowel impaction. Hemorrhoids may be worsened.

Less frequent side effects are abdominal pain and bloating, bleeding in the stomach or intestine, belching, gas, nausea, vomiting, diarrhea, heartburn, and appetite loss. Your stool may have an unusual appearance because of a high fat level.

Other side effects include Vitamin A and D deficiency, rashes, irritation of the tongue and anus, osteoporosis, black stools, stomach ulcers, dental bleeding, hiccups, a sour taste, pancreas inflammation, ulcer attack, gallbladder attack, bleeding, black-and-blue marks, itching and rash, backache, muscle and joint pains, arthritis, headache, anxiety, dizziness, fatigue, ringing or buzzing in the ears, fainting, tingling in the hands or feet, blood in the urine, frequent or painful urination, an unusual urine odor, eye irritation, weight changes, increased sex drive, swollen glands, swelling of the arms or legs, shortness of breath.

Drug Interactions

This medication interferes with the absorption of virtually all other medicines taken by mouth. Take other medicines at least 1 hour before or 4 to 6 hours after Colestipol. Some drugs for which this effect has been proven are: Cephalexin, Chenodiol, Clindamycin, corticosteroids, digitalis drugs, iron, Penicillins, Phenobarbital, Phenylbutazone, Tetracycline, thiazide diuretics, thyroid drugs, Trimethoprim, Vitamins A, D, E, and K, Warfarin.

Food Interactions

Take this medication before meals. It may be mixed with soda, water, juice, applesauce, or crushed pineapple.

Usual Dose

15 to 30 grams (3 to 6 packets) per day in 2 to 4 divided doses.

Overdosage

The most severe effect of Colestipol overdose is bowel impaction. Take the overdose victim to a hospital emergency room for evaluation and treatment. ALWAYS bring the medicine container with you.

Special Information

Do not swallow the granules in their dry form; mix it with soda, water, or juice and drink as a liquid.

Constipation, stomach gas, nausea, and heartburn may occur and then disappear with continued use of this medication. Call your doctor if these side effects continue or if you develop unusual problems such as bleeding from the gums or rectum.

Prepare each packet of powder by mixing it with a liquid, soup, cereal, or pulpy fruit. Alternatively, the powder may be added to a glass of 6 ounces or more of liquid or carbonated beverage.

Some Colestipol may stick to the sides of the glass; this material should be rinsed with water or juice and drunk.

If you miss a dose, skip it and continue on your regular dose schedule. Do not double any doses.

Brand Name

Combipres

Ingredients

Chlorthalidone
Clonidine

Type of Drug

Antihypertensive.

Prescribed for

High blood pressure.

General Information

This drug is a combination of two effective antihypertensive drugs. One of them works by causing the dilation of certain blood vessels. The other is a diuretic which lowers blood pressure through its effect on body ions (sodium and potassium). Although it is convenient to take the two drugs in one tablet, it may not be in your best interest. If you need more or less of one of the ingredients than are available in the Combipres tablets, you must take the drugs as separate pills. Often, doctors are able to lower your blood pressure most effectively by manipulating the doses of one drug or the other.

Cautions and Warnings

Do not take Combipres if you are allergic to either of the ingredients or to sulfa-type drugs.

Some people develop a tolerance to the effect of one of the ingredients in this product. If this happens, your blood pressure may increase and you may require a change of dose or medicine.

Pregnancy/Breast-feeding

This drug should not be taken by women planning to become pregnant, pregnant women, or nursing mothers. Chlorthalidone, if used during pregnancy, may cause side effects in the newborn infant; they are jaundice, blood problems, and low potassium. Chlorthalidone passes into breast milk. Nursing mothers should use an alternate feeding method.

Seniors

Older adults may be more likely to be sensitive to this drug's effects and should be treated with a lower dosage than younger adults.

Possible Side Effects

One of the ingredients in this drug can cause loss of potassium from the body (hypokalemia). The signs of this problem are dryness of the mouth, weakness, lethargy, drowsiness, restlessness, muscle pains or cramps, muscular tiredness, stomach upset, nausea and vomiting, and abnormal heart rhythms. To prevent or treat hypokalemia, potassium supplements, in the form of tablets, powders, or liquids, are given every day. You may increase your potassium intake naturally by eating more bananas, citrus fruits, melons, or tomatoes.

Combipres may also cause constipation or headache.

Less common side effects: loss of appetite, feeling of ill health, nausea, vomiting, weight gain, breast enlargement, adverse effects on the heart, changes in dream patterns, nightmares, difficulty sleeping, anxiety, depression, rash, hives, itching, thinning or loss of hair, dryness or burning of the eyes, sexual impotence. Other possible adverse effects from this combination are tingling of the toes or fingers, changes in blood composition, sensitivity to sunlight, difficulty in breathing, drug allergy, dizziness when rising quickly from a sitting or lying position, muscle spasms, weariness, blurred vision.

Drug Interactions

May interact with Digitalis to cause abnormal heart rhythms. The effect of an oral antidiabetic medicine may be altered by Combipres. People taking Lithium drugs should be careful about also taking Combipres since the combination may lead to Lithium toxicity. Avoid alcohol, barbiturates, sedatives, and tranquilizers while taking Combipres. Their action may be increased by one of the ingredients in Combipres.

Food Interactions

You may take this medicine without regard to food, although medicine is, generally, best taken on an empty stomach.

Usual Dose

2 tablets per day (of either strength). The dose of this drug must be tailored to your individual needs for maximum effectiveness.

Overdosage

Symptoms are excessive urination, fatigue, and extreme lowering of blood pressure. The patient should be taken immediately to a hospital emergency room. ALWAYS bring the medicine bottle.

Special Information

Avoid over-the-counter drugs containing stimulant drugs. If you are unsure which ones to avoid, ask your pharmacist.

One of the ingredients in Combipres causes drowsiness in about 35 percent of those who take it. Be extremely careful while driving or operating any equipment. This effect is most prominent during the first few weeks of therapy.

Do not suddenly stop taking this medication.

If you forget a dose of Combipres, take it as soon as you remember. If it is almost time for your next dose, skip the one you forgot and continue with your regular schedule. Do not take a double dose of Combipres.

Generic Name

Conjugated Estrogens

Brand Names

Conjugated Estrogenic	Premarin
Substances	Progens
Estrocon	

(Also available in generic form)

Other Estrogen Products

Esterified Estrogens	Estratab
Estraderm	Menest
Estradiol Transdermal System	

Type of Drug

Estrogen.

Prescribed for

Moderate to severe symptoms associated with menopause and prevention of postmenopausal osteoporosis. There is no evidence that this drug is effective for nervous symptoms or depression occurring during menopause: it should not be used to treat this condition. Conjugated Estrogens may also be used to treat various types of cancer in selected patients and other conditions where supplementation of normal estrogenic substances is required.

General Information

Because of the potential development of secondary disease after a long period of taking Conjugated Estrogens, the decision to take this medication chronically should be made cautiously by you and your doctor.

Cautions and Warnings

Estrogens have been reported to increase the risk of certain types of cancer in postmenopausal women taking this type of drug for prolonged periods of time: the risk tends to depend upon the duration of treatment and the dose of the estrogen being taken. When long-term estrogen therapy is indicated for the treatment of menopausal symptoms, the lowest effective dose should be used. If you have to take Conjugated Estrogens for extended periods of time, you should see your doctor at least twice a year so that he can assess your current condition and your need to continue the drug therapy.

If you are taking an estrogenic product and experience vaginal bleeding of a recurrent, abnormal, or persistent nature, contact your doctor immediately.

If you have active thrombophlebitis or any other disorder associated with the formation of blood clots, you probably should not take this drug. If you feel that you have a disorder associated with blood clots and you have been taking Conjugated Estrogens or a similar product, you should contact your doctor immediately so that he can evaluate your situation and decide about stopping the drug therapy.

Prolonged continuous administration of estrogenic substances to certain animal species has increased the frequency of cancer in these animals, and there is evidence that these drugs may increase the risk of various cancers in humans. This drug should be taken with caution by women with a strong family history of breast cancer or those who have breast nodules, fibrocystic disease of the breast, or abnormal mammogram. Furthermore, long-term taking of Conjugated Estrogens may expose a woman to a two- to threefold increase in chances of developing gallbladder disease. It is possible that women taking Conjugated Estrogens for extended periods of time may experience some of the same development of long-term adverse effects as women who have taken oral contraceptives for extended periods of time. These long-term problems may include thromboembolic disease or the development of various disorders associated with the development of blood clots, liver cancer or other liver tumors, high blood pressure, glucose intolerance or a development of a symptom similar to diabetes or the aggravation of diabetes in patients who had this disease before they started the estrogen, and high blood levels of calcium in certain classes of patients.

Pregnancy/Breast-feeding

If you are pregnant do not use this or any other estrogenic substance, since these drugs, if used during the earlier stages of pregnancy, may seriously damage the offspring. Estrogens may reduce the flow of breast milk and the effects on nursing infants are not predictable.

Seniors

The risk of some side effects increases with age, especially if you smoke.

Possible Side Effects

Breakthrough bleeding, spotting, changes in menstrual flow, dysmenorrhea, premenstrual-type syndrome, amenorrhea, swelling of the ankles and legs, vaginal infection with candida, cystitislike syndrome, enlargement or tenderness of the breasts, nausea, vomiting, abdominal cramps, feeling of bloatedness, jaundice or yellowing of the skin or whites of the eyes, rash, loss of scalp hair, development of new hairy areas. Lesions of the eye have been associated with estrogen therapy. If you wear contact lenses and are taking estrogen, it is possible that you will become intolerant to the lenses. You may also experience headache—possibly migraine headache—dizziness, depression, weight changes, retention of water, and changes in sex drive.

Other side effects include stroke, blood clot formation, dribbling or sudden passage of urine, loss of coordination, chest pains, leg pains, difficulty breathing, slurred speech, vision changes, skin rash, skin irritation and redness.

Drug Interactions

Vitamin C (in doses of 1 gram a day or more) may increase the effect of estrogen.

Phenytoin, Ethotoin, and Mephenytoin may interfere with estrogen effects.

Estrogens may force a dosage change in oral anticoagulant (blood-thinning) drugs, which your doctor can do with a simple blood test.

Estrogens may increase the side effects of antidepressants and phenothiazine tranquilizers. Low estrogen doses may increase estrogen effectiveness.

Food Interactions

This drug may be taken with food to reduce upset stomach.

Usual Dose

0.3 to 3.75 milligrams per day, depending on the disease and patient's response.

Estradiol skin patches: 1 patch twice a week for 3 weeks. Rest 1 week, then start again.

Overdosage

Overdosage may cause nausea and withdrawal bleeding in adult females. Accidental overdosage in children has not resulted in serious adverse side effects.

Special Information

Call your doctor if you develop chest pain, difficulty breathing, pain in the groin or calves, unusual vaginal bleeding, missed menstrual period, lumps in the breast, sudden severe headaches, dizziness or fainting, disturbances in speech or vision, weakness or numbness in the arms or legs, abdominal pains, depression, yellowing of the skin or whites of the eyes. Call your doctor if you think you are pregnant.

Cigarette smoking increases the chance of cardiovascular side effects, including stroke and blood clotting.

Estrogen skin patches should be applied to a clean area, preferably on the abdomen. Do not apply to your breasts. The application site should be rotated and each site should have a 7-day patch-free period.

Different brands of Conjugated Estrogen tablets may not produce the same effects; therefore they are not considered medically interchangeable. Do not switch to a different brand without your doctor's knowledge.

Brand Name

Cortisporin Otic

Ingredients

Hydrocortisone
Neomycin Sulfate
Polymyxin-B

Other Brand Names

AK Spore HC Otic	Ortega Otic M
Cortatrigen Modified Ear Drops	Otocort
Drotic	Otomycin Hpn Otic
My Cort Otic	Otoreid HC

(Also available in generic form)

Type of Drug

Steroidal antibiotic combination product.

Prescribed for

Superficial infections, inflammation, itching, and other problems involving the outer ear.

General Information

Cortisporin Otic contains a steroid drug to reduce inflammation and two antibiotics to treat local infections. This combination can be quite useful for local infections and inflammations of the ear because of its dual method of action and its relatively broad, nonspecific applicability.

Cautions and Warnings

This product is specifically designed to be used in the ear. It can be very damaging if accidentally placed into your eye.

Pregnancy/Breast-feeding

Pregnant and breast-feeding women may use this product with no restriction.

Seniors

Older adults may use this product with no restriction.

Possible Side Effects

Local irritation such as itching or burning can occur if you are sensitive or allergic to one of the ingredients in this drug.

Usual Dose

2 to 4 drops in the affected ear 3 to 4 times per day.

Special Information

Use only when specifically prescribed by a physician. Overuse of this or similar products can result in the growth of other organisms such as fungi. If new infections or new problems appear during the time you are using this medication, stop using the drug and contact your doctor.

Generic Name

Cyclandelate

Brand Names

Cyclan
Cyclospasmol

(Also available in generic form)

Type of Drug

Vasodilator.

Prescribed for

Nighttime leg cramps. Also prescribed to dilate large blood vessels in the brain so that more blood can be delivered to it and to treat Raynaud's phenomenon (spasms of blood vessels usually associated with cold temperatures).

General Information

Cyclandelate relaxes various smooth muscles: it slows their normal degree of responsiveness but does not paralyze muscle cells. Cyclandelate may directly widen blood vessels in the brain and other areas, increasing the flow of blood and oxygen to these areas.

These actions should be considered as possibly effective. There is considerable doubt among experts that this drug produces the effects claimed for it.

Cautions and Warnings

Do not take Cyclandelate if you are allergic or sensitive to it. Do not take Cyclandelate if you have a history of glaucoma, or of heart or other disease in which major blood vessels have been partly or completely blocked.

Pregnancy/Breast-feeding

This drug has not been found to cause birth defects. Pregnant women, or those who might become pregnant while taking this drug, should not take it without their doctor's approval. When the drug is considered essential by your doctor, the potential risk of taking the medicine must be carefully weighed against the benefit it might produce.

This drug has caused no problems among breast-fed infants. You must consider the potential effect on the nursing infant if breast feeding while taking this medicine.

Seniors

Older adults may take this medication without special consideration.

Possible Side Effects

The most common side effect of Cyclandelate is mild stomach upset, but this can be avoided by taking the medicine with food or antacid. Cyclandelate can produce mild flushing, particularly in the face and extremities. It can also cause headache, feeling of weakness, and rapid heartbeat, especially during the first few weeks of therapy.

Less common side effects: Cyclandelate can make you feel weak, dizzy, or faint when you rise quickly from a lying or sitting position. This is called orthostatic hypotension and is caused by a sudden drop in the amount of blood being supplied to your brain. You can usually avoid orthostatic hypotension by getting up slowly. If the symptom becomes a problem, contact your doctor so that he can adjust your dose or prescribe a different medicine for you.

Drug Interactions

Avoid taking over-the-counter drugs for cough, cold or allergy as some of these drugs can aggravate heart disease or other diseases related to blocked blood vessels. Contact your doctor or pharmacist for more specific information about over-the-counter products which could be a problem.

Food Interactions

This drug may be taken with food or antacids to reduce stomach upset.

Usual Dose

Starting dose, 1200 to 1600 milligrams per day in divided doses before meals and at bedtime. As you begin to respond to the medication, the dose may be reduced to a lowest effective level of, usually, 400 to 800 milligrams per day given in 2 to 4 divided doses. Improvement takes several weeks to appear; do not look for immediate benefits. Use of this medication for less than several weeks is usually of little or no value and certainly of no permanent value.

Special Information

If you miss a dose of Cyclandelate, take it as soon as possible. Do not double any doses, but continue your regular dose schedule.

Generic Name

Cyclosporine

Brand Name

Sandimmune

Type of Drug

Immunosuppressant.

Prescribed for

Prevention of the body's rejection of a transplanted kidney, heart, or liver. Used with or without corticosteroids for those who have previously been given other drug treatments. Cyclosporine has had limited success in bone marrow, heart-lung, and pancreas transplants, all of which are considered nonapproved uses for the drug.

Many researchers think that Cyclosporine may help in the treatment of other immunologic diseases such as diabetes, psoriasis, myasthenia gravis, multiple sclerosis, rheumatoid arthritis, lupus, and others. The drug is not approved by the FDA for treating these conditions.

General Information

Cyclosporine is the first new drug approved in the United States in over 20 years to prevent rejection of transplanted organs. A product of fungus metabolism, Cyclosporine was proved a potent immunosuppressant in 1972. First given to human kidney- and bone-marrow-transplant patients in 1978, it selectively inhibits cells known as T-lymphocytes and prevents the production of a compound known as interlukein-II, which activates T-lymphocyte cells. T-lymphocytes are an integral part of the body's defense mechanism that actually destroy invading cells.

Cautions and Warnings

This drug should be prescribed only by doctors experienced in immunosuppressive therapy and the care of organ-transplant patients. It is always used with adrenal corticosteroid drugs. Cyclosporine should not be given with other immunosuppressants since oversuppression of the immune system can result in lymphoma or extreme susceptibility to infection.

The oral form of the drug is poorly and erratically absorbed into the bloodstream. Because of this, it must be taken in doses 3 times larger than the injectable dose. People taking this drug orally over a period of time should have their blood checked for Cyclosporine levels so that the dose can be adjusted, if necessary.

Pregnancy/Breast-feeding

This drug should be avoided by pregnant women or women who may become pregnant while using it. In those situations where it is deemed essential, the potential risk of the drug must be carefully weighed against any benefit it might produce. Cyclosporine passes into breast milk. Nursing mothers who take this medicine should use an alternative feeding method.

Seniors

Older adults may take this medicine without special precautions.

Possible Side Effects

Kidney toxicity: Cyclosporine is known to be extremely toxic to the kidneys. This effect is seen in 25 percent of all kidney transplants, 38 percent of heart transplants, and 37 percent of liver transplants where the drug is used. Mild toxicity is generally seen 2 to 3 months after the transplant and is often reversed by reducing the Cyclosporine dose.

Severe toxicity usually develops soon after transplantation and may be difficult to differentiate from organ rejection. Drug toxicity responds to a reduction in Cyclosporine dosage, while rejection does not. If the toxic effect does not respond to dosage reduction, your doctor will probably switch to a different drug. All people treated with Cyclosporine should be tested periodically for kidney function.

Liver toxicity: This is much less common than kidney toxicity, but still occurs in many people receiving Cyclosporine. Liver toxicity is usually present in 4 percent of kidney transplants, 7 percent of heart transplants, and 4 percent of liver transplants, usually during the first month of therapy, when doses tend to be the highest.

Lymphoma may develop in people whose immune systems are excessively suppressed. Almost 85 percent of all people treated with this medicine will develop an infection, compared with 94 percent on other forms of immunosuppressive therapy.

Other frequent Cyclosporine side effects are: high blood pressure, increased hair growth, growth of the gums, tremors, cramps, acne, brittle hair or fingernails, convulsions, headache, confusion, diarrhea, nausea and vomiting, tingling in the hands or feet, facial flushing, reduction in blood counts of white cells and platelets, sinus inflammation, swollen and painful male breasts, drug allergy, conjunctivitis (redeye), fluid retention and swelling, ringing or buzzing in the ears, hearing loss, high blood sugar, muscle pains.

Rare side effects include: blood in the urine, heart attack, itching, anxiety, depression, lethargy, weakness, mouth sores, difficulty swallowing, intestinal bleeding, constipation, pancreas inflammation, night sweats, chest pain, joint pains, visual disturbances, weight loss.

Drug Interactions

Cyclosporine should be used carefully with other drugs known to be toxic to the kidneys. Phenytoin, for seizure disorders, reduces Cyclosporine blood levels.

Excessive immunosuppression may result from the use of Cyclosporine with any immune-suppressing drug other than a corticosteroid.

Cyclosporine's effect and the chance of drug side effects are increased when it is taken together with male hormones, Cimetidine, Danazol, Erythromycin, Ketoconazole, Miconazole.

Cyclosporine increases blood potassium. Excessive blood potassium levels can be reached if it is taken together with a potassium-sparing diuretic (like Spironolactone), salt substitutes, potassium supplements, or foods high in potassium.

Food Interactions

The oral form of this drug comes in an oily base derived from castor oil. You should mix it in a glass (not a paper or plastic cup) with whole milk, chocolate milk, or orange juice at room temperature to make it taste better. Drink immediately after mixing, add more of the diluent, and drink that to be sure that the entire dose has been taken.

Cyclosporine is best taken on an empty stomach but may be taken with food if it upsets your stomach.

Usual Dose

The usual oral dose of Cyclosporine is 6.8 milligrams per pound of body weight per day, given 4 to 12 hours before the transplant operation. This dosage is continued after the operation for a week or two and then gradually reduced (5 percent per week) to 2.25 to 4.5 milligrams per pound of body weight. Use the method described in "Food Interactions." Injectable Cyclosporine is given to people who can't take or tolerate the oral form, in ⅓ the dose of the oral liquid.

Overdosage

Victims of Cyclosporine overdose can be expected to develop drug side effects and symptoms of extreme immunosuppression. Patients taking an overdose of this drug must be made to vomit with Syrup of Ipecac (available at any pharmacy) to remove any remaining drug from the stomach. Call your doctor or a poison control center before doing this. If you must go to a hospital emergency room, ALWAYS bring the medicine bottle.

Special Information

Call your doctor at the first sign of fever, sore throat, tiredness, unusual bleeding, or bruising.

This medicine should be continued as long as prescribed by the doctor. Do not stop taking it because of side effects or other problems. If you cannot tolerate the oral form, it can be given by injection.

Do not keep the oral liquid in the refrigerator. After the bottle is opened, use it within 2 months.

Generic Name

Cyproheptadine Hydrochloride

Brand Name

Periactin

(Also available in generic form)

Type of Drug

Phenothiazine-type antihistamine.

Prescribed for

Relief of symptoms associated with allergies, drug allergies, colds or upper respiratory infections, infection or itching of the extremities, insect bites, and general itching.

It has also been used to stimulate appetite and for the treatment of headaches.

General Information

Cyproheptadine Hydrochloride is an antihistamine. Any effect it exerts is due to its ability to counteract the effects of histamine, a chemical released by the body as part of allergic or sensitivity reactions. Histamine is also released as a part of the body's reaction to the common cold or similar respiratory infections. Cyproheptadine Hydrochloride is especially useful in treating symptoms of allergy, itching, and the common cold. It has been reported to cause weight gain and has even been tried as an appetite stimulant.

Cautions and Warnings

Do not take Cyproheptadine Hydrochloride if you are allergic to it or to other phenothiazine-type drugs such as Chlorpromazine and Prochlorperazine. Signs of allergies to the phenothiazines include sore throat, fever, unusual bleeding or bruising, rash, blurred vision, and yellowing of the skin.

Although this drug is usually not a problem for people with heart, liver, and stomach problems, they would do well to avoid taking it.

Pregnancy/Breast-feeding

Antihistamines have not been proven to be a cause of birth defects or other problems in pregnant women, although studies in animals have shown that some drugs (Meclizine and Cyclizine), used mainly against nausea and vomiting, may cause birth defects. Do not take any antihistamine without your doctor's knowledge. Small amounts of antihistamine medicines pass into breast milk and may affect a nursing infant. Nursing mothers should avoid antihistamines or use alternate feeding methods while taking the medicine.

Seniors

Seniors are more sensitive to antihistamine side effects. Confusion, difficult or painful urination, dizziness, drowsiness, a faint feeling, dry mouth, nose, or throat, nightmares or excitement, nervousness, restlessness, or irritability are more likely to occur among older adults.

Possible Side Effects

Most frequent: sedation, sleeplessness, dizziness, disturbed coordination. Less common: itching, rash, drug allergy, sensitivity to sunlight, excessive perspiration, chills, dryness of the mouth, nose, and throat.

Other possible side effects: lowered blood pressure, headache, palpitations, rapid heartbeat, effects on the blood system, confusion, restlessness, excitation, nervousness, irritability, sleeplessness, euphoria, tingling in the hands and feet, blurred vision, double vision, ringing in the ears, convulsions, stomach upset, loss of appetite, vomiting, nausea, diarrhea, constipation, thickening of mucus and other bronchial secretions resulting in tightness in the chest, wheezing, stuffy nose. Cyproheptadine Hydrochloride may also produce adverse effects common to the phenothiazine class of drugs, such as tremors, a spastic, uncontrollable motion, and (rarely) a form of jaundice (yellowing of the skin and eyes).

Drug Interactions

Alcohol will increase the drowsiness or sleepiness that can be produced by Cyproheptadine Hydrochloride, so avoid drinking excessive amounts of alcoholic beverages. Taking Cyproheptadine Hydrochloride with another sedative, tranquilizer, barbiturate, or hypnotic drug can increase drowsiness and other symptoms of depression.

Cyproheptadine Hydrochloride can influence the effectiveness of any high blood pressure medicine you are taking.

If you have Parkinson's disease, you probably should not be taking this type of antihistamine; it is known to produce specific adverse drug effects in people with Parkinson's disease. An MAO inhibitor may interact with Cyproheptadine Hydrochloride to prolong the drying effect of the antihistamine, causing dry mouth and blurred vision.

Usual Dose

Adult: 4 to 20 milligrams daily.
Child (age 7 to 14): 4 milligrams 2 to 3 times per day.
Child (age 2 to 6): 2 to 3 milligrams per day.

The maximum daily dose for adults is 32 milligrams; for children age 7 to 14, 16 milligrams; for children age 2 to 6, 12 milligrams.

Overdosage

Symptoms are depression or stimulation (especially in children), dry mouth, fixed or dilated pupils, flushing of the skin, and stomach upset. Take the patient to a hospital emergency room immediately. ALWAYS bring the medicine container to the hospital. Do not induce vomiting. After having taken this drug the patient might breathe in the vomit, causing serious lung damage.

Special Information

Cyproheptadine Hydrochloride can produce sleepiness. Be careful if you are driving or operating hazardous machinery.

The liquid form of this medicine is very bitter. To improve the taste you can mix it with fruit juice, milk, or a carbonated beverage.

If you forget to take a dose of Cyproheptadine, take it as

soon as you remember. If it's almost time for your next
dose, skip the one you forgot and continue with your regular
schedule. Do not take a double dose of Cyproheptadine.

Brand Name

Darvocet-N

Ingredients

Acetaminophen
Propoxyphene Napsylate

Other Brand Names

The following products contain the same ingredients in different concentrations:

Dolene-AP 65	Propacet N
DOXApap N	Prox/APAP
Genagesic	Wygesic
Lorcet	

(Also available in generic form)

Type of Drug

Analgesic.

Prescribed for

Relief of mild to moderate pain.

General Information

Propoxyphene Napsylate, the major ingredient in this product, is a chemical derivative of Methadone, a narcotic used
for pain relief. It is estimated that Propoxyphene Napsylate
is about ½ to ⅔ as strong a pain reliever as Codeine and about
as effective as Aspirin.

Cautions and Warnings

Do not take this drug if you are allergic to either ingredient.
It may produce physical or psychological drug dependence
(addiction) after long periods of time. The major sign of

dependence is anxiety when the drug is suddenly stopped. Darvocet-N abuse can lead to toxic effects on the kidneys and liver from the Acetaminophen ingredient of this drug (see "Possible Side Effects" below).

Pregnancy/Breast-feeding

This drug crosses into the blood circulation of a developing baby. It has not been found to cause birth defects. Pregnant women, or those who might become pregnant while taking this drug, should not take it without their doctor's approval. When the drug is considered essential by your doctor, the potential risk of taking the medicine must be carefully weighed against the benefit it might produce.

This drug passes into breast milk, but has caused no problems among breast-fed infants. You must consider the potential effect on the nursing infant if breast-feeding while taking this medicine.

Seniors

Older adults may be more sensitive to the side effects of this medicine and should use it with caution.

Possible Side Effects

Dizziness, sedation, nausea, vomiting. These effects usually disappear if you lie down and relax for a few moments.

Less common side effects: constipation, abdominal pain, skin rash, light-headedness, weakness, headache, euphoria, and minor visual disturbances. Long-term use may lead to adverse effects caused by the Acetaminophen portion of Darvocet-N: anemias and changes in the composition of blood. Allergic reactions are rash, itching, and fever.

Drug Interactions

Interaction with alcohol, tranquilizers, sedatives, hypnotics, or antihistamines may produce tiredness, dizziness, light-headedness, and other signs of depression.

Food Interactions

Take with a full glass of water or with food to reduce the possibility of stomach upset.

Usual Dose

1 to 2 tablets every 4 hours to relieve pain.

Overdosage

Symptoms are restlessness and difficulty in breathing, leading to stupor or coma, blue color of the skin, anemia, yellowing of the skin and/or whites of the eyes, rash, fever, stimulation, excitement, and delirium followed by depression, coma, and convulsions. The patient should be taken to a hospital emergency room immediately. ALWAYS bring the medicine bottle.

Special Information

Do not drink excessive amounts of alcohol when taking this medicine. Be extra careful when driving or operating machinery.

If you forget a dose of Darvocet-N, skip it and continue with your regular schedule. Do not take a double dose of Darvocet-N.

Brand Name

Darvon Compound-65

Ingredients

Aspirin
Caffeine
Propoxyphene Hydrochloride

Other Brand Names

Bexophene
Dolene Compound 65
Doxaphene Compound

Propoxyphene Hydrochloride
Compound

(Also available in generic form)

Type of Drug

Analgesic combination.

Prescribed for

Relief of mild to moderate pain.

General Information

Propoxyphene Hydrochloride, the major ingredient in this product, is a chemical derivative of Methadone, a narcotic used for pain relief. It is estimated that Propoxyphene Hydrochloride is about ½ to ⅔ as strong a pain reliever as Codeine and about as effective as Aspirin.

Cautions and Warnings

Do not take Darvon Compound-65 if you know you are allergic or sensitive to it. Long-term use of this medicine may cause drug dependence or addiction. Use this drug with extreme caution if you suffer from asthma or other breathing problems. Darvon Compound-65 affects the central nervous system, producing sleepiness, tiredness, and/or inability to concentrate.

Pregnancy/Breast-feeding

Darvon has been shown to cause birth defects in animals, but we don't know if this occurs in humans. When a woman takes large amounts of narcotic drugs during pregnancy or breast-feeding, the baby may become dependent on the narcotic. Narcotics may also cause breathing problems in the infant during delivery. Do not take this medicine if you are pregnant or think you may be pregnant.

Nursing mothers should consider alternate feeding methods or observe their infants for possible drug side effects.

Seniors

Older adults may be more likely to develop drug side effects and should take this medicine with caution.

Possible Side Effects

Most frequent: light-headedness, dizziness, sleepiness, nausea, vomiting, loss of appetite, sweating. If these effects occur, consider calling your doctor and asking him about lowering the dose you are taking. Usually the side effects disappear if you simply lie down.

More serious side effects of Darvon Compound-65 are shallow breathing or difficulty in breathing.

Less common side effects: euphoria (feeling high), weakness, sleepiness, headache, agitation, uncoordinated muscle movement, minor hallucinations, disorientation and visual disturbances, dry mouth, loss of appetite, constipation, flushing of the face, rapid heartbeat, palpitations, faintness, urinary difficulties or hesitancy, reduced sex drive and/or potency, itching, skin rashes.

Drug Interactions

Interaction with alcohol, tranquilizers, barbiturates, or sleeping pills produces tiredness, sleepiness, or inability to concentrate, and seriously increases the depressive effect of Darvon Compound-65.

The Aspirin component of Darvon Compound-65 can affect anticoagulant (blood-thinning) therapy. Be sure to discuss this with your doctor so that the proper dosage adjustment can be made.

Food Interactions

Take with food or ½ glass of water to prevent stomach upset.

Usual Dose

1 capsule every 4 hours as needed for pain.

Overdosage

Symptoms are depression of respiration (breathing), extreme tiredness progressing to stupor and then coma, cold and clammy skin, slowing down of the heartbeat, convulsions, and cardiac arrest. The patient should be taken to a hospital emergency room immediately. ALWAYS bring the medicine bottle.

Special Information

Drowsiness may occur: be careful when driving or operating machinery.

Do not drink excessive amounts of alcohol when taking this medicine.

If you forget a dose of Darvon Compound-65, skip it and continue with your regular schedule. Do not take a double dose.

Generic Name

Demeclocycline

Brand Name

Declomycin

Type of Drug

Broad-spectrum antibiotic effective against gram-positive and gram-negative organisms. It belongs to the general class of antibiotics known as Tetracycline.

Prescribed for

Bacterial infections such as gonorrhea, infections of the mouth, gums, and teeth, Rocky Mountain spotted fever and other fevers caused by ticks and lice from a variety of carriers, urinary tract infections, and respiratory system infections such as pneumonia and bronchitis.

These diseases are produced by gram-positive and gram-negative organisms such as diplococci, staphylococci, streptococci, gonococci, *E. coli,* and *Shigella.*

Demeclocycline has also been used successfully to treat some skin infections, but it is not considered the first-choice antibiotic for the treatment of general skin infections or wounds.

Demeclocycline has been used experimentally to treat the disease syndrome of inappropriate antidiuretic hormone (SIADH), where excess amounts of antidiuretic hormone are produced by the body.

General Information

Demeclocycline works by interfering with the normal growth cycle of the invading bacteria, preventing them from reproducing and thus allowing the body's normal defenses to fight off the infection. This process is referred to as bacteriostatic action. Demeclocycline has also been used along with other medicines to treat amoebic infections of the intestinal tract, known as amoebic dysentery. It is also prescribed for diseases caused by ticks, fleas, and lice.

Demeclocycline has been successfully used for the treatment of adolescent acne, in small doses over a long period of time. Adverse effects or toxicity in this type of therapy are almost unheard of.

Since the action of this antibiotic depends on its concentration within the invading bacteria, it is imperative that you completely follow your doctor's directions.

Cautions and Warnings

Demeclocycline should not be given to people with known liver disease or kidney or urine excretion problems. You should avoid taking high doses of Demeclocycline or undergoing extended Demeclocycline therapy if you will be exposed to sunlight for a long period, because this antibiotic can interfere with your body's normal sun-screening mechanism, possibly causing a severe sunburn. If you have a known history of allergy to Demeclocycline, you should avoid taking this drug or other drugs within this category such as Aureomycin, Terramycin, Rondomycin, Vibramycin, Tetracycline, and Minocycline.

This drug is very likely to cause skin sensitivity, which has the appearance of a severe sunburn.

Pregnancy/Breast-feeding

You should not use Demeclocycline if you are pregnant, especially during the last 4½ months. Do not use while breast-feeding because Demeclocycline may have an adverse effect on the formation of an infant's bones and teeth. Demeclocycline, when used in children, has been shown to interfere with the development of the long bones and may retard growth.

Exceptions would be when Demeclocycline is the only effective antibiotic available and all risk factors have been known to the patient.

Seniors

Older adults, especially those with poor kidney function, may be more likely to develop side effects if taking this drug for a long period of time.

Possible Side Effects

As with other antibiotics, the common side effects of Demeclocycline are stomach upset, nausea, vomiting, diarrhea, and rash. Less common side effects include hairy tongue and itching and irritation of the anal and/or vaginal region. If these symptoms appear, consult your physician immediately. Periodic physical examinations and laboratory tests should be given to patients who are on long-term Demeclocycline.

Less common side effects: loss of appetite, peeling of the skin, sensitivity to the sun, fever, chills, anemia, possible brown spotting of the skin, decrease in kidney function, weakness, thirst, excessive urination, damage to the liver.

Drug Interactions

Demeclocycline (a bacteriostatic drug) may interfere with the action of bactericidal agents such as Penicillin. It is not advisable to take both during the same course of therapy.

Don't take multivitamin products containing minerals at the same time as Demeclocycline, or you may reduce the antibiotic's effectiveness. You may take these two medicines at least 2 hours apart.

People receiving anticoagulation therapy (blood-thinning agents) should consult their doctor, since Demeclocycline will interfere with this form of therapy. An adjustment in the anticoagulant dosage may be required.

Food Interactions

The antibacterial effect of Demeclocycline is neutralized when taken with food, some dairy products, including milk and cheese, and antacids.

Usual Dose

Adult: 600 milligrams per day.

Child (age 8 and over): 3 to 6 milligrams per pound per day.

Child (under age 8): should avoid Demeclocycline, as it has been shown to produce serious discoloration of the permanent teeth.

Take on an empty stomach 1 hour before or 2 hours after meals.

Special Information

Do *not* take after the expiration date on the label. The decomposition of Demeclocycline produces a highly toxic substance which can cause serious kidney damage. Demeclocycline can be stored at room temperature.

If you forget to take a dose of Demeclocycline, take it as soon as you remember. If it is almost time for your next dose and you take 2 doses per day, take the missed dose and then the next dose 5 to 6 hours later. If you take 4 doses per day, double your next dose or take the missed dose and then the next dose 2 to 4 hours later. Go back to your regular dose schedule after making up for the missed dose.

Generic Name

Desipramine

Brand Names

Norpramin
Pertofrane

Type of Drug

Antidepressant.

Prescribed for

Depression with or without symptoms of anxiety.

General Information

Desipramine and other members of this group are effective in treating symptoms of depression. They can elevate mood, increase physical activity and mental alertness, improve appetite and sleep patterns in a depressed patient. These drugs are mild sedatives and therefore useful in treating mild forms of depression associated with anxiety. You should not expect instant results with this medicine: benefits are usually seen after 1 to 4 weeks. If symptoms are not affected after 6 to 8 weeks, contact your doctor. Occasionally this drug and other members of the group of drugs have been used in treating nighttime bed-wetting in young children but they do not produce long-lasting relief, and therapy with one of them for nighttime bed-wetting is of questionable value.

Cautions and Warnings

Do not take Desipramine if you are allergic or sensitive to this or other members of this class of drug: Doxepin, Nortriptyline, Imipramine, Protriptyline, and Amitriptyline. The drugs should not be used if you are recovering from a heart attack. Desipramine may be taken with caution if you have a history of epilepsy or other convulsive disorders, difficulty in urination, glaucoma, heart disease, or thyroid disease. Desipramine can interfere with your ability to perform tasks which require concentration, such as driving or operating machinery.

Pregnancy/Breast-feeding

This drug, like other antidepressants, crosses into your developing baby's circulation and may cause birth defects if taken during the first 3 months of pregnancy. There have been reports of newborn infants suffering from heart, breathing, and urinary problems after their mothers had taken an antidepressant of this type immediately before the delivery. You should avoid taking this medication while pregnant.

Antidepressants of this type are known to pass into breast milk and may affect a breast-feeding infant, although this has not been proven. Nursing mothers should consider alternate feeding methods if taking this medicine.

Seniors

Older adults are more sensitive to the effects of this drug and often require a lower dose than a younger adult to do the same job. Follow your doctor's directions and report any side effects at once.

Possible Side Effects

Changes in blood pressure (both high and low), abnormal heart rates, heart attack, confusion, especially in elderly patients, hallucinations, disorientation, delusions, anxiety, restlessness, excitement, numbness and tingling in the extremities, lack of coordination, muscle spasms or tremors, seizures and/or convulsions, dry mouth, blurred vision, constipation, inability to urinate, rash, itching, sensitivity to bright light or sunlight, retention of fluids, fever, allergy, changes in composition of blood, nausea, vomiting, loss of appetite, stomach upset, diarrhea, enlargement of the breasts in males and females, increased or decreased sex drive, increase or decrease of blood sugar.

Less common side effects: agitation, inability to sleep, nightmares, feeling of panic, peculiar taste in the mouth, stomach cramps, black coloration of the tongue, yellowing eyes and/or skin, changes in liver function, increased or decreased weight, perspiration, flushing, frequent urination, drowsiness, dizziness, weakness, headache, loss of hair, nausea, not feeling well.

Drug Interactions

Interaction with monoamine oxidase (MAO) inhibitors can cause high fevers, convulsions, and occasionally death. Don't take MAO inhibitors until at least 2 weeks after Desipramine has been discontinued. Certain patients may require concomitant use of Desipramine and an MAO inhibitor, and in these cases close medical observation is warranted.

Desipramine interacts with Guanethidine, a drug used to treat high blood pressure: if your doctor prescribes Desipramine and you are taking medicine for high blood pressure, be sure to discuss this with him.

Desipramine increases the effects of barbiturates, tranquilizers, other depressive drugs, and alcohol. Don't drink alcohol if you take this medicine.

Taking Desipramine and thyroid medicine will enhance the effects of the thyroid medicine. The combination can cause abnormal heart rhythms.

Large doses of Vitamin C (Ascorbic Acid) can reduce the effect of Desipramine. Drugs such as Bicarbonate of Soda or Acetazolamide will increase the effect of Desipramine.

Food Interactions

This drug is best taken on an empty stomach but may be taken with food if it upsets your stomach.

Usual Dose

Adult: 75 to 300 milligrams per day. The dose of this drug must be tailored to patient's need. Patients taking high doses of this drug should have regular heart examinations to check for side effects.

Adolescent and senior: lower doses are recommended, usually 25 to 150 milligrams per day.

Child (under age 12): this drug should not be used.

Overdosage

Symptoms are confusion, inability to concentrate, hallucinations, drowsiness, lowered body temperature, abnormal heart rate, heart failure, large pupils of the eyes, convulsions, severely lowered blood pressure, stupor, and coma (as well as agitation, stiffening of body muscles, vomiting, and high fever). The patient should be taken to a hospital emergency room immediately. ALWAYS bring the medicine bottle.

Special Information

Avoid alcohol and other drugs that depress the nervous system while taking this antidepressant. Do not stop taking this medicine unless your doctor has specifically told you to do so. Abruptly stopping this medicine may cause nausea, headache, and a sickly feeling. This medicine can cause drowsiness, dizziness, and blurred vision. Be careful when driving or operating complicated machinery. Avoid exposure to the sun or sun lamps for long periods of time. Call your doctor if dry mouth, difficulty urinating, or excessive sedation develops.

If you take more than 1 dose of Desipramine per day and forget to take a dose, take the missed dose as soon as possible. If it is almost time for your next dose, skip the missed dose and continue your usual dose schedule. If you take Desipramine once a day and don't remember until the next day, skip the forgotten dose and continue with your regular schedule. Do not double any doses.

Generic Name

Dexamethasone Tablet/Liquid

Brand Names

Decadron   Dexone
Dexameth   Hexadrol

(Also available in generic form)

Type of Drug

Adrenal corticosteroid.

Prescribed for

Reduction of inflammation. There is a wide range of disorders for which Dexamethasone is prescribed, from skin rash to cancer. The drug may be used as a treatment for adrenal gland disease, since one of the hormones produced by the adrenal gland is very similar to Dexamethasone. If patients are not producing sufficient adrenal hormones, Dexamethasone may be used as replacement therapy. It may also be prescribed for the treatment of bursitis, arthritis, severe skin reactions such as psoriasis or other rashes, several allergic conditions, asthma, drug or serum sickness, severe, acute, or chronic allergic inflammation of the eye and surrounding areas such as conjunctivitis, respiratory diseases including pneumonitis, blood disorders, gastrointestinal diseases including ulcerative colitis, and inflammation of the nerves, heart, or other organs.

General Information

Dexamethasone is one of many adrenal corticosteroids used in medical practice today. The major differences between Dexamethasone and other adrenal corticosteroids are potency of medication and variation in some secondary effects. Choice of an adrenal corticosteroid to be used for a specific disease is usually a matter of doctor preference and past experience. Other adrenal corticosteroids include Cortisone, Hydrocortisone, Prednisolone, Triamcinolone, Methylprednisolone, Meprednisone, Paramethasone, Fluprednisolone, Prednisone, Betamethasone, and Fludrocortisone.

Dexamethasone may be used as eyedrops, eye ointment, topical cream, intranasal spray, or for oral inhalation as well as in an oral tablet.

Cautions and Warnings

Because of the effect of Dexamethasone on your adrenal gland, it is essential that the dose be tapered from a large dose down to a small dose over a period of time. Do not stop taking this medication suddenly and/or without the advice of your doctor. If you do, you may cause a failure of the adrenal gland with extremely serious consequences.

Dexamethasone has a strong anti-inflammatory effect, and may mask some signs of infection. If new infections appear during the use of Dexamethasone therapy, they may be difficult to diagnose and may grow more rapidly due to your decreased resistance. If you think you are getting an infection during the time that you are taking Dexamethasone, you should contact your doctor, who will prescribe appropriate therapy.

If you are taking Dexamethasone, you should not be vaccinated against any infectious diseases, because of inability of the body to produce the normal reaction to vaccination. Discuss this with your doctor before he administers any vaccination.

Dexamethasone may stop or slow the growth of children and adolescents. This is particularly true if used for long time periods.

Pregnancy/Breast-feeding

Studies have shown that corticosteroids applied to the skin in large amounts or over long periods of time can be the cause of birth defects. Pregnant women, or those who might become pregnant while using this medicine, should not do so unless they are under a doctor's care.

Corticosteroid drugs taken by mouth pass into breast milk and large drug doses may interfere with the growth of a nursing infant. Steroids applied to the skin are not likely to cause problems but you should not use the medicine unless under a doctor's care.

Seniors

Older adults are more likely to develop high blood pressure while taking this medicine (by mouth). Also, older women

have a greater chance of being suceptible to bone degeneration (osteoporosis) associated with large doses of this class
of medicines.

Possible Side Effects

Stomach upset is one of the more common side effects of
Dexamethasone, which may in some cases cause gastric or
duodenal ulcers. If you notice a slight stomach upset when
you take your dose of Dexamethasone, take this medication
with food or a small amount of antacid. If stomach upset
continues or bothers you, notify your doctor. Other side
effects: water retention, heart failure, potassium loss, muscle weakness, loss of muscle mass, loss of calcium which
may result in bone fractures and a condition known as aseptic necrosis of the femoral and humoral heads (this means
the ends of the large bones in the hip may degenerate from
loss of calcium), slowing down of wound healing, black-and-
blue marks on the skin, increased sweating, allergic skin
rash, itching, convulsions, dizziness, headache.

Less common side effects are: irregular menstrual cycles,
slowing down of growth in children, particularly after the
medication has been taken for long periods of time, depression of the adrenal and/or pituitary glands, development of
diabetes, increased pressure of the fluid inside the eye, hypersensitivity or allergic reactions, blood clots, insomnia,
weight gain, increased appetite, nausea, and feeling of ill
health. Psychic derangements may appear which range from
euphoria to mood swings, personality changes, and severe
depression. Dexamethasone may also aggravate existing emotional instability.

Drug Interactions

Dexamethasone and other adrenal corticosteroids may interact with Insulin and oral antidiabetic drugs, causing an increased requirement of the antidiabetic drugs.

Interaction with Phenobarbital, Ephedrine, and Phenytoin
may reduce the effect of Dexamethasone by increasing its
removal from the body.

If a doctor prescribes Dexamethasone you should discuss
any oral anticoagulant (blood-thinning) drugs you are taking: their dose may have to be changed.

Interaction with diuretics such as Hydrochlorothiazide may

cause you to lose blood potassium. Be aware of signs of lowered potassium level such as weakness, muscle cramps, and tiredness, and report them to your physician. Eat high-potassium foods such as bananas, citrus fruits, melons, and tomatoes.

Food Interactions

You may take oral doses of this medicine with food if it upsets your stomach. Drinking alcoholic beverages while you are on this medicine may increase the chance of developing a stomach ulcer.

Usual Dose

Initial dose, 0.75 to 9 milligrams per day. The dose of this medicine must be individualized to the patient's need, although it is always desirable to take the lowest effective dose of Dexamethasone. Stressful situations may cause a need for a temporary increase in your Dexamethasone dose. This drug must be tapered off slowly and not stopped abruptly. This drug may be taken every other day instead of every day. It is best to take Dexamethasone in the morning, if prescribed once a day.

Overdosage

There is no specific treatment for overdosage of adrenal corticosteroids. Symptoms are anxiety, depression, and/or stimulation, stomach bleeding, increased blood sugar, high blood pressure, and retention of fluid. The patient should be taken to a hospital emergency room immediately, where stomach pumping, oxygen, intravenous fluids, and other supportive treatments are available. ALWAYS bring the medicine bottle.

Special Information

Do not stop taking this medicine on your own. Suddenly stopping this or any other corticosteroid drug can have severe consequences; the dosage should be gradually reduced by your doctor.

If you are on a multiple-dose schedule, take the doses at evenly spaced time intervals throughout the day. If you are on an every-other-day or once-a-day dose schedule, take the dose early in the morning, preferably before 9 A.M.

If you miss taking a dose of Dexamethasone and you take several doses per day, take the missed dose as soon as you remember and continue with your regular dose schedule. If it is almost time for the next dose, double up and skip the missed dose.

If you take 1 dose a day and you forget to take it, skip the missed dose and go back to your regular dose schedule.

If you take 1 dose every other day, take the missed dose as soon as you remember early in the same day and then go back to your regular dose schedule. If it is too late to take the missed dose, wait until the next day and continue with the every-other-day dose schedule.

Generic Name

Dexchlorpheniramine Maleate

Brand Names

Dexchlor   Polaramine
Poladex T.D.   Polargen

(Also available in generic form)

Type of Drug

Antihistamine.

Prescribed for

Seasonal allergy, stuffed and runny nose, itching of the eyes, scratchy throat caused by allergy, and other allergic symptoms such as itching, rash, or hives.

General Information

Antihistamines generally, and Dexchlorpheniramine Maleate specifically, act by antagonizing at the site where histamine works. This site is often called the H_1 histamine receptor. Antihistamines work by drying up the secretions of the nose, throat, and eyes.

Cautions and Warnings

Dexchlorpheniramine Maleate should not be used if you are

allergic to this drug. It should be avoided or used with extreme care if you have narrow-angle glaucoma (pressure in the eye), stomach ulcer or other stomach problems, enlarged prostate, or problems passing urine. It should not be used by people who have deep-breathing problems such as asthma.

Use with care if you have a history of thyroid disease, heart disease, high blood pressure, or diabetes.

Pregnancy/Breast-feeding

Dexchlorpheniramine has not been proven to be a cause of birth defects or other problems in pregnant women, although studies in animals have shown that some antihistamines (Meclizine and Cyclizine), used mainly against nausea and vomiting, may cause birth defects. Do not take any antihistamine without your doctor's knowledge.

Small amounts of antihistamine medicines pass into breast milk and may affect a nursing infant. Nursing mothers should avoid antihistamines or use alternate feeding methods while taking the medicine.

Seniors

Seniors are most sensitive to antihistamine side effects. Confusion, difficult or painful urination, dizziness, drowsiness, a faint feeling, dry mouth, nose, or throat, nightmares or excitement, nervousness, restlessness, or irritability are more likely to occur among older adults.

Possible Side Effects

Occasional: itching, rash, sensitivity to light, excessive perspiration, chills, dryness of mouth, nose, and throat, lowering of blood pressure, headache, rapid heartbeat, sleeplessness, dizziness, disturbed coordination, confusion, restlessness, nervousness, irritability, euphoria (feeling high), tingling of the hands and feet, blurred vision, double vision, ringing in the ears, stomach upset, loss of appetite, nausea, vomiting, constipation, diarrhea, difficulty in urination, tightness of the chest, wheezing, nasal stuffiness.

Drug Interactions

Dexchlorpheniramine Maleate should not be taken with MAO inhibitors.

Interaction with tranquilizers, sedatives, and sleeping medication will increase the effects of these drugs: it is extremely important that you discuss this with your doctor so that doses of these drugs can be properly adjusted.

Be extremely cautious when drinking while taking Dexchlorpheniramine Maleate, which will enhance the intoxicating effect of alcohol. Alcohol also has a sedative effect.

Usual Dose

Adult: 2 milligrams every 4 to 6 hours. Repeat-action tablets: 4 to 6 milligrams every 8 to 10 hours and at bedtime.

Child (age 6 to 12): 1 milligram every 4 to 6 hours. Repeat-action tablets: 4 milligrams once a day and at bedtime.

Child (age 2 to 5): 0.5 milligram every 4 to 6 hours. Do not use the repeat-action tablets.

Overdosage

Symptoms are depression or stimulation (especially in children), dry mouth, fixed or dilated pupils, flushing of the skin, and stomach upset. Take the patient to a hospital emergency room immediately, if you cannot make him vomit. ALWAYS bring the medicine bottle.

Special Information

Antihistamines produce a depressing effect: be extremely cautious when driving or operating heavy equipment.

If you forget a dose of Dexchlorpheniramine Maleate, take it as soon as you remember. If it is almost time for your next dose, skip the forgotten dose and continue with your regular schedule. Do not take a double dose.

Generic Name

Dextroamphetamine (D-Amphetamine)

Brand Names

Dexampex	Oxydess
Dexedrine	Spancap
Ferndex	

(Also available in generic form)

Type of Drug

Central nervous-system stimulant.

Prescribed for

Short-term (a couple of months) aid to diet control, abnormal behavioral syndrome in children, narcolepsy (uncontrollable and unpredictable desire to sleep).

General Information

When taking this medicine as part of a weight control program it is usual to experience a decrease in drug effectiveness because your body is breaking down the drug faster. Do not increase the amount of drug you are taking: simply stop taking the medicine.

The use of D-Amphetamine (as well as other drugs) in the treatment of minimal brain dysfunction in children is extremely controversial and must be judged by a physician qualified to treat the disorder. Children whose problems are judged to have been produced by their surroundings or by primary psychiatric disorders may not be helped by D-Amphetamine.

Cautions and Warnings

D-Amphetamine is highly abusable and addictive. It must be used with extreme caution. People with hardening of the arteries (arteriosclerosis), heart disease, high blood pressure, thyroid disease, or glaucoma, or who are sensitive or allergic to any amphetamine, should not take this medication.

Pregnancy/Breast-feeding

Amphetamines should be avoided by women who are or might become pregnant. Amphetamine use early in pregnancy has been associated with some birth defects, and animal studies suggest that amphetamines can be the source of other birth defects as well. Infants born to mothers taking amphetamines have a lower birth weight and an increased risk of premature delivery. They may experience drug withdrawal symptoms immediately after birth.

It is not known if amphetamines pass into breast milk. The potential risk of affecting your nursing infant must be taken into account when deciding to breast-feed while on an amphetamine diet pill.

Seniors

Older adults are more sensitive to the effects of this drug. Follow your doctor's directions and report any side effects at once.

Possible Side Effects

Palpitations, restlessness, overstimulation, dizziness, sleeplessness, increased blood pressure, rapid heartbeat.

Less common side effects: euphoria, hallucinations, muscle spasms and tremors, headache, dryness of the mouth, unpleasant taste, diarrhea, constipation, stomach upset, itching, loss of sex drive, (rarely) psychotic drug reactions.

Drug Interactions

D-Amphetamine should not be given at the same time as, or within 14 days following the use of, MAO inhibitors. This may cause severe lowering of the blood pressure.

D-Amphetamine may also decrease the effectiveness of Guanethidine.

If D-Amphetamine is taken with Insulin, Insulin requirements may be altered.

Food Interactions

Take this medicine with food if it upsets your stomach.

Usual Dose

Narcolepsy: 5 to 60 milligrams per day, depending on individual need.

Abnormal behavior syndrome: 2.5 to 40 milligrams per day, depending on child's age and response to the drug.

Weight control: 5 to 30 milligrams per day in divided doses ½ to 1 hour before meals; or, as a long-acting dose, once in the morning.

Overdosage

Symptoms are tremors, muscle spasms, restlessness, exaggerated reflexes, rapid breathing, hallucinations, confusion, panic, and overaggressive behavior, followed by depression and exhaustion after the central nervous system stimulation wears off, as well as abnormal heart rhythms, changes in blood pressure, nausea, vomiting, diarrhea, convulsions, and coma. The patient should be taken to a hospital emergency room immediately. ALWAYS bring the medicine container.

Special Information

Take this medicine at least 6 to 8 hours before you plan to go to sleep, or it will interfere with a sound and restful night's sleep.

Do not crush or chew the sustained-release formulations.

If you miss a dose, take it as early as possible to avoid sleeping problems. If you take 1 dose per day, it may be best to skip the missed dose and resume your dose schedule the next day. If you take 2 to 3 doses per day and you remember the missed dose within an hour or so, take it right away. If you remember too late, skip the missed dose and go back to your regular dose schedule the next day. Do not double any doses.

Generic Name

Dextrothyroxine Sodium

Brand Name

Choloxin

Type of Drug

Antihyperlipidemic.

Prescribed for

Lowering blood cholesterol levels. Triglyceride levels may also be affected by Dextrothyroxine Sodium. May also be used to treat thyroid disease in patients who cannot take other thyroid drugs.

General Information

This drug is interesting in that it is a close cousin to Levothyroxine Sodium, a thyroid drug. It is thought to lower blood cholesterol by stimulating the liver to remove more cholesterol from the blood than usual. The lowering of blood cholesterol levels may have an effect on the development of heart disease, although no one knows for sure. This drug is only part of the therapy for high blood cholesterol levels. Diet and weight control are also very important. Remember, this medicine is not a substitute for dietary restrictions or other activities prescribed by your doctor.

Cautions and Warnings

Dextrothyroxine Sodium should not be taken by people with heart disease of any kind, severe high blood pressure, advanced liver or kidney disease, or a history of iodism.

This drug is not meant to help people lose weight. In large doses, it will not reduce appetite but can cause serious side effects.

This drug should be discontinued for 2 weeks before surgery. It could interact with the general anesthetic drugs to cause heart problems.

Pregnancy/Breast-feeding

Although no serious effects have been reported, this drug should not be used by women who are pregnant or breast-feeding unless it is absolutely necessary.

Seniors

Older adults are more sensitive to the effects of this drug. Follow your doctor's directions and report any side effects at once.

Possible Side Effects

The fewest side effects from Dextrothyroxine Sodium are experienced by people with normal thyroid function and no heart disease. The risk of side effects is increased if you have an underactive thyroid gland and is greatest if you have both thyroid and heart disease.

The most common side effects are heart palpitations and other effects related to heart function. Other side effects include sleeplessness, nervousness, weight loss, sweating, flushing, increased body temperature, hair loss, menstrual irregularity, and an unusual need to urinate. Dextrothyroxine Sodium can also cause upset stomach, nausea and vomiting, constipation, diarrhea, and loss of appetite.

Less common side effects: headache, change in sex drive (increase or decrease), hoarseness, dizziness, ringing or buzzing in the ears, swelling of the arms and legs, not feeling well, tiredness, visual disturbances, psychic changes, tingling in the hands or feet, muscle pain, rashes. Some rather bizarre subjective complaints have been linked to this drug.

Drug Interactions

May interact with digitalis drugs to yield adverse effects on the heart. Dextrothyroxine Sodium may increase the effects of oral anticoagulant drugs like Warfarin. Some patients may need their anticoagulant dose reduced by 30 percent. Dextrothyroxine Sodium will increase the effect of other drugs being given for underactive thyroid.

The drug may increase blood sugar levels in diabetic patients. Diabetics may need an adjustment in their Insulin or oral antidiabetic drug therapy while taking Dextrothyroxine Sodium.

Food Interactions

Take this medicine with food if it upsets your stomach.

Usual Dose

Adult: up to 8 milligrams per day.

Child: up to 4 milligrams per day; approximately 0.05 milligrams per pound.

Overdosage

Symptoms are headache, irritability, nervousness, sweating, and rapid heartbeat, with unusual stomach rumbling with or without cramps, chest pains, heart failure, and shock. The patient should be taken to a hospital emergency room immediately. ALWAYS bring the medicine bottle.

Special Information

Contact your doctor if you develop chest pain, heart palpitations, sweating, diarrhea, or a rash.

If you forget a dose of Dextrothyroxine, take it late in the day. If you don't remember until the next day, skip the forgotten dose and continue with your regular schedule. Do not take a double dose.

Generic Name

Diazepam

Brand Names

Valium
Valrelease
Zetran

(Also available in generic form)

Type of Drug

Minor tranquilizer.

Prescribed for

Relief of symptoms of anxiety, tension, fatigue, or agitation.

General Information

Diazepam is a member of the group of drugs known as
benzodiazepines. These drugs are used as either antianxiety
agents, anticonvulsants, or sedatives (sleeping pills). They
exert their effects by relaxing the large skeletal muscles and
by a direct effect on the brain. In doing so, they can relax
you and make you either more tranquil or sleepier, depending
on the drug and how much you use. Many doctors prefer
Diazepam and the other members of this class to other
drugs that can be used for the same effect. Their reason is
that the benzodiazepines tend to be safer, have fewer side
effects, and are usually as, if not more, effective.

These drugs are generally used in any situation where
they can be a useful adjunct.

Benzodiazepine tranquilizing drugs can be abused if taken
for long periods of time and it is possible to develop
withdrawal symptoms if you discontinue the therapy abruptly.
Withdrawal symptoms include tremor, muscle cramps,
stomach cramps, vomiting, insomnia, agitation, sweating,
and even convulsions.

Cautions and Warnings

Do not take Diazepam if you know you are sensitive or
allergic to this drug or to other benzodiazepines such as

Chlordiazepoxide, Oxazepam, Clorazepate, Lorazepam, Prazepam, Flurazepam, Clonazepam, and Temazepam.

Diazepam and other members of this drug group may aggravate narrow-angle glaucoma, but if you have open-angle glaucoma you may take the drugs. In any case, check this information with your doctor. Diazepam can cause tiredness, drowsiness, inability to concentrate, or similar symptoms. Be careful if you are driving, operating machinery, or performing other activities which require concentration.

Pregnancy/Breast-feeding

Avoid taking this drug during the first 3 months of pregnancy except under strict supervision of your doctor. Taken during the first 3 months of pregnancy, Diazepam has been shown to increase the chance of birth defects. The baby may become dependent on Diazepam if it is used continually during pregnancy. If used during the last weeks of pregnancy or during breast-feeding, the baby may be overly tired or short of breath, or have a low heartbeat. Use during labor may cause weakness in the newborn.

Members of the benzodiazepine family pass into breast milk. Since infants break the drug down more slowly than adults, it is possible for the medicine to accumulate and have an undesired effect on the baby.

Seniors

Older adults are more sensitive to the effects of this drug, especially dizziness and drowsiness. Follow your doctor's directions and report any side effects at once.

Possible Side Effects

Most common: mild drowsiness during the first few days of therapy. If drowsiness persists, contact your doctor.

Less common side effects are: confusion, depression, lethargy, disorientation, headache, inactivity, slurred speech, stupor, dizziness, tremor, constipation, dry mouth, nausea, inability to control urination, changes in sex drive, irregular menstrual cycle, changes in heart rhythm, lowered blood pressure, retention of fluids, blurred or double vision, itching, rash, hiccups, nervousness, inability to fall asleep, (occasional) liver dysfunction. If you experience any of these reactions stop taking the medicine and contact your doctor immediately.

Drug Interactions

Diazepam is a central nervous system depressant. Avoid alcohol, tranquilizers, narcotics, barbiturates, MAO inhibitors, antihistamines, and other medicines used to relieve depression. Smoking may reduce the effectiveness of Diazepam. The effects of Diazepam may be prolonged when taken together with Cimetidine.

Usual Dose

Adult: 2 to 40 milligrams per day as individualized for maximum benefit, depending on symptoms and response to treatment.

Senior: will usually require less of the drug to control tension and anxiety.

Child (6 months and over): 1 to 2.5 milligrams 3 to 4 times per day; possibly more if needed to control anxiety and tension.

Infant (under 6 months): this drug should not be used.

Overdosage

Symptoms are confusion, sleep or sleepiness, lack of response to pain such as a pin stick, shallow breathing, lowered blood pressure, and coma. The patient should be taken to a hospital emergency room immediately. ALWAYS bring the medicine bottle.

Special Information

Do not drink alcohol or take other depressive drugs, such as tranquilizers, sleeping pills, narcotics, or barbiturates, when taking Diazepam.

Do not crush or chew the sustained-release preparation (Valrelease).

If you miss a dose and it is within an hour or so of your usual dose time, take it right away. If over an hour has passed, skip the missed dose and go back to your regular dose schedule. Do not double any doses.

Generic Name

Diclofenac

Brand Name
Voltaren

Type of Drug
Nonsteroidal anti-inflammatory.

Prescribed for
Rheumatoid arthritis and osteoarthritis.

General Information
Diclofenac is one of many nonsteroidal anti-inflammatory drugs sold in the United States to reduce inflammation, relieve pain and fever, and relieve menstrual cramps and discomfort. The choice of one member of this group over another often depends on your individual response to a specific drug. Because of this, it is common to try several of these drugs before you find the one that is right for you. Diclofenac starts working in about 30 minutes and will remain effective for about 3 hours. Approved in the United States in late 1988, Diclofenac is used all over the world and holds the distinction of having been one of the most widely prescribed nonsteroidal anti-inflammatory drugs in the world before it was approved in the United States.

Cautions and Warnings
Do not take this product if you are allergic to Aspirin or to any other nonsteroidal anti-inflammatory drug. This drug can worsen stomach ulcers or cause a new ulcer to develop. It should be used with caution if you have kidney disease. Diclofenac may cause liver inflammation.

Pregnancy/Breast-feeding
This drug may cross into the blood circulation of a developing baby. It has not been found to cause birth defects. Pregnant women, or those who might become pregnant while taking this drug, should not take it without their doctor's approval. When the drug is considered essential by your

doctor, the potential risk of taking the medicine must be carefully weighed against the benefit it might produce.

This drug passes into breast milk, but has caused no problems among breast-fed infants. You must consider the potential effect on the nursing infant if breast-feeding while taking this medicine.

Seniors

Older adults are more sensitive to the stomach, kidney, and liver effects of this drug. Some doctors recommend that persons 70 years of age and older take ½ the usual dose, although Diclofenac's rapid elimination from the body may make it more useful for older adults. Follow your doctor's directions and report any side effects at once.

Possible Side Effects

Most common: upset stomach, dizziness, headache, drowsiness, ringing in the ears.

Other side effects include heartburn, nausea, vomiting, bloating, stomach gas or pain, diarrhea, constipation, dark stools, nervousness, sleeplessness, depression, confusion, tremor, loss of appetite, fatigue, itching, rash, double or blurred vision, dry or irritated eyes, heart failure, palpitations, abnormal heart rhythms, anemia or other changes in the composition of your blood, changes in liver function, hair loss, tingling in the hands or feet, fever, enlarged breasts, blood in the urine, urinary tract irritation, thirst, frequent urination, kidney damage, low blood sugar, asthma, difficulty breathing, skin rash, itching, swelling, black-and-blue marks.

Drug Interactions

Aspirin causes this drug to be eliminated from the body more rapidly than normal. Do not take Diclofenac together with Methotrexate, which is used to treat cancers and severe rheumatoid arthritis. This drug may increase the effectiveness of anticoagulant (blood-thinning) drugs. It can increase blood-clotting time by 3 to 4 minutes. Taking this drug together with a thiazide diuretic increases the chances for kidney failure.

Diclofenac may increase the effects of sulfa drugs, antidiabetes drugs, and Phenytoin or other drugs for seizure disorders.

Food Interactions

You may take this drug with food if it upsets your stomach.

Usual Dose

Adult: 100 to 200 milligrams per day divided into 2, 3, or 4 doses.

Senior: probably should start with ½ to ⅓ the usual dose.

Overdosage

Symptoms may include drowsiness, dizziness, confusion, disorientation, lethargy, tingling in the hands or feet, numbness, nausea, vomiting, upset stomach, stomach pains, headache, ringing or buzzing in the ears, sweating, and blurred vision. Take the victim to a hospital emergency room at once for treatment. ALWAYS bring the medicine bottle with you.

Special Information

Avoid Aspirin and alcoholic beverages while taking this medication. You may become dizzy or drowsy while taking this medicine. Be careful while driving or operating complex equipment. Call your doctor if you develop a skin rash, itching, swelling, visual disturbances, black stools, or a persistent headache while taking this medication.

If you forget to take a dose of Diclofenac, take it as soon as you remember. If it is almost time for your next dose, skip the forgotten dose and continue with your regular schedule.

Generic Name

Dicloxacillin Sodium

Brand Names

Dicloxacil   Dynapen
Dycill   Pathocil

(Also available in generic form)

Type of Drug

Penicillin-type antibiotic.

Prescribed for

Gram-positive bacterial infections. Gram-positive bacteria (pneumococci, streptococci, and staphylococci) are organisms which usually cause diseases such as pneumonia, infections of the tonsils and throat, venereal disease, meningitis (infection of the spinal column), and septicemia (general infection of the bloodstream). This drug is best used to treat certain infections resistant to Penicillin, although it may be used as initial treatment for some patients.

General Information

Penicillin-type antibiotics fight infection by killing bacteria. They do this by destroying the cell wall of invading bacteria. Other antibiotics simply prevent bacteria from reproducing. Many infections can be treated by almost any member of this family, but some infections can only be treated by certain penicillin-type antibiotics.

   Penicillins cannot treat a cold, flu, or any virus infection and should never be taken unless prescribed by a doctor for a specific illness. Always take your antibiotic exactly according to your doctor's directions for use, including the number of pills to take every day and the number of days to take the medicine. If you do not follow directions, you may not get the antibiotic's full benefit.

Cautions and Warnings

If you have a known history of allergy to penicillin, do not take Dicloxacillin. The drugs are similar. The most common allergic reaction to Dicloxacillin Sodium, as well as to the other penicillins, is a hivelike rash over the body with itching and redness. It is important to tell your doctor if you have ever taken this drug or any other penicillin before and if you have experienced any adverse reaction to the drug such as rash, itching, or difficulty in breathing.

Pregnancy/Breast-feeding

Although Dicloxacillin Sodium has not been shown to harm the developing fetus, the drug should be used during pregnancy only if considered essential. This medicine is excreted in breast milk and should be used with caution by nursing mothers.

Seniors

Seniors may take this medicine without special precautions.

Possible Side Effects

Common: stomach upset, nausea, vomiting, diarrhea, possible rash. Less common: hairy tongue, itching or irritation around the anus and/or vagina, stomach pain with or without bleeding.

Drug Interactions

The effects of Dicloxacillin Sodium can be significantly reduced when taken with other antibiotics. Consult your doctor if you are taking both during the same course of therapy. Otherwise, Dicloxacillin Sodium is generally free of interactions with other medications.

Food Interactions

To ensure the maximum effect, you should take the medication on an empty stomach, either 1 hour before or 2 hours after meals.

Usual Dose

Adult and child (88 pounds or more): 125 to 250 milligrams every 6 hours. In severe infections, 500 milligrams may be needed.

Child (less than 88 pounds): 5.5 to 11 milligrams per pound of body weight per day in divided doses.

Overdosage

Dicloxacillin overdose is unlikely but may result in diarrhea or upset stomach.

Special Information

Do not take this medicine after the expiration date on the label. Be sure to take this medicine exactly according to your doctor's directions.

Stop taking the medicine and call your doctor if any of the following side effects develop: skin rash, hives, itching, wheezing. Other side effects that demand your doctor's attention are: blood in the urine, passage of large amounts of light-colored urine, swelling of the face or ankles, trouble breathing, unusual weakness or tiredness.

If you miss a dose of Dicloxacillin Sodium, take it as soon as possible. Take the rest of that day's doses at regularly spaced time intervals. Go back to your regular schedule the next day.

Dicloxacillin Sodium capsules can be stored at room temperature. The liquid should be kept in the refrigerator and shaken well before use.

Generic Name

Diethylpropion Hydrochloride

Brand Names

Depletite
Tenuate
Tenuate Dospan

Tepanil
Tepanil Ten Tab

(Also available in generic form)

Type of Drug

Nonamphetamine appetite depressant.

Prescribed for

Suppression of appetite and treatment of obesity.

General Information

Although Diethylpropion Hydrochloride is not an amphetamine, it can produce the same adverse effects as the amphetamine appetite suppressants.

Cautions and Warnings

Do not use Diethylpropion Hydrochloride if you have heart disease, high blood pressure, thyroid disease, or glaucoma, or if you are sensitive or allergic to this or similar drugs. Furthermore, do not use this medication if you are emotionally agitated or have a history of drug abuse.

Pregnancy/Breast-feeding

Other drugs similar to Diethylpropion Hydrochloride have caused birth defects. However, in animal and human studies, Diethylpropion Hydrochloride has not been shown to cause these effects. Check with your doctor before taking it if you are, or might be, pregnant.

This medicine passes into breast milk and can affect a nursing infant.

Seniors

Older adults should not take this medicine unless prescribed by a doctor. It can aggravate diabetes and high blood pressure, conditions common to older adults.

Possible Side Effects

Common side effects are a false sense of well-being, nervousness, overstimulation, restlessness, and trouble sleeping. Other side effects are palpitations, high blood pressure, drowsiness, sedation, weakness, dizziness, tremor, headache, dry mouth, nausea, vomiting, diarrhea and other intestinal disturbances, rash, itching, changes in sex drive, hair loss, muscle pain, difficulty in passing urine, sweating, chills, blurred vision, fever.

Usual Dose

25 milligrams 3 times per day 1 hour before meals; an additional tablet may be given in midevening, if needed to suppress the desire for midnight snacks.

Sustained-release tablets or capsules of 75 milligrams (Tenuate Dospan, Tepanil Ten-Tab): 1 per day usually in midmorning.

Overdosage

Symptoms are restlessness, tremor, shallow breathing, confusion, hallucinations, and fever, followed by fatigue and depression, with additional symptoms such as high or possibly low blood pressure, cold and clammy skin, nausea, vomiting, diarrhea, and stomach cramps. The patient should be taken to a hospital emergency room immediately. ALWAYS bring the medicine bottle.

Special Information

Use for no more than 12 weeks as an adjunct to diet, under strict supervision of your doctor.

Medicine alone will not take off weight. You must limit and modify your food intake, preferably under medical supervision.

This drug can cause dry mouth, which can be relieved by sugarless candy, gum, or shaved ice.

Do not crush or chew sustained-release products.

The long-acting preparations should be taken at least 10 to 14 hours before your bed time to help avoid sleeping troubles.

If you forget to take a dose of Diethylpropion Hydrochloride, take it as soon as you remember. If it is almost time for your next regularly scheduled dose, skip the one you forgot and continue with your regular schedule. Do not take a double dose.

Generic Name

Diethylstilbestrol

Brand Name

DES

(Also available in generic form)

Type of Drug

Estrogen.

Prescribed for

Hormone replacement, some cases of cancer of the prostate or breast. In emergencies, DES has been prescribed as a postcoital contraceptive.

General Information

Diethylstilbestrol is an estrogen, or female hormone. Estrogens are natural substances required for regulation of the menstrual cycle and for normal sexual development.

Because of the potential development of secondary disease after a long period of taking Diethylstilbestrol, the decision to take this medication chronically should be made cautiously by you and your doctor.

Cautions and Warnings

Estrogens have been reported to increase the risk of certain types of cancer in postmenopausal women taking this type of drug for prolonged periods of time: this risk tends to depend upon the duration of treatment and on the dose of the estrogen being taken. When long-term estrogen therapy is indicated for the treatment of menopausal symptoms, the lowest effective dose should be used. If you have to take Diethylstilbestrol for extended periods of time, you should see your doctor at least twice a year so that he can assess your current condition and your need to continue the drug therapy. If you are taking an estrogenic product and experience vaginal bleeding of a recurrent, abnormal, or persistent nature, contact your doctor immediately.

If you have active thrombophlebitis or any other disorder associated with the formation of blood clots, you probably should not take this drug. If you feel that you have a disorder associated with blood clots and you have been taking Diethylstilbestrol or a similar product, you should contact your doctor immediately so that he can evaluate your situation and decide about stopping the drug therapy.

Prolonged continuous administration of estrogenic substances to certain animal species has increased the frequency of cancer in these animals, and there is evidence that these drugs may increase the risk of various cancers in humans. This drug should be taken with caution by women with a strong family history of breast cancer or those who have breast nodules, fibrocystic disease of the breast, or abnormal mammogram. Furthermore, long-term use of Diethylstilbestrol may expose a woman to a two- to threefold increase in chance of developing gallbladder disease. It is possible that women taking Diethylstilbestrol for extended periods of time may experience some of the same development of long-term adverse effects as women who have taken oral contraceptives for extended periods of time. These long-term problems may include thromboembolic disease or the development of various disorders associated with the development of blood clots, liver cancer or other liver tumors, high blood pressure, glucose intolerance or a development of a symptom similar to diabetes or the aggravation of diabetes in patients who had this disease before they started the estrogen, and high blood levels of calcium in certain classes of patients.

Pregnancy/Breast-feeding

Do not use this or any other estrogenic substance if you are pregnant, since these drugs, if used during the earlier stages of pregnancy, may seriously damage the offspring, or cause spontaneous abortion.

Estrogens may reduce the flow of breast milk. If estrogen is considered essential for a nursing mother, she should use an alternative method of feeding her infant.

Seniors

Older adults are more susceptible to drug side effects, especially if you smoke.

Possible Side Effects

Breakthrough bleeding, spotting, changes in menstrual flow, dysmenorrhea, premenstrual-type syndrome, resumption of menorrhea, vaginal infection with candida, cystitislike syndrome, enlargement or tenderness of the breasts, swelling of the feet or ankles, nausea, vomiting, abdominal cramps, feeling of bloatedness, jaundice or yellowing of the skin or whites of the eyes, skin rash, loss of scalp hair, development of new hairy areas. Lesions of the eye have been associated with estrogen therapy. If you wear contact lenses and are taking estrogens, it is possible that you will become intolerant to the lenses. You may also experience headache—possibly migraine—dizziness, depression, weight changes, retention of water, and changes in sex drive.

Other side effects include stroke, blood clot formation, dribbling or sudden passage of urine, loss of coordination, chest pains, leg pains, difficulty breathing or catching a breath, slurred speech, vision change, skin rash, skin irritation and redness.

Drug Interactions

Vitamin C (in doses of 1 gram a day or more) may increase the effect of estrogen.

Phenytoin, Ethotoin, and Mephenytoin may interfere with estrogen effects.

Estrogens may force a dosage change in oral anticoagulant (blood-thinning) drugs, which your doctor can do with a simple blood test.

Estrogens may increase the side effects of antidepressants and phenothiazine-type tranquilizers. Low estrogen doses may increase estrogen effectiveness.

Food Interactions

This drug may be taken without regard to food or meals.

Usual Dose

0.2 to 3 milligrams per day, depending upon the disease being treated and patient's response. Some diseases or patients may require up to 15 milligrams per day.

Overdosage

Overdose may cause nauséa and withdrawal bleeding in adult females. Serious adverse effects have not been reported after accidental overdosage in children.

Special Information

If you forget to take a dose of Diethylstilbestrol, take it as soon as you remember. If it is almost time for your next regularly scheduled dose, skip the one you forgot and continue with your regular schedule. Do not take a double dose.

Generic Name

Diflunisal

Brand Name

Dolobid

Type of Drug

Nonsteroidal anti-inflammatory.

Prescribed for

Relief of mild or moderate pain, rheumatoid arthritis, osteoarthritis.

General Information

This drug is derived from salicylic acid but is chemically

different from Aspirin. It reduces pain and inflammation but we do not know exactly how the medicine works. Part of the drug's action may be due to its ability to inhibit a hormone called prostaglandin, a property it shares with other nonsteroidal anti-inflammatory drugs (NSAIDs). It is quickly absorbed into the bloodstream and produces pain relief in about 1 hour. Its maximum effect is seen within 2 to 3 hours. People taking Diflunisal generally have a good pain-relieving effect 8 to 12 hours after taking their medicine. Usually it takes 3 to 4 days of therapy to reach an acceptable level of pain relief.

A single 500-milligram tablet of Diflunisal is about equal in its ability to relieve pain to 650 milligrams of Aspirin or Acetaminophen (2 regular tablets) or to 1 tablet of Darvon-N 100. Two 500-milligram tablets of Diflunisal are about equal to 600 milligrams of Acetaminophen with 60 milligrams of Codeine (Tylenol with Codeine #4) in pain relief.

Cautions and Warnings

People who are allergic to Diflunisal, Aspirin, other NSAIDs, and those with a history of asthma attacks brought on by another NSAID or by Aspirin, should not take Diflunisal. This medicine can cause gastrointestinal bleeding. People with a history of active gastrointestinal bleeding should be cautious about taking Diflunisal.

This drug can affect blood clotting at high doses and should be avoided by people with clotting problems and those taking Warfarin.

People with heart problems who use this medicine may find their arms and legs or feet become swollen.

Pregnancy/Breast-feeding

This drug crosses into the blood circulation of a developing baby. It has not been found to cause birth defects, but may affect a developing infant's heart during the last 3 months of pregnancy. Pregnant women, or those who might become pregnant while taking this drug, should not take it without their doctor's approval. When the drug is considered essential by your doctor, the potential risk of taking the medicine must be carefully weighed against the benefit it might produce.

This drug passes into breast milk, but has caused no prob-

lems among breast-fed infants. You should either stop breast-feeding while taking this medicine or use an alternative feeding method.

Seniors

Older adults, especially those with poor kidney function, may be more susceptible to the side effects of this drug.

Possible Side Effects

Common side effects include diarrhea, stomach gas, headache, sleeplessness, rash.

Less common side effects are nausea, upset stomach, vomiting, constipation, stomach ulcers, gastrointestinal bleeding, loss of appetite, hepatitis, gallbladder attacks, painful urination, poor kidney function, kidney inflammation, blood and protein in the urine, dizziness, fainting, nervousness, depression, hallucinations, confusion, disorientation, tingling in the hands or feet, light-headedness, itching, sweating, dry nose and mouth, heart palpitations, chest pain, difficulty breathing, and muscle cramps.

A small number of people taking Diflunisal have experienced severe allergic reactions, including closing of the throat, fever and chills, changes in liver function, jaundice, kidney failure. These people must be treated in a hospital emergency room or doctor's office.

Severe dermatologic reactions like erythema multiforme and Stevens-Johnson syndrome have occurred to people taking this medication.

Drug Interactions

Diflunisal can increase the effects of oral anticoagulant drugs such as Warfarin. You may take this combination, but your doctor may have to adjust your anticoagulant dose to take this effect into account.

The combination of Diflunisal and a thiazide diuretic increases the amount of diuretic in your blood.

Taking antacids together with Diflunisal may decrease the amount of Diflunisal absorbed into the bloodstream. This effect is especially important if you take antacids on a continuous basis for hyperacidity or an ulcer.

Diflunisal increases the amount of Acetaminophen in your blood by about 50 percent. It also increases the amount of

Indomethacin in your blood; the combination of Indomethacin and Diflunisal has resulted in a fatal gastrointestinal
hemorrhage.

Food Interactions

Take this medicine with food if it upsets your stomach.

Usual Dose

500 to 1000 milligrams to start, then 250 to 500 milligrams
every 8 to 12 hours. Do not take more than 1500 milligrams
per day.

Overdosage

People have died from an overdose of 15 grams of Diflunisal.
The most common signs of overdose are drowsiness, nausea, vomiting, diarrhea, rapid breathing, rapid heartbeat,
sweating, ringing or buzzing in the ears, disorientation, stupor, and coma.

Take the victim to a hospital emergency room at once for
treatment. ALWAYS remember to bring the medicine bottle
with you.

Special Information

Do not take any nonprescription products with Aspirin or
Acetaminophen while taking Diflunisal, unless directed to do
so by your doctor. Do not crush or chew the tablets.

Contact your doctor if you develop any unusual side effects or if side effects become intolerable.

If you forget to take a dose of Diflunisal, take it as soon as
you remember. If it is almost time for your next regularly
scheduled dose, skip the one you forgot and continue with
your regular schedule. Do not take a double dose.

Generic Name

Digitoxin

Brand Names

Crystodigin
Purodigin

(Also available in generic form)

Type of Drug

Cardiac glycoside.

Prescribed for

Congestive heart failure and other heart abnormalities.

General Information

Digitoxin directly affects the heart muscle (myocardium), depending on the dose you are taking. Digitoxin improves your heart's pumping ability or helps to control its beating rhythm. Patients with heart problems very often notice swelling of the feet, ankles, and hands. Digitalis drugs improve this symptom by improving drug circulation.

Digitoxin is more useful than Digoxin in patients who have kidney problems. Digitoxin is not removed from the body by the kidneys but mostly by the liver.

This medication is generally used for long periods of time.

Cautions and Warnings

Do not use this drug if you know you are allergic or sensitive to Digitalis. Long-term use of Digitoxin can cause the body to lose potassium, especially since Digitoxin is generally used in combination with a diuretic drug. For this reason, be sure to eat a well-balanced diet and emphasize foods which are high in potassium such as bananas, citrus fruits, melons, and tomatoes.

Pregnancy/Breast-feeding

This drug crosses into the blood circulation of a developing baby. It has not been found to cause birth defects. Pregnant women, or those who might become pregnant while taking this drug, should not take it without their doctor's approval. When the drug is considered essential by your doctor, the potential risk of taking the medicine must be carefully weighed against the benefit it might produce.

This drug passes into breast milk, but has caused no problems among breast-fed infants. You must consider the potential effect on the nursing infant if breast-feeding while taking this medicine.

Seniors

Older adults are more sensitive to the effects of this drug, especially loss of appetite. Follow your doctor's directions and report any side effects at once.

Possible Side Effects

Most common: loss of appetite, nausea, vomiting, diarrhea, blurred or disturbed vision. If you experience any of these problems, discuss them with your doctor immediately.

Less common side effects: Enlargement of the breasts has been reported after long-term use of Digitoxin, but this is uncommon. Allergy or sensitivity to Digitoxin is also uncommon.

Drug Interactions

Barbiturates, Phenytoin, antidiabetic drugs, Phenylbutazone, and Rifampin will counteract the effectiveness of Digitoxin by stimulating its breakdown by your liver.

The absorption of this medication into your bloodstream is reduced by taking it together with antacids, kaolin-pectin mixtures, cholestyramine, Colestipol. Other drugs that can prevent Digitoxin from being absorbed are: oral Kanamycin, Metoclopramide, oral Neomycin.

Drugs that may increase the effect of Digitoxin are anticholinergic drugs, Erythromycin and Tetracycline, Hydroxychloroquine, Nifedipine, and Verapamil.

Low blood potassium, a common side effect of thiazide diuretics, Furosemide, Ethacrynic acid and Bumetanide, will increase Digitoxin's effect and increase the chance of developing a toxic side effect. Spironolactone can either increase or decrease the effect of Digitoxin. The effect is unpredictable.

Quinidine may increase the amount of Digitoxin in your

blood by 2 to 3 times, beginning 1 to 3 days after the Quinidine is started. The effects of Digitoxin on your heart may be additive to those of the Ephedrine, Epinephrine and other stimulants, beta blockers, calcium salts, Procainamide, Rauwolfia drugs.

Thyroid drugs will change your Digitoxin requirement. Your doctor will have to make a dosage adjustment if you start taking a thyroid drug.

Food Interactions

Take each day's dose after your morning meal.

Usual Dose

Adult: the first dose—known as the digitalizing dose—is 2 milligrams over about 3 days, or 0.4 milligram per day for 4 days. Maintenance dose ranges from 0.05 to 0.03 milligram daily.

Senior: lower doses, as seniors are more sensitive to adverse effects.

Infant and child: the first dose depends on age but can be from 0.01 milligram per pound to 0.02 milligram per pound. Maintenance dose is 1/10 the first dose.

Overdosage

Symptoms are loss of appetite, nausea, vomiting, diarrhea, headache, weakness, apathy, blurred vision, yellow or green spots before the eyes, yellowing of the skin and eyes, or changes in heartbeat. Contact your doctor immediately if any of these symptoms appear. An early sign of overdose in children is change in heart rhythm. Vomiting, diarrhea, and eye trouble are frequently seen in older people.

Special Information

Do not stop taking this medicine unless your doctor tells you to. Avoid nonprescription medicine containing stimulants. Your pharmacist can tell you which nonprescription medicine is safe for you. Call your doctor if you develop loss of appetite, stomach pains, nausea, or vomiting, diarrhea, unusual tiredness or weakness, visual disturbances, or mental depression. There are considerable variations among Digitoxin tablets made by different manufacturers. Do not change brands of Digitoxin without telling your doctor.

If you forget to take a dose of Digitoxin, do not take the forgotten dose. Skip the dose and go back to your regular schedule. Do not take a double dose. Call your doctor if you forget to take your medicine for 2 or more days.

Generic Name

Digoxin

Brand Names

Lanoxicaps
Lanoxin

(Also available in generic form)

Type of Drug

Cardiac glycoside.

Prescribed for

Congestive heart failure, and other heart abnormalities.

General Information

Digoxin directly affects the heart muscle (myocardium), depending on the dose you are taking. Digoxin improves your heart's pumping ability or helps to control its beating rhythm. Patients with heart problems very often notice swelling of the feet, ankles, and hands. Digitalis drugs improve this symptom by improving drug circulation.

This medication is generally used for long periods of time.

Cautions and Warnings

Do not use this drug if you know you are allergic or sensitive to Digitalis. Long-term use of Digoxin can cause the body to lose potassium, especially since Digoxin is generally used in combination with a diuretic drug. For this reason, be sure to eat a well-balanced diet and emphasize foods which are high in potassium, such as bananas, citrus fruits, melons, and tomatoes.

Pregnancy/Breast-feeding

This drug crosses into the blood circulation of a developing baby. It has not been found to cause birth defects. Pregnant women, or those who might become pregnant while taking this drug, should not take it without their doctor's approval. When the drug is considered essential by your doctor, the potential risk of taking the medicine must be carefully weighed against the benefit it might produce. However, digitalis drugs have been given to pregnant women to treat heart problems of the unborn child.

This drug passes into breast milk, but has caused no problems among breast-fed infants. You must consider the potential effect on the nursing infant if breast-feeding while taking this medicine.

Seniors

Older adults are more sensitive to the effects of this drug, especially loss of appetite. Follow your doctor's directions and report any side effects at once.

Possible Side Effects

Most common: loss of appetite, nausea, vomiting, diarrhea, blurred or disturbed vision. If you experience any of these problems, discuss them with your doctor immediately.

Less common side effects: enlargement of the breasts has been reported after long-term use of Digoxin, but this is uncommon. Allergy or sensitivity to Digoxin is also uncommon.

Drug Interactions

The absorption of this medication into your bloodstream is reduced by taking it together with antacids, kaolin-pectin mixtures, cholestyramine, Colestipol. Other drugs that can prevent Digoxin from being absorbed are: oral Kanamycin, Metoclopramide, oral Neomycin.

Drugs that may increase the effect of Digoxin are anticholinergic drugs, Erythromycin and Tetracycline, Hydroxychloroquine, Nifedipine, and Verapamil.

Low blood potassium, a common side effect of thiazide diuretics, Furosemide, Ethacrynic acid and Bumetanide, will increase Digoxin's effect and increase the chance of developing a toxic side effect. Spironolactone can either increase or decrease the effect of Digoxin. The effect is unpredictable.

Quinidine increases the amount of Digoxin in your blood by 2 to 3 times beginning 1 to 3 days after the Quinidine is started. The effects of Digoxin on your heart may be additive to those of the Ephedrine, Epinephrine and other stimulants, beta blockers, calcium salts, Procainamide, Rauwolfia drugs.

Thyroid drugs will change your Digoxin requirement. Your doctor will have to make a dosage adjustment if you start taking a thyroid drug.

Food Interactions

Taking Digoxin with foods high in fiber content may decrease the absorption of Digoxin. Take your dose after your morning meal.

Usual Dose

Adult: the first dose—known as the digitalizing dose—is 1 to 1.5 milligrams. Maintenance dose ranges from 0.125 to 0.5 milligram.

Senior: lower dose, as the elderly are more sensitive to adverse effects.

Infant and child: substantially lower dose.

Overdosage

If symptoms of loss of appetite, nausea, vomiting, diarrhea, headache, weakness, feeling of not caring, blurred vision, yellow or green spots before the eyes, yellowing of the skin and eyes, or changes in heartbeat appear, contact your doctor immediately. An early sign of overdose in children is change in heart rhythm. Vomiting, diarrhea, and eye trouble are frequently seen in older people.

Special Information

Do not stop taking this medicine unless your doctor tells you to. Avoid nonprescription medicine containing stimulants. Your pharmacist can tell you which nonprescription medicine is safe for you. Call your doctor if you develop loss of appetite, stomach pains, nausea or vomiting, diarrhea, unusual tiredness or weakness, visual disturbances, or mental depression. There are considerable variations among Digoxin tablets made by different manufacturers. Do not change brands of Digoxin without telling your doctor.

If you forget to take a dose of Digoxin, do not take the forgotten dose. Skip the dose and go back to your regular schedule. Do not take a double dose. Call your doctor if you forget to take your medicine for 2 or more days.

Generic Name

Diltiazem Hydrochloride

Brand Name

Cardizem

Type of Drug

Calcium channel blocker.

Prescribed for

Angina pectoris; high blood pressure, and to prevent a reoccurrence of some kinds of heart attack.

General Information

Diltiazem Hydrochloride is one of three calcium channel blockers sold in the United States, the others being Nifedipine and Verapamil. These drugs work by slowing the passage of calcium into muscle cells. This causes muscles in the blood vessels that supply your heart to open wider, allowing more blood to reach heart tissues. The drugs also decrease muscle spasm In those blood vessels. Diltiazem Hydrochloride also reduces the speed at which electrical impulses are carried through heart tissue, adding to its ability to slow the heart and prevent the pain of angina. This drug can help to reduce high blood pressure by causing blood vessels throughout the body to widen, allowing blood to flow more easily through them, especially when combined with a diuretic, beta blocker, or other blood-pressure-lowering drug.

Cautions and Warnings

Diltiazem Hydrochloride can slow your heart and interfere with normal electrical conduction. For people with a condition called sick sinus syndrome, this can result in temporary heart stoppage; most people will not develop this effect.

Diltiazem Hydrochloride can cause severe liver damage and should be taken with caution if you have had hepatitis or any other liver condition. Caution should also be exercised if you have a history of kidney problems, although no clear tendency toward causing kidney damage exists.

Pregnancy/Breast-feeding

Animal studies with Diltiazem Hydrochloride have revealed a definite potential to harm a developing fetus, usually at doses greater than the usual human dose. As the dose was increased, adverse effects became more frequent and more severe. Diltiazem Hydrochloride should not be taken by pregnant women or women who may become pregnant while using it. In those situations where it is deemed essential, the potential risk of the drug must be carefully weighed against any benefit it might produce.

Nursing mothers should use an alternative feeding method, since Diltiazem Hydrochloride passes into breast milk. Diltiazem Hydrochloride's safety in children has not been established.

Seniors

Older adults are more sensitive to the effects of this drug, because it takes longer to pass out of their bodies. Follow your doctor's directions and report any side effects at once.

Possible Side Effects

Abnormal heart rhythms, fluid accumulation in the hands, legs, or feet, headache, fatigue, nausea, and rash.

Less common side effects: low blood pressure, dizziness, fainting, changes in heart rate (increase or decrease), heart failure, light-headedness, nervousness, tingling in the hands or feet, hallucinations, temporary memory loss, difficulty sleeping, weakness, diarrhea, vomiting, constipation, upset stomach, itching, unusual sensitivity to sunlight, painful or stiff joints, liver inflammation, and increased urination, especially at night.

Drug Interactions

Taking Diltiazem Hydrochloride together with a beta-blocking drug for high blood pressure is usually well tolerated, but may lead to heart failure in people with already weakened hearts.

Calcium channel blockers, including Diltiazem Hydrochloride, may add to the effects of Digoxin, although this effect is not observed with any consistency and only affects people with a lot of Digoxin already in their systems.

Food Interactions

Diltiazem Hydrochloride is best taken on an empty stomach, at least 1 hour before or 2 hours after meals.

Usual Dose

30 to 60 milligrams 4 times per day.

Overdosage

The two major symptoms of Diltiazem Hydrochloride overdose are very low blood pressure and reduced heart rate. Patients poisoned with this drug must be made to vomit within 30 minutes of the actual dose with Syrup of Ipecac (available at any pharmacy) to remove the drug from the stomach. If overdose symptoms have developed or more than 30 minutes have passed, vomiting is of little value. You must go to a hospital emergency room for treatment. ALWAYS bring the medicine bottle.

Special Information

Call your doctor if you develop any of the following symptoms: swelling of the hands, legs, or feet, severe dizziness, constipation or nausea, or very low blood pressure.

If you forget to take a dose of Diltiazem Hydrochloride, take it as soon as you remember. If it is almost time for your next regularly scheduled dose, skip the one you forgot and continue with your regular schedule. Do not take a double dose.

Generic Name

Dimenhydrinate

Brand Names

Calm-X   Marmine
Dimentabs   Motion-Aid
Dramamine

(Also available in generic form)

Type of Drug

Antihistamine.

Prescribed for

Prevention or treatment of nausea, vomiting, or dizziness associated with motion sickness.

General Information

Dimenhydrinate is a mixture of Diphenhydramine, an antihistamine, and another ingredient, although the antihistamine is believed to be the active ingredient. Dimenhydrinate depresses middle ear function, but the way in which it actually prevents nausea, vomiting, or dizziness is not known. Dimenhydrinate tablets and liquid are available without a prescription.

Cautions and Warnings

People with a prostate condition, some types of stomach ulcers, bladder problems, difficulty urinating, glaucoma, asthma, or abnormal heart rhythms should only use Dimenhydrinate while under a doctor's care.

　　Because it controls nausea and vomiting, Dimenhydrinate can hide the symptoms of overdose of other medicines or the symptoms of appendicitis. Your doctor may have difficulty reaching an accurate diagnosis in these conditions unless he or she knows you are taking Dimenhydrinate.

Pregnancy/Breast-feeding

Antihistamines have not been proven to be a cause of birth defects or other problems in pregnant women, although studies in animals have shown that some drugs (Meclizine and Cyclizine), used mainly against nausea and vomiting, may cause birth defects. Do not take any antihistamine without your doctor's knowledge.

Small amounts of antihistamines pass into breast milk and may affect a nursing infant. Dimenhydrinate may inhibit milk production. Nursing mothers should avoid antihistamines or use alternate feeding methods while taking the medicine.

Seniors

Seniors are more sensitive to antihistamine side effects.

Possible Side Effects

The most common side effect of Dimenhydrinate is dizziness. Other, less frequent side effects are blurred vision, difficult or painful urination, dry mouth, nose, or throat, increased sensitivity to the sun, loss of appetite, nightmares, rash, ringing or buzzing in the ears.

Drug Interactions

Taking Dimenhydrinate together with alcoholic beverages, other antihistamines, tranquilizers, or other nervous system depressants can result in excessive dizziness, drowsiness, or other signs of nervous system depression.

Food Interactions

Take this medicine with food or milk if it upsets your stomach.

Usual Dose

Adult: 50 to 100 milligrams (1 to 2 tablets or 4 to 8 teaspoons) every 4 to 6 hours.

Child (age 6 to 12): 25 to 50 milligrams (½ or 1 tablet or 2 to 4 teaspoons) every 6 to 8 hours. No more than 3 doses a day.

Child (age 2 to 5): up to 25 milligrams (½ tablet or 2 teaspoons) every 6 to 8 hours. No more than 3 doses a day.

Child (under age 2): see your doctor.

Overdosage

The usual effect of an overdose is drowsiness, clumsiness, and unsteadiness. Dry mouth, nose, and throat, a faint feeling, and facial flushing can also occur. Convulsions, coma, and breathing difficulty can develop after a massive overdose of Dimenhydrinate.

Overdose victims should be taken to a hospital emergency room for treatment. ALWAYS remember to bring the medicine bottle with you.

Special Information

For maximum effectiveness against motion sickness, take your dose of Dimenhydrinate 1 to 2 hours before traveling. Dimenhydrinate may still be effective if taken 30 minutes before traveling.

Dimenhydrinate and other antihistamines can cause dry mouth, nose, or throat. Sugarless candy, gum, or ice chips can relieve this symptom, which is only temporary. Contact your doctor if excessive dryness lasts more than 2 weeks.

If you forget to take a dose of Dimenhydrinate, take it as soon as you remember. If it is almost time for your next regularly scheduled dose, skip the one you forgot and continue with your regular schedule. Do not take a double dose.

Generic Name

Diphenhydramine Hydrochloride

Brand Names

Aller May	Fenylhist
Beaphen	Hydramine
Beldin	Nervine Nighttime Sleep-Aid
Belix	Nordryl
Benadryl	Nytol
Benylin Cough	Phen-Amin
Bydramine	Sleep-Eze
Compōz	Sominex
Diahist	Tusstat
Diphen Cough	Twilite
Dormarex-2	Valdrene

(Also available in generic form)

Type of Drug

Antihistamine.

Prescribed for

Seasonal allergy, stuffed and runny nose, Itching of the eyes, scratchy throat caused by allergy, and other allergic symptoms such as itching, rash, or hives. In addition, Diphenhydramine Hydrochloride has been used for motion sickness and, with other drugs, for Parkinson's disease and as a nighttime aid.

General Information

Antihistamines generally, and Diphenhydramine Hydrochloride specifically, act by antagonizing histamine at the site of the H_1 histamine receptor.

Antihistamines work by drying up the secretions of the nose, throat, and eyes. They relieve itch and will help you go to sleep.

Cautions and Warnings

Diphenhydramine Hydrochloride should not be used if you are allergic to this drug. It should be avoided or used with extreme care if you have narrow-angle glaucoma (pressure in the eye), stomach ulcer or other stomach problems, enlarged prostate, or problems passing urine. It should not be used by people who have deep-breathing problems such as asthma.

Use with care if you have a history of thyroid disease, heart disease, high blood pressure, or diabetes.

Pregnancy/Breast-feeding

Antihistamines have not been proven to be a cause of birth defects or other problems in pregnant women, although studies in animals have shown that some drugs (Meclizine and Cyclizine), used mainly against nausea and vomiting, may cause birth defects. Do not take any antihistamine without your doctor's knowledge.

Small amounts of antihistamine medicines pass into breast milk and may affect a nursing infant. Nursing mothers should avoid antihistamines or use alternative feeding methods while taking the medicine.

Seniors

Seniors are more sensitive to antihistamine side effects. Confusion, difficult or painful urination, dizziness, drowsiness, a faint feeling, dry mouth, nose, or throat, nightmares or excitement, nervousness, restlessness, or irritability are more likely to occur among older adults.

Possible Side Effects

Occasional: itching, rash, sensitivity to light, perspiration, chills, dryness of the mouth, nose, and throat, lowering of blood pressure, headache, rapid heartbeat, sleeplessness, dizziness, disturbed coordination, confusion, restlessness, nervousness, irritability, euphoria (feeling high), tingling of the hands and feet, blurred vision, double vision, ringing in the ears, stomach upset, loss of appetite, nausea, vomiting, constipation, diarrhea, difficulty in urination, tightness of the chest, wheezing, nasal stuffiness.

Drug Interactions

Diphenhydramine Hydrochloride should not be taken with MAO inhibitors.

Interaction with tranquilizers, sedatives, and sleeping medication will increase the effects of these drugs; it is extremely important that you discuss this with your doctor so that doses of these drugs can be properly adjusted.

Be extremely cautious when drinking while taking Diphenhydramine Hydrochloride, which will enhance the intoxicating effect of the alcohol. Alcohol also has a sedative effect.

Food Interactions

Take this drug with food if it upsets your stomach.

Usual Dose

Adult: 25 to 50 milligrams 3 to 4 times times per day.

Child (over 20 pounds): 12.5 to 25 milligrams 3 to 4 times per day.

For sleep: 25 to 50 milligrams at bedtime.

Overdosage

Symptoms are depression or stimulation (especially in children), dry mouth, fixed or dilated pupils, flushing of the skin, and stomach upset. Take the patient to a hospital emergency room immediately, if you cannot make him vomit. ALWAYS bring the medicine bottle.

Special Information

Diphenhydramine Hydrochloride produces a depressant effect: be extremely cautious when driving or operating heavy equipment.

If you forget to take a dose of Diphenhydramine Hydrochloride, take it as soon as you remember. If it is almost time for your next regularly scheduled dose, skip the one you forgot and continue with your regular schedule. Do not take a double dose.

Generic Name

Dipyridamole

Brand Names

Persantine
Pyridamole

(Also available in generic form)

Type of Drug

Antianginal agent; anticoagulant.

Prescribed for

Prevention of attacks of angina pectoris; generally used for chronic treatment of angina, not for the immediate pain of an attack. Also used for the prevention of myocardial reinfarction and stroke.

The action of this drug should be considered as "possibly effective." There is considerable doubt among medical experts that this drug produces the effects claimed for it.

The only fully approved use for Dipyridamole is as an anticoagulant, in combination with Warfarin, for people who have received replacement heart valves.

General Information

Dipyridamole has been used in the treatment of angina and is also being studied as a possible addition to the treatment of stroke. In such studies, the drug is examined for its possible ability to affect platelets, a component of blood involved in clotting. It appears that the use of this drug will decline gradually and be limited to use as an anticoagulant for people who have received new heart valves or blood vessels.

Pregnancy/Breast-feeding

This drug has not been found to cause birth defects. Pregnant women, or those who might become pregnant while taking this drug, should not take it without their doctor's approval. When the drug is considered essential by your doctor, the potential risk of taking the medicine must be carefully weighed against the benefit it might produce.

This drug has caused no problems among breast-fed infants. You must consider the potential effect on the nursing infant if breast-feeding while taking this medicine.

Seniors

Older adults are more sensitive to the effects of this drug, especially dizziness and fainting. Follow your doctor's directions and report any side effects at once.

Possible Side Effects

Headache, dizziness, light-headedness, fainting, nausea, flushing, weakness, mild stomach upset, possible skin rash.

Dipyridamole has, on rare occasions, been reported to aggravate angina pectoris.

Drug Interactions

May interact with anticoagulant (blood-thinning drugs); patients taking anticoagulants and Dipyridamole should be checked periodically by their physician. Aspirin has an effect similar to Dipyridamole on the platelets and may increase the chances of bleeding due to loss of platelet effectiveness when taken with Dipyridamole.

Food Interactions

Dipyridamole should be taken 1 hour before or 2 hours after

meals with a full glass of water. Take it with food or milk if it upsets your stomach.

Usual Dose

Anti-angina: 50 milligrams 3 times per day.

For heart valve replacement: 75 to 100 milligrams 4 times a day.

Special Information

If you miss a dose of Dipyridamole, take it as soon as you can. If it is 4 hours or less until your next regular dose, skip the missed dose and go back to your regular dose schedule. Do not double any doses of Dipyridamole.

Generic Name

Disopyramide

Brand Names

Napamide
Norpace
Norpace CR

(Also available in generic form)

Type of Drug

Antiarrhythmic.

Prescribed for

Abnormal heart rhythms.

General Information

Disopyramide slows the rate at which nerve impulses are carried through heart muscle, reducing the response of heart muscle to those impulses. It acts on the heart similarly to the more widely used antiarrhythmic medicines, Procainamide Hydrochloride and Quinidine Sulfate. Disopyramide is often used as an alternative to one of these medications for people who do not respond to other antiarrhythmic drugs. It may be prescribed for people who have had a heart attack (infarction) because it helps infarcted areas to respond more like adjacent, healthy heart tissue to nerve impulses.

Cautions and Warnings

This drug can exacerbate heart failure or produce severe reductions in blood pressure. It should only be used in combination with another antiarrhythmic agent or beta blocker, such as Propranolol Hydrochloride, when single-drug treatment has not been effective or the arrhythmia may be life-threatening.

In rare instances, Disopyramide has caused a reduction in blood-sugar levels. Because of this, the drug should be used with caution by diabetics, older adults (who are more susceptible to this effect), and people with poor kidney or liver function. Blood-sugar levels should be measured periodically in people with heart failure, liver or kidney disease, those who are malnourished, and those taking a beta-blocking drug.

Disopyramide should be used with caution by people who have severe difficulty urinating (especially men with a severe prostate condition), glaucoma, or myasthenia gravis.

Pregnancy/Breast-feeding

Do not take this drug if you are pregnant or planning to become pregnant while using it, because it will pass from mother to child. If Disopyramide is considered essential, discuss the potential risks of taking it with your doctor. Nursing women should not take Disopyramide, as it passes into breast milk.

Seniors

Older adults are more sensitive to the effects of this drug, especially urinary difficulty and dry mouth. Follow your doctor's directions and report any side effects at once.

Possible Side Effects

Heart failure, low blood pressure, and urinary difficulty are the most serious side effects of this drug. Other frequent side effects are dry mouth, constipation, blurred vision, dry nose, eyes, and throat, frequent urination and feeling a need to urinate frequently, dizziness, fatigue, headache, nervousness, difficulty breathing, chest pain, nausea, stomach bloating, gas, and pain, loss of appetite, diarrhea, vomiting, itching, rashes, muscle weakness, generalized aches and pains, a feeling of ill health, low blood levels of potassium, increases in blood cholesterol and triglyceride levels.

Less common: male impotence, painful urination, stomach pain, reduction in heart activity, anemia (reduced levels of blood hemoglobin and hematocrit), reduced white-blood-cell counts (rare), sleeplessness, depression, psychotic reactions (rare), liver inflammation and jaundice, numbness and tingling in the hands or feet, elevated blood urea nitrogen (BUN) and creatinine (blood tests for kidney function), low blood sugar, fever, swollen, painful male breasts, drug allergy, glaucoma.

Drug Interactions

Phenytoin and Rifampin may increase the rate at which your body removes Disopyramide from the blood. Your doctor may need to alter your Disopyramide dose if this combination is used. Other drugs known to increase drug breakdown by the liver, such as barbiturates and Primidone, may also have this effect.

Food Interactions

Disopyramide may cause symptoms of low blood sugar: anxiety, chills, cold sweats, cool, pale skin, drowsiness, excessive hunger, nausea, nervousness, rapid pulse, shakiness, unusual weakness, or tiredness. If this happens to you, eat some chocolate candy or other high-sugar food and call your doctor at once. Disopyramide should be taken 1 hour before or 2 hours after meals.

Usual Dose

Adult: 200 to 300 milligrams every 6 hours. In severe cases, 400 milligrams every 4 hours may be required. The long-acting preparation is taken every 12 hours.

People with reduced kidney function: reduced dosage, depending on the degree of kidney failure present.

People with liver failure: 400 milligrams per day.

Child: 2.5 to 14 milligrams per pound of body weight per day, depending on age and condition.

Overdosage

Symptoms are breathing difficulty, abnormal heart rhythms, unconsciousness, and, in severe cases, death. Patients taking an overdose of this drug must be made to vomit with Syrup of Ipecac (available at any pharmacy) to remove any remaining drug from the stomach. Call your doctor or a poison control center before doing this. If you must go to a hospital emergency room, ALWAYS bring the medicine bottle. Prompt and vigorous treatment can make the difference between life and death in severe overdose cases.

Special Information

Disopyramide can cause dry mouth, urinary difficulty, constipation, and blurred vision. Call your doctor if these symptoms become severe or intolerable, but don't stop taking this medicine without your doctor's knowledge and approval.

If you forget to take a dose of Disopyramide, take it as soon as possible. However, if it is within 4 hours of your next dose, skip the forgotten dose and go back to your regular schedule. Do not take a double dose.

If Disopyramide is required for a child and capsules are not appropriate, your pharmacist, with your doctor's permission, can make a liquid product. Do not do this at home, because Disopyramide requires special preparation. The liquid should be refrigerated and protected from light, and should be thrown away after 30 days.

Brand Name

Diupres

Ingredients

Chlorothiazide
Reserpine

Other Brand Names

Chlorserpine
Diurigen with Reserpine

(Also available in generic form)

Type of Drug

Antihypertensive.

Prescribed for

High blood pressure.

General Information

Diupres is a good example of a drug taking advantage of a drug interaction. Each of the drug ingredients works by different mechanisms to lower your blood pressure. The Chlorothiazide relaxes the muscles in your veins and arteries and also helps reduce the volume of blood flowing through those blood vessels. Reserpine works on the nervous system to reduce the efficiency of nerve transmissions which are contributing to the increased pressure. These drugs complement each other so that their combined effect is better than the effect of either one alone.

It is essential that you take your medicine exactly as prescribed for maximum benefit.

An ingredient in this drug may cause excessive loss of potassium, which may lead to a condition called hypokalemia. Warning signs are dryness of mouth, excessive thirst, weakness, drowsiness, restlessness, muscle pains or cramps, muscular fatigue, lack of urination, abnormal heart rhythms, and upset stomach. If warning signs occur, call your doctor. You may need potassium from some outside source. This may be done by either taking a potassium supplement or by eating foods such as bananas, citrus fruits, melons, and tomatoes, which have high concentrations of potassium.

Cautions and Warnings

Do not take this drug if you have a history of mental depression, active peptic ulcer, or ulcerative colitis, or if you are sensitive or allergic to either of its ingredients, to similar drugs of the Chlorothiazide group, or to sulfa drugs. If you have a history of allergy or bronchial asthma, you may also have a sensitivity or allergy to the Chlorothiazide ingredient.

Pregnancy/Breast-feeding

Although Chlorothiazide has been used to treat specific conditions in pregnancy, unsupervised use by pregnant women should be avoided; the drug will cross the placenta and pass into the unborn child, possibly causing problems. Chlorothiazide will also pass into the breast milk of nursing mothers.

Seniors

Older adults are more sensitive to the effects of this drug. Follow your doctor's directions and report any side effects at once.

Possible Side Effects

Loss of appetite, stomach irritation, nausea, vomiting, cramps, diarrhea, constipation, dizziness, headache, tingling in the arms and legs, restlessness, chest pains, abnormal heart rhythms, drowsiness, depression, nervousness, anxiety, nightmares, glaucoma, blood disorders, itching, fever, difficulty in breathing, muscle spasms, gout, weakness, high blood sugar, sugar in urine, blurred vision, stuffy nose, dryness of the mouth, rash. Occasional: impotence or decreased sex drive.

Drug Interactions

Interaction with Digitalis or Quinidine may cause abnormal heart rhythms.

Interaction with drugs containing Lithium may lead to toxic effects of Lithium.

Avoid over-the-counter cough, cold, or allergy remedies containing stimulant drugs which may raise your blood pressure.

Food Interactions

If you take Diupres once a day, take it after breakfast. Do not take the medicine after 6 P.M. The medicine may be taken with food or milk if it upsets your stomach.

Usual Dose

Must be individualized to patient's response.

Special Information

This drug should be stopped at the first sign of despondency, early morning insomnia, loss of appetite, or sexual impotence. Drug-induced depression may persist for several months after the drug has been discontinued; it has been known to be severe enough to result in suicide attempts. This drug should be used with care by women of childbearing age.

If you forget to take a dose of Diupres, take it as soon as you remember. If it is almost time for your next regularly scheduled dose, skip the one you forgot and continue with your regular schedule. Do not take a double dose.

Brand Name

Donnatal

Ingredients

Atropine Sulfate
Hyoscyamine Hydrobromide

Phenobarbital
Scopolamine Hydrobromide

(Liquids also contain alcohol)

Other Brand Names

Barophen
Bellastal
Donnamor
Donnapine
Hyosophen
Malatal
Myphentol

Relaxadon
Seds
Spaslin
Spasmolin
Spasquid
Susano

(Also available in generic form)

The following products contain the same ingredients in different concentrations:

Barbidonna
Donphen Tablets
Hybephen

Kinesed
Spasmophen

(Also available in generic form)

Type of Drug

Anticholinergic combination.

Prescribed for

Symptomatic relief of stomach spasm and other forms of cramps. Donnatal may also be prescribed for the treatment of motion sickness.

The actions of this drug should be considered as "possibly effective." There is considerable doubt among medical experts that this drug produces the effects claimed for it.

General Information

Donnatal is a mild antispasmodic sedative drug. It is only used to relieve symptoms, not to treat the cause of the symptoms. In addition to the brand names listed above, there are 40 to 50 other drug products which are anticholinergic combinations with the same properties. All are used to relieve cramps, and all are about equally effective. Some have additional ingredients to reduce or absorb excess gas in the stomach, to coat the stomach, or to control diarrhea.

Cautions and Warnings

Donnatal should not be used by people with glaucoma, rapid heartbeat, severe intestinal disease such as ulcerating colitis, serious kidney or liver disease, or a history of allergy to any of the ingredients of this drug. Donnatal and other drugs of this class can reduce the patient's ability to sweat. Therefore if you take this type of medication, avoid extended heavy exercise and the excessive high temperature of summer.

Pregnancy/Breast-feeding

This drug may cause birth defects or interfere with your baby's development. Check with your doctor before taking it if you are, or might be, pregnant. Regular use of Donnatal during the last 3 months of pregnancy may cause drug dependency of the newborn. Labor may be prolonged, delivery may be delayed, and the newborn may have breathing problems if Donnatal is used.

Breast-feeding while using Donnatal may cause increased tiredness, shortness of breath, or a slow heartbeat in the baby. Donnatal may decrease the flow of breast milk. Nursing mothers should use alternate feeding methods.

Seniors

Older adults are more sensitive to the effects of this drug, especially excitement, confusion, drowsiness, agitation, constipation, dry mouth, and urinary problems. Memory may be impaired and glaucoma worsened. Follow your doctor's directions and report any side effects at once.

Possible Side Effects

Most common: blurred vision, dry mouth, difficulty in urination, flushing, dry skin.

Infrequent: rapid or unusual heartbeat, increased sensitivity to strong light, loss of taste sensation, headache, difficulty in passing urine, nervousness, tiredness, weakness, dizziness, inability to sleep, nausea, vomiting, fever, stuffy nose, heartburn, loss of sex drive, decreased sweating, constipation, bloated feeling, allergic reactions such as fever and rash.

Drug Interactions

Although Donnatal contains only a small amount of Phenobarbital, it is wise to avoid excessive amounts of alcohol or other drugs which have a sedative effect. Be careful when driving or operating equipment. Other Phenobarbital interactions are probably not important, but are possible with anticoagulants, adrenal corticosteroids, tranquilizers, narcotics, sleeping pills, Digitalis or other cardiac glycosides, and antihistamines.

Some phenothiazine drugs, tranquilizers, antidepressants, and narcotics may increase the side effects of the Atropine Sulfate contained in Donnatal, causing dry mouth, difficulty in urination, and constipation.

Food Interactions

Take this drug about 30 to 60 minutes before meals.

Usual Dose

Adult: 1 to 2 tablets, capsules, or teaspoons 3 to 4 times per day.

Child: half the adult dose, if necessary.

Overdosage

Symptoms are dry mouth, difficulty in swallowing, thirst,

blurred vision, sensitivity to strong light, flushed, hot dry skin, rash, fever, abnormal heart rate, high blood pressure, difficulty in urination, restlessness, confusion, delirium, and difficulty in breathing. The patient should be taken to a hospital emergency room immediately. ALWAYS bring the medicine bottle.

Special Information

Dry mouth from Donnatal can be relieved by chewing gum, or sucking hard candy or ice chips; constipation can be treated with a stool-softening laxative.

If you forget to take a dose of Donnatal, take it as soon as you remember. If it is almost time for your next regularly scheduled dose, skip the one you forgot and continue with your regular schedule. Do not take a double dose.

Donnatal is also available in a longer-acting preparation called Donnatal Extentabs.

Generic Name

Doxepin Hydrochloride

Brand Names

Adapin
Sinequan

(Also available in generic form)

Type of Drug

Antidepressant.

Prescribed for

Primary depression or depression secondary to disorders such as alcoholism, major organic diseases such as cancer, or other illnesses which may have a strong psychological impact on a patient.

General Information

Doxepin Hydrochloride and other members of this group are effective in treating symptoms of depression. They can elevate your mood, increase physical activity and mental alertness, and improve appetite and sleep patterns in a depressed patient. The drugs are mild sedatives and therefore useful in treating mild forms of depression associated with anxiety. You should not expect instant results with this medicine: benefits are usually seen after 1 to 4 weeks of therapy. If symptoms are not changed after 6 to 8 weeks, contact your doctor.

Cautions and Warnings

Unlike other tricyclic antidepressants, Doxepin Hydrochloride should not be given to children under age 12 and cannot be used to treat nighttime bed-wetting. Do not take Doxepin Hydrochloride if you are allergic or sensitive to this or other members of this class of drug: Imipramine, Nortriptyline, Amitriptyline, Desipramine, and Protriptyline. The drugs should not be used if you are recovering from a heart attack. Doxepin Hydrochloride may be taken with caution if you have a history of epilepsy or other convulsive disorders, difficulty in urination, glaucoma, heart disease, or thyroid disease.

Pregnancy/Breast-feeding

This drug, like other antidepressants, crosses into your developing baby's circulation and may cause birth defects if taken during the first 3 months of pregnancy. There have been reports of newborn infants suffering from heart, breathing, and urinary problems after their mothers had taken an antidepressant of this type immediately before delivery. You should avoid taking this medication while pregnant.

Antidepressants of this type are known to pass into breast milk and may affect a breast-feeding infant, although this has not been proven. Nursing mothers should consider alternative feeding methods if taking this medicine.

Seniors

Older adults are more sensitive to the effects of this drug and often require a lower dose than a younger adult to do the same job. Follow your doctor's directions and report any side effects at once.

Possible Side Effects

Changes in blood pressure (both high and low), abnormal heart rate, heart attack, confusion, especially in elderly patients, hallucinations, disorientation, delusions, anxiety, restlessness, excitement, numbness and tingling in the extremities, lack of coordination, muscle spasm or tremors, seizures and/or convulsions, dry mouth, blurred vision, constipation, inability to urinate, rash, itching, sensitivity to bright light or sunlight, changes in composition of blood, nausea, vomiting, loss of appetite, stomach upset, diarrhea, enlargement of the breasts in males and females, increased or decreased sex drive, and increased or decreased blood sugar.

Less common side effects: agitation, inability to sleep, nightmares, feeling of panic, peculiar taste in the mouth, stomach cramps, black coloration of the tongue, yellowing eyes and/or skin, changes in liver function, increased or decreased weight, excessive perspiration, flushing, frequent urination, drowsiness, dizziness, weakness, headache, loss of hair, nausea, not feeling well.

Drug Interactions

Interaction with MAO inhibitors can cause high fevers, convulsions, and (occasionally) death. Don't take MAO inhibitors until at least 2 weeks after Doxepin Hydrochloride has been discontinued.

Certain patients may require concomitant use of Doxepin Hydrochloride and an MAO inhibitor, and in these cases close medical observation is warranted.

Doxepin Hydrochloride interacts with Guanethidine and Clonidine, drugs used to treat high blood pressure: if your doctor prescribes Doxepin Hydrochloride and you are taking medicine for high blood pressure, be sure to discuss this with him.

Doxepin Hydrochloride increases the effects of barbiturates, tranquilizers, other depressive drugs, and alcohol. Don't drink alcoholic beverages if you take Doxepin Hydrochloride.

Taking Doxepin Hydrochloride and thyroid medicine will enhance the effects of the thyroid medicine. The combination can cause abnormal heart rhythms. The combination of Doxepin Hydrochloride and Reserpine may cause overstimulation.

Large doses of Vitamin C (Ascorbic Acid), oral contraceptives, or smoking can reduce the effect of Doxepin Hydrochloride. Drugs such as Bicarbonate of Soda, Acetazolamide, Quinidine, or Procainamide will increase the effect of Doxepin Hydrochloride. Ritalin and phenothiazine drugs such as Thorazine and Compazine block the metabolism of Doxepin Hydrochloride, causing it to stay in the body longer. This can cause possible overdose.

The combination of Doxepin Hydrochloride with large doses of the sleeping pill Ethchlorvynol has caused patients to experience passing delirium.

Food Interactions

This drug is best taken on an empty stomach but you can take it with food if it upsets your stomach.

Usual Dose

Adult: initial dose is a moderate 10 to 25 milligrams 3 times per day; the low dose reduces drowsiness during the first few days. The doctor may then increase or decrease the dose according to individual response, giving 50 to 300 milligrams per day.

Child (under age 12): this drug should not be used.

Overdosage

Symptoms are confusion, inability to concentrate, hallucinations, drowsiness, lowered body temperature, abnormal heart rate, heart failure, large pupils of the eyes, convulsions, severely lowered blood pressure, stupor, and coma (as well as agitation, stiffening of body muscles, vomiting, and high fever). The patient should be taken to a hospital emergency room immediately. ALWAYS bring the medicine bottle.

Special Information

Doxepin Hydrochloride can interfere with your ability to perform tasks which require concentration, such as driving or operating machinery. Do not stop taking this medicine without first discussing it with your doctor, since stopping may cause you to become nauseated, weak, and headachy.

Liquid Doxepin Hydrochloride should not be diluted until just before use. Dilute in about 4 ounces of water or juice just before you take it. Do not mix with grape juice.

Avoid alcohol and other drugs that depress the nervous system while taking this antidepressant. This medicine can cause drowsiness, dizziness, and blurred vision. Be careful when driving or operating complicated machinery. Avoid exposure to the sun or sun lamps for long periods of time. Call your doctor if dry mouth, difficulty urinating, or excessive sedation develops.

If you take Doxepin Hydrochloride several times a day and forget a dose, take it as soon as you remember. If it is almost time for your next regularly scheduled dose, skip the one you forgot and continue with your regular schedule. If you take it once a day at bedtime and forget, don't take it when you get up and go back to your regular schedule. Call your doctor if you skip 2 or more days of medication. Never take a double dose.

Generic Name

Doxycycline

Brand Names

AK-Ramycin   Doxy-Lemmon
AK-Ratabs   Vibramycin
Doryx   Vibra-Tabs
Doxy-Caps   Vivox
Doxychel

Type of Drug

Broad-spectrum antibiotic effective against gram-positive and gram-negative organisms; tetracycline-type antibiotic.

Prescribed for

Bacterial infections such as gonorrhea, infections of the mouth, gums, and teeth, pelvic inflammatory disease, Rocky Mountain spotted fever and other fevers caused by ticks and lice from a variety of carriers, urinary tract infections, and respiratory system infections such as pneumonia and bronchitis.

These diseases may be produced by gram-positive or gram-negative organisms such as diplococci, staphylococci, streptococci, gonococci, *E. coli,* and *Shigella.*

Doxycycline has also been used successfully to treat some skin infections, but is not considered the first-choice antibiotic for the treatment of general skin infections or wounds. It may be used to prevent "traveler's diarrhea."

General Information

Doxycycline works by interfering with the normal growth cycle of the invading bacteria, preventing them from reproducing and thus allowing the body's normal defenses to fight off the infection. This process is referred to as bacteriostatic action. Doxycycline has also been used along with other medicines to treat amoebic infections of the intestinal tract, known as amoebic dysentery. It is also prescribed for diseases caused by ticks, fleas, and lice.

Doxycycline has been successfully used for the treatment of adolescent acne, in small doses over a long period of time. Adverse effects or toxicity in this type of therapy are almost unheard of.

Since the action of this antibiotic depends on its concentration within the invading bacteria, it is imperative that you completely follow the doctor's directions.

Cautions and Warnings

In general, children up to age 8 should avoid Doxycycline as it has been shown to produce serious discoloration of the permanent teeth. Doxycycline when used in children has been shown to interfere with the development of long bones and may retard growth.

Exceptions would be when Doxycycline is the only effective antibiotic available and all risk factors have been made known to the patient.

Doxycycline should not be given to people with known liver disease. You should avoid taking high doses of Doxycycline therapy if you will be exposed to sunlight for a long period because this antibiotic may interfere with your body's normal sun-screening mechanism, possibly causing severe sunburn. If you have a known history of allergy to Doxycycline you should avoid taking this drug or other drugs within this category such as Aureomycin, Terramycin, Rondomycin, Vibramycin, Demeclocycline, Tetracycline, and Minocycline.

Pregnancy/Breast-feeding

You should not use Doxycycline if you are pregnant. Doxycycline is not recommended for use during the last half of pregnancy or during breast-feeding, when the infant's bones and teeth are being formed.

Nursing mothers should not take this medication.

Seniors

This drug may be taken without special precautions.

Possible Side Effects

As with other antibiotics, the common side effects of Doxycycline are stomach upset, nausea, vomiting, diarrhea, and rash. Less common side effects include hairy tongue and itching and irritation of the anal and/or vaginal region. If these symptoms appear, consult your physician immediately. Periodic physical examinations and laboratory tests should be given to patients who are on long-term Doxycycline.

Less common side effects: loss of appetite, peeling of the skin, sensitivity to the sun, fever, chills, anemia, possible brown spotting of the skin, decrease in kidney function, damage to the liver.

Drug Interactions

Doxycycline (a bacteriostatic drug) may interfere with the action of bactericidal agents such as Penicillin. It is not advisable to take both.

Don't take multivitamin products containing minerals at the same time as Doxycycline, or you will reduce the antibiotic's effectiveness. Space the taking of these two medicines at least 2 hours apart.

People receiving anticoagulation therapy (blood-thinning agents) should consult their doctor, since Doxycycline will interfere with this form of therapy. An adjustment in the anticoagulant dosage may be required.

Anticonvulsant drugs such as Carbamazepine, Phenytoin, and barbiturates may increase the elimination of Doxycycline from the body, requiring higher or more frequent doses of the antibiotic.

Food Interactions

You may take Doxycycline with food or milk to reduce stomach upset.

Usual Dose

Adult and child (101 pounds and over): first day, 200 milligrams given as 100 milligrams every 12 hours. Maintenance, 100 milligrams per day in 1 to 2 doses. The maintenance dose may be doubled for severe infections.

Child (under 101 pounds): first day, 2 milligrams per pound of body weight divided in 2 doses. Maintenance, 1 milligram per pound as a single daily dose. Double the maintenance dose for severe infections.

Gonorrhea: 300 milligrams in one dose and then a second 300-milligram dose in 1 hour.

Syphilis: 300 milligrams a day for not less than 10 days.

An increased incidence of side effects is observed if the dose is over 200 milligrams per day.

Special Information

Do not take after the expiration date on the label.

Doxycycline can be stored at room temperature.

If you forget a dose of Doxycycline, take it as soon as possible. Space the next 2 doses 10 to 12 hours apart if you usually take it once a day and then go back to your regular schedule. If you take the medicine twice a day, space the next 2 doses 5 to 6 hours apart, then go back to your regular schedule.

Brand Name

Drixoral

Ingredients

Dexbrompheniramine Maleate
Pseudoephedrine Sulfate

Other Brand Names

Bromfed   Disobrom
Brompheril   Disophrol/Chronotabs

(Also available in generic form)

Type of Drug

Combination antihistamine–decongestant.

Prescribed for

Relief of sneezing, runny nose, and nasal congestion associated with the common cold, allergy, or other upper respiratory condition.

General Information

Drixoral is one of many products marketed to relieve the symptoms of the common cold. Most of these products contain ingredients to relieve nasal congestion or to dry up runny noses or relieve a scratchy throat; and several of them may contain ingredients to suppress cough, or to help eliminate unwanted mucus. All these products are good only for the relief of symptoms and do not treat the underlying problem, such as a cold virus or other infections. Drixoral tablets are a long-acting preparation, while the syrup is not.

Cautions and Warnings

This drug can cause you to become overly anxious and nervous and may interfere with your sleep. It should be avoided if you have diabetes, heart disease, high blood pressure, thyroid disease, glaucoma, or a prostate condition.

Pregnancy/Breast-feeding

This drug crosses into the blood circulation of a developing

baby. It has not been found to cause birth defects. Pregnant women, or those who might become pregnant while taking this drug, should not take it without their doctor's approval. When the drug is considered essential by your doctor, the potential risk of taking the medicine must be carefully weighed against the benefit it might produce.

This drug passes into breast milk, but has caused no problems among breast-fed infants. You must consider the potential effect on the nursing infant if breast-feeding while taking this medicine.

Seniors

Older adults are more sensitive to the effects of this drug. Follow your doctor's directions and report any side effects at once.

Possible Side Effects

Mild drowsiness has been seen in patients taking Drixoral.

Infrequent: restlessness, tension, nervousness, tremor, weakness, inability to sleep, headache, palpitations, elevation of blood pressure, sweating, sleeplessness, loss of appetite, nausea, vomiting, dizziness, constipation.

Drug Interactions

Interaction with alcoholic beverages may cause excessive drowsiness and/or sleepiness, or inability to concentrate. Also avoid sedatives, tranquilizers, antihistamines, sleeping pills, thyroid medicine, or antihypertensive drugs such as Reserpine or Guanethidine.

Do not self-medicate with over-the-counter drugs for the relief of cold symptoms: taking Drixoral with such drugs may aggravate high blood pressure, heart disease, diabetes, or thyroid disease.

Do not take Drixoral if you are taking or suspect you may be taking a monoamine oxidase (MAO) inhibitor; severe elevation in blood pressure may result.

Food Interactions

If this drug upsets your stomach it should be taken with food.

Usual Dose

Tablet:

Adult and child (age 12 and over): 1 tablet morning and night.

Child (under age 12): not recommended.

Liquid:

Adult and child (age 12 and over): 2 teaspoons every 4 to 6 hours.

Child (under age 12): not recommended.

Special Information

Since drowsiness may occur during use of Drixoral, be cautious while performing mechanical tasks requiring alertness.

If you forget to take a dose of Drixoral, take it as soon as you remember. If it is almost time for your next regularly scheduled dose, skip the one you forgot and continue with your regular schedule. Do not take a double dose.

Generic Name

Dronabinol

Brand Name

Marinol

Type of Drug

Antinauseant.

Prescribed for

Relief of nausea and vomiting associated with cancer chemotherapy. Has been studied as a treatment for glaucoma.

General Information

Dronabinol is the first legal form of marijuana available to the American public. The psychoactive chemical ingredient in marijuana, it is also known as delta-9-THC. It has been studied for several years as an antinauseant in people receiving cancer chemotherapy who have not responded to other antinausea drugs. Dronabinol has all of the psychological effects of marijuana and is, therefore, considered to be a highly abusable drug. Its ability to cause personality changes, feelings of detachment, hallucinations, and euphoria has made Dronabinol relatively unacceptable among older adults and others who feel they must be in control of their environment at all times. Younger adults have reported greater success rate with Dronabinol, probably because they are able to tolerate these effects.

Most people start on Dronabinol while in the hospital because the doctor needs to monitor closely their response to the medication and possible adverse effects.

Cautions and Warnings

Dronabinol should not be used to treat nausea and vomiting caused by anything other than cancer chemotherapy. It should not be used by people who are allergic to it, to marijuana, or to sesame oil. Dronabinol has a profound effect on its users' mental status and will impair your ability to operate complex equipment, or engage in any activity that requires intense concentration, sound judgment, and coordination.

Like other abusable drugs, Dronabinol produces a definite set of withdrawal symptoms. Tolerance to the drug's effects develops after a month of use. Withdrawal symptoms can develop within 12 hours of the drug's discontinuation and include restlessness, sleeplessness, and irritability. Within a day after the drug has been stopped, stuffy nose, hot flashes, sweating, loose stools, hiccups, and appetite loss may be evident. The symptoms will subside within 4 days.

Dronabinol should be used with caution by people with a manic-depressive or schizophrenic history because of the possibility that Dronabinol will aggravate the underlying disease.

Dronabinol causes reduced fertility in animal studies and may have a similar effect on women. It may also affect the potency of male sperm, actually reducing the number of sperm produced.

Pregnancy/Breast-feeding

Studies of Dronabinol in pregnant animals taking doses 10 to 400 times the human dose have shown no adverse effects on the developing fetus. However, Dronabinol should not be taken by a pregnant woman unless it is absolutely neces-

sary. Dronabinol passes into breast milk and can affect a
nursing infant. Nursing mothers either should not use the
drug or should change the method of feeding their child.

Seniors

Older adults are more sensitive to the effects of this drug.
Follow your doctor's directions and report any side effects at
once.

Possible Side Effects

Most frequent: drowsiness, a "high" feeling (easy laughing,
elation, and heightened awareness), dizziness, anxiety, muddled thinking, perceptual difficulties, poor coordination, irritability, a weird feeling, depression, weakness, sluggishness,
headache, hallucinations, memory lapse, loss of muscle coordination, unsteadiness, paranoia, depersonalization, disorientation and confusion, rapid heartbeat, dizziness when
rising from a sitting or lying position.

Less common: difficulty talking, flushing of the face, perspiring, nightmares, ringing or buzzing in the ears, speech
slurring, fainting, diarrhea, loss of ability to control bowel
movement, muscle pains.

Drug Interactions

Dronabinol will increase the psychological effects of alcoholic beverages, tranquilizers, sleeping pills, sedatives, and
other depressants. It will also enhance the effects of other
psychoactive drugs.

Usual Dose

5 to 15 milligrams 1 to 3 hours before starting chemotherapy
treatment, repeated every 2 to 4 hours after chemotherapy
has been given, for a total of 4 to 6 doses per day. The daily
dose may be increased up to 30 milligrams a day if needed,
but psychiatric side effects increase dramatically at higher
doses.

Overdosage

Overdosage symptoms can occur at usual doses or at higher
doses taken if the drug is being abused. The primary symptoms of overdosage are the psychiatric symptoms listed

under "Possible Side Effects." No deaths have been caused by either marijuana or Dronabinol. Dronabinol treatment may be restarted at lower doses if other antinauseants are ineffective.

Special Information

Avoid alcoholic beverages, tranquilizers, sleeping pills, and other depressants while taking Dronabinol.

Dronabinol may impair your ability to drive a car, to perform complex tasks, or to operate complex equipment.

Dronabinol can cause acute psychiatric or psychological effects and you should be aware of this possibility while taking the drug. Be sure to remain in close contact with your doctor and call him or her if any such side effects develop.

Dronabinol capsules must be stored in the refrigerator.

If you forget to take a dose of Dronabinol, take it as soon as you remember. If it is almost time for your next regularly scheduled dose, skip the one you forgot and continue with your regular schedule. Do not take a double dose.

Brand Name

Dyazide

Ingredients

Hydrochlorothiazide
Triamterene

Other Brand Name

The following product contains the same ingredients in different concentrations:

Maxzide

(Also available in generic form)

Type of Drug

Diuretic.

Prescribed for

High blood pressure or any condition where it is desirable to eliminate excess water from the body.

General Information

Dyazide is a combination of two diuretics and is a convenient, effective approach for the treatment of diseases where the elimination of excess water is required. One of the ingredients in Dyazide has the ability to hold potassium in the body while producing a diuretic effect. This balances off the other ingredient, Hydrochlorothiazide, which normally causes a loss of body potassium. Combination drugs like Dyazide should only be used when you need the exact amounts of ingredients in the product and when your doctor feels you would benefit from taking fewer pills each day.

Cautions and Warnings

Do not use Dyazide if you have nonfunctioning kidneys, if you may be allergic to this drug or any sulfa drug, or if you have a history of allergy or bronchial asthma.

Do not take any potassium supplements together with Dyazide unless specifically directed to do so by your doctor.

Pregnancy/Breast-feeding

Dyazide may be used to treat specific conditions in pregnant women, but the decision to use this medication by pregnant women should be weighed carefully because the drug may cross the placental barrier into the blood of the unborn child. Dyazide may appear in the breast milk of nursing mothers. Be sure your baby doctor knows you are taking Dyazide.

Seniors

Older adults are more sensitive to the effects of this drug, especially dizziness because of potassium loss. Closely follow your doctor's directions and report any side effects at once.

Possible Side Effects

Loss of appetite, drowsiness, lethargy, headache, gastrointestinal upset, cramping and diarrhea. Less common side effects of Dyazide are rash, mental confusion, fever, feeling of ill health, inability to achieve or maintain erection in males, bright red tongue, burning inflamed feeling in the tongue, headache, tingling in the toes and fingers, restlessness, anemias or other effects on components of the blood, unusual sensitivity to sunlight, dizziness when rising quickly from a sitting position. Dyazide can also produce muscle spasms, gout, weakness, and blurred vision.

Drug Interactions

Dyazide will increase the effect of other blood-pressure-lowering drugs. This is good and is the reason why many people with high blood pressure take more than one medicine.

The possibility of developing imbalances in body fluids (electrolytes) is increased if you take other medications such as Digitalis and adrenal corticosteroids while you are taking Dyazide.

If you are taking an oral antidiabetic drug and begin taking Dyazide, the antidiabetic dose may have to be altered.

Lithium Carbonate should not be taken with Dyazide because the combination may increase the risk of Lithium toxicity.

Avoid over-the-counter cough, cold, or allergy remedies containing stimulant drugs which can aggravate your condition.

Food Interactions

Take this drug with food if it upsets your stomach.

Usual Dose

1 capsule twice per day.

Overdosage

Signs can be tingling in the arms, or legs, weakness, fatigue, changes in your heartbeat, a sickly feeling, dry mouth, restlessness, muscle pains or cramps, urinary difficulty, nausea, or vomiting. Take the overdose victim to a hospital emergency room for treatment at once. ALWAYS bring the prescription bottle and any remaining medicine.

Special Information

Take Dyazide exactly as prescribed. This drug can make you drowsy. Be careful if you drive or operate machinery. Call

your doctor if you develop muscle or stomach cramps, drowsiness, nausea, diarrhea, unusual thirst, headache, rash.

If you forget to take a dose of Dyazide, take it as soon as
you remember. If it is almost time for your next regularly
scheduled dose, skip the one you forgot and continue with
your regular schedule. Do not take a double dose.

Generic Name

Dyphylline

Brand Names

Dilor   Luphylline
Dyphlex   Neothyline

(Also available in generic form)

Type of Drug

Bronchodilator.

Prescribed for

Relief of bronchial asthma and breathing difficulty associated with emphysema, bronchitis, and other diseases.

General Information

Dyphylline is one of several drugs known as xanthine derivatives which are the mainstay of therapy for bronchial asthma
and similar diseases. Other members of this group include
Aminophylline, Oxtriphylline, and Theophylline. Although the
dosage for each of these drugs is different, they all work by
relaxing bronchial muscles and helping reverse spasms in
these muscles.

Timed-release products allow Dyphylline to act continuously throughout the day. This permits you to decrease the
total number of doses to be taken every day.

Cautions and Warnings

Do not take this medicine if you are allergic or sensitive to it
or any other xanthine drug. Dyphylline can aggravate stomach ulcers or heart disease.

Pregnancy/Breast-feeding

Dyphylline passes into the circulation of the developing baby.
It does not cause birth defects but may result in dangerous
drug levels in the infant's bloodstream. Babies born of mothers taking this medication may be nervous, jittery, and irritable, and may gag and vomit when fed. Women who must
use this medication to control asthma or other conditions
should talk with their doctor about the relative risks of using
this medication and the benefits it will produce for them.

Very large quantities of Dyphylline pass into breast milk
and may cause a nursing infant to have difficulty sleeping
and be nervous or irritable. Use an alternative feeding method
if you must take this medicine.

Seniors

Older adults may take longer to clear this drug from their
bodies than younger adults. Older adults with heart failure or
other cardiac conditions, chronic lung disease, a virus infection
with fever, or reduced liver function may require a lower
dosage of this medication to account for the clearance effect.

Possible Side Effects

Nausea, vomiting, stomach pain, diarrhea, irritability, restlessness, difficulty sleeping, excitability, muscle twitching or
spasms, palpitations, abnormal heart rhythms, changes in
heart rate, low blood pressure, rapid breathing, and local
irritation (if the suppository is used).

Infrequent: vomiting blood, fever, headache, dehydration.

Drug Interactions

Taking this drug together with another xanthine drug can
increase side effects. Don't do it unless your doctor has
directed you to.

Theophylline is often taken together with a stimulant like
Ephedrine to treat asthma. Such combinations may result in
excessive stimulation and should only be used if directed by
your doctor.

Erythromycin, flu vaccine, Allopurinol, and Cimetidine will
increase the amount of Dyphylline in your blood and increase the chances for drug side effects. Cigarette or marijuana smoking decreases the effectiveness of Dyphylline.

Food Interactions

This drug is best taken on an empty stomach, 1 hour before or 2 hours after meals. It may be taken with food or meals if it upsets your stomach.

Diet can influence the way this drug works in your body. For example, charcoal-broiled beef may increase the amount of Dyphylline eliminated from your body through the urine. Low-carbohydrate/high-protein diets also produce this effect and may reduce Dyphylline's effectiveness.

Caffeine (another xanthine derivative) may add to drug side effects. Avoid large quantities of caffeine-containing foods including coffee, cola beverages, tea, cocoa, and chocolate.

Usual Dose

Up to 7 milligrams per pound of body weight 4 times a day.

Dyphylline dosage must be tailored to your specific needs and the severity of your disease. The best dose for you is the lowest dose that will control your symptoms.

Overdosage

The first symptoms are loss of appetite, nausea, vomiting, difficulty sleeping, and restlessness, followed by unusual behavior patterns, frequent vomiting, and extreme thirst with delirium, convulsions, and very high temperature. Some overdose victims collapse.

Overdoses of oral tablets or liquid rarely produce serious symptoms. Most often, the overdose victim loses his/her appetite, or experiences nausea, vomiting, and stimulation. Take the victim to a hospital emergency room at once for treatment. ALWAYS bring the medicine bottle with you.

Special Information

If you forget to take a dose of Dyphylline, take it as soon as you remember. If it is almost time for your next regularly scheduled dose, skip the one you forgot and continue with your regular schedule. Do not take a double dose.

Generic Name

Econazole Nitrate

Brand Name

Spectazole

Type of Drug

Antifungal.

Prescribed for

Fungus infections of the skin, including those responsible for athlete's foot and many other common infections.

General information

This drug is similar to another antifungal agent, Miconazole Nitrate. However, unlike Miconazole Nitrate, Econazole Nitrate is available only as a cream for application to the skin. Very small amounts of Econazole Nitrate are absorbed into the bloodstream, but quite a bit of the drug penetrates to the middle and inner layers of the skin, where it can kill fungus organisms that may have penetrated to deeper layers.

Cautions and Warnings

This product is generally safe, but belongs to a family known to cause liver damage. Therefore, the long-term application of this product to large areas of skin might produce an adverse effect on the liver.

Pregnancy/Breast-feeding

When the drug was given by mouth to pregnant animals in doses 10 to 40 times the amount normally applied to the skin, Econazole Nitrate was found to be toxic to the developing fetus. Because of this, Econazole Nitrate should be avoided by women during the first 3 months of pregnancy. It should be used during the last 6 months of pregnancy only if absolutely necessary.

It is not known if Econazole Nitrate passes into human breast milk. However, animals given this drug by mouth did show passage of the drug and its breakdown products into milk. As a precaution, nursing mothers either should not use the drug or should change the method of feeding their children.

Seniors

Older adults may take this medicine without restriction.

Possible Side Effects

Burning, itching, stinging, and redness in the areas to which the cream has been applied.

Usual Dose

Apply enough of the cream to cover affected areas once or twice a day.

Overdosage

This cream should not be swallowed. If it is swallowed, the victim may be nauseated and have an upset stomach. Other possible effects are drowsiness, liver inflammation and damage. Little is known about Econazole Nitrate overdose, and you should call your local poison control center for more information.

Special Information

Clean the affected areas before applying Econazole Nitrate cream, unless otherwise directed by your doctor.

Call your doctor if the affected area burns, stings, or becomes red after using this product.

This product is quite effective and can be expected to relieve symptoms within a day or two after you begin using it. Follow your doctor's directions for the complete 2-to-4-week course of treatment to gain maximum benefit from the product. Stopping it too soon may not completely eliminate the fungus and can lead to a relapse.

If you forget to take a dose of Econazole Nitrate, apply it as soon as you remember. If it is almost time for your next regularly scheduled dose, skip the one you forgot and continue with your regular schedule. Do not apply a double dose.

Generic Name

Enalapril

Brand Name

Vasotec

Type of Drug

Antihypertensive.

Prescribed for

High blood pressure. Low doses may be used to treat mild to moderate blood pressure. This medicine may be taken alone or with a thiazide-type diuretic.

General Information

This medicine belongs to a relatively new class of drugs, ACE inhibitors, which work by preventing the conversion of a potent hormone called Angiotensin I. This directly affects the production of other hormones and enzymes which participate in the regulation of blood pressure. The effect is to lower blood pressure within 1 to 1½ hours after taking the medicine.

Cautions and Warnings

This drug can cause kidney problems, especially loss of protein in the urine. Patients taking Enalapril should have the amount of protein in the urine measured during the first month of treatment and monthly for the next few months. The drug can also cause a reduction in white-blood-cell count, leading to a potential for increased susceptibility to infection. Enalapril should be used with caution by people who have kidney disease or diseases of the immune/collagen system (particularly lupus erythematosus), or who have taken other drugs that affect the white-blood-cell count.

Pregnancy/Breast-feeding

The effect of Enalapril on a developing fetus is not known. Women who are, or might become, pregnant while taking this drug should discuss the matter with their doctor.

It is not known if Enalapril passes into breast milk and if it will affect a nursing infant.

Seniors

Older adults may be *less* sensitive to the blood-pressure-lowering effects of this drug than younger adults. But, they may be *more* sensitive to its side effects. Dosage must be individualized to your needs.

Possible Side Effects

Dizziness, tiredness, headache, diarrhea, rash (usually mild), and cough are the most common side effects.

Less common drug side effects are itching, fever, temporary loss of taste perception, stomach irritation, chest pain, low blood pressure, heart palpitations, difficulty sleeping, tingling in the hands or feet, nausea, vomiting, jaundice and liver damage, excessive sweating, muscle cramps, (male) impotence, and muscle weakness. Some people experience unusual reactions after taking the first dose of the drug which can include facial flushing and swelling, swelling of the arms and legs, and closing of the throat.

Drug Interactions

The blood-pressure-lowering effect of Enalapril is additive with diuretic drugs and the beta blockers. Other drugs that cause rapid drops in blood pressure should be used with extreme caution because of a possible severe drop when taken together with Enalapril.

Enalapril may increase potassium levels in your blood, especially when given with potassium-sparing diuretics and/or potassium supplements.

Food Interactions

This drug is best taken on an empty stomach, usually 1 hour before or 2 hours after a meal.

Usual Dose

2½ to 40 milligrams once a day. Some people may take their total daily dosage in 2 divided doses. People with poor kidney function have to take less medicine to achieve reduced blood pressure.

Overdosage

The primary effect of Enalapril overdosage is a rapid drop in blood pressure, as evidenced by dizziness or fainting. Take the overdose victim to a hospital emergency room immediately. ALWAYS remember to bring the medicine bottle.

Special Information

Call your doctor if you develop fever, sore throat, mouth sores, abnormal heartbeat, chest pain, or if you have a persistent rash or loss of taste perception.

Enalapril may cause dizziness when quickly rising from a lying or sitting position.

Avoid strenuous exercise and/or very hot weather as heavy sweating and/or dehydration can cause a rapid drop in blood pressure.

Do not stop taking this medicine without your doctor's knowledge.

Avoid nonprescription medicines such as diet pills, decongestants, and stimulants that can raise your blood pressure.

If you forget to take a dose of Enalapril, take it as soon as you remember. If it is almost time for your next regularly scheduled dose, skip the one you forgot and continue with your regular schedule. Do not take a double dose.

Generic Name

Encainide

Brand Name

Enkaid

Type of Drug

Antiarrhythmic.

Prescribed for

Abnormal heart rhythms.

General Information

Encainide is one of the newest antiarrhythmic drugs to be approved for use in the United States. It is prescribed for situations where the abnormal rhythm is so severe as to be life threatening and does not respond to other drug treatments. Encainide works by affecting the movement of nervous impulses within the heart. It produces a proportionally greater effect in areas of the heart that are oxygen starved than in normal cells. This effect could equalize the function of these two kinds of cells, treating abnormal rhythms that commonly develop in oxygen-starved tissues.

Encainide's effects may not become apparent for 3 to 5 days after you start taking it. Since Encainide therapy is often started while you are in the hospital, especially if you are being switched from another antiarrhythmic drug to Encainide, your doctor will be able to closely monitor how well the drug is working for you.

Cautions and Warnings

Do not take Encainide if you are allergic or sensitive to it or if you have heart block.

Encainide can cause new arrhythmias or worsen others that already exist in people taking this drug. The chance of Encainide causing or worsening arrhythmias increases with certain kinds of underlying heart disease and an increasing dose of the drug. Occasionally, Encainide will worsen heart failure in people taking the drug because it tends to reduce the force and rate of each heartbeat.

Abnormal blood potassium (either high or low) can alter the effects of Encainide. Your doctor should be sure that your blood potassium remains in the normal range while you are taking Encainide.

Encainide and the products of Encainide metabolism in the body are released through the kidneys. People with reduced kidney function will experience toxic drug effects unless their dosage is altered to account for their poor kidney function. Reduced liver function affects the body's ability to break down Encainide. Your dose of Encainide may have to be altered, but the exact amount of dosage adjustment must be individualized to each person's situation.

Pregnancy/Breast-feeding

It is not known if Encainide passes into the blood circulation of a developing baby. Pregnant women should carefully review the benefits to be obtained by taking this drug, and the potential dangers, with their doctor.

Encainide passes into mother's milk, but it is not known if

this will be harmful to a nursing infant. Nursing others who must take this drug should use bottle-feeding to avoid any possible complications in their babies.

Seniors

Older adults with poor kidney function are more likely to develop drug side effects and require a lower dosage than people with normal kidneys.

Possible Side Effects

The most common side effects of Encainide are dizziness, vision disturbances, and headache. In studies of this drug, only 7 percent of people taking Encainide developed a drug side effect.

Less common side effects are weakness and tiredness, chest pain, pains in the arms or legs, tingling in the hands or feet, heart failure, palpitations, bloating, worsening of some abnormal heart rhythms, fainting, constipation, abdominal pain, diarrhea, dry mouth, upset stomach, nausea, vomiting, loss of appetite, sleeplessness, nervousness, tremors, coughing, difficulty breathing, skin rash, taste changes, ringing or buzzing in the ears.

Rare side effects include a sickly feeling, blood pressure changes, confusion, muscle weakness, changes in your walk, nightmares, unusual sensations or feelings, double vision, unusual sensitivity to bright lights, and swelling around the eyes.

Drug Interactions

Cimetidine increases the amount of Encainide in the bloodstream by reducing the liver's ability to break down the drug. This combination should be used with caution.

Food Interactions

Encainide should be taken on an empty stomach, but can be taken with food or meals if it upsets your stomach. Food delays the absorption of Encainide into your bloodstream but does not affect the total amount your body absorbs.

Usual Dose

The usual starting dose is 25 milligrams every 8 hours. Your dose can be increased to 35 milligrams and then 50 milligrams every 8 hours, but increases should be spaced by at least 3 to 5 days. The maximum dose of Encainide depends on your response to the drug, your kidney function, and the specific arrhythmia being treated, but can go up to 300 milligrams a day. People who take 50 milligrams or less a day may be able to take Encainide only twice a day.

Overdosage

The effects of Encainide overdosage are low blood pressure and changes in heart function. Victims of Encainide overdose may die from this drug and should be taken to a hospital emergency room for treatment. ALWAYS remember to bring the medicine bottle with you.

Special Information

Encainide can make you dizzy, light-headed, or disoriented. Take care while driving a car or performing any complex tasks.

Call your doctor if you develop chest pains, an abnormal heartbeat, difficulty breathing, bloating in your feet or legs, tremors, fever, chills, sore throat, unusual bleeding or bruising, or any other unusual side effect.

If you forget to take a dose of Encainide and remember within 4 hours, take it as soon as possible. If you don't remember until later, skip the forgotten dose and continue with your regular schedule. Call your doctor if you forget 2 or more doses in a row. Do not take a double dose of Encainide.

Brand Name
Entex LA

Ingredients
Guaifenesin
Phenylpropanolamine

Other Brand Names
Dura-Vent
Rymed TR
Utex S/R

The following product contains the same ingredients in different concentrations and can be bought without a prescription:

Head and Chest

Type of Drug

Decongestant-expectorant combination.

Prescribed for

Relief of some symptoms of the common cold, allergy, or other upper respiratory condition, including nasal congestion and stuffiness and runny nose. The ingredient Guiafenesin is supposed to help loosen thick mucus that may contribute to your feeling of chest congestion. But the effectiveness of this and other expectorant drugs has not been established.

General Information

Entex LA and its generic equivalent products are only a few of the several hundred cold and allergy remedies available on both a prescription-only and a nonprescription basis. There are a variety of different formulas employed in these products, such as the combination used in Entex LA. The decongestant ingredient, Phenylpropanolamine, will produce the most dramatic effect in reducing congestion and stuffiness. The expectorant, Guiafenesin, may help relieve chest congestion. There are other products using this same general formula, an expectorant plus a decongestant, on the market, but they use different decongestants or a combination of decongestants in combination with the expectorant Guiafenesin.

These products should not be used over extended periods to treat a persistent or chronic cough, especially one that may be caused by cigarette smoking, asthma, or emphysema. Information on other decongestant-expectorant combinations can be obtained from your pharmacist.

Since nothing can cure a cold or an allergy, the best you can hope to achieve from taking this or any other cold or allergy remedy is symptom relief.

Cautions and Warnings

Entex LA can cause you to become overly anxious and nervous and may interfere with your sleep.

Do not use these products if you have diabetes, heart disease, high blood pressure, thyroid disease, glaucoma, or a prostate condition.

Pregnancy/Breast-feeding

Entex LA should be avoided by pregnant women or women who may become pregnant while using it. Discuss the potential risks with your doctor.

Nursing mothers must observe for any possible drug effects on their infants while taking Entex LA, since the decongestant Phenylpropanolamine may pass into breast milk.

Seniors

Older adults are more sensitive to the effects of this drug. Follow your doctor's directions and report any side effects at once.

Possible Side Effects

Fear, anxiety, restlessness, sleeplessness, tenseness, excitation, nervousness, dizziness, drowsiness, headaches, tremors, hallucinations, psychological disturbances, and convulsions.

Less common: nausea, vomiting, upset stomach, low blood pressure, heart palpitations, chest pain, rapid heartbeat, abnormal heart rhythms, irritability, feeling "high," eye irritation and tearing, hysterical reactions, reduced appetite, difficulty urinating in men with a prostate condition, weakness, loss of facial color, and breathing difficulty.

Drug Interactions

This product should be avoided if you are taking an MAO inhibitor for depression or high blood pressure because the MAO inhibitor may cause a very rapid rise in blood pressure or increase some side effects (dry mouth and nose, blurred vision, abnormal heart rhythms).

The decongestant portion of this product may interfere with the normal effects of blood-pressure-lowering medicines. It can also aggravate diabetes, heart disease, hyperthyroid disease, high blood pressure, a prostate condition, stomach ulcers, and urinary blockage.

Food Interactions

Take this medicine with food if it causes an upset stomach.

Usual Dose

1 tablet (Entex LA) or capsule (Dura-Vent) 2 times per day.

Overdosage

The main symptoms of overdose are sedation, sleepiness, sweating, and increased blood pressure. Hallucinations, convulsions, and nervous-system depression are particularly prominent in older adults, and breathing may become more difficult. Most cases of overdose are not severe. Patients taking an overdose of this drug must be made to vomit with Syrup of Ipecac (available at any pharmacy) to remove any remaining drug from the stomach. Call your doctor or a poison control center before doing this. If you must go to a hospital emergency room, ALWAYS bring the medicine bottle.

Special Information

Call your doctor if your side effects are severe or gradually become intolerable.

If you forget to take a dose of Entex LA, take it as soon as you remember. If it is almost time for your next regularly scheduled dose, skip the one you forgot and continue with your regular schedule. Do not take a double dose.

Brand Name

Equagesic

Ingredients

Aspirin
Meprobamate

Other Brand Names

Epromate   Meprogesic-Q
Equazine-M   Micrainin

(Also available in generic form)

Type of Drug

Analgesic combination.

Prescribed for

Pain relief in patients who suffer muscle spasms, sprains, strains, or bad backs.

General Information

Equagesic is a combination product containing a tranquilizer and Aspirin; it is used for the relief of pain associated with muscle spasms. The tranquilizer (Meprobamate) in this combination opens it to many drug interactions, especially with other tranquilizers or depressant drugs, which can result in habituation and possible drug dependence. Equagesic may be effective in providing temporary relief from pain and muscle spasm. If you are taking Equagesic, you must follow any other instructions your doctor gives you to help treat the basic problem.

Cautions and Warnings

Do not take Equagesic if you are allergic to any of the ingredients contained in it.

Pregnancy/Breast-feeding

This drug crosses into the blood circulation of a developing baby. It has not been found to cause birth defects, although Meprobamate, an ingredient in Equagesic, increases the chance of birth defects if taken during the first 3 months of pregnancy. Pregnant women, or those who might become pregnant while taking this drug, should not take it without their doctor's approval. When the drug is considered essential by your doctor, the potential risk of taking the medicine must be carefully weighed against the benefit it might produce.

This drug passes into breast milk, but has caused no problems among breast-fed infants. You must consider the potential effect on the nursing infant if breast-feeding while taking this medicine.

Seniors

Older adults are more sensitive to the effects of Equagesic. Follow your doctor's directions and report any side effects at once.

Possible Side Effects

Most frequent: nausea, vomiting, stomach upset, dizziness,

drowsiness. Less frequent: allergy, itching, rash, fever, fluid in the arms and/or legs, occasional fainting spells, spasms of bronchial muscles leading to difficulty in breathing.

Less common: People taking Equagesic have occasionally experienced effects on components of the blood system. Equagesic has also caused blurred vision.

Drug Interactions

Meprobamate may cause sleepiness, drowsiness, or, in high doses, difficulty in breathing. Avoid interaction with other drugs that produce the same effect, for example, barbiturates, narcotics, tranquilizers, sleeping pills, and some antihistamines. Do not drink alcoholic beverages with Equagesic, because the depressive effect of the alcohol will be increased.

If you are taking an anticoagulant (blood-thinning medication) and have been given a new prescription for Equagesic, be sure that your doctor is aware that there is Aspirin in Equagesic. Aspirin affects the ability of your blood to clot and can necessitate a change in the dose of your anticoagulant.

Food Interactions

If you experience stomach upset with Equagesic, take each dose with food or water.

Usual Dose

1 or 2 tablets 3 to 4 times per day as needed for the relief of pain associated with skeletal muscle spasms.

Overdosage

Equagesic overdoses are serious. Symptoms are drowsiness, feeling of light-headedness, desire to go to sleep, nausea, and vomiting. The patient should be taken to a hospital emergency room immediately. ALWAYS bring the medicine bottle.

Special Information

If you forget to take a dose of Equagesic, take it as soon as you remember. If it is almost time for your next regularly scheduled dose, skip the one you forgot and continue with your regular schedule. Do not take a double dose.

Generic Name

Ergoloid Mesylates

Brand Names

Deapril-ST	Hydergine-LC
Gerimal	Hydroloid-G
Hydergine	Niloric

(Also available in generic form)

Type of Drug

Psychotherapeutic.

Prescribed for

Alzheimer's disease; depression, confusion, forgetfulness, antisocial behavior, and dizziness in the elderly.

General Information

Ergoloid Mesylates has improved the supply of blood to the brain in test animals and reduces heart rate and muscle tone in blood vessels. Some studies have shown the drug to be very effective in relieving mild symptoms of mental impairment, while others have found it to be only moderately effective. It has been most beneficial in patients whose symptoms are due to the effects of high blood pressure in the brain.

Cautions and Warnings

Do not use this drug if you are allergic or sensitive to Ergoloid Mesylates or any of its derivatives.

Pregnancy/Breast-feeding

This drug may interfere with your baby's development. Check with your doctor before taking it if you are or might be pregnant.

Seniors

Older adults are more likely to develop some drug side effects, especially low body temperature (hypothermia).

Possible Side Effects

Ergoloid Mesylates does not produce serious side effects. Since some forms of this drug are taken under the tongue, you may experience some irritation, nausea, or stomach upset. Some other side effects are drowsiness, slow heartbeat, and rash.

Usual Dose

1 milligram 3 times a day.

Overdosage

Symptoms are blurred vision, dizziness, fainting, flushing, headache, loss of appetite, nausea, vomiting, stomach cramps, stuffed nose. Take the victim to a hospital emergency room for treatment. ALWAYS remember to take the medicine bottle with you.

Special Information

The results of this drug are gradual. Frequently they are not seen for 3 to 4 weeks.

Dissolve sublingual tablets under the tongue: they are not effective if swallowed whole.

If you forget to take a dose of Ergoloid Mesylates, do not take the forgotten dose. Skip the dose and go back to your regular schedule. Do not take a double dose. Call your doctor if you forget to take your medicine for 2 or more days.

Generic Name

Erythromycin

Brand Names

E.E.S.	Erythromycin Ethyl-succinate
E.E.S. 400	Erythromycin Stearate
E-Mycin	Ethril
E-Mycin E	Ilosone
Eramycin	Ilotycin
ERYC	PCE
Erypar	Pediamycin
EryPed	Pfizer-E
Ery-Tab	Robimycin
Erythrocin	Wyamycin
Erythromycin Base	Wyamycin E
Erythromycin Estolate	

(Also available in generic form)

Other Preparations

Ak-Mycin
Eye Ointment
Topical Ointment

Topical Solutions

Akne-Mycin	Erymax
A/T/S	E-Solve
C-Solve 2	GTS
Erycette	Staticin
Eryderm	T-Stat

Type of Drug

Bacteriostatic antibiotic, effective against gram-positive organisms such as streptococcus, staphylococcus, and gonococcus.

Prescribed for

Infections of the upper and lower respiratory tract; infections of the mouth, gums, and teeth; infections of the nose, ears, and sinuses. May be used for mild to moderate skin infections, but is not considered the antibiotic of choice. Can also be effective against amoebas of the intestinal tract, which cause amoebic dysentery and legionnaire's disease.

Erythromycin is a relatively safe antibiotic. It is used instead of Penicillin for mild to moderate infections in people who are allergic to the penicillin class of antibiotics.

Erythromycin eye ointment is used to prevent newborn gonococcal or chlamydial infections of the eye. Erythromycin topical solution and ointment are used to control acne.

Note: Erythromycin is not the antibiotic of choice for severe infections.

General Information

Erythromycin works by interfering with the normal growth cycle of the invading bacteria, preventing them from reproducing and thus allowing the body's normal defenses to fight off the infection. This process is referred to as bacteriostatic action.

Erythromycin is absorbed from the gastrointestinal tract, but it is deactivated by the acid content of the stomach. Because of this, the tablet form of this drug is formulated in such a way as to bypass the stomach and dissolve in the intestine.

Erythromycin is used primarily for infections of the mouth, nose, ears, sinuses, throat, and lungs. It can also be used to treat venereal disease and pelvic inflammatory disease in people who have allergies and/or sensitivity to the penicillin class of antibiotics.

Because the action of this antibiotic depends on its concentration within the invading bacteria, it is imperative that you follow the doctor's directions regarding the spacing of the doses as well as the number of days you should continue taking the medication. The effect of the antibiotic is severely reduced if these instructions are not followed.

Cautions and Warnings

Erythromycin is excreted primarily through the liver. People with liver disease or damage should exercise caution. Those on long-term therapy with Erythromycin are advised to have periodic blood tests.

Erythromycin is available in a variety of formulations. One formula, Erythromycin Estolate, has occasionally produced fatigue, nausea, vomiting, abdominal cramps, and fever. If you are susceptible to stomach problems, Erythromycin may cause mild to moderate stomach upset. Discontinuing the drug will reverse this condition.

Pregnancy/Breast-feeding

Pregnant and breast-feeding women may use this product with no restriction.

Seniors

Older adults may use this product with no restriction.

Possible Side Effects

Most common: nausea, vomiting, stomach cramps, diarrhea. Less common: hairy tongue, itching, irritation of the anal and/or vaginal region. If any of these symptoms appear, consult your physician immediately.

Erythromycin should not be given to people with known sensitivity to this antibiotic. It may cause a yellowing of the skin and eyes. If this occurs, discontinue the drug and notify your doctor immediately.

Drug Interactions

Erythromycin is relatively free of interactions with other medicines. However, there seems to be a neutralizing effect between it and Lincomycin and Clindamycin. Erythromycin interferes with the elimination of Theophylline from the body. This may cause toxic effects of Theophylline overdose.

Food Interactions

Food in the stomach will decrease the absorption rate of some Erythromycin products. In general, Erythromycin is best taken on an empty stomach.

Usual Dose

Adult: 250 to 500 milligrams every 6 hours.

Child: 50 to 200 milligrams per pound of body weight per day in divided doses, depending upon age, weight, and severity of infection.

Take 1 hour before or 2 hours after meals.

Eye ointment: ½-inch ribbon, 2 to 3 times per day.

Topical solution: Apply morning and night.

Doses of E.E.S., Pediamycin, and Wyamycin are 60 percent higher, due to different chemical composition of the Erythromycin formulation.

Special Information

Erythromycin products should be stored at room temperature, except for oral liquids and topical liquids. These should be kept in the refrigerator.

If you forget a dose of oral Erythromycin, take it as soon as you remember. If it is almost time for your next dose, space the next 2 doses over 4 to 6 hours, then go back to your regular schedule.

Generic Name

Ethacrynic Acid

Brand Name

Edecrin

Type of Drug

Diuretic.

Prescribed for

Congestive heart failure, cirrhosis of the liver, kidney dysfunction, high blood pressure, and other conditions where it may be desirable to rid the body of excess fluid.

General Information

Ethacrynic Acid is a potent diuretic that works in the same way as Furosemide and Bumetanide. Not only do these drugs affect the same part of the kidney as the more commonly used thiazide-type diuretics, they also affect the portion of the kidney known as the Loop of Henle. This double action makes Ethacrynic Acid and the other "loop" diuretics extremely potent drugs. All three "loop" diuretics can be used for the same purposes, but their doses are quite different.

Cautions and Warnings

Excessive quantities of Ethacrynic Acid can lead to dehydration and severe imbalance in your body levels of potassium, sodium, and chloride. Warning signs of dehydration are dry mouth, excessive thirst, loss of appetite, weakness, lethargy, drowsiness, restlessness, tingling in the hands or feet, muscle weakness, pain or cramps, low blood pressure, reduced urine volume, rapid heartbeat, abnormal heart rhythms, nausea, and vomiting.

Do not use Ethacrynic Acid if you have had an allergic reaction to it in the past. People who are allergic to or cannot tolerate Ethacrynic Acid may receive a prescription for Bumetanide as an alternative diuretic.

People with severe kidney or liver disease who take this medicine should maintain close contact with their doctor because the drug can accentuate some conditions affecting these organs.

Pregnancy/Breast-feeding

Ethacrynic Acid is not recommended during pregnancy because it may cause abnormalities in the developing baby. Pregnant women who require a potent diuretic may be given Furosemide or Bumetanide, but only under their doctor's supervision. It is not known if Ethacrynic Acid passes into breast milk. Nursing mothers who take this drug must watch for any possible drug effects on their infants while taking this medication; however, it is recommended that women taking Ethacrynic Acid use alternative feeding methods.

Seniors

Older adults may be more sensitive to Ethacrynic Acid side effects than younger adults and should be treated with doses at the low end of the recommended range.

Possible Side Effects

Loss of appetite, nausea, vomiting, diarrhea, inflammation of the pancreas, yellowing of the skin or whites of the eyes, dizziness, headaches, blurred vision, ringing or buzzing in the ears, reduction of blood-platelet and white-blood-cell levels.

Less common side effects: Ethacrynic Acid may worsen

liver or kidney disease, cause abdominal pains, dry mouth, impotence, muscle weakness or cramps, arthritislike pains in the joints, low blood pressure, changes in heart rhythm, and chest pains. The "loop" diuretics have been associated with a sense of fullness in the ears, diminished hearing, and hearing loss. But these side effects are rare and usually only follow rapid intravenous injection of these drugs.

Drug Interactions

Ethacrynic Acid may increase the effects of blood-pressure-lowering drugs. This is a beneficial interaction that doctors may use in treating high blood pressure. It increases the side effects of Lithium by interfering with the elimination of that drug from the body.

Alcohol, barbiturate-type sleeping pills, and narcotic pain relievers can cause excessive low blood pressure when taken with potent diuretics like Ethacrynic Acid.

The possibility of losing body potassium with Ethacrynic Acid is accentuated by combining it with Digoxin (for the heart) and the adrenal corticosteroids (for inflammation). Also, potassium loss increases the chances of Digoxin side effects.

Probenecid reduces the effectiveness of Ethacrynic Acid by interfering with its action on the kidneys. Indomethacin and other nonsteroid anti-inflammatory drugs like Naproxen, Sulindac, and Ibuprofen may also reduce Ethacrynic Acid effectiveness.

People taking Ethacrynic Acid for high blood pressure or heart failure should take care to avoid nonprescription medicines that might aggravate their condition such as decongestants, cold and allergy treatments, and diet pills, all of which can contain stimulants. If you are unsure about which medicine to choose, ask your pharmacist.

Food Interactions

Ethacrynic Acid may cause loss of body potassium (hypokalemia), a complication that can be avoided by adding foods rich in potassium to your diet. Some potassium-rich foods are tomatoes, citrus fruits, melons, and bananas. Hypokalemia can also be prevented by taking a potassium supplement in pill, powder, or liquid form. This product may be taken with food or meals if it upsets your stomach.

Usual Dose

Adults: 50 to 200 milligrams taken every day or every other day.

Child: starting dose, 25 milligrams. Increase slowly.

Overdosage

The major symptoms of overdose are related to the potent diuretic effect of Ethacrynic Acid: lethargy, weakness, dizziness, confusion, cramps, loss of appetite, and vomiting. Victims of Ethacrynic Acid overdose should be taken to a hospital emergency room for treatment. ALWAYS remember to bring the medicine bottle with you.

Special Information

Take your daily dose no later than 10 A.M.. If taken later in the day, this potent diuretic could interfere with your sleep by keeping you up to go to the bathroom.

Call your doctor if any warning signs of dehydration develop while you are taking Ethacrynic Acid. They are dry mouth, excessive thirst, loss of appetite, weakness, lethargy, drowsiness, restlessness, tingling in the hands or feet, muscle weakness, pain, or cramps, low blood pressure, reduced urinary volume, rapid heartbeat, abnormal heart rhythms, nausea, and vomiting.

If you forget to take a dose of Ethacrynic Acid, take it as soon as you remember. If it is almost time for your next regularly scheduled dose, skip the one you forgot and continue with your regular schedule. Do not take a double dose.

Generic Name

Ethosuximide

Brand Name

Zarontin

Type of Drug

Anticonvulsant.

Prescribed for

Control of petit mal seizures.

General Information

Ethosuximide and the other succinimide-type anticonvulsants control petit mal seizures (sometimes known as absence seizures) by slowing the transmission of impulses through certain areas of the brain. The succinimides are first choice of treatment for this type of seizure, which may then be treated by Clonazepam if the succinimides are not sufficient.

Cautions and Warnings

Ethosuximide may be associated with severe reductions in white-blood-cell and platelet counts. Your doctor should perform periodic blood counts while you are taking this medicine.

In patients with grand mal and petit mal, succinimide-type anticonvulsants, when used alone, may increase the number of grand mal seizures, necessitating more medicine to control those seizures.

Abrupt withdrawal of any anticonvulsant may lead to severe seizures. It is important that your dosage be gradually reduced by your doctor.

Pregnancy/Breast-feeding

This drug should be avoided by women who may become pregnant while using it and by pregnant and nursing mothers, since it will cross into the developing infant, and possible adverse effects on the infant are not known. In those situations where it is deemed essential, the potential risk of the drug must be carefully weighed against any benefit it might produce.

Recent reports suggest a strong association between the use of anticonvulsant drugs and birth defects. Although most of the information pertains to Phenytoin and Phenobarbital, not Ethosuximide, other reports indicate a general association between all anticonvulsant-drug treatments and birth defects. It is possible that the epileptic condition itself or genetic factors common to people with seizure disorders may also figure in the higher incidence of birth defects. Mothers taking Ethosuximide should not breast-feed because of the possibility that the drug will pass into their breast milk and affect the baby. Use an alternative feeding method.

Seniors

Older adults may take this drug without restriction. Be sure to follow your doctor's directions.

Possible Side Effects

Nausea, vomiting, upset stomach, stomach cramps and pain, loss of appetite, diarrhea, constipation, weight loss, drowsiness, dizziness, and poor muscle control.

Less common: reductions in white-blood-cell and platelet counts, nervousness, hyperactivity, sleeplessness, irritability, headache, blurred vision, unusual sensitivity to bright lights, hiccups, a euphoric feeling, a dreamlike state, lack of energy, fatigue, confusion, mental instability, mental slowness, depression, sleep disturbances, nightmares, loss of the ability to concentrate, aggressiveness, constant concern with well-being and health, paranoid psychosis, suicidal tendencies, increased sex drive, rash, itching, frequent urination, kidney damage, blood in the urine, swelling around the eyes, hair loss, hairiness, muscle weakness, nearsightedness, vaginal bleeding, and swelling of the tongue and/or gums.

Drug Interactions

The depressant effects of Ethosuximide are increased by tranquilizers, sleeping pills, narcotic pain relievers, antihistamines, alcohol, MAO inhibitors, antidepressants, and other anticonvulsants.

Ethosuximide may increase the action of Phenytoin by increasing the blood levels of that drug. Your doctor should be sure that your dosages of the two drugs are appropriate to your condition.

Carbamazepine, another medicine prescribed to treat seizure disorders, may interfere with Ethosuximide action by increasing the rate at which it is removed from the body.

The action of Ethosuximide may be increased by Isoniazid, prescribed to prevent tuberculosis, and by Valproic Acid, another anticonvulsant drug, possibly leading to an increase in drug side effects when both drugs are taken together.

Avoid alcoholic beverages, which increase the depressant effects of this medicine.

Food Interactions

Ethosuximide is best taken on an empty stomach but may be taken with food if it upsets your stomach.

Usual Dose

Adult and child (over age 6): 500 milligrams per day to start.

Child (age 3 to 6): 250 milligrams per day to start.

The dose is increased in steps of 250 milligrams every 4 to 7 days until seizures are controlled or side effects develop. The maximum daily dose is 1500 milligrams.

Dosage adjustments may be required for people with reduced kidney or liver function.

Overdosage

Ethosuximide overdose will cause exaggerated side effects. If the overdose is discovered immediately, it may be helpful to make the victim vomit with Syrup of Ipecac to remove any remaining medicine from the stomach. But all victims of Ethosuximide overdose must be taken to a hospital emergency room for treatment. ALWAYS bring the prescription bottle with you.

Special Information

Call your doctor if side effects become intolerable. Especially important are sore throat, joint pains, unexplained fever, rashes, unusual bleeding or bruising, drowsiness, dizziness, and blurred vision. Be sure to tell your doctor if you become pregnant while taking this medicine.

Ethosuximide may interfere with your ability to drive a car or perform other complex tasks because it can cause drowsiness and difficulty concentrating.

If you forget to take a dose of Ethosuximide and remember within 4 hours, take it as soon as possible. Then go back to your regular schedule. Do not take a double dose.

Your doctor should perform periodic blood counts while you are taking this drug to check for possible adverse drug effects.

Do not suddenly stop taking the medicine, since this can result in severe seizures. The dosage must be discontinued gradually by your doctor.

Carry identification or wear a bracelet indicating that you suffer from a seizure disorder for which you take Ethosuximide.

Generic Name

Famotidine

Brand Name

Pepcid

Type of Drug

Antiulcer, histamine H_2 antagonist.

Prescribed for

Ulcers of the stomach and upper intestine (duodenum). Also prescribed for other conditions characterized by the production of large amounts of gastric fluids.

General Information

Famotidine is the newest histamine H_2 antagonist to be released in the United States. It works against ulcers and other gastrointestinal conditions by actually turning off the system that produces stomach acid.

Cautions and Warnings

Do not take Famotidine if you have had an allergic reaction to it in the past.

Pregnancy/Breast-feeding

Although studies with laboratory animals have revealed no damage to a developing fetus, it is recommended that Famotidine be avoided by pregnant women, or women who might become pregnant while using it. In those situations where it is deemed essential, Famotidine's potential risk must be carefully weighed against any benefit it might produce.

Famotidine may pass into breast milk. Animal studies revealed that nursing infants experienced growth problems. No problems have been identified in nursing human babies, but breast-feeding mothers must consider the possibility of a drug effect while nursing their infants.

Seniors

Older adults respond well to Famotidine but may need less medication than a younger adult to achieve the desired response, since the drug is eliminated through the kidneys and kidney function tends to decline with age. Older adults may be more susceptible to some drug side effects.

Possible Side Effects

The most common side effects of Famotidine are mild diarrhea, dizziness, and constipation.

Less common side effects are anxiety, decrease in sexual drive, headache, drowsiness, dry mouth or skin, joint or muscle pains, loss of appetite, depression, nausea or vomiting, ringing or buzzing in the ears, skin rash or itching, stomach pains, temporary hair loss, changes in taste perception.

Rarely, the medicine has caused fever, swelling of the eyelids, chest tightness, rapid heartbeat, unusual bleeding or bruising, and unusual tiredness or weakness.

Drug Interactions

Enteric-coated tablets should not be taken with Famotidine. The change in stomach acidity will cause the tablets to disintegrate prematurely in the stomach.

Famotidine may inhibit the absorption of Ketoconazole into the bloodstream.

Vitamin B_{12} absorption may be inhibited by Famotidine.

Food Interactions

Famotidine may be taken on an empty stomach or with food or meals. Food may slightly increase the amount of drug absorbed, but this difference is of no consequence.

Usual Dose

The usual adult dosage is either 20 to 40 milligrams at bedtime, or 20 milligrams twice a day.

Overdosage

There is little information on Famotidine overdosage. Overdose victims might be expected to show exaggerated side effect symptoms, but little else is known. Your local poison control center may advise giving the victim Syrup of Ipecac to cause vomiting and remove any remaining drug from the stomach. Victims who have definite symptoms should be taken to a hospital emergency room for observation and possible treatment. ALWAYS remember to bring the prescription bottle with you.

Special Information

You must take this medicine exactly as directed and follow your doctor's instructions for diet and other treatments in order to get the maximum benefit from it. Cigarettes are known to be associated with stomach ulcers and will reverse effect of Famotidine on stomach acid.

Call your doctor at once if any unusual side effects develop. Especially important are unusual bleeding or bruising, unusual tiredness, diarrhea, dizziness, or rash. Black, tarry stools or vomiting "coffee-ground" material may indicate your ulcer is bleeding.

If you forget to take a dose of Famotidine, take it as soon as you remember. If it is almost time for your next regularly scheduled dose, skip the one you forgot and continue with your regular schedule. Do not take a double dose.

Generic Name

Fenoprofen Calcium

Brand Name

Nalfon

Type of Drug

Nonsteroidal anti-inflammatory.

Prescribed for

Relief of pain and inflammation of joints and muscles; arthritis, both rheumatoid and osteoarthritis; mild to moderate pain of menstrual cramps; dental surgery and extractions; and athletic injuries such as sprains and strains.

General Information

Fenoprofen Calcium is one of several nonsteroidal anti-inflammatory drugs (NSAIDs) used to reduce inflammation, relieve pain, or reduce fever. NSAIDs share the same side effects and may be used by patients who cannot tolerate Aspirin. Choice of one of these drugs over another depends on disease response, side effects seen in a particular patient, convenience of times to be taken, and cost. Different drugs or different doses of the same drug may be tried to produce the greatest effectiveness with the fewest side effects.

Cautions and Warnings

Do not take Fenoprofen Calcium if you are allergic or sensitive to this drug, Aspirin, or other NSAIDs. Fenoprofen Calcium may cause stomach ulcers. This drug should not be used by patients with severe kidney disease.

Pregnancy/Breast-feeding

This drug crosses into the blood circulation of a developing baby. It has not been found to cause birth defects. Pregnant women, or those who might become pregnant while taking this drug, should not take it without their doctor's approval. When the drug is considered essential by your doctor, the potential risk of taking the medicine must be carefully weighed against the benefit it might produce.

This drug passes into breast milk, but has caused no problems among breast-fed infants. You must consider the potential effect on the nursing infant if breast-feeding while taking this medicine.

Seniors

Older adults are more sensitive to the stomach, kidney, and liver effects of this drug. Some doctors recommend that persons 70 and older take ½ the usual dose. Follow your doctor's directions and report any side effects at once.

Possible Side Effects

Most frequent: stomach upset, dizziness, headache, drowsiness, ringing in the ears. Others: heartburn, nausea, vomiting, bloating, gas in the stomach, stomach pain, diarrhea, constipation, dark stool, nervousness, insomnia, depression, confusion, tremor, loss of appetite, fatigue, itching, rash, double vision, abnormal heart rhythm, anemia or other changes in the composition of the blood, changes in liver function, loss of hair, tingling in the hands and feet, fever, breast enlargement, lowered blood sugar, effects on the kidneys. If symptoms appear, stop taking the medicine and see your doctor immediately.

Drug Interactions

Fenoprofen Calcium increases the action of Phenytoin, sulfa drugs, drugs used to control diabetes, and drugs used to thin the blood. If you are taking any of these medicines, be sure to discuss it with your doctor, who will probably change the dose of the other drug.

An adjustment in the dose of Fenoprofen Calcium may be needed if you take Phenobarbital.

Food Interactions

Take this medicine with food if it upsets your stomach.

Usual Dose

Adult: 300 to 600 milligrams 4 times per day to start. Mild to moderate pain: 200 milligrams every 4 to 6 hours.
Child: not recommended.
Arthritis: 300 to 600 milligrams 3 to 4 times per day; up to 3200 milligrams per day.

Overdosage

Symptoms may include drowsiness, dizziness, confusion, disorientation, lethargy, tingling in the hands or feet, numbness, nausea, vomiting, upset stomach, stomach pains, headache, ringing or buzzing in the ears, sweating and blurred vision, low blood pressure, and rapid heartbeat. Take the victim to a hospital emergency room at once for treatment. ALWAYS bring the medicine bottle with you.

Special Information

Avoid Aspirin and alcoholic beverages while taking this medication. You may become dizzy or drowsy while taking this medicine. Be careful while driving or operating complex equipment. Call your doctor if you develop a skin rash, itching, swelling, visual disturbances, black stools, or a persistent headache while taking this medication.

If you forget to take a dose of Fenoprofen Calcium, take it as soon as you remember. If it is almost time for your next regularly scheduled dose, skip the one you forgot and continue with your regular schedule. Do not take a double dose.

Generic Name

Ferrous Sulfate

Brand Names

Feosol	Ferralyn Lanacaps
Fer-In-Sol	Ferra TD
Fer Iron	Mol-Iron
Fero-Gradumet	Slow FE
Ferospace	

(Also available in generic form)

Type of Drug

Iron-containing product.

Prescribed for

Iron deficiency of the blood.

General Information

Ferrous Sulfate is used to treat anemias due to iron deficiency. Other anemias will not be affected by this drug. Ferrous Sulfate works by being incorporated into red blood cells where it can help carry oxygen throughout the body. Iron is absorbed only in a small section of the gastrointestinal tract called the duodenum. Sustained-release preparations of iron should only be used to help minimize the stomach discomfort that Ferrous Sulfate can cause, since any drug which passes the duodenum (in the upper part of the small intestine) cannot be absorbed.

Other drugs may also provide a source of iron to treat iron deficiency anemia. The iron in these products may be combined with other vitamins or with special extracts as in the product Triniscon, where iron is combined with Vitamin B_{12}, Folic Acid, and Intrinsic Factor.

Cautions and Warnings

Do not take Ferrous Sulfate if you have a history of stomach upset, peptic ulcer, or ulcerative colitis.

Pregnancy/Breast-feeding

This drug has been found to be safe for use during pregnancy and breast-feeding. Remember, you should check with your doctor before taking any drug if you are pregnant.

Seniors

Older adults may require larger doses than younger adults to correct an iron deficiency since the ability to absorb iron decreases with age.

Possible Side Effects

Stomach upset and irritation, nausea, diarrhea, constipation.

Drug Interactions

Ferrous Sulfate will interfere with absorption of oral Tetracycline. Separate the doses by at least 2 hours.

   Antacids will interfere with the absorption of iron; again, separate doses by 2 hours.

   In either case, avoid taking iron supplements (unless absolutely necessary) until your other medical condition clears up.

Food Interactions

Iron salts and iron-containing products are best absorbed on an empty stomach; but if they upset your stomach, take with meals or immediately after meals.

Usual Dose

1 to 3 tablets per day.

Overdosage

Symptoms appear after 30 minutes to several hours: lethargy (tiredness), vomiting, diarrhea, stomach upset, change in pulse to weak and rapid, and lowered blood pressure—or, after massive doses, shock, black and tarry stools due to massive bleeding in the stomach or intestine, and pneumonia. Quickly induce vomiting and feed the patient eggs and milk until he can be taken to a hospital for stomach pumping. Be sure to call a doctor right away. The patient must be taken to the hospital as soon as possible, since stomach pumping should not be performed after the first hour of iron ingestion because there is a danger of perforation of the stomach wall. In the hospital emergency room measures to treat shock, loss of water, loss of blood, and respiratory failure may be necessary. ALWAYS bring the medicine bottle.

Special Information

Iron salts impart a black color to stools and are slightly constipating. If stools become black and tarry in consistency, however, there may be some bleeding in the stomach or intestine. Discuss it with your doctor.

If you forget to take a dose of Ferrous Sulfate, take it as soon as you remember. If it is almost time for your next regularly scheduled dose, skip the one you forgot and continue with your regular schedule. Do not take a double dose.

Brand Name
Fiorinal

Ingredients

Aspirin
Butalbital
Caffeine

Other Brand Names

Butalbital Compound   Lanorinal
Fiorgen PF   Marnal
Isollyl Improved

(Also available in generic form)

Type of Drug

Nonnarcotic analgesic combination.

Prescribed for

Relief of headache pain or other types of pain.

General Information

Fiorinal is one of many combination products containing barbiturates and analgesics. These products often also contain tranquilizers or narcotics. Products such as Esgic and Fioricet substitute Acetaminophen for Aspirin.

Cautions and Warnings

Fiorinal can cause drug dependence or addiction. Use this drug with caution if you have asthma or problems in breathing. It can affect your ability to drive a car or operate machinery. Do not drink alcoholic beverages while taking Fiorinal. The Aspirin component in this drug can interfere with the normal coagulation of blood. This is especially important if you are taking blood-thinning medication.

Pregnancy/Breast-feeding

There is an increased chance of birth defects while using Fiorinal during pregnancy. Fiorinal may be required to be used if a serious situation arises which threatens the mother's life.

Regularly using Fiorinal during the last 3 months of pregnancy may cause drug dependency of the newborn. Pregnant women using Fiorinal may experience prolonged labor and delayed delivery, and breathing problems may afflict the newborn. If taken during the last 2 weeks of pregnancy, Fiorinal may cause bleeding problems in the newborn child. Problems may also be seen in the mother herself, including bleeding.

Breast-feeding while using Fiorinal may cause increased tiredness, shortness of breath, or a slow heartbeat in the baby.

Caffeine can cause birth defects in animals but has not been shown to cause problems in humans.

Seniors

The Butalbital in this combination product may have more of a depressant effect on seniors than younger adults. Other effects that may be more prominent are dizziness, light-headedness, or fainting when rising suddenly from a sitting or lying position.

Possible Side Effects

Major: light-headedness, dizziness, sedation, nausea, vomiting, sweating, stomach upset, loss of appetite, (possible) mild stimulation.

Less common side effects: weakness, headache, sleeplessness, agitation, tremor, uncoordinated muscle movements, mild hallucinations, disorientation, visual disturbances, feeling high, dry mouth, loss of appetite, constipation, flushing of the face, changes in heart rate, palpitations, faintness, difficulty in urination, skin rashes, itching, confusion, rapid breathing, diarrhea.

Drug Interactions

Interaction with alcohol, tranquilizers, barbiturates, sleeping pills, or other drugs that produce depression can cause tiredness, drowsiness, and inability to concentrate.

Interaction with Prednisone, steroids, Phenylbutazone, or alcohol can irritate your stomach.

The dose of anticoagulant (blood-thinning) drugs will have to be changed by your physician if you begin taking Fiorinal, which contains Aspirin.

Food Interactions

Take with a full glass of water or with food to reduce the possibility of stomach upset.

Usual Dose

1 to 2 tablets or capsules every 4 hours or as needed. Maximum of 6 doses per day.

Overdosage

Symptoms are difficulty in breathing, nervousness progressing to stupor or coma, pinpointed pupils of the eyes, cold clammy skin and lowered heart rate and/or blood pressure, nausea, vomiting, dizziness, ringing in the ears, flushing, sweating and thirst. The patient should be taken to a hospital emergency room immediately. ALWAYS bring the medicine bottle.

Special Information

Drowsiness may occur.

If you forget to take a dose of Fiorinal, take it as soon as you remember. If it is almost time for your next regularly scheduled dose, skip the one you forgot and continue with your regular schedule. Do not take a double dose.

Brand Name

Fiorinal with Codeine

Ingredients

Aspirin   Caffeine
Butalbital   Codeine Phosphate

Other Brand Names

BAC Tablets
Fiorgen with Codeine

(Also available in generic form)

Type of Drug

Narcotic analgesic combination.

Prescribed for

Relief of headache pain or other types of pain.

General Information

Fiorinal with Codeine is one of many combination products containing barbiturates and analgesics. These products often also contain tranquilizers or narcotics, and Acetaminophen may be substituted for Aspirin.

Cautions and Warnings

Fiorinal with Codeine can cause drug dependence or addiction. Use this drug with caution if you have asthma or problems in breathing. It can affect your ability to drive a car or operate machinery.

Pregnancy/Breast-feeding

There is an increased chance of birth defects while using Fiorinal with Codeine during pregnancy. Fiorinal with Codeine may be required to be used if a serious situation arises which threatens the mother's life.

Regularly using Fiorinal with Codeine during the last 3 months of pregnancy may cause drug dependency of the newborn. Pregnant women using Fiorinal with Codeine may experience prolonged labor and delayed delivery, and breathing problems may afflict the newborn. If taken during the last 2 weeks of pregnancy, Fiorinal with Codeine may cause bleeding problems in the newborn child. Problems may also be seen in the mother herself, including bleeding.

Breast-feeding while using Fiorinal with Codeine may cause increased tiredness, shortness of breath, or a slow heartbeat in the baby.

Caffeine can cause birth defects in animals but has not been shown to cause problems in humans.

Codeine can cause addiction in the unborn child if used regularly during pregnancy.

Seniors

The Codeine and Butalbital in this combination product may have more of a depressant effect on seniors than younger adults. Other effects that may be more prominent are dizziness, light-headedness or fainting when rising suddenly from a sitting or lying position.

Possible Side Effects

Major: light-headedness, dizziness, sedation, nausea, vomiting, sweating, stomach upset, loss of appetite, (possible) mild stimulation.

Less common side effects: weakness, headache, sleeplessness, agitation, tremor, uncoordinated muscle movements, mild hallucinations, disorientation, visual disturbances, feeling high, dry mouth, loss of appetite, constipation, flushing of the face, changes in heart rate, palpitations, faintness, difficulty in urination, rashes, itching, confusion, rapid breathing, diarrhea.

Drug Interactions

Interaction with alcohol, tranquilizers, barbiturates, sleeping pills, or other drugs that produce depression can cause tiredness, drowsiness, and inability to concentrate.

Interaction with Prednisone, steroids, Phenylbutazone, or alcohol can irritate your stomach.

The dose of anticoagulant (blood-thinning) drugs will have to be changed by your physician if you begin taking Fiorinal with Codeine, which contains Aspirin.

Food Interactions

Take with a full glass of water or with food to reduce the possibility of stomach upset.

Usual Dose

1 to 2 tablets or capsules every 4 hours or as needed. Maximum of 6 doses per day.

Overdosage

Symptoms are difficulty in breathing, nervousness progressing to stupor or coma, pinpointed pupils of the eyes, cold clammy skin and lowered heart rate and/or blood pressure, nausea, vomiting, dizziness, ringing in the ears, flushing, sweating, and thirst. The patient should be taken to a hospital emergency room immediately. ALWAYS bring the medicine bottle.

Special Information

Drowsiness may occur. If you forget to take a dose of Fiorinal with Codeine, take it as soon as you remember. If it is almost time for your next regularly scheduled dose, skip the one you forgot and continue with your regular schedule. Do not take a double dose.

Generic Name

Flecainide

Brand Name

Tambocor

Type of Drug

Antiarrhythmic.

Prescribed for

Abnormal heart rhythm.

General Information

Flecainide is one of the newer antiarrhythmic drugs to be approved for use in the United States. It is prescribed for situations where the abnormal rhythm is so severe as to be life threatening and does not respond to other drug treatments. Flecainide, like other antiarrhythmic drugs, works by affecting the movement of nervous impulses within the heart.

Flecainide's effects may not become apparent for 3 to 4 days after you start taking it. Since Flecainide therapy is often started while you are in the hospital, especially if you are being switched from another antiarrhythmic drug to Flecainide, your doctor will be able to closely monitor how well the drug is working for you.

Cautions and Warnings

Do not take Flecainide if you are allergic or sensitive to it or if you have heart block.

Flecainide can cause new arrhythmias or worsen others that already exist in 7 percent of people who take this drug. The chance of Flecainide causing or worsening arrhythmias increases with certain kinds of underlying heart disease and an increasing dose of the drug. Flecainide may cause or worsen heart failure in about 5 percent of people taking the drug because it tends to reduce the force and rate of each heartbeat.

Flecainide is broken down extensively in the liver. People with poor liver function should not take Flecainide unless the benefits of taking it clearly outweigh the possible risks of drug toxicity.

Pregnancy/Breast-feeding

Animal studies have shown Flecainide to damage a developing fetus at doses 4 times the normal human dose, although it is not known if Flecainide passes into the blood circulation of a developing baby. Pregnant women should carefully review the benefits to be obtained by taking this drug versus the potential dangers with their doctors. It is not known if Flecainide will affect the labor and delivery process.

It is not known if Flecainide passes into mother's milk. Nursing mothers who must take this drug should use bottle-feeding to avoid any potential complications in their babies.

Seniors

Older adults with reduced kidney and/or liver function are more likely to develop drug side effects and require a lower dosage than people with normal liver and kidneys.

Possible Side Effects

The most common side effects of Flecainide are dizziness, light-headedness, faintness, unsteadiness, visual disturbances W(blurred vision, spots before the eyes), difficulty breathing, headache, nausea, fatigue, heart palpitations, chest pain, tremors, weakness, constipation, bloating, and abdominal pain.

Less common side effects are: new or worsened heart arrhythmias or heart failure, heart block, slowed heart rate, vomiting, diarrhea, upset stomach, loss of appetite, stomach gas, a bad taste in your mouth, dry mouth, tingling in the hands or feet, partial or temporary paralysis, loss of muscle control, flushing, sweating, ringing or buzzing in the ears, anxiety, sleeplessness, depression, feeling sick, twitching, weakness, convulsions, speech disorders, stupor, memory loss, personality loss, nightmares, a feeling of apathy, eye pain, unusual sensitivity to bright light, sagging eyelids, reduced white-blood-cell or blood-platelet counts, male impotence, reduced sex drive, frequent urination, urinary difficulty, itching, rash, fever, swollen lips, tongue, and mouth, muscle aches, closing of the throat.

Drug Interactions

The combination of Propranolol and Flecainide can cause an exaggerated decrease in heart rate. Other drugs that slow the heart may also interact with Flecainide to produce an excessive slowing of heart rate.

The pacing of Flecainide out of your body through the kidneys is affected by the acid nature of your urine. Less acidity increases the amount of drug released and more acidity, such as can occur with megadoses of Vitamin C, decreases the amount you release. Extreme changes in urine acid content can expose you to increased side effects (more acid) or loss of drug effect (less acid).

Food Interactions

Flecainide can be taken without regard to food or meals.

Usual Dose

The usual starting dose for all patients is 100 milligrams every 12 hours. Your doctor can increase your dose by 50 milligrams each time every several days, if needed. The maximum dose of Flecainide depends on your response to the drug, your kidney function, and the specific arrhythmia being treated, but can go up to 600 milligrams a day.

Overdosage

The effects of Flecainide overdosage are changes in heart function. Victims of Flecainide overdose should be taken to a hospital emergency room for treatment. ALWAYS remember to bring the medicine bottle with you.

Special Information

Flecainide can make you dizzy, light-headed, or disoriented. Take care while driving a car or performing any complex tasks.

Call your doctor if you develop chest pains, an abnormal heartbeat, difficulty breathing, bloating in your feet or legs, tremors, fever, chills, sore throat, unusual bleeding or bruising, yellowing of the whites of your eyes, or any other side effect that you feel is intolerable.

If you forget to take a dose of Flecainide and remember within 6 hours, take it as soon as possible. If you don't remember until later, skip the forgotten dose and continue with your regular schedule. Do not take a double dose of Flecainide.

Generic Name

Flunisolide

Brand Names

AeroBid Inhaler
Nasalide Inhaler

Type of Drug

Adrenal corticosteroid.

Prescribed for

Chronic asthma or other respiratory condition. Relieves symptoms of seasonal inflammation of the nasal membranes.

General Information

The Flunisolide used in this product works in the same way as other adrenal corticosteroids applied to the skin or taken by mouth as a tablet. Flunisolide inhaler relieves the symptoms of asthma for people who require regular steroid treatment by mouth. Using the aerosol generally allows a reduction in the oral dose or elimination of oral steroids all together. It works by reducing the inflammation of the mucosal lining within the bronchi, making it easier to breathe. This product should be used only as part of a preventive therapy program. It will not treat an asthma attack. The nasal inhaler acts directly in the nose, reducing inflammation. This relieves the symptoms of seasonal rhinitis.

Cautions and Warnings

Flunisolide oral inhalation should not be used if your asthma can be controlled by other steroid medicines. It is meant only for people taking Prednisone or another steroid by mouth and other asthma medicines but are still not under control. Do not use a Flunisolide inhaler if you are allergic to it or to any other steroid drug. During stressful periods, you may have to go back to taking steroids by mouth if your asthma is not controlled.

Pregnancy/Breast-feeding

Large amounts of Flunisolide used during pregnancy or breast-feeding may slow the growth of a developing baby. Steroids can cause birth defects or interfere with the developing fetus. Check with your doctor if you are, or might be, pregnant.

Flunisolide may pass into breast milk and cause unwanted effects in a nursing infant.

Seniors

Older adults may use this medicine without special precaution. Be sure your doctor knows if you have any bone disease, colitis, diabetes, bowel disease, glaucoma, fungus infection, heart disease, herpes infection, high blood pressure, high blood cholesterol, kidney disease, or underactive thyroid.

Possible Side Effects

Most common: dry mouth, hoarseness.

Less common: fungus infections of the mouth or throat.

Rare: deaths due to failure of the adrenal gland have occurred during the process of switching from an oral product. Aerosol Flunisolide is given in a much smaller dose than the oral tablets, reducing the chance for side effects. However, if the drug is used in very large amounts for a long period of time, you may develop a variety of other side effects. Information on those can be found under Prednisone on page 727.

Food Interactions

Do not use this product if you have any food in your mouth.

Usual Dose

Oral:

Adult: 2 inhalations (0.5 milligrams) 2 times a day, morning and evening. Do not take more than 8 inhalations a day. Allow at least 1 minute between inhalations. People with more severe asthma may start out with a higher dose.

Child (age 6 to 15): 2 inhalations twice a day, morning and night.

Child (under age 6): not recommended.

Nasal:

Adult: 2 sprays (0.5 milligrams) in each nostril 2 times a day up to 8 times per day in each nostril.

Child (age 6 to 15): 1 spray in each nostril 3 times a day or 2 sprays 2 times per day.

Child (under age 6): not recommended.

Special Information

Follow the instructions that come with your inhaler. Do not exceed the maximum dose per day.

If you use a bronchodilator inhaler (Isoproterenol, Metaproterenol, etc.) at the same time as your Flunisolide inhaler, use the bronchodilator first to open your bronchial tree and increase the amount of Flunisolide that gets into your lungs.

If you forget a dose of Flunisolide and remember within an hour of the normal time, use it right away. If you don't remember until later skip the forgotten dose and go back to your regular schedule. Do not take a double dose.

Generic Name

Fluocinolone Acetonide

Brand Names

Fluocet	Synalar
Fluonid	Synalar-HP
Flurosyn	Synemol

(Also available in generic form)

Type of Drug

Topical corticosteroid.

Prescribed for

Relief of local skin inflammation, itching, or other skin problems.

General Information

Fluocinolone Acetonide is one of many adrenal corticosteroids used in medical practice today. The major differences between Fluocinolone Acetonide and other adrenal corticosteroids are potency of medication and variation in some

secondary effects. In most cases the choice of adrenal corticosteroids to be used in a specific disease is a matter of doctor
preference and past experience. Other topical adrenal corticosteroids include Hydrocortisone, Triamcinolone, Methylprednisolone, Paramethasone, Dexamethasone, Betamethasone,
Amcinonide, Desoximetasone, Diflorasone Diacetate, Fluocinonide, Halcinonide, Clocortolone Pivalate, and Desonide.

Cautions and Warnings

Fluocinolone Acetonide should not be used if you have viral
diseases of the skin (herpes), fungal infections of the skin
(athlete's foot), or tuberculosis of the skin, nor should it be
used in the ear if the eardrum is perforated. People with a
history of allergies to any of the components of the ointment,
cream, or gel should not use this drug.

Pregnancy/Breast-feeding

Studies have shown that corticosteroids applied to the skin
in large amounts or over long periods of time can be the
cause of birth defects. Pregnant women or those who might
become pregnant while using this medicine should not do
so unless they are under a doctor's care.

Corticosteroid drugs taken by mouth pass into breast milk,
and large drug doses may interfere with the growth of a
nursing infant. Steroids applied to the skin are not likely to
cause problems, but you should not use the medicine unless
under a doctor's care.

Seniors

Older adults are more likely to develop high blood pressure
while taking this medicine (by mouth). Also, older women
have a greater chance of being susceptible to bone degeneration (osteoporosis) associated with large doses of this class
of medicine.

Possible Side Effects

Itching, irritation, dryness, and redness of the skin.

Special Information

Clean the skin before applying Fluocinolone Acetonide to
prevent secondary infection. Apply in a very thin film (effec-

tiveness is based on contact area and not on the thickness of the layer applied).

If you forget to apply a dose of Fluocinolone Acetonide, apply it as soon as you remember. If it is almost time for your next regularly scheduled dose, skip the one you forgot and continue with your regular schedule. Do not apply a double dose.

Generic Name

Fluocinonide Ointment/Cream/Gel

Brand Names

Lidex
Lidex-E

Type of Drug

Topical corticosteroid.

Prescribed for

Relief of local skin inflammation, itching, or other skin problems.

General Information

Fluocinonide, one of the most potent topical steroids available today, is used to relieve the symptoms of any itching, rash, or inflammation of the skin. It does not treat the underlying cause of the skin problem, only the symptom. It exerts this effect by interfering with natural body mechanisms that produce the rash, itching, etc., in the first place. If you use this drug without finding the cause of the problem, the condition may return after you stop using the drug. Fluocinonide should not be used without your doctor's consent because it could cover an important reaction, one that may be valuable to him in treating you.

Cautions and Warnings

Fluocinonide should not be used if you have viral diseases of the skin (herpes), fungal infections of the skin (athlete's foot), or tuberculosis of the skin, nor should it be used in the ear if the eardrum is perforated. People with a history of allergies to any of the components of the ointment, cream, or gel should not use this drug.

Pregnancy/Breast-feeding

Studies have shown that corticosteroids applied to the skin in large amounts or over long periods of time can be the cause of birth defects. Pregnant women or those who might become pregnant while using this medicine should not do so unless they are under a doctor's care.

Corticosteroid drugs taken by mouth pass into breast milk, and large drug doses may interfere with the growth of a nursing infant. Steroids applied to the skin are not likely to cause problems, but you should not use the medicine unless under a doctor's care.

Seniors

Older adults are more likely to develop high blood pressure while taking this medicine (by mouth). Also, older women have a greater chance of being susceptible to bone degeneration (osteoporosis) associated with large doses of this class of medicines.

Possible Side Effects

Itching, irritation, dryness and redness of the skin.

Special Information

Clean the skin before applying Fluocinonide to prevent secondary infection. Apply a very thin film (effectiveness is based on contact area and not on the thickness of the layer applied).

If you forget to apply a dose of Fluocinonide, apply it as soon as you remember. If it is almost time for your next regularly scheduled dose, skip the one you forgot and continue with your regular schedule. Do not apply a double dose.

Generic Name

Fluoxetine Hydrochloride

Brand Name

Prozac

Type of Drug

Antidepressant.

Prescribed for

Depression.

General Information

Fluoxetine Hydrochloride is chemically unrelated to the older tricyclic and tetracyclic antidepressant medicines. It works by allowing the passage of a neurohormone, serotonin, into nervous system cells. The drug is effective in treating common symptoms of depression. It can help improve your mood and mental alertness, increase physical activity, and improve sleep patterns. The drug takes about 4 weeks to work and stays in the body for several weeks, even after you stop taking it. This may be important when your doctor starts or stops treatment.

Unlike other antidepressants, Fluoxetine Hydrochloride can cause people taking the drug to experience weight loss. This is particularly true in underweight depressed people. In one study, 13 percent of people taking this drug lost more than 5 percent of their body weight. This property of the drug earned a lot of publicity during its initial period of evaluation, but the drug has not been studied as a weight-loss treatment.

Cautions and Warnings

Do not take Fluoxetine Hydrochloride if you are allergic to it. Allergies to other antidepressants should not prevent you from taking Fluoxetine Hydrochloride because the drug is chemically different from other antidepressants.

People with severe liver or kidney disease should be cautious about taking this drug and should be treated with doses that are lower than normal.

Pregnancy/Breast-feeding

Animal studies showed no evidence that Fluoxetine Hydrochloride will harm a developing fetus. However, there is no information showing that this drug is safe to take during pregnancy. Do not take this drug if you are, or might become, pregnant without first seeing your doctor and reviewing the benefits of therapy against the risk of taking Fluoxetine Hydrochloride. It is not known if Fluoxetine Hydrochloride passes into breast milk.

Seniors

Fluoxetine Hydrochloride has been studied in older adults. Several hundred seniors took the drug during its study phase without any unusual adverse effect, but any person with liver or kidney disease, problems that are more common among seniors, must receive a lower dose than an otherwise healthy person. Be sure to report any unusual side effects to your doctor.

Possible Side Effects

The most common side effects of Fluoxetine Hydrochloride are anxiety, nervousness, sleeplessness, drowsiness, tiredness, weakness, tremors, sweating, dizziness, light-headedness, dry mouth, upset or irritated stomach, appetite loss, nausea, vomiting, diarrhea, stomach gas, rash, and itching.

Less common side effects include changes in sex drive, abnormal ejaculation, impotence, abnormal dreams, difficulty concentrating, increased appetite, acne, hair loss, dry skin, chest pains, allergy, runny nose, bronchitis, abnormal heart rhythms, bleeding, blood pressure changes, headaches, fainting when rising suddenly from a sitting position, bone pain, bursitis, twitching, breast pain, fibrocystic disease of the breast, cystitis, urinary pain, double vision, eye or ear pain, conjunctivitis, anemia, swelling, low blood sugar, low thyroid activity.

In addition, many other side effects affecting virtually every body system have been reported by people taking this medicine. They are too numerous to mention here but are considered infrequent or rare and affect only a small number of people.

In studies of the drug before it was released in the United

States, 15 percent of people taking it had to stop because of drug side effects. Be sure to report anything unusual to your doctor at once.

Drug Interactions

Fluoxetine Hydrochloride may prolong the effects of Diazepam and other benzodiazepine-type drugs in your body.

Little is known about taking Fluoxetine Hydrochloride and other nervous-system-active agents together. Report any unusual occurrences to your doctor. At least 2 weeks should elapse between taking Fluoxetine Hydrochloride and an MAO-inhibitor drug.

People taking Warfarin or Digoxin may experience an increase in that drug's effect if they start taking Fluoxetine Hydrochloride. Your doctor will have to reevaluate your Warfarin or Digoxin dosage.

People taking Tryptophan and Fluoxetine Hydrochloride together may develop agitation, restlessness, and upset stomach.

Food Interactions

Fluoxetine Hydrochloride may be taken without regard to food or meals.

Usual Dose

20 to 80 milligrams per day. Seniors, people with kidney or liver disease, and those taking several different medicines should take a lower dosage.

Overdosage

Two people have died after taking a Fluoxetine Hydrochloride overdose. Symptoms of overdose may include seizures, nausea, vomiting, agitation, restlessness, and nervous system excitation. There is no specific antidote for Fluoxetine Hydrochloride overdose.

Any person suspected of having taken a Fluoxetine Hydrochloride overdose should be taken to a hospital emergency room for treatment at once. ALWAYS take the medicine bottle with you.

Special Information

Fluoxetine Hydrochloride can make you dizzy or drowsy.

Take care when driving or doing other tasks that require alertness and concentration.

Be sure your doctor knows if you are pregnant, breast-feeding, taking other medications, or drinking alcohol while taking this drug. Notify your doctor of any unusual side effects, if rash or hives develop, if you become excessively nervous or anxious while taking Fluoxetine Hydrochloride, or if you lose your appetite (especially if you are already underweight!).

If you forget a dose of Fluoxetine Hydrochloride, take it as soon as you remember. If it is almost time for your next dose, skip the forgotten dose and continue with your regular schedule. Do not take a double dose of Fluoxetine Hydrochloride.

Generic Name

Fluoxymesterone

Brand Names

Android-F
Halotestin
Ora-Testryl

(Also available in generic form)

Type of Drug

Androgenic (male) hormone.

Prescribed for

Diseases in which male hormone replacement or augmentation is needed; male menopause.

General Information

This is a member of the androgenic or male hormone group, which includes Testosterone, Methyl Testosterone, Calusterone, and Dromostanolone Propionate. (The last two are used primarily to treat breast cancer in women.) Females taking any androgenic drug should be careful to watch for deepening of the voice, oily skin, acne, hairiness, increased libido, and menstrual irregularities, effects related to the so-called virilizing effects of these hormones. Virilization is a sign that the drug is starting to produce changes in secondary sex characteristics. The drugs should be avoided if possible by young boys who have not gone through puberty.

Cautions and Warnings

Men with unusually high blood levels of calcium, known or suspected cancer of the prostate, or prostate destruction or disease, cancer of the breast, or with liver, heart, or kidney disease should not use this medication.

Pregnancy/Breast-feeding

Fluoxymesterone is not recommended for use during pregnancy or breast-feeding. Fluoxymesterone may cause unwanted problems in babies such as the development of male features in female babies.

Seniors

Older men treated with this medicine run an increased risk of prostate enlargement or prostate cancer.

Possible Side Effects

In males: inhibition of testicle function, impotence, chronic erection of the penis, enlargement of the breast.

In females: unusual hairiness, baldness in a pattern similar to that seen in men, deepening of the voice, enlargement of the clitoris. These changes are usually irreversible once they have occurred. Females also experience increases in blood calcium and menstrual irregularities.

In both sexes: changes in libido, flushing of the skin, acne, habituation, excitation, chills, sleeplessness, water retention, nausea, vomiting, diarrhea. Symptoms resembling stomach ulcer may develop. Fluoxymesterone may affect levels of blood cholesterol.

Drug Interactions

Fluoxymesterone may increase the effect of oral anticoagulants; dosage of the anticoagulant may have to be decreased. It may have an effect on the glucose tolerance test, a blood test used to screen for diabetes mellitus.

Food Interactions

Take with meals if the drug upsets your stomach.

Usual Dose

2 to 30 milligrams per day, depending upon the disease being treated and patient's response.

Special Information

Fluoxymesterone and other androgens are potent drugs. They must be taken only under the close supervision of your doctor and never used casually. The dosage and clinical effects of the drug vary widely and require constant monitoring.

If you forget to take a dose of Fluoxymesterone, take it as soon as you remember. If it is almost time for your next regularly scheduled dose, skip the one you forgot and continue with your regular schedule. Do not take a double dose.

Generic Name

Fluphenazine Hydrochloride

Brand Names

Permitil
Prolixin

Type of Drug

Phenothiazine antipsychotic.

Prescribed for

Psychotic disorders, moderate to severe depression with anxiety, control of agitation or aggressiveness of disturbed children, alcohol withdrawal symptoms, intractable pain, and senility.

General Information

Fluphenazine Hydrochloride and other members of the phenothiazine group act on a portion of the brain called the hypothalamus. The drugs affect parts of the hypothalamus that control metabolism, body temperature, alertness, muscle tone, hormone balance, and vomiting, and may be used to treat problems related to any of these functions.

Cautions and Warnings

Fluphenazine Hydrochloride should not be taken if you are allergic to one of the drugs in the broad classification of phenothiazine drugs. Do not take it if you have blood, liver, kidney, or heart disease, very low blood pressure, or Parkinson's disease. This medication is a tranquilizer and can have a depressive effect, especially during the first few days of therapy. Care should be taken when performing activities requiring a high degree of concentration, such as driving.

Pregnancy/Breast-feeding

Infants born to women taking this medication have experienced drug side effects (liver jaundice, nervous system effects) immediately after birth. Check with your doctor about taking this medicine if you are or might become pregnant.

This drug may pass into breast milk and affect a nursing infant. Consider alternative feeding methods if you must take this medicine.

Seniors

Older adults are more sensitive to the effects of this medication than younger adults and usually require a lower dosage to achieve a desired effect. Also, older adults are more likely to develop drug side effects. Some experts feel that elderly people should be treated with ½ to ¼ the usual adult dose.

Possible Side Effects

Most common: drowsiness, especially during the first or second week of therapy. If the drowsiness becomes troublesome, contact your doctor.

Can cause jaundice (yellowing of the whites of the eyes or skin), usually in 2 to 4 weeks. The jaundice usually goes away when the drug is discontinued, but there have been cases when it did not. If you notice this effect or if you develop symptoms such as fever and generally not feeling well, contact your doctor immediately. Less frequent: changes in components of the blood including anemias, raised or lowered blood pressure, abnormal heart rate, heart attack, feeling faint or dizzy.

Phenothiazines can produce "extrapyramidal effects," such as spasms of the neck muscles, severe stiffness of the back muscles, rolling back of the eyes, convulsions, difficulty in swallowing, and symptoms associated with Parkinson's disease. These effects look very serious, but disappear after the drug has been withdrawn; however, symptoms of the face, tongue, and jaw may persist for as long as several years, especially in the elderly with a history of brain damage. If you experience extrapyramidal effects, contact your doctor immediately.

Fluphenazine Hydrochloride may cause an unusual increase in psychotic symptoms or may cause paranoid reactions, tiredness, lethargy, restlessness, hyperactivity, confusion at night, bizarre dreams, inability to sleep, depression, and euphoria. Other reactions are itching, swelling, unusual sensitivity to bright lights, red skin, and rash. There have been cases of breast enlargement, false positive pregnancy tests, changes in menstrual flow in females, and impotence and changes in sex drive in males. Fluphenazine Hydrochloride may also cause dry mouth, stuffy nose, headache, nausea, vomiting, loss of appetite, change in body temperature, loss of facial color, excessive salivation, excessive perspiration, constipation, diarrhea, changes in urine and stool habits, worsening of glaucoma, blurred vision, weakening of eyelid muscles, and spasms in bronchial and other muscles, as well as increased appetite, fatigue, excessive thirst, and changes in the coloration of skin, particularly in exposed areas.

Drug Interactions

Fluphenazine Hydrochloride should be taken with caution in combination with barbiturates, sleeping pills, narcotics, or any other medication which may produce a depressive effect. Avoid alcohol.

Usual Dose

Adult: 0.5 to 10 milligrams per day in divided doses. (The lowest effective dose should be used.) Few people will require more than 3 milligrams per day, although some have required 20 milligrams or more per day.

Senior: Older patients usually require lower doses of this drug than younger adults because they metabolize it more slowly.

Overdosage

Symptoms are depression, extreme weakness, tiredness, desire to go to sleep, coma, lowered blood pressure, uncontrolled muscle spasms, agitation, restlessness, convulsions, fever, dry mouth, and abnormal heart rhythms. The patient should be taken to a hospital emergency room immediately. ALWAYS bring the medicine bottle.

Special Information

This medication may cause drowsiness. Use caution when driving or operating complex equipment, and avoid alcoholic beverages while taking the medicine.

The drug may also cause unusual sensitivity to the sun and can turn your urine reddish-brown to pink.

If dizziness occurs, avoid sudden changes in posture and avoid climbing stairs.

Use caution in hot weather. This medicine may make you more prone to heat stroke.

If you take Fluphenazine Hydrochloride once a day and forget your dose, take it as soon as possible. If you don't remember until the next day, skip the forgotten dose and continue with your regular schedule. If you take the medicine more than once a day and forget a dose, take the forgotten dose as soon as possible. If it is almost time for your next dose, skip the forgotten dose and go on with your regular schedule.

Generic Name

Flurandrenolide

Brand Names

Cordran Ointment/Lotion/Tape
Cordran SP Cream

(Also available in generic form)

Type of Drug

Corticosteroid.

Prescribed for

Relief of local inflammation of the skin, itching, or other skin problems.

General Information

Flurandrenolide is used to relieve the symptom of any itching, rash, or inflammation of the skin. It does not treat the underlying cause of the skin problem, only the symptom. It exerts this effect by interfering with natural body mechanisms that produced the rash, itching, etc., in the first place. If you use this drug without finding the cause of the problem, the condition may return after you stop using the drug. Flurandrenolide should not be used without your doctor's consent because it could cover an important reaction, one that may be valuable to him in treating you.

Cautions and Warnings

Flurandrenolide should not be used if you have viral diseases of the skin (herpes), fungal infections of the skin (athlete's foot), or tuberculosis of the skin, nor should it be used in the ear if the eardrum has been perforated. Don't use this medicine if you are allergic to any of the components of the ointment, cream, lotion, or tape.

Pregnancy/Breast-feeding

Studies have shown that corticosteroids applied to the skin in large amounts or over long periods of time can be the cause of birth defects. Pregnant women or those who might become pregnant while using this medicine should not do so unless they are under a doctor's care.

Corticosteroid drugs taken by mouth pass into breast milk and large drug doses may interfere with the growth of a nursing infant. Steroids applied to the skin are not likely to cause problems, but you should not use the medicine unless under a doctor's care.

Seniors

Older adults are more likely to develop high blood pressure

while taking this medicine (by mouth). Also, older women
have a greater chance of being susceptible to bone degeneration (osteoporosis) associated with large doses of this class
of medicines.

Possible Side Effects

Burning sensations, itching, irritation, dryness of the skin,
secondary infection.

Special Information

Clean the skin before applying Flurandrenolide in a very thin
film (effectiveness is based on contact area and not on the
thickness of the layer applied). Flurandrenolide tape comes
with specific directions for use; follow them carefully.

If you forget to take a dose of Flurandrenolide, take it as
soon as you remember. If it is almost time for your next
regularly scheduled dose, skip the one you forgot and continue with your regular schedule. Do not take a double dose.

Generic Name

Flurazepam

Brand Name

Dalmane

(Also available in generic form)

Type of Drug

Sedative-sleeping medicine.

Prescribed for

Insomnia or sleeplessness, frequent nighttime awakening, or
waking up too early in the morning.

General Information

Flurazepam is a member of the group of drugs known as
benzodiazepines. These drugs are used as either antianxiety
agents, anticonvulsants, or sedatives (sleeping pills). They
exert their effects by relaxing the large skeletal muscles and

by a direct effect on the brain. In doing so, they can relax you and make you either more tranquil or sleepier, depending on the drug and how much you use. Many doctors prefer Flurazepam and the other members of this class to other drugs that can be used for the same effect. Their reason is that the benzodiazepines tend to be safer, have fewer side effects, and are usually as, if not more, effective.

These drugs are generally used in any situation where they can be a useful adjunct.

Benzodiazepine tranquilizing drugs can be abused if taken for long periods of time, and it is possible to develop withdrawal symptoms if you discontinue the therapy abruptly. Withdrawal symptoms include convulsions, tremor, muscle cramps, stomach cramps, insomnia, agitation, diarrhea, vomiting, sweating.

Cautions and Warnings

Do not take Flurazepam if you know you are sensitive or allergic to this drug or to other benzodiazepines such as Chlordiazepoxide, Oxazepam, Clorazepate, Diazepam, Lorazepam, Prazepam, Clonazepam, and Temazepam.

Flurazepam and other members of this drug group may aggravate narrow-angle glaucoma, but if you have openangle glaucoma you may take the drugs. In any case, check this information with your doctor. Flurazepam can cause tiredness, drowsiness, inability to concentrate, or similar symptoms. Be careful if you are driving, operating machinery, or performing other activities which require concentration.

Pregnancy/Breast-feeding

Avoid taking this drug during the first 3 months of pregnancy except under strict supervision of your doctor.

The baby may become dependent on Flurazepam, if it is used continually during pregnancy. If used during the last weeks of pregnancy or during breast-feeding the baby may be overly tired, be short of breath, or have a slow heartbeat.

Use during labor may cause weakness in the newborn.

Seniors

Older adults are more sensitive to the effects of this drug, especially dizziness and drowsiness. Follow your doctor's directions and report any side effects at once.

Possible Side Effects

Most common: mild drowsiness during the first few days of therapy, especially in the elderly or debilitated. If drowsiness persists, contact your doctor.

Less common side effects: confusion, depression, lethargy, disorientation, headache, lack of activity, slurred speech, stupor, dizziness, tremor, constipation, dry mouth, nausea, inability to control urination, changes in sex drive, irregular menstrual cycle, changes in heart rhythm, lowered blood pressure, retention of fluids, blurred or double vision, itching, rash, hiccups, nervousness, inability to fall asleep, (occasional) liver dysfunction. If you experience any of these reactions stop taking the medicine and contact your doctor immediately.

Drug Interactions

Flurazepam is a central nervous system depressant. Avoid alcohol, tranquilizers, narcotics, sleeping pills, barbiturates, MAO inhibitors, antihistamines, and other medicines used to relieve anxiety.

Cimetidine may increase the effect of Flurazepam.

Food Interactions

Flurazepam is best taken on an empty stomach, but may be taken with food if it upsets your stomach.

Usual Dose

Adult: 15 to 30 milligrams at bedtime. Must be individualized for maximum benefit.

Senior: initiate therapy with 15 milligrams at bedtime.

Overdosage

Symptoms are confusion, sleep or sleepiness, lack of response to pain such as a pin stick, shallow breathing, lowered blood pressure, and coma. The patient should be taken to a hospital emergency room immediately. ALWAYS bring the medicine bottle.

Special Information

If you forget to take a dose of Flurazepam and you remember within about an hour of your regular time, take it right away. If you do not remember until later, skip the forgotten dose and go back to your regular schedule. Do not take a double dose.

Your sleep may be disturbed for 1 or 2 nights after you stop taking the medication regularly.

Generic Name
Flurbiprofen

Brand Name
Ansaid

Type of Drug
Nonsteroidal anti-inflammatory.

Prescribed for
Rheumatoid and osteoarthritis.

General Information
Flurbiprofen is one of many nonsteroidal anti-inflammatory drugs (NSAIDs) sold in the United States to reduce inflammation, relieve pain and fever, and relieve menstrual cramps and discomfort. The choice of one member of this group over another often depends on your individual response to a specific drug. It is common to try several of these drugs before you find the one that is right for you. People who cannot tolerate or do not respond to other NSAIDs may respond to Flurbiprofen.

Cautions and Warnings
Do not take this product if you are allergic to Aspirin or any other NSAID. This drug can worsen a stomach ulcer or cause a new ulcer to develop. It should be used with caution if you have kidney disease.

Pregnancy/Breast-feeding
Flurbiprofen may cross into the blood circulation of a devel-

oping baby. It has not been found to cause birth defects. Pregnant women or those who might become pregnant while taking Flurbiprofen should not take it without their doctor's approval. When the drug is considered essential by your doctor, the potential risk of taking the medicine must be carefully weighed against the benefit it might produce.

Flurbiprofen may pass into breast milk but has caused no problems among breast-fed infants. You must consider the potential effect on the nursing infant if you are breast-feeding while taking this medicine.

Seniors

Older adults are more sensitive to the stomach, kidney, and liver effects of this drug. Some doctors recommend that persons 70 years of age and older take one half the usual dose. Follow your doctor's directions and report any side effects at once.

Possible Side Effects

Most frequent: upset stomach, dizziness, headache, drowsiness, ringing in the ears, rash.

Other side effects include heartburn, nausea, vomiting, bloating, stomach gas or pain, diarrhea, constipation, dark stools, nervousness, sleeplessness, depression, confusion, tremor, loss of appetite, fatigue, itching, double or blurred vision, dry or irritated eyes, heart failure, palpitations, abnormal heart rhythms, anemia or other changes in the composition of the blood, changes in liver function, hair loss, tingling in the hands or feet, fever, enlarged breasts, blood in the urine, urinary irritation, thirst, frequent urination, kidney damage, low blood sugar, asthma, difficulty breathing, skin rash, itching, swelling, black and blue marks.

Drug Interactions

Aspirin causes this drug to be eliminated from the body more rapidly than normal.

Flurbiprofen may increase the effectiveness of Lithium and sulfa, anticoagulant (blood-thinning), antidiabetes, and anti-seizure drugs.

People taking Methotrexate should not take Flurbiprofen or any other NSAID. Four people have died from combining Methotrexate and an NSAID.

Flurbiprofen may reduce the effects of beta blocking drugs such as Propranolol and Atenolol.

Food Interactions

You may take this drug with food if it upsets your stomach.

Usual Dose

200 to 300 milligrams per day. Senior citizens and those with kidney problems should start with a lower dose.

Overdosage

Symptoms may include drowsiness, dizziness, confusion, disorientation, lethargy, tingling in the hands or feet, numbness, nausea, vomiting, upset stomach, stomach pains, headache, ringing or buzzing in the ears, sweating, and blurred vision. Take the victim to a hospital emergency room at once for treatment. ALWAYS bring the medicine bottle with you.

Special Information

Avoid Aspirin and alcoholic beverages while taking this medication.

You may become dizzy or drowsy while taking this medicine. Be careful while driving or operating complex equipment.

Call your doctor if any of the following symptoms develop: skin rash, itching, swelling, visual disturbances, black stools, or a persistent headache.

If you forget to take a dose of Flurbiprofen, take it as soon as you remember. If it is almost time for your next dose, skip the forgotten dose and continue with your regular schedule.

Generic Name

Furosemide

Brand Name

Lasix

(Also available in generic form)

Type of Drug

Diuretic.

Prescribed for

Congestive heart failure, cirrhosis of the liver, kidney dysfunction, high blood pressure, and other conditions where it may be desirable to rid the body of excess fluid.

General Information

Furosemide causes the production of urine by affecting the kidneys. It may also cause lowered blood pressure. Furosemide is particularly useful as a very strong drug with great diuretic potential, when a drug with less diuretic potential would fail to produce the desired therapeutic effect.

Cautions and Warnings

Furosemide if given in excessive quantities will cause depletion of water and electrolytes. It should not be taken without constant medical supervision and unless the dose has been adjusted to your particular needs. You should not take this drug if your production of urine has been decreased abnormally by some type of kidney disease, or if you feel you may be allergic to it or if you have experienced an allergic reaction to it in the past.

Excessive use of Furosemide will result in dehydration or reduction in blood volume, and may cause circulatory collapse and other related problems, particularly in the elderly. In addition, because of the potent effect that this drug has on the electrolytes in the blood—potassium, sodium, carbon dioxide, and others—frequent laboratory evaluations of these electrolytes should be performed during the few months of therapy, and periodically afterward.

Pregnancy/Breast-feeding

Although Furosemide has been used to treat specific conditions in pregnancy, it should generally not be used to treat a pregnant woman because of its potential effects on the unborn child. Although this effect has not been seen in humans, Furosemide can cause kidney problems in unborn animals if given to animals during pregnancy. If your doctor feels that your case warrants the use of Furosemide, the decision to use this drug must be made by you and your doctor based on the potential benefits derived from this drug as opposed to the potential problems that may be associated with its use. If you must take this drug during the period that you are nursing a newborn baby, you should stop nursing and feed the baby prepared formulas.

Seniors

Older adults are more sensitive to the effects of this drug. Follow your doctor's directions and report any side effects at once.

Possible Side Effects

If you are taking Furosemide you should be aware that changes may develop in potassium and other electrolyte concentrations in your body. In the case of lower potassium produced by Furosemide (hypokalemia), you may observe these warning signs: dryness of the mouth, thirst, weakness, lethargy, drowsiness, restlessness, muscle pains or cramps, muscular tiredness, low blood pressure, decreased frequency of urination and decreased amount of urine produced, abnormal heart rate, and stomach upset including nausea and vomiting. To treat this, potassium supplements are given in the form of tablets, liquids, or powders, or by increased consumption of potassium-rich foods such as bananas, citrus fruits, melons, and tomatoes.

Furosemide may alter the metabolism of sugar in your body. If you have diabetes mellitus, you may develop high blood sugar or sugar in the urine while you are taking the drug. To treat this problem, the dose of drugs that you are taking to treat your diabetes will have to be altered.

In addition, people taking Furosemide have experienced one or more of the following side effects: abdominal discomfort, nausea, vomiting, diarrhea, rash, dizziness, lightheadedness, weakness, headache, blurred vision, fatigue, jaundice or yellowing of the skin or whites of the eyes, acute attacks of gout, ringing in the ears, reversible periodic impairment in hearing. There have also been some reported cases of irreversible hearing loss.

Other side effects are: dermatitis, unusual skin reactions, tingling in the extremities, postural hypotension (or dizziness on rising quickly from a sitting or lying position), anemia of

various types. Rare: a sweet taste in the mouth, burning
feeling in the stomach and/or mouth, thirst, increased perspiration, frequent urination.

Drug Interactions

Furosemide will increase (potentiate) the action of other blood-
pressure-lowering drugs. This is beneficial, and is frequently
used to help lower blood pressure in patients with hypertension.

The possibility of developing electrolyte imbalances in body
fluids is increased if you take other medications such as
Digitalis and adrenal corticosteroids while you are taking
Furosemide.

If you are taking Furosemide because of congestive heart
failure and are also taking Digitalis, loss of potassium may
significantly affect the toxicity of Digitalis.

If you are taking an oral antidiabetic drug and begin taking
Furosemide, the antidiabetic dose may have to be altered.

If you are taking Lithium Carbonate, you should probably
not take a diuretic, which by reducing the elimination of
Lithium from the blood adds a high risk of Lithium toxicity.

Interaction with aminoglycoside antibiotics may cause periodic hearing losses; make sure your doctor knows you are
taking Furosemide before he gives you an injection of an
aminoglycoside.

If you are taking high doses of Aspirin to treat arthritis or
similar diseases, and you begin to take Furosemide, you
may have to lower the dose of Aspirin because of the effect
Furosemide has on passage of Aspirin through the kidneys.

If you are taking Furosemide for the treatment of high
blood pressure or congestive heart failure, avoid over-the-
counter drug products for the treatment of coughs, colds,
and allergies which may contain stimulant drugs. Check with
your pharmacist, who can give you accurate information
about any over-the-counter drug and its potential interactions with Furosemide.

Food Interactions

Foods that are high in potassium, including bananas, citrus
fruits, melons, and tomatoes, should be given high priority
in your daily diet.

Usual Dose

Adult: 20 to 80 milligrams per day, depending on disease and patient's response. Doses of 600 milligrams per day or even more have been prescribed.

Infant and child: 4 to 5 milligrams per pound of body weight daily in a single dose. If therapy is not successful, the dose may be increased by steps of 2 to 5 milligrams, but not to more than 14 to 15 milligrams per day.

Maintenance doses are adjusted to the minimum effective level.

Special Information

If the amount of urine you produce each day is dropping or if you suffer from significant loss of appetite, muscle weakness, tiredness, or nausea while taking this drug, contact your doctor immediately.

Furosemide is usually taken once a day, after breakfast. If a second dose is needed, it should be taken no later than 2 in the afternoon. This is to avoid waking up during the night to urinate.

If you forget to take a dose of Furosemide, take it as soon as you remember. If it is almost time for your next regularly scheduled dose, skip the one you forgot and continue with your regular schedule. Do not take a double dose.

Brand Name

Gaviscon

Ingredients

Alginic Acid	Magnesium Trisilicate
Aluminum Hydroxide Dried Gel	Sodium Bicarbonate

Other Brand Names

Algenic Alka Liquid
Parviscon

(Also available in generic form)

Type of Drug

Antacid.

Prescribed for

Heartburn, acid indigestion, or sour stomach.

General Information

Gaviscon is one of many commercial antacid products on the market. Antacids are used by many people for the relief of temporary symptoms associated with indigestion caused by drugs, food, or disease. For more information on antacids, see pages 60–65.

Cautions and Warnings

Do not use this antacid if you are on a sodium-restricted diet.

Pregnancy/Breast-feeding

Check with your doctor before taking this drug if you are, or might be, pregnant, or if you are breast-feeding.

Seniors

Older adults may use this product without restriction. Do not exceed package directions without your doctor's permission.

Possible Side Effects

Occasional constipation or diarrhea if taken in large quantities.

Drug Interactions

Do not take this drug at the same time as a Tetracycline derivative, antibiotic, Digoxin, Phenytoin, Quinidine, Warfarin, or oral iron supplement. The antacid may interfere with the effective absorption of these drugs.

Take other drugs 1 hour before or 2 hours after taking an antacid.

Usual Dose

Chew 2 to 4 tablets 4 times per day, as needed. Do not take more than 16 tablets per day.

Overdosage

Take the patient to an emergency facility. ALWAYS bring the medication bottle.

Special Information

Do not swallow these tablets whole—they must be chewed.
   Gaviscon-2 contains twice as much medication as Gaviscon. Only ½ as many tablets are needed.
   Store the medication at room temperature in a dry place.

Generic Name

Gemfibrozil

Brand Name

Lopid

Type of Drug

Antihyperlipidemic (blood-fat reducer).

Prescribed for

People with excessively high levels of blood triglycerides.

General Information

Gemfibrozil consistently reduces blood triglyceride levels, but is usually prescribed only for people with very high blood-fat levels who have not responded to dietary changes or other therapies. Normal levels range between 50 and 200 milligrams. People with very high levels of blood triglycerides are likely to have severe abdominal pains and pancreas inflammation. Gemfibrozil usually has little effect on blood cholesterol levels, although it may reduce blood cholesterol in some people.
   Gemfibrozil works by affecting the breakdown of body fats and by reducing the amount of triglyceride manufactured by the liver. However, it is not known if these two mechanisms are solely responsible for the drug's effect on triglyceride levels.

Cautions and Warnings

Gemfibrozil should not be taken by people with severe liver or kidney disease or by those who have had allergic reactions to the drug. Gemfibrozil users may have an increased chance of developing gallbladder disease and should realize that this drug, like other blood-fat reducers including Clofibrate and Probucol, has not been proven to reduce the chances of fatal heart attacks.

Long-term studies of male rats in which the animals were given between 1 and 10 times the maximum human dose showed a definite increase in liver tumors, both cancerous and noncancerous. Other studies on male rats, in which 3 to 10 times the human dose was given for 10 weeks, showed that the drug reduced sperm activity, although this effect has not been reported in humans.

Pregnancy/Breast-feeding

There are no Gemfibrozil studies involving pregnant women. However, it should be avoided by pregnant women or women who may become pregnant while using it. In those situations where its use is considered essential, the potential risk of the drug must be carefully weighed against any benefit it might produce. Because of the tumor-stimulating effect of Gemfibrozil, it is recommended that nursing mothers consider bottle-feeding while taking this drug.

Seniors

Older adults may be more likely to develop drug side effects since the drug primarily passes out of the body through your kidneys and kidney function declines with age.

Possible Side Effects

Most common: abdominal and stomach pains and gas, diarrhea, nausea, and vomiting.

Less common side effects: rash and itching, dizziness, blurred vision, anemia, reduced levels of certain white blood cells, increased blood sugar, and muscle pains, especially in the arms and legs. Other adverse reactions are dry mouth, constipation, loss of appetite, upset stomach, sleeplessness, tingling in the hands or feet, ringing or buzzing in the ears, back pains, painful muscles and/or joints, swollen joints, fatigue, a feeling of ill health, reduction in blood potassium, and abnormal liver function. People taking this drug may be more susceptible to the common cold or other viral or bacterial infections.

Drug Interactions

Gemfibrozil increases the effects of oral anticoagulant (blood-thinning) drugs, and your doctor will have to reduce your anticoagulant dosage when Gemfibrozil treatment is started.

Food Interactions

Follow your doctor's instructions for dietary restrictions.

Gemfibrozil is best taken on an empty stomach 30 minutes before meals, but may be taken with food if it upsets your stomach.

Usual Dose

900 to 1500 milligrams per day, in 2 divided doses taken 20 minutes before breakfast and the evening meal.

Overdosage

There are no reports of Gemfibrozil overdosage, but victims might be expected to develop exaggerated versions of the drug's side effects. Patients taking an overdose of this drug must be made to vomit with Syrup of Ipecac (available at any pharmacy) to remove any remaining drug from the stomach. Call your doctor or a poison control center before doing this. If you must go to a hospital emergency room, ALWAYS bring the medicine bottle.

Special Information

Your doctor should perform periodic blood counts during the first year of Gemfibrozil treatment to check for anemia or other blood effects. Liver-function tests are also necessary. Blood-sugar levels should be checked periodically while you are taking Gemfibrozil, especially if you are diabetic or have a family history of diabetes.

Gemfibrozil may cause dizziness or blurred vision. Use caution while driving or doing anything else that requires concentration and alertness.

Call your doctor if any drug side effects become severe or

intolerable, especially diarrhea, nausea, vomiting, or stomach pains and/or gas. These may disappear by reducing the drug dose.

If you forget to take a dose of Gemfibrozil, take it as soon as you remember. If it is almost time for your next regularly scheduled dose, skip the one you forgot and continue with your regular schedule. Do not take a double dose.

Generic Name

Glipizide

Brand Name

Glucotrol

Type of Drug

Oral antidiabetic.

Prescribed for

Diabetes mellitus (high sugar levels in the blood and urine) that develops during adulthood.

General Information

Glipizide is a "second-generation" antidiabetes drug that was sold in Europe and Canada for several years before the F.D.A. approved its use in the United States. It belongs to the same chemical class as earlier oral antidiabetic drugs, but is more potent, so that less medication is required to accomplish the same effect as the other products. Other minor differences between the first- and second-generation drugs are not considered clinically important at this time. Glipizide and the other second-generation drug, Glyburide, offer no advantage over first-generation agents (Acetohexamide, Chlorpropamide, Tolazamide, and Tolbutamide) available in the United States.

The major differences among all antidiabetes drugs are in the time it takes for the drugs' action to begin and the duration of their effect. All oral antidiabetes drugs work by stimulating the cells in the pancreas that release Insulin into the blood to increase their production. These antidiabetics require a functioning pancreas to produce their effect. However, they may be used together with Insulin injections in certain cases.

Cautions and Warnings

Mild stress, such as infection, minor surgery, or emotional upset, reduces the effectiveness of Glipizide. Remember that while you are taking this medication, you should be under your doctor's continuous care.

The long-term (several years) use of oral antidiabetes drugs has been associated with more heart disease than has treatment with diet or diet plus Insulin. For this reason, many physicians consider diet or diet plus Insulin to be superior to an oral antidiabetes drug.

Glipizide is an aid to, not a substitute for, dietary control. Dietary restriction is still of primary importance in treating diabetes. Follow the diet plan your doctor has prescribed.

Glipizide and the other oral antidiabetes drugs are not oral Insulin, nor are they a substitute for Insulin; they do not lower blood sugar by themselves.

Treating diabetes is your responsibility. Following all of your doctor's instructions with regard to diet, body weight, exercise, personal hygiene, and measures to avoid infection is of paramount importance.

Glipizide should not be used if you have severe kidney, liver, or endocrine (hormone) system disease.

Pregnancy/Breast-feeding

This drug should be avoided by pregnant women and by those who may become pregnant while using it. In those situations where it is deemed essential, the potential risk of the drug must be carefully weighed against any benefit it might produce. Bear in mind that diabetic mothers are known to be 3 to 4 times more likely to have children with birth defects than are nondiabetic women.

If you are pregnant or nursing, attempts should be made to control your diabetes with diet and/or Insulin during this time. If you take Glipizide during pregnancy, it should be stopped at least 1 month before the expected birth date to avoid very low blood sugar in your newborn baby.

This drug may pass into breast milk. Nursing mothers who

must take this drug should consider alternative feeding methods.

Seniors

Older adults with reduced kidney function may be more sensitive to drug side effects because of a reduced ability to eliminate it from the body. Low blood sugar, the major sign of drug overdose, may be more difficult to identify in older adults than in younger adults. Also, low blood sugar is more likely to be a cause of nervous system side effects in older adults.

Older adults taking antidiabetes drugs must keep in close touch with their doctor and closely follow his/her directions.

Possible Side Effects

Most common: appetite loss, nausea, vomiting, heartburn, and upset stomach. You may experience tingling in your hands or feet and itching and rash. These effects can be treated by reducing the daily Glipizide dose or switching to another antidiabetes drug.

Less common side effects: Glipizide can produce abnormally low blood-sugar levels if too much is taken. Other factors that can contribute to low blood sugar are age, kidney or liver disease, malnutrition, consumption of alcoholic beverages, and glandular disorders.

Glipizide may produce liver inflammation shown by a yellow discoloration of your skin or the whites of your eyes, but this is rare. Other side effects are relatively infrequent, but can include weakness, fatigue, dizziness, headache, loss of some kidney function, mild reduction in levels of white blood cells and platelets (involved in clotting), and drug allergy (itching and rash).

Drug Interactions

The action of Glipizide may be enhanced by Insulin, sulfa drugs, Oxyphenbutazone, Phenylbutazone, Clofibrate, Aspirin and other Salicylates, Probenecid, Dicumarol, Bishydroxycoumarin, Warfarin, Phenyramidol, and MAO inhibitor drugs, requiring a reduction in Glipizide dosage.

Thiazide-type diuretics, corticosteroids, phenothiazine tranquilizers, drugs for underactive thyroids, estrogens, oral contraceptives, Phenytoin, Nicotinic Acid, calcium channel blockers, Isoniazid, and the stimulant ingredients added for their decongestant effects to many nonprescription cough, cold, and allergy medicines can increase blood-sugar levels, calling for a possible increase in Glipizide dosage. Check with your doctor or pharmacist before taking any such over-the-counter products.

Beta blockers, prescribed for high blood pressure and some forms of heart disease, may counteract the effects of oral antidiabetes drugs. The outward signs of low blood sugar may also be reversed by these drugs.

Alcoholic beverages can either increase or decrease blood-sugar levels and should be avoided. Also, alcoholic beverages can interact with this medication to cause flushing of the face and body, throbbing pain in the head and neck, breathing difficulty, nausea, vomiting, sweating, chest pains, thirst, low blood pressure, heart palpitations, weakness, dizziness, blurred vision, and confusion. Contact your doctor at once if you experience any of these symptoms.

Food Interactions

Dietary restriction is an essential part of the treatment of diabetes. Be sure to follow the diet your doctor prescribes. Glipizide is best taken on an empty stomach but may be taken with food if it upsets your stomach.

Usual Dose

5 milligrams once per day.

Overdosage

Mild Glipizide overdosage lowers blood sugar and can be treated by consuming sugar in such forms as candy and orange juice. More serious overdosage must be treated in a hospital emergency room. ALWAYS bring the prescription bottle with you.

Special Information

This medicine should not be discontinued without your doctor's knowledge and advice. It should be taken as a part of a program for the treatment of your condition, including diet, exercise, personal hygiene, measures to avoid infection, and periodic testing of your urine for sugar and ketones. Your doctor may also want you to measure blood sugar periodically, which can be conveniently accomplished at home using an appropriate device.

Contact your doctor if you are not feeling well or if you develop symptoms such as yellowing of the skin or whites of the eyes, an abnormally light-colored stool, low-grade fever, unusual bleeding or bruising, sore throat, or diarrhea.

Abnormally low blood sugar may be evidenced by fatigue, hunger, profuse sweating, and numbness in your hands or feet.

Abnormally high blood sugar may be evidenced by excessive thirst and/or frequent urination, and very high levels of sugar or ketones in your urine.

If you forget to take a dose of Glipizide, take it as soon as you remember. If it is almost time for your next regularly scheduled dose, skip the one you forgot and continue with your regular schedule. Do not take a double dose.

Generic Name

Glyburide

Brand Names

DiaBeta
Micronase

Type of Drug

Oral antidiabetic.

Prescribed for

Diabetes mellitus (high sugar levels in the blood and urine) that develops during adulthood.

General Information

Glyburide is a "second-generation" antidiabetes drug that was sold in Europe and Canada for several years before the F.D.A. approved its use in the United States. It belongs to the same chemical class as earlier oral antidiabetic drugs, but is more potent, so that less medication is required to accomplish the same effect as the other products. Other minor differences between the first- and second-generation drugs are not considered clinically important at this time. Glyburide and the other second-generation drug, Glipizide, offer no advantage over first-generation agents (Acetohexamide, Chlorpropamide, Tolazamide, and Tolbutamide) available in the United States.

The major differences among all antidiabetes drugs are in the time it takes for the drugs' action to begin and the duration of their effect. All currently available antidiabetes drugs work by stimulating the cells in the pancreas that release Insulin into the blood to increase their production. These antidiabetics require a functioning pancreas to produce their effect. However, they may be used together with Insulin in certain cases.

Cautions and Warnings

Mild stress, such as infection, minor surgery, or emotional upset, reduces the effectiveness of Glyburide. Remember that while you are taking this medication, you should be under your doctor's continuous care.

The long-term (several years) use of oral antidiabetes drugs has been associated with more heart disease than has treatment with diet or diet plus Insulin. For this reason, many physicians consider diet or diet plus Insulin to be superior to an oral antidiabetes drug.

Glyburide is an aid to, not a substitute for, dietary control. Dietary restriction is still of primary importance in treating diabetes. Follow the diet plan your doctor has prescribed.

Glyburide and the other oral antidiabetes drugs are not oral Insulin, nor are they a substitute for Insulin. They do not lower blood sugar on their own.

Treating diabetes is your responsibility. Following all of your doctor's instructions with regard to diet, body weight, exercise, personal hygiene, and measures to avoid infection is of paramount importance.

Glyburide should not be used if you have severe kidney, liver, or endocrine (hormone) system disease.

Pregnancy/Breast-feeding

Unlike the older oral antidiabetes drugs, Glyburide has been tested in animals and found to produce no damage to the developing fetus. Other oral antidiabetes drugs produce birth defects but the exact relationship is unclear because children of diabetic mothers are 3 to 4 times more prone to birth defects than are children of nondiabetic women. Nevertheless, there is no corresponding proof of safety in humans, and Glyburide should be taken with extreme caution if you are pregnant, might become pregnant during its use, or are nursing. Attempts should be made to control your diabetes with diet and/or Insulin during this time. If you take Glyburide during pregnancy, it should be stopped at least 2 weeks before the expected birth to avoid very low blood sugar in the newborn baby.

This drug may pass into breast milk. Nursing mothers who must take this medicine should consider alternate feeding methods.

Seniors

Older adults with reduced kidney function may be more sensitive to drug side effects because of a reduced ability to eliminate it from the body. Low blood sugar, the major sign of drug overdose, may be more difficult to identify in older adults than in younger adults. Also, low blood sugar is more likely to be a cause of nervous system side effects in older adults.

Older adults taking antidiabetes drugs must keep in close touch with their doctor and closely follow his/her directions.

Possible Side Effects

Most common: appetite loss, nausea, vomiting, heartburn, and upset stomach. You may experience tingling in your hands or feet and itching and rash. These effects can be treated by reducing the daily Glyburide dose or switching to another antidiabetes drug.

Less common side effects: Glyburide can produce abnormally low blood-sugar levels if too much is taken. Other factors that can contribute to low blood sugar are age, kidney or liver disease, malnutrition, consumption of alcoholic beverages, and glandular disorders.

Glyburide may produce liver inflammation shown by a yellow discoloration of your skin or the whites of your eyes, but this is rare. Other side effects are relatively infrequent, but can include weakness, fatigue, dizziness, headache, loss of some kidney function, mild reduction in levels of white blood cells and platelets (involved in clotting), and drug allergy (itching and rash).

Drug Interactions

The action of Glyburide may be enhanced by Insulin, sulfa drugs, Oxyphenbutazone, Phenylbutazone, Clofibrate, Aspirin and other Salicylates, Probenecid, Dicumarol, Bishydroxycoumarin, Warfarin, Phenyramidol, and MAO inhibitor drugs, requiring a reduction in Glyburide dosage.

Thiazide-type diuretics, corticosteroids, phenothiazine tranquilizers, drugs for underactive thyroids, estrogens, oral contraceptives, Phenytoin, Nicotinic Acid, calcium channel blockers, Isoniazid, and the stimulant ingredients added for their decongestant effects to many nonprescription cough, cold, and allergy medicines can increase blood-sugar levels, calling for a possible increase in Glyburide dosage. Check with your doctor or pharmacist before taking any such over-the-counter products.

Beta blockers, prescribed for high blood pressure and some forms of heart disease, may counteract the effects of oral antidiabetes drugs. The outward signs of low blood sugar may also be reversed by these drugs.

Alcoholic beverages can either increase or decrease blood-sugar levels and should be avoided. Also, alcoholic beverages can interact with this medication to cause flushing of the face and body, throbbing pain in the head and neck, breathing difficulty, nausea, vomiting, sweating, chest pains, thirst, low blood pressure, heart palpitations, weakness, dizziness, blurred vision, and confusion. Contact your doctor at once if you experience any of these symptoms.

Food Interactions

This medicine is best taken on an empty stomach, but may be taken with food. Dietary management is an important part of the treatment of diabetes. Be sure to follow your doctor's directions about the foods you should avoid.

Usual Dose

2.5 to 20 milligrams once per day, usually with breakfast or the first main meal.

Overdosage

Mild Glyburide overdosage lowers blood sugar and can be treated by consuming sugar in such forms as candy and orange juice. More serious overdosage must be treated in a hospital emergency room. ALWAYS bring the prescription bottle with you.

Special Information

This medicine should not be discontinued without your doctor's knowledge and advice. It should be taken as a part of a program for the treatment of your condition, including diet, exercise, personal hygiene, measures to avoid infection, and periodic testing of your urine for sugar and ketones. Your doctor may also want you to measure blood sugar periodically, which can be conveniently accomplished at home using an appropriate device.

Contact your doctor if you are not feeling well or if you develop symptoms such as yellowing of the skin or whites of the eyes, an abnormally light-colored stool, low-grade fever, unusual bleeding or bruising, sore throat, or diarrhea.

Abnormally low blood sugar may be evidenced by fatigue, hunger, profuse sweating, and numbness in your hands or feet.

Abnormally high blood sugar may be evidenced by excessive thirst and/or frequent urination, and very high levels of sugar or ketones in your urine.

If you forget to take a dose of Glyburide, take it as soon as you remember. If it is almost time for your next regularly scheduled dose, skip the one you forgot and continue with your regular schedule. Do not take a double dose.

Generic Name

Guanabenz Acetate

Brand Name

Wytensin

Type of Drug

Antihypertensive.

Prescribed for

High blood pressure.

General Information

This drug works by stimulating certain nerve receptors in the central nervous system, resulting in a lessening of general nervous-system stimulation by the brain. The immediate blood-pressure reduction occurs without a major effect on blood vessels. However, chronic use of Guanabenz Acetate can result in widening of blood vessels and a slight reduction in pulse rate. It can be taken alone or in combination with a thiazide diuretic.

Cautions and Warnings

Do not take Guanabenz Acetate if you are sensitive to it.

Pregnancy/Breast-feeding

Reports of the effects of this drug in pregnant women have yielded conflicting results. Because it may adversely affect a developing baby, this drug should be avoided by pregnant women or women who may become pregnant while using it. In those situations where it is deemed essential, the potential risk of the drug must be carefully weighed against any benefit it might produce.

Nursing mothers should not use this drug, since it is not known if it passes into breast milk. Consider an alternative feeding method if you must take Guanabenz Acetate.

Seniors

Older adults are more sensitive to the sedative and blood-pressure-lowering effects of this drug. Follow your doctor's directions and report any side effects at once.

Possible Side Effects

The incidence and severity of side effects increase with increases in the daily dosage. The side effects are drowsiness, sedation, dry mouth, dizziness, weakness, and headache.

Less common side effects are: chest pains, swelling in the hands, legs, or feet, heart palpitations and abnormal heart rhythms, stomach and abdominal anxiety, pains and discomfort, nausea, diarrhea, vomiting, constipation, anxiety, poor muscle control, depression, difficulty sleeping, stuffy nose, blurred vision, muscle aches and pains, difficulty breathing, frequent urination, male impotence, unusual taste in the mouth, and swollen and painful male breasts.

Drug Interactions

The effect of this drug is increased by taking it together with other blood-pressure-lowering agents. Its sedative effects will be increased by taking it together with tranquilizers, sleeping pills, or other nervous system depressants.

People taking Guanabenz Acetate for high blood pressure should avoid nonprescription medicines that might aggravate hypertension, such as decongestants, cold and allergy treatments, and diet pills, all of which may contain stimulants. If you are unsure about which medicine to choose, ask your pharmacist.

Food Interactions

This drug is best taken on an empty stomach but may be taken with food if it upsets your stomach.

Usual Dose

4 milligrams 2 times per day to start, with a gradual increase to a maximum of 32 milligrams twice per day, although doses this large are rarely needed.

Overdosage

Guanabenz Acetate will cause sleepiness, lethargy, low blood pressure, irritability, pinpoint pupils, and reduced heart rate.

Patients taking an overdose of this drug must be made to

vomit with Syrup of Ipecac (available at any pharmacy) to remove any remaining drug from the stomach. Call your doctor or a poison control center before doing this. If you must go to a hospital emergency room, ALWAYS bring the medicine bottle.

Special Information

Take this drug exactly as prescribed for maximum benefit. If any side effects become severe or intolerable, contact your doctor, who may reduce your daily dosage to eliminate the side effect.

If you forget to take a dose of Guanabenz Acetate, take it as soon as you remember. If it is almost time for your next regularly scheduled dose, skip the one you forgot and continue with your regular schedule. Do not take a double dose. Call your doctor if you miss 2 or more consecutive doses.

Generic Name

Guanadrel Sulfate

Brand Name

Hylorel

Type of Drug

Antihypertensive.

Prescribed for

High blood pressure.

General Information

This drug is similar to Guanethidine Sulfate and works by preventing the release of the neurohormone norepinephrine from nervous-system storage sites. This relaxes blood-vessel muscles and lowers blood pressure by preventing blood-vessel constriction. Guanadrel Sulfate is usually taken with other medicines, such as diuretics.

Cautions and Warnings

Guanadrel Sulfate must not be taken by people who are

sensitive or allergic to its effects, who have heart failure (the drug can cause you to retain salt and water), or those with a tumor of the adrenal glands known as pheochromocytoma. Asthmatics and people with stomach ulcers may find their conditions are worsened by this drug.

Pregnancy/Breast-feeding

This drug should be avoided by pregnant women or women who may become pregnant while using it. In those situations where it is deemed essential, the potential risk of the drug must be carefully weighed against any benefit it might produce.

Nursing mothers should watch for any possible drug effect on their infants while taking this medication. It is not known if Guanadrel Sulfate passes into breast milk.

Seniors

Older adults are more sensitive to the blood-pressure-lowering effects of this drug. Follow your doctor's directions and report any side effects at once.

Possible Side Effects

Difficulty breathing with or without physical exertion, heart palpitations, chest pains, coughing, fatigue, headache, feeling faint, drowsiness, visual disturbances, tingling in the hands or feet, confusion, increased bowel movements, gas pains, indigestion, constipation, loss of appetite, inflammation of the tongue, nausea, vomiting, frequent urination, a feeling that you need to urinate, nighttime urination, fluid retention and swelling in the arms, legs, or feet, male impotence, aching arms or legs, leg cramps, and excessive changes in body weight (up or down).

Other side effects are: psychological changes, depression, difficulty sleeping, fainting, dry mouth, dry throat, blood in the urine, joint pains or inflammation, backache, and neckache.

Drug Interactions

Guanadrel Sulfate should be discontinued 2 to 3 days before surgery to avoid potentially severe interaction with anesthetic agents.

It should not be taken together with MAO inhibitor drugs

or within a week of MAO inhibitor therapy because of the possible enhancement of MAO side effects.

The effects of Guanadrel Sulfate may be reversed by tricyclic antidepressant drugs, Ephedrine, Phenylpropanolamine, and the phenothiazine tranquilizers. Avoid nonprescription medicines that might aggravate your condition, such as decongestants, cold and allergy treatments, asthma remedies, and diet pills, all of which may contain stimulants. If you are unsure about which medicine to choose, ask your pharmacist.

Guanadrel Sulfate's effects may be increased by beta-blocking drugs and Reserpine.

Alcoholic beverages are likely to increase the chances of dizziness and fainting associated with Guanadrel Sulfate.

Food Interactions

This drug is best taken on an empty stomach but may be taken with food if it upsets your stomach.

Usual Dose

5 milligrams twice per day to start. The daily dosage will be increased in small steps until blood-pressure control is achieved or side effects become intolerable. Most people require between 20 and 75 milligrams per day. Larger daily amounts may be required but should be divided into 3 or 4 doses per day.

Overdosage

Extreme dizziness and blurred vision are the hallmarks of Guanadrel Sulfate overdose. Lie down until the symptoms subside. If the symptoms are more severe and include a rapid drop in blood pressure, take the victim to the hospital at once for treatment. ALWAYS bring the prescription bottle with you.

Special Information

It may seem odd, but Guanadrel Sulfate is only available in a 10-milligram or 25-milligram tablet. If you are required to take 5 milligrams twice a day, you must break a 10-milligram tablet in half. This tablet is designed for this.

Guanadrel Sulfate frequently causes weakness and dizziness in someone who has been sitting or lying down and then rises quickly. This is more likely to happen early in the morning, during hot weather, if you have been sitting or reclining for a long period of time, or if you have been drinking alcoholic beverages. You can minimize this reaction by getting up as slowly as possible. When you get up from lying down, sit on the edge of your bed for several minutes with your feet dangling, then stand slowly. Call your doctor if the problem continues; your daily drug dosage may have to be reduced.

People taking this drug for long periods of time may become tolerant to its effects. If this happens, your doctor will increase your daily dose slightly to achieve the same degree of blood-pressure control.

If you forget to take a dose of Guanadrel Sulfate, take it as soon as you remember. If it is almost time for your next regularly scheduled dose, skip the one you forgot and continue with your regular schedule. Do not take a double dose.

Generic Name

Guanethidine Sulfate

Brand Name

Ismelin Sulfate

(Also available in generic form)

Type of Drug

Antihypertensive.

Prescribed for

High blood pressure.

General Information

Guanethidine Sulfate affects the section of the nervous system which controls pressure in the major blood vessels. Its blood-pressure-lowering effect is enhanced when taken along with other medicines, such as diuretics.

Cautions and Warnings

Patients who may be allergic to this drug, who are taking an MAO inhibitor, or who also have a tumor called a pheochromocytoma should not take Guanethidine Sulfate.

Pregnancy/Breast-feeding

This drug may cross into the blood circulation of a developing baby. It has not been found to cause birth defects. Pregnant women, or those who might become pregnant while taking this drug, should not take it without their doctor's approval. When the drug is considered essential by your doctor, the potential risk of taking the medicine must be carefully weighed against the benefit it might produce.

This drug has caused no problems among breast-fed infants. You must consider the potential effect on the nursing infant if breast-feeding while taking this medicine.

Seniors

Older adults are more sensitive to the blood-pressure-lowering effects of this drug. Follow your doctor's directions and report any side effects at once.

Possible Side Effects

Dizziness, weakness, especially on rising quickly from a sitting or prone position, slowed heartbeat, increased bowel movements, possibly severe diarrhea, male impotence (difficult ejaculation), retention of fluid in the body.

Less common side effects: difficulty in breathing, fatigue, nausea, vomiting, increased frequency of nighttime urination, difficulty in controlling urinary function, itching, rash, loss of scalp hair, dry mouth, involuntary lowering of eyelids, blurred vision, muscle aches and spasms, mental depression, chest pains (angina pectoris), tingling in the chest, stuffy nose, weight gain, asthma in some patients. This drug may affect kidney function.

Drug Interactions

Guanethidine Sulfate may interact with digitalis drugs to slow heart rates excessively. When taken with other blood-pressure-lowering drugs it can lower pressure excessively.

Otherwise, this is a useful interaction that is sometimes used in treating hypertension (high blood pressure).

Drugs with stimulant properties (antidepressants, decongestants), oral contraceptives, and some antipsychotic drugs (phenothiazines, etc.) may reduce the effectiveness of Guanethidine Sulfate. The drug should not be taken together with MAO inhibitors, which should be stopped at least 1 week before taking Guanethidine Sulfate.

Avoid over-the-counter cough, cold, or allergy medicines which may contain stimulants. Check with your doctor or pharmacist before combining these medicines.

Guanethidine should be taken with caution if you also take an antidiabetes drug. The combination will increase antidiabetic activity and may cause your blood sugar to be too low.

Food Interactions

This medicine is best taken on an empty stomach, but you may take it with food if it upsets your stomach.

Usual Dose

Adult: 10 milligrams per day to start. Dose is adjusted according to patient's need. Average daily dose is 25 to 50 milligrams.

Child: 0.09 milligrams per pound of body weight per day. Maximum daily dose is 1.36 milligrams per pound of body weight.

Overdosage

Symptoms are basically exaggerated or prolonged side effects, including dizziness, weakness, slowed heartbeat, and possible diarrhea. Call your doctor immediately if the symptoms appear or if you think you have these symptoms.

Special Information

Do not stop taking this medication unless specifically directed to. Call your doctor if you develop frequent diarrhea or are often dizzy or faint. Alcoholic beverages, heat, and strenuous exercise may increase the chances of dizziness or faintness developing.

If you forget to take a dose of Guanethidine Sulfate, take it as soon as you remember. If it is almost time for your next regularly scheduled dose, skip the one you forgot and continue with your regular schedule. Do not take a double dose.

Generic Name

Halazepam

Brand Name

Paxipam

Type of Drug

Minor tranquilizer.

Prescribed for

Relief of symptoms of anxiety, tension, fatigue, and agitation.

General Information

Halazepam is a member of the group of drugs known as benzodiazepines. These drugs are used either as antianxiety agents, anticonvulsants, or sedatives (sleeping pills.) They exert their effects by relaxing the large skeletal muscles and by a direct effect on the brain. In doing so, they can relax you and make you either more tranquil or sleepier, depending upon which drug you use and how much you take. Many doctors prefer the benzodiazepines to other drugs that can be used for the same effects. Their reason is that these drugs tend to be safer, have fewer side effects, and are usually as, if not more, effective. The benzodiazepines are generally prescribed in any situation where they can be a useful adjunct.

The benzodiazepines, including Halazepam, can be abused if taken for long periods of time and it is possible to experience withdrawal symptoms if you stop taking the drug abruptly. Withdrawal symptoms include tremor, muscle cramps, stomach cramps, vomiting, insomnia, and convulsions.

Cautions and Warnings

Do not take Halazepam if you know you are sensitive or allergic to this drug or other benzodiazepines such as Diazepam, Oxazepam, Chlorazepate, Lorazepam, Prazepam, Flurazepam, Temazepam, and Clonazepam. Halazepam and other members of this group can aggravate narrow-angle glaucoma, but if you have open-angle glaucoma you may take the drug. In any case, check with your doctor. Halazepam can cause tiredness, drowsiness, inability to concentrate, or similar symptoms. Be careful if you are driving, operating machinery, or performing other activities which require concentration.

Pregnancy/Breast-feeding

This drug may cause birth defects or interfere with your baby's development. Check with your doctor before taking it if you are, or might be, pregnant.

If used during breast-feeding the baby may be overly tired, be short of breath, or have a slow heartbeat.

Seniors

Older adults are more sensitive to the effects of this drug, especially dizziness and drowsiness, and require a lower daily dose, usually 20 to 40 milligrams. Follow your doctor's directions and report any side effects at once.

Possible Side Effects

Most common: mild drowsiness during the first few days of therapy. If drowsiness persists, contact your doctor.

Less common side effects: confusion, depression, lethargy, disorientation, headache, inactivity, slurred speech, stupor, dizziness, tremor, constipation, dry mouth, nausea, inability to control urination, changes in sex drive, irregular menstrual cycle, changes in heart rhythm, lowered blood pressure, fluid retention, blurred or double vision, itching, rash, hiccups, nervousness, inability to fall asleep, and occasional liver dysfunction. If you experience any of these symptoms, stop taking the medicine and contact your doctor immediately.

Drug Interactions

Halazepam is a central nervous system depressant. Avoid alcohol, other tranquilizers, narcotics, barbiturates, MAO inhibitors, antihistamines, and medicine used to relieve depression. Taking Halazepam with these drugs may result in excessive depression, tiredness, sleepiness, difficulty breathing, or similar symptoms. Smoking may reduce the effectiveness of Halazepam by increasing the rate at which it is broken down in the body. The effects of Halazepam may be prolonged when taken together with Cimetidine.

Food Interactions

Halazepam is best taken on an empty stomach but may be taken with food.

Usual Dose

The dose must be tailored to the individual needs of the patient.

Adult: 60 to 160 milligrams per day.

Senior and debilitated patient: require less of the drug to control anxiety and tension.

Child: this drug should not be used.

Overdosage

Symptoms are confusion, sleepiness, lack of response to pain such as a pin stick, shallow breathing, lowered blood pressure, and coma. The patient should be taken to a hospital emergency room. ALWAYS bring the medicine bottle.

Special Information

Do not drink alcoholic beverages or take other depressive drugs, such as tranquilizers, sleeping pills, narcotics, or barbiturates when taking Halazepam. Tell your doctor if you become pregnant or are nursing an infant. Take care while driving or operating machinery.

If you forget to take a dose of Halazepam and you remember within about an hour of your regular time, take it right away. If you do not remember until later, skip the forgotten dose and go back to your regular schedule. Do not take a double dose.

Generic Name

Haloperidol

Brand Name

Haldol

(Also available in generic form)

Type of Drug

Butyrophenone antipsychotic.

Prescribed for

Psychotic disorders and to help control an unusual disorder: Gilles de la Tourette's syndrome; short-term treatment of hyperactive children.

General Information

Haloperidol is one of many nonphenothiazine agents used in the treatment of psychosis. The drugs in this group are usually about equally effective when given in therapeutically equivalent doses. The major differences are in type and severity of side effects. Some patients may respond well to one and not at all to another: this variability is not easily explained and is thought to result from inborn biochemical differences.

Cautions and Warnings

Haloperidol should not be used by patients who are allergic to it. Patients with blood, liver, kidney, or heart disease, very low blood pressure, or Parkinson's disease should avoid this drug.

Pregnancy/Breast-feeding

Avoid this drug if you are pregnant. Haloperidol has not been studied in pregnant women; however, serious problems have been seen in pregnant animals given large amounts of Haloperidol. Nursing baby animals have also shown problems such as tiredness and body movement problems. Haloperidol is not recommended during nursing.

Seniors

Older adults are more sensitive to the effects of this medication than younger adults and usually require a lower dosage to achieve a desired effect. Also, older adults are more likely to develop drug side effects. Some experts feel that elderly people should be treated with ½ to ¼ the usual adult dose.

Possible Side Effects

Most common: drowsiness, especially during the first or second week of therapy. If the drowsiness becomes troublesome, contact your doctor.

Less common side effects: Haloperidol can cause jaundice (yellowing of the whites of the eyes or skin), usually in 2 to 4 weeks. The jaundice usually goes away when the drug is discontinued, but there have been cases when it did not. If you notice this effect or if you develop fever and generally do not feel well, contact your doctor immediately. Other less common side effects: changes in components of the blood including anemias, raised or lowered blood pressure, abnormal heartbeat, heart attack, feeling faint or dizzy.

Butyrophenone drugs can produce extrapyramidal effects such as spasms of the neck muscles, severe stiffness of the back muscles, rolling back of the eyes, convulsions, difficulty in swallowing, and symptoms associated with Parkinson's disease. These effects look very serious but disappear after the drug has been withdrawn; however, symptoms of the face, tongue, and jaw may persist for several years, especially in the elderly with a long history of brain disease. If you experience these extrapyramidal effects contact your doctor immediately.

Haloperidol may cause an unusual increase in psychotic symptoms or may cause paranoid reactions, tiredness, lethargy, restlessness, hyperactivity, confusion at night, bizarre dreams, inability to sleep, depression, or euphoria. Other reactions are itching, swelling, unusual sensitivity to bright lights, red skin, and rash. There have been cases of breast enlargement, false positive pregnancy tests, changes in menstrual flow in females, impotence and changes in sex drive in males.

Haloperidol may also cause dry mouth, stuffy nose, headache, nausea, vomiting, loss of appetite, change in body temperature, loss of facial color, excessive salivation, excessive perspiration, constipation, diarrhea, changes in urine and stool habits, worsening of glaucoma, blurred vision, weakening of eyelid muscles, and spasms of bronchial and other muscles, as well as increased appetite, fatigue, excessive thirst, and changes in the coloration of skin, particularly in exposed areas.

Drug Interactions

Haloperidol should be taken with caution in combination with barbiturates, sleeping pills, narcotics, or any other medication which produces a depressive effect. Avoid alcohol.

Haloperidol may increase the need for anticonvulsant medicine in patients who must take both drugs. It may interfere with oral anticoagulant drugs. Any dosage adjustment necessary can easily be made by your doctor.

Food Interactions

This medicine is best taken on an empty stomach, but you may take it with food if it upsets your stomach.

Usual Dose

Adult: 0.5 to 2 milligrams 2 to 3 times per day. Dose may be increased according to patient's need up to 100 milligrams per day.

Child: not recommended.

Overdosage

Symptoms are depression, extreme weakness, tiredness, desire to go to sleep, comas, lowered blood pressure, uncontrolled muscle spasms, agitation, restlessness, convulsions, fever, dry mouth, and abnormal heart rhythms. The patient should be taken to a hospital emergency room immediately. ALWAYS bring the medicine bottle.

Special Information

This medication may cause drowsiness. Use caution when driving or operating complex equipment and avoid alcoholic beverages while taking the medicine.

The drug may also cause unusual sensitivity to the sun and can turn your urine reddish-brown to pink.

If dizziness occurs, avoid sudden changes in posture and avoid climbing stairs.

Use caution in hot weather. This medicine may make you more prone to heat stroke.

If you forget to take a dose of Haloperidol, take it as soon as you remember. Take the rest of the day's doses evenly spaced throughout the day. Do not take a double dose.

Generic Name

Hydralazine Hydrochloride

Brand Names

Alazine
Apresoline

(Also available in generic form)

Type of Drug

Antihypertensive.

Prescribed for

Aortic insufficiency, congestive heart failure, essential hypertension (high blood pressure), heart valve replacement.

General Information

Although the mechanism of action is not completely understood, it is felt that Hydralazine Hydrochloride lowers blood pressure by enlarging the blood vessels throughout the body. This also helps to improve heart functions and blood flow to the kidneys and brain.

Cautions and Warnings

Long-term administration of large doses of Hydralazine Hydrochloride may produce an arthritislike syndrome in some people, although symptoms of this problem usually disappear when the drug is discontinued. Fever, chest pain, not feeling well, or other unexplained symptoms should be reported to your doctor.

Pregnancy/Breast-feeding

This drug crosses into the blood circulation of a developing baby. It has not been found to cause human birth defects. Pregnant women, or those who might become pregnant while taking this drug, should not take it without their doctor's approval. When the drug is considered essential by your doctor, the potential risk of taking the medicine must be carefully weighed against the benefit it might produce.

This drug passes into breast milk, but has caused no problems among breast-fed infants. You must consider the potential effect on the nursing infant if breast-feeding while taking this medicine.

Seniors

Older adults are more sensitive to the blood-pressure-lowering effects of this drug and to the drug's side effects, especially low body temperature. Follow your doctor's directions and report any side effects at once.

Possible Side Effects

Common: headache, loss of appetite, nausea, vomiting, diarrhea, rapid heartbeat, chest pain.

Less common side effects: stuffy nose, flushing, tearing in the eyes, itching and redness of the eyes, numbness and tingling of the hands and feet, dizziness, tremors, muscle cramps, depression, disorientation, anxiety, itching, rash, fever, chills, (occasional) hepatitis, constipation, difficulty in urination, adverse effects on the normal composition of the blood.

Drug Interactions

Hydralazine Hydrochloride should be used with caution by patients who are taking MAO inhibitors.

Nonsteroid anti-inflammatory drugs, especially Indomethacin, estrogens, and drugs with stimulant properties, will reduce the effects of Hydralazine.

The combination of Hydralazine with other blood-pressure-lowering drugs can produce very low blood pressure.

Food Interactions

Hydralazine Hydrochloride may antagonize Vitamin B_6, pyridoxine, which can result in peripheral neuropathy including tremors, tingling and numbness of the fingers, toes, or other extremities. If these occur, your doctor may consider pyridoxine supplementation.

Take Hydralazine Hydrochloride with food.

Usual Dose

Tailored to your needs, like other antihypertensive drugs.

Adult: Most people begin with 40 milligrams per day for the first few days, then increase to 100 milligrams per day for the rest of the first week. Dose increases until the maximum effect is seen.

Child: 0.34 milligrams per pound of body weight per day and up to 200 milligrams per day.

Overdosage

If symptoms of extreme lowering of blood pressure, rapid heartbeat, headache, generalized skin flushing, chest pains, and poor heart rhythms appear, contact your doctor immediately.

Special Information

Take this medicine exactly as prescribed.

Do not self-medicate with over-the-counter cough, cold, or allergy remedies whose stimulant ingredients will increase blood pressure.

If you forget to take a dose of Hydralazine Hydrochloride, take it as soon as you remember. If it is almost time for your next regularly scheduled dose, skip the one you forgot and continue with your regular schedule. Do not take a double dose.

Generic Name

Hydrochlorothiazide

Brand Names

Aquazide	Hydromal
Chlorzide	Hydro-t
Diaqua	Hydro-Z
Diu-Scrip	Mictrin
Esidrix	Oretic
Hydro-Chlor	Thiuretic
HydroDIURIL	Zide

(Also available in generic form)

Type of Drug

Diuretic.

Prescribed for

Congestive heart failure, cirrhosis of the liver, kidney mal-function, high blood pressure, and other conditions where it is necessary to rid the body of excess water.

General Information

This drug is a member of the class known as thiazide diuretics. Thiazides act on the kidneys to stimulate the production of large amounts of urine. They also cause you to lose bicarbonate, chloride, and potassium ions from the body. They are used as part of the treatment of any disease where it is desirable to eliminate large quantities of body water. These diseases include heart failure, some kidney diseases, and liver disease. Thiazide drugs are often taken together with other medicines to treat high blood pressure.

Cautions and Warnings

Do not take Hydrochlorothiazide if you are allergic or sensi-tive to this drug, similar drugs of this group, or sulfa drugs. If you have a history of allergy or bronchial asthma, you may also have a sensitivity or allergy to Hydrochlorothiazide.

Pregnancy/Breast-feeding

Although this drug has been used to treat specific conditions in pregnancy, unsupervised use by pregnant patients should be avoided. Hydrochlorothiazide will cross the placenta and can cause side effects in the newborn infant, such as jaundice, blood problems, and low potassium. Birth defects have not been seen in animal studies. Hydrochlorothiazide passes into breast milk. No problems have been reported in nursing infants, but nursing mothers should consider an alternate feeding method.

Seniors

Older adults are more sensitive to the effects of this drug, especially dizziness. They should closely follow their doctor's directions and report any side effects at once.

Possible Side Effects

Hydrochlorothiazide will cause a loss of body potassium. Signs of low potassium are dryness of the mouth, thirst, weakness, lethargy, drowsiness, restlessness, muscle pains or cramps, muscular tiredness, low blood pressure, decreased frequency of urination and decreased amount of urine produced, abnormal heart rate, stomach upset including nausea and vomiting.

To treat this, potassium supplements are given in the form of tablets, liquids, or powders, or by increased consumption of foods such as bananas, citrus fruits, melons, and tomatoes.

Less common side effects are: loss of appetite, stomach upset, nausea, vomiting, cramping, diarrhea, constipation, dizziness, headache, tingling of the toes and fingers, restlessness, changes in blood composition, sensitivity to sun light, rash, itching, fever, difficulty in breathing, allergic reactions, dizziness when rising quickly from a sitting or lying position, muscle spasms, weakness, blurred vision.

Drug Interactions

Hydrochlorothiazide will increase (potentiate) the action of other blood-pressure-lowering drugs. This is good and is the reason why people with high blood pressure often take more than one medicine.

The possibility of developing imbalances in body fluids

(electrolytes) is increased if you take medications such as Digitalis and adrenal corticosteroids while you take Hydrochlorothiazide.

If you are taking an oral antidiabetic drug and begin taking Hydrochlorothiazide, the antidiabetic dose may have to be altered.

Lithium Carbonate taken with Hydrochlorothiazide should be monitored carefully by a doctor as there may be an increased risk of Lithium toxicity.

Usual Dose

Adult: 25 to 200 milligrams per day, depending on condition treated. Maintenance dose, 25 to 100 milligrams per day; some patients may require up to 200 milligrams per day. It is recommended that you take this drug early in the morning, thus avoiding the possibility of your sleep being disturbed by the need to urinate.

Child (age 6 months and over): 1 milligram per pound of body weight per day in 2 doses.

Infant (under age 6 months): 1.5 milligrams per pound per day in 2 doses.

The dose, individualized to your response, must be altered until maximum therapeutic response at minimum effective dose is reached.

Overdosage

Signs can be tingling in the arms or legs, weakness, fatigue, changes in your heartbeat, a sickly feeling, dry mouth, restlessness, muscle pains or cramps, urinary difficulty, nausea, or vomiting. Take the overdose victim to a hospital emergency room for treatment at once. ALWAYS bring the prescription bottle and any remaining medicine.

Special Information

If you are taking Hydrochlorothiazide for the treatment of high blood pressure or congestive heart failure, avoid over-the-counter medicines for the treatment of coughs, colds, and allergies: such medicines may contain stimulants. If you are unsure about them, ask your pharmacist.

If you forget to take a dose of Hydrochlorothiazide, take it as soon as you remember. If it is almost time for your next regularly scheduled dose, skip the one you forgot and continue with your regular schedule. Do not take a double dose.

Brand Name

Hydropres

Ingredients

Hydrochlorothiazide
Reserpine

Other Brand Names

Hydro-Serp	Hydrotensin
Hydroserpine	Mallopress

(Also available in generic form)

Type of Drug

Antihypertensive.

Prescribed for

High blood pressure.

General Information

Hydropres is a good example of a drug taking advantage of a drug interaction. Each of the drug ingredients works by different mechanisms to lower your blood pressure. The Hydrochlorothiazide relaxes the muscles in your veins and arteries and also helps reduce the volume of blood flowing through those blood vessels. Reserpine works on the nervous system to reduce the efficiency of nerve transmissions which are contributing to the increased pressure. These drugs complement each other so that their combined effect is better than the effect of either one alone.

It is essential that you take your medicine exactly as prescribed for maximum benefit.

An ingredient in this drug may cause excessive loss of potassium, which may lead to a condition called hypokalemia.

Warning signs are dryness of mouth, excessive thirst, weakness, drowsiness, restlessness, muscle pains or cramps, muscular fatigue, lack of urination, abnormal heart rhythms, and upset stomach. If warning signs occur, call your doctor.

This drug should be stopped at the first sign of despondency, early morning insomnia, loss of appetite, or sexual impotence. Drug-induced depression may persist for several months after the drug has been discontinued; it has been known to be severe enough to result in suicide attempts.

Cautions and Warnings

Do not take this drug if you have a history of mental depression, active peptic ulcer, or ulcerative colitis, or if you are sensitive or allergic to either of its ingredients, to similar drugs of the Hydrochlorothiazide group, or to sulfa drugs. If you have a history of allergy or bronchial asthma, you may also have a sensitivity or allergy to the Hydrochlorothiazide ingredient.

Pregnancy/Breast-feeding

Although the Hydrochlorothiazide ingredient has been used to treat specific conditions in pregnancy, unsupervised use by pregnant women should be avoided; the drug will cross the placenta and pass into the unborn child, possibly causing problems such as jaundice and low potassium. The Hydrochlorothiazide ingredient will pass into breast milk of nursing mothers, who should consider alternate feeding methods.

Seniors

Older adults are more sensitive to the blood-pressure-lowering effects of this drug. Follow your doctor's directions and report any side effects at once.

Possible Side Effects

Loss of appetite, stomach irritation, nausea, vomiting, cramps, diarrhea, constipation, dizziness, headache, tingling in the arms and legs, restlessness, chest pains, abnormal heart rhythms, drowsiness, depression, nervousness, anxiety, nightmares, glaucoma, blood disorders, rash, itching, fever, difficulty in breathing, muscle spasms, gout, weakness, high blood sugar, sugar in urine, blurred vision, stuffy nose, dryness of the mouth. Occasional: impotence or decreased sex drive.

Drug Interactions

Interaction with Digitalis or Quinidine may cause abnormal heart rhythms.

Interaction with drugs containing Lithium may lead to toxic effects of Lithium.

Avoid over-the-counter cough, cold, or allergy remedies containing stimulant drugs which may raise your blood pressure.

Food Interactions

You may need potassium from some outside source. This may be done by either taking a potassium supplement or by eating foods such as bananas, citrus fruits, melons, and tomatoes, which have high concentrations of potassium.

Usual Dose

Must be individualized to patient's response.

Special Information

Avoid over-the-counter medicines for the treatment of coughs, colds, and allergies: such medicines may contain stimulants. If you are unsure about them, ask your pharmacist.

If you forget to take a dose of Hydropres, take it as soon as you remember. If it is almost time for your next regularly scheduled dose, skip the one you forgot and continue with your regular schedule. Do not take a double dose.

Generic Name

Hydroxyzine

Brand Names

Anxanil	Hydroxyzine Pamoate
Atarax	Hy-Pam
Atozine	Vamate
Durrax	Vistaril
Hydroxyzine Hydrochloride	

(Also available in generic form)

Type of Drug

Antihistamine.

Prescribed for

Nausea and vomiting; the management of emotional stress such as anxiety, tension, agitation, or itching caused by allergies.

General Information

Hydroxyzine Hydrochloride may be of value in relieving temporary anxiety such as stress of dental or other minor surgical procedures, acute emotional problems, and the management of anxiety associated with stomach and digestive disorders, skin problems, and behavior difficulties in children. This drug has also been used in the treatment of alcoholism.

Cautions and Warnings

Hydroxyzine Hydrochloride should not be used if you know you are sensitive or allergic to this drug.

Pregnancy/Breast-feeding

Antihistamines have not been proven to be a cause of birth defects or other problems in pregnant women, although studies in animals have shown that Hydroxyzine may cause birth defects during the first months of pregnancy. Do not take any antihistamine without your doctor's knowledge.

Small amounts of antihistamine medicines pass into breast milk and may affect a nursing infant. Nursing mothers should avoid antihistamines or use alternate feeding methods while taking the medicine.

Seniors

Seniors are more sensitive to antihistamine side effects. Confusion, difficult or painful urination, dizziness, drowsiness, a faint feeling, dry mouth, nose, or throat, nightmares or excitement, nervousness, restlessness, or irritability are more likely to occur among older adults.

Possible Side Effects

The primary side effect of Hydroxyzine Hydrochloride is drowsiness, but this disappears in a few days or when the dose is reduced. At higher doses, you may experience dry mouth and occasional tremors or convulsions.

Drug Interactions

Hydroxyzine Hydrochloride has a depressive effect on the nervous system, producing drowsiness and sleepiness. It should not be used with alcohol, sedatives, tranquilizers, antihistamines, or other depressants.

Usual Dose

Adult: 25 to 100 milligrams 3 to 4 times per day.

Child (age 6 and over): 5 to 25 milligrams 3 to 4 times per day.

Child (under age 6): 5 to 10 milligrams 3 to 4 times per day.

Special Information

Be aware of the depressive effect of Hydroxyzine Hydrochloride: be careful when driving or operating heavy or dangerous machinery.

If you forget to take a dose of Hydroxyzine Hydrochloride, take it as soon as you remember. If it is almost time for your next regularly scheduled dose, skip the one you forgot and continue with your regular schedule. Do not take a double dose.

Generic Name

Ibuprofen

Brand Names

Motrin
Pamprin-B
Rufen

The following products are available without a prescription:

Advil   Midol 200
Haltran   Nuprin
Ibuprin   Trendar
Medipren

(Also available in generic form)

Type of Drug

Nonsteroidal anti-inflammatory.

Prescribed for

Relief of pain and inflammation of joints and muscles, fever, arthritis, mild to moderate pain of menstrual cramps, dental surgery and extractions, and athletic injuries such as sprains and strains.

General Information

Ibuprofen is one of several nonsteroidal anti-inflammatory drugs (NSAIDs) used to reduce inflammation, relieve pain, or reduce fever. All NSAIDs share the same side effects and may be used by patients who cannot tolerate Aspirin. Choice of one of these drugs over another depends on disease response, side effects seen in a particular patient, convenience of times to be taken, and cost. Different drugs or different doses of the same drug may be tried until the greatest effectiveness is seen with the fewest side effects.

In 1984 a reduced strength, 200 milligrams of Ibuprofen, became available without a prescription (Advil or Nuprin). These products are intended for the relief of mild to moderate pain and fever reduction, much the same way Aspirin would be used.

Cautions and Warnings

Do not take Ibuprofen if you are allergic or sensitive to this drug, Aspirin, or other NSAIDs. Ibuprofen may cause stomach ulcers. This drug should not be used by patients with severe kidney disease.

Pregnancy/Breast-feeding

This drug crosses into the blood circulation of a developing baby. It has not been found to cause birth defects. Pregnant women, or those who might become pregnant while taking this drug, should not take it without their doctor's approval. When the drug is considered essential by your doctor, the potential risk of taking the medicine must be carefully weighed against the benefit it might produce. Ibuprofen may also make labor longer.

This drug passes into breast milk, but has caused no problems among breast-fed infants. You must consider the potential effect on the nursing infant if breast-feeding while taking this medicine.

Seniors

Older adults are more sensitive to the stomach, kidney, and liver effects of this drug. Some doctors recommend that persons 70 and older take ½ the usual dose. Follow your doctor's directions and report any side effects at once.

Possible Side Effects

Most frequent: stomach upset, dizziness, headache, drowsiness, ringing in the ears. Others: heartburn, nausea, vomiting, bloating, gas in the stomach, stomach pain, diarrhea, constipation, dark stool, nervousness, insomnia, depression, confusion, tremor, loss of appetite, fatigue, itching, rash, double vision, abnormal heart rhythm, anemia or other changes in the composition of the blood, changes in liver function, loss of hair, tingling in the hands and feet, fever, breast enlargement, lowered blood sugar, effects on the kidneys. If symptoms appear, stop taking the medicine and see your doctor immediately.

Drug Interactions

Ibuprofen increases the action of Phenytoin, sulfa drugs, drugs used to control diabetes, and drugs used to thin the blood. If you are taking any of these medicines, be sure to discuss it with your doctor, who will probably change the dose of the other drug.

An adjustment in the dose of Ibuprofen may be needed if you take Phenobarbital.

Food Interactions

Take with meals to reduce stomach upset.

Usual Dose

800 to 1600 or even 3200 milligrams per day.

Overdosage

Symptoms may include drowsiness, dizziness, confusion, disorientation, lethargy, tingling in the hands or feet, numbness, nausea, vomiting, upset stomach, stomach pains, headache, ringing or buzzing in the ears, sweating and blurred vision. Take the victim to a hospital emergency room at once for treatment. ALWAYS bring the medicine bottle with you.

Special Information

Avoid Aspirin and alcoholic beverages while taking this medication. You may become dizzy or drowsy while taking this medicine. Be careful while driving or operating complex equipment. Call your doctor if you develop a skin rash, itching, swelling, visual disturbances, black stools, or a persistent headache while taking this medication.

If you forget to take a dose of Ibuprofen, take it as soon as you remember. If it is almost time for your next regularly scheduled dose, skip the one you forgot and continue with your regular schedule. Do not take a double dose.

Generic Name

Imipramine

Brand Names

Janimine

Tipramine

Tofranil

Tofranil-PM (long-acting
dosage form)

(Also available in generic form)

Type of Drug

Antidepressant.

Prescribed for

Depression with or without symptoms of anxiety.

General Information

Imipramine and other members of this group are effective in treating symptoms of depression. They can elevate your mood, increase physical activity and mental alertness, improve appetite and sleep patterns. These drugs are mild sedatives and therefore useful in treating mild forms of depression associated with anxiety. You should not expect instant results with this medicine: benefits are usually seen after 1 to 4 weeks. If symptoms are not affected after 6 to 8 weeks, contact your doctor. Occasionally this drug and other members of the group of drugs have been used in treating nighttime bed-wetting in young children, but they do not produce long-lasting relief, and therapy with one of them for nighttime bed-wetting is of questionable value.

Cautions and Warnings

Do not take Imipramine if you are allergic or sensitive to this or other members of this class of drug: Doxepin, Nortriptyline, Amitriptyline, Desipramine, and Protriptyline. The drugs should not be used if you are recovering from a heart attack. Imipramine may be taken with caution if you have a history of epilepsy or other convulsive disorders, difficulty in urination, glaucoma, heart disease, or thyroid disease. Imipramine can interfere with your ability to perform tasks which require concentration, such as driving or operating machinery. Do not stop taking this medicine without first discussing it with your doctor, since stopping may cause you to become nauseated, weak, and headachy.

Pregnancy/Breast-feeding

This drug, like some other antidepressants, crosses into your developing baby's circulation and may cause birth defects if taken during the first 3 months of pregnancy. There have been reports of newborn infants suffering from heart, breathing, and urinary problems after their mothers had taken an antidepressant of this type immediately before delivery. You should avoid taking this medication while pregnant.

Antidepressants of this type are known to pass into breast milk and may affect a breast-feeding infant, although this has not been proven. Nursing mothers should consider alternate feeding methods if taking this medicine.

Seniors

Older adults are more sensitive to the effects of this drug and often require a lower dose than a younger adult to do the same job. Follow your doctor's directions and report any side effects at once.

Possible Side Effects

Changes in blood pressure (both high and low), abnormal heart rates, heart attack, confusion, especially in elderly patients, hallucinations, disorientation, delusions, anxiety, restlessness, excitement, numbness and tingling in the extremities, lack of coordination, muscle spasms or tremors, seizures and/or convulsions, dry mouth, blurred vision, constipation, inability to urinate, rash, itching, sensitivity to bright light or sunlight, retention of fluids, fever, allergy, changes in composition of blood, nausea, vomiting, loss of appetite, stomach upset, diarrhea, enlargement of the breasts in males and females, increased or decreased sex drive, increased or decreased blood sugar.

Less common side effects: agitation, inability to sleep, nightmares, feeling of panic, peculiar taste in the mouth, stomach cramps, black coloration of the tongue, yellowing eyes and/or skin, changes in liver function, increased or decreased weight, perspiration, flushing, frequent urination, drowsiness, dizziness, weakness, headache, loss of hair, nausea, not feeling well.

Drug Interactions

Interaction with monoamine oxidase (MAO) inhibitors can cause high fevers, convulsions, and occasionally death. Don't take MAO inhibitors until at least 2 weeks after Imipramine has been discontinued.

Imipramine interacts with Guanethidine and Clonidine, drugs used to treat high blood pressure: if your doctor prescribes Imipramine and you are taking medicine for high blood pressure, be sure to discuss this with him.

Imipramine increases the effects of barbiturates, tranquilizers, other depressive drugs, and alcohol. Don't drink alcoholic beverages if you take this medicine.

Taking Imipramine and thyroid medicine will enhance the effects of the thyroid medicine. The combination can cause abnormal heart rhythms. The combination of Imipramine and Reserpine may cause overstimulation.

Large doses of Vitamin C (Ascorbic Acid), oral contraceptives, or smoking can reduce the effect of Imipramine. Drugs such as Bicarbonate of Soda, Acetazolamide, Quinidine, or Procainamide will increase the effect of Imipramine. Ritalin and phenothiazine drugs such as Thorazine and Compazine block the metabolism of Imipramine, causing it to stay in the body longer. This can cause possible overdose.

The combination of Imipramine with large doses of the sleeping pill Ethchlorvynol has caused patients to experience passing delirium.

Food Interactions

This drug is best taken on an empty stomach but you can take it with food if it upsets your stomach.

Usual Dose

Adult: initial dose, about 75 milligrams per day in divided doses; then increased or decreased as judged necessary by your doctor. The individualized dose may be less than 75 or up to 200 milligrams. Long-term patients being treated for depression may be given extended-acting medicine daily at bedtime or several times per day.

Adolescent and senior: initial dose, 30 or 40 milligrams per day. These patients require less of the drug because of increased sensitivity. Maintenance dose is usually less than 100 milligrams per day.

Child: dose for nighttime bed-wetting is 25 milligrams per day (age 6 and over), an hour before bedtime. If relief of bed-wetting does not occur within 1 week, the dose is increased to a daily 50 to 75 milligrams, depending on age; often in midafternoon and at bedtime. (A dose greater than 75 milligrams will increase side effects without increasing effectiveness.) The medication should be gradually tapered off; this may reduce the probability that the bed-wetting will return.

Overdosage

Symptoms are confusion, inability to concentrate, hallucinations, drowsiness, lowered body temperature, abnormal heart rate, heart failure, large pupils of the eyes, convulsions, severely lowered blood pressure, stupor, and coma (as well as agitation, stiffening of body muscles, vomiting, and high fever). The patient should be taken to a hospital emergency room immediately. ALWAYS bring the medicine bottle.

Special Information

Avoid alcohol and other drugs that depress the nervous system while taking this antidepressant. Do not stop taking this medicine unless your doctor has specifically told you to do so. Abruptly stopping this medicine may cause nausea, headache, and a sickly feeling. This medicine can cause drowsiness, dizziness, and blurred vision. Be careful when driving or operating complicated machinery. Avoid exposure to the sun or sun lamps for long periods of time. Call your doctor if dry mouth, difficulty urinating, or excessive sedation develops.

If you take Imipramine several times a day and forget a dose, take it as soon as you remember. If it is almost time for your next regularly scheduled dose, skip the one you forgot and continue with your regular schedule. If you take it once a day at bedtime and forget, don't take it when you get up; go back to your regular schedule. Call your doctor if you skip 2 or more days of medication. Never take a double dose.

Generic Name

Indapamide

Brand Name

Lozol

Type of Drug

Diuretic.

Prescribed for

Congestive heart failure, cirrhosis of the liver, high blood pressure, and other conditions where it is necessary to rid the body of excess water.

General Information

This diuretic is most similar to the thiazide diuretics in its action and effects on the body. Thiazides work on the kidneys to promote the release of sodium from the body, carrying water with it. They also cause you to lose potassium ions, chloride, and bicarbonate. There are no major differences between Indapamide and other thiazide diuretics.

Cautions and Warnings

Do not take Indapamide if you are allergic or sensitive to it or to any other thiazide drug or any sulfa drug. If you have a history of allergy or bronchial asthma, you may also have a sensitivity or allergy to Indapamide. Do not take this drug if you have kidney or liver disease.

Pregnancy/Breast-feeding

This drug should not be taken by pregnant women, or women who may become pregnant while using it, since it will pass into the blood system of the fetus. In those situations where it is deemed essential, the potential risk of the drug must be carefully weighed against any benefit it might produce. Thiazide diuretics are known to pass into breast milk. Nursing mothers should either not take the drug or change their feeding method.

Seniors

Older adults are more sensitive to the effects of this drug. Follow your doctor's directions and report any side effects at once.

Possible Side Effects

Loss of body potassium, leading to dry mouth, thirst, weakness, drowsiness, restlessness, muscle pains, cramps, or tiredness, low blood pressure, decreased frequency of urination, abnormal heart rhythm, and upset stomach. Other side effects are loss of appetite, nausea, vomiting, stomach bloating or cramps, diarrhea, constipation, yellowing of the skin or whites of the eyes, pancreas inflammation, liver inflammation (hepatitis), frequent urination (especially at night), headache, dizziness, fatigue, loss of energy, tiredness, a feeling of ill health, numbness in the hands or feet, nervousness, tension, anxiety, irritability, and agitation.

Less common side effects: kidney inflammation, impotence, reduced sex drive, light-headedness, drowsiness, fainting, difficulty sleeping, depression, tingling in the hands or feet, blurred vision, reduced levels of white blood cells and platelets, dizziness when rising quickly from a sitting or lying position, heart palpitations, chest pain, gout attacks, chills, stuffy nose, facial flushing, and weight loss.

Drug Interactions

Indapamide increases the effects of other blood-pressure-lowering drugs. This interaction is beneficial and often used to help treat people with high blood pressure.

The chances of losing body potassium are increased if you take Indapamide with Digoxin or with a corticosteroid anti-inflammatory drug. If you are taking medicine to treat diabetes and begin taking Indapamide, the dose of your diabetes medicine may have to be adjusted.

Indapamide will increase the effects of Lithium and the chances of developing Lithium toxicity by preventing it from passing out of your body.

People taking Indapamide for high blood pressure or heart failure should take care to avoid nonprescription medicines that might aggravate those conditions, such as decongestants, cold and allergy treatments, and diet pills, all of which may contain stimulants. If you are unsure about which medicine to choose, ask your pharmacist.

Dizziness when rising from a sitting or lying position may be worsened by taking Indapamide with alcoholic beverages, barbiturate-type sleeping pills, or narcotic pain relievers.

The effects of Indapamide may be counteracted by Indomethacin because of its effect on the kidneys. Colestipol Hydrocholoride or Cholestyramine, taken at the same time as Indapamide, will reduce the drug's effect by preventing it from being absorbed into the bloodstream.

Taking more than one diuretic drug at a time can result in an excessive and prolonged diuretic effect. This is especially true when a thiazide diuretic is combined with a "loop" diuretic such as Bumetanide, Ethacrynic Acid, or Furosemide.

Taking Indapamide and other thiazide-type diuretics with calcium or Vitamin D could result in excessive levels of calcium in the blood.

Sulfa drugs may increase the effects of Indapamide by increasing the amount of diuretic drug in the bloodstream.

Indapamide may increase the effect of Quinidine, taken for abnormal heart rhythms, by interfering with its release from the body via the kidneys.

Food Interactions

Indapamide may cause loss of body potassium (hypokalemia), a complication that can be avoided by adding foods high in potassium to your diet. Some potassium-rich foods are tomatoes, citrus fruits, melons, and bananas. Hypokalemia can also be prevented by taking a potassium supplement in pill, powder, or liquid form. Indapamide may be taken with food or meals if it upsets your stomach.

Usual Dose

2.5 to 5 milligrams per day.

Overdosage

The primary symptom of overdose is potassium deficiency and dehydration: confusion, dizziness, muscle weakness, upset stomach, excessive thirst, loss of appetite, lethargy (rare), drowsiness, restlessness (rare), tingling in the hands or feet, rapid heartbeat, nausea, and vomiting. Patients taking an overdose of this drug must be made to vomit with Syrup of Ipecac (available at any pharmacy) to remove any remaining drug from the stomach. Call your doctor or a poison control center before doing this. If you must go to a hospital emergency room, ALWAYS bring the medicine bottle. If overdose symptoms have developed or more than 1 hour has passed since the overdose was taken, do not make the victim vomit, just go to an emergency room.

Special Information

Always take your daily dose of Indapamide by 10:00 A.M. Taking it later in the day will increase the chances that you will be kept awake at night by the need to urinate frequently.

Call your doctor if muscle weakness, cramps, nausea, dizziness, or other severe side effects develop.

If you forget to take a dose of Indapamide, take it as soon as you remember. If it is almost time for your next regularly scheduled dose, skip the one you forgot and continue with your regular schedule. Do not take a double dose.

Brand Name

Inderide

Ingredients

Hydrochlorothiazide
Propranolol

(Also available in generic form)

Type of Drug

Antihypertensive.

Prescribed for

High blood pressure.

General Information

Inderide is a combination of two proven antihypertensive drugs. One of these works by directly affecting the dilation of the blood vessels; the other works by affecting the nerves which control the dilating of the blood vessels. The more dilated (open) these vessels are, the lower the blood pressure. This combination is good so long as both ingredients are present in the right amounts. If you need more or less of one ingredient than the other, you must take the ingredients as separate pills. Often, doctors are able to lower your blood pressure most effectively by manipulating the doses of one drug or the other. Inderide is also available in a long-acting combination known as Inderide LA.

Cautions and Warnings

Do not take this drug if you are allergic to either of the active ingredients or to sulfa drugs. If you have a history of heart failure, asthma, or upper respiratory disease, Inderide may aggravate the situation.

Pregnancy/Breast-feeding

This drug may cause birth defects or interfere with your baby's development. Check with your doctor before taking it if you are, or might be, pregnant.

If this drug is considered essential for a nursing mother, she should change the method of feeding her infant.

Seniors

Older adults are more sensitive to the effects of this drug. Follow your doctor's directions and report any side effects at once.

Possible Side Effects

May decrease the heart rate, aggravate heart failure or some other heart diseases, cause a tingling in the hands or feet, light-headedness, depression, sleeplessness, weakness, tiredness, feeling of not caring, hallucinations, visual disturbances, disorientation, loss of short-term memory, nausea, vomiting, upset stomach, cramps, diarrhea, constipation, allergic reactions including: sore throat, rash, and fever. Inderide can also cause adverse effects on the blood.

Inderide can cause a lowering of body potassium (hypokalemia). The signs of this include dryness of the mouth, weakness, thirst, lethargy, drowsiness, restlessness, muscle pains or cramps, muscle tiredness, low blood pressure, decreased frequency of urination. To treat this, potassium supplements are given as tablets, liquids, or powders.

Less common side effects include loss of appetite, dizziness, headache, increased sensitivity to the sun, dizziness when rising quickly from a sitting or lying position, muscle spasms, and loss of hearing (it comes back after the drug has been stopped).

Drug Interactions

Inderide may interact with Reserpine and similar drugs to cause very low blood pressure, slowed heart rate, and dizziness.

Inderide may cause a need for the alteration of your daily dose of oral antidiabetic drug.

Inderide should not be taken with Lithium drugs since there is an increased possibility of Lithium toxicity. This drug may interact with digitalis drugs to cause abnormal heart rhythms. This effect results from potassium loss and may be prevented by taking extra potassium.

Food Interactions

You may increase your natural consumption of potassium by eating more bananas, citrus fruits, melons, or tomatoes.

Usual Dose

4 tablets of either strength per day. The dose of this drug must be tailored to your needs for maximum benefit.

Overdosage

In case of overdosage contact your doctor or poison control center immediately. The patient may have to be taken to a hospital emergency room for treatment. ALWAYS bring the medicine bottle with you.

Special Information

Do not stop taking this medicine unless your doctor tells you to.

If you develop rash, severe muscle pains, or difficulty in breathing, call your doctor.

Avoid any over-the-counter drugs containing stimulants. If you are unsure which ones to avoid, ask your pharmacist.

If you forget to take a dose of Inderide, take it as soon as possible. However, if it is within 4 hours of your next dose (8 hours for Inderide LA), skip the forgotten dose and go back to your regular schedule. Do not take a double dose.

Generic Name

Indomethacin

Brand Names

Indameth
Indocin
Indocin SR (long-acting capsules)

(Also available in generic form)

Type of Drug

Nonsteroidal anti-inflammatory.

Prescribed for

Arthritis and other forms of inflammation of joints and muscles.

General Information

Indomethacin has pain-relieving, fever-lowering, and inflammation-reducing effects, but we do not know exactly how these effects are produced. Part of these actions may be due to Indomethacin's prostaglandin-inhibitory effects. It also can produce serious side effects at high doses. For this reason, the drug should be taken with caution. It is not a simple analgesic, like Aspirin or Ibuprofen.

Cautions and Warnings

Use Indomethacin with extra caution if you have a history of ulcers, bleeding diseases, or allergic reaction to Aspirin. It should be avoided by children under age 14, and patients with nasal polyps. This drug is not a simple pain reliever; it should be used only under the strict supervision of your doctor.

Pregnancy/Breast-feeding

This drug crosses into the blood circulation of a developing baby and may cause birth defects especially during the last 3 months of your pregnancy. Pregnant women, or those who might become pregnant while taking this drug, should not take it without their doctor's approval. When the drug is considered essential by your doctor, the potential risk of taking the medicine must be carefully weighed against the benefit it might produce.

This drug passes into breast milk and has caused problems in at least one breast-fed infant. You must consider the potential effect on the nursing infant if breast-feeding while taking this medicine.

Seniors

Older adults are more sensitive to the side effects of this drug, especially those affecting your stomach, liver, kidneys, and nervous system. Some doctors recommend persons 70 and older take ½ the usual dose. Follow your doctor's directions and report any side effects at once.

Possible Side Effects

Indomethacin may produce severe stomach upset or other reactions. It has caused ulcers in all portions of the gastrointestinal tract, including the esophagus, stomach, small intestine, and large intestine. For this reason any unusual stomach upset, nausea, vomiting, loss of appetite, gas, gaseous feeling, or feeling of being bloated must be reported immediately to your doctor. Indomethacin may cause blurred vision: this is an important side effect and must be reported to your doctor immediately. If you develop a persistent headache while taking Indomethacin, report this to your doctor immediately and stop taking the drug.

Indomethacin may aggravate preexisting psychiatric disturbances, epilepsy, or Parkinson's disease. It may cause reduction in mental alertness and coordination which can affect you particularly while driving, operating a machine or appliance, or engaging in any activity requiring alertness and concentration.

On rare occasions Indomethacin can cause effects on the liver, and anemia or other effects on components of the blood. People who are allergic to the drug can develop reactions including a rapid fall in blood pressure, difficulty in breathing, itching, and rashes. It has also caused ringing in the ears, retention of fluids in the body, elevation of blood pressure, passing of blood in the urine, loss of hair (occasional), vaginal bleeding, and increased blood sugar.

Drug Interactions

Avoid alcohol, which will aggravate any problem with drowsiness or lack of alertness.

Probenecid (Benemid) increases the amount of Indomethacin in your blood by reducing its elimination from the body. This interaction will reduce the amount of Indomethacin required.

If you are taking an anticoagulant (blood-thinning) drug and start taking Indomethacin, you probably will experience no serious interaction, but your doctor should know that you are taking both drugs so he can monitor the anticoagulant during the first week or two of Indomethacin therapy, in case dosage adjustment may be required.

Indomethacin increases the effect of antidiabetes drugs, digitalis drugs, Sulfinpyrazone, Lithium, and Verapamil.

Indomethacin may reduce the effects of some blood-pressure-lowering drugs.

Food Interactions

Since Indomethacin causes stomach upset in many patients and can be a source of ulcers, it should be taken with food or antacids. Adrenal corticosteroids, Aspirin, or other drugs may aggravate this problem. Space Indomethacin and such drugs at least 2 to 3 hours apart to minimize irritating effects on the stomach.

Usual Dose

50 to 150 milligrams per day, individualized to patient's needs.

Overdosage

Symptoms may include drowsiness, dizziness, confusion, disorientation, lethargy, tingling in the hands or feet, numbness, nausea, vomiting, upset stomach, stomach pains, headache, ringing or buzzing in the ears, sweating, and blurred vision. Take the victim to the hospital emergency room at once for treatment. ALWAYS bring the medicine bottle with you.

Special Information

Avoid Aspirin and alcoholic beverages while taking this medication. You may become dizzy or drowsy while taking this medicine. Be careful while driving or operating complex equipment. Call your doctor if you develop a skin rash, itching, swelling, visual disturbances, black stools, or a persistent headache while taking this medication.

The sustained-release capsules should not be crushed or chewed.

If you forget to take a dose of Indomethacin and you remember within about an hour of your regular time, take it right away. If you do not remember until later, skip the forgotten dose and go back to your regular schedule. Do not take a double dose.

Generic Name

Insulin

Brand Names

Insulin for Injection

Beef Regular Iletin II	Pork Regular Iletin II
Humulin BR	Regular Iletin
Humulin R	Regular Insulin
Novolin R	Regular Purified Pork Insulin
Novoline R PenFill	Velosulin

Insulin Zinc Suspension

Humulin L	Lente Insulin
Lente Iletin	Lente Purified Pork Insulin
Lente Iletin II	Novolin L

Insulin Zinc Suspension, Extended

Ultralente Iletin
Ultralente Insulin
Ultralente Purified Beef

Insulin Zinc Suspension, Prompt

Semilente Iletin
Semilente Insulin
Semilente Purified Pork

Isophane Insulin Suspension and Insulin Injection

Mixtard
Novolin 70/30

Isophane Insulin Suspension (NPH)

Beef NPH Iletin II   NPH Iletin
Humulin N   NPH Insulin
Insulatard NPH   NPH Purified Pork
Novolin N   Pork NPH Iletin II

Protamine Zinc Insulin Suspension

Protamine Zinc and   Protamine Zinc and
   Iletin (Beef and Pork)   Iletin II (Pork)
Protamine Zinc and
   Iletin II (Beef)

Type of Drug

Antidiabetic.

Prescribed for

Diabetes mellitus that cannot be controlled by dietary restriction. Insulin may also be used in a hospital to treat
hyperkalemia (high blood potassium levels).

General Information

Insulin is a complex hormone normally produced by the pancreas. Diabetes develops when we do not make enough
Insulin or when the Insulin we do make is not effective in our
bodies. At the present, most of the Insulin we use as a drug
we get from animals. Insulin derived from pork is closer in
chemical structure to our own Insulin than that derived from
beef. It causes fewer reactions.

Insulin used for injection is the unmodified material derived from the animal source. It starts to work quickly, and
lasts only 6 to 8 hours. People using only Insulin injection
must take several injections per day. Pharmaceutical scien-

tists have been able to add on to the Insulin molecule so as to help extend the time over which the drug can exert its effect. Insulin Zinc Suspension, like Insulin for injection, is considered rapid-acting. It starts to work in 30 to 60 minutes and lasts 12 to 16 hours.

Intermediate-acting Insulin starts working 1 to 1½ hours after injection and continues to work for 24 hours. Isophane Insulin Suspension and Insulin Zinc Suspension are intermediate-acting forms of Insulin. Long-acting Insulin begins working 4 to 8 hours after injection and its effect lasts for 36 hours or more. Protamine Zinc Insulin Suspension and Insulin Zinc Suspension (Extended) are long-acting types of Insulin.

Other factors have a definite influence on patients' response to Insulin: diet, amount of regular exercise, and other medicines being used.

Because Insulin is derived from a natural source, there are a number of normal contaminants in the products. In recent years, processes have been developed to remove many of these contaminants. The first process resulted in single-peak Insulin, with only one high point of drug effect, making the action of the drug more predictable and therefore safer. Today, all Insulin sold in the United States is single-peak. The second refinement resulted in purified Insulin. Several purified Insulin products are available. The advantage of purified Insulin over single-peak is that it produces fewer reactions at the injection site.

Recent developments in recombinant DNA research have led to the production of human Insulin. This product has fewer allergic reactions as compared to older Insulins manufactured from pork and/or beef sources. Human insulins may also be produced by semi-synthetic processes. These semi-synthetic insulins, however, start with an animal product and may contain some of the same impurities.

Cautions and Warnings

Patients taking Insulin *must* also follow the diet that has been prescribed. Be sure to take exactly the dose prescribed. Too much Insulin will cause lowering of the blood sugar and too little will not control the diabetes. Avoid alcoholic beverages.

Pregnancy/Breast-feeding

This drug has been found to be safe for use during pregnancy and breast-feeding. Remember, you should check with your doctor before taking any drug if you are pregnant. Pregnant diabetic women must exactly follow their doctor's directions for Insulin use.

Seniors

Older adults may use Insulin without special restriction. Be sure to follow your doctor's directions for medication and diet.

Possible Side Effects

Allergic reactions.

Drug Interactions

Insulin may affect blood-potassium levels and can therefore affect digitalis drugs. Patients on Insulin who begin taking oral contraceptive pills, adrenal corticosteroids (by mouth), Epinephrine, or thyroid hormones may have an increased need for Insulin. Thiazide diuretic drugs can raise blood-sugar levels and cause a need for more Insulin. The blood-sugar-lowering effects of Insulin can be increased by MAO inhibitor drugs, Phenylbutazone, Sulfinpyrazone, Tetracycline, alcoholic beverages, and anabolic steroid drugs (Oxymetholone, Oxandrolone, Methandrostenolone, Ethylestrenol, Stanozolol, Nandrolone). Patients taking these drugs may require a decrease in their Insulin dosage.

Food Interactions

Follow your doctor's directions for diet restrictions. Diet is a key element in controlling your disease.

Usual Dose

The dose and kind of Insulin must be individualized to the patient's need. Insulin is generally injected ½ hour before meals; the longer-acting forms are taken ½ hour before breakfast. Since Insulin can only be given by injection, patients must learn to give themselves their Insulin subcutaneously (under the skin) or have a family member or friend give them their injection. Hospitalized patients may receive Insulin injection directly into a vein.

One manufacturer has developed a device to aid in injecting Insulin. The device looks like a pen and is easily used. Another type of injection convenience device is the Insulin infusion pump. The infusion pump automatically administers a predetermined amount of regular Insulin. Consult your doctor or pharmacist for complete details on either of these devices.

Special Information

You may develop low blood sugar if you take too much Insulin, work or exercise more strenuously than usual, skip a meal, take Insulin too long before a meal, or vomit before a meal. Signs of low blood sugar may be fatigue, headache, drowsiness, nausea, tremulous feeling, sweating, or nervousness. If you develop any of these signs while taking Insulin, your blood sugar may be too low. The usual treatment for low blood sugar is eating a candy bar or lump of sugar, which diabetics should carry with them at all times. If the signs of low blood sugar do not clear up within 30 minutes, call your doctor. You may need further treatment.

If your Insulin is in suspension form, you must evenly distribute the suspended particles throughout the liquid before taking the dose out. Do this by rotating the vial and turning it over several times. Do not shake the vial too strenuously.

Insulin products are generally stable at room temperatures for about 2 years. They must be kept away from direct sunlight and extreme temperatures. Most manufacturers, however, still recommend that Insulin be stored in a refrigerator or a cool place whenever possible. Insulin should not be put in a freezer or exposed to very high temperatures; this can affect its stability. Partly used vials of Insulin should be thrown away after several weeks if not used.

Some Insulin products can be mixed. Do it only if so directed by your doctor. Insulin for injection may be mixed with Isophane Insulin Suspension and Protamine Zinc Insulin in any proportion. Insulin Zinc Suspension, Insulin Zinc Suspension (Prompt), and Insulin Zinc Suspension (Extended) may also be mixed in any proportions. Insulin for injection and Insulin Zinc Suspension must be mixed immediately before using. You should consistently use the same type and brand of Insulin syringes to prevent measuring errors and possible dosing errors.

Generic Name

Isosorbide Dinitrate

Brand Names

Dilatrate-SR	Isordil Titradose
Iso-Bid	Isotrate Timecelles
Isonate	Onset
Isordil	Sorate
Isordil Sublingual	Sorbitrate
Isordil Tembids	Sorbitrate SA

(Also available in generic form)

Type of Drug

Antianginal agent.

Prescribed for

Relief of heart or chest pain associated with angina pectoris; also, control or prevention of recurrence of chest or heart pain, and in reducing heart work in congestive heart failure and other similar conditions.

General Information

Isosorbide Dinitrate belongs to the class of drugs known as nitrates, which are used to treat pain associated with heart problems. The exact nature of their action is not fully understood. However, they are believed to relax muscles of veins and arteries.

Cautions and Warnings

If you know that you are allergic or sensitive to this drug or other drugs for heart pain such as Nitroglycerin, do not use Isosorbide Dinitrate. Anyone who has a head injury or has recently had a head injury should use this drug with caution.

Pregnancy/Breast-feeding

This drug crosses into the blood circulation of a developing baby. It has not been found to cause birth defects. Pregnant women, or those who might become pregnant while taking this drug, should not take it without their doctor's approval.

When the drug is considered essential by your doctor, the potential risk of taking the medicine must be carefully weighed against the benefit it might produce.

This drug passes into breast milk, but has caused no problems among bread-fed infants. You must consider the potential effect on the nursing infant if breast-feeding while taking this medicine.

Seniors

Older adults may take this medicine without restriction. Be sure to follow your doctor's directions for use.

Possible Side Effects

Flushing of the skin and headache are common, but should disappear after your body has had an opportunity to get used to the drug. You may experience dizziness and weakness in the process.

There is a possibility of blurred vision and dry mouth; if this happens stop taking the drug and call your physician.

Less common side effects include nausea, vomiting, weakness, sweating, rash with itching, redness, possible peeling. If these signs appear, discontinue the medication and consult your physician.

Drug Interactions

If you take Isosorbide Dinitrate, do not self-medicate with over-the-counter cough and cold remedies, since many of them contain ingredients which may aggravate heart disease.

Interaction with large amounts of whiskey, wine, or beer can cause rapid lowering of blood pressure resulting in weakness, dizziness, and fainting.

Food Interactions

Take Isosorbide Dinitrate on an empty stomach unless you get a headache which cannot be controlled by the usual means. If this occurs, the medication can be taken with meals.

Usual Dose

Average daily dose, 10 to 20 milligrams 4 times per day. The drug may be given in doses from 5 milligrams to 40 milligrams 4 times per day.

Sustained-release: 40 to 80 milligrams every 8 to 12 hours.

Special Information

If you take this drug sublingually (under the tongue) be sure the tablet is fully dissolved before swallowing the drug. Do not crush or chew the sustained-release capsules or tablets.

Call your doctor if you develop a headache, dizziness, facial flushing, blurred vision, or dry mouth.

If you forget to take a dose of Isosorbide Dinitrate, take it as soon as you remember. If it is almost time for your next regularly scheduled dose, skip the one you forgot and continue with your regular schedule. Do not take a double dose.

Generic Name

Isotretinoin

Brand Name

Accutane

Type of Drug

Antiacne.

Prescribed for

Severe cystic acne that has not responded to other treatment, including medicines applied to the skin and antibiotics.

Isotretinoin has been used experimentally to treat a variety of other skin disorders involving the process of keratinization, or hardening of skin cells, and a condition known as mycosis fungoides that begins in the skin and can progress to a form of leukemia. Isotretinoin treatment is usually successful for these conditions, but relatively high doses are usually needed.

General Information

Isotretinoin was one of the first specialized products of vitamin research to be released for prescription by doctors. Researchers have long known that several vitamins, including A and D, have special properties that make them attractive treatments for specific conditions. However, the vitamins themselves are not appropriate treatments for these conditions because of the side effects that would develop if you took the quantities needed to produce the desired effects.

It is not known exactly how Isotretinoin works in cases of severe cystic acne. But its effect is to reduce the amount of sebum (the oily substance that serves as the skin's natural lubricant) in the skin, shrink the skin glands that produce sebum, and inhibit the process of keratinization, in which skin cells become hardened and block the flow of sebum onto the skin. Keratinization is key to the problem of severe acne because it leads to the buildup of sebum within skin follicles and causes the formation of closed comedones (whiteheads). Sebum production may be permanently reduced after Isotretinoin treatment, but no one knows why it has this effect.

Cautions and Warnings

People allergic or sensitive to Vitamin A, any Vitamin A product, or to Paraben preservatives used in Accutane should not use Isotretinoin.

Isotretinoin has been associated with several cases of increased fluid pressure inside the head. The symptoms of this condition, known as pseudotumor cerebri, are severe headaches, nausea, vomiting, and visual disturbances. Isotretinoin may cause temporary opaque spots on the cornea of your eye, causing visual disturbances. These generally go away by themselves within 2 months after the drug has been stopped. Several cases of severe bowel inflammation, indicated by abdominal discomfort and pain, severe diarrhea, or bleeding from the rectum, have developed in people taking Isotretinoin.

Pregnancy/Breast-feeding

This product should never be used by women who are pregnant or who might become pregnant while using it because it is known to cause harm to the developing baby when taken during pregnancy. Specifically, Isotretinoin can cause abnormalities of the head, brain, eye, ear, and hearing mechanisms. Several cases of spontaneous abortion have been linked to Isotretinoin.

Before taking this drug, women of childbearing age or potential should take a simple urinary pregnancy test to confirm that they are not pregnant. Also, you must be absolutely certain that effective birth control is used for 1 month before and during, and 1 month after Isotretinoin treatment. Accidental pregnancy during Isotretinoin therapy should be considered possible grounds for a therapeutic abortion. *Discuss this with your doctor immediately*. Nursing mothers should not take Isotretinoin because of the possibility that it will affect the nursing infant. It is not known if Isotretinoin passes into breast milk.

Seniors

Older adults may take this medication without special restriction. Follow your doctor's directions and report any side effects at once.

Possible Side Effects

The frequency of side effects increases with your daily dose, the most severe effects occurring at daily doses above 0.45 milligrams per pound of body weight per day. The most common side effects are dry, chapped, and inflamed lips, dry mouth, dry nose, nosebleeds, eye irritation and conjunctivitis (red-eye), dry and flaky skin, rash, itching, peeling of skin from the face, palms of the hands, and soles of the feet, unusual sensitivity to sunlight, temporary skin discoloration, dry mucous membranes of the mouth and nose, brittle nails, inflammation of the nailbed or bone under the nail of either the hands or feet, temporary thinning of the hair, nausea, vomiting, and abdominal pains, tiredness, lethargy, sleeplessness, headache, tingling in the hands or feet, dizziness, protein, blood, and white blood cells in the urine, blurred vision, urinary difficulty, bone and joint aches and pains, muscle pains, and stiffness.

Isotretinoin causes extreme elevations of blood triglycerides and milder elevations of other blood fats, including cholesterol. It also can cause an increased blood-sugar and uric-acid level and an increase in liver-function-test values.

Less common side effects: crusting over wounds caused by an exaggerated healing response stimulated by the drug, hair problems other than thinning, loss of appetite, upset stomach or intestinal discomfort, severe bowel inflammation, stomach or intestinal bleeding, weight loss, visual disturbances, pseudotumor cerebri (see "Cautions and Warnings" for symptoms), mild bleeding or easy bruising, fluid retention, infections of the lungs or respiratory system; several people taking Isotretinoin have developed widespread herpes simplex infections.

Drug Interactions

Supplemental Vitamin A increases Isotretinoin side effects and must be avoided while you are taking this medicine.

Alcohol should be avoided while you are taking Isotretinoin since the combination can cause severe elevations of blood triglyceride levels.

People taking Isotretinoin who have developed pseudotumor cerebri have usually been taking a Tetracycline antibiotic. Although the link has not been definitely established, you should avoid Tetracycline antibiotics while taking this medicine.

Food Interactions

Isotretinoin should be taken with food or meals.

Avoid eating beef liver, calf's liver, or chicken liver while taking Isotretinoin. Liver contains extremely large amounts of Vitamin A. Foods with moderate amounts of Vitamin A that you need not avoid but should limit your intake of are apricots, broccoli, cantaloupe, carrots, endive, persimmon, pumpkin, spinach, and winter squash.

Usual Dose

0.22 to 0.9 milligrams per pound of body weight per day, in 2 divided doses for 15 to 20 weeks. Lower doses may be effective, but relapses are more common. Since Isotretinoin, like Vitamin A, dissolves in body fat, people weighing more than 155 pounds may need doses at the high end of the usual range.

If the total cyst count drops by 70 percent before 15 to 20 weeks, the drug may be stopped. Treatment should stop for 2 months after the 15-to-20 week treatment. A second course of treatment may be given if the acne doesn't clear up.

Overdosage

Isotretinoin overdose is likely to cause nausea, vomiting, lethargy, and other frequent side effects. Patients taking an

overdose of this drug must be made to vomit with Syrup of
Ipecac (available at any pharmacy) to remove any remaining
drug from the stomach. Call your doctor or a poison control
center before doing this. If you must go to a hospital emergency room, ALWAYS bring the medicine bottle.

Special Information

You may become unusually sensitive to sunlight while taking this drug. Use a sunscreen and wear protective clothing
until your doctor can determine if you are likely to develop
this effect.

Be sure your doctor knows if you are pregnant or plan to
become pregnant while taking Isotretinoin, if you are breast-
feeding a baby, if you are a diabetic, if you are taking a
Vitamin A supplement (as a multivitamin or Vitamin A alone),
or if you or any family member has a history of high blood
triglyceride levels.

Call your doctor if any severe side effects develop. Abdominal pain, bleeding from the rectum, severe diarrhea,
headache, nausea and vomiting, visual difficulty of any kind,
severe muscle or bone and joint aches or pains, and unusual
sensitivity to sunlight or to ultraviolet light are especially
important.

Sometimes, acne actually gets a little worse when Isotretinoin treatment begins, but subsequently it starts to improve.
Don't be alarmed if this happens, but be sure to tell your
doctor, who will want to know.

Do not donate blood during Isotretinoin treatment or for
up to 30 days after you have stopped because of risk to a
developing fetus of a pregnant woman who might receive
the blood.

If you forget to take a dose of Isotretinoin, take it as soon
as you remember. If it is almost time for your next regularly
scheduled dose, skip the one you forgot and continue with
your regular schedule. Do not take a double dose.

Generic Name

Ketoconazole

Brand Names

Nizoral
Nizoral Cream

Type of Drug

Antifungal.

Prescribed for

Thrush and other systemic fungus infections, including candidiasis, histoplasmosis, and blastomycosis. Ketoconazole may also be prescribed for fungus infections of the skin, fingernails, and vagina.

General Information

This medicine is effective against a wide variety of fungus organisms. It works by disrupting the fungus cell's membrane, ultimately destroying the cell.

Cautions and Warnings

Ketoconazole has been associated with liver inflammation and damage. At least 1 of every 10,000 people who take the drug will develop this condition. In most cases, the inflammation subsides when the drug is discontinued. Do not take Ketoconazole if you have had an allergic reaction to it. It should not be used to treat fungus infections of the nervous system because only small amounts of the drug will enter that part of the body.

Pregnancy/Breast-feeding

Animals given doses of Ketoconazole larger than the maximum human dose have shown some damage in their developing offspring. This drug should be avoided by pregnant women or women who may become pregnant while using it. In those situations where it is deemed essential, the potential risk of the drug must be carefully weighed against any benefit it might produce. Nursing mothers who must take Ketoconazole should find an alternative method of feeding their infants since the drug passes into breast milk.

Seniors

Older adults may take this medication without special restriction. Follow your doctor's directions and report any side effects at once.

Possible Side Effects

Nausea, vomiting, upset stomach, abdominal pain or discomfort, itching, swelling of male breasts. Most of these side effects are mild, and only a small number of people (1.5 percent) have to stop taking the drug because of severe side effects.

Less common side effects: headache, dizziness, drowsiness or tiredness, fever, chills, unusual sensitivity to bright lights, diarrhea, reduced sperm count, male impotence, and reduced levels of blood platelets.

Drug Interactions

Antacids, histamine H_2 antagonists, and other drugs that reduce the amount of acid in the stomach will counteract the effects of Ketoconazole by preventing it from being absorbed. This drug requires an acid environment to pass into the blood.

When Ketoconazole is taken together with Rifampin, both drugs lose their effectiveness.

The combination of Isoniazid and Ketoconazole causes a neutralization of the Ketoconazole's effect. These interactions occur even when drug doses are separated by 12 hours.

Ketoconazole increases the amount of Cyclosporine in your blood and the chances for kidney damage caused by Cyclosporine. It also increases the effect of oral anticoagulant drugs.

Taking Ketoconazole and Phenytoin can affect the amount of either medicine in your blood, increasing or decreasing either drug's effect.

Food Interactions

Ketoconazole should be taken with food or meals to increase the amount absorbed into the blood. This happens because food stimulates acid release, and Ketoconazole is absorbed much more efficiently when there is acid in the stomach.

Usual Dose

Tablets:
Adult: 200 to 400 milligrams taken once per day. Dosage may continue for several months, depending on the type of infection being treated.
Child (age 2 and up): 1.5 to 3 milligrams per pound of body weight once per day.
Child (under age 2): this drug should not be used.
Cream: Apply to affected and immediate surrounding areas 1 or 2 times a day for 14 days.

Overdosage

The most likely effects of Ketoconazole overdose are liver damage and exaggerated versions of the drug's side effects. Victims of Ketoconazole overdose should be immediately given Bicarbonate of Soda or any other antacid to reduce the amount of drug absorbed into the blood. Call your local poison control center for more information. If you take the victim to a hospital emergency room for treatment, ALWAYS bring the prescription bottle.

Special Information

If you must take antacids or other ulcer treatments, separate doses of those medicines from Ketoconazole doses by at least 2 hours. Anything that reduces your stomach-acid levels will reduce the amount of Ketoconazole absorbed into the blood.

Use caution while doing anything that requires intense concentration, like driving a car, or operating machinery. This drug can cause headaches, dizziness, and drowsiness.

Call your doctor if you develop pains in the stomach or abdomen, severe diarrhea, a high fever, unusual tiredness, loss of appetite, nausea, vomiting, yellow discoloration of the skin or whites of the eyes, pale stools, or dark urine.

If you forget to take a dose of Ketoconazole, take it as soon as you remember. If it is almost time for your next regularly scheduled dose, space the missed dose and the next dose 10 to 12 hours apart. Then go back to your regular schedule.

Generic Name

Ketoprofen

Brand Name

Orudis

Type of Drug

Nonsteroidal anti-inflammatory.

Prescribed for

Rheumatoid and osteoarthritis; pain associated with amenorrhea.

General Information

Ketoprofen is one of many nonsteroidal anti-inflammatory drugs (NSAIDs) sold in the United States to reduce inflammation, relieve pain and fever, and relieve menstrual cramps and discomfort. The choice of one member of this group over another often depends on your individual response to a specific drug. Because of this, it is common to try several of these drugs before you find the one that is right for you. Ketoprofen starts working in about ½ hour and will last for about 3 hours.

Cautions and Warnings

Do not take this product if you are allergic to Aspirin or to any other NSAID. This drug can worsen stomach ulcers or cause a new ulcer to develop. It should be used with caution if you have kidney disease.

Pregnancy/Breast-feeding

This drug crosses into the blood circulation of a developing baby. It has not been found to cause birth defects. Pregnant women, or those who might become pregnant while taking this drug, should not take it without their doctor's approval. When the drug is considered essential by your doctor, the potential risk of taking the medicine must be carefully weighed against the benefit it might produce.

This drug passes into breast milk, but has caused no problems among breast-fed infants. You must consider the potential effect on the nursing infant if breast-feeding while taking this medicine.

Seniors

Older adults are more sensitive to the stomach, kidney, and liver effects of this drug. Some doctors recommend that persons 70 years of age and older take ½ the usual dose. Follow your doctor's directions and report any side effects at once.

Possible Side Effects

Most frequent: upset stomach, dizziness, headache, drowsiness, ringing in the ears.

Other side effects include heartburn, nausea, vomiting, bloating, stomach gas or pain, diarrhea, constipation, dark stools, nervousness, sleeplessness, depression, confusion, tremor, loss of appetite, fatigue, itching, rash, double or blurred vision, dry or irritated eyes, heart failure, palpitations, abnormal heart rhythms, anemia or other changes in the composition of your blood, changes in liver function, hair loss, tingling in the hands or feet, fever, enlarged breasts, blood in the urine, urinary irritation, thirst, frequent urination, kidney damage, low blood sugar, asthma, difficulty breathing, skin rash, itching, swelling, black-and-blue marks.

Drug Interactions

Aspirin causes this drug to be eliminated from the body more rapidly than normal. Do not take this drug together with Methotrexate, used to treat cancers. One person died from the combination. This drug may increase the effectiveness of anticoagulant (blood-thinning) drugs. It can increase blood-clotting time by 3 to 4 minutes. Taking this drug together with a thiazide diuretic increases the chances for kidney failure.

Ketoprofen may increase the effects of sulfa drugs, antidiabetes drugs, and Phenytoin or other drugs for seizure disorders.

Food Interactions

You may take this drug with food if it upset your stomach.

Usual Dose

50 to 75 milligrams 3 or 4 times a day. No more than 300 milligrams per day.

Senior and patient with kidney problems: start with ½ to ⅓ the usual dose.

Overdosage

Symptoms may include drowsiness, dizziness, confusion, disorientation, lethargy, tingling in the hands or feet, numbness, nausea, vomiting, upset stomach, stomach pains, headache, ringing or buzzing in the ears, sweating, and blurred vision. Take the victim to a hospital emergency room at once for treatment. ALWAYS bring the medicine bottle with you.

Special Information

Avoid Aspirin and alcoholic beverages while taking this medication. You may become dizzy or drowsy while taking this medicine. Be careful while driving or operating complex equipment. Call your doctor if you develop a skin rash, itching, swelling, visual disturbances, black stools, or a persistent headache while taking this medication.

If you forget to take a dose of Ketoprofen, take it as soon as you remember. If it is almost time for your next regularly scheduled dose, skip the one you forgot and continue with your regular schedule. Do not take a double dose.

Generic Name

Labetalol Hydrochloride

Brand Names

Normodyne
Trandate

Type of Drug

Alpha-beta–adrenergic blocking agent.

Prescribed for

High blood pressure.

General Information

This drug, first studied for its effect as a beta blocker, is a unique approach to high-blood-pressure treatment because it selectively blocks both alpha and beta adrenergic impulses. This combination of actions contributes to its ability to reduce your blood pressure. It may be better than other beta-blocking drugs because it rarely affects heart rate. Other drugs can increase or decrease heart rate.

Cautions and Warnings

People with asthma, severe heart failure, reduced heart rate, and heart block should not take Labetalol Hydrochloride.

People with angina who take Labetalol Hydrochloride for high blood pressure should have their dose reduced gradually over a 1-to-2-week period, instead of having it discontinued suddenly, to avoid possible aggravation of the angina.

Labetalol Hydrochloride should be used with caution if you have liver disease because your ability to eliminate the drug from your body may be impaired.

Pregnancy/Breast-feeding

This drug crosses into the blood circulation of a developing baby. It has not been found to cause birth defects. Pregnant women, or those who might become pregnant while taking this drug, should not take it without their doctor's approval. When the drug is considered essential by your doctor, the potential risk of taking the medicine must be carefully weighed against the benefit it might produce.

This drug passes into breast milk, but has caused no problems among breast-fed infants. You must consider the potential effect on the nursing infant if breast-feeding while taking this medicine.

Seniors

Senior citizens may be more or less sensitive to the effects of this medicine. Your dosage of this drug must be adjusted to your individual needs by your doctor. Seniors may be more likely to suffer from cold hands and feet and reduced body temperature, chest pains, a general feeling of ill health, sudden difficulty breathing, sweating, or changes in heartbeat because of this medicine.

Possible Side Effects

Most Labetalol Hydrochloride side effects develop early in the course of treatment and increase with larger doses. Side effects include dizziness, tingling of the scalp, nausea, vomiting, upset stomach, taste distortion, fatigue, sweating, male impotence, urinary difficulty, diarrhea, bile-duct blockage, bronchial spasm, breathing difficulty, muscle weakness, cramps, dry eyes, blurred vision, rash, swelling of the face, and loss of hair.

Less frequent adverse effects of Labetalol Hydrochloride include aggravation of lupus erythematosus, a disease of body connective tissue, and stuffy nose. Because this drug is a beta blocker, it has the potential to cause mental depression, confusion and disorientation, loss of short-term memory, emotional instability, colitis, drug allergy (fever, sore throat, breathing difficulty), and reduction in the levels of white blood cells and blood platelets.

Drug Interactions

Labetalol Hydrochloride may prevent normal signs of low blood sugar from appearing and can also interfere with the action of oral antidiabetes drugs.

The combination of Labetalol Hydrochloride and a tricyclic antidepressant drug can cause tremor.

This drug may interfere with the effectiveness of some antiasthma drugs, especially Ephedrine, Isoproterenol, and other beta stimulants.

Cimetidine increases the amount of Labetalol Hydrochloride absorbed into the bloodstream from oral tablets.

Labetalol Hydrochloride may increase the blood-pressure-lowering effect of Nitroglycerin.

Food Interactions

This medicine may be taken with food if it upsets your stomach because it is unaffected by food in the stomach. In fact, food increases the amount of Labetalol Hydrochloride absorbed into your blood.

Usual Dose

The usual starting dose is 100 milligrams taken twice per day. The dosage may be increased gradually to as much as

1200 milligrams twice per day, but the usual maintenance dose is in the range of 200 to 400 milligrams twice daily.

Overdosage

Labetalol Hydrochloride overdose slows your heart rate and causes an excessive drop in blood pressure. The possible consequences of these effects can be treated only in a hospital emergency room. ALWAYS bring the medicine bottle with you.

Special Information

This medication is meant to be taken on a continuing basis. Do not stop it unless instructed to do so by your doctor. Weakness, breathing difficulty, or other side effects should be reported to your doctor as soon as possible. Most side effects are not serious, but a small number of people (about 7 in 100) have to switch to another medicine because of drug side effects.

If you forget to take a dose of Labetalol Hydrochloride, take it as soon as possible. However, if it is within 8 hours of your next dose, skip the forgotten dose and go back to your regular schedule. Do not take a double dose.

Generic Name

Levobunolol

Brand Name

Betagan

Type of Drug

Beta-adrenergic blocking agent.

Prescribed for

Open-angle glaucoma (increased fluid pressure inside the eye).

General Information

When applied to the eye, Levobunolol eye drops work in the same way as the other beta-blocker eye drops, Timolol and

Betaxolol. It reduces fluid pressure inside the eye by reducing the production of eye fluids and slightly increasing the rate at which fluids flow through and leave the eye. Beta-blocking eye drops produce a greater drop in eye pressure than either Pilocarpine or Epinephrine but may be combined with these or other drugs to produce a more pronounced drop in eye pressure.

Cautions and Warnings

Levobunolol should not be used if you have asthma or other severe lung disease, heart failure, heart block, or a very slow heart rate. Your doctor should give careful consideration to the use of Levobunolol if you have diabetes or overactive thyroid because Levobunolol may mask important signs of low blood sugar or overactive thyroid. Emphysema and other chronic (lung) diseases should be considered as a reason to avoid this drug because it can, if absorbed into your blood, cause spasm of the bronchial muscles and may counteract the effect of drugs used to treat these diseases.

Pregnancy/Breast-feeding

This drug may cross into the blood circulation of a developing baby. It has not been found to cause birth defects. Pregnant women, or those who might become pregnant while using these eye drops, should not take them without their doctor's approval. When the drug is considered essential by your doctor, the potential risk of taking the medicine must be carefully weighed against the benefit it might produce.

It is not known if Levobunolol passes into breast milk. Levobunolol has caused no problems among breast-fed infants. You must consider the potential effect on the nursing infant if breast-feeding while taking this medicine.

Seniors

Senior citizens may be more or less sensitive to the effects of this medication. Your dosage of Levobunolol must be adjusted to your individual need by your doctor. Seniors are more likely to suffer from drug side effects.

Possible Side Effects

The more common side effects of Levobunolol include tearing, stinging of the eye, and redness or inflammation of the eye.

Less common side effects include headache, dizziness, poor muscle control, lethargy and, rarely, a skin rash. If Levobunolol is absorbed into your bloodstream, it can cause the same side effects as Timolol eye drops (see page 853).

Drug Interactions

Levobunolol should be used with caution if you are taking another beta-blocking drug by mouth. If Levobunolol is absorbed into your bloodstream it can increase the effects of that oral drug on your body and also increase the chance for drug side effects.

If Levobunolol is absorbed into the blood, it can mask the effects of antidiabetes medicine and can enhance the effects of Reserpine, producing very low blood pressure, dizziness, and possible fainting.

Food Interactions

Levobunolol eye drops may be used without regard to meals.

Usual Dose

One drop in the affected eye 1 or 2 times a day.

Overdosage

Possible symptoms are very slow heartbeat, heart failure, low blood pressure, and spasms of the bronchial muscles, making it hard to breathe. Take the victim to a hospital emergency room for treatment. ALWAYS bring the medicine container with you.

Special Information

To administer the eye drop, lie down or tilt your head backward and look at the ceiling. Hold the dropper above your eye and drop the medicine inside your lower lid while looking up. To prevent possible infection, don't allow the dropper to touch your fingers, eyelid, or any surface. Release the lower lid and keep your eye open. Don't blink for about 30 seconds. Press gently on the bridge of your nose at the inside corner of your eye for about a minute. This will help circulate the medicine around your eye. Wait at least 5 minutes before using any other eye drops.

If you forget to instill a dose of Levobunolol, do it as soon as you remember. If it is almost time for your next regularly scheduled dose, skip the one you forgot and continue with your regular schedule. Do not instill a double dose.

If you use Levobunolol once a day and forget to take it for an entire day, skip the forgotten dose and follow your regular schedule.

Generic Name

Levodopa (L-Dopa)

Brand Names

Dopar
Larodopa

(Also available in generic form)

Type of Drug

Anti-Parkinsonian.

Prescribed for

Parkinson's disease; relief of pain associated with Shingles (Herpes Zoster).

General Information

Parkinson's disease can develop as a result of changes in the utilization of dopamine in the brain or damage to the central nervous system caused by carbon monoxide poisoning or manganese poisoning. It usually develops in the elderly because of hardening of the arteries. In many cases, the cause of Parkinson's disease is not known. Levodopa works by entering into the brain where it is converted to dopamine, a chemical found in the central nervous system. The new dopamine replaces what is deficient in people with Parkinson's disease. Another drug used to treat Parkinson's disease is Amantadine (Symmetrel). It has been shown to increase the amount of dopamine released in the brain.

Cautions and Warnings

Patients with severe heart or lung disease, asthma, or kidney, liver, or hormone diseases should be cautious about using this drug. Do not take it if you have a history of stomach ulcer. People with a history of psychosis must be treated with extreme care; this drug can cause depression with suicidal tendencies.

Pregnancy/Breast-feeding

Levodopa has not been studied in humans; however, studies show problems with the babies' growth in pregnant and nursing animals. Pregnant women should take this drug only if it is absolutely necessary. Women taking this drug must not breast-feed their infants.

High doses of Amantadine (Symmetrel), another drug used to treat Parkinson's disease, have been shown to cause birth defects and harm the unborn child.

Nursing while using Amantadine is not recommended since it can cause skin rashes, vomiting, or urination problems in the baby.

Seniors

Older adults may require smaller doses of Levodopa than younger adults because they are less tolerant to the drug's effects. Also, the body enzyme that breaks the drug down decreases with age, so a large dose is not needed.

Seniors who respond to Levodopa treatments, especially those with osteoporosis, should resume activity gradually. Sudden increases in mobility lead to a greater possibility of broken bones than a gradual return to physical activity.

Seniors, especially those with heart disease, are more likely to develop abnormal heart rhythms and other cardiac side effects of Levodopa.

Possible Side Effects

Muscle spasms, inability to control arms, legs, or facial muscles, loss of appetite, nausea, vomiting (with or without stomach pain), dry mouth, difficulty eating, dribbling saliva from the corners of the mouth (due to poor muscle control), tiredness, hand tremors, headache, dizziness, numbness, weakness and a faint feeling, confusion, sleeplessness, grinding of the teeth, nightmares, euphoria, hallucinations, delusions, agitation and anxiousness, feeling of general ill health.

Less common side effects: heart irregularities or palpitations, dizziness when standing or arising in the morning, mental changes (depression, with or without suicidal tendencies; paranoia; loss of some intellectual function), difficulty urinating, muscle twitching, burning of the tongue, bitter taste, diarrhea, constipation, unusual breathing patterns, double or blurred vision, hot flashes, weight gain or loss, darkening of the urine, or sweat.

Rare adverse effects include stomach bleeding, development of an ulcer, high blood pressure, convulsions, adverse effects on the blood, difficulty controlling the eye muscles, feeling of being stimulated, hiccups, loss of hair, hoarseness, decreasing size of male genitalia, and retention of fluids.

Drug Interactions

The effect of Levodopa is increased when it is used together with an anticholinergic drug (such as Trihexyphenidyl). If one of these drugs is stopped, the change must be gradual to allow for adjustments in the other one. Levodopa can interact with drugs for high blood pressure to cause further lowering of pressure. Dosage adjustments in the high blood pressure medication may be needed. Methyldopa (a drug for high blood pressure) may increase the effects of Levodopa.

The effects of Levodopa may be antagonized by Reserpine, benzodiazepine drugs, phenothiazine-type tranquilizing drugs, Phenytoin, Papaverine, and Vitamin BF.

Patients taking MAO inhibitor drugs should stop taking them 2 weeks before starting to take Levodopa.

Levodopa may increase the effects of stimulants such as amphetamines, Ephedrine, Epinephrine, Isoproterenol, and the tricyclic antidepressant drugs.

Levodopa will affect the blood sugar of diabetic patients. Adjustments in dosages of antidiabetic medicine may be needed.

Food Interactions

Do not take vitamin preparations which contain Vitamin B_6, pyridoxine. Vitamin B_6 will decrease the effectiveness of Levodopa.

This drug can cause upset stomach; each dose should be taken with food.

Usual Dose

0.5 to 8 grams per day. Dosage must be individualized to patient's need.

Overdosage

People taking an overdose of Levodopa must be treated in a hospital emergency room. ALWAYS bring the prescription bottle with you.

Special Information

Be careful while driving or operating any machinery.

Call your doctor *immediately* if any of the following occur: abnormal urine test for sugar (diabetics), uncontrollable movement of the face, eyelids, mouth, tongue, neck, arms, hands, or legs, mood changes, palpitations or irregular heartbeats, difficulty urinating, severe nausea or vomiting.

If you forget to take a dose of Levodopa, take it as soon as possible. However, if it is within 2 hours of your next dose, skip the forgotten dose and go back to your regular schedule. Do not take a double dose.

Generic Name

Levothyroxine Sodium

Brand Names

Levothroid
Synthroid

(Also available in generic form)

Type of Drug

Thyroid replacement.

Prescribed for

Replacement of thyroid hormone or low output of hormone from the thyroid gland.

General Information

Levothyroxine Sodium is one of several thyroid replacement

products available. The major difference between these products is in effectiveness in treating certain phases of thyroid disease.

Although several different companies make generic versions of this drug, you should not switch between brands unless your doctor knows about it. This applies to all brands and generic versions of Levothyroxine tablets.

Cautions and Warnings

If you have hyperthyroid disease or high output of thyroid hormone you should not use Levothyroxine Sodium. Symptoms of hyperthyroid disease include headache, nervousness, sweating, rapid heartbeat, chest pains, and other signs of central nervous system stimulation. If you have heart disease or high blood pressure, thyroid therapy should not be used unless it is clearly indicated and supervised by your physician. If you develop chest pains or other signs of heart disease while you are taking thyroid medication, contact your doctor immediately.

Pregnancy/Breast-feeding

Small amounts of the thyroid hormones will find their way into the bloodstream of a developing fetus. However, they have not been associated with birth defects or other problems when used in the dosages required to maintain normal thyroid function in the mother.

Small amounts of the thyroid hormones pass into breast milk but have not been associated with problems in nursing infants.

Seniors

Older adults are more sensitive to the effects of the thyroid hormones. The usual dosage of thyroid hormones should be reduced by about 25 percent after age 60.

Possible Side Effects

Most common: palpitations of the heart, rapid heartbeat, abnormal heart rhythms, weight loss, chest pains, shaking of the hands, headache, diarrhea, nervousness, menstrual irregularity, inability to sleep, sweating, inability to stand heat. These symptoms may be controlled by adjusting the dose of the medication. If you are suffering from one or more side effects, you must contact your doctor immediately so that the proper dose adjustment can be made.

Drug Interactions

Taking a thyroid hormone together with Colestipol or Cholestyramine can reduce the effect of the thyroid product by preventing its passage into your bloodstream. Separate doses of these 2 medicines by 4 to 5 hours.

The combination of Maprotiline and a thyroid hormone may increase the chances for abnormal heart rhythms. Your doctor may have to adjust the dose of your thyroid hormone.

Aspirin and other salicylate products may increase the effectiveness of your thyroid hormone by releasing more drug into the blood from body storage sites.

Estrogen drugs may increase your need for thyroid hormones.

Avoid taking over-the-counter products containing stimulant drugs, such as many drugs used to treat coughs, colds, or allergies, which will affect your heart and may cause symptoms of overdosage.

Thyroid replacement therapy may increase the effect of anticoagulant (blood-thinning) drugs such as Warfarin or Bishydroxycoumarin. Be sure you report this to your physician as it will be necessary to reduce the dose of your anticoagulant drug by approximately one-third at the beginning of thyroid therapy (to avoid hemorrhage). Further adjustments may be made later after your doctor reviews your blood tests.

Diabetics may have to increase their dose of Insulin or oral antidiabetic drugs. Changes in dose must be made by a doctor.

Food Interactions

This drug is best taken on an empty stomach but may be taken with food.

Usual Dose

Initial dose, as little as 25 micrograms per day; then increased in steps of 25 micrograms once every 3 to 4 weeks, depending upon response, with final dose of 100 to 200 micrograms per day, or even 300 to 400 micrograms if needed to achieve normal function.

Overdosage

Symptoms are headache, irritability, nervousness, sweating, rapid heartbeat with unusual stomach rumbling and with or without cramps, chest pains, heart failure, and shock. The patient should be taken to a hospital emergency room immediately. ALWAYS bring the medicine bottle.

Special Information

Thyroid replacement therapy is usually lifelong treatment. Be sure you have a fresh supply of your medication and always remember to take it according to your doctor's directions. Don't stop taking the medicine unless instructed to do so by your doctor.

Call your doctor if you develop nervousness, diarrhea, excessive sweating, chest pains, increased pulse rate, heart palpitations, intolerance to heat, or any other unusual occurrence.

Children beginning on thyroid treatment may lose some hair during the first few months, but this is only temporary and the hair generally grows back.

If you forget to take a dose of Levothyroxine Sodium, take it as soon as you remember. If it is almost time for your next regularly scheduled dose, skip the one you forgot and continue with your regular schedule. Do not take a double dose. Call your doctor if you forget 2 or more doses in a row.

Brand Name

Librax

Ingredients

Chlordiazepoxide
Clidinium Bromide

(Also available in generic form)

Other Brand Names

Clindex
Clinoxide
Clipoxide

Type of Drug

Anticholinergic combination.

Prescribed for

Anxiety and spasms associated with gastrointestinal disease. Librax may be specifically prescribed as an adjunct in the treatment of organic or functional gastrointestinal disorders and in the management of peptic ulcers, gastritis, irritable bowel syndrome, spastic colon, and mild ulcerative colitis.

The actions of this drug should be considered as "possibly effective." There is considerable doubt among medical experts that this drug produces the effects claimed for it.

General Information

Librax is one of many combinations of this class containing an anticholinergic or antispasmodic drug and a minor tranquilizer such as Chlordiazepoxide. All the drugs in this class will provide symptomatic relief only, and will not treat an underlying disease: it is important that you realize while taking this medication that you should actively pursue the treatment of the underlying cause of this problem if one is present and can be found.

Cautions and Warnings

Librax should not be used if you know you are sensitive or allergic to either of its ingredients, Chlordiazepoxide (Librium) and Clidinium Bromide (Quarzan), or to any benzodiazepine drug, which is related to Chlordiazepoxide. Do not use this medicine if you have glaucoma, or if you have a history of prostatic hypertrophy and bladder-neck obstruction.

Some people may develop dependence on Librax because of its tranquilizer components.

Pregnancy/Breast-feeding

This drug may cause birth defects or interfere with your baby's development. Check with your doctor before taking it if you are, or might be, pregnant. Chlordiazepoxide may pass into breast milk and affect your baby. Clidinium may reduce the amount of breast milk you produce.

Seniors

Older adults are more likely to develop excitement, agitation, drowsiness, or confusion at the normal dosages of this drug.

If you develop dry mouth, constipation, and difficulty passing urine (especially men), you should probably stop taking the drug. Check with your doctor.

The Clidinium component in this combination drug can bring on or worsen glaucoma, if already present. It can also severely affect your memory because it blocks a hormone in the brain (acetylcholine) that is responsible for many memory processes.

Possible Side Effects

Most common: mild drowsiness (usually experienced during the first few days of therapy), dry mouth, difficulty in urination, constipation. These side effects may be accentuated in the elderly or debilitated person. If they persist, discuss these problems with your doctor, since it is possible that you may be taking too much of the drug for your system—or the side effects may be so bothersome as to suggest the possibility of using a different medication.

Infrequent: confusion, depression, lethargy, disorientation, headache, lack of activity, slurring of speech, stupor, dizziness, tremor, constipation, nausea, difficulty in urination, changes in sex drive, menstrual irregularity, changes in heart rhythm, stuffy nose, fever, heartburn, suppression of lactation in females, bloated feeling, drug allergy or allergic reaction to the drug including itching, rash, and less common manifestations. Most people taking Librax experience few truly bothersome effects and although the effects listed may be a problem, in most patients they do not constitute a severe difficulty.

Drug Interactions

The central nervous system depressant (tranquilizer) or the atropine-like drug (anticholinergic) in Librax may interact with alcoholic beverages or depressant drugs such as other tranquilizers, narcotics, barbiturates, or even antihistamines, causing excessive tiredness or sleepiness.

Both Librax ingredients may be potentiated (increased in effect) by MAO inhibitors: you may wish to discuss with your doctor the possibility of avoiding the combination.

The anticholinergic ingredient in Librax may be inhibited by certain drugs used to treat high blood pressure, including Guanethidine (Ismelin) and Reserpine. Discuss this with your doctor.

Cimetidine may exaggerate the effects expected from Chlordiazepoxide.

Food Interactions

This medication is best taken on an empty stomach, but may be taken with food if it irritates your stomach.

Usual Dose

1 to 2 capsules 3 to 4 times per day, usually before meals and at bedtime. Amount and scheduling of medication may vary according to disease and patient's response.

Overdosage

Symptoms are dry mouth, difficulty in swallowing, thirst, blurred vision, inability to tolerate bright lights, flushed, hot dry skin, rash, high temperatures, palpitations and other unusual heart rhythms, feeling that you must urinate but difficulty in doing so, restlessness or depression, confusion, delirium, possible coma and/or lack of reflexes, and lowered respiration (breathing) and blood pressure. The patient should be taken to a hospital emergency room immediately. ALWAYS bring the medicine bottle.

Special Information

Avoid alcoholic beverages while you are taking this medicine. Sleeping pills, narcotics, barbiturates, other tranquilizers, or other drugs causing nervous system depression should be used with caution while you are taking the medication. Tell your doctor if you become pregnant or are breast-feeding.

If you forget to take a dose of Librax, take it as soon as you remember. If it is almost time for your next regularly scheduled dose, skip the one you forgot and continue with your regular schedule. Do not take a double dose.

Brand Name

Limbitrol

Ingredients

Amitriptyline
Chlordiazepoxide

Type of Drug

Antianxiety-antidepressant combination.

Prescribed for

Moderate to severe anxiety and depression.

General Information

This combination contains two drugs often used by themselves. Some reports have stated that this combination takes effect sooner than other treatments. Symptoms that may respond to this treatment are sleeplessness, feelings of guilt or worthlessness, agitation, anxiety, suicidal thoughts, and appetite loss.

Cautions and Warnings

Do not take this drug if you are allergic to either of the ingredients or related drugs. It should be used with caution if you have a history of heart disease, epilepsy, or other convulsive disorder, difficulty urinating, glaucoma, or thyroid disease.

This combination can cause drowsiness or dizziness. While taking this drug, drive and operate equipment with extreme caution. Avoid alcoholic beverages.

Pregnancy/Breast-feeding

This drug may cause birth defects or interfere with your baby's development. Check with your doctor before taking it if you are, or might be, pregnant.

If Limbitrol is used during breast-feeding the baby may be overly tired, be short of breath, or have a low heartbeat.

Seniors

Older adults are more sensitive to the side effects of this drug, especially those people with cardiac problems, glaucoma, urinary and stomach problems. Follow your doctor's directions and report any side effects at once.

Possible Side Effects

Mild drowsiness, changes in blood pressure, abnormal heart rates, heart attacks, confusion (especially in elderly patients), hallucinations, disorientation, delusions, anxiety, restlessness, lethargy, depression, inactivity, slurred speech, stupor, dizziness, excitement, numbness and tingling in the extremities, blurred vision, constipation, difficult urination, lack of coordination, muscle spasms, seizures or convulsions, dry mouth, blurred vision, rash, itching, sensitivity to the sun or bright light, retention of fluids, fever, drug allergy, changes in blood composition, nausea, vomiting, loss of appetite, stomach upset, diarrhea, enlargement of the breasts, changes in sex drive, changes in blood sugar.

Less common side effects are: headache, changes in menstrual cycle, blurred or double vision, inability to fall asleep, nightmares, feeling of panic, peculiar taste in the mouth, stomach cramps, black coloration of the tongue, yellowing of the eyes or skin, changes in liver function, changes in weight, sweating, flushing, loss of hair, feeling of ill health.

Drug Interactions

Avoid MAO inhibitors while taking this combination. The addition of MAO inhibitors can cause fever and convulsions. Do not take this drug together with Guanethidine. If you are taking high blood pressure medicine with this combination, consult your doctor. Do not take this combination with alcohol, sleeping pills, or other depressive drugs.

Large doses of Vitamin C can reduce the effect of Amitriptyline, one ingredient of Limbitrol.

Food Interactions

This medication is best taken on an empty stomach but may be taken with food if it irritates your stomach.

Usual Dose

1 to 2 tablets 3 to 4 times per day.

Overdosage

May cause confusion, drowsiness, difficulty concentrating, abnormal heart rate, convulsions, and coma. Bring the patient to a hospital emergency room and ALWAYS bring the medicine bottle.

Special Information

Avoid alcoholic beverages while you are taking this medicine. Sleeping pills, narcotics, barbiturates, other tranquilizers, or other drugs causing nervous system depression should be used with caution while you are taking the medication. Tell your doctor if you become pregnant or are breast feeding.

If you forget to take a dose of Limbitrol, do not take the forgotten dose. Skip the dose and go back to your regular schedule. Do not take a double dose.

Generic Name

Lindane

Brand Names

G-Well   Lindane
Kwell   Scabene
Kwildane

(Also available in generic form)

Type of Drug

Parasiticide.

Prescribed for

Topical treatment of head lice, crab lice, and scabies.

General Information

Lindane is considered to be the most effective agent against lice and scabies by many authorities. It should only be used when prescribed by a physician because it cannot prevent infestation, it can only treat it. Also, this medication is extremely irritating, particularly when applied to the eyelids and genital areas. If allowed to remain in contact with the skin for too long, Lindane will be absorbed directly into the bloodstream, causing signs of drug overdose.

Cautions and Warnings

Lindane is poisonous. Don't let any of it get into your eyes or mouth or in any open cut or scratch. Use rubber gloves if applying Lindane to another person. Call your doctor if you develop a rash or irritation while using this medicine, become clumsy or unsteady, if you have an unexplained seizure, become nervous, restless, irritable, vomit, or develop a very fast heartbeat.

Pregnancy/Breast-feeding

Lindane is absorbed through the skin and may cause unwanted effects in both pregnant mother and unborn baby. It is not recommended for use during pregnancy. It also passes into breast milk in small amounts. Use an alternative feeding method while using Lindane.

Seniors

Older adults should follow the same precautions as all others when using Lindane.

Possible Side Effects

Skin rash.

Usual Dose

For head lice: pour 1 ounce of shampoo on the affected area; rub vigorously; be sure to wet all hairy areas. Wet hair with warm water and work into a full lather for at least 4 minutes. Rinse hair thoroughly and rub with a dry towel. Comb with a fine-tooth comb to remove any remaining nit shells. A second application is usually not needed, but may be made after 24 hours if necessary. The drug should not be used more than twice in 1 week. The shampoo may also be used for crab lice.

For crab lice: after a bath or shower, apply a thin layer of lotion to hairy areas and over the skin of adjacent areas. Leave on for 12 to 24 hours, then wash thoroughly and put on freshly laundered or dry-cleaned clothing. Repeat after 4 days if necessary.

For scabies: after a bath or shower, apply a thin layer of the lotion over the entire skin surface. Leave on for 24 hours, then wash thoroughly. If necessary, a second and third weekly application may be made.

Overdosage

Anyone who ingests this drug accidentally should be taken to a hospital emergency room immediately. When taken internally, Lindane is a stimulant; the patient may require Phenobarbital or a similar depressant to neutralize the effect.

If contact with your eyes occurs during shampoo or other use, flush the eyes and surrounding area with water. If irritation or sensitization occurs, discontinue use and call a doctor.

Special Instructions

Do not apply to face. Flush thoroughly with water if medication comes in contact with eyes. Do not exceed prescribed dose.

Generic Name

Liothyronine

Brand Names

Cyronine
Cytomel

(Also available in generic form)

Type of Drug

Thyroid replacement.

Prescribed for

Replacement of thyroid hormone or low output from the thyroid gland.

General Information

Liothyronine is one of several thyroid replacement products available in the United States. The major difference between these products is the fact that they are actually different thyroid hormones and may be better at treating different phases of thyroid disease.

Cautions and Warnings

Do not take this product if you have hyperthyroid disease or high output of thyroid hormone. Symptoms of hyperthyroidism are headache, nervousness, sweating, rapid heartbeat, chest pain, and stimulation of the nervous system. If you have heart disease or high blood pressure, thyroid-replacement therapy should not be used unless it is clearly needed and supervised by your doctor.

Pregnancy/Breast-feeding

Small amounts of the thyroid hormones will find their way into the bloodstream of a developing fetus. However, they have not been associated with birth defects or other problems when used in the dosages required to maintain normal thyroid function in the mother.

Small amounts of the thyroid hormones pass into breast milk but have not been associated with problems in nursing infants.

Seniors

Older adults are more sensitive to the effects of the thyroid hormones. The usual dosage of thyroid hormones should be reduced by about 25 percent after age 60.

Possible Side Effects

Most common: heart palpitations, rapid heartbeat, abnormal heart rhythms, weight loss, chest pains, shaking of the hands, headache, diarrhea, nervousness, menstrual irregularity, difficulty sleeping, excessive sweating, intolerance to heat. These symptoms may be controlled by adjusting the dose of your medication. If you are suffering from one or more side effects, contact your doctor so that the proper dosage adjustment can be made.

Drug Interactions

Avoid over-the-counter products containing stimulant drugs, including many products sold to treat symptoms of the common cold or allergies. The stimulant-thyroid combination can affect your heart and may cause symptoms of overdosage.

Thyroid-replacement therapy may increase the effect of anticoagulant (blood-thinning) drugs such as Warfarin or Bishydroxycoumarin. Be sure your doctor knows if you are taking both drugs because it will be necessary to reduce your anticoagulant dosage by ⅓ at the beginning of your thyroid therapy to avoid hemorrhage. Further adjustments may be needed later after your doctor reviews your blood tests.

Diabetics may have to increase their dose of Insulin or antidiabetic medicine. Dosage changes must be made by your doctor.

Taking a thyroid hormone together with Colestipol or Cholestyramine can reduce the effect of the thyroid product by preventing its passage into your bloodstream. Separate doses of these 2 medicines by 4 to 5 hours.

The combination of Maprotiline and a thyroid hormone may increase the chances for abnormal heart rhythms. Your doctor may have to adjust the dose of your thyroid hormone.

Aspirin and other salicylate products may increase the effectiveness of your thyroid hormone by releasing more drug into the blood from body storage sites.

Estrogen drugs may increase your need for thyroid hormones.

Food Interactions

This drug is best taken on an empty stomach but may be taken with food.

Usual Dose

Adult: 5 to 100 micrograms per day, depending on the condition being treated and your response to therapy.

Child and senior: begin at the low end of the dosage range and increase slowly until the desired effect has been achieved.

Overdosage

Symptoms are: headache, irritability, nervousness, sweating, rapid heartbeat, unusual stomach rumbling with or without cramps, chest pains, heart failure, shock. Take the victim to a hospital emergency room at once for treatment. ALWAYS bring the medicine bottle with you.

Special Information

Thyroid-replacement therapy is usually lifelong treatment. Be sure you have a fresh supply of your medication and always remember to take it according to your doctor's directions. Don't stop taking the medicine unless instructed to do so by your doctor.

Call your doctor if you develop nervousness, diarrhea, excessive sweating, chest pains, increased pulse rate, heart palpitations, intolerance to heat, or any other unusual occurrence.

Children beginning on thyroid treatment may lose some hair during the first few months, but this is only temporary and hair generally grows back.

If you forget to take a dose of Liothyronine, take it as soon as you remember. If it is almost time for your next regularly scheduled dose, skip the one you forgot and continue with your regular schedule. Do not take a double dose. Call your doctor if you forget to take 2 or more doses in a row.

Generic Name

Liotrix

Brand Names

Euthroid
Thyrolar

Type of Drug

Thyroid replacement.

Prescribed for

Replacement of thyroid hormone or low output from the thyroid gland.

General Information

Liotrix is one of several thyroid-replacement products available in the United States. It is unique in that it is a mixture of two synthetic thyroid hormones (Liothyronine and Levothyroxine). Some doctors feel that this mixture is superior to single hormone or natural thyroid products.

Cautions and Warnings

Do not take this product if you have hyperthyroid disease or high output of thyroid hormone. Symptoms of hyperthyroidism are headache, nervousness, sweating, rapid heartbeat, chest pain, and stimulation of the nervous system. If you have heart disease or high blood pressure, thyroid-replacement therapy should not be used unless it is clearly needed and supervised by your doctor.

Pregnancy/Breast-feeding

Small amounts of the thyroid hormones will find their way into the bloodstream of a developing fetus. However, they have not been associated with birth defects or other problems when used in the dosages required to maintain normal thyroid function in the mother.

Small amounts of the thyroid hormones pass into breast milk but have not been associated with problems in nursing infants.

Seniors

Older adults are more sensitive to the effects of the thyroid hormones. The usual dosage of thyroid hormones should be reduced by about 25 percent after age 60.

Possible Side Effects

Most common: heart palpitations, rapid heartbeat, abnormal heart rhythms, weight loss, chest pains, shaking of the hands, headache, diarrhea, nervousness, menstrual irregularity, difficulty sleeping, excessive sweating, intolerance to heat. These symptoms may be controlled by adjusting the dose of your medication. If you are suffering from one or more side effects, contact your doctor so that the proper dosage adjustment can be made.

Drug Interactions

Avoid over-the-counter products containing stimulant drugs, including many products sold to treat symptoms of the common cold or allergies. The stimulant-thyroid combination can affect your heart and may cause symptoms of overdosage.

Thyroid-replacement therapy may increase the effect of anticoagulant (blood-thinning) drugs such as Warfarin or Bishydroxycoumarin. Be sure your doctor knows if you are taking both drugs because it will be necessary to reduce your anticoagulant dosage by ⅓ at the beginning of your thyroid therapy to avoid hemorrhage. Further adjustments may be needed later after your doctor reviews your blood tests.

Diabetics may have to increase their dose of Insulin or antidiabetic medicine. Dosage changes must be made by your doctor.

Taking a thyroid hormone together with Colestipol or Cholestyramine can reduce the effect of the thyroid product by preventing its passage into your bloodstream. Separate doses of these 2 medicines by 4 to 5 hours.

The combination of Maprotiline and a thyroid hormone may increase the chances for abnormal heart rhythms. Your doctor may have to adjust the dose of your thyroid hormone.

Aspirin and other salicylate products may increase the effectiveness of your thyroid hormone by releasing more drug into the blood from body storage sites.

Estrogen drugs may increase your need for thyroid hormones.

Food Interactions

This drug is best taken before breakfast but may be taken with food.

Usual Dose

Adult: a single "¼" to "2" tablet each day (see "Special Information" below for an explanation), depending on the condition being treated and your response to therapy.

Child and senior: begin at the low end of the dosage range and increase slowly until the desired effect has been achieved.

Overdosage

Symptoms are: headache, irritability, nervousness, sweating, rapid heartbeat, unusual stomach rumbling with or without cramps, chest pains, heart failure, shock. Take the victim to a hospital emergency room at once for treatment. ALWAYS bring the medicine bottle with you.

Special Information

Liotrix tablets are rated according to their approximate equivalent to thyroid hormone. A "½" tablet is roughly equal to 30 milligrams of thyroid hormone, a "1" tablet to 60 milligrams, a "2" tablet to 120 milligrams, and so on.

Thyroid-replacement therapy is usually lifelong treatment. Be sure you have a fresh supply of your medication and always remember to take it according to your doctor's directions. Don't stop taking the medicine unless instructed to do so by your doctor.

Call your doctor if you develop nervousness, diarrhea, excessive sweating, chest pains, increased pulse rate, heart palpitations, intolerance to heat, or any other unusual occurrence.

Children beginning on thyroid treatment may lose some hair during the first few months, but this is only temporary and the hair generally grows back.

If you forget to take a dose of Liotrix, take it as soon as you remember. If it is almost time for your next regularly scheduled dose, skip the one you forgot and continue with your regular schedule. Do not take a double dose. Call your doctor if you forget to take 2 or more doses in a row.

Generic Name

Lisinopril

Brand Names

Prinivil
Zestril

Type of Drug

Antihypertensive; ACE inhibitor.

Prescribed for

High blood pressure. Low doses may be used to treat mild

to moderate blood pressure. This medicine may be taken
alone or with a thiazide-type diuretic.

General Information

This medicine belongs to a relatively new class of drugs,
ACE inhibitors, which work by preventing the conversion of
a potent hormone called Angiotensin 1. This directly affects
the production of other hormones and enzymes which participate in the regulation of blood pressure. Lisinopril starts
lowering blood pressure within 1 hour after taking the
medicine.

Cautions and Warnings

This drug can cause kidney problems, especially loss of
protein in the urine. Patients taking Lisinopril should have
the amount of protein in the urine measured during the first
month of treatment and monthly for the next few months.
The drug can also cause a reduction in white-blood-cell count,
leading to a potential for increased susceptibility to infection. Lisinopril should be used with caution by people who
have kidney disease or diseases of the immune/collagen
system (particularly lupus erythematosus) or who have taken
other drugs that affect the white-blood-cell count.

Pregnancy/Breast-feeding

The effect of Lisinopril on a developing fetus is not known.
However, animal studies indicate that Lisinopril may affect a
developing fetus. Women who are, or might become, pregnant while taking this drug should discuss the matter with
their doctor.

It is not known if Lisinopril passes into breast milk or if it
will affect a nursing infant.

Seniors

Older adults are as sensitive to the blood-pressure-lowering
effects of this drug as younger adults, but they absorb twice
as much of the drug. Dosage must be individualized to your
needs.

Possible Side Effects

Dizziness, tiredness, headache, diarrhea, nausea, low blood

pressure, cough, rash (usually mild), and cough are the most common side effects.

Less common drug side effects are itching, fever, temporary loss of taste perception, stomach irritation, chest pain, heart palpitations, difficulty sleeping, tingling in the hands or feet, vomiting, jaundice and liver damage, excessive sweating, muscle cramps, joint and muscle pains, (male) impotence, and muscle weakness. Some people experience unusual reactions after taking the first dose of the drug which can include facial flushing and swelling, swelling of the arms and legs, and closing of the throat.

Drug Interactions

The blood-pressure-lowering effect of Lisinopril is additive with diuretic drugs and the beta blockers. Other drugs that cause rapid drops in blood pressure should be used with extreme caution because of a possible severe drop when taken together with Lisinopril.

Lisinopril may increase potassium levels in your blood, especially when given with potassium-sparing diuretics and/or potassium supplements.

Food Interactions

This drug is best taken on an empty stomach, usually 1 hour before or 2 hours after a meal.

Usual Dose

10 to 40 milligrams once a day. Some people may take their total daily dosage in 2 divided doses.

People with poor kidney function have to take less medicine to achieve reduced blood pressure.

Overdosage

The primary effect of Lisinopril overdosage is a rapid drop in blood pressure, as evidenced by dizziness or fainting. Take the overdose victim to a hospital emergency room immediately. ALWAYS remember to bring the medicine bottle.

Special Information

Call your doctor if you develop fever, sore throat, mouth sores, abnormal heartbeat, or chest pain, or if you have persistent rash or loss of taste perception.

Lisinopril may cause dizziness when quickly rising from a lying or sitting position.

Avoid strenuous exercise and/or very hot weather as heavy sweating and/or dehydration can cause a rapid drop in blood pressure.

Do not stop taking this medicine without your doctor's knowledge.

Avoid nonprescription medicines such as diet pills, decongestants, and stimulants that can raise your blood pressure.

If you forget to take a dose of Lisinopril, take it as soon as you remember. If it is almost time for your next dose, skip the forgotten dose and go back to your regular schedule.

Generic Name
Lithium

Brand Names

Cibalith-S Syrup	Lithium Citrate Syrup
Eskalith	Lithobid
Eskalith-CR	Lithonate
Lithane	Lithotabs
Lithium Carbonate	

(Also available in generic form)

Type of Drug

Antipsychotic, antimanic.

Prescribed for

Treatment of the manic phase of manic-depressive illness.

Lithium has also been used in cancer treatment; for migraine headaches, premenstrual tension, bulimia, alcoholism, and overactive thyroid; and as a lotion for genital herpes and dandruff.

General Information

Lithium is the only medicine which is effective as an antimanic drug. It reduces the level of manic episodes and may produce normal activity within the first 3 weeks of treatment. Typical manic symptoms include rapid speech, elation, hyperactive movements, need for little sleep, grandiose ideas, poor judgment, aggressiveness, and hostility.

Cautions and Warnings

This drug should not be given to patients with heart or kidney disease, dehydration, low blood sodium, or to patients who take diuretic drugs. If such patients require Lithium they must be very closely monitored by their doctors.

Lithium may affect routine mental or physical activity. Take care while driving or operating machinery.

Pregnancy/Breast-feeding

Lithium can cause heart and thyroid birth defects, especially if taken during the first 3 months of pregnancy. It can affect the newborn infant if present in your blood during your delivery. Talk with your doctor about the risk of taking this drug during your pregnancy versus any benefit it will produce for you.

Lithium passes readily into breast milk and can affect a nursing infant. Signs of these effects are weak muscle tone, low body temperature, bluish discoloration of the skin, and abnormal heart rhythms in the nursing infant. Use an alternative feeding method while taking this medicine.

Seniors

Older adults are more sensitive to the effects of Lithium because they cannot clear it out of the body through their kidneys as rapidly as younger adults. Lithium is potentially toxic to the central nervous system in the elderly, even when Lithium blood levels are in the desired range. Also, older adults are more likely to develop an underactive thyroid because of Lithium treatment.

Possible Side Effects

Side effects of Lithium are directly associated with the amount of this drug in the blood. At usual doses, the patient may develop a fine hand tremor, thirst, and excessive urination. Mild nausea and discomfort may be present during the first few days of treatment. At higher levels, diarrhea, vomiting, drowsiness, muscle weakness and poor coordination, giddiness, ringing in the ears, and blurred vision may occur.

The following body systems can be affected by Lithium,

producing symptoms which tend to become worse with more
of this drug in the body: muscles, nerves, central nervous
system (blackouts, seizures, dizziness, incontinence, slurred
speech, coma), heart and blood vessels, stomach and intestines, kidney and urinary tract, skin, thyroid gland. Lithium
can also cause changes in tests used to monitor heart-brain
function and can cause dry mouth and blurred vision.

Drug Interactions

When combined with Haloperidol, Lithium may cause an
unusual set of symptoms including weakness, tiredness, fever, and confusion. In a few patients these symptoms have
been followed by permanent brain damage.

Lithium may reduce the effect of Chlorpromazine.

The drug is counteracted by Sodium Bicarbonate, Acetazolamide, Urea, Mannitol, and Aminophylline, which increase
the rate at which Lithium is released from the body.

Long-term use of thiazide diuretic drugs may decrease
the clearance of Lithium from the body. Salt (sodium chloride) is directly related to this drug in the body. You will
retain more of the drug than normal if the salt level in
your body is low, and will hold less if you have a high salt
level.

Food Interactions

It is essential to maintain a normal diet, including salt and
fluid intake, while taking Lithium, since it can cause a natural
reduction in body salt levels. Lithium should be taken immediately after meals or with food or milk.

Usual Dose

Must be individualized to each patient's need. Most patients
will respond to 600 milligrams 3 times per day at first, then
will require 300 milligrams 3 to 4 times per day.

Slow release: 900 milligrams twice a day.

Overdosage

Toxic blood levels of Lithium are only slightly above the
levels required for treatment. If diarrhea, vomiting, tremors,
drowsiness, or poor coordination occur, stop taking the medicine and call your doctor immediately.

Special Information

Lithium may cause drowsiness. If you are taking this drug be cautious while driving or operating any machinery.

If you forget to take a dose of Lithium, take it as soon as possible. However, if it is within 2 hours of your next dose (6 hours if you take a long-acting form of Lithium), skip the forgotten dose and go back to your regular schedule. Do not take a double dose.

Brand Name

Lomotil

Ingredients

Atropine Sulfate
Diphenoxylate

Other Brand Names

Diphenatol   Lonox
Lofene   Lo-Trol
Logen   Low-Quel
Lomanate   Nor-Mil

(Also available in generic form)

Type of Drug

Antidiarrheal.

Prescribed for

Symptomatic treatment of diarrhea.

General Information

Lomotil and other antidiarrheal agents should only be used for short periods: they will relieve the diarrhea, but not its underlying causes. Sometimes these drugs should not be used even though there is diarrhea present: people with some kinds of bowel, stomach, or other disease may be harmed by taking antidiarrheal drugs. Obviously, the decision to use Lomotil must be made by your doctor. Do not use Lomotil without his advice.

Cautions and Warnings

Do not take Lomotil if you are allergic to this medication or
any other medication containing Atropine Sulfate, or if you
are jaundiced (yellowing of the whites of the eyes and/or
skin) or are suffering from diarrhea caused by antibiotics
such as Clindamycin or Lincomycin.

Pregnancy/Breast-feeding

This drug crosses into the blood circulation of a developing
baby. It has not been found to cause birth defects. Pregnant
women, or those who might become pregnant while taking
this drug, should not take it without their doctor's approval.
When the drug is considered essential by your doctor, the
potential risk of taking the medicine must be carefully weighed
against the benefit it might produce.

This drug passes into breast milk, but has caused no problems among breast-fed infants. You must consider the potential effect on the nursing infant if breast-feeding while
taking this medicine.

Seniors

Older adults are more sensitive to the side effects of this
drug, especially breathing difficulty. Follow your doctor's
directions and report any side effects at once.

Possible Side Effects

Most common: dryness of the skin inside the nose or mouth,
flushing or redness of the face, fever, unusual heart rates,
inability to urinate.

Less commonly, people taking Lomotil for extended periods may experience abdominal discomforts, swelling of the
gums, interference with normal breathing, feeling of numbness in the extremities, drowsiness, restlessness, rashes,
nausea, sedation, vomiting, headache, dizziness, depression,
feeling unwell, lethargy, loss of appetite, euphoria, itching,
and coma.

Drug Interactions

Lomotil, a depressant on the central nervous system, may
cause tiredness or inability to concentrate, and may thus
increase the effect of sleeping pills, tranquilizers, and alco-

hol. Avoid drinking large amounts of alcoholic beverages while taking Lomotil.

Usual Dose

Adult: 4 tablets per day until diarrhea has stopped; then reduce to the lowest level that will control diarrhea (usually 2 tablets per day or less).

The liquid form, supplied with a dropper calibrated to deliver medication as desired in milliliters, is used for children age 2 to 12.

Child (age 8 to 12, or about 60 to 80 pounds): 4 milliliters 5 times per day.

Child (age 5 to 8, or about 45 to 60 pounds): 4 milliliters 4 times per day.

Child (age 2 to 5, or about 26 to 45 pounds): 4 milliliters 3 times per day.

Child (under age 2): not recommended.

Overdosage

Lomotil overdose is generally accidental: patients, feeling that the prescribed amount has not cured their diarrhea, will take more medication on their own. Symptoms of overdosage (particularly effects on breathing) may not be evident until 12 to 30 hours after the medication has been taken. Symptoms are dryness of skin, mouth, and/or nose, flushing, fever and abnormal heart rates with possible lethargy, coma, or depression of breathing. The patient should be taken to a hospital emergency room immediately. ALWAYS bring the medicine bottle.

Special Information

Lomotil may cause drowsiness and difficulty concentrating: be careful while driving or operating any appliance or equipment. Notify your doctor if heart palpitations occur.

If you forget to take a dose of Lomotil, take it as soon as you remember. If it is almost time for your next regularly scheduled dose, skip the one you forgot and continue with your regular schedule. Do not take a double dose.

Generic Name

Loperamide

Brand Name

Imodium
Imodium-AD

Type of Drug

Antidiarrheal.

Prescribed for

Symptomatic treatment of diarrhea.

General Information

Loperamide and other antidiarrheal agents should only be
used for short periods: they will relieve the diarrhea, but not
its underlying causes. Sometimes these drugs should not be
used even though there is diarrhea present: people with
some kinds of bowel, stomach, or other disease may be
harmed by taking antidiarrheal drugs. A low-dose version of
Loperamide can be purchased without a prescription as
Imodium-AD.

Cautions and Warnings

Do not use Loperamide if you are allergic or sensitive to it or
if you suffer from diarrhea associated with colitis. Also, do
not use when intestinal toxins from bacteria such as *E. coli,*
Salmonella, or *Shigella* are present (as in most forms of
traveler's diarrhea) or with certain drugs such as Clindamycin.
Loperamide is not known to be addictive.

Pregnancy/Breast-feeding

This drug crosses into the blood circulation of a developing
baby. It has not been found to cause birth defects. Pregnant
women, or those who might become pregnant while taking
this drug, should not take it without their doctor's approval.
When the drug is considered essential by your doctor, the
potential risk of taking the medicine must be carefully weighed
against the benefit it might produce.

  This drug passes into breast milk, but has caused no prob-

lems among breast-fed infants. You must consider the potential effect on the nursing infant if breast-feeding while taking this medicine.

Seniors

Older adults are more sensitive to the constipating effects of this drug. Follow your doctor's directions and report any side effects at once.

Possible Side Effects

The incidence of side effects from Loperamide is low. Stomach and abdominal pain, bloating or other discomfort, constipation, dryness of the mouth, dizziness, tiredness, nausea and vomiting, and rash are possible.

Drug Interactions

Loperamide, a depressant on the central nervous system, may cause tiredness and inability to concentrate, and may thus increase the effect of sleeping pills, tranquilizers, and alcohol. Avoid drinking large amounts of alcoholic beverages while taking Loperamide.

Usual Dose

Adult and child (age 12 and over): 2 capsules to start, followed by 1 capsule after each loose stool, up to 8 capsules per day maximum. Improvement should be seen in 2 days. People with long-term (chronic) diarrhea usually need 2 to 4 capsules per day. This drug usually is effective within 10 days or not at all.

Child (under age 12): not recommended.

Overdosage

Symptoms are constipation, irritation of the stomach, and tiredness. Large doses cause vomiting. The patient should be taken to the emergency room immediately. ALWAYS bring the medicine bottle.

Special Information

Loperamide may cause drowsiness and difficulty concentrating: be careful while driving or operating any appliance or equipment.

If you forget to take a dose of Loperamide, do not take the forgotten dose. Skip the dose and go back to your regular schedule. Do not take a double dose.

Generic Name
Lorazepam

Brand Names
Alzapam
Ativan

(Also available in generic form)

Type of Drug
Minor tranquilizer.

Prescribed for
Relief of symptoms of anxiety, tension, fatigue, or agitation.

General Information
Lorazepam is a member of the group of drugs known as benzodiazepines. These drugs are used as either antianxiety agents, anticonvulsants, or sedatives (sleeping pills). They exert their effects by relaxing the large skeletal muscles and by a direct effect on the brain. In doing so, they can relax you and make you either more tranquil or sleepier, depending on the drug and how much you use. Many doctors prefer Lorazepam and other members of this class to other drugs that can be used for the same effect. Their reason is that the benzodiazepines tend to be safer, have fewer side effects, and are usually as, if not more, effective.

These drugs are generally used in any situation where they can be a useful adjunct.

Benzodiazepine tranquilizing drugs can be abused if taken for long periods of time and it is possible to develop withdrawal symptoms if you discontinue the therapy abruptly. Withdrawal symptoms include convulsions, tremor, muscle cramps, stomach cramps, vomiting, and sweating.

Cautions and Warnings

Do not take Lorazepam if you know you are sensitive or allergic to this drug or to other benzodiazepines such as Chlordiazepoxide, Oxazepam, Clorazepate, Diazepam, Praze-pam, Flurazepam, Clonazepam, and Temazepam.

Lorazepam and other members of this drug group may aggravate narrow-angle glaucoma, but if you have open-angle glaucoma you may take the drugs. In any case, check this information with your doctor. Lorazepam can cause tired-ness, drowsiness, inability to concentrate, or similar symp-toms. Be careful if you are driving, operating machinery, or performing other activities which require concentration.

Pregnancy/Breast-feeding

Avoid taking this drug during the first 3 months of preg-nancy except under strict supervision of your doctor. The baby may become dependent on Lorazepam if it is used continually during pregnancy. If used during the last weeks of pregnancy or during breast-feeding, the baby may be overly tired, be short of breath, or have a low heartbeat. Use during labor may cause weakness in the newborn.

Seniors

Older adults are more sensitive to the effects of this drug, especially dizziness and drowsiness. They should closely follow their doctor's directions and report any side effects at once.

Possible Side Effects

Most common: mild drowsiness during the first few days of therapy, especially in the elderly or debilitated. If drowsiness persists, contact your doctor.

Less common side effects: confusion, depression, leth-argy, disorientation, headache, lack of activity, slurred speech, stupor, dizziness, tremor, constipation, dry mouth, nausea, inability to control urination, changes in sex drive, irregular menstrual cycle, changes in heart rhythm, lowered blood pres-sure, retention of fluids, blurred or double vision, itching, rash, hiccups, nervousness, inability to fall asleep, (occasional) liver dysfunction. If you experience any of these reactions stop taking the medicine and contact your doctor immediately.

Drug Interactions

Lorazepam is a central nervous system depressant. Avoid alcohol, tranquilizers, narcotics, sleeping pills, barbiturates, MAO inhibitors, antihistamines, and other medicines used to relieve depression.

Food Interactions

Lorazepam is best taken on an empty stomach, but may be taken with food.

Usual Dose

Adult: 2 to 10 milligrams per day as individualized for maximum benefit, depending on symptoms and response to treatment, which may call for a dose outside the range given. Most people require 2 to 6 milligrams per day. 2 to 4 milligrams may be taken at bedtime for sleep.

Senior: usually requires less of the drug to control anxiety and tension.

Child: not recommended.

Overdosage

Symptoms are confusion, sleep or sleepiness, lack of response to pain such as a pin stick, shallow breathing, lowered blood pressure, and coma. The patient should be taken to a hospital emergency room immediately. ALWAYS bring the medicine bottle.

Special Information

Do not drink alcoholic beverages while taking Lorazepam. Sleeping pills, narcotics, other tranquilizers, or any other drug producing nervous-system depression should be used with caution while taking Lorazepam.

If you forget to take a dose of Lorazepam and you remember within about an hour of your regular time, take it right away. If you do not remember until later, skip the forgotten dose and go back to your regular schedule. Do not take a double dose.

Brand Name

Lotrisone

Ingredients

Betamethasone
Clotrimazole

Type of Drug

Steroid-antifungal combination.

Prescribed for

Severe fungal infection or rash.

General Information

Lotrisone cream is used to relieve the symptoms of itching,
rash, or skin inflammation associated with a severe fungus
infection. It may treat the underlying cause of the skin problem by killing the fungus and relieves inflammation that may
be associated with the infection. This combination product
should only be used on your doctor's prescription. A combination such as this may be less effective than applying either
Clotrimazole cream or Betamethasone cream to the skin.

Improvement usually occurs within the first week of treatment. If you don't get better after using Lotrisone for 4
weeks, your doctor should reevaluate your condition and
prescribe a different medicine.

Cautions and Warnings

Do not use Lotrisone if you are sensitive or allergic to either
of its two active ingredients. Do not apply Lotrisone to the
eye, or to the ear if the eardrum is perforated, unless specifically directed to do so by your doctor.

Check with your doctor before using the contents of an old
tube of Lotrisone for a new skin problem.

Pregnancy/Breast-feeding

Pregnant women should not use this product, especially
during the first 3 months, because it can affect the development of the fetus.

Seniors
Seniors may use Lotrisone without special precaution.

Possible Side Effects
Itching, stinging, burning, skin peeling, swelling.

Drug Interactions
None known.

Food Interactions
None known.

Usual Dose
Apply twice daily to affected areas of skin.

Special Information
Apply a thin film of Lotrisone to affected area(s). Washing or soaking the skin before applying the medicine may increase the amount that penetrates your skin.

Stop using the medicine and call your doctor if Lotrisone causes itching, burning, or skin irritation.

Generic Name

Lovastatin

Brand Name
Mevacor

Type of Drug
Cholesterol-lowering agent.

Prescribed for
High blood-cholesterol levels, in conjunction with a low-cholesterol diet program.

General Information
The value of Lovastatin and other drugs that reduce blood cholesterol lies in the assumption that reducing levels of

blood fats reduces the chance of heart disease. Studies conducted by the National Heart, Lung, and Blood Institute have identified high levels of blood fats (cholesterol and LDL) as a cause of heart and blood-vessel disease. Drugs that can reduce the amounts of either or both of these blood fats can reduce the risk of deaths and nonfatal heart attacks.

Lovastatin reduces both total cholesterol and LDL-cholesterol counts. A significant response is seen after 2 weeks of treatment. Blood-fat levels reach their lowest levels within 4 to 6 weeks after you start taking this medication and remain at or close to that level so long as you continue to take the medicine.

Cautions and Warnings

People with a history of liver disease should avoid this medication because of the possibility that the drug itself can aggravate or cause liver disease. Your doctor should take a blood sample to test your liver function every month or so during the first year of treatment to be sure that the drug is not adversely affecting you.

Lovastatin causes muscle aches in a small number of people that can be a sign of a more serious condition.

Pregnancy/Breast-feeding

Pregnant women should not take Lovastatin. Laboratory studies have show that daily doses of Lovastatin 500 times the maximum recommended human dose cause malformations of the skeleton in fetal laboratory animals. Because hardening of the arteries is a chronic, long-term process, temporarily stopping this medication during pregnancy should cause no problem. If you become pregnant while taking Lovastatin, stop the drug immediately and call your doctor.

Lovastatin passes into breast milk. Women taking this medication should not breast-feed their infants.

Seniors

Lovastatin is only likely to be prescribed for an older adult with severely elevated blood cholesterol. However, the drug may be taken in the same doses as by a younger adult. Be sure to report any side effects to your doctor.

Possible Side Effects

Most people who take Lovastatin tolerate it very well. Stud-

ies of the drug revealed that only 2 out of every 100 had to
stop taking it because of intolerable side effects.

The most common side effect of Lovastatin is headache.
Other common side effects are constipation, diarrhea, stomach gas, abdominal pain or cramps, itching, and rash. Other
side effects include upset stomach, nausea, and muscle aches.

Rare side effects include heartburn, muscle cramps, blurred
vision, changes in taste perception, and changes in the lens
of your eye.

Drug Interactions

The cholesterol-lowering effects of Lovastatin and Cholestyramine are additive when the two drugs are taken together.

Food Interactions

Take Lovastatin with meals to reduce the chance of upset
stomach or intestinal side effects. Continue your low-cholesterol diet while taking Lovastatin.

Usual Dose

Adult: The usual dose of Lovastatin is 20 to 80 milligrams
per day. Your daily dosage should be adjusted about once a
month, based on your doctor's assessment of how well the
drug is working to reduce your blood cholesterol.

Child: the effect of Lovastatin in children has not been
studied.

Overdosage

Persons suspected of having taken an overdose of Lovastatin
should be taken to a hospital emergency room for evaluation and treatment. The effects of overdose are not well
known.

Special Information

Lovastatin causes muscle aches in a small number of people. Call your doctor if this happens to you.

Although the manufacturer of this drug recommends a
maximum daily dose of 80 milligrams, studies have shown
that the cholesterol-lowering effect of Lovastatin continues
to increase up to a daily dose of 120 milligrams.

If you forget to take a dose of Lovastatin, take it as soon as

you remember. If it is almost time for your next regularly
scheduled dose, skip the one you forgot and continue with
your regular schedule. Do not take a double dose.

Generic Name

Maprotiline

Brand Name

Ludiomil

Type of Drug

Antidepressant.

Prescribed for

Depression with or without symptoms of anxiety.

General Information

Maprotiline and other members of this group are effective in
treating symptoms of depression. They can elevate your
mood, increase physical activity and mental alertness, improve appetite and sleep patterns. These drugs are mild
sedatives and therefore useful in treating mild forms of depression associated with anxiety. You should not expect
instant results with this medicine: benefits are usually seen
after 1 to 4 weeks. If symptoms are not affected after 6 to 8
weeks, contact your doctor. Occasionally, other members of
this group of drugs have been used in treating nighttime
bed-wetting in the young child, but they do not produce
long-lasting relief, and therapy with one of them for nighttime bed-wetting is of questionable value.

Cautions and Warnings

Do not take Maprotiline if you are allergic or sensitive to this
or other members of this class of drug: Doxepin, Nortriptyline, Imipramine, Desipramine, Protriptyline, and Amitriptyline. The drugs should not be used if you are recovering
from a heart attack. Maprotiline may be taken with caution if
you have a history of epilepsy or other convulsive disorders,

difficulty in urination, glaucoma, heart disease, or thyroid
disease. Maprotiline can interfere with your ability to perform tasks which require concentration, such as driving or
operating machinery.

Pregnancy/Breast-feeding

This drug, like other antidepressants, crosses into your developing baby's circulation and may cause birth defects if taken
during the first 3 months of pregnancy. There have been
reports of newborn infants suffering from heart, breathing,
and urinary problems after their mothers had taken an antidepressant of this type immediately before delivery. You
should avoid taking this medication while pregnant.

Antidepressants of this type are known to pass into breast
milk and may affect a breast-feeding infant, although this
has not been proven. Nursing mothers should consider alternate feeding methods if taking this medicine.

Seniors

Older adults are more sensitive to the effects of this drug
and often require a lower dose than a younger adult to do
the same job. Follow your doctor's directions and report any
side effects at once.

Possible Side Effects

Changes in blood pressure (both high and low), abnormal
heart rates, heart attack, confusion, especially in elderly
patients, hallucinations, disorientation, delusions, anxiety,
restlessness, excitement, numbness and tingling in the extremities, lack of coordination, muscle spasms or tremors,
seizures and/or convulsions, dry mouth, blurred vision, constipation, inability to urinate, rash, itching, sensitivity to bright
light or sunlight, retention of fluids, fever, allergy, changes
in composition of blood, nausea, vomiting, loss of appetite,
stomach upset, diarrhea, enlargement of the breasts in males
and females, increased or decreased sex drive, increased or
decreased blood sugar.

Less common side effects: agitation, inability to sleep,
nightmares, feeling of panic, development of a peculiar taste
in the mouth, stomach cramps, black coloration of the tongue,
yellowing eyes and/or skin, changes in liver function, in-

creased or decreased weight, increased perspiration, flushing, frequent urination, drowsiness, dizziness, weakness, headache, loss of hair, nausea, not feeling well.

Drug Interactions

Interaction with monoamine oxidase (MAO) inhibitors can cause high fevers, convulsions, and occasionally death. Don't take MAO inhibitors until at least 2 weeks after Maprotiline has been discontinued.

Maprotiline interacts with Guanethidine, a drug used to treat high blood pressure: if your doctor prescribes Maprotiline and you are taking medicine for high blood pressure, be sure to discuss this with him.

Maprotiline increases the effects of barbiturates, tranquilizers, other depressive drugs, and alcohol. Don't drink alcoholic beverages if you take this medicine.

Taking Maprotiline and thyroid medicine will enhance the effects of the thyroid medicine. The combination can cause abnormal heart rhythms.

Large doses of Vitamin C (Ascorbic Acid) can reduce the effect of Maprotiline. Drugs such as Bicarbonate of Soda or Acetazolamide will increase the effect of Maprotiline.

Food Interactions

This drug is best taken on an empty stomach but can be taken with food if it upsets your stomach.

Usual Dose

Adult: 75 to 225 milligrams per day. Hospitalized patients may need up to 300 milligrams per day. The dose of this drug must be tailored to patient's need.

Senior: lower doses are recommended for people over 60 years of age, usually 50 to 75 milligrams per day.

Overdosage

Symptoms are confusion, inability to concentrate, hallucinations, drowsiness, lowered body temperature, abnormal heart rate, heart failure, large pupils of the eyes, convulsions, severely lowered blood pressure, stupor, and coma (as well as agitation, stiffening of body muscles, vomiting, and high fever). The patient should be taken to a hospital emergency room immediately. ALWAYS bring the medicine bottle.

Special Information

Avoid alcohol and other drugs that depress the nervous system while taking this antidepressant. Do not stop taking this medicine unless your doctor has specifically told you to do so. Abruptly stopping this medicine may cause nausea, headache, and a sickly feeling. This medicine can cause drowsiness, dizziness, and blurred vision. Be careful when driving or operating complicated machinery. Avoid exposure to the sun or sun lamps for long periods of time. Call your doctor if dry mouth, difficulty urinating, or excessive sedation develops.

If you forget to take a dose of Maprotiline, take it as soon as you remember. If it is almost time for your next regularly scheduled dose, skip the one you forgot and continue with your regular schedule. Do not take a double dose. If you take Maprotiline at bedtime and forget the dose, skip it and continue with your regular schedule.

Brand Name

Marax

Ingredients

Ephedrine Sulfate
Hydroxyzine Hydrochloride
Theophylline

Other Brand Names

Hydrophed
T.E.H. Compound
Theofedral

(Also available in generic form)

Type of Drug

Antiasthmatic combination product.

Prescribed for

Relief of asthma symptoms or other upper respiratory disorders.

The actions of this drug should be considered as "possibly effective." There is considerable doubt among medical experts that this drug produces the effects claimed for it.

General Information

Marax is one of several antiasthmatic combination products prescribed for the relief of asthmatic symptoms and other breathing problems. These products contain drugs which help relax the bronchial muscles, drugs which increase the diameter of the breathing passages, and a mild tranquilizer to help relax the patient. Other products in this class may contain similar ingredients along with other medicine to help eliminate mucus from the breathing passages.

Cautions and Warnings

This drug should not be taken if you have severe kidney or liver disease.

Pregnancy/Breast-feeding

This drug crosses into the blood circulation of a developing baby. It has not been found to cause birth defects. Pregnant women, or those who might become pregnant while taking this drug, should not take it without their doctor's approval. When the drug is considered essential by your doctor, the potential risk of taking the medicine must be carefully weighed against the benefit it might produce.

This drug passes into breast milk, but has caused no problems among breast-fed infants. You must consider the potential effect on the nursing infant if breast-feeding while taking this medicine.

Seniors

Older adults may take longer to clear Theophylline, an ingredient in this combination, from their bodies than younger adults. Older adults with heart failure or other cardiac conditions, chronic lung disease, a virus infection with fever, or reduced liver function may require a lower dosage of this medication to account for the clearance effect.

Possible Side Effects

Large doses of Marax can produce excitation, shakiness,

sleeplessness, nervousness, rapid heartbeat, chest pains, irregular heartbeat, dizziness, dryness of the nose and throat,
headache, and sweating. Occasionally people have been
known to develop hesitation or difficulty in urination. Marax
may also cause stomach upset, diarrhea, and possible bleeding, so you are advised to take this drug with food.

Less frequent side effects: excessive urination, heart stimulation, drowsiness, muscle weakness, muscle twitching, unsteady walk. These effects can usually be controlled by having
your doctor adjust the dose.

Drug Interactions

Marax may cause sleeplessness or drowsiness. Do not take
this drug with alcoholic beverages.

Taking Marax or similar medicines with an MAO inhibitor
can produce severe interaction. Consult your doctor first.

Marax or similar products taken together with Lithium
Carbonate will increase the excretion of Lithium; they have
neutralized the effect of Propranolol. Erythromycin and similar antibiotics cause the body to hold Theophylline, leading
to possible side effects.

Food Interactions

Take the drug with food to help prevent stomach upset.

Actions and side effects of Marax may be enhanced by
ingestion of caffeine from sources which include various
teas, coffee, chocolate, and soft drinks.

Usual Dose

Tablet:
Adult: 1 tablet 2 to 4 times per day.
Child (over age 5): ½ tablet 2 to 4 times per day.
Syrup:
Child (over age 5): 1 teaspoon 3 to 4 times per day.
Child (age 2 to 5): ½ teaspoon 3 to 4 times per day.

Take doses at least 4 hours apart. The dose is adjusted to
severity of disease and patient's ability to tolerate side effects.

Special Information

If you forget to take a dose of Marax, take it as soon as you
remember. If it is almost time for your next regularly sched-

uled dose, skip the one you forgot and continue with your regular schedule. Do not take a double dose.

Generic Name

Mazindol

Brand Names

Mazanor
Sanorex

Type of Drug

Nonamphetamine appetite suppressant.

Prescribed for

Short-term (2 to 3 months) appetite suppression, treating obesity.

General Information

Although this medicine is not an amphetamine, it has many of the same effects as amphetamine drugs and suppresses appetite by working on specific areas in the brain. Each dose of Mazindol works for 8 to 15 hours.

Cautions and Warnings

Do not take Mazindol if you have heart disease, high blood pressure, thyroid disease, or glaucoma, or if you are sensitive or allergic to this or other appetite suppressants. Do not use this medicine if you are prone to emotional agitation or drug abuse.

Pregnancy/Breast-feeding

Studies have shown that large doses of Mazindol may damage an unborn baby. The use of this and other appetite suppressants should be avoided by women who are or could become pregnant, unless the potential benefit outweighs any possible drug hazard.

It is not known if Mazindol passes into breast milk. Nursing mothers should not take this or any other appetite suppressant.

Seniors

Older adults should not take this medicine unless prescribed
by a doctor. It can aggravate diabetes or high blood pressure, conditions common to older adults.

Possible Side Effects

Common side effects are a false sense of well-being, nervousness, overstimulation, restlessness, and trouble sleeping. Other, less common side effects are palpitations, high
blood pressure, drowsiness, sedation, weakness, dizziness,
tremor, headache, dry mouth, nausea, vomiting, diarrhea,
and other intestinal disturbances, rash, itching, changes in
sex drive, hair loss, muscle pains, difficulty urinating, sweating, chills, blurred vision, and fever.

Drug Interactions

Taking other stimulants together with Mazindol may result
in excessive stimulation. Taking this medicine within 14 days
of any MAO inhibitor drug may result in severe high blood
pressure.

Appetite suppressants may reduce the effects of some
medicines used to treat high blood pressure. One case of
Lithium toxicity occurred in a person taking Mazindol.

Food Interactions

Do not crush or chew this product. Mazindol can be taken on
a full stomach to reduce upset stomach caused by the drug.

Usual Dose

1 milligram 3 times a day, 1 hour before meals, or 2 milligrams once a day, before lunch.

Overdosage

Symptoms of overdose are restlessness, tremor, shallow
breathing, confusion, hallucinations, and fever, followed by
fatigue and depression. Additional symptoms are changes in
blood pressure, cold and clammy skin, nausea, vomiting,
diarrhea, and stomach cramps. Take the victim to a hospital
emergency room immediately. ALWAYS bring the medicine
bottle.

Special Information

Do not take this medicine for more than 12 weeks as part of a weight-control program and take it only under a doctor's supervision. This medicine will not reduce body weight by itself. You must limit or modify your food intake.

This drug can cause dry mouth which can be relieved by sugarless candy or gum or by ice chips.

If you forget to take a dose of Mazindol, do not take the forgotten dose. Skip the dose and go back to your regular schedule. Do not take a double dose.

Generic Name

Meclizine

Brand Names

Antivert   Motion Cure
Antrizine   Ru Vert M
Bonine   Wehvert
Dizmiss

(Also available in generic form)

Type of Drug

Antiemetic, antivertigo agent.

Prescribed for

Relief of nausea, vomiting, and dizziness associated with motion sickness or disease affecting the middle ear.

General Information

Meclizine is an antihistamine used to treat or prevent nausea, vomiting, and motion sickness. It takes a little longer to start working than most other drugs of this type but its effects last much longer (1 to 2 days). The specific method by which Meclizine acts on the brain to prevent dizziness and the nausea associated with it is not fully understood. In general, Meclizine does a better job of preventing motion sickness than of treating the symptoms once they are present.

Use with caution in children as a treatment for vomiting or nausea. This drug may obscure symptoms important in reaching the diagnosis of underlying disease. Meclizine is one of several drugs prescribed for the relief of nausea, vomiting, or dizziness that do not cure any underlying problems.

Cautions and Warnings

Do not take this medication if you think you are allergic to it or other antihistamines.

Pregnancy/Breast-feeding

Meclizine may cause birth defects or other problems in pregnant women. Do not take this medicine without your doctor's knowledge.

Small amounts of antihistamine medicines pass into breast milk and may affect a nursing infant. Nursing mothers should avoid antihistamines or use alternate feeding methods while taking the medicine.

Seniors

Seniors are more sensitive to antihistamine side effects. Confusion, difficult or painful urination, dizziness, drowsiness, a faint feeling, dry mouth, nose, or throat, nightmares or excitement, nervousness, restlessness, or irritability are more likely to occur among older adults.

Possible Side Effects

Most common: drowsiness, dry mouth, blurred vision.

Infrequent: difficulty in urination, constipation. Adverse effects are usually not cause for great concern. If they become serious, discuss them with your doctor.

Drug Interactions

Meclizine may cause sleepiness, tiredness, or inability to concentrate. Avoid tranquilizers, sleeping pills, alcoholic beverages, barbiturates, narcotics, and antihistamines, which can add to these effects.

Usual Dose

Adult: 25 to 50 milligrams 1 hour before travel; repeat every 24 hours for duration of journey. For control of dizziness (diseases affecting middle ear, etc.), 25 to 100 milli-grams per day in divided doses.

Child: this drug should not be used.

Special Information

Meclizine may cause tiredness, sleepiness, and inability to concentrate. Be extremely careful while driving or operating any machinery, appliances, or delicate equipment.

If you forget to take a dose of Meclizine, take it as soon as you remember. If it is almost time for your next regularly scheduled dose, skip the one you forgot and continue with your regular schedule. Do not take a double dose.

Generic Name

Meclofenamate Sodium

Brand Name

Meclomen

(Also available in generic form)

Type of Drug

Nonsteroidal anti-inflammatory.

Prescribed for

Arthritis, mild to moderate pain of menstrual cramps, dental surgery and extractions, and athletic injuries such as sprains and strains.

General Information

Meclofenamate Sodium is one of many nonsteroidal anti-inflammatory drugs (NSAIDs) available in the United States for the treatment of pain and inflammation of arthritis and osteoarthritis. Many people find they must try several of these NSAIDs before they find the one that is right for their condition. Meclofenamate Sodium must be taken for several days before it exerts any effect and will take 2 to 3 weeks for the maximum effect to develop.

As a group, these drugs reduce inflammation and ease

pain via the same mechanism and share many side effects, the most common of which are stomach upset and irritation. In fact, the potential effect of Meclofenamate Sodium on your stomach and intestines is so severe that it is recommended for use only after other medications have proven ineffective for controlling your symptoms. Many doctors also prescribe the NSAIDs to treat mild to moderate pain, menstrual cramps and pain, dental pain, and strains and sprains. However, you should check with your doctor before using Meclofenamate Sodium for any of these purposes.

Cautions and Warnings

Do not use Meclofenamate Sodium if you have had an allergic reaction to it or to any other nonsteroid anti-inflammatory drugs. Also, people allergic to Aspirin should not take Meclofenamate Sodium.

People with reduced kidney function should also receive lower than the usual dose because their ability to remove the drug from the body is impaired. Also, their kidney function should be monitored by periodic measurements of blood creatinine levels.

Pregnancy/Breast-feeding

This drug should be avoided by pregnant women, women who may become pregnant while using it, and nursing mothers, since this drug passes into breast milk. In those situations where it is deemed essential, the potential risk of the drug must be carefully weighed against any benefit it might produce.

Seniors

Older patients should be treated with a reduced daily dosage because they are more likely to be sensitive to the side effects. Report any side effects to your doctor at once.

Possible Side Effects

Most common: nausea, vomiting, and diarrhea, which may be severe. Other possible side effects are heartburn, stomach pain and discomfort, stomach ulcer, bleeding in the stomach or intestines, liver inflammation and jaundice, dizziness, headache, and rashes.

Less common side effects: light-headedness, nervousness, tension, fainting, tingling in the hands or feet, muscle weakness and aches, tiredness, a feeling of ill health, difficulty sleeping, drowsiness, strange dreams, confusion, loss of the ability to concentrate, depression, personality changes, stuffy nose, changes in taste perception, heart failure, low blood pressure, fluid retention, cystitis, urinary infection, changes in kidney function, nosebleeds, hemorrhage, easy bruising, reduction in the count of some white blood cells, itching, hair loss, appetite and body-weight changes, increased sugar in the blood or urine, increased need for Insulin in diabetic patients, flushing or sweating, menstrual difficulty, vaginal bleeding.

Drug Interactions

Meclofenamate Sodium may enhance the activity of oral anticoagulants (blood-thinning agents), Phenytoin and other antiseizure drugs, oral antidiabetes drugs, and sulfa drugs by increasing the amounts of these agents in the bloodstream. People taking Meclofenamate Sodium in combination with any of these medications may require a reduction in the dosage of their anticoagulant, antiseizure, sulfa, or antidiabetes drug.

Aspirin reduces the effectiveness of Meclofenamate Sodium. These two drugs should never be taken together.

Probenecid may increase the action of Meclofenamate Sodium in your blood and cause side effects. People taking this drug in combination should report any side effects or adverse effects to their doctor at once.

Food Interactions

Meclofenamate Sodium may be taken with food or meals if it upsets your stomach. If your stomach is still irritated, your dosage may have to be reduced, or you may have to change to another nonsteroid anti-inflammatory drug.

Usual Dose

200 to 400 milligrams per day.

Overdosage

The primary symptom of overdosage is acute stomach and intestinal distress. Symptoms generally develop within an hour of the overdose and resolve on their own within another 24 hours. Patients taking an overdose of this drug must be made to vomit with Syrup of Ipecac (available at any pharmacy) to remove any remaining drug from the stomach if the overdose was taken within the past hour. Call your doctor or a poison control center before doing this. If more than an hour has passed, go to a hospital emergency room. ALWAYS bring the medicine bottle.

Special Information

Meclofenamate Sodium may cause blurred vision or drowsiness. Because of this, you should be especially careful while driving or doing anything else that requires concentration.

Call your doctor if you develop severe stomach or intestinal irritation, sudden weight gain, rash, itching, swelling, black or tarry bowel movements, or intense headaches.

If you forget to take a dose of Meclofenamate Sodium, take it as soon as you remember. If it is almost time for your next regularly scheduled dose, skip the one you forgot and continue with your regular schedule. Do not take a double dose.

Generic Name

Medroxyprogesterone Acetate

Brand Names

Amen
Curretab
Provera

(Also available in generic form)

Type of Drug

Progestogen.

Prescribed for

Irregular menstrual bleeding.

General Information

Because of the potential development of secondary disease

after a long period of taking Medroxyprogesterone Acetate, the decision to take this medication chronically should be made cautiously by you and your doctor. Your continued need for chronic therapy with Medroxyprogesterone Acetate should be evaluated at least every 6 months to be sure that this therapy is absolutely necessary.

Cautions and Warnings

Do not take this drug if you have a history of blood clots or similar disorders, a history of convulsions, liver disease, known or suspected breast cancer, undiagnosed vaginal bleeding, or miscarriage.

Pregnancy/Breast-feeding

This drug is known to cause birth defects or interfere with your baby's development. It is not considered safe for use during pregnancy.

This drug passes into breast milk, but has caused no problems among breast-fed infants. You must consider the potential effect on the nursing infant if breast-feeding while taking this medicine.

Seniors

Older adults with severe liver disease are more sensitive to the effects of this drug. Follow your doctor's directions and report any side effects at once.

Possible Side Effects

Breakthrough bleeding, spotting, changes in or loss of menstrual flow, retention of water, increase or decrease in weight, jaundice, rash (with or without itching), mental depression.

A significant association has been demonstrated between the use of progestogen drugs and the following serious adverse effects: development of blood clots in the veins, lungs, or brain. Other possible adverse effects: changes in libido or sex drive, changes in appetite and mood, headache, nervousness, dizziness, tiredness, backache, loss of scalp hair, growth of hair in unusual quantities or places, itching, symptoms similar to urinary infections, unusual rashes.

Food Interactions

This medicine is best taken on an empty stomach, but you may take it with food if it upsets your stomach.

Usual Dose

5 to 10 milligrams per day for 5 to 10 days beginning on what is assumed to be the 16th to 21st day of the menstrual cycle.

Special Information

At the first sign of sudden, partial, or complete loss of vision, leg cramps, water retention, unusual vaginal bleeding, migraine headache, or depression, or if you think you have become pregnant, stop the drug immediately and call your doctor.

If you forget to take a dose of Medroxyprogesterone Acetate, take it as soon as you remember. If it is almost time for your next regularly scheduled dose, skip the one you forgot and continue with your regular schedule. Do not take a double dose.

Generic Name

Megestrol Acetate

Brand Names

Megace
Pallace

Type of Drug

Progestational hormone.

Prescribed for

Cancer of the breast or endometrium.

General Information

Megestrol Acetate has been used quite successfully in the treatment of the cancers cited above. It exerts its effect by acting as a hormonal counterbalance in areas rich in estrogen (breast and endometrium). Other progestational hormones such as Norethindrone (Norlutin, Norlutate) may be used to treat cancer of the endometrium or uterus or to correct hormone imbalance.

Cautions and Warnings

This drug should only be used for its two specifically approved indications. The use of this drug should be accompanied by close, continued contact with your doctor.

Pregnancy/Breast-feeding

This drug passes into breast milk, but has caused no problems among breast-fed infants. You must consider the potential effect on the nursing infant if breast-feeding while taking this medicine.

Seniors

Older adults with severe liver disease are more sensitive to the effects of this drug. Follow your doctor's directions and report any side effects at once.

Possible Side Effects

Back or stomach pain, headache, nausea, vomiting. If any of these symptoms appear, contact your doctor immediately. This drug should be used with caution if you have a history of blood clots in the veins.

Food Interactions

This medicine is best taken on an empty stomach, but you may take it with food if it upsets your stomach.

Usual Dose

40 to 320 milligrams per day.

Special Information

2 months of continued treatment is usually required to determine if Megestrol is effective treatment for your condition.

If you forget to take a dose of Megestrol Acetate, take it as soon as you remember. If it is almost time for your next regularly scheduled dose, skip the one you forgot and continue with your regular schedule. Do not take a double dose.

Generic Name

Meperidine

Brand Names

Demerol
Meperidine Hydrochloride
Pethadol

(Also available in generic form)

Type of Drug

Narcotic analgesic.

Prescribed for

Moderate to severe pain.

General Information

Meperidine is a narcotic drug with potent pain-relieving effect. It is also used before surgery to reduce patient anxiety and help bring the patient into the early stages of anesthesia. Meperidine is probably the most commonly used narcotic analgesic in American hospitals. Its effects compare favorably with those of Morphine Sulfate, the standard against which other narcotics are judged.

Meperidine is a narcotic drug with some pain-relieving and cough-suppressing activity. As an analgesic it is useful for mild to moderate pain. 25 to 50 milligrams of Meperidine are approximately equal in pain-relieving effect to 2 Aspirin tablets (650 milligrams). Meperidine may be less active than Aspirin for types of pain associated with inflammation, since Aspirin reduces inflammation and Meperidine does not. Meperidine suppresses the cough reflex but does not cure the underlying cause of the cough. In fact, sometimes it may not be desirable to overly suppress cough, because cough suppression reduces your ability to naturally eliminate excess mucus produced during a cold or allergy attack.

Cautions and Warnings

The side effects of narcotic drugs are exaggerated when the patient has a head injury, brain tumor, or other head prob-

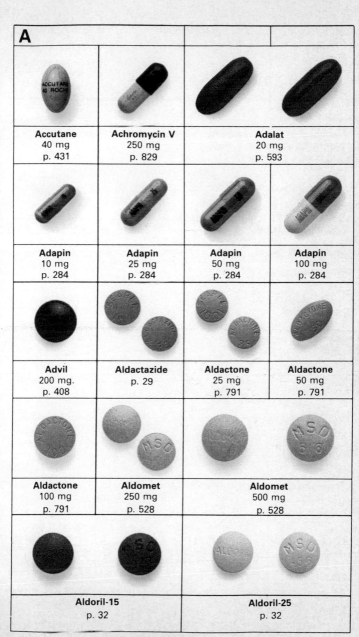

Accutane 40 mg p. 431	**Achromycin V** 250 mg p. 829	**Adalat** 20 mg p. 593	
Adapin 10 mg p. 284	**Adapin** 25 mg p. 284	**Adapin** 50 mg p. 284	**Adapin** 100 mg p. 284
Advil 200 mg. p. 408	**Aldactazide** p. 29	**Aldactone** 25 mg p. 791	**Aldactone** 50 mg p. 791
Aldactone 100 mg p. 791	**Aldomet** 250 mg p. 528	**Aldomet** 500 mg p. 528	
Aldoril-15 p. 32		**Aldoril-25** p. 32	

A

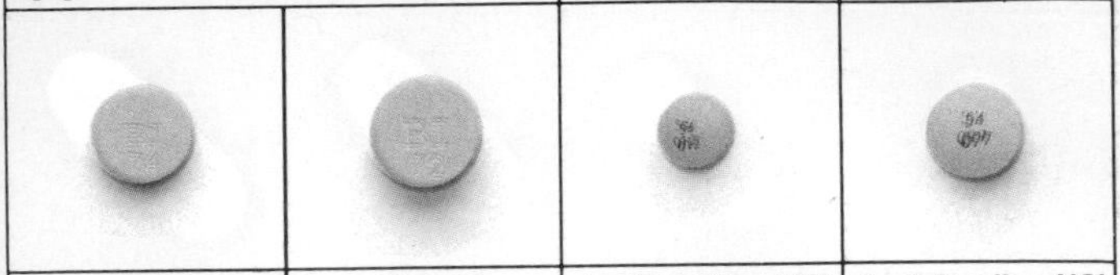

Alupent 10 mg p. 513	**Alupent** 20 mg p. 513	**Amitriptyline HCl** 25 mg p. 47	**Amitriptyline HCl** 50 mg p. 47
Amoxil 250 mg p. 54	**Amoxil** 500 mg p. 54	**Amoxil Chewable** 250 mg p. 54	**Ampicillin** 250 mg p. 57
Ampicillin 500 mg p. 57	**Anaprox** 275 mg p. 580		**Antivert** 12.5 mg p. 493
Antivert/25 p. 493	**Armour Thyroid** 1 gr p. 849	**Armour Thyroid** 2 gr p. 849	**Atarax** 25 mg p. 406
Ativan 0.5 mg p. 478	**Ativan** 1 mg p. 478	**Ativan** 2 mg p. 478	**Atromid-S** 500 mg p. 177

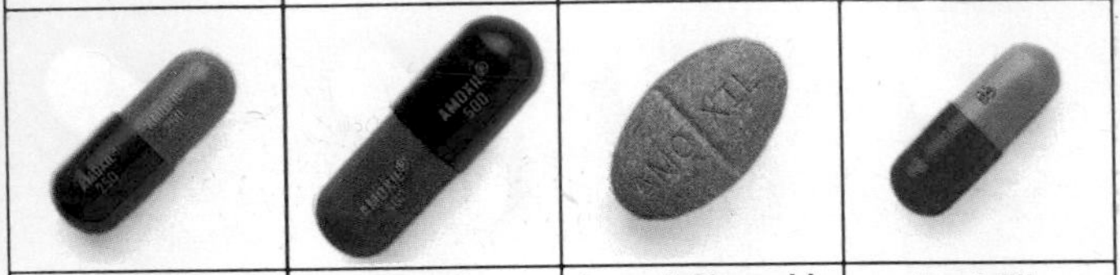

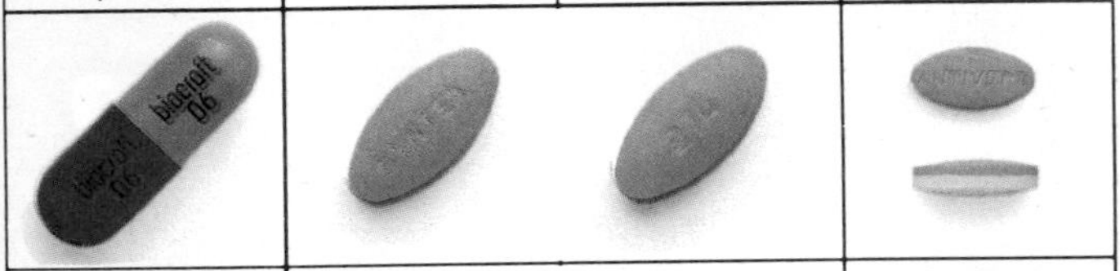

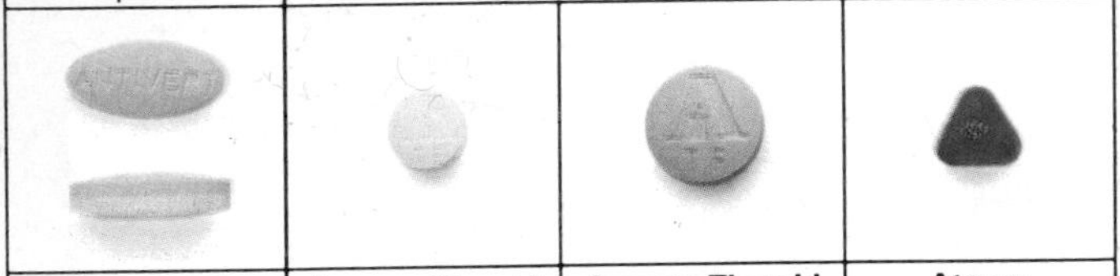

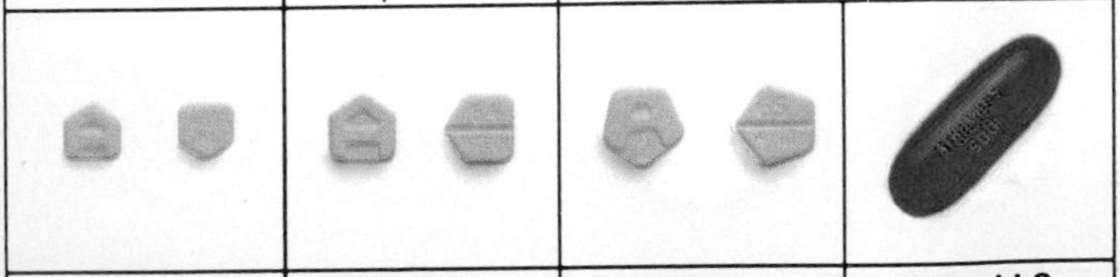

A

B

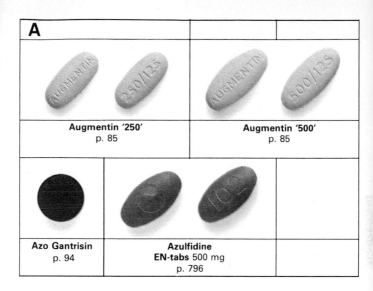

A

Augmentin '250' p. 85		Augmentin '500' p. 85	

Azo Gantrisin p. 94	Azulfidine EN-tabs 500 mg p. 796	

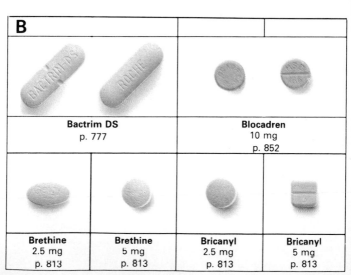

B

Bactrim DS p. 777		Blocadren 10 mg p. 852	

Brethine 2.5 mg p. 813	Brethine 5 mg p. 813	Bricanyl 2.5 mg p. 813	Bricanyl 5 mg p. 813

C

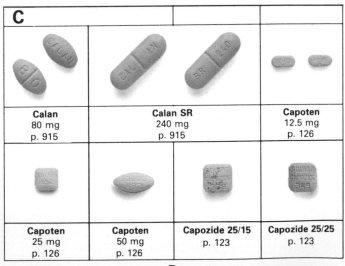

B

Bumex 0.5 mg p. 115	**Bumex** 1 mg p. 115	**BuSpar** 5 mg p. 118	**Butazolidin** 100 mg p. 699
Butazolidin 100 mg p. 699			

C

Calan 80 mg p. 915	**Calan SR** 240 mg p. 915		**Capoten** 12.5 mg p. 126
Capoten 25 mg p. 126	**Capoten** 50 mg p. 126	**Capozide 25/15** p. 123	**Capozide 25/25** p. 123

D

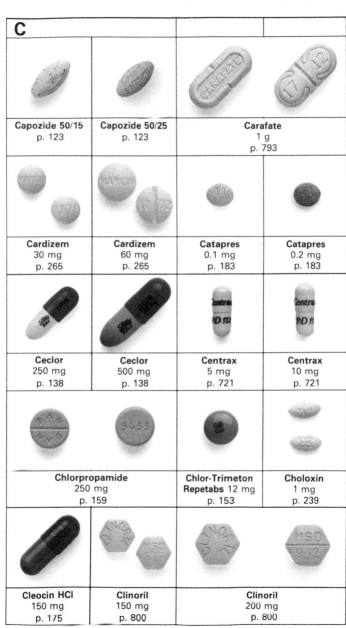

C			
Capozide 50/15 p. 123	**Capozide 50/25** p. 123	**Carafate** 1 g p. 793	
Cardizem 30 mg p. 265	**Cardizem** 60 mg p. 265	**Catapres** 0.1 mg p. 183	**Catapres** 0.2 mg p. 183
Ceclor 250 mg p. 138	**Ceclor** 500 mg p. 138	**Centrax** 5 mg p. 721	**Centrax** 10 mg p. 721
Chlorpropamide 250 mg p. 159		**Chlor-Trimeton Repetabs** 12 mg p. 153	**Choloxin** 1 mg p. 239
Cleocin HCl 150 mg p. 175	**Clinoril** 150 mg p. 800	**Clinoril** 200 mg p. 800	

E

C

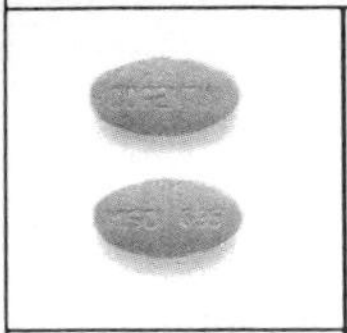

Cogentin 1 mg p. 103	Cogentin 2 mg p. 103	Compazine 5 mg p. 738	Compazine 10 mg p. 738

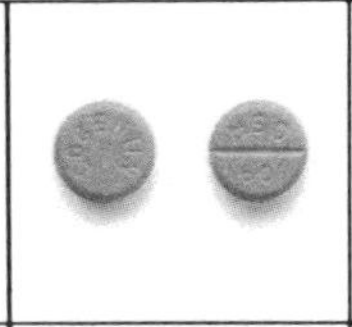

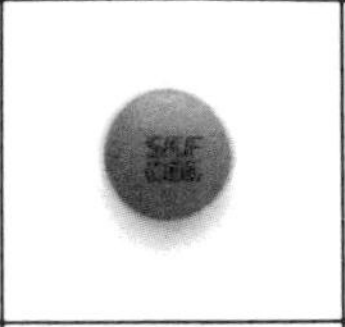

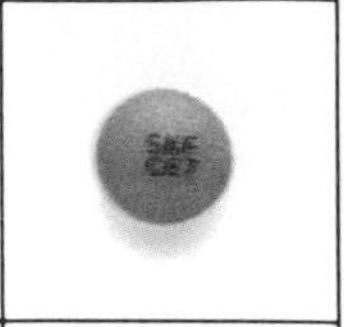

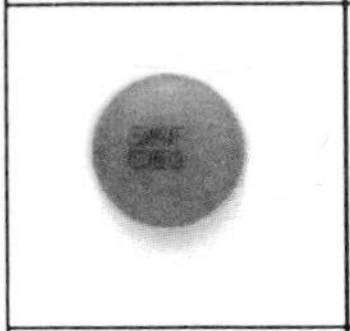

Compazine 25 mg p. 738	Corgard 40 mg p. 574	Corgard 80 mg p. 574	

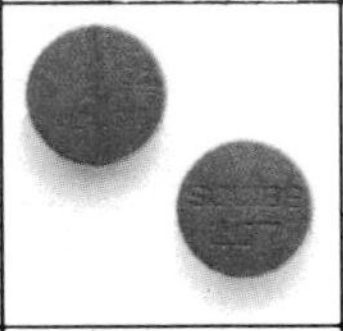

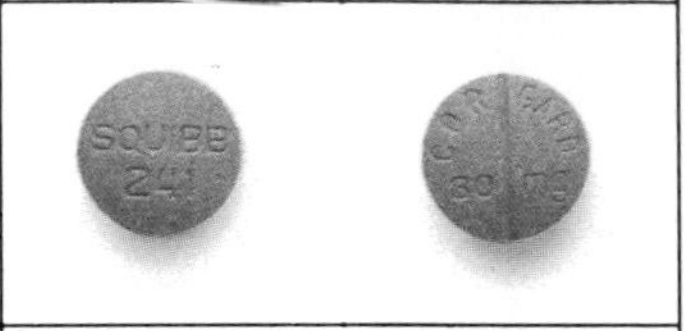

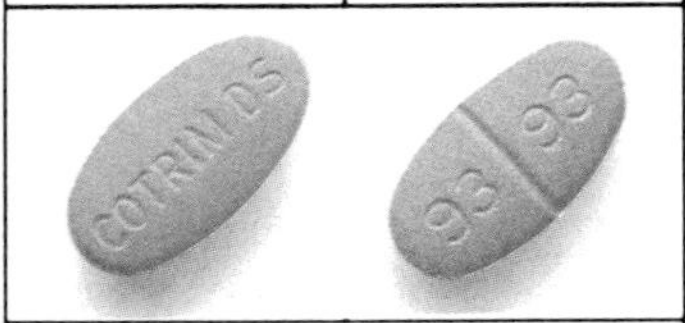

Cotrim DS p. 777	Coumadin 2.5 mg p. 921	Coumadin 5 mg p. 921

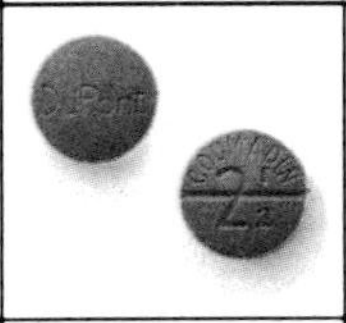

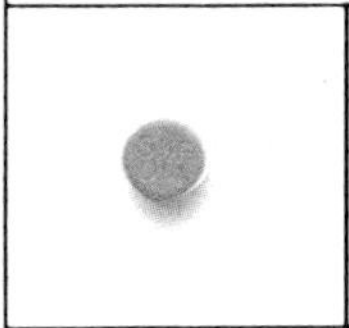

Cytomel 5 mcg p. 461	Cytomel 25 mcg p. 461	Cytomel 50 mcg p. 461	

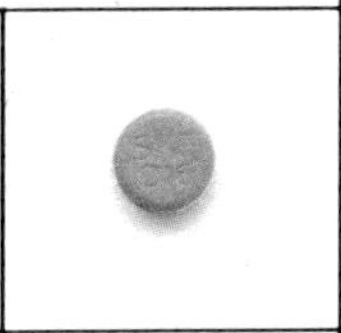

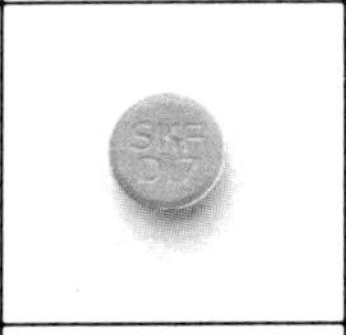

F

D

Dalmane 15 mg p. 360	**Dalmane** 30 mg p. 360	**Darvocet-N 100** p. 218	**Darvon** Compound-65 p. 220
Decadron 0.25 mg p. 230	**Decadron** 0.5 mg p. 230	**Decadron** 0.75 mg p. 230	**Decadron** 1.5 mg p. 230
Decadron 4 mg p. 230	**Deconamine SR** p. 65	**Deltasone** 5 mg p. 727	**Demerol HCl** 50 mg p. 502
Demulen 1/35-21 p. 617	**Demulen 1/50-21** p. 617	**Depakene** 250 mg p. 910	**Desyrel** 50 mg p. 870
Desyrel 100 mg p. 870	**Desyrel Dividose** 150 mg p. 870	**Dexamethasone** 0.25 mg p. 230	**Dexamethasone** 0.5 mg p. 230

G

D			
Dexamethasone 0.75 mg p. 230	Dexamethasone 1.5 mg p. 230	Dexamethasone 4 mg p. 230	DiaBeta 5 mg p. 378
Diabinese 100 mg p. 159	Diabinese 250 mg p. 159	Diamox 125 mg p. 20	Dilantin Infatabs 50 mg p. 702
Dilantin Kapseals 100 mg p. 702	Dipyridamole 25 mg p. 273	Dipyridamole 50 mg p. 273	Dipyridamole 75 mg p. 273
Ditropan 5 mg p. 633		Diulo 2.5 mg p. 542	Diulo 5 mg p. 542
Diulo 10 mg p. 542	Diuril 250 mg p. 150	Diuril 500 mg p. 150	Dolobid 500 mg p. 255

H

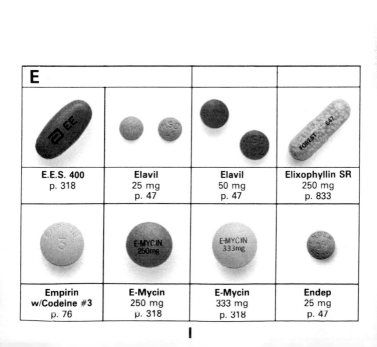

D			
Donnatal p. 281	**Dopar** 250 mg p. 447	**Dopar** 500 mg p. 447	**Doxycycline** **Hyclate** 100 mg p. 288
Dramamine 50 mg p. 268	**Drixoral** p. 292	**Duricef** 500 mg p. 138	**Dyazide** p. 297

E			
E.E.S. 400 p. 318	**Elavil** 25 mg p. 47	**Elavil** 50 mg p. 47	**Elixophyllin SR** 250 mg p. 833
Empirin w/Codeine #3 p. 76	**E-Mycin** 250 mg p. 318	**E-Mycin** 333 mg p. 318	**Endep** 25 mg p. 47

I

E

 **Endep** 50 mg p. 47	 **Endep** 75 mg p. 47	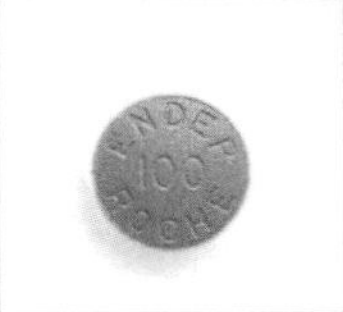 **Endep** 100 mg p. 47	 **Enduron** 5 mg p. 525
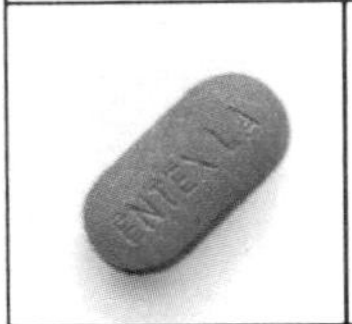 **Entex LA** p. 310	 **Equagesic** p. 313		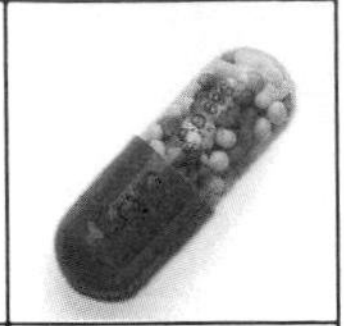 **ERYC** 250 mg p. 318
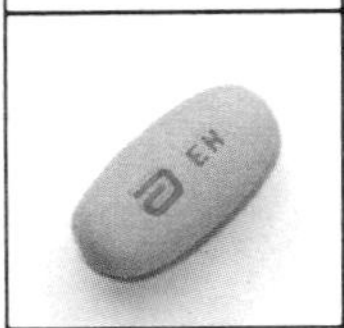 **Ery-Tab** 333 mg p. 318	 **Erythrocin** **Stearate** 250 mg p. 318	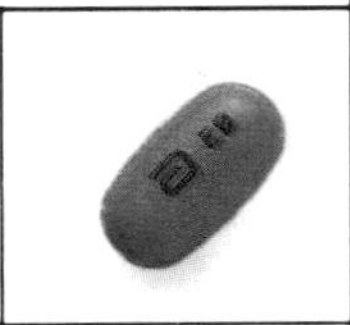 **Erythromycin** **Base** 250 mg p. 318	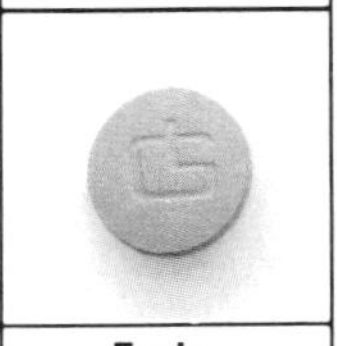 **Esgic** p. 336
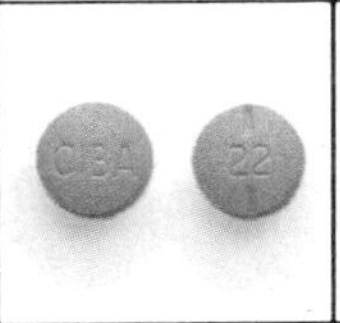 **Esidrix** 25 mg p. 400	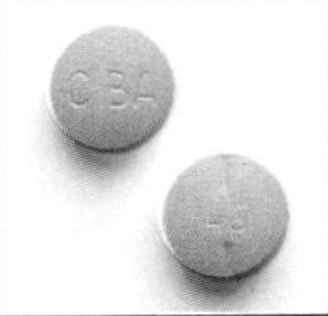 **Esidrix** 50 mg p. 400	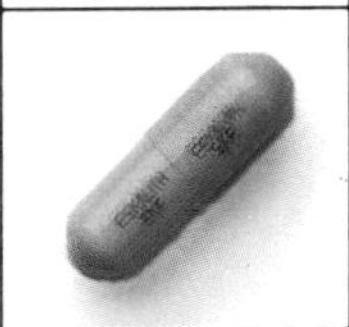 **Eskalith** 300 mg p. 470	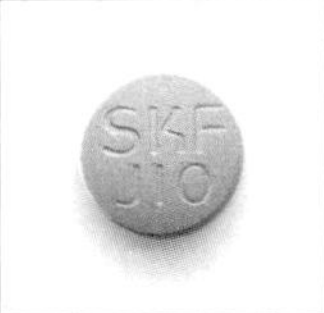 **Eskalith CR** 450 mg p. 470
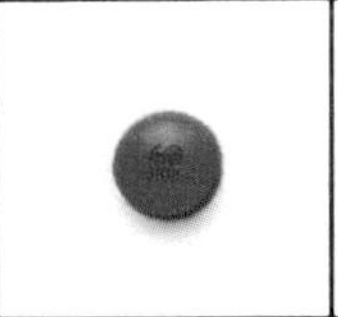 **Etrafon** p. 879			

J

F

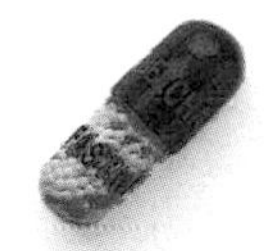

Fastin 30 mg p. 696	**Feldene** 20 mg p. 714	**Fioricet** p. 336	

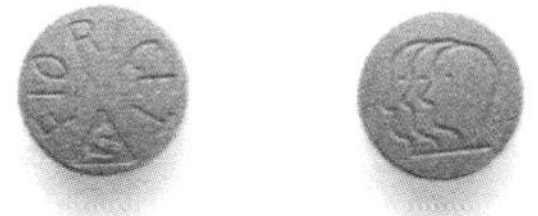

Fiorinal p. 335	**Fiorinal** p. 335	**Fiorinal** w/Codeine #3 p. 338

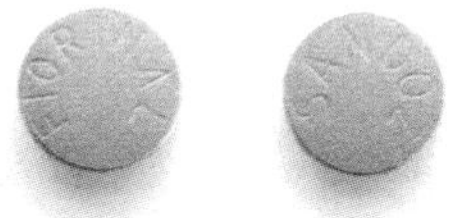

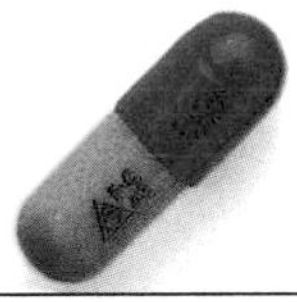

Flagyl 250 mg p. 549	**Flagyl** 500 mg p. 549

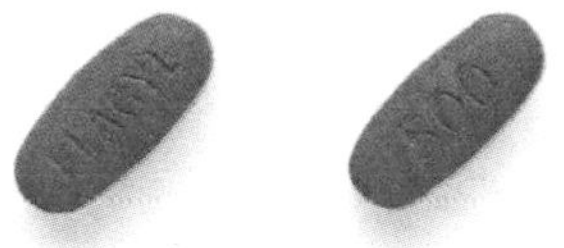

Furosemide 20 mg p. 365	**Furosemide** 40 mg p. 365

K

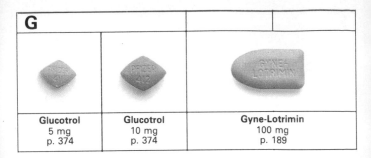

G			

| **Glucotrol** 5 mg p. 374 | **Glucotrol** 10 mg p. 374 | **Gyne-Lotrimin** 100 mg p. 189 | |

H			
Halcion 0.125 mg p. 883	**Halcion** 0.25 mg p. 883	**Haldol** 1 mg p. 394	**Halotestin** 2 mg p. 353
Halotestin 5 mg p. 353	**Halotestin** 10 mg p. 353	**Hydrochloro-thiazide** 25 mg p. 400	**Hydrochloro-thiazide** 50 mg p. 400
Hydrocodone Bitartrate w/APAP p. 918	**HydroDIURIL** 50 mg p. 400	**Hydropres 25** p. 403	**Hydropres 50** p. 403

L

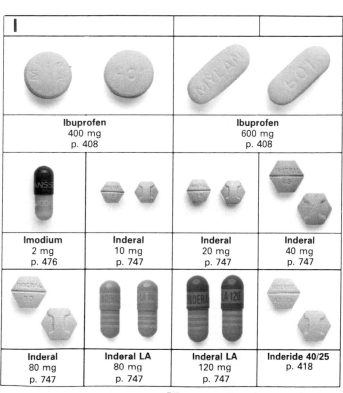

H			
Hydroxyzine HCl 25 mg p. 406	**Hygroton** 25 mg p. 162	**Hygroton** 50 mg p. 162	

I			
Ibuprofen 400 mg p. 408		**Ibuprofen** 600 mg p. 408	
Imodium 2 mg p. 476	**Inderal** 10 mg p. 747	**Inderal** 20 mg p. 747	**Inderal** 40 mg p. 747
Inderal 80 mg p. 747	**Inderal LA** 80 mg p. 747	**Inderal LA** 120 mg p. 747	**Inderide 40/25** p. 418

M

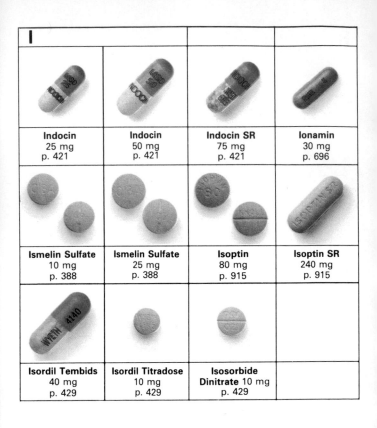

I			
Indocin 25 mg p. 421	**Indocin** 50 mg p. 421	**Indocin SR** 75 mg p. 421	**Ionamin** 30 mg p. 696
Ismelin Sulfate 10 mg p. 388	**Ismelin Sulfate** 25 mg p. 388	**Isoptin** 80 mg p. 915	**Isoptin SR** 240 mg p. 915
Isordil Tembids 40 mg p. 429	**Isordil Titradose** 10 mg p. 429	**Isosorbide Dinitrate** 10 mg p. 429	

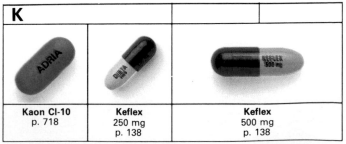

K			
Kaon Cl-10 p. 718	**Keflex** 250 mg p. 138	**Keflex** 500 mg p. 138	

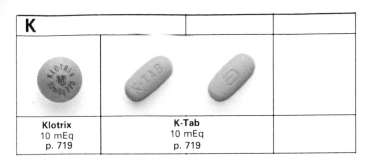

K			
Klotrix 10 mEq p. 719	K-Tab 10 mEq p. 719		

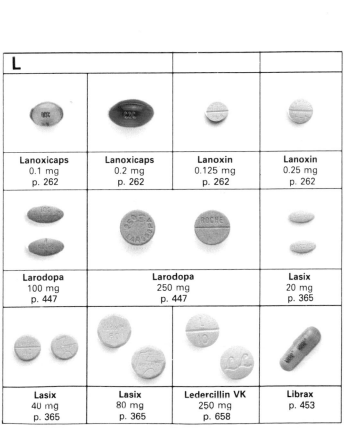

L			
Lanoxicaps 0.1 mg p. 262	Lanoxicaps 0.2 mg p. 262	Lanoxin 0.125 mg p. 262	Lanoxin 0.25 mg p. 262
Larodopa 100 mg p. 447	Larodopa 250 mg p. 447		Lasix 20 mg p. 365
Lasix 40 mg p. 365	Lasix 80 mg p. 365	Ledercillin VK 250 mg p. 658	Librax p. 453

O

L			
Libritabs 10 mg p. 147	**Librium** 10 mg p. 147	**Limbitrol** p. 457	**Lithobid** 300 mg p. 470
Lithonate 300 mg p. 470	**Lomotil** p. 473	**Lo/Ovral-21** p. 617	**Lopid** 300 mg p. 371
Lopressor 50 mg p. 546	**Lopressor** 100 mg p. 546	**Lorelco** 250 mg p. 733	**Lozol** 2.5 mg p. 415
Ludiomil 25 mg p. 485	**Ludiomil** 50 mg p. 485	**Ludiomil** 75 mg p. 485	

P

M			
Macrodantin 50 mg p. 599	**Macrodantin** 100 mg p. 599	**Marax** p. 488	
Maxzide p. 297	**Mazanor** 1 mg p. 491	**Meclizine HCl** 25 mg p. 493	**Meclomen** 50 mg p. 495
Meclomen 100 mg p. 495	**Medrol** 4 mg p. 534	**Megace** 20 mg p. 500	**Megace** 40 mg p. 500
Mellaril 25 mg p. 839	**Methyldopa** 250 mg p. 528		**Micro-K Extencaps** 8mEq p. 719
Micro-K 10 Extencaps p. 719	**Micronase** 2.5 mg p. 378	**Micronase** 5 mg p. 378	**Micronor** p. 618

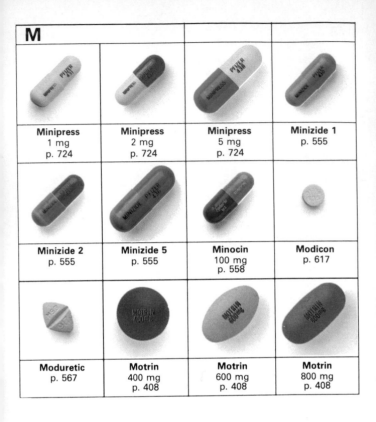

M			
Minipress 1 mg p. 724	**Minipress** 2 mg p. 724	**Minipress** 5 mg p. 724	**Minizide 1** p. 555
Minizide 2 p. 555	**Minizide 5** p. 555	**Minocin** 100 mg p. 558	**Modicon** p. 617
Moduretic p. 567	**Motrin** 400 mg p. 408	**Motrin** 600 mg p. 408	**Motrin** 800 mg p. 408

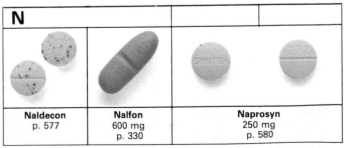

N			
Naldecon p. 577	**Nalfon** 600 mg p. 330	**Naprosyn** 250 mg p. 580	

R

Naprosyn 375 mg p. 580		**Naprosyn** 500 mg p. 580	
Nicorette 2 mg p. 587	**Nizoral** 200 mg p. 436	**Nolvadex** 10 mg p. 805	**Nordette-21** p. 617
Norgesic Forte p. 607		**Norinyl 1+35** **21-Day** p. 617	**Norinyl 1+50** **21-Day** p. 617
Normodyne 200 mg p. 441	**Norpace** 100 mg p. 275	**Norpace** 150 mg p. 275	**Norpace CR** 100 mg p. 275
Norpramin 25 mg p. 226	**Norpramin** 50 mg p. 226	**Novafed A** p. 65	**Nuprin** 200 mg p. 408

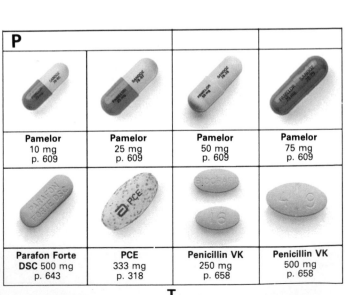

O			
Omnipen 250 mg p. 57	**Omnipen** 500 mg p. 57	**Orinase** 500 mg p. 864	**Ortho-Novum 1/35 21** p. 617
Ortho-Novum 1/50 21 p. 617	**Orudis** 75 mg p. 439	**Ovral** p. 617	

P			
Pamelor 10 mg p. 609	**Pamelor** 25 mg p. 609	**Pamelor** 50 mg p. 609	**Pamelor** 75 mg p. 609
Parafon Forte DSC 500 mg p. 643	**PCE** 333 mg p. 318	**Penicillin VK** 250 mg p. 658	**Penicillin VK** 500 mg p. 658

T

P

Pentids '400' p. 656	**Pentids '800'** p. 656	**Pen-Vee K** 500 mg p. 658	**Pepcid** 40 mg p. 328
Percocet p. 668	**Percodan** p. 671	**Persantine** 25 mg p. 273	**Persantine** 50 mg p. 273
Persantine 75 mg p. 273	**Phenaphen w/Codeine #3** p. 17	**Phenaphen w/Codeine #4** p. 17	**Phenobarbital** 30 mg p. 690
Plegine 35 mg p. 677	**Polycillin** 250 mg p. 57	**Polymox** 250 mg p. 54	**Polymox** 500 mg p. 54
Poly-Vi-Flor w/Iron 1 mg p. 716	**Prednisone** 5 mg p. 727	**Premarin** 0.3 mg p. 203	**Premarin** 0.625 mg p. 203

U

P

Premarin 1.25 mg p. 203	**Principen '250'** p. 57	**Principen '500'** p. 57	**Procan SR** 500 mg p. 736
Procardia 10 mg p. 593	**Procardia** 20 mg p. 593		**Prolixin** 1 mg p. 355
Prolixin 5 mg p. 355	**Prolixin** 10 mg p. 355	**Proloid** 32 mg p. 845	**Proloid** 65 mg p. 845
Proloid 100 mg p. 845	**Proloid** 130 mg p. 845	**Proloid** 200 mg p. 845	**Pronestyl** 375 mg p. 736
Pronestyl 500 mg p. 736	**Pronestyl-SR** 500 mg p. 736	**Propoxyphene** **Napsylate/APAP** p. 744	**Propranolol HCl** 20 mg p. 747

V

P			
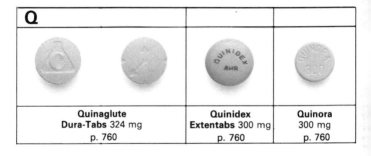			
Propranolol HCl 40 mg p. 747	**Proventil** 2 mg p. 26	**Provera** 10 mg p. 498	**Pyridium** 200 mg p. 676

Q			
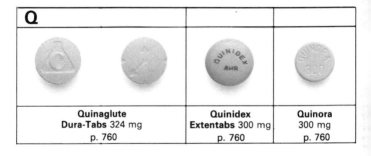			
Quinaglute Dura-Tabs 324 mg p. 760		**Quinidex Extentabs** 300 mg p. 760	**Quinora** 300 mg p. 760

R			
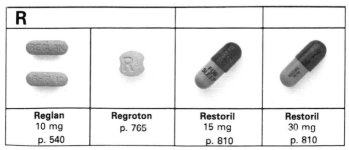			
Reglan 10 mg p. 540	**Regroton** p. 765	**Restoril** 15 mg p. 810	**Restoril** 30 mg p. 810

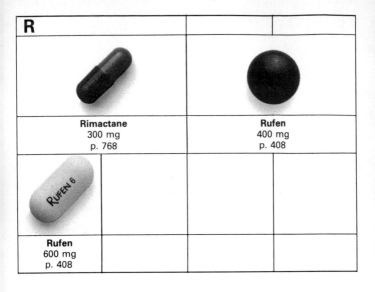

R		
Rimactane 300 mg p. 768	Rufen 400 mg p. 408	
Rufen 600 mg p. 408		

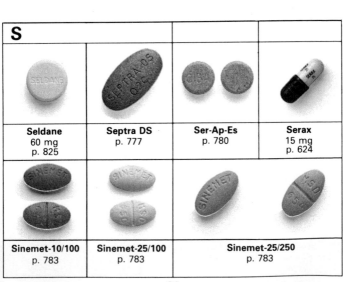

S			
Seldane 60 mg p. 825	Septra DS p. 777	Ser-Ap-Es p. 780	Serax 15 mg p. 624
Sinemet-10/100 p. 783	Sinemet-25/100 p. 783	Sinemet-25/250 p. 783	

X

S

Sinequan 25 mg p. 284	**Sinequan** 50 mg p. 284	**Slo-bid Gyrocaps** 200 mg p. 833	**Slo-bid Gyrocaps** 300 mg p. 833
Slo-Phyllin Gyrocaps 125 mg p. 833	**Slo-Phyllin Gyrocaps** 250 mg p. 833	**Slow-K** 8 mEq p. 719	
Sorbitrate 5 mg p. 429		**Sorbitrate** 10 mg p. 429	
Sorbitrate 20 mg p. 429	**Sorbitrate** 30 mg p. 429	**Sorbitrate SA** 40 mg p. 429	
Spectrobid 400 mg p. 97		**Stelazine** 1 mg p. 886	**Stelazine** 2 mg p. 886

Y

S

Stelazine 5 mg p. 886	**Stelazine** 10 mg p. 886	**Sudafed** 30 mg p. 754	**Sumycin '250'** p. 829
Sumycin '500' p. 829	**Surmontil** 25 mg p. 896	**Surmontil** 50 mg p. 896	**Symmetrel** 100 mg p. 447
Synalgos-DC p. 803	**Synthroid** 0.05 mg p. 450	**Synthroid** 0.1 mg p. 450	**Synthroid** 0.15 mg p. 450
Synthroid 0.2 mg p. 450			

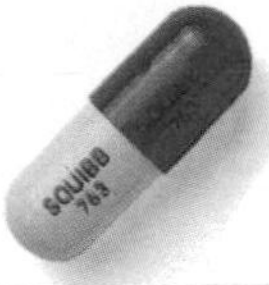

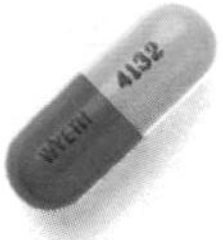

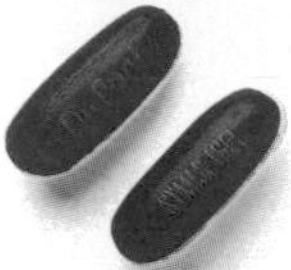

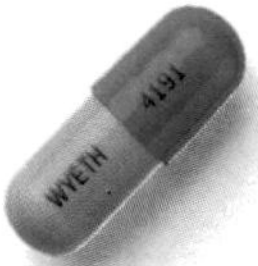

Z

T			
Tagamet 300 mg p. 169	**Tagamet** 400 mg p. 169	**Tagamet** 800 mg p. 169	**Talwin NX** p. 661
Tavist-1 1.34 mg p. 172	**Tavist-D** p. 66		**Tedral SA** p. 808
Tegopen 500 mg p. 191	**Tegretol** 200 mg p. 129	**Teldrin** 12 mg p. 153	**Tenoretic 50** p. 816
Tenormin 50 mg p. 82	**Tenormin** 100 mg p. 82	**Tenuate Dospan** 75 mg p. 250	**Tetracycline HCl** 250 mg p. 829
Theo-Dur 200 mg p. 833	**Theo-Dur** 300 mg p. 833	**Theolair** 125 mg p. 833	

T			
Thorazine 75 mg p. 156	**Thorazine** 150 mg p. 156	**Thorazine** 300 mg p. 156	**Thorazine** 10 mg p. 156
Thorazine 25 mg p. 156	**Thorazine** 50 mg p. 156	**Thorazine** 100 mg p. 156	**Thorazine** 200 mg p. 156
Tigan 100 mg p. 892	**Tofranil** 10 mg p. 411	**Tofranil** 25 mg p. 411	**Tofranil** 50 mg p. 411
Tofranil-PM 75 mg p. 411	**Tofranil-PM** 100 mg p. 411	**Tofranil-PM** 125 mg p. 411	**Tofranil-PM** 150 mg p. 411
Tolectin DS 400 mg p. 867	**Tolinase** 250 mg p. 861	**Tonocard** 400 mg p. 858	**Tonocard** 600 mg p. 858

T			
Trandate 100 mg p. 441	**Trandate** 200 mg p. 441	**Trandate** 300 mg p. 441	**Tranxene** 3.75 mg p. 186
Tranxene 7.5 mg p. 186	**Trental** 400 mg p. 666	**Triavil 2-10** p. 879	**Triavil 2-25** p. 879
Tuss-Ornade p. 907		**Tylenol** w/Codeine #2 p. 17	
Tylenol w/Codeine #3 p. 17		**Tylenol** w/Codeine #4 p. 17	

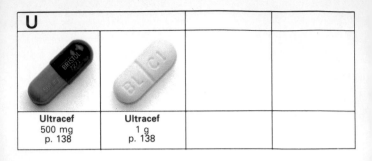

U			
Ultracef 500 mg p. 138	**Ultracef** 1 g p. 138		

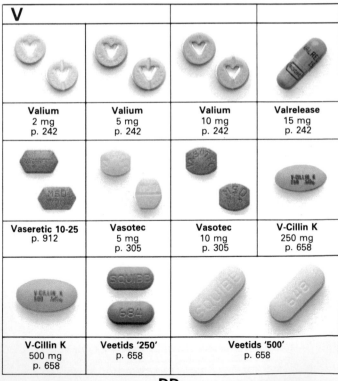

V			
Valium 2 mg p. 242	**Valium** 5 mg p. 242	**Valium** 10 mg p. 242	**Valrelease** 15 mg p. 242
Vaseretic 10-25 p. 912	**Vasotec** 5 mg p. 305	**Vasotec** 10 mg p. 305	**V-Cillin K** 250 mg p. 658
V-Cillin K 500 mg p. 658	**Veetids '250'** p. 658	**Veetids '500'** p. 658	

DD

V			
Velosef 250 mg p. 138	**Velosef** 500 mg p. 138	**Ventolin** 2 mg p. 26	**Ventolin** 4 mg p. 26
Vibra-Tabs 100 mg p. 288	**Vicodin** p. 918	**Visken** 5 mg p. 708	**Vivactil** 5 mg p. 751
Vivactil 10 mg p. 751			

W			
Wymox 250 mg p. 54	**Wymox** 500 mg p. 54	**Wytensin** 4 mg p. 383	

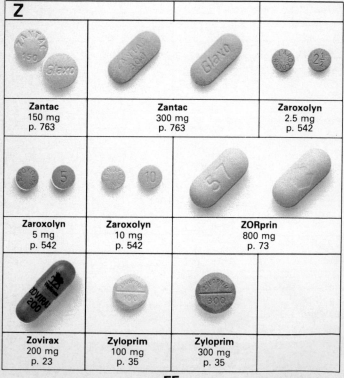

X–Y

Xanax
0.25 mg
p. 38

Xanax
0.5 mg
p. 38

Xanax
1 mg
p. 38

Yutopar
10 mg
p. 770

Z

Zantac
150 mg
p. 763

Zantac
300 mg
p. 763

Zaroxolyn
2.5 mg
p. 542

Zaroxolyn
5 mg
p. 542

Zaroxolyn
10 mg
p. 542

ZORprin
800 mg
p. 73

Zovirax
200 mg
p. 23

Zyloprim
100 mg
p. 35

Zyloprim
300 mg
p. 35

FF

lem. Narcotics can also hide the symptoms of head injury. They should be used with extreme caution in patients with head injuries.

Pregnancy/Breast-feeding

No studies of this medication have been done in women and no reports of human birth defects exist, but animal studies show that high doses of the drug can cause problems in a developing fetus. Pregnant women, or women who might become pregnant while using this drug, should talk to their doctor about the risk of taking this medicine versus the benefits it can provide.

This drug passes into breast milk, but no problems in nursing infants have been seen. Breast-feeding women should consider the possibility of adverse effects on their nursing infant. Choose another feeding method if you must take this medicine.

Seniors

Seniors are more likely to be sensitive to side effects of this drug and should be treated with smaller dosages than younger adults.

Possible Side Effects

Most frequent: light-headedness, dizziness, sleepiness, nausea, vomiting, loss of appetite, sweating. If these occur, consider calling your doctor and asking him about lowering your present dose of Meperidine. Usually the side effects disappear if you simply lie down.

More serious side effects of Meperidine are shallow breathing or difficulty in breathing.

Less common side effects: euphoria (feeling high), weakness, sleepiness, headache, agitation, uncoordinated muscle movement, minor hallucinations, disorientation and visual disturbances, dry mouth, loss of appetite, constipation, flushing of the face, rapid heartbeat, palpitations, faintness, urinary difficulties or hesitancy, reduced sex drive and/or potency, itching, skin rashes, anemia, lowered blood sugar, and a yellowing of the skin and/or whites of the eyes. Narcotic analgesics may aggravate convulsions in those who have had convulsions in the past.

Drug Interactions

Because of its depressant effect and potential effect on breathing, Meperidine should be taken with extreme care in combination with alcohol, sleeping medicine, tranquilizers, or other depressant drugs.

Food Interactions

This drug may be taken with food to reduce stomach upset.

Usual Dose

Adult: 50 to 150 milligrams every 3 to 4 hours as needed.
Child: 0.5 to 0.8 milligrams per pound every 3 to 4 hours as needed, up to the adult dose.

Overdosage

Symptoms are depression of respiration (breathing), extreme tiredness progressing to stupor and then coma, pinpointed pupils of the eyes, no response to stimulation such as a pin stick, cold and clammy skin, slowing down of the heartbeat, lowering of blood pressure, convulsions, and cardiac arrest. The patient should be taken to a hospital emergency room immediately. ALWAYS bring the medicine bottle.

Special Information

If you are taking Meperidine, be extremely careful while driving or operating machinery. Avoid alcoholic beverages. Call your doctor if this drug makes you very nauseated or constipated or if you have trouble breathing.

If you forget to take a dose of Meperidine, take it as soon as you remember. If it is almost time for your next regularly scheduled dose, skip the one you forgot and continue with your regular schedule. Do not take a double dose.

Generic Name

Meprobamate

Brand Names

Equanil	Neurate
Meprospan	Sedabamate
Miltown	Tranmep
Neuramate	

(Also available in generic form)

Type of Drug

Minor tranquilizer.

Prescribed for

Relief of anxiety and tension, and to promote sleep in anxious or tense patients.

General Information

Meprobamate and the other drugs in its chemical group are used as either antianxiety agents, anticonvulsants, or sedatives (sleeping pills). This drug exerts effects by relaxing the large skeletal muscles and by a direct effect on the brain. In doing so, it can relax you and make you either more tranquil or sleepier, depending on the drug and how much you use.

Meprobamate is generally used in any situation where it can be a useful adjunct.

Meprobamate can be abused if taken for long periods of time and it is possible to develop withdrawal symptoms if you discontinue the therapy abruptly. Withdrawal symptoms include convulsions, tremor, muscle or stomach cramps, vomiting, and sweating.

Cautions and Warnings

You should not take Meprobamate if you are allergic to it or if you feel that you may be allergic to a related drug such as Carisoprodol, Mebutamate, or Carbromal. Severe physical and psychological dependence has been experienced by people taking Meprobamate for long periods of time. The drug can produce chronic intoxication after prolonged use or if used in greater than recommended doses, leading to adverse effects such as slurred speech, dizziness, and general sleepiness or depression. Sudden withdrawal of Meprobamate after prolonged and excessive use may result in drug withdrawal symptoms including severe anxiety, loss of appetite, sleeplessness, vomiting, tremors, muscle twitching, severe sleepiness, confusion, hallucinations, and possibly convulsions. Such withdrawal symptoms usually begin 12 to 48 hours after Meprobamate has been stopped and may last 1 to 4 days. When someone has taken this medication in excessive quantities for weeks, months, or longer, the medication must be gradually reduced over a period of 1 or 2 weeks in order to avoid these withdrawal symptoms.

If you are taking Meprobamate you should be aware that this drug may cause inability to perform usual tasks which require coordination, such as driving or operating machinery, and you must be extremely careful when performing such tasks.

Pregnancy/Breast-feeding

Use with extreme caution if you are in the first 3 months of pregnancy or if you suspect that you may be pregnant; Meprobamate has been shown to increase the chance of birth defects and may cause tiredness in nursing infants. If you are pregnant and are taking this medication, you should discuss it with your doctor.

Meprobamate passes into breast milk. Its effect on nursing infants is unknown.

Seniors

Older adults are more sensitive to the effects of this drug. Follow your doctor's directions and report any side effects at once.

Possible Side Effects

Most common: drowsiness, sleepiness, dizziness, slurred speech, headache, weakness, tingling in the arms and legs, euphoria, and possibly excitement or paradoxical reactions such as overstimulation.

Infrequent: nausea, vomiting, diarrhea, abnormal heart rhythms, low blood pressure, itching, rash, effects on various components of the blood. Quite rarely there has been severe hypersensitivity or allergic reactions producing high fever, chills, closing of the throat (bronchospasm), loss of urinary function, and other severe symptoms.

Drug Interactions

Interactions with other drugs that produce depression of the central nervous system can cause sleepiness, tiredness, and tranquilization. Interaction with other tranquilizers, alcoholic beverages in excessive quantities, narcotics, barbiturates and other sleeping pills, or antihistamines can cause excessive depression, sleepiness, and fatigue.

Food Interactions

This medicine is best taken on an empty stomach, but you may take it with food if it upsets your stomach.

Usual Dose

Adult (when used as a tranquilizer): 1200 to 1600 milligrams per day in divided doses; maximum permissible, 2400 milligrams per day.

Child (age 6 to 12): 100 to 200 milligrams 2 to 3 times per day.

Child (under age 6): this drug should not be used.

Overdosage

In attempted suicide or accidental overdose, symptoms are extreme drowsiness, lethargy, stupor, and coma, with possible shock and respiratory collapse (breathing stops).

The overdosed patient must be taken to a hospital emergency room immediately. ALWAYS bring the medicine bottle. Some people have died after taking 30 tablets, others have survived after taking 100.

The overdose is much worse if there is interaction with alcohol or another depressant: a much smaller dose of Meprobamate can produce fatal results.

After a large overdose, the patient will go to sleep very quickly and blood pressure, pulse, and breathing levels will be greatly reduced. After the patient is taken to the hospital his stomach should be pumped and respiratory assistance and other supportive therapy given.

Special Information

Avoid alcohol and other drugs that depress the nervous system while taking this sleeping pill. Be sure to take this medicine according to your doctor's direction. Do not change your dose without your doctor's approval. This drug causes drowsiness, poor concentration, and makes it more difficult to drive a car, operate machinery, or perform complicated activities.

Call your doctor at once if you develop fever, sore throat, nosebleeds, mouth sores, unexplained black-and-blue marks, easy bruising or bleeding.

If you forget to take a dose of Meprobamate and you remember within about an hour of your regular time, take it right away. If you do not remember until later, skip the forgotten dose and go back to your regular schedule. Do not take a double dose.

Generic Name

Mesalamine

Brand Name

Rowasa

Type of Drug

Anti-inflammatory.

Prescribed for

Ulcerative colitis, proctitis, or proctosigmoiditis.

General Information

Sulfasalazine, a widely used treatment for ulcerative colitis and other inflammatory conditions, is broken down in the colon to Mesalamine. It is thought that Mesalamine is the active agent in treating the symptoms of bowel inflammation. No one knows how Mesalamine produces its effect, but it is thought to be a direct effect in the bowel, not one involving the rest of the body.

Little of the drug is absorbed into the blood; 70 to 90 percent of the drug stays in the colon.

Cautions and Warnings

Mesalamine may cause cramping, sudden abdominal pain, and bloody diarrhea. Fever, headache, and a rash may also occur. The symptoms may occur suddenly and are reason to call your doctor and stop taking the drug at once.

People who are sensitive to Sulfasalazine have been able to tolerate Mesalamine because so little of the drug is absorbed into the blood.

Pregnancy/Breast-feeding

Animal studies have revealed no indication that Mesalamine can harm a developing fetus. Pregnant women should consult with their doctor before using this medication. It is not known if Mesalamine passes into breast milk.

Seniors

Seniors may use this drug without special precaution. Be sure to report any unusual side effects to your doctor.

Possible Side Effects

Mesalamine is generally well tolerated with few side effects. Among those that do occur, the most common are abdominal pain, cramps, and discomfort, headache, intestinal gas, nausea, flu, feeling tired or weak, not feeling well, fever, and rash.

Less common side effects are common cold, sore throat, diarrhea, joint and leg pains, dizziness, bloating, back pain, pain on inserting the enema tip, hemorrhoids, itching, rectal pain, soreness or burning, constipation, hair loss, swelling of the arms and legs, urinary burning, urinary infections, weakness, and sleeplessness.

Usual Dose

One rectal enema (1 bottle) at bedtime every night for 3 to 6 weeks. The enema liquid should be retained for about 8 hours.

Special Information

Shake the bottle well and remove the protective sheath from the applicator tip. Lie on your left side with your lower leg extended and the upper leg flexed to maintain balance. Gently insert the applicator tip in the rectum pointing toward your navel. Steadily squeezing the bottle will discharge most of the contents into your colon.

Call your doctor if you forget a dose of Mesalamine.

Generic Name

Mesoridazine

Brand Name

Serentil

Type of Drug

Phenothiazine antipsychotic.

Prescribed for

Psychotic disorders, moderate to severe depression with anxiety, control of agitation or aggressiveness of disturbed children, alcohol withdrawal symptoms, intractable pain, and senility.

General Information

Mesoridazine and other members of the phenothiazine group act on a portion of the brain called the hypothalamus. They affect parts of the hypothalamus that control metabolism, body temperature, alertness, muscle tone, hormone balance, and vomiting, and may be used to treat problems related to any of these functions.

Cautions and Warnings

Mesoridazine should not be taken if you are allergic to one of the drugs in the broad classification known as phenothiazine drugs. Do not take Mesoridazine if you have any blood, liver, kidney, or heart disease. This medication is a tranquilizer and can have a depressive effect, especially during the first few days of therapy. Care should be taken when performing activities requiring a high degree of concentration, such as driving.

This drug should be used with caution and under strict

supervision of your doctor if you have glaucoma, epilepsy, ulcers, or difficulty passing urine.

Avoid exposure to extreme heat because this drug can impair your ability to accommodate to high temperatures.

Pregnancy/Breast-feeding

Infants born to women taking this medication have experienced drug side effects (liver jaundice, nervous system effects) immediately after birth. Check with your doctor about taking this medicine if you are or might become pregnant.

This drug may pass into breast milk and affect a nursing infant. Consider alternate feeding methods if you take this medicine.

Seniors

Older adults are more sensitive to the effects of this medication than younger adults and usually require a lower dosage to achieve a desired effect. Also, older adults are more likely to develop drug side effects. Some experts feel that elderly people should be treated with ½ to ¼ the usual adult dose.

Possible Side Effects

Most common: drowsiness, especially during the first or second week of therapy. If the drowsiness becomes troublesome, contact your doctor.

Mesoridazine can cause jaundice (yellowing of the whites of the eyes of skin), usually in 2 to 4 weeks. The jaundice usually goes away when the drug is discontinued, but there have been cases when it did not. If you notice this effect or if you develop symptoms such as fever and generally not feeling well, contact your doctor immediately. Less frequent: changes in components of the blood including anemias, raised or lowered blood pressure, abnormal heart rates, heart attack, feeling faint or dizzy.

Phenothiazines can produce "extrapyramidal effects," such as spasm of the neck muscles, rolling back of the eyes, convulsions, difficulty in swallowing, and symptoms associated with Parkinson's disease. These effects look very serious but go away after the drug has been withdrawn; however, symptoms of the face, tongue, and jaw may persist for as long as several years, especially in the elderly with a history of brain damage. If you experience extrapyramidal effects, contact your doctor immediately.

Mesoridazine may cause an unusual increase in psychotic symptoms or may cause paranoid reactions, tiredness, lethargy, restlessness, hyperactivity, confusion at night, bizarre dreams, inability to sleep, depression, and euphoria. Other reactions are itching, swelling, unusual sensitivity to bright lights, red skin (particularly in exposed areas), and rash. There have been cases of breast enlargement, false positive pregnancy tests, changes in menstrual flow in females, and impotence and changes in sex drive in males, stuffy nose, headache, nausea, vomiting, loss of appetite, change in body temperature, loss of facial color, excessive salivation and perspiration, constipation, diarrhea, changes in urine and stool habits, worsening of glaucoma, blurred vision, weakening of eyelid muscles and spasms in bronchial and other muscles, increased appetite, and excessive thirst.

Drug Interactions

Mesoridazine should be avoided in combination with barbiturates, sleeping pills, narcotics, other tranquilizers, or any other medication which may produce a depressive effect. Avoid alcohol.

Usual Dose

30 to 400 milligrams per day, depending on the condition being treated.

Overdosage

Symptoms are depression, extreme weakness, tiredness, desire to go to sleep, coma, lowered blood pressure, uncontrolled muscle spasms, agitation, restlessness, convulsions, fever, dry mouth, and abnormal heart rhythms. The patient should be taken to a hospital emergency room immediately. ALWAYS bring the medicine bottle.

Special Information

This medication may cause drowsiness. Use caution when driving or operating complex equipment and avoid alcoholic beverages while taking the medicine.

The drug may also cause unusual sensitivity to the sun and can turn your urine reddish-brown to pink.

If dizziness occurs, avoid sudden changes in posture and avoid climbing stairs.

Use caution in hot weather. This medicine may make you more prone to heat stroke.

If you take Mesoridazine once a day and forget your dose, take it as soon as possible. If you don't remember until the next day, skip the forgotten dose and continue with your regular schedule.

If you take the medicine more than once a day and forget a dose, take the forgotten dose as soon as possible. If it is almost time for your next dose, skip the forgotten dose and go on with your regular schedule.

Generic Name

Metaproterenol

Brand Names

Alupent
Metaprel

(Also available in generic form)

Type of Drug

Bronchodilator.

Prescribed for

Asthma and spasm of the bronchial muscles.

General Information

Metaproterenol can be taken both by mouth as a tablet or syrup and by inhalation. This drug may be used together with other drugs to produce the desired relief from asthmatic symptoms. Oral Metaproterenol begins working 15 to 30 minutes after a dose and its effects may last for up to 4 hours. Metaproterenol inhalation begins working in 1 to 5 minutes and lasts for 3 to 4 hours.

Cautions and Warnings

This drug should be used with caution by patients who have

angina, heart disease, high blood pressure, a history of stroke or seizures, diabetes, thyroid disease, prostate disease, or glaucoma. Excessive use of Metaproterenol inhalant could lead to worsening of your condition.

Pregnancy/Breast-feeding

This drug should be used by women who are pregnant or breast-feeding only when absolutely necessary. The potential hazard to the unborn child or nursing infant is not known at this time. However, it has caused birth defects when given in large amounts to pregnant animals. It is not known if Metaproterenol passes into breast milk.

Seniors

Older adults are more sensitive to the effects of this drug. They should closely follow their doctor's directions and report any side effects at once.

Possible Side Effects

Restlessness, anxiety, fear, tension, sleeplessness, tremors, convulsions, weakness, dizziness, headache, flushing, pallor, sweating, nausea; also vomiting, loss of appetite, muscle cramps, urinary difficulties.

Less common side effects: Metaproterenol can cause some side effects on the heart and cardiovascular system, such as high blood pressure, abnormal heart rhythms, and angina. It is less likely to cause these effects than some of the older drugs.

Drug Interactions

The effect of this drug may be increased by antidepressant drugs, some antihistamines, Levothyroxine, and MAO inhibitor drugs. This drug may antagonize the effects of Reserpine or Guanethidine.

Food Interactions

If the tablets cause an upset stomach, they may be taken with food.

Usual Dose

Oral:

Adult and child (over 60 pounds, or over age 9): 60 to 80 milligrams per day.

Child (under 60 pounds, or age 6 to 9): 30 to 40 milligrams per day.

Inhalation:

Adult and child (over age 12): 2 to 3 puffs every 3 to 4 hours.

Child (under age 12): not recommended.

Each canister contains about 300 inhalations. Do not use more than 12 puffs per day.

Overdosage

Symptoms of Metaproterenol overdose are palpitation, abnormal heart rhythms, rapid or slow heartbeat, chest pain, high blood pressure, fever, chills, cold sweat, blanching of the skin, nausea, vomiting, sleeplessness, delirium, tremor, pinpoint pupils, convulsions, coma, and collapse. If you or someone you know has taken an overdose of this drug call your doctor or bring the patient to a hospital emergency room. ALWAYS remember to bring the prescription bottle or inhaler with you.

Special Information

Be sure to follow your doctor's instructions for this drug. Using more of it than was prescribed can lead to drug tolerance and actually cause your condition to worsen.

Metaproterenol inhalation should be used during the second half of your inward breath, since this allows it to reach more deeply into your lungs.

Call your doctor immediately if you develop chest pain, palpitations, rapid heartbeat, muscle tremors, dizziness, headache, facial flushing, urinary difficulty, or if you still have trouble breathing after using this medicine.

If you miss a dose of Metaproterenol, take it as soon as possible. Take the rest of that day's dose at regularly spaced time intervals. Go back to your regular schedule the next day.

Generic Name

Methenamine

Brand Names

Hiprex	Methenamine Hippurate
Mandameth	Methenamine Mandelate
Mandelamine	Urex

(Also available in generic form)

Type of Drug

Urinary anti-infective.

Prescribed for

Chronic urinary tract infections.

General Information

This drug and other methenamine salts work by turning into formaldehyde and ammonia when the urine is acidic. It is the formaldehyde that kills the bacteria in the urinary tract. These drugs do not break down in the blood. Acidification of the urine may be necessary with 4 to 12 grams per day of Ascorbic Acid (Vitamin C) or Ammonium Chloride tablets.

Cautions and Warnings

Patients with kidney disease, dehydration, or severe liver disease should not use this drug.

Pregnancy/Breast-feeding

This drug crosses into the blood circulation of a developing baby. It has not been found to cause birth defects. Pregnant women, or those who might become pregnant while taking this drug, should not take it without their doctor's approval. When the drug is considered essential by your doctor, the potential risk of taking the medicine must be carefully weighed against the benefit it might produce.

This drug passes into breast milk, but has caused no problems among breast-fed infants. You must consider the potential effect on the nursing infant if breast-feeding while taking this medicine.

Seniors

Older adults may take this medication without special restriction. Follow your doctor's directions and report any side effects at once.

Possible Side Effects

Large doses for long periods of time may cause bladder irritation, painful and frequent urination, and protein or blood in the urine. This drug may cause elevation in liver enzymes.
Less common: upset stomach, rash.

Drug Interactions

Do not take this with sulfa drugs, since the sulfas can form a precipitate in the urine when mixed with Methenamine, which may lead to a kidney stone.
Sodium Bicarbonate and Acetazolamide will decrease the effect of Methenamine by making the drug less acidic.

Food Interactions

The action of Methenamine will be decreased by foods which reduce urine acidity, including milk and dairy products. Avoid these agents in large quantities when taking Methenamine.
Take Methenamine with food to minimize upset stomach.

Usual Dose

Adult: 1 gram 2 to 4 times a day.
Child (age 6 to 12): 0.5 to 1 gram 2 to 4 times per day.

Special Information

Take each dose with at least 8 ounces of water. Call your doctor if you develop pain when urinating or severe upset stomach.
If you miss a dose of Methenamine, take it as soon as possible. Take the rest of that day's doses at regularly spaced time intervals. Go back to your regular schedule the next day.

Generic Name

Methotrexate

Brand Names

Methotrexate
MTX
Rheumatrex

(Also available in generic form)

Type of Drug

Antimetabolite, antiarthritis, anti-inflammatory.

Prescribed for

Cancer chemotherapy, psoriasis, rheumatoid arthritis, severe asthma.

General Information

Methotrexate and other antimetabolites were among the first drugs found to be effective against certain cancers in the late 1940s. More recent research applying smaller doses of this drug to other diseases has resulted in its acceptance as a treatment for psoriasis, rheumatoid arthritis, and severe asthma. Methotrexate doses differ dramatically for each use of the drug, but you should be aware that Methotrexate can be extremely toxic, even in the relatively low doses prescribed for rheumatoid arthritis.

Methotrexate should be considered last-resort therapy for rheumatoid arthritis, to be used only for severe cases that have not responded satisfactorily to any other form of therapy.

Methotrexate should be prescribed only by doctors who are familiar with the drug and its potential for producing toxic effects. It may be effective after 3 to 6 weeks of treatment, and improvement in the condition may continue for another 12 weeks or more. Although the drug clearly reduces arthritis symptoms, it does not alter the basic course of the disease. Arthritis improvements have been maintained for 2 years or more by people who continued their Methotrexate therapy. Unfortunately, the benefits of Methotrexate are lost after use of the drug is discontinued.

Cautions and Warnings

Methotrexate can trigger a unique and dangerous form of lung disease any time during your course of therapy. This reaction can occur at doses as low as 7.5 milligrams a week, which is the antiarthritis dose of Methotrexate. Symptoms of this condition are cough, respiratory infection, difficulty breathing, abnormal chest x-ray, and low blood concentration oxygen. Any change in your breathing or lung status while taking Methotrexate should be reported to your doctor.

Methotrexate can cause severe liver damage, but this usually occurs only after taking the drug for a long period of time. Changes in liver enzyme values (measured by a blood test) are common.

Methotrexate should be used with caution, and the dosage should be reduced for people with kidney disease and those who have lost some kidney function.

Methotrexate can cause severe reduction in red and white blood cell and blood platelet counts.

Your doctor should test your blood periodically for cell counts and liver enzyme measurements while you are taking Methotrexate. Kidney function should also be tested.

Methotrexate can cause severe diarrhea, stomach irritation, and mouth or gum sores. Death can result from intestinal perforation caused by Methotrexate.

Pregnancy/Breast-feeding

Methotrexate can cause the death of a developing fetus or severe birth defects in a surviving fetus. This drug should not be taken by pregnant women. Women who might become pregnant and who must take Methotrexate should be careful to use effective birth control during their treatment. Women should not attempt to become pregnant during their Methotrexate treatment or for at least one menstrual cycle after the treatment is completed.

Nursing mothers who must take Methotrexate should use an alternative feeding method because of the possibility of serious Methotrexate reactions in the nursing infant.

Methotrexate can also affect sperm. Men should not attempt to father a child during Methotrexate treatment or for 3 months after treatment has been completed to avoid possible birth defects.

Seniors

Not much is known about the specific reaction of Methotrexate in the bodies of older adults, who may be more susceptible to drug side effects. People with kidney and/or liver disease require smaller doses than those with normal kidneys and livers to obtain the same effect.

The relatively low doses of Methotrexate prescribed for rheumatoid arthritis may be well tolerated by seniors, but they should be closely monitored by their doctor while taking Methotrexate.

Possible Side Effects

The most common side effects of Methotrexate are liver irritation, loss of some kidney function, reduction in blood cell counts, nausea, vomiting, diarrhea, stomach upset and irritation, itching, rash, hair loss, dizziness, and increased susceptibility to infection.

Less common side effects include reduced blood hematocrit (a measure of red blood cell count), unusual sensitivity to the sun, acne, headache, drowsiness, blurred vision, respiratory infection and breathing problems, loss of appetite, muscle aches, chest pain, coughing, painful urination, eye discomfort, nose bleeds, fever, infections, blood in the urine, sweating, ringing or buzzing in the ears, defective sperm production, reduced sperm count, menstrual dysfunction and vaginal discharge, convulsions, and slight paralysis.

Drug Interactions

Fatal reactions have developed in people taking Methotrexate together with some NSAIDs (Ketoprofen, Naproxen, Indomethacin, and Phenylbutazone). Do not take any other anti-inflammatory or antiarthritis drug (even Ibuprofen, which can be bought without a prescription) together with Methotrexate unless specifically directed to do so by your doctor.

Aspirin and other salicylates, Probenecid, and sulfa drugs can increase the therapeutic and toxic effects of Methotrexate. Avoid these combinations.

Food Interactions

Food slows the rate at which Methotrexate is absorbed into the blood from your stomach. It is best taken on an empty stomach or 2 hours after meals, but you may take it with food if it upsets your stomach.

Usual Dose

Methotrexate dosage varies with the condition being treated. Some cancers can be treated with 10 to 30 milligrams per day, while others are treated with hundreds or thousands of milligrams given by intravenous injection in the hospital.

The starting Methotrexate dose for rheumatoid arthritis is 7.5 milligrams a week by mouth, either as a single dose or in 3 separate doses of 2.5 milligrams taken every 12 hours. Weekly dosage may be increased gradually up to 20 milligrams. Doses above 20 milligrams a week are more likely to cause severe side effects.

Overdosage

Methotrexate overdose can be serious and life-threatening. Every Methotrexate overdose victim should be taken at once to a hospital emergency room for treatment. A specific antidote to the effects of Methotrexate, Calcium Leucovorin, is available in every hospital. ALWAYS remember to bring the prescription container with you.

Special Information

If you vomit after taking a dose of Methotrexate, do not take a replacement dose unless instructed to do so by your doctor.

Call your doctor immediately if you develop diarrhea, fever or chills, reddening of the skin, mouth or lip sores, stomach pain, unusual bleeding or bruising, blurred vision, seizures, cough, difficulty breathing.

These symptoms are less severe but should stilll be reported to the doctor: back pain, darkened urine, dizziness, drowsiness, headache, unusual tiredness or sickness, yellowing of the eyes or skin.

If you forget to take a dose of Methotrexate, skip the forgotten dose and continue with your regular schedule. Tell your doctor about the dose you forgot to take. Do not take a double dose of Methotrexate.

Generic Name

Methsuximide

Brand Name
Celontin

Type of Drug
Anticonvulsant.

Prescribed for
Control of petit mal seizures.

General Information
Methsuximide and the other succinimide-type anticonvulsants control petit mal seizures by slowing the transmission of impulses through certain areas of the brain. The succinimides are first choice of treatment for this type of seizure, although Methsuximide is used only after Ethosuximide has been tried. If Methsuximide doesn't work, the condition may be treated with Clonazepam.

Cautions and Warnings
Methsuximide may be associated with severe reductions in white-blood-cell and platelet counts. Your doctor should perform periodic blood counts while you are taking this medicine.

In patients with grand mal and petit mal, succinimide-type anticonvulsants, when used alone, may increase the number of grand mal seizures and necessitate more medicine to control those seizures.

Abrupt withdrawal of any anticonvulsant may lead to severe seizures. It is important that your dosage be gradually reduced by your doctor.

Pregnancy/Breast-feeding
This drug should be avoided by women who may become pregnant while using it and by pregnant and nursing mothers, since it will cross into the developing infant's circulation, and possible adverse effects on the infant are not known. In those situations where it is deemed essential, the potential

risk of the drug must be carefully weighed against any benefit it might produce.

Recent reports suggest a strong association between the use of anticonvulsant drugs and birth defects. Although most of the information pertains to Phenytoin and Phenobarbital, not Methsuximide, other reports indicate a general association between all anticonvulsant drug treatments and birth defects. It is possible that the epileptic condition itself or genetic factors common to people with seizure disorders may also be a factor in the higher incidence of birth defects. Mothers taking Methsuximide should not breast-feed because of the possibility that the drug will pass into their breast milk and affect the baby. Use an alternative feeding method.

Seniors

Older adults may take this medication without special restriction. Follow your doctor's directions and report any side effects at once.

Possible Side Effects

Nausea, vomiting, upset stomach, stomach cramps and pain, loss of appetite, diarrhea, constipation, weight loss, drowsiness, dizziness, and poor muscle control.

Less common: reductions in white-blood-cell and platelet counts, nervousness, hyperactivity, sleeplessness, irritability, headache, blurred vision, unusual sensitivity to bright lights, hiccups, a euphoric feeling, a dreamlike state, lack of energy, fatigue, confusion, mental instability, mental slowness, depression, sleep disturbances, nightmares, loss of the ability to concentrate, aggressiveness, constant concern with well-being and health, paranoid psychosis, suicidal tendencies, increased sex drive, itching, frequent urination, kidney damage, blood in the urine, swelling around the eyes, hair loss, hairiness, muscle weakness, nearsightedness, vaginal bleeding, and swelling of the tongue and/or gums.

Drug Interactions

The depressant effects of Methsuximide are increased by tranquilizers, sleeping pills, narcotic pain relievers, antihistamines, alcohol, MAO inhibitors, antidepressants, and other anticonvulsants.

Methsuximide may increase the action of Phenytoin by increasing the blood levels of that drug. Your doctor should be sure that your dosages of the two drugs are appropriate to your condition.

Carbamazepine, another medicine prescribed to treat seizure disorders, may interfere with Methsuximide action by increasing the rate at which it is removed from the body.

The action of Methsuximide may be increased by Isoniazid, prescribed to prevent tuberculosis, and by Valporic Acid, another anticonvulsant drug, possibly leading to an increase in drug side effects when both drugs are taken together.

Avoid alcoholic beverages, which increase the depressant effects of this medicine.

Food Interactions

Methsuximide is best taken on an empty stomach but may be taken with food if it upsets your stomach.

Usual Dose

300 milligrams per day to start. If needed, the dose may be increased in steps of 300 milligrams every 7 days until seizures are controlled or side effects develop. The maximum daily dose is 1200 milligrams.

Dosage adjustments may be required for people with reduced kidney or liver function.

Overdosage

Methsuximide overdose will cause exaggerated side effects. If the overdose is discovered immediately, it may be helpful to induce vomiting with Syrup of Ipecac to remove any remaining medicine from the stomach. But all victims of Methsuximide overdose must be taken to a hospital emergency room for treatment. ALWAYS bring the prescription bottle with you.

Special Information

Call your doctor if side effects become intolerable. Especially important are sore throat, joint pains, unexplained fever, rashes, unusual bleeding or bruising, drowsiness, dizziness, and blurred vision. Be sure to tell your doctor if you become pregnant while taking this medicine.

Methsuximide may interfere with your ability to drive a car or perform other complex tasks because it can cause drowsiness and difficulty concentrating.

Your doctor should perform periodic blood counts while you are taking this drug to check for possible adverse drug effects.

Do not suddenly stop taking the medicine, since to do so can result in severe seizures. The dosage must be discontinued gradually by your doctor.

Carry identification or wear a bracelet indicating that you suffer from a seizure disorder for which you take Methsuximide.

If you forget to take a dose of Methsuximide, take it as soon as possible, unless it is within 4 hours of your next dose. If that is the case, skip the forgotten dose and go back to your regular schedule. Do not take a double dose.

Generic Name

Methyclothiazide

Brand Names

Aquatensen
Enduron
Ethon

(Also available in generic form)

Type of Drug

Diuretic.

Prescribed for

Congestive heart failure, cirrhosis of the liver, kidney malfunction, high blood pressure, and other conditions where it is necessary to rid the body of excess water.

General Information

This drug is a member of the class known as thiazide diuretics. Thiazides act on the kidneys to stimulate the production of large amounts of urine. They also cause you to lose bicarbonate, chloride, and potassium ions from the body.

They are used as part of the treatment of any disease where it is desirable to eliminate large quantities of body water. These diseases include heart failure, some kidney diseases, and liver disease. Thiazide drugs are often taken together with other medicines to treat high blood pressure.

Cautions and Warnings

Do not take Methyclothiazide if you are allergic or sensitive to this drug, similar drugs of this group, or sulfa drugs. If you have a history of allergy or bronchial asthma, you may also have a sensitivity or allergy to Methyclothiazide.

Pregnancy/Breast-feeding

This drug may interfere with your baby's development, although it may rarely be prescribed during pregnancy. Check with your doctor before taking it if you are, or might be, pregnant. Methyclothiazide passes into breast milk but has not caused problems in nursing infants.

Seniors

Older adults are more sensitive to the effects of this drug, especially dizziness. They should closely follow their doctor's directions and report any side effects at once.

Possible Side Effects

Methyclothiazide will cause a loss of potassium in the body. Signs of low potassium levels are dryness of the mouth, thirst, weakness, lethargy, drowsiness, restlessness, muscle pains or cramps, muscular tiredness, low blood pressure, decreased frequency of urination and decreased amount of urine produced, abnormal heart rate, and stomach upset including nausea and vomiting.

To treat this, potassium supplements are given in the form of tablets, liquids, or powders, or by increased consumption of foods such as bananas, citrus fruits, melons, and tomatoes.

Less common side effects are: loss of appetite, stomach upset, nausea, vomiting, cramping, diarrhea, constipation, dizziness, headache, tingling of the toes and fingers, restlessness, changes in blood composition, sensitivity to sunlight, rash, itching, fever, difficulty in breathing, allergic reactions, dizziness when rising quickly from a sitting position, muscle spasms, weakness, blurred vision.

Drug Interactions

Methyclothiazide will increase the action of other blood-pressure-lowering drugs. This is good, and is the reason why people with high blood pressure often take more than one medicine.

The possibility of developing imbalances in body fluids (electrolytes) is increased if you take medications such as Digitalis and adrenal corticosteroids while you take Methyclothiazide.

If you are taking an oral antidiabetic drug and begin taking Methyclothiazide, the antidiabetic drug dose may have to be altered.

Lithium Carbonate should not be taken with Methyclothiazide because the combination may increase the risk of Lithium toxicity.

If you are taking this drug for the treatment of high blood pressure or congestive heart failure, avoid over-the-counter medicines for the treatment of coughs, colds, and allergies: such medicines may contain stimulants. If you are unsure about them, ask your pharmacist.

Usual Dose

2.5 to 10 milligrams per day, in the morning. Thiazide diuretic doses must be adjusted toward maximum effect with minimum medication. Eventual dose is often 5 milligrams or less.

Overdosage

Signs can be tingling in the arms or legs, weakness, fatigue, changes in your heartbeat, a sickly feeling, dry mouth, or vomiting. Take the overdose victim to a hospital emergency room for treatment at once. ALWAYS bring the prescription bottle and any remaining medicine.

Special Information

If you forget to take a dose of Methyclothiazide, take it as soon as you remember. If it is almost time for your next regularly scheduled dose, skip the one you forgot and continue with your regular schedule. Do not take a double dose.

Generic Name

Methyldopa

Brand Name

Aldomet

(Also available in generic form)

Type of Drug

Antihypertensive.

Prescribed for

High blood pressure.

General Information

Methyldopa's mechanism of action in the body is quite complicated and not well understood. It takes about 2 days of
treatment to reach Methyldopa's maximal antihypertensive
effect.

Methyldopa is usually prescribed with one or more of the
other high blood pressure medications or a diuretic.

This does not cure high blood pressure, but helps to control it.

Cautions and Warnings

You should not take Methyldopa if you have hepatitis or
active cirrhosis or if you have ever developed a reaction to
Methyldopa.

Pregnancy/Breast-feeding

This drug crosses into the blood circulation of a developing
baby. It has not been found to cause birth defects. Pregnant
women, or those who might become pregnant while taking
this drug, should not take it without their doctor's approval.
When the drug is considered essential by your doctor, the
potential risk of taking the medicine must be carefully weighed
against the benefit it might produce.

This drug passes into breast milk, but has caused no problems among breast-fed infants. You must consider the po-

tential effect on the nursing infant if breast-feeding while
taking this medicine.

Seniors

Older adults are more sensitive to the sedative and blood-
pressure-lowering effects of this drug. Follow your doctor's
directions and report any side effects at once.

Possible Side Effects

Most people have little trouble with Methyldopa, but it can
cause transient sedation during the first few weeks of therapy or when the dose is increased. Transient headache or
weakness are other possible early symptoms.

Less common side effects: dizziness, light-headedness, tingling in the extremities, unusual muscle spasms, decreased
mental acuity, and psychic disturbances including nightmares,
mild psychosis, or depression; also changes in heart rate,
increase of pain associated with angina pectoris, retention of
water, resulting weight gain, and orthostatic hypotension
(dizziness when rising suddenly from a sitting or lying position), as well as nausea, vomiting, constipation, diarrhea,
mild dryness of the mouth, and sore and/or black tongue.
The drug may cause liver disorders: you may develop jaundice (yellowing of the skin and/or whites of the eyes), with or
without fever, in the first 2 to 3 months of therapy. If you are
taking Methyldopa for the first time, be sure your doctor
checks your liver function, especially during the first 6 to 12
weeks of therapy. If you develop fever or jaundice, stop
taking the drug and contact your physician immediately: if
the reactions are due to Methyldopa, your temperature and/or
liver abnormalities will reverse toward normal as soon as
the drug is discontinued. Still other adverse effects are stuffy
nose, breast enlargement, lactation (in females), impotence
or decreased sex drive, mild symptoms of arthritis, and skin
reactions.

Drug Interactions

Methyldopa will increase the effect of other blood-pressure-
lowering drugs. This is a desirable interaction which benefits
patients with high blood pressure.

Avoid over-the-counter cough, cold and allergy preparations containing stimulant drugs that can aggravate your high blood pressure. Information on over-the-counter drugs that are safe for you can be obtained from your pharmacist.

Methyldopa may increase the blood sugar, lowering effect of Tolbutamine or other oral antidiabetic drugs. If given together, with phenoxybenzamine, inability to control one's bladder (urinary incontinence) may result. The combination of Methyldopa and Lithium may cause symptoms of Lithium overdose, even though blood levels of Lithium do not change. Methyldopa when given together with Haloperidol may produce irritability, aggressiveness, assaultive behavior, or other psychiatric symptoms.

Food Interactions

This medicine is best taken on an empty stomach, but you may take it with food if it upsets your stomach.

Usual Dose

Adult: starting dose, 250-milligram tablet 2 to 3 times per day for first 2 days. Dosage may be increased or decreased until blood-pressure control is achieved. Maintenance dose, 500 milligrams to 3000 milligrams per day in 2 to 4 divided doses, per patient's needs.

Child: 5 milligrams per pound of body weight per day in 2 to 4 divided doses per patient's needs. Maximum dose, 30 milligrams per pound of body weight per day, up to 3 grams per day.

Special Information

Take this drug exactly as prescribed by your doctor so you can maintain maximum control over your high blood pressure.

A mild sedative effect is to be expected from Methyldopa and will resolve within several days.

Do not stop taking this medicine unless you are told to by your doctor. Avoid nonprescription cough and cold medicines or diet pills which contain stimulants. Your pharmacist can give you more information on those nonprescription drugs to be avoided. Call your doctor if you develop fever, prolonged general tiredness, or unusual dizziness.

If you forget to take a dose of Methyldopa, take it as soon as you remember. If it is almost time for your next regularly scheduled dose, skip the one you forgot and continue with your regular schedule. Do not take a double dose.

Generic Name

Methylphenidate

Brand Names

Ritalin
Ritalin-SR (long-acting form)

(Also available in generic form)

Type of Drug

Central nervous system stimulant.

Prescribed for

Attention deficit syndrome in children; psychological, educational, or social disorders; narcolepsy and mild depression.

General Information

Chronic or abusive use of Methylphenidate can cause the development of drug dependence or addiction; also the drug can cause severe psychotic episodes. The primary use for Methylphenidate is the treatment of minimal brain dysfunction or attention deficit disorders in children. Common signs of this disease are short attention span, easy distractibility, emotional instability, impulsiveness, and moderate to severe hyperactivity. Children who suffer from this disorder will find it difficult to learn. There are many who feel that Methylphenidate is only a temporary solution because it does not permanently change patterns of behavior. When Methylphenidate is used, it must be used with other special measures.

Cautions and Warnings

Do not take Methylphenidate if you are extremely tense or agitated, have glaucoma, are allergic to this drug, have high blood pressure, or have a history of epilepsy or other seizures.

Pregnancy/Breast-feeding

This drug crosses into the blood circulation of a developing baby. It has not been found to cause birth defects. Pregnant women, or those who might become pregnant while taking this drug, should not take it without their doctor's approval. When the drug is considered essential by your doctor, the potential risk of taking the medicine must be carefully weighed against the benefit it might produce.

This drug passes into breast milk, but has caused no problems among breast-fed infants. You must consider the potential effect on the nursing infant if breast-feeding while taking this medicine.

Seniors

Older adults may take this medication without special restriction. Follow your doctor's directions and report any side effects at once.

Possible Side Effects

Most common in adults: nervousness and inability to sleep, which are generally controlled by reducing or eliminating the afternoon or evening dose. Most common in children: loss of appetite, stomach pains, weight loss (especially during prolonged periods of therapy), difficulty sleeping, and abnormal heart rhythms.

Infrequent in adults: skin rash, itching, fever, symptoms similar to arthritis, loss of appetite, nausea, dizziness, abnormal heart rhythms, headache, drowsiness, changes in blood pressure or pulse, chest pains, stomach pains, psychotic reactions, effects on components of the blood, loss of some scalp hair.

Drug Interactions

Methylphenidate will decrease the effectiveness of Guanethidine, a drug used to treat high blood pressure.

Interaction with MAO inhibitors may vastly increase the effect of Methylphenidate and cause problems.

If you take Methylphenidate regularly, avoid alcoholic beverages; they will add to the drowsiness problem.

Interaction with anticoagulants (blood-thinning drugs), some drugs used to treat epilepsy or other kinds of convulsions,

Phenylbutazone and Oxyphenbutazone, and antidepressant drugs will slow the rate at which these drugs are broken down by the body, making more of them available in the bloodstream. Thus it may be necessary to lower the dose of them.

Food Interactions

This medicine is best taken on an empty stomach, but you may take it with food if it upsets your stomach.

Usual Dose

Doses should be tailored to individual needs; the doses listed here are only guidelines.

Adult: 10 or 20 to 30 or even 60 milligrams per day in divided doses 2 to 3 times per day, preferably 30 to 45 minutes before meals.

Child (over age 6): initial dose, 5 milligrams before breakfast and lunch; then increase in steps of 5 to 10 milligrams each week as required, but not to exceed 60 milligrams per day.

Overdosage

Symptoms are stimulation of the nervous system such as vomiting, agitation, tremors (uncontrollable twitching of the muscles), convulsions followed by coma, euphoria, confusion, hallucinations, delirium, sweating, flushing (face, hands, and extremities will be red), headache, high fever, abnormal heart rate, high blood pressure, and dryness of the mouth and nose. The patient should be taken to a hospital emergency room. ALWAYS bring the medicine bottle.

Special Information

Methylphenidate can mask the signs of temporary drowsiness or fatigue: be careful while driving or operating an automobile, machine, or appliance.

You should take the last daily dose of Methylphenidate by 6 P.M., to avoid sleeping problems.

If you miss a dose of Methylphenidate, take it as soon as possible. Take the rest of that day's doses at regularly spaced time intervals. Go back to your regular schedule the next day.

Generic Name

Methylprednisolone

Brand Names

Medrol
Meprolone

(Also available in generic form)

Type of Drug

Adrenal corticosteroid.

Prescribed for

Reduction of inflammation. The variety of disorders for which Methylprednisolone is prescribed is almost endless, from skin rash to cancer. The drug may be used as a treatment for adrenal gland disease, since one of the hormones produced by the adrenal gland is very similar to Methylprednisolone. If patients are not producing sufficient adrenal hormones, Methylprednisolone may be used as replacement therapy. It may also be prescribed for the treatment of bursitis, arthritis, severe skin reactions such as psoriasis or other rashes, severe allergic conditions, asthma, drug or serum sickness, severe acute or chronic allergic inflammation of the eye and surrounding areas such as conjunctivitis, respiratory diseases including pneumonitis, blood disorders, gastrointestinal diseases including ulcerative colitis, and inflammation of the nerves, heart, or other organs.

General Information

Methylprednisolone is one of many adrenal corticosteroids used in medical practice today. The major differences between Methylprednisolone and other adrenal corticosteroids are potency of medication (which differs from the milligram strength) and variation in some secondary effects. In most cases the choice of adrenal corticosteroids to be used in a specific disease is a matter of doctor preference and past experience. Other oral adrenal corticosteroids include Cortisone, Hydrocortisone, Prednisone, Prednisolone,

Triamcinolone, Meprednisone, Paramethasone, Fluprednisolone, Dexamethasone, and Betamethasone.

Cautions and Warnings

Because of the effect of Methylprednisolone on your adrenal
gland, it is essential that the dose be tapered from a large
dose down to a small dose over a period of time. Do not
stop taking this medication suddenly and/or without the advice of your doctor. If you do, you may cause a failure of the
adrenal gland with extremely serious consequences. Methylprednisolone has a strong anti-inflammatory effect, and may
mask some signs of infections. If new infections appear
during the use of Methylprednisolone therapy, they may be
difficult to discover and may grow more rapidly due to your
decreased resistance. If you think you are getting any kind of
infection during the time that you are taking Methylprednisolone, you should contact your doctor, who will prescribe
appropriate therapy.

If you are taking Methylprednisolone you should not be
vaccinated against infectious disease, because of a potential
inability of the body to produce the normal reaction to the
vaccination. Discuss this with your doctor before taking any
vaccination.

Pregnancy/Breast-feeding

Corticosteroid drugs taken by mouth pass into breast milk,
and large drug doses may interfere with the growth of a
nursing infant. Methylprednisolone, like other oral glucocorti-
coids, can cause problems in the newborn infant, such as
slower growth. Animal studies have shown birth defects or
other unwanted effects.

Seniors

Older adults are more likely to develop high blood pressure
while taking this medicine (by mouth). Also, older women
have a greater chance of being susceptible to bone degeneration (osteoporosis) associated with large doses of this class
of medicines.

Possible Side Effects

Stomach upset is one of the more common side effects of

Methylprednisolone, which may in some cases cause gastric or duodenal ulcers. Other side effects: retention of water, heart failure, potassium loss, muscle weakness, loss of muscle mass, loss of calcium from bones which may result in bone fractures and a condition known as aseptic necrosis of the femoral and humoral heads (this means the ends of the large bones in the hip may degenerate from loss of calcium), slowing down of wound healing, black-and-blue marks on the skin, increased sweating, allergic skin rash, itching, convulsions, dizziness, headache.

Less common side effects: irregular menstrual cycles, slowing down of growth in children, particularly after the medication has been taken for long periods of time, depression of the adrenal and/or pituitary glands, development of diabetes, increased pressure of the fluid inside the eye, hypersensitivity or allergic reactions, blood clots, insomnia, weight gain, increased appetite, nausea, and feeling of ill health. Psychic derangements may appear which range from euphoria to mood swings, personality changes, and severe depression. Methylprednisolone may also aggravate existing emotional instability.

Drug Interactions

Methylprednisolone and other adrenal corticosteroids may interact with Insulin or oral antidiabetic drugs, causing an increased requirement of the antidiabetic drugs.

Interaction with Phenobarbital, Ephedrine, and Phenytoin may reduce the effect of Methylprednisolone by increasing its removal from the body.

If a doctor prescribes Methylprednisolone you should discuss any oral anticoagulant (blood-thinning) drugs you are taking; their dose may have to be changed.

Interaction with diuretics such as Hydrochlorothiazide may cause you to lose blood potassium. Be aware of signs of lowered potassium level such as weakness, muscle cramps, and tiredness, and report them to your physician.

Food Interactions

If you notice a slight stomach upset when you take your dose of Methylprednisolone, take this medication with food or with a small amount of antacid. If stomach upset continues, notify your doctor.

It is recommended that you eat high-potassium foods such as bananas, citrus fruits, melons, and tomatoes.

Usual Dose

Initial dose, 4 to 48 milligrams. Maintenance dose is determined by your doctor based on your response.

Overdosage

There is no specific treatment for overdosage of adrenal corticosteroids. Symptoms are anxiety, depression and/or stimulation, stomach bleeding, increased blood sugar, high blood pressure, and retention of fluid. The patient should be taken to a hospital emergency room immediately, where stomach pumping, oxygen, intravenous fluids, and other supportive treatment are available.

Special Information

Do not stop taking this medicine on your own. Suddenly stopping this or any other corticosteroid drug can have severe consequences; the dosage will be gradually reduced by your doctor.

If you take Methylprednisolone once a day and forget your dose, take it as soon as possible. If you don't remember until the next day, skip the forgotten dose and continue with your regular schedule.

If you take the medicine more than once a day and forget a dose, take the forgotten dose as soon as possible. If it is almost time for your next dose, skip the forgotten dose and go on with your regular schedule.

Generic Name

Methyltestosterone

Brand Names

Android	Oreton Methyl
Metandren	Testred
Methyl	Virilon

(Also available in generic form)

Type of Drug

Androgenic (male) hormone.

Prescribed for

Diseases in which male hormone replacement or augmentation is needed; male menopause.

General Information

This is a member of the androgenic or male hormone group, which includes Testosterone, Calusterone, and Dromostanolone Propionate. (The last two are used primarily to treat breast cancer in women.) Females taking any androgenic drug should watch for deepening of the voice, oily skin, acne, hairiness, increased libido, and menstrual irregularities, which may be related to the so-called virilizing effects of these hormones. Virilization is a sign that the drug is starting to produce changes in secondary sex characteristics. The drugs should be avoided if possible by boys who have not gone through puberty.

Cautions and Warnings

Men who have an unusually high blood level of calcium, known or suspected cancer of the prostate, or prostate destruction or disease, cancer of the breast, liver, heart, or kidney disease should not use this medication.

Pregnancy/Breast-feeding

Women who are pregnant or breast-feeding should not use Methyltestosterone, since it may cause unwanted problems in babies, such as the development of male features in female babies.

Seniors

Older men treated with this drug run an increased risk of developing prostate enlargement or prostate cancer.

Possible Side Effects

In males: inhibition of testicle function, impotence, chronic erection of the penis, enlargement of the breast.

In females: unusual hairiness, baldness in a pattern similar to that seen in men, deepening of the voice, enlargement of the clitoris. These changes are usually irreversible once they have occurred. Females also experience menstrual irregularities and increases in blood calcium.

In both sexes: changes in libido, flushing of the skin, acne, mild dependence on the drug, excitation, chills, sleeplessness, water retention, nausea, vomiting, diarrhea. Symptoms resembling stomach ulcer may develop. Methyltestosterone may affect level of blood cholesterol.

Drug Interactions

Methyltestosterone may increase the effect of oral anticoagulants; dosage of the anticoagulant may have to be decreased. The drug may have an effect on the glucose tolerance test, a blood test used to screen people for diabetes mellitus.

Usual Dose

5 to 200 milligrams per day, depending upon the disease being treated and patient's response.

Special Information

Methyltestosterone and other androgens are potent drugs. They must be taken only under the close supervision of your doctor and never used casually. The dosage and clinical effects of the drug vary widely and require constant monitoring.

Buccal tablets are intended to be dissolved between the cheek and gum. While buccal tablets are in your mouth you should refrain from eating, smoking, or drinking.

If you take Methyltestosterone once a day and forget your dose, take it as soon as possible. If you don't remember until the next day, skip the forgotten dose and continue with your regular schedule.

If you take the medicine more than once a day and forget a dose, take the forgotten dose as soon as possible. If it is almost time for your next dose, skip the forgotten dose and go on with your regular schedule.

Generic Name

Metoclopramide

Brand Names

Clopra   Reclomide
Maxolon   Reglan
Octamide

(Also available in generic form)

Type of Drug

Gastrointestinal stimulant.

Prescribed for

Symptoms of diabetic gastroparesis (stomach paralysis), including nausea, vomiting, fullness after meals, and loss of appetite. Also used to facilitate certain X-ray diagnostic procedures. Used for the relief of nausea and vomiting. This drug is also used by nursing mothers to improve lactation and is used to treat certain cases of stomach ulcers and anorexia nervosa.

General Information

This drug stimulates movement of the upper gastrointestinal tract but does not stimulate excess stomach acids or other secretions. It has been investigated in the United States as an antinauseant for patients receiving anticancer drugs. It has been used extensively for this purpose in Europe and South America. Although it is not known exactly how the drug works, its results may be caused by the direct effect of Metoclopramide on special receptors in the brain. Its value as an antiemetic is about the same as that of other currently available drugs.

Cautions and Warnings

This drug should not be used where stimulation of the gastrointestinal tract could be dangerous (bleeding ulcers, etc.) and should not be used if you are allergic to the drug. This drug can cause "extrapyramidal" side effects similar to those caused by phenothiazine drugs. Do not take the two classes of drugs together. Extrapyramidal effects occur in only about 0.2 percent of the people taking the drug and usually include restlessness and involuntary movements of arms and legs, face, tongue, lips, or other parts of the body.

Pregnancy/Breast-feeding

This drug crosses into the blood circulation of a developing baby. It has not been found to cause birth defects. Pregnant women, or those who might become pregnant while taking this drug, should not take it without their doctor's approval. When the drug is considered essential by your doctor, the potential risk of taking the medicine must be carefully weighed against the benefit it might produce.

This drug passes into breast milk, but has caused no problems among breast-fed infants. You must consider the potential effect on the nursing infant if breast-feeding while taking this medicine.

Seniors

Older adults are more sensitive to the "extrapyramidal" effects of this drug discussed above under "Cautions and Warnings." Follow your doctor's directions and report any side effects at once.

Possible Side Effects

Restlessness, drowsiness, tiredness.

Less common side effects: sleeplessness, headache, dizziness, nausea, upset stomach.

Drug Interactions

The effects of Metoclopramide on the stomach are antagonized by narcotics and anticholinergic drugs. Metoclopramide may interact with alcohol, sedatives, or other depressant drugs to produce excessive sleepiness or tiredness. Because of its effects on the gastrointestinal tract, this drug may affect the passage of drugs through the stomach or intestines into the bloodstream.

Food Interactions

When taking this drug for nausea, be sure to take the medicine 30 minutes before meals and at bedtime.

Usual Dose

Adult: 1 to 2 tablets before meals and at bedtime. Single doses of 1 to 2 tablets are used before X-ray diagnostic procedures.

Child (age 6 to 14): ¼ to ½ the adult dose.

Child (under age 6): 0.05 milligrams per pound of body weight per dose.

Overdosage

Symptoms are drowsiness, disorientation, restlessness, or uncontrollable muscle movements. Symptoms usually disappear within 24 hours after the drug has been stopped. Anticholinergic drugs will antagonize these symptoms.

Special Information

If you forget to take a dose of Metoclopramide, take it as soon as you remember. If it is almost time for your next regularly scheduled dose, skip the forgotten dose and continue with your regular schedule. Do not take a double dose.

Generic Name

Metolazone

Brand Names

Diulo
Zaroxolyn

Type of Drug

Diuretic.

Prescribed for

Congestive heart failure, cirrhosis of the liver, high blood pressure, and other conditions where it is necessary to rid the body of excess water.

General Information

This diuretic is most similar to the thiazide diuretics in its action and effects on the body. It works on the kidneys to promote the release of sodium from the body, and to stimulate the production of large amounts of urine. Thiazides also cause you to lose potassium, chloride, and bicarbonate from the body. There are no major differences between Metolazone and other thiazide diuretics.

Cautions and Warnings

Do not take Metolazone if you are allergic or sensitive to it or to any other thiazide drug or any sulfa drug. If you have a history of allergy or bronchial asthma, you may also have a sensitivity or allergy to Metolazone. Avoid this drug if you have kidney or liver disease.

Pregnancy/Breast-feeding

This drug should not be taken by pregnant women or women who may become pregnant while using it since it will pass into the blood system of the fetus. In those situations where it is deemed essential, the potential risk of the drug must be carefully weighed against any benefit it might produce. Nursing mothers who must take thiazide-type drugs should consider an alternative method of feeding their infants since these diuretics are known to pass into breast milk. No problems have been reported in nursing infants with this medicine.

Seniors

Older adults are more sensitive to the effects of this drug, especially dizziness. They should closely follow their doctor's directions and report any side effects at once.

Possible Side Effects

Loss of body potassium, leading to dry mouth, thirst, weakness, drowsiness, restlessness, muscle pains and cramps or tiredness, low blood pressure, decreased frequency of urination, abnormal heart rhythm, and upset stomach. Less common side effects: loss of appetite, nausea, vomiting, stomach bloating or cramps, diarrhea, constipation, yellowing of the skin or whites of the eyes, pancreas inflammation, liver inflammation (hepatitis), frequent urination (especially at night), headache, dizziness, fatigue, loss of energy, a feeling of ill health, numbness in the hands or feet, nervousness, tension, anxiety, irritability, and agitation.

Other uncommon side effects are kidney inflammation, male impotence, reduced sex drive, light-headedness, drowsiness, fainting, difficulty sleeping, depression, tingling in the hands or feet, blurred vision, reduced levels of white blood cells and platelets, dizziness when rising quickly from a sitting or lying position, heart palpitations, chest pain, gout attacks, chills, stuffy nose, facial flushing, and weight loss.

Drug Interactions

Metolazone increases the effects of other blood-pressure-lowering drugs. This interaction is good and is the reason why people with high blood pressure often take more than one medicine.

The chances of losing body potassium are increased if you take Metolazone with Digoxin or with a corticosteroid anti-inflammatory drug. If you are taking medicine to treat diabetes and begin taking Metolazone, the dose of your diabetes medicine may have to be adjusted.

Metolazone will enhance the effects of Lithium and increase the chances of developing Lithium toxicity by preventing it from passing out of your body.

People taking Metolazone for high blood pressure or heart failure should take care to avoid nonprescription medicines that might aggravate your condition, such as decongestants, cold or allergy treatments, and diet pills, all of which may contain stimulants. If you are unsure about which medicine to choose, ask your pharmacist.

Dizziness when rising from a sitting or lying position may be worsened by taking Metolazone with alcoholic beverages, barbiturate-type sleeping pills, and narcotic pain relievers.

The effects of Metolazone may be counteracted by Indomethacin because of its effect on the kidneys. Taking Colestipol or Cholestyramine (cholesterol-lowering drugs) at the same time as Metolazone will reduce the drug's effect by preventing it from being absorbed into the bloodstream.

Taking more than one diuretic drug at a time can result in an excessive and prolonged diuretic effect. This is especially true when a thiazide-type diuretic is combined with a "loop" diuretic such as Bumetanide, Ethacrynic Acid, or Furosemide.

Taking Metolazone and other thiazide-type diuretics with calcium or Vitamin D could result in excessive levels of calcium in the blood.

Sulfa drugs may increase the effects of Metolazone by increasing the amount of diuretic drug in the bloodstream.

Metolazone may increase the effect of Quinidine, for abnormal heart rhythms, by interfering with its release from the body via the kidneys.

Food Interactions

Metolazone may cause loss of body potassium (hypokalemia), a complication that can be avoided by adding foods rich in potassium to your diet. Some potassium-rich foods are tomatoes, citrus fruits, melons, and bananas. Hypokalemia can also be prevented by taking a potassium supplement in pill, powder, or liquid form. Metolazone may be taken with food or meals if it upsets your stomach.

Usual Dose

2.5 to 10 milligrams per day.

Overdosage

The primary symptom of overdose is potassium deficiency by dehydration: confusion, dizziness, muscle weakness, upset stomach, excessive thirst, loss of appetite, lethargy (rare), drowsiness, restlessness (rare), tingling in the hands or feet, rapid heartbeat, nausea, and vomiting. Patients taking an overdose of this drug must be made to vomit with Syrup of Ipecac (available at any pharmacy) to remove any remaining drug from the stomach, if the overdose was taken within the past hour. Call your doctor or a poison control center before doing this. If more than an hour has passed, go to a hospital emergency room. ALWAYS bring the medicine bottle.

Special Information

Always take your daily dose of Metolazone by 10 A.M. Taking it later in the day will increase the chances of being kept awake at night by the need to urinate frequently.

Call your doctor if muscle weakness, cramps, nausea, dizziness, or other severe side effects develop.

If you forget to take a dose of Metolazone, take it as soon as you remember. If it is almost time for your next regularly scheduled dose, skip the forgotten dose and continue with your regular schedule. Do not take a double dose.

Generic Name

Metoprolol

Brand Name
Lopressor

Type of Drug
Beta-adrenergic blocking agent.

Prescribed for
High blood pressure, preventing a second heart attack.

General Information
This drug is very much like Propranolol but it has a more specific effect on the heart and a less specific effect on receptors in the blood vessels and respiratory tract. This means that the drug causes fewer problems in asthmatics and has a more specific effect on heart functions.

Cautions and Warnings
Metoprolol should be used with care if you have a history of asthma, upper respiratory disease, or seasonal allergy, which may be made worse by the effects of this drug.

Pregnancy/Breast-feeding
Drugs similar to Metoprolol have been shown to cause problems during pregnancy in animal studies when used in very high amounts. Pregnant and breast-feeding women should use this drug only if it is essential.

Seniors
Senior citizens may be more or less sensitive to the effects of this medication. Your dosage of this drug must be adjusted to your individual needs by your doctor. Seniors may be more likely to suffer from cold hands and feet and reduced body temperature, chest pains, a general feeling of ill health, sudden difficulty breathing, sweating, or changes in heartbeat because of this medicine.

Possible Side Effects

Metoprolol may decrease the heart rate; may aggravate a condition of congestive heart failure; and may produce lowered blood pressure, tingling in the extremities, light-headedness, mental depression including inability to sleep, weakness, and tiredness. It may also produce a mental depression which is reversible when the drug is withdrawn, visual disturbances, hallucinations, disorientation, and short-term memory loss. Patients taking Metoprolol may experience nausea, vomiting, stomach upset, abdominal cramps and diarrhea, or constipation. If you are allergic to this drug, you may show typical reactions associated with drug allergies, including sore throat, fever, difficulty in breathing, and various effects on the blood system. Metoprolol may induce bronchospasms (spasms of muscles in the bronchi), which will make any existing asthmatic condition or any severe upper respiratory disease worse.

Occasionally, patients taking Metoprolol experience emotional instability, or a feeling of detachment or personality change, or the drug may produce unusual effects on the blood system.

Drug Interactions

This drug will interact with any psychotropic drug, including the MAO inhibitors, that stimulates one of the adrenergic segments of the nervous system. Since this information is not generally known, you should discuss the potential problem of using Metoprolol with your doctor if you are taking any psychotropic or psychiatric drug.

Metoprolol may cause increased effectiveness of Insulin or oral antidiabetic drugs. If you are diabetic, discuss the situation with your doctor; a reduction in dose of antidiabetic medication will probably be made.

Metoprolol may reduce the effectiveness of Digitalis on your heart. Any dose of Digitalis medication will have to be altered. If you are taking Digitalis for a purpose other than congestive heart failure, the effectiveness of the Digitalis may be increased by Metoprolol, and the dose of Digitalis may have to be reduced.

Metoprolol may interact with certain other drugs to produce lowering of blood pressure. This interaction often has positive results in the treatment of patients with high blood pressure.

Do not self-medicate with over-the-counter cold, cough, or allergy remedies which may contain stimulant drugs that will aggravate certain types of heart disease and high blood pressure, or other ingredients that may antagonize the effects of Metoprolol. Double-check with your doctor or pharmacist before taking any over-the-counter medication.

Food Interactions

Take this medicine with food if it upsets your stomach.

Usual Dose

100 to 450 milligrams per day. The dosage of this drug must be tailored to the patient's need.

Overdosage

Symptoms are slowed heart rate, heart failure, lowered blood pressure, and spasms of the bronchial muscles which make it difficult to breathe. The patient should be taken to a hospital emergency room where proper therapy can be given. ALWAYS bring the medicine bottle with you.

Special Information

This drug may make you tired, so take care when driving or when operating machinery. Call your doctor if you become dizzy or develop diarrhea. Do not stop taking this medicine abruptly unless you are told to do so by your doctor, or serious heart pain (angina) may develop.

If you forget to take a dose of Metoprolol, take it as soon as possible. However, if it is within 8 hours of your next dose, skip the forgotten dose and go back to your regular schedule. Do not take a double dose.

Generic Name

Metronidazole

Brand Names

Femazole   Metryl
Flagyl   Protostat
Metizol   Satric

(Also available in generic form)

Type of Drug

Amoebicide and antibiotic.

Prescribed for

Acute amoebic dysentery; vaginal infections (trichomonas); diseases caused by some parasites; any specific types of bacterial infections.

General Information

Metronidazole may be prescribed for asymptomatic disease when the doctor feels that the use of this drug is indicated; specifically, asymptomatic females may be treated with this drug when vaginal examination shows evidence of trichomonas. Because trichomonas infection of the vaginal area is a venereal disease, asymptomatic sexual partners of treated patients should be treated simultaneously if the organism has been found to be present in the woman's genital tract, in order to prevent reinfection of the partner. The decision to treat an asymptomatic male partner who does not have the organism present is an individual one and must be made by the doctor.

Cautions and Warnings

If you have a history of blood disease or if you know that you are sensitive or allergic to Metronidazole you should not use this drug.

Metronidazole has been shown to be carcinogenic (cancer-inducing) in mice and possibly in rats. This drug should not be used unnecessarily and should only be used in specific conditions for which it is normally prescribed.

Pregnancy/Breast-feeding

This drug may cause birth defects or interfere with your baby's development. Check with your doctor before taking it if you are, or might be, pregnant.

Breast-feeding while taking Metronidazole may cause unwanted side effects in your infant. If you must take Metronidazole, you should temporarily stop nursing and discard pumped breast milk. Nursing can resume 1 or 2 days after stopping Metronidazole.

Seniors

Older adults with severe liver disease are more sensitive to the effects of this drug. Follow your doctor's directions and report any side effects at once.

Possible Side Effects

Most common: symptoms in the gastrointestinal tract, including nausea (sometimes accompanied by headache), loss of appetite, occasional vomiting, diarrhea, stomach upset, abdominal cramping, and constipation. A sharp, unpleasant metallic taste is also associated with the use of this drug. Dizziness and, rarely, incoordination have been reported. Numbness or tingling in the extremities and occasional joint pains have been associated with Metronidazole therapy as have confusion, irritability, depression, inability to sleep, and weakness. Itching and a sense of pelvic pressure have been reported.

Rarely: fever, increased urination, incontinence, decrease of libido.

Drug Interactions

Avoid alcoholic beverages: interaction with Metronidazole may cause abdominal cramps, nausea, vomiting, headaches, and flushing. Modification of the taste of alcoholic beverages has also been reported.

People taking oral anticoagulant (blood-thinning) drugs such as Warfarin will have to have their dose of Warfarin changed, because Metronidazole increases the effect of anticoagulants.

Food Interactions

This medicine is best taken on an empty stomach, but you may take it with food if it upsets your stomach.

Usual Dose

Adult: for the treatment of amoebic dysentery, 500 to 750 milligrams 3 times per day for 5 to 10 days.

Child: amoebic dysentery, 16 to 23 milligrams per pound of body weight daily divided in 3 equal doses, for 10 days.

For trichomonal infections: 250 milligrams 3 times per day for 7 days, or 2 grams in 1 dose.

Special Information

Follow your doctor's dosage instructions faithfully and don't stop until the full course of therapy has been taken.

The occasional darkening of urine of patients taking Metronidazole is of uncertain clinical significance and is probably not important.

If you forget to take a dose of Metronidazole, take it as soon as you remember. If it is almost time for your next regularly scheduled dose, skip the forgotten dose and continue with your regular schedule. Do not take a double dose.

Generic Name

Mexiletene

Brand Name

Mexitil

Type of Drug

Antiarrhythmic.

Prescribed for

Abnormal heart rhythms.

General Information

Mexiletene is one of the newest antiarrhythmic drugs available in the United States and is generally prescribed only after other drugs have been tried. When Mexiletene is replacing other drug treatments, it may be given 6 to 12 hours after the last dose of Quinidine or Disopyramide, 3 to 6

hours after the last dose of Procainamide, or 12 hours after
the last dose of Tocainide.

Cautions and Warnings

Since this drug is broken down by your liver and the drug
can cause some liver problems of its own, people with severe liver disease must be cautious while taking this medicine. A small number of people taking this drug (0.2 percent)
develop convulsions while taking Mexiletene. Almost a third
of those who developed a convulsion stopped taking the
drug because of that problem.

Pregnancy/Breast-feeding

This drug crosses into the blood circulation of a developing
baby. It has not been found to cause birth defects. Pregnant
women, or those who might become pregnant while taking
this drug, should not take it without their doctor's approval.
When the drug is considered essential by your doctor, the
potential risk of taking the medicine must be carefully weighed
against the benefit it might produce.

This drug passes into breast milk, but has caused no problems among breast-fed infants. You must consider the potential effect on the nursing infant if breast-feeding while
taking this medicine.

Seniors

Older adults with severe liver disease are more sensitive to
the effects of this drug. Follow your doctor's directions and
report any side effects at once.

Possible Side Effects

Most common side effects seen during drug studies: nausea, vomiting, diarrhea, constipation, tremors, dizziness, light-
headedness, nervousness, and poor coordination. These side
effects were reversed if the drug dose was reduced, if the
medicine was taken with food or antacids, or if the drug was
stopped.

Other common side effects: heart palpitations, chest pains,
angina, changes in appetite, abdominal pains or cramps,
stomach ulcers and bleeding, difficulty swallowing, dry mouth,
altered taste, changes in the saliva and mucous membranes

of your mouth, tingling or numbness in the hands or feet, weakness, fatigue, ringing or buzzing in the ears, depression, speech difficulties, rash, difficulty breathing, swelling.

Less common or rare side effects: abnormal heart rhythms, memory loss, hallucinations and other psychological problems, fainting, low blood pressure, slow heartbeat, swelling, hot flashes, high blood pressure, shock, joint pains, fever, sweating, hair loss, impotence, decreased sex drive, feeling sickly, difficulty urinating, hiccups, and dry skin.

Drug Interactions

The effects of Mexiletene are reduced by Phenytoin, Rifampin, Phenobarbital, and other drugs that stimulate the liver to break down drugs more rapidly.

Cimetidine raises blood levels of this drug. This combination can lead to an increase in Mexiletene side effects.

Food Interactions

Taking this drug with food reduces the rate at which it is absorbed into your blood and can reduce the incidence of some very common side effects, especially those related to your stomach and intestine.

Usual Dose

600 to 1200 milligrams per day in 3 divided doses.

Overdosage

Symptoms of overdose can be found under "Possible Side Effects." The most dangerous are those that affect the nervous system. Take the overdose victim to a hospital emergency room at once for treatment. ALWAYS bring the medicine bottle with you.

Special Information

Call your doctor if you develop tiredness, yellow skin or eyes, sore throat, unexplained bruising or bleeding, or if any side effect becomes bothersome or intolerable.

Avoid diets that can change the acidity of your urine. A high-acid diet will increase the rate at which Mexiletene is removed from your body, and a basic diet will cause the drug to be retained in your body.

If you miss a dose of Mexiletine, take it as soon as you can. If it is more than 4 hours past your dose time, skip the missed dose and go back to your usual dose schedule.

Generic Name

Miconazole Nitrate

Brand Names

Micatin	Monistat-7
Monistat-3	Monistat-Derm

(Also available in generic form)

Type of Drug

Antifungal.

Prescribed for

Treatment of fungus infections in the vagina, on the skin, and in the blood.

General Information

Miconazole Nitrate is used as a vaginal cream, vaginal suppositories, or topical cream, powder, or lotion, or by intravenous injection. When given as an injection to hospitalized patients, it is effective against serious fungal infections. When used for vaginal or topical infections, it is effective against several nonfungus types of organisms, as well as fungus-type infections. On the skin, it is used for common fungus infections such as athlete's foot or jock itch.

Cautions and Warnings

Do not use Miconazole Nitrate if you know you are allergic to it.

Pregnancy/Breast-feeding

Pregnant women should avoid using the vaginal cream during the first 3 months of pregnancy. They should use it during the next 6 months only if it is absolutely necessary.

Miconazole Nitrate has not been shown to cause problems in breast-fed infants.

Seniors

Older adults may take this medication without special restriction. Follow your doctor's directions and report any side effects at once.

Possible Side Effects

After intravenous injection: vein irritation, itching, rash, nausea, vomiting, fever, drowsiness, diarrhea, loss of appetite, flushing. After vaginal administration: itching, burning or irritation, pelvic cramps, hives, rash, headache. After application to the skin: irritation, burning.

Usual Dose

Intravenous: 200 to 3600 milligrams per day.

Vaginal suppository or cream: One applicatorful or suppository into the vagina at bedtime for 3 to 7 days.

Topical: apply to affected areas of skin twice a day for up to 1 month.

Special Information

When using the vaginal cream, insert the whole applicatorful of cream high into the vagina and be sure to complete the full course of treatment prescribed for you. Call your doctor if you develop burning or itching.

If you forget to take a dose of Miconazole Nitrate, take it as soon as you remember. If it is almost time for your next regularly scheduled dose, skip the forgotten dose and continue with your regular schedule. Do not take a double dose.

Brand Name

Minizide

Ingredients

Polythiazide
Prazosin Hydrochloride

Type of Drug

Antihypertensive combination.

Prescribed for

High blood pressure.

General Information

This is one of many fixed-dose combinations available to treat high blood pressure. It is a combination of two popular medicines often prescribed individually and offers the advantage of allowing the patient to take only one capsule per dose. These combinations are useful only when you require the exact dosage of each ingredient contained in the product. Minizide is available in 3 different strength combinations to allow proper dosage adjustment.

Cautions and Warnings

Prazosin Hydrochloride can cause dizziness and fainting, usually because of an effect called "postural hypotension" where blood supply to the brain is reduced when you rise suddenly from a sitting or lying position. This usually occurs after taking the first dose of Prazosin.

Pregnancy/Breast-feeding

Polythiazide, an ingredient in this combination, may cross into the blood circulation of a developing baby. The combination has not been found to cause birth defects, but may cause other problems in the newborn. Pregnant women, or those who might become pregnant while taking this drug, should not take it without their doctor's approval. When the drug is considered essential by your doctor, the potential risk of taking the medicine must be carefully weighed against the benefit it might produce.

Polythiazide, an ingredient in this combination, may pass into breast milk. The combination has caused no problems among breast-fed infants, but you must consider the potential effect on the nursing infant if breast-feeding while taking this medicine.

Seniors

Older adults should use this combination with caution because of greater sensitivity to drug side effects. Also, older adults are more likely to develop low body temperature (hypothermia) caused by Prazosin Hydrochloride.

Possible Side Effects

The most common side effects of this combination are dizziness, headache, drowsiness, lack of energy, weakness, heart palpitations, and nausea.

Less common side effects: loss of appetite, vomiting, diarrhea, constipation, upset stomach, stomach pains, swelling of the arms or legs, shortness of breath, fainting, rapid heartbeat, chest pains (angina), muscle spasms, nervousness, depression, tingling in the hands or feet, unusual sensitivity to the sun, rash, itching, frequent urination, loss of urinary control, impotence (men), blurred vision, eye redness, ringing or buzzing in the ears, stuffed nose, sweating, dry mouth.

Drug Interactions

Minizide's effectiveness may be lessened when it is taken together with anti-inflammatory pain relievers, especially Indomethacin, with estrogen-containing drugs, or drugs with stimulant properties such as decongestants and diet pills.

Minizide's effectiveness is increased when combined with other antihypertensive medicines.

Food Interactions

Take this medicine with food if it upsets your stomach.

Usual Dose

1 capsule 2 to 3 times per day.

Overdosage

Symptoms can be very low blood pressure, drowsiness, slow reflexes, weakness, tingling in the arms or legs, changes in heartbeat, dry mouth, a sickly feeling, restlessness, muscle pains or cramps, urinary difficulty, nausea, or vomiting. Take the victim to a hospital emergency room at once for treatment. ALWAYS remember to bring the medicine bottle with you.

Special Information

Take this medication exactly as prescribed and don't stop

taking it without your doctor's permission, even if you feel perfectly well. High blood pressure has few symptoms and most people with high blood pressure feel fine.

Avoid over-the-counter diet pills, decongestants, and products for the common cold that contain a stimulant and can raise your pressure. Ask your pharmacist to suggest a product you can safely take.

This product can cause dizziness, drowsiness, and headache. Avoid driving or operating complex equipment if this happens to you. You may want to take the first dose of medicine before you go to bed. If you get extremely dizzy, lie down and let the episode pass.

If you forget to take a dose of Minizide, take it as soon as you remember. If it is almost time for your next regularly scheduled dose, skip the forgotten dose and continue with your regular schedule. Do not take a double dose.

Generic Name
Minocycline

Brand Name
Minocin

Type of Drug
Broad-spectrum tetracycline-type antibiotic.

Prescribed for
Sexually transmitted diseases such as gonorrhea, syphilis, and chlamydia; infections of the mouth, gums, teeth, Rocky Mountain spotted fever and other fevers caused by ticks and lice from a variety of carriers, urinary tract infections; and respiratory system infections such as pneumonia and bronchitis.

These diseases are produced by gram-positive and gram-negative organisms such as diplococci, staphylococci, streptococci, gonococci, *E. coli,* and *Shigella.*

Minocycline has also been successfully used to treat some skin infections, but it is not considered the first-choice antibiotic for the treatment of general skin infections or wounds.

General Information

Minocycline works by interfering with the normal growth cycle of the invading bacteria, preventing them from reproducing and thus allowing the body's normal defenses to fight off the infection. This process is referred to as bacteriostatic action. Minocycline has also been used along with other medicines to treat amoebic infections of the intestinal tract, known as amoebic dysentery. It is also prescribed for diseases caused by ticks, fleas, and lice.

Minocycline has been successfully used for the treatment of adolescent acne, in small doses over a long period of time. Adverse effects or toxicity in this type of therapy are almost unheard of.

Since the action of this antibiotic depends on its concentration within the invading bacteria, it is imperative that you completely follow your doctor's directions.

Cautions and Warnings

Minocycline should not be given to people with known liver disease or kidney or urine excretion problems. You should avoid taking high doses of Minocycline or undergoing extended Minocycline therapy if you will be exposed to sunlight for a long period because this antibiotic can interfere with your body's normal sun-screening mechanism, possibly causing a severe sunburn. If you have a known history of allergy to Minocycline you should avoid taking this drug or other drugs within this category such as Aureomycin, Terramycin, Rondomycin, Vibramycin, Demeclocycline, and Tetracycline.

Pregnancy/Breast-feeding

You should not use Minocycline if you are pregnant, especially during the last half of pregnancy, or during breast-feeding when bones and teeth are being formed. Minocycline when used in children has been shown to interfere with the development of the long bones and may retard growth.

Exceptions would be when Minocycline is the only effective antibiotic available and all risk factors have been made known to the patient.

Seniors

Older adults may take this drug without special precaution.

Possible Side Effects

As with other antibiotics, the common side effects of Minocycline are stomach upset, nausea, vomiting, diarrhea, and skin rash. Less common side effects include hairy tongue and itching and irritation of the anal and/or vaginal region. If these symptoms appear, consult your physician immediately. Periodic physical examinations and laboratory tests should be given to patients who are on long-term Minocycline.

Other uncommon side effects: loss of appetite, peeling of the skin, sensitivity to the sun, fever, chills, anemia, possible brown spotting of the skin, decrease in kidney function, damage to the liver.

Drug Interactions

Minocycline (a bacteriostatic drug) may interfere with the action of bactericidal agents such as Penicillin. It is not advisable to take both during the same course of therapy.

Don't take multivitamin products containing minerals at the same time as Minocycline, or you may reduce the antibiotic's effectiveness. You may take these two medicines at least 2 hours apart.

People receiving anticoagulation therapy (blood-thinning agents) should consult their doctor, since Minocycline will interfere with this form of therapy. An adjustment in the anticoagulant dosage may be required.

Food Interactions

Minocycline may be taken with food or milk if it upsets your stomach.

Usual Dose

Adult: first dose, 200 milligrams, followed by 100 milligrams every 12 hours. Or 100 to 200 milligrams may be given to start, followed by 50 milligrams 4 times per day.

Child (age 9 and over): approximately 2 milligrams per pound of body weight initially, followed by 1 milligram per pound every 12 hours.

Child (up to age 8): not recommended, as the drug has been shown to produce serious discoloration of the permanent teeth.

Special Information

Minocycline can be stored at room temperature. Do *not* take after the expiration date on the label. The decomposition of Minocycline produces a highly toxic substance which can cause serious kidney damage. Call your doctor if your side effects become intolerable, especially if you become dizzy or unsteady.

If you miss a dose of Minocycline, take it as soon as possible. If it is almost time for your next dose and you take the medication once a day, space the next two doses 10 to 12 hours apart, then go back to your regular daily schedule. If it is almost time for your next dose and you take the medicine twice a day, space the next two doses 5 to 6 hours apart, then go back to your regular schedule.

Generic Name

Minoxidil

Brand Names

Loniten
Rogaine Lotion

(Also available in generic form)

Type of Drug

Antihypertensive; hair growth stimulant.

Prescribed for

Severe high blood pressure not controllable with other drugs. Early male-pattern baldness.

General Information

The oral form of this drug can cause severe adverse effects on the heart. It is usually given together with a beta-blocking antihypertensive drug (Propranolol, Metoprolol, Nadolol, etc.) to prevent rapid heartbeat and a diuretic to prevent fluid accumulation. Some patients may have to be hospitalized when treatment with this drug is started, to avoid too rapid a drop in blood pressure.

Minoxidil works by dilating peripheral blood vessels and allowing more blood to flow through arms and legs. This increased blood flow reduces the resistance levels in central vessels (heart, lungs, kidneys, etc.) and therefore reduces blood pressure. Its effect on blood pressure can be seen ½ hour after a dose is taken and lasts up to 3 days. Patients usually take the medicine once or twice a day. Maximum drug effect occurs as early as 3 days after the drug is started, if the dose is large enough (40 milligrams per day).

Researchers have formulated 1 and 5 percent solutions of Minoxidil for application to the scalp to treat male-pattern baldness, taking advantage of the side effect of causing hair growth. The ideal strength of Minoxidil in lotion is 2%. Applying this solution does not work for all people who try it and it is necessary to continue Minoxidil applications to maintain any new hair growth stimulated by the drug. This form of Minoxidil was approved by the FDA in mid-1988. Since a standardized formula is now commercially available in the United States, the Food and Drug Administration is discouraging preparation of Minoxidil topical lotion from the tablets.

The ideal candidate for Minoxidil's hair restoring effect is a man just starting to lose his hair. Women may be helped by Minoxidil lotion. The drug won't help unless hair in the balding area is at least ½ inch long and it takes 4 to 6 months of application before an effect can be expected. Regime must be followed cautiously. Stopping the medication will nullify any benefit you have gained and any hair you have grown will fall out. Some men who used Rogaine continuously for a year found they continued to go bald, but the rate of hair loss was slowed.

Cautions and Warnings

This drug should not be used by people with pheochromocytoma, a rare tumor in which extra body stimulants (catecholamines) are made. Minoxidil may cause the accumulation of water and sodium in the body, leading to heart failure. It also increases heart rate. To protect you from these side effects, Minoxidil must be given with other drugs, a diuretic and a beta-adrenergic blocker.

It has not been carefully studied in patients who have suffered a heart attack within the past month.

Pregnancy/Breast-feeding

This drug crosses into the blood circulation of a developing baby. It has not been found to cause birth defects. Pregnant women, or those who might become pregnant while taking this drug, should not take it without their doctor's approval. When the drug is considered essential by your doctor, the potential risk of taking the medicine must be carefully weighed against the benefit it might produce.

This drug passes into breast milk, but has caused no problems among breast-fed infants. You must consider the potential effect on the nursing infant if breast-feeding while taking this medicine.

Seniors

Older adults are more sensitive to the blood-pressure-lowering effects of this drug because of a normal loss of some kidney capacity to clear the drug from your body. Follow your doctor's directions and report any side effects at once.

Possible Side Effects

Water and sodium retention can develop, leading to heart failure. Also, some patients taking this drug may develop fluid in the sacs surrounding the heart. This is treated with diuretic drugs.

Eighty percent of people taking this drug experience thickening, elongation, and darkening of body hair within 3 to 6 weeks after starting Minoxidil. This is usually first noticed on the temples, between the eyebrows, between the eyebrows and hairline, or on the upper cheek. Later on it will extend to the back, arms, legs, and scalp. This effect stops when the drug is stopped and symptoms will disappear in 1 to 6 months. Electrocardiogram changes occur in 60 percent of patients but are usually not associated with any symptoms. Some other laboratory tests (blood, liver, kidney) may be affected by Minoxidil. Local irritation has occurred when Minoxidil has been used topically.

People using 2% Minoxidil lotion may experience irritation or itching. The amount of Minoxidil absorbed into the scalp is too small to affect blood pressure or cause other serious side effects.

Drug Interactions

Minoxidil may interact with Guanethidine to produce dizziness when rising from a sitting or lying position.

Do not take over-the-counter drugs containing stimulants. If you are unsure which drugs to avoid, ask your pharmacist.

Food Interactions

This drug may be taken at any time. It is not affected by food or liquid intake.

Usual Dose

Adult and child (age 12 and over): 5 milligrams to start; may be increased to 40 milligrams per day. Do not take more than 100 milligrams per day. The daily dose of Minoxidil must be tailored to each patient's needs.

Child (under age 12): 0.1 milligrams per pound per day to start; may be increased to 0.5 milligrams per pound per day. Do not use more than 50 milligrams per day. The daily dose of Minoxidil must be tailored to each patient's needs.

Minoxidil is usually given together with a diuretic (Hydrochlorothiazide, 100 milligrams per day; Chlorthalidone, 50 to 100 milligrams per day; or Furosemide, 80 milligrams per day) and a beta-adrenergic blocker (Propranolol, 80 to 160 milligrams per day; or the equivalent dose of another drug). People who cannot take a beta-adrenergic blocker may take Methyldopa, 500 to 1500 milligrams per day, instead. 0.2 to 0.4 milligrams per day of Clonidine may also be used.

Minoxidil lotion: Apply to scalp twice a day.

Overdosage

Symptoms may be those associated with too low blood pressure. Contact your doctor or poison control center if an overdose of Minoxidil occurs.

Special Information

Since Minoxidil is usually given with two other medications, a beta-adrenergic blocker and a diuretic, do not discontinue any of these drugs unless told to do so by your doctor. Take all medication exactly as prescribed.

The effect of this drug on body hair (see "Possible Side

Effects'') is a nuisance but not dangerous. Do not stop taking Minoxidil because of it.

Call your doctor if you experience an increase in your pulse of 20 or more beats per minute, weight gain of more than 5 pounds, unusual swelling of your arms and/or legs, face, or stomach, chest pain, difficulty in breathing, dizziness, or fainting spells.

If you forget to take a dose of Minoxidil, take it as soon as you remember. If it is almost time for your next regularly scheduled dose, skip the forgotten dose and continue with your regular schedule. Do not take a double dose.

Generic Name

Misoprostol

Brand Name

Cytotec

Type of Drug

Antiulcer.

Prescribed for

Prevention of stomach ulcers associated with taking nonsteroidal anti-inflammatory drugs (for arthritis).

General Information

Misoprostol, approved by the FDA in late 1988, is intended to prevent severe stomach irritation or ulcers in people taking a nonsteroidal anti-inflammatory drug (NSAID) for arthritis. It does not prevent duodenal ulcers. Like Cimetidine and some other antiulcer drugs, Misoprostol supresses stomach acid. It has shown an ability to protect the stomach lining from damage, although the exact way that the drug produces this effect is not known. Misoprostol may stimulate the body to produce more stomach lining, increase the thickness of the protective gel layer that lines the stomach, increase blood flow in the stomach lining, making it repair itself more quickly, or increase the production of bicarbonate, a "natural antacid," in the stomach.

Misoprostol is likely to be an effective ulcer treatment for people who have not responded to Cimetidine, Ranitidine, or Lisinopril, or who cannot take one of these drugs because of interaction with another drug or side effects.

Cautions and Warnings

This drug may make men and women less fertile.

Pregnancy/Breast-feeding

Misoprostol can cause spontaneous miscarriage. Women who are, or might become, pregnant while taking Misoprostol should not take this medicine. The chances of a woman of childbearing age taking this medicine are rather small, since it is generally intended for older adults who take anti-arthritis medicine on a regular basis. Nevertheless, this caution should be kept in mind. Do not take Misoprostol if you are nursing.

Seniors

Older adults absorb more Misoprostol than younger people do, although adverse effects usually do not accompany this phenomenon. The dosage of Misoprostol should be reduced if intolerable side effects develop. This drug is intended for seniors and others with a history of ulcer or stomach disease or those who have been unable to tolerate anti-arthritis drugs in the past.

Possible Side Effects

The most common side effects of Misoprostol are diarrhea, nausea, vomiting, upset stomach, stomach pain, and stomach gas. Most cases of diarrhea are mild and last a maximum of 2 to 3 days.

Misoprostol can cause spontaneous miscarriage in pregnant women, and the drug should be avoided by women who are, or might become, pregnant.

Drug Interactions

Misoprostol reduces stomach acid and may interfere with the absorption of drugs such as Diazepam and Theophylline, which may depend upon the presence of stomach acid for their absorption.

Food Interactions

Misoprostol should be taken with food.

Usual Dose

800 micrograms per day.

Overdosage

The toxic dose of Misoprostol in humans is not known. Up to 1600 micrograms per day have been taken with only minor discomfort. Overdose symptoms are sedation, tremor, convulsions, breathing difficulty, stomach pain, diarrhea, fever, changes in heart rate (very fast or very slow), and low blood pressure. Animals given much larger doses have developed liver, kidney, heart, and testicular damage.

Overdose victims should be taken to a hospital emergency room for treatment. ALWAYS remember to bring the prescription bottle with you.

Special Information

Do not stop taking Misoprostol without your doctor's knowledge.

Do not share this drug with anyone else, especially a woman of childbearing age.

If you forget to take a dose of Misoprostol, take it as soon as you remember. If you don't remember until it is almost time to take your next dose, skip the forgotten dose and continue with your regular schedule.

Brand Name

Moduretic

Ingredients

Amiloride
Hydrochlorothiazide

Type of Drug

Diuretic.

Prescribed for

High blood pressure or any condition where it is desirable to eliminate excess water from the body.

General Information

Moduretic is a combination of two diuretics and is a convenient, effective approach for the treatment of diseases where the elimination of excess water is required. One of the ingredients in Moduretic, Amiloride, holds potassium in the body while producing a diuretic effect. This balances the Hydrochlorothiazide, which often causes a loss of body potassium.

Combination drugs such as Moduretic should only be used when you need the exact amount of ingredients contained in the product and when your doctor feels you would benefit from taking fewer pills per day.

Cautions and Warnings

This drug should not be used by people with diabetes or severe kidney disease or those who are allergic to either of these ingredients or to sulfa drugs. This drug may cause abnormally high blood-potassium levels. Since too much potassium in your blood can be fatal, your doctor should test blood-potassium levels periodically.

Pregnancy/Breast-feeding

This drug should only be used by pregnant women or nursing mothers if absolutely necessary. It may cause birth defects or interfere with your baby's development. Check with your doctor before taking it if you are, or might be, pregnant.

Seniors

Older adults are more sensitive to the effects of this drug. They should closely follow their doctor's directions and report any side effects at once.

Possible Side Effects

Headache, weakness, tiredness, dizziness, difficulty in breathing, abnormal heart rhythms, nausea, loss of appetite, diarrhea, stomach and abdominal pains, decrease in blood potassium, rash, itching, leg pains.

Less common side effects: feeling sick, chest and back

pain, heart palpitations, dizziness when rising from a sitting or lying position, angina pain, constipation, stomach bleeding, stomach upset, appetite changes, feeling of being bloated, hiccups, thirst, vomiting, stomach gas, gout, dehydration, flushing, muscle cramps or spasms, joint pain, tingling in the arms or legs, feeling of numbness, stupor, sleeplessness, nervousness, depression, sleepiness, confusion, visual disturbances, bad taste in the mouth, stuffy nose, sexual impotence, urinary difficulties, dry mouth, adverse effects on the blood system, fever, shock, allergic reactions, jaundice, liver damage, sugar in the blood or urine, unusual sensitivity to the sun, restlessness.

Drug Interactions

Moduretic will add to (potentiate) the action of other blood-pressure-lowering drugs. Since this is beneficial, it is frequently used to help lower blood pressure in patients with hypertension.

The possibility of developing imbalances in body fluids (electrolytes) is increased if you take other medications such as Digitalis and adrenal corticosteroids while you are taking Moduretic.

If you are taking an oral antidiabetic drug and begin taking Moduretic, the antidiabetic dose may have to be altered.

Lithium Carbonate should not be taken with Moduretic because the combination may increase the risk of Lithium toxicity.

Avoid over-the-counter cough, cold, or allergy remedies containing stimulant drugs which can aggravate your condition.

Moduretic may interfere with the oral blood-thinning drugs such as Warfarin by making the blood more concentrated (thicker).

Food Interactions

Take Moduretic with food if it upsets your stomach.

Usual Dose

1 to 2 tablets per day.

Overdosage

Signs are tingling in the arms or legs, weakness, fatigue,

slow heartbeat, a sickly feeling, dryness of the mouth, lethargy, restlessness, muscle pains or cramps, low blood pressure, rapid heartbeat, urinary difficulty, nausea, or vomiting. A patient who has taken a Moduretic overdose should be taken to a hospital emergency room. ALWAYS bring the medicine bottle.

Special Information

This drug can affect your concentration. Do not drive or operate machinery while taking it. Call your doctor if you develop muscle or stomach cramps, nausea, diarrhea, unusual thirst, headache, or rash.

Moduretic should be taken in the morning, no later than 10 A.M.

If you forget to take a dose of Moduretic, take it as soon as you remember. If it is almost time for your next regularly scheduled dose, skip the forgotten dose and continue with your regular schedule. Do not take a double dose.

Generic Name

Monoctanoin

Brand Name

Moctanin

Type of Drug

Gallstone dissolver.

Prescribed for

Gallstones.

General Information

This drug, given only by injection directly into the bile duct, is used by your doctor to remove cholesterol gallstones only after other methods of removing the gallstones have failed. The next step after trying this drug is surgery.

Cautions and Warnings

Monoctanoin should not be used if you have jaundice (yellow skin or eyes), infection in the bile tract, or a recent ulcer.

Pregnancy/Breast-feeding

This drug has not been found to cause birth defects. When the drug is considered essential by your doctor, the potential risk of taking the medicine must be carefully weighed against the benefit it might produce.

This drug may pass into breast milk. You must consider the potential effect on the nursing infant if breast-feeding while taking this medicine.

Seniors

Older adults may use this medication without special restriction. Follow your doctor's directions and report any side effects at once.

Possible Side Effects

Most common: abdominal pain and discomfort, nausea, vomiting, diarrhea.

Other side effects: indigestion, loss of appetite, fever.

Rare side effects include fever, itching, lethargy, chills, sweating, depression, headache, low blood potassium, drug allergy.

Usual Dose

This drug is administered by your doctor directly into the bile duct. Treatment may have to continue for up to 10 days.

Generic Name

Nabilone

Brand Name

Cesamet

Type of Drug

Antinauseant.

Prescribed for

Nausea and vomiting associated with cancer chemotherapy.

General Information

Nabilone is a synthetic, chemically pure form of marijuana used for its effect in the prevention and treatment of nausea and vomiting caused by cancer chemotherapy. Nabilone is most useful for people who have not responded to other antinauseant drugs. As you might expect, Nabilone has all of the psychological effects of marijuana and is, therefore, considered to be a highly abusable drug. Its ability to cause personality changes, feelings of detachment, hallucinations, and euphoria have made Nabilone relatively unacceptable among older adults and others who feel they must be in control of their environment at all times. Younger adults have reported a greater success rate with Nabilone and other marijuana derivatives (known as cannabinoids) probably because they are able to tolerate these effects.

Many people starting on Nabilone will begin while in the hospital because of the need for their doctor to closely monitor their response to the medication and possible adverse effects.

Cautions and Warnings

Nabilone should not be used to treat nausea and vomiting caused by anything other than cancer chemotherapy.

It should not be used by people who are allergic to it, to marijuana, or to sesame oil. Nabilone has a profound effect on its users' mental status and will impair the ability to operate complex equipment, or engage in any activity that requires intense concentration, sound judgment, and complete coordination.

Nabilone should be used with caution by people with a manic depressive or schizophrenic history because of the possibility that Nabilone will aggravate the underlying disease.

Like other abusable drugs, Nabilone produces a definite set of withdrawal symptoms. Tolerance to the drug's effects develops after a month of use. Withdrawal symptoms can develop within 12 hours of the drug's discontinuation and include restlessness, sleeplessness, and irritability. Within a day after the drug has been stopped, stuffy nose, hot flashes, sweating, loose stools, hiccups, and appetite loss may occur. The symptoms will subside within 4 days.

Pregnancy/Breast-feeding

Animal studies of Nabilone have shown no adverse effects on the developing fetus. However, Nabilone should NOT be taken by a pregnant woman unless it is absolutely necessary.

Nabilone may pass into breast milk and affect a nursing infant. Nabilone may reduce the amount of milk produced by a nursing mother.

Seniors

Older adults are more likely to be susceptible to the side effects of Nabilone, especially disorientation, euphoria, and other psychological symptoms.

Possible Side Effects

The most common side effects of Nabilone include dry mouth, drowsiness, a "high" feeling (easy laughing, elation, and heightened awareness), dizziness, muddled thinking, perceptual difficulties, depression, headache, memory loss, nightmares, appetite changes, sleep disturbances, and dizziness when rising from a sitting or lying position.

Other side effects are poor coordination, irritability, a queer feeling, weakness, sluggishness, hallucinations, memory lapse, loss of muscle coordination, unsteadiness, paranoia, depersonalization, disorientation and confusion, rapid heartbeat, difficulty talking, flushing of the face, perspiring, ringing or buzzing in the ears, speech slurring, fainting, diarrhea, loss of ability to control bowel movement, muscle pains.

Drug Interactions

Nabilone will increase the psychological effects of alcoholic beverages, tranquilizers, sleeping pills, sedatives, and other depressants. It will also enhance the effects of other psychoactive drugs.

Usual Dose

1 or 2 milligrams twice a day. On chemotherapy treatment day, take the initial dose before your treatment. Do not take more than 6 milligrams a day.

Overdosage

Overdose symptoms can occur at usual doses or at higher doses taken if the drug is being abused. The primary symptoms of overdose are the psychiatric symptoms found in the "Possible Side Effects" section of this drug profile. No deaths have been caused by either marijuana or nabilone. Nabilone treatment may be restarted at lower doses if other antinauseants are ineffective.

Special Information

Avoid alcoholic beverages, tranquilizers, sleeping pills, and other depressants while taking Nabilone.

Nabilone may impair your ability to drive a car, to perform complex tasks, or to operate complex equipment.

Nabilone can cause acute psychiatric or psychological effects, and you should be aware of this possibility while taking the drug. Be sure to remain in close contact with your doctor and call him or her if any such side effects develop.

If you forget to take a dose of Nabilone, take it as soon as you remember. If it is almost time for your next dose, skip the forgotten capsule and continue with your regular schedule. Do not take a double dose of Nabilone.

Generic Name

Nadolol

Brand Name

Corgard

Type of Drug

Beta-adrenergic blocking agent.

Prescribed for

High blood pressure; angina pectoris (a specific type of chest pain).

General Information

This drug is quite similar to Propranolol, another beta-blocking

agent. It has not been studied in as many kinds of problems
as Propranolol, but it is very useful because it can be taken
once a day. When used for high blood pressure, it is usually
given with a diuretic such as Hydrochlorothiazide.

Cautions and Warnings

Nadolol should be used with care if you have a history of
asthma or other upper respiratory disease or of heart failure.
You should stop taking the drug several days before major
surgery, if possible. Do not do this without telling your doctor. Nadolol can hide some symptoms of diabetes or thyroid
disease.

Pregnancy/Breast-feeding

This drug crosses into the blood circulation of a developing
baby. It has not been found to cause birth defects. Pregnant
women, or those who might become pregnant while taking
this drug, should not take it without their doctor's approval.
When the drug is considered essential by your doctor, the
potential risk of taking the medicine must be carefully weighed
against the benefit it might produce.

This drug passes into breast milk, but has caused no problems among breast-fed infants. You must consider the potential effect on the nursing infant if breast-feeding while
taking this medicine.

Seniors

Senior citizens may be more or less sensitive to the effects
of this medication. Your dosage of this drug must be adjusted to your individual needs by your doctor. Seniors may
be more likely to suffer from cold hands and feet and reduced body temperature, chest pains, a general feeling of ill
health, sudden difficulty breathing, sweating, or changes in
heartbeat because of this medicine.

Possible Side Effects

Nadolol may decrease the heart rate; may aggravate a condition of congestive heart failure; and may produce lowered
blood pressure, tingling in the extremities, light-headedness,
mental depression including inability to sleep, weakness,
and tiredness. It may also produce a mental depression

which is reversible when the drug is withdrawn, visual disturbances, hallucinations, disorientation, and short-term memory loss. Patients taking Nadolol may experience nausea, vomiting, stomach upset, abdominal cramps and diarrhea, or constipation. If you are allergic to this drug, you may show typical reactions associated with drug allergies, including sore throat, fever, difficulty in breathing, and various effects on the blood system. Nadolol may induce bronchospasms (spasms of muscles in the bronchi), which will make any existing asthmatic condition or any severe upper respiratory disease worse.

Occasionally, patients taking Nadolol may experience emotional instability, or a feeling of detachment or personality change, or the drug may produce unusual effects on the blood system.

Drug Interactions

This drug will interact with any psychotropic drug, including the MAO inhibitors, that stimulates one of the adrenergic segments of the nervous system. Since this information is not generally known, you should discuss the potential problem of using Nadolol with your doctor if you are taking any psychotropic or psychiatric drug.

Nadolol may cause increased effectiveness of Insulin or oral antidiabetic drugs. If you are diabetic, discuss the situation with your doctor; a reduction in dose of antidiabetic medication will probably be made.

Nadolol may reduce the effectiveness of Digitalis on your heart. Any dose of Digitalis medication will have to be altered. If you are taking Digitalis for a purpose other than congestive heart failure, the effectiveness of the Digitalis may be increased by Nadolol, and the dose of Digitalis may have to be reduced.

Nadolol may interact with certain other drugs to lower blood pressure. This interaction often has positive results in the treatment of patients with high blood pressure.

Do not self-medicate with over-the-counter cold, cough, or allergy remedies which may contain stimulant drugs that will aggravate certain types of heart disease and high blood pressure, or other ingredients that may antagonize the effects of Nadolol. Double-check with your doctor or pharmacist before taking any over-the-counter medication.

Food Interactions

Take this medicine with food if it upsets your stomach.

Usual Dose

40 to 240 milligrams per day.

Patients with bad kidneys may take their medication dosage as infrequently as once every 60 hours.

Overdosage

Symptoms are slowed heart rate, heart failure, lowered blood pressure, and spasms of the bronchial muscles which make it difficult to breathe. The patient should be taken to a hospital emergency room where proper therapy can be given. ALWAYS bring the medicine bottle with you.

Special Information

Nadolol may be taken at any time, without regard to meals. Since this drug is taken only once a day, be sure to take it at the same time every day. Do not stop taking the drug abruptly unless your doctor tells you to, or serious heart pain and other effects can occur. Call your doctor if you have trouble breathing when you exert yourself or are lying down, have a nighttime cough, or develop swollen ankles, arms, or legs.

If you forget to take a dose of Nadolol, take it as soon as possible. However, if it is within 8 hours of your next dose, skip the forgotten dose and go back to your regular schedule. Do not take a double dose.

Brand Name

Naldecon Tablets

Ingredients

Chlorpheniramine Maleate
Phenylephrine Hydrochloride
Phenylpropanolamine Hydrochloride
Phenytoloxamine Citrate

Other Brand Names

Amaril "D"	New-Decongest
Decongestabs	Sinocon
Histaminic H/S	Tri-phen-chlor T.D.
Nalgest	Vasominic T.D.

(Also available in generic form)

Type of Drug

Long-acting combination antihistamine-decongestant.

Prescribed for

Relief of sneezing, runny nose, and nasal congestion associated with the common cold, allergy, or other upper respiratory condition.

General Information

Naldecon Tablets are one of many products marketed to relieve the symptoms of the common cold. Most of these products contain ingredients to relieve nasal congestion or to dry up runny noses or relieve a scratchy throat; and several of them may contain ingredients to suppress cough, or to help eliminate unwanted mucus. All these products are good only for the relief of symptoms and do not treat the underlying problem such as a cold virus or other infections.

Cautions and Warnings

This drug can cause you to become overly anxious and nervous, and may interfere with your sleep. It should be avoided if you have diabetes, heart disease, high blood pressure, thyroid disease, glaucoma, or a prostate condition.

Pregnancy/Breast-feeding

This drug crosses into the blood circulation of a developing baby. It has not been found to cause birth defects. Pregnant women, or those who might become pregnant while taking this drug, should not take it without their doctor's approval. When the drug is considered essential by your doctor, the potential risk of taking the medicine must be carefully weighed against the benefit it might produce.

This drug passes into breast milk, but has caused no prob-

lems among breast-fed infants. You must consider the potential effect on the nursing infant if breast-feeding while taking this medicine.

Seniors

Older adults are more sensitive to the effects of this drug. Follow your doctor's directions and report any side effects at once.

Possible Side Effects

Mild drowsiness.

Infrequent: restlessness, tension, nervousness, tremor, weakness, inability to sleep, headache, palpitations, elevation of blood pressure, sweating, sleeplessness, loss of appetite, nausea, vomiting, dizziness, constipation.

Drug Interactions

Interaction with sedatives, tranquilizers, antihistamines, sleeping pills, thyroid medicine, and antihypertensive drugs such as Reserpine or Guanethidine may produce excessive drowsiness and/or sleepiness, or inability to concentrate.

Do not self-medicate with over-the-counter drugs for the relief of cold symptoms; taking Naldecon Tablets with such drugs may aggravate high blood pressure, heart disease, diabetes, or thyroid disease.

Do not take Naldecon Tablets if you are taking or suspect you may be taking a monoamine oxidase (MAO) inhibitor: severe elevation in blood pressure may result.

Naldecon and other similar cold products interact with alcoholic beverages and can cause excessive drowsiness.

Food Interactions

Take this medicine with food if it upsets your stomach.

Usual Dose

Adult and child (age 12 and over): 1 tablet 3 times per day.

Child (under age 12): not recommended.

Special Information

Since drowsiness may occur during use of Naldecon Tablets, be cautious while performing mechanical tasks requiring alertness.

If you forget to take a dose of Naldecon, take it as soon as you remember. If it is almost time for your next regularly scheduled dose, skip the forgotten dose and continue with your regular schedule. Do not take a double dose.

Generic Name

Naproxen

Brand Names

Anaprox
Anaprox DS
Naprosyn

(Also available in generic form)

Type of Drug

Nonsteroidal anti-inflammatory.

Prescribed for

Relief of pain and inflammation of joints and muscles; mild to moderate pain of menstrual cramps, dental surgery and extractions, rheumatoid arthritis and osteoarthritis, ankylosing spondylitis, tendonitis, bursitis, and acute gout. Naproxen has also been prescribed for the fever that occurs in pediatric cancer patients.

General Information

Naproxen is one of several nonsteroidal anti-inflammatory drugs (NSAIDs) used to reduce inflammation, relieve pain, or reduce fever. All NSAIDs share the same side effects and may be used by patients who cannot tolerate Aspirin. Choice of one of these drugs over another depends on disease response, side effects seen in a particular patient, convenience of times to take it, and cost. Different drugs or different doses of the same drug may be tried until the greatest effectiveness is seen with the fewest side effects.

Naproxen is the only one of 2 NSAIDs available in an oral suspension form.

Cautions and Warnings

Do not take Naproxen if you are allergic or sensitive to this drug, Aspirin, or other NSAIDs. Naproxen may cause stomach ulcers. This drug should not be used by patients with severe kidney or liver disease.

Pregnancy/Breast-feeding

This drug crosses into the blood circulation of a developing baby. It has not been found to cause birth defects, but it may cause unwanted effects on the heart or blood flow of the newborn. It may also prolong labor or cause other problems during delivery. Pregnant women, or those who might become pregnant while taking this drug, should not take it without their doctor's approval. When the drug is considered essential by your doctor, the potential risk of taking the medicine must be carefully weighed against the benefit it might produce.

This drug passes into breast milk, but has caused no problems among breast-fed infants. You must consider the potential effect on the nursing infant if breast-feeding while taking this medicine.

Seniors

Older adults are more sensitive to the stomach, kidney, and liver effects of this drug. Some doctors recommend that persons 70 and older take ½ the usual dose. Follow your doctor's directions and report any side effects at once.

Possible Side Effects

Most frequent: stomach upset, dizziness, headache, drowsiness, ringing in the ears. Others: heartburn, nausea, vomiting, bloating, gas in the stomach, stomach pain, diarrhea, constipation, dark stool, nervousness, insomnia, depression, confusion, tremor, loss of appetite, fatigue, itching, rash, double vision, abnormal heart rhythm, anemia or other changes in the composition of the blood, changes in liver function, loss of hair, tingling in the hands and feet, fever, breast enlargement, lowered blood sugar, effects on the

kidneys. If symptoms appear, stop taking the medicine and
see your doctor immediately.

Drug Interactions

Naproxen increases the action of Phenytoin, sulfa drugs,
drugs used to control diabetes, and drugs used to thin the
blood. If you are taking any of these medicines, be sure to
discuss it with your doctor, who will probably change the
dose of the other drug.

An adjustment in the dose of Naproxen may be needed if
you take Phenobarbital.

Do not take Aspirin while you are taking Naproxen. This
combination offers no advantages and may be detrimental.

Food Interactions

Take this medicine with food or an antacid if it upsets your
stomach.

Usual Dose

Adult: 250 milligrams to 375 milligrams morning and night,
to start. Dose may be adjusted up to 1250 milligrams per
day, if needed. Mild to moderate pain: 250 milligrams every
6 to 8 hours.

Child: 4.5 milligrams per pound of body weight divided
into 2 doses per day.

Overdosage

Symptoms may include drowsiness, dizziness, confusion,
disorientation, lethargy, tingling in the hands or feet, numbness, nausea, vomiting, upset stomach, stomach pains, headache, ringing or buzzing in the ears, sweating, and blurred
vision. Take the victim to a hospital emergency room at once
for treatment. ALWAYS bring the medicine bottle with you.

Special Information

Avoid Aspirin and alcoholic beverages while taking this medication. You may become dizzy or drowsy taking this medicine. Be careful while driving or operating complex equipment.
Call your doctor if you develop a skin rash, itching, swelling,
visual disturbances, black stools, or a persistent headache
while taking this medication.

NEOSPORIN OPHTHALMIC SOLUTION

If you forget to take a dose of Naproxen, take it as soon as you remember. If it is almost time for your next regularly scheduled dose, skip the forgotten dose and continue with your regular schedule. Do not take a double dose.

Brand Name

Neosporin Ophthalmic Solution

Ingredients

Gramicidin
Neomycin Sulfate
Polymyxin-B Sulfate

(Also available in generic form)

Type of Drug

Topical antibiotic for use in the eye.

Prescribed for

Superficial infections of the eye.

General Information

Neosporin Ophthalmic Solution is a combination of antibiotics which are effective against the most common eye infections. It is most useful when the infecting organism is one known to be sensitive to one of the three antibiotics contained in Neosporin Ophthalmic Solution. It is also useful when the infecting organism is not known, because of the drug's broad range of coverage.

Prolonged use of any antibiotic product in the eye should be avoided because of the possibility of developing sensitivity to the antibiotic. Frequent or prolonged use of antibiotics in the eye may result in the growth of other organisms such as fungi. If the infection does not clear up within a few days, contact your doctor.

Neosporin (or its generic equivalent) is also available as an eye ointment with a minor formula change. Both the eye drops and eye ointment are used for the same things.

Cautions and Warnings

Neosporin Ophthalmic Solution should not be used if you know you are sensitive to or have an allergy to this product or to any of the ingredients in it.

Pregnancy/Breast-feeding

This drug has been found to be safe for use during pregnancy or breast-feeding. Remember, you should check with your doctor before taking any drug if you are pregnant.

Seniors

Older adults may take this medication without special restriction. Follow your doctor's directions and report any side effects at once.

Possible Side Effects

Occasional local irritation after application to the eye.

Usual Dose

1 to 2 drops in the affected eye or eyes 2 to 4 times per day; more frequently if the infection is severe.

Special Information

Tilt the head backward when applying the eye drops. Pull the lower eyelid away from the eye to form a pouch. After applying the drop, keep the eye closed for a minute or so. This allows the medication to come in contact with the infection.

If you forget to take a dose of Neosporin, take it as soon as you remember. If it is almost time for your next regularly scheduled dose, skip the forgotten dose and continue with your regular schedule. Do not take a double dose.

Generic Name

Nicardipine

Brand Name

Cardene

Type of Drug

Calcium channel blocker.

Prescribed for

Angina pectoris; high blood pressure.

General Information

Nicardipine is one of several calcium channel blockers available in the United States; some others are Diltiazem, Nifedipine, and Verapamil. These drugs work by slowing the passage of calcium into muscle cells. This causes the muscles in the blood vessels that supply your heart with blood to open wider, allowing more blood to reach heart tissues. They also decrease muscle spasm in those blood vessels. Nicardipine also reduces the speed at which electrical impulses are carried through heart tissue, adding to its ability to slow the heart and prevent the pain of angina. It can help to reduce high blood pressure by causing blood vessels throughout the body to widen, allowing blood to flow more easily through them, especially when combined with a diuretic, beta blocker, or other blood-pressure-lowering drug.

Cautions and Warnings

Nicardipine can slow your heart rate and interfere with normal electrical conduction in heart muscle. For some people, this can result in temporary heart stoppage; people whose hearts are otherwise healthy will not develop this effect.

Pregnancy/Breast-feeding

Large doses of calcium channel blockers may cause prolonged pregnancy and harm to the fetus, including poor bone development and stillbirths. Nicardipine should be avoided by pregnant women or women who may become pregnant while using it. In situations where it is deemed essential, the potential risk of the drug must be carefully weighed against any benefit it might produce.

Nursing mothers should watch their babies for any possible drug effect. It is not known if Nicardipine passes into breast milk.

Seniors

Older adults may be more sensitive to the side effects of Nicardipine.

Because of the possibility of reduced kidney and/or liver function in older adults, they should receive smaller doses than younger adults, beginning with 20 milligrams 2 to 3 times a day and continuing with carefully increased doses.

Possible Side Effects

The most common side effects of Nicardipine are abnormal heart rhythms, fluid accumulation in the hands, legs, or feet, headache, fatigue, nausea, and skin rash.

Less common side effects include low blood pressure, dizziness, fainting, changes in heart rate (increase or decrease), heart failure, light-headedness, nervousness, tingling in the hands or feet, hallucinations, temporary memory loss, difficulty sleeping, weakness, diarrhea, vomiting, constipation, upset stomach, itching, unusual sensitivity to the sun, painful or stiff joints, liver inflammation, and increased urination, especially at night.

Drug Interactions

Taking Nicardipine with a beta blocking drug to treat high blood pressure is usually well tolerated but may lead to heart failure in susceptible people.

Calcium channel blockers, including Nicardipine, may add to the effects of Digoxin, although this is not observed with any consistency and occurs only in people with a large amount of Digoxin already in their systems.

Blood levels of cyclosporine may be increased by Nicardipine, increasing the chance for cyclosporine-related kidney damage.

The effect of Quinidine may be altered by Nicardipine.

Food Interactions

Nicardipine is best taken on an empty stomach, at least 1 hour before or 2 hours after meals, but it may be taken with food or milk if it upsets your stomach.

Usual Dose

60 to 120 milligrams per day.

Overdosage

The two major symptoms of Nicardipine overdose are very low blood pressure and reduced heart rate. Nicardipine can be removed from the stomach by giving the victim Syrup of Ipecac to induce vomiting, but this must be done within 30 minutes of the actual overdose, before the drug can be absorbed into the blood. Once symptoms develop or if more than 30 minutes have passed since the overdose, the victim must be taken to a hospital emergency room for treatment.

Special Information

Call your doctor if you develop any of the following symptoms: swelling of the hands, legs, or feet, severe dizziness, constipation or nausea, or very low blood pressure.

Some people may experience a slight increase in blood pressure just before their next dose is due. You will be able to see this effect only if you use a home blood pressure monitoring device. If this happens, contact your doctor at once.

If you forget to take a dose of Nicardipine, take it as soon as you remember. If it is almost time for your next dose, skip the forgotten dose and continue with your regular schedule.

Generic Name

Nicotine

Brand Name

Nicorette Chewing Gum

Type of Drug

Smoking deterrent.

Prescribed for

People addicted to cigarettes who need another source of their drug (Nicotine) to help break the smoking habit.

General Information

Nicotine is known to affect many brain functions, including improving memory, increasing one's ability to perform a number of different tasks, reducing hunger, and increasing tolerance to pain. This chewing gum, a source of noninhaled Nicotine, makes cigarette withdrawal much easier for many people. Although this product is designed to fulfill a specific need in those trying to quit smoking, there are a great many other social and psychological needs filled by smoking. These must be dealt with through counseling or other psychological support in order for a program to be successful.

You may be addicted to Nicotine if you smoke more than 15 cigarettes per day; prefer unfiltered cigarettes or those with a high nicotine content; usually inhale the smoke; have your first cigarette within 30 minutes of getting up in the morning; find the first morning cigarette the hardest to give up; smoke most frequently in the morning hours; find it hard to obey "no smoking" signs or rules; smoke even when you are sick in bed.

Cautions and Warnings

Nicotine Chewing Gum should not be used by nonsmokers or others who are not addicted to the effects of this drug. It should not be used during the period immediately following a heart attack or if severe abnormal heart rhythms, angina pains, or severe temperomandibular joint (TMJ) disease are present. People with other heart conditions must be evaluated by a cardiologist (heart doctor) before starting treatment with Nicotine Chewing Gum.

This product should be used with caution by diabetics being treated with Insulin or people with an overactive thyroid, pheochromocytoma, high blood pressure, stomach ulcers, and chronic dental problems that might be worsened by Nicotine Chewing Gum.

It is possible for Nicotine addiction to be transferred from cigarettes to the gum or for the addiction actually to worsen while using the product.

Pregnancy/Breast-feeding

This product should not be used by women who are pregnant, or who might become pregnant, because Nicotine is known to harm the developing baby when taken during the last 3 months of pregnancy. Nicotine, whether from cigarettes or chewing gum, interferes with the newborn baby's ability to breathe properly. Additionally, one miscarriage has occurred in a woman using Nicotine Chewing Gum. Mothers should not breast-feed while using this product since Nicotine passes into breast milk and can be harmful to a growing infant.

Seniors

Older adults with severe liver damage may be more sensitive to the effects of this drug. Follow your doctor's directions and report any side effects at once.

Possible Side Effects

Injury to gums, jaw, or teeth; stomach growling due to swallowing air. Other common systemic side effects are nausea, vomiting, hiccups, and upset stomach.

Less common: excessive salivation, dizziness, light-headedness, irritability, headache, increased bowel movement, diarrhea, constipation, gas pains, dry mouth, hoarseness, facial flushing, sneezing, coughing, feeling "high," and sleeplessness.

Drug Interactions

Heavy smokers who suddenly stop smoking may experience an increase in the effects of a variety of drugs whose breakdowns are known to be stimulated by cigarettes. If you are taking any of the following medications, your dosage may have to be reduced to account for this effect: Theophylline, Imipramine, Pentazocine, Furosemide, Propranolol, Propoxyphene Hydrochloride.

Smoking increases the rate at which your body breaks down caffeine. Stopping Nicotine may make you more sensitive to the effects of the caffeine in coffee or tea.

Usual Dose

1 piece of gum whenever you feel the urge for a cigarette, not more than 30 per day. Each piece contains 2 milligrams of Nicotine.

Overdosage

Nicotine overdosage can be deadly. Symptoms include salivation, nausea, vomiting, diarrhea, abdominal pains, headache, cold sweats, dizziness, hearing and visual disturbances,
weakness, and confusion. If untreated, these symptoms will
be followed by fainting, very low blood pressure, a pulse
that is weak, rapid, and irregular, convulsions, and death by
paralysis of the muscles that control breathing. The lethal
dose of Nicotine is about 50 milligrams.

Nicotine stimulates the brain's vomiting center, making
this reaction common, but not automatic. Spontaneous vomiting may be sufficient to remove the poison from the victim's system. If this has not occurred, call your doctor or
poison control center for instructions on how to make the
victim vomit by giving Syrup of Ipecac. If the victim must be
treated in a hospital emergency room, ALWAYS bring the
chewing gum package with you.

Special Information

Follow the instructions on the patient-information sheet included in each package of the gum.

Chew each piece of the gum slowly and intermittently for
about 30 minutes to promote slow and even absorption of
the Nicotine through the tissues in your mouth. Too-rapid
chewing releases the Nicotine too quickly and can lead to
side effects of nausea, hiccups, or throat irritation.

You will learn to control your daily dose of Nicotine chewing gum so that your smoking habit is broken and side
effects are minimized. Do not chew more than 30 pieces of
gum per day. The amount of gum chewed each day should
be gradually reduced after 3 months of successful treatment.

Nicotine Chewing Gum is not recommended for more than
6 months at a time.

Generic Name

Nicotinic Acid (Niacin)

Brand Names

Niac	Nicolar
Niacels	Nico-Span
Nicobid	Nicotinex
Nico 400	Span-Niacin

(Also available in generic form)

Type of Drug

Vitamin.

Prescribed for

Treatment of Nicotinic Acid deficiency (pellagra). Also, pre-scribed to help lower high blood levels of lipids or fats, and to help dilate or enlarge certain blood vessels.

General Information

Nicotinic Acid or Niacin, also known as Vitamin B_3, is essen-tial to normal body function through the part it plays in enzyme activity. It is effective in lowering blood levels of fats and can help enlarge or dilate certain blood vessels, but we do not know exactly how it does these things. Normally, individual requirements of Nicotinic Acid are easily supplied in a well-rounded diet.

Cautions and Warnings

Do not take this drug if you are sensitive or allergic to it or to any related drugs or if you have liver disease, stomach ulcer, severely low blood pressure, gout, or hemorrhage (bleeding).

Pregnancy/Breast-feeding

When used in normal doses Nicotinic Acid can be taken by pregnant women, but if it is used in high doses (to help lower blood levels of fats) there may be some problems. Although Niacin has not been shown to cause birth defects or problems in breast-fed infants, if you are pregnant or nursing consult with your doctor.

Seniors

Older adults may take this medication without special restriction. Follow your doctor's directions and report any side effects at once.

Possible Side Effects

Most common: flushing (redness and a warm sensation in the face and hands).

Less common side effects: decreased sugar tolerance in diabetics, activation of stomach ulcers, jaundice (yellowing of the whites of the eyes and skin), stomach upset, oily skin, dry skin, possible aggravation of skin conditions such as acne, itching, high blood levels of uric acid, low blood pressure, temporary headache, tingling feeling, skin rash, abnormal heartbeats, dizziness.

Drug Interactions

Nicotinic Acid, which can enlarge blood vessels, can intensify the effect of antihypertensive (blood-pressure-lowering) drugs, causing postural hypotension (getting dizzy when you rise quickly from a sitting or lying position).

If you are diabetic, large doses of Nicotinic Acid can throw your blood sugar slightly out of control and your doctor may have to adjust either your diet or your drug therapy.

Usual Dose

Supplementary vitamin product: 25 milligrams per day.

Treatment of high blood levels of lipids or fats: initial dose, 500 milligrams to 3 grams per day with or after meals (take with cold water to assist in swallowing). If 3 grams does not prove effective the dose may be increased slowly to a maximum of 6 grams per day.

The dose should be built up slowly so you can watch carefully for common side effects: flushing or redness of the face and extremities, itching, and stomach upset.

Overdosage

Overdose victims experience drug side effects. Take the victim to an emergency room for treatment. Bring the medicine bottle with you.

Special Information

If you forget to take a dose of Nicotinic Acid, take it as soon as you remember. If it is almost time for your next regularly scheduled dose, skip the forgotten dose and continue with your regular schedule. Do not take a double dose.

Generic Name

Nifedipine

Brand Names

Adalat
Procardia

Type of Drug

Calcium channel blocker.

Prescribed for

Angina pectoris, Prinzmetal's angina, and high blood pressure.
It has also been prescribed to treat asthma, Raynaud's Disease, and preterm labor.

General Information

Nifedipine was the first member of this new drug group to be marketed in the United States. It works by blocking the passage of calcium into heart and smooth muscle. Since calcium is an essential factor in muscle contraction, any drug that affects calcium in this way will interfere with the contraction of these muscles. When this happens the amount of oxygen used by the muscles is also reduced. Therefore, Nifedipine is used in the treatment of angina, a type of heart pain related to poor oxygen supply to the heart muscles. Also, Nifedipine dilates (opens) the vessels that supply blood to the heart muscles and prevents spasm of these arteries. Nifedipine only affects the movement of calcium into muscle cells. It does not have any affect on calcium in the blood.

Cautions and Warnings

Nifedipine may cause lowered blood pressure in some patients. Patients taking a beta-blocking drug who begin taking Nifedipine may develop heart failure or increased angina pain. Do not take this drug if you have had an allergic reaction to it.

Pregnancy/Breast-feeding

This drug crosses into the blood circulation of a developing baby. It has not been found to cause human birth defects. Pregnant women, or those who might become pregnant while taking this drug, should not take it without their doctor's approval. When the drug is considered essential by your doctor, the potential risk of taking the medicine must be carefully weighed against the benefit it might produce.

This drug may pass into breast milk, but has caused no problems among breast-fed infants. You must consider the potential effect on the nursing infant if breast-feeding while taking this medicine.

Seniors

Older adults are more sensitive to the effects of this drug, because it takes longer to pass out of their bodies. Follow your doctor's directions and report any side effects at once.

Possible Side Effects

Dizziness, light-headedness, flushing, a feeling of warmth, headache, weakness, nausea, heartburn, muscle cramps, tremors, swelling of the arms or legs, nervousness, mood changes, heart palpitations, difficulty breathing, coughs, wheezing, stuffy nose, sore throat.

Less common side effects: shortness of breath, diarrhea, cramps, stomach gas, muscle cramps, stiffness and inflammation of the joints, shakiness, jitteriness, blurred vision, difficulty sleeping, difficulty maintaining balance, itching, rash, fever, sweating, chills, sexual difficulties. In addition, some patients taking Nifedipine have experienced heart attack, heart failure, fluid in the lungs, and abnormal heart rhythms. The occurrence of these serious effects has not been directly related to taking Nifedipine. Future research may tell us whether Nifedipine actually causes these problems or if the occurrence is merely coincidental. Nifedipine can cause increases in certain blood enzyme tests.

Drug Interactions

Nifedipine may interact with the beta-blocking drugs to cause heart failure, very low blood pressure, or an increased incidence of angina pain. However, in many cases these drugs have been taken together with no problem. Nifedipine may cause a lowering of blood pressure in patients already taking medicine to control their high blood pressure through interaction with the other antihypertensive drugs.

Food Interactions

Take this drug 1 hour before or 2 hours after meals.

Usual Dose

30 to 120 milligrams per day. No patient should take more than 180 milligrams per day.

Do not stop taking the drug abruptly. The dosage should be gradually reduced over a period of time.

Overdosage

Overdose of Nifedipine can cause low blood pressure. If you think you have taken an overdose of Nifedipine, call your doctor or go to a hospital emergency room. ALWAYS bring the medicine bottle.

Special Information

Call your doctor if you develop swelling in the arms or legs, difficulty breathing, increased heart pains, dizziness or lightheadedness, or lowered blood pressure.

If you forget to take a dose of Nifedipine, take it as soon as you remember. If it is almost time for your next regularly scheduled dose, skip the forgotten dose and continue with your regular schedule. Do not take a double dose.

Generic Name

Nimodipine

Brand Name

Nimotop

Type of Drug

Calcium channel blocker.

Prescribed for

Functional losses following a stroke. Nimodipine may also be prescribed for migraine and cluster headaches.

General Information

Nimodipine is one of several calcium channel blockers available in the United States. Unlike the other members of this group, Nimodipine has a negligible effect on the heart. It is unique because it is the only calcium channel blocker proven effective as a drug to help improve neurological symptoms after a stroke. Calcium channel blockers work by slowing the passage of calcium into cells. This causes muscles in the blood vessels that supply your heart and other tissues to open wider, allowing more blood to flow through them. They also decrease muscle spasm in those blood vessels.

Nimodipine readily dissolves in fatty tissues and reaches very high concentrations in the brain and spinal fluid. Because of this, it has a greater effect on blood vessels in the brain than on those in other parts of the body. Nimodipine relieves stroke symptoms but does not reduce spasms in brain blood vessels. A great deal of research still needs to be done to discover exactly how this drug works.

Cautions and Warnings

Nimodipine should not be taken if you are sensitive or allergic to it or if you have a condition called aortic stenosis, in which the aorta becomes stiffer and less flexible than normal. Animals given Nimodipine developed a high rate of testicular and uterine cancer. It is not known if the drug has this effect on humans.

Liver disease, including cirrhosis, may slow the breakdown of Nimodipine by the body. This can produce a need to take a lower than normal dose of the drug.

Pregnancy/Breast-feeding

Animal studies have shown that Nimodipine can cause malformation of a fetus. Very high doses can cause poor fetal growth, death of the fetus, and fetal bone problems. Nimodipine should be avoided by pregnant women or women who may become pregnant while using it. In situations where the drug is deemed essential by your doctor, the potential risk of the drug must be carefully weighed against any benefit it might produce.

Nimodipine has been shown, in animal studies, to pass into breast milk. Women who must use Nimodipine should use an alternative feeding method.

Seniors

Older adults, especially those with severe liver disease, may be more sensitive to the side effects of Nimodipine.

Possible Side Effects

The most common side effects of Nimodipine are diarrhea and headache.

Less common side effects include swelling of the arms or legs, changes in blood pressure (low or high), heart failure, rapid heartbeat, changes in the electrocardiogram, depression, memory loss, psychosis, paranoid feelings, hallucinations, nausea, itching, acne, rash, anemia, bleeding or bruising, abnormal blood clotting, flushing, breathing difficulty, stomach bleeding, and muscle cramps.

Rare side effects include dizziness, heart attack, liver inflammation or jaundice, vomiting, and sexual difficulties.

Drug Interactions

Calcium channel blockers may cause bleeding when taken alone or together with Aspirin.

Cimetidine may increase the effects of Nimodipine by decreasing the rate at which Nimodipine is broken down by the liver.

Taking Nimodipine together with a beta-blocking drug is usually well-tolerated but may lead to heart failure in susceptible people.

Calcium channel blockers, including Nimodipine, may add
to the effects of Digoxin, although this effect is not observed
with any consistency and only affects people with a large
amount of Digoxin already in their system.

Food Interactions

Nimodipine is best taken on an empty stomach—at least 1
hour before or 2 hours after meals—but may be taken with
food or milk if it upsets your stomach.

Usual Dose

60 milligrams 4 times a day beginning within 96 hours after
the stroke and continuing for 21 days.

Overdosage

The major symptoms of Nimodipine overdose are nausea,
weakness, dizziness, drowsiness, confusion, and slurred
speech. Blood pressure and heart rate may also be affected.
Nimodipine can be removed from a victim's stomach by
giving Syrup of Ipecac to induce vomiting, but this should
be done only under a doctor's supervision or direction. Once
symptoms develop, the victim must be taken to a hospital
emergency room for treatment.

Special Information

Call your doctor if you develop any of the following symptoms: swelling of the arms or legs, breathing difficulty, severe dizziness, constipation, or nausea.

Patients who are unable to swallow Nimodipine capsules
because of their condition may have the liquid withdrawn
from the capsule with a syringe and mixed with other liquids
to be given orally or through a feeding tube.

If you forget to take a dose of Nimodipine, take it as soon
as you remember. If it is almost time for your next dose, skip
the forgotten dose and continue with your regular schedule.
Call your doctor if you miss more than 2 doses.

Generic Name

Nitrofurantoin

Brand Names

Furadantin	Furanite
Furalan	Macrodantin (Macro Crystals)
Furan	Nitrofan

(Also available in generic form)

Type of Drug

Urinary anti-infective.

Prescribed for

Urinary tract infections by organisms susceptible to Nitrofurantoin. These organisms cause pyelonephritis, pyelitis, and cystitis.

General Information

Nitrofurantoin, like several other drugs (including Naladixic Acid [NegGram]), is of value in treating urinary tract infections because it appears in large amounts in the urine. It should not be used to treat infections in other parts of the body.

Cautions and Warnings

Do not take Nitrofurantoin if you have kidney disease, or if you are allergic to this agent.

Pregnancy/Breast-feeding

Nitrofurantoin should not be taken by pregnant women because it can interfere with your developing baby's immature enzyme systems and cause a blood problem called hemolytic anemia.

This medicine passes into breast milk and may affect some nursing infants. Check with your doctor about the need for using an alternative feeding method while taking this medication.

Seniors

Older adults with kidney disease may be more sensitive to the effects of this drug. Follow your doctor's directions and report any side effects at once.

Possible Side Effects

Loss of appetite, nausea, vomiting, stomach pain, diarrhea. Some people develop hepatitis symptoms.

Side effects are less prominent when Macrodantin (large crystal form of Nitrofurantoin) is used rather than Furadantin (regular crystal size).

Less common side effects: fever, chills, cough, chest pain, difficulty in breathing, development of fluid in the lungs; if these occur in the first week of therapy they can generally be resolved by stopping the medication. If they develop after a longer time they can be more serious because they develop more slowly and are more difficult to associate with the drug. If you develop chest pains or difficulty in breathing while taking Nitrofurantoin, report the effects to your physician immediately. Other adverse effects: rashes, itching, asthmatic attacks in patients with history of asthma, drug fever, symptoms similar to arthritis, jaundice (yellowing of the whites of the eyes and/or skin), effects on components of the blood, headache, dizziness, drowsiness, temporary loss of hair. The oral liquid form of Nitrofurantoin can stain your teeth if you don't swallow the medicine rapidly.

This drug is known to cause changes in the blood. Therefore, it should be used only under strict supervision by your doctor.

Food Interactions

Nitrofurantoin may be taken with food to help decrease stomach upset, loss of appetite, nausea, or other gastrointestinal symptoms. Avoid eating citrus fruits or milk products while taking Nitrofurantoin. These can change the acidity of your urine and affect the drug's action.

Usual Dose

Adult: 50 to 100 milligrams 4 times per day.

Child (over age 3 months): 2 to 3 milligrams per pound of body weight in 4 divided doses.

Child (under age 3 months): not recommended.

Nitrofurantoin may be used in lower doses over a long period by people with chronic urinary infections.

Continue to take this medicine at least 3 days after you stop experiencing symptoms of urinary tract infection.

Special Information

Nitrofurantoin may give your urine a brownish color: this is usual and not dangerous.

If you miss a dose of Nitrofurantoin, take it as soon as possible. If it is almost time for your next dose and you take the medicine 3 or more times a day, space the missed dose and your next dose by 2 to 4 hours or double your next dose and then continue with your regular schedule.

Generic Name

Nitroglycerin

Brand Names

Klavikordal	Nitrolin
Niong	Nitrolingual Spray
Nitro-Bid Ointment	Nitrol Ointment
Nitro-Bid Plateau Caps	Nitronet
Nitrocap TD	Nitrong
Nitrodisc Patches	Nitrospan
Nitro-Dur Patches	Nitrostat
Nitrogard	NTS Patches
Nitroglyn	Transderm Nitro Patches

(Also available in generic form)

Type of Drug

Antianginal agent.

Prescribed for

Prevention and treatment of chest pains associated with angina pectoris.

General Information

Nitroglycerin is available in several dosage forms, including sublingual tablets (which are taken under the tongue and are allowed to dissolve), capsules (which are swallowed), transmucosal tablets (which are placed between lip or cheek and gum and are allowed to dissolve), an oral spray (sprayed directly on the inside of the cheek), patches (which deliver Nitroglycerin through the skin over a 24-hour period), and ointment (which is usually spread over the chest wall, although it can be spread on any area of the body). Frequently patients may take one or more dosage forms of Nitroglycerin to prevent and/or treat the attack of chest pain associated with angina.

Cautions and Warnings

You should not take Nitroglycerin if you are known to be allergic to it. Also, because Nitroglycerin will increase the pressure of fluid inside your head, it should be taken with great caution if head trauma or bleeding in the head is present.

Pregnancy/Breast-feeding

This drug crosses into the blood circulation of a developing baby. It has not been found to cause birth defects. Pregnant women, or those who might become pregnant while taking this drug, should not take it without their doctor's approval. When the drug is considered essential by your doctor, the potential risk of taking the medicine must be carefully weighed against the benefit it might produce.

This drug passes into breast milk, but has caused no problems among breast-fed infants. You must consider the potential effect on the nursing infant if breast-feeding while taking this medicine.

Seniors

Older adults may take Nitroglycerin without special restriction. Be sure to follow your doctor's directions for use.

Possible Side Effects

The most frequent side effect of Nitroglycerin is flushing of the skin. Headache is common and may be severe or persistent. Once in a while, episodes of dizziness and weakness have been associated with the use of Nitroglycerin. There is a possibility that you will experience blurred vision. If this occurs, stop taking the drug and call your physician.

Less common side effects: Occasionally an individual exhibits a marked sensitivity to the blood-pressure-lowering effect of Nitroglycerin, causing severe responses of nausea, vomiting, weakness, restlessness, loss of facial color or pallor, perspiration, and collapse even with the usual therapeutic dose. Drug rash occasionally occurs.

Drug Interactions

If you are taking Nitroglycerin continuously, avoid excessive alcohol intake, which may cause lowering of blood pressure and resulting faintness and dizziness.

Avoid over-the-counter drugs containing stimulants, which may aggravate your heart disease. Such drugs are used to treat coughs, colds, and allergies, and as appetite suppressants.

Food Interactions

Do not use any oral form of Nitroglycerin with food or gum in your mouth. Nitroglycerin pills intended for swallowing (most are *not*) are best taken on an empty stomach.

Usual Dose

Only as much as is necessary to control chest pains. Since the sublingual dosage form (tablet taken under the tongue) acts within 10 to 15 seconds of being taken, the drug is only taken when necessary.

Long-acting (sustained-release) capsules or tablets: generally used to prevent chest pains associated with angina, with the dose being 1 capsule or tablet every 8 to 12 hours.

Ointment: 1 to 2 inches of ointment are squeezed from the tube onto a prepared piece of paper with markings on it. (Some patients may require as much as 4 to 5 inches.) The ointment is spread on the skin every 3 to 4 hours as needed for control of chest pains. The drug is absorbed through the skin. Application sites should be rotated to prevent skin inflammation and rash.

Patches: placed on the chest once a day and left on for 24 hours.

Aerosol: delivers a premeasured dose. Spray 1 or 2 doses under or on your tongue and repeat as needed to relieve an angina attack.

Special Information

The sublingual form should be acquired from your pharmacist only in the original, unopened bottle, and the tablets must not be transferred to a secondary bottle or container; otherwise the tablets may lose potency. Close the bottle tightly after each use or the drug may evaporate from the tablets.

The sublingual form should produce a burning sensation under the tongue, which indicates that the drug is potent and will produce the desired effect. If there is no such sensation you must have the tablets replaced immediately.

When applying Nitroglycerin ointment, do not rub or massage into the skin. Any excess ointment should be washed from hands after application.

Orthostatic hypotension, where more blood stays in the extremities and less becomes available to the brain, resulting in light-headedness or faintness if you stand up suddenly, can be a problem if you take Nitroglycerin over a long period of time. Avoid prolonged standing and be careful to stand up slowly.

Generic Name

Norfloxacin

Brand Name

Noroxin

Type of Drug

Urinary anti-infective.

Prescribed for

Urinary infections. This medicine does not work against the common cold, flu, or other virus infections.

General Information

Norfloxacin is the first of a new class of antibacterial drugs, called Fluoroquinolones, to be marketed in the United States. This drug works against many organisms that traditional treatments like antibiotics have trouble killing. It is chemically related to an older antibacterial called Nalidixic Acid, but works better than that drug against urinary infections.

Cautions and Warnings

Do not take Norfloxacin if you have had an allergic reaction to it in the past, or if you have had a reaction to a related medication like Nalidixic Acid.

Pregnancy/Breast-feeding

Pregnant women should not take this medication. Studies in monkeys have shown that this drug can reduce your chances for a successful pregnancy and that doses 10 times greater than the maximum human dose can cause spontaneous abortion. The drug has not caused birth defects in animals given up to 50 times the human dose.

It is not known if Norfloxacin passes into breast milk. Nursing mothers should avoid taking Norfloxacin unless it is absolutely necessary because of the chance that the drug might pass into breast milk. Be sure your doctor knows if you are breast-feeding.

Seniors

Studies in healthy senior citizens showed that Norfloxacin was released from their bodies more slowly than from younger adults because of decreased kidney function.

Norfloxacin dosage must be adjusted according to kidney function. Since most seniors have lost some kidney function, your doctor will take this factor into account by giving you a lower daily dosage of Norfloxacin.

Possible Side Effects

The most common side effects of Norfloxacin are headache, dizziness, and light-headedness.

Other side effects: rash, fatigue, drowsiness, depression, difficulty sleeping, upset stomach, abdominal pains, stomach gas, constipation, and heartburn.

Rare side effects include dry mouth, diarrhea, fever, and vomiting. Visual disturbances such as blurred or double vision, changes in color perception, halos around lights, and sensitivity to bright lights are rare but should be reported to your doctor.

Drug Interactions

Antacids will decrease the amount of Norfloxacin absorbed into the blood. If you must take them, separate your antacid dosage from Norfloxacin by at least 2 hours.

Probenecid will decrease the amount of Norfloxacin released through your kidneys and may increase the chance of drug side effects.

Nitrofurantoin may antagonize Norfloxacin's antibacterial effects. Do not take these two drugs together.

Food Interactions

Take this medicine with a full glass of water either 1 hour before or 2 hours after meals. Food interferes with the absorption of this drug into the bloodstream.

Usual Dose

400 to 800 milligrams per day.

Overdosage

The symptoms of Norfloxacin overdose are the same as those found under "Possible Side Effects." Overdose victims should be taken to a hospital emergency room for treatment of those symptoms. However, you may induce vomiting with Syrup of Ipecac to remove excess drug from the victim's stomach. Consult your poison control center or hospital emergency room for specific instructions.

Special Information

Take each dose with a full glass of water and be sure to drink at least 8 glasses of water a day while taking Norfloxacin. This will promote removal of the drug from your system and help to avoid side effects.

Call your doctor if depression, visual disturbances, dizziness, headache, or light-headedness, or any intolerable side effect develop.

It is essential that you take this medicine according to your doctor's directions. Do not stop taking it if you begin to feel better a few days after you start treatment, unless directed to do so by your doctor.

Since Norfloxacin can cause visual changes, dizziness, drowsiness or light-headedness, it can affect your ability to drive a car or do other things requiring full concentration and attention.

If you forget to take a dose of Norfloxacin, take it as soon as you remember. If it is almost time for your next regularly scheduled dose, skip the forgotten dose and continue with your regular schedule. Do not take a double dose.

Brand Name

Norgesic Forte

Ingredients

Aspirin
Caffeine
Orphenadrine Citrate

Type of Drug

Muscle relaxant combination.

Prescribed for

Muscle spasms.

General Information

The primary ingredient in Norgesic Forte is Orphenadrine Citrate, a derivative of the antihistamine Diphenhydramine Hydrochloride (Benadryl). It is a moderately effective muscle relaxant which works by exerting a general sedative effect. The Aspirin in Norgesic Forte is there only for pain relief.

Norgesic Forte cannot solve the problems of pain due to muscle spasm: it can only temporarily relieve the pain. You must follow any additional advice given regarding exercise, diet, or immobilization to help solve the underlying problem.

Cautions and Warnings

Norgesic Forte should not be used if you have a history of glaucoma, stomach ulcer, intestinal obstruction, difficulty in passing urine, or known sensitivity or allergy to this drug or any of its ingredients. It should not be used by children.

Pregnancy/Breast-feeding

This product has not been studied for its effect on a developing baby. However, too much Aspirin late in a pregnancy can decrease a newborn's weight and cause other problems. Pregnant women, or those who might become pregnant while taking this drug, should not do so without their doctor's approval. When the drug is considered essential by your doctor, the potential risk of taking the medicine must be carefully weighed against the benefit it might produce.

It is not known if this drug passes into breast milk, but you must consider the potential effect on the nursing infant if breast-feeding while taking this medicine.

Seniors

Older adults may be more sensitive to the side effects of this medication.

Possible Side Effects

Dryness of the mouth is usually the first side effect to appear. As the daily dose increases, other possible side effects include rapid heartbeat, palpitations, difficulty in urination, blurred vision, enlarged pupils, weakness, nausea, vomiting, headache, dizziness, constipation, drowsiness, rash, itching, runny or stuffy nose, hallucinations, agitation, tremor, and stomach upset. Elderly patients taking this drug may occasionally experience some degree of mental confusion. Large doses or prolonged therapy may result in Aspirin intoxication with symptoms of ringing in the ears, headache, dizziness, fever, confusion, sweating, thirst, drowsiness, dimness of vision, rapid breathing, increased pulse rate, or diarrhea.

Drug Interactions

One of the ingredients in Norgesic Forte is Aspirin, which may significantly affect the effectiveness of oral anticoagulant (blood-thinning) drugs, may increase the effect of Probenecid, and may increase the blood-sugar-lowering effects of oral antidiabetic drugs such as Chlorpropamide and Tolbutamide.

Interaction with Propoxyphene (Darvon) may cause confusion, anxiety, tremors, or shaking.

Long-term users should avoid excessive alcohol intake, which may aggravate stomach upset and bleeding.

Food Interactions

Take with food or at least ½ glass of water to prevent stomach upset.

Usual Dose

½ to 1 tablet 3 to 4 times per day.

Overdosage

2 to 3 grams of Orphenadrine (40 to 60 Norgesic Forte tablets) is lethal to adults. Large overdoses can be rapidly fatal. The victim must be taken to a hospital emergency room as quickly as possible for treatment. ALWAYS bring the medicine bottle with you.

Special Information

Norgesic Forte may make you drowsy. Take care while driving or operating complex equipment.

Avoid alcoholic beverages, which can enhance the irritating effect of this product on your stomach and its depressive effect.

If you forget to take a dose of Norgesic Forte and you remember within about an hour of your regular time, take the dose right away. If you do not remember until later, skip the forgotten dose and go back to your regular schedule. Do not take a double dose.

Generic Name

Nortriptyline

Brand Names

Aventyl
Pamelor

Type of Drug

Antidepressant.

Prescribed for

Depression with or without symptoms of anxiety.

General Information

Nortriptyline and other members of this group are effective in treating symptoms of depression. They can elevate your mood, increase physical activity and mental alertness, improve appetite and sleep patterns. These drugs are mild sedatives and therefore useful in treating mild forms of depression associated with anxiety. You should not expect instant results with this medicine: benefits are usually seen after 1 to 4 weeks. If symptoms are not affected after 6 to 8 weeks, contact your doctor. Occasionally this drug and other members of the group of drugs have been used in treating nighttime bed-wetting in young children, but they do not produce long-lasting relief and therapy with one of them for nighttime bed-wetting is of questionable value.

Cautions and Warnings

Do not take Nortriptyline if you are allergic or sensitive to this or other members of this class of drug: Doxepin, Protriptyline, Imipramine, Desipramine, and Amitriptyline. The drugs should not be used if you are recovering from a heart attack. Nortriptyline may be taken with caution if you have a history of epilepsy or other convulsive disorders, difficulty in urination, glaucoma, heart disease, or thyroid disease. Nortriptyline can interfere with your ability to perform tasks which require concentration, such as driving or operating machinery.

Pregnancy/Breast-feeding

This drug, like other antidepressants, crosses into your developing baby's circulation and may cause birth defects if taken during the first 3 months of pregnancy. There have been reports of newborn infants suffering from heart, breathing, and urinary problems after their mothers had taken an antidepressant of this type immediately before delivery. You should avoid taking this medication while pregnant.

Antidepressants of this type are known to pass into breast milk and may affect a breast-feeding infant, although this has not been proven. Nursing mothers should consider alternate feeding methods if taking this medicine.

Seniors

Older adults are more sensitive to the effects of this drug and often require a lower dose than a younger adult to do the same job. Follow your doctor's directions and report any side effects at once.

Possible Side Effects

Changes in blood pressure (both high and low), abnormal heart rates, heart attack, confusion (especially in elderly patients), hallucinations, disorientation, delusions, anxiety, restlessness, excitement, numbness and tingling in the extremities, lack of coordination, muscle spasms or tremors, seizures and/or convulsions, dry mouth, blurred vision, constipation, inability to urinate, rash, itching, sensitivity to bright light or sunlight, retention of fluids, fever, allergy, changes in composition of blood, nausea, vomiting, loss of appetite, stomach upset, diarrhea, enlargement of the breasts in males and females, increased or decreased sex drive, increased or decreased blood sugar.

Less common side effects: agitation, inability to sleep, nightmares, feeling of panic, development of a peculiar taste in the mouth, stomach cramps, black coloration of the tongue, yellowing eyes and/or skin, changes in liver function, increased or decreased weight, perspiration, flushing, frequent urination, drowsiness, dizziness, weakness, headache, loss of hair, nausea, not feeling well.

Drug Interactions

Interaction with monoamine oxidase (MAO) inhibitors can cause high fevers, convulsions, and occasionally death. Don't take MAO inhibitors until at least 2 weeks after Nortriptyline has been discontinued.

In patients who require concomitant use of Nortriptyline and an MAO inhibitor, close medical observation is warranted.

Nortriptyline interacts with Guanethidine and Clonidine, drugs used to treat high blood pressure: if your doctor prescribes Nortriptyline and you are taking medicine for high blood pressure, be sure to discuss this with him.

Nortriptyline increases the effects of barbiturates, tranquilizers, other sedative drugs, and alcohol. Don't drink alcoholic beverages if you take this medicine.

Taking Nortriptyline and thyroid medicine will enhance the effects of the thyroid medicine. The combination can cause abnormal heart rhythms. The combination of Nortriptyline and Reserpine may cause overstimulation.

Large doses of Vitamin C (Ascorbic Acid), oral contraceptives, or smoking can reduce the effect of Nortriptyline. Drugs such as Bicarbonate of Soda, Acetazolamide, Quinidine, or Procainamide will increase the effect of Nortriptyline. Ritalin and phenothiazine drugs such as Thorazine and Compazine block the metabolism of Nortriptyline, causing it to stay in the body longer. This can cause possible overdose.

The combination of Nortriptyline with large doses of the sleeping pill Ethchlorvynol has caused patients to experience passing delirium.

Food Interactions

Take this drug on an empty stomach. If it upsets your stomach you may take it with food.

Usual Dose

Adult: 25 milligrams 3 times per day, which may be increased to 150 milligrams per day if necessary. The medication must be tailored to the needs of the patient.

Adolescent and senior: lower doses are recommended—generally, 30 to 50 milligrams per day.

Overdosage

Symptoms are confusion, inability to concentrate, hallucinations, drowsiness, lowered body temperature, abnormal heart rate, heart failure, enlarged pupils of the eyes, convulsions, severely lowered blood pressure, stupor, and coma (as well as agitation, stiffening of body muscles, vomiting, and high fever). The patient should be taken to a hospital emergency room immediately. ALWAYS bring the medicine bottle.

Special Information

Avoid alcohol and other drugs that depress the nervous system while taking this antidepressant. Do not stop taking this medicine unless your doctor has specifically told you to do so. Abruptly stopping this medicine may cause nausea, headache, and a sickly feeling. This medicine can cause drowsiness, dizziness, and blurred vision. Be careful when driving or operating complicated machinery. Avoid exposure to the sun or sun lamps for long periods of time. Call your doctor if dry mouth, difficulty urinating, or excessive sedation develops.

If you take Nortriptyline several times a day and forget a dose, take it as soon as you remember. If it is almost time for your next regularly scheduled dose, skip the forgotten dose and continue with your regular schedule.

If you take it once a day at bedtime and forget, don't take it when you get up; go back to your regular schedule. Call your doctor if you skip 2 or more days of medication. Never take a double dose.

Brand Name

Novahistine Elixir

Ingredients

Chlorpheniramine Maleate
Phenylephrine Hydrochloride

Other Brand Names

Alamine Liquid
Dallergy D Syrup
Dihistine Elixir
Histor-D Syrup

Myhistine Elixir
Phenhist Elixir
Ru-Tuss Liquid

The following product contains the same ingredients at twice the concentration:

Tussanil Syrup

(Also available in generic form)

Type of Drug

Decongestant combination.

Prescribed for

Relief of cough, nasal congestion, runny nose, and other

symptoms associated with the common cold, viruses, or other upper respiratory diseases. The drug may also be used to treat allergies, asthma, ear infections, or sinus infections.

General Information

Novahistine Elixir is one of more than 100 products marketed to relieve the symptoms of the common cold and other upper respiratory infections. These products may contain medicine to relieve congestion, act as an antihistamine, relieve or suppress cough, and help you to cough up mucus. They may contain medicine for a single purpose, or may contain a combination of medicines. Some combinations leave out the antihistamine, the decongestant, or the expectorant. You must realize while taking Novahistine Elixir or similar products that these drugs are only for the relief of symptoms and will not treat the underlying problem, such as a cold virus or other infections. Novahistine Elixir and similar products may be obtained without a prescription.

Cautions and Warnings

This drug can cause you to become overly anxious and nervous and may interfere with your sleep. It should be avoided if you have diabetes, heart disease, high blood pressure, thyroid disease, glaucoma, or a prostate condition.

Pregnancy/Breast-feeding

This drug crosses into the blood circulation of a developing baby. It has not been found to cause birth defects. Pregnant women, or those who might become pregnant while taking this drug, should not take it without their doctor's approval. When the drug is considered essential by your doctor, the potential risk of taking the medicine must be carefully weighed against the benefit it might produce.

This drug passes into breast milk, but has caused no problems among breast-fed infants. You must consider the potential effect on the nursing infant if breast-feeding while taking this medicine.

Seniors

Older adults are more sensitive to the effects of this drug. Follow your doctor's directions and report any side effects at once.

Possible Side Effects

Dry mouth, blurred vision, difficulty passing urine, headache, palpitations, (possibly) constipation, nervousness, dizziness, restlessness, or even inability to sleep.

Drug Interactions

Taking Novahistine Elixir with MAO inhibitors can produce severe interaction. Consult your doctor first.

Novahistine Elixir contains Chlorpheniramine. Drinking alcoholic beverages while taking this drug may produce excessive drowsiness and/or sleepiness, or inability to concentrate.

Food Interactions

Take this medicine with food if it upsets your stomach.

Usual Dose

1 to 2 teaspoons every 4 to 6 hours.

Special Information

Take with a full glass of water to reduce stomach upset and help remove excessive mucus from the throat.

If you forget to take a dose of Novahistine, take it as soon as you remember. If it is almost time for your next regularly scheduled dose, skip the forgotten dose and continue with your regular schedule. Do not take a double dose.

Generic Name

Nystatin Vaginal Tablets

Brand Names

Mycostatin
Nilstat
O-V Statin

(Also available in generic form)

Type of Drug

Vaginal anti-infective.

Prescribed for

Fungal infection of the vagina.

General Information

Generally you will have relief of symptoms in 1 to 3 days. Nystatin Vaginal Tablets effectively control troublesome and unpleasant symptoms such as itching, inflammation, and discharge. In most cases, 2 weeks of therapy is sufficient for treatment, but prolonged treatment may be necessary. It is important that you continue using this medicine during menstruation. This drug has been used to prevent thrush or candida infection in the newborn infant by treating the mother for 3 to 6 weeks before her due date. At times the vaginal tablet has been used to treat candida infections of the mouth: the vaginal tablet is used as a lozenge and is allowed to be dissolved in the mouth and then swallowed.

O-V Statin is packaged in a "therapy pak." This package contains both vaginal and oral tablets for dual treatment when required.

Cautions and Warnings

Do not take this drug if you know you may be sensitive or allergic to Nystatin Vaginal Tablets.

Pregnancy/Breast-feeding

Pregnant and breast-feeding women may use this product with no restriction.

Seniors

Older adults may use this product with no restriction.

Possible Side Effects

Nystatin Vaginal Tablets are virtually nontoxic, and are generally well tolerated. The only side effect reported has been intravaginal irritation: If this occurs, discontinue the drug and contact your doctor.

Usual Dose

1 tablet inserted high in the vagina daily for 2 weeks.

Special Information

Do not stop taking the medication just because you begin to feel better. All the medication prescribed must be taken for at least 2 days after the relief of symptoms.

Some of the brands of Nystatin Vaginal Tablets require storage in the refrigerator. Ask your pharmacist for specific instructions.

If you forget a dose of Nystatin, take it as soon as you remember. If it is almost time for your next regularly scheduled dose, skip the one you forgot and continue with your regular schedule. Do not take a double dose.

Generic Name

Oral Contraceptives (Combination)

Brand Names

Low Dose Single-Phase Combinations (by estrogen content)

Brevicon	Lo/Ovral
Demulen 1/35	Modicon
Levlen	Nordette
Loestrin 1.5/30	Norinyl 1 + 35
Loestrin 1/20	Ortho-Novum 1/35
Loestrin Fe 1.5/30	Ovcon-35
Loestrin Fe 1/20	

Regular Dose Single-Phase Combinations (by estrogen content)

Demulen 1/50	Norlestrin Fe 2.5/50
Norinyl 1 + 50	Ortho-Novum 1/50
Norlestrin 1/50	Ovcon-50
Norlestrin 2.5/50	Ovral
Norlestrin Fe 1/50	

Low Dose Two-Phase Combinations (by estrogen content)

Ortho-Novum 10/11

Triple-Phase Combinations

Ortho-Novum 7/7/7	Tri-Norinyl
Tri Levlen	TriPhasil

Progestin-only Products (mini-pill)

Low Dose:	High Dose:
Ovrette	Micronor
	Nor-Q.D.

Type of Drug

Oral contraceptive.

Prescribed for

Prevention of pregnancy. Postcoital (morning after) pill, endometriosis, and cyclic withdrawal bleeding.

General Information

Oral contraceptives (the Pill) are synthetic hormones, either Progestin alone or Progestin combined with Estrogen. These hormones are similar to natural female hormones that control the menstrual cycle and prepare a woman's body to accept a fertilized egg. The natural hormones cannot be used as contraceptives because very large doses would be needed. Once a fertilized egg is accepted (implanted in the womb) no more eggs may be released from the ovaries until the pregnancy is over. Oral contraceptives interfere with these natural processes; they may not allow sperm to reach the unfertilized egg; not allow the acceptance of a fertilized egg and/or not allow ovulation (the release of an unfertilized egg).

Oral contraceptives provide a very high-rated protection from pregnancy. They are from 97 to 99 percent effective, depending upon which product is used and your compliance with taking the Pill regularly. Using no contraceptive at all is only about 20 to 40 percent effective.

The many different combination products available contain different amounts of Estrogen and Progestin. Products containing the least amount of Estrogen may be less effective in some women than others. In general, the product that contains the lowest amount of hormones but is effective and keeps side effects to a minimum is preferred.

The mini-pill, Progestin-only products, may cause irregular menstrual cycles and may be less effective than combination products. Mini-pills may be used in older women or women who should avoid Estrogens. (See "Cautions and Warnings.")

Single-phase products provide a fixed amount of Estrogen and Progestin throughout the entire pill cycle.

In the two-phase combination, the amount of Progestin first increases and then decreases. This is supposed to allow normal changes to take place in the uterus. The amount of Estrogen remains at a steady low level throughout the cycle. The newest combination products are triple-phase in design. Throughout the cycle, the Estrogen portion remains the same, but the Progestin changes to create a wave pattern in three parts. The three-phase products are supposed to act like normal hormones and reduce breakthrough bleeding. Breakthrough bleeding may be seen with the older combination products beginning with the eighth through sixteenth days. The amount of Estrogen in these new products is considered to be in the low category.

Every woman taking or thinking of taking the Pill should be fully aware of the problems associated with this type of contraception. The highest risk is in women over 35 who smoke and have high blood pressure.

Cautions and Warnings

You should not use oral contraceptives if you have or have had blood clots of the veins or arteries, have a disease affecting blood coagulation, have known or suspected cancer of the breast or sex organs, irregular or scanty menstrual periods, or suspect you are pregnant.

Women who should avoid Estrogen-containing products are those with a history of headaches, high blood pressure, and varicose veins. Older women and women who have experienced side effects from Estrogen also should not take Estrogen products.

Pregnancy/Breast-feeding

This drug is known to cause birth defects or interfere with your baby's development. It is not considered safe for use during pregnancy.

Oral contraceptives reduce the amount of breast milk you make and can affect its quality. Some of the hormone passes into your breast milk, but the effect on a nursing infant is not known. Do not breast-feed while you are taking oral contraceptives.

Possible Side Effects

Nausea, abdominal cramps, bloating, vaginal bleeding, change in menstrual flow, possible infertility after coming off the Pill, breast tenderness, weight change, headaches, rash, vaginal itching and burning, general vaginal infection, nervousness, dizziness, formation of eye cataract, changes in sex drive, changes in appetite, loss of hair.

Rare side effects: Women who take oral contraceptives are more likely to develop several serious conditions including the formation of blood clots in the deep veins, stroke, heart attack, liver cancer, gallbladder disease, and high blood pressure. Women who smoke cigarettes are much more likely to develop some of these adverse effects.

Drug Interactions

Interaction with Rifampin decreases the effectiveness of oral contraceptives. The same may be true of barbiturates, Phenylbutazone, Phenytoin, Ampicillin, Neomycin, Penicillin V, Tetracycline, Chloramphenicol, sulfa drugs, Nitrofurantoin, tranquilizers, and antimigraine medication.

Another interaction reduces the effect of anticoagulant (blood-thinning) drugs. Discuss this with your doctor.

The Pill can also increase blood cholesterol (fat), and can interfere with blood tests for thyroid function and blood sugar.

Usual Dose

The first day of bleeding is the first day of the menstrual cycle. At the start, 1 tablet, beginning on the fifth day of the menstrual cycle, is taken every day for 20 to 21 days according to the number of contraceptive tablets supplied by the manufacturer. If 7 days after taking the last tablet menstrual flow has not begun, begin the next month's cycle of pills. Progestin-only mini-pills are taken every day, 365 days a year.

Overdosage

Overdosage may cause nausea and withdrawal bleeding in adult females. Accidental overdosage in children who take their mother's pills has not shown serious adverse effects.

Special Information

Some manufacturers have included 7 blank or 7 iron pills in their packages, to be taken on days when the Pill is not taken. These pills have the number 28 as part of the brand name and a pill should be taken every day.

If you forget to take the Pill for 1 day, take 2 pills the following day. If you miss 2 consecutive days, take 2 pills for the next 2 days. Then continue to take 1 pill daily. If you miss 3 consecutive days, don't take any more pills for the next 7 days and use another form of contraception; then start a new cycle.

Forgetting to take the Pill reduces your protection: if you keep forgetting to take it, you should consider other means of birth control.

All oral contraceptive prescriptions must come with a "patient package insert" for you to read. It gives detailed information about the drug and is required by federal law.

Generic Name

Oxacillin Sodium

Brand Names

Bactocill
Prostaphlin

(Also available in generic form)

Type of Drug

Broad-spectrum antibiotic.

Prescribed for

Gram-positive bacterial infections. Gram-positive bacteria (pneumococci, streptococci, and staphylococci) are organisms which usually cause diseases such as pneumonia, infections of the tonsils and throat, venereal disease, meningitis (infection of the spinal column), and septicemia (infection of the bloodstream). This drug is best used to treat infections resistant to Penicillin, although it may be used as initial treatment for some patients.

General Information

Penicillin-type antibiotics fight infection by killing bacteria. They do this by destroying the cell wall of invading bacteria. Other antibiotics simply prevent bacteria from reproducing. Many infections can be treated by almost any member of this family, but some infections can only be treated by certain penicillin-type antibiotics.

Penicillins cannot treat against a cold, flu, or any virus infection, and should never be taken unless prescribed by a doctor for a specific illness. Always take your antibiotic exactly according to your doctor's directions for use, including the number of pills to take every day and the number of days to take the medicine. If you do not follow directions, you may not get the antibiotic's full benefit.

Cautions and Warnings

Do not take Oxacillin if you have a known history of allergy to Penicillin. The drugs are similar. The most common allergic reaction to Oxacillin Sodium, as well as to the other penicillins, is a hivelike rash over the body with itching and redness. It is important to tell your doctor if you have ever taken Oxacillin Sodium or penicillins before and if you have experienced any adverse reaction to the drug such as rash, itching, or difficulty in breathing.

Pregnancy/Breast-feeding

Oxacillin has not caused birth defects. Be sure to check with your doctor before taking this or any other medicine. Oxacillin passes into breast milk and may affect a nursing infant.

Seniors

Seniors may take this medicine without special precaution.

Possible Side Effects

Common: stomach upset, nausea, vomiting, diarrhea, possible rash. Less common: hairy tongue, itching or irritation around the anus and/or vagina. If these symptoms occur, contact your doctor immediately.

Drug Interactions

The effect of Oxacillin Sodium can be significantly reduced

when it is taken with other antibiotics. Consult your doctor if you are taking both during the same course of therapy. Otherwise, Oxacillin Sodium is generally free of interactions with other medications.

Food Interactions

To ensure the maximum effect, you should take the medication on an empty stomach, either 1 hour before or 2 hours after meals.

Usual Dose

Adult and child (88 pounds or more): 500 to 1000 milligrams every 4 to 6 hours.

Child (less than 88 pounds): 20 to 40 milligrams per pound of body weight per day in divided doses.

This drug is frequently used in higher doses when given intravenously. It must be given intravenously for serious infections because of the unusually high doses required.

Overdosage

Oxacillin overdose is unlikely but can result in diarrhea or upset stomach.

Special Information

Oxacillin capsules can be stored at room temperature. The liquid requires refrigeration. Do not take this medicine after the expiration date on the label. Be sure to take this medicine exactly according to your doctor's directions.

Stop taking the medicine and call your doctor if any of the following side effects develop: skin rash, hives, itching, wheezing. Other side effects that demand your doctor's attention are: blood in the urine, passage of large amounts of light-colored urine, swelling of the face or ankles, trouble breathing, unusual weakness or tiredness. If you miss a dose of Oxacillin, take it as soon as possible. If it is almost time for your next dose and you take the medicine twice a day, space the next two doses 5 to 6 hours apart and then go back to your regular schedule.

If it is almost time for your next dose and you take the medicine 3 or more times a day, space the missed dose and your next dose by 2 to 4 hours and then continue with your regular schedule.

Generic Name

Oxazepam

Brand Name

Serax

(Also available in generic form)

Type of Drug

Tranquilizer.

Prescribed for

Relief of symptoms of anxiety, tension, fatigue, or agitation.

General Information

Oxazepam is a member of the group of drugs known as benzodiazepines. These drugs are used as either antianxiety agents, anticonvulsants, or sedatives (sleeping pills). They exert their effects by relaxing the large skeletal muscles and by a direct effect on the brain. In doing so, they can relax you and make you either more tranquil or sleepier, depending on the drug and how much you use. Many doctors prefer Oxazepam and the other members of this class to other drugs that can be used for the same effect. Their reason is that the benzodiazepines tend to be safer, have fewer side effects, and are usually as, if not more, effective.

These drugs are generally used in any situation where they can be a useful adjunct.

Benzodiazepine tranquilizing drugs can be abused if taken for long periods of time and it is possible to develop withdrawal symptoms if you discontinue the therapy abruptly. Withdrawal symptoms include convulsions, tremor, muscle cramps, stomach cramps, vomiting, and sweating.

Cautions and Warnings

Do not take Oxazepam if you know you are sensitive or allergic to this drug or other benzodiazepines such as Chlordiazepoxide, Prazepam, Clorazepate, Diazepam, Lorazepam, Flurazepam, and Clonazepam.

Oxazepam and other members of this drug group may

aggravate narrow-angle glaucoma, but if you have open-angle glaucoma you may take the drugs. In any case, check this information with your doctor. Oxazepam can cause tiredness, drowsiness, inability to concentrate, or similar symptoms. Be careful if you are driving, operating machinery, or performing other activities which require concentration.

Pregnancy/Breast-feeding

Do not take Oxazepam if you are planning to become pregnant and avoid taking it if you are pregnant or nursing. An increased chance of birth defects has not been seen; however, there is a risk factor to be considered. Other drugs similar to Oxazepam have been shown to cause birth defects.

The baby may become dependent on Oxazepam if it is used continually during pregnancy. If used during the last weeks of pregnancy or during breast-feeding, the baby may be overly tired, be short of breath, or have a low heartbeat.

Use during labor may cause weakness in the newborn.

Seniors

Older adults are more sensitive to the effects of this drug, especially dizziness and drowsiness. They should closely follow their doctor's directions and report any side effects at once.

Possible Side Effects

Most common: mild drowsiness during the first few days of therapy, especially in the elderly or debilitated. If drowsiness persists, contact your doctor.

Less common side effects: confusion, depression, lethargy, disorientation, headache, lack of activity, slurred speech, stupor, dizziness, tremor, constipation, dry mouth, nausea, inability to control urination, changes in sex drive, irregular menstrual cycle, changes in heart rhythm, lowered blood pressure, retention of fluids, blurred or double vision, itching, rash, hiccups, nervousness, inability to fall asleep, (occasional) liver dysfunction. If you experience any of these reactions stop taking the medicine and contact your doctor immediately.

Drug Interactions

Oxazepam is a central nervous system depressant. Avoid alcohol, tranquilizers, narcotics, sleeping pills, barbiturates,

MAO inhibitors, antihistamines, and other medicines used to relieve depression.

Food Interactions

Oxazepam is best taken on an empty stomach, but may be taken with food.

Usual Dose

Adult: 10 to 120 milligrams per day as individualized for maximum benefit, depending on symptoms and response to treatment, which may require a dose outside the range given.

Senior: usually requires less of the drug to control anxiety and tension.

Overdosage

Symptoms are confusion, sleep or sleepiness, lack of response to pain such as a pin stick, shallow breathing, lowered blood pressure, and coma. The patient should be taken to a hospital emergency room immediately. ALWAYS bring the medicine bottle.

Special Information

Do not drink alcoholic beverages while taking Oxazepam. Sleeping pills, narcotics, barbiturates, other tranquilizers, or other drugs which produce nervous system depression should be used with caution while taking Oxazepam.

If you forget to take a dose of Oxazepam and you remember within about an hour of your regular time, take it right away. If you do not remember until later, skip the forgotten dose and go back to your regular schedule. Do not take a double dose.

Generic Name

Oxprenolol

Brand Names

Slow-Trasicor
Trasicor

Type of Drug

Beta-adrenergic blocker.

Prescribed for

High blood pressure, angina pains, abnormal heart rhythms. It may also be prescribed by your doctor to treat anxiety, tremors, overactive thyroid, and mitral valve prolapse, and to prevent heart attacks in people who have already had one.

General Information

Oxprenolol is a relatively weak beta blocker and is given in larger doses than some other beta-blocking drugs available in the United States. Otherwise, Oxprenolol is remarkably similar to other beta blockers in its ability to lower blood pressure and treat abnormal heart rhythms and other conditions, and it may cause fewer side effects because of the drug's mild stimulating effect.

Cautions and Warnings

You should be cautious about taking Oxprenolol if you have asthma, severe heart failure, very slow heart rate or heart block because the drug can worsen these conditions. People with angina who take Oxprenolol for high blood pressure should have their drug dosage reduced gradually over 1 to 2 weeks rather than suddenly discontinued. This will avoid possible aggravation of the angina. Oxprenolol should be used with caution if you have liver disease because your ability to eliminate the drug from your body will be impaired.

Pregnancy/Breast-feeding

Animal studies in which rats and rabbits were given amounts of medicine greater than normal human doses revealed no adverse effects of Oxprenolol on the developing baby. However, Oxprenolol should be avoided by pregnant women or women who might become pregnant while taking it. When the drug is considered essential by your doctor, the potential risk of taking the medicine must be carefully weighed against the benefit it might produce. Small amounts of Oxprenolol may pass into your breast milk. Nursing mothers taking this drug must observe their infants for possible drug-related side effects.

Seniors

Senior citizens may be more or less sensitive to the effects of Oxprenolol, and may need more or less of the drug than younger adults to achieve the same effect. This means that your dosage of Oxprenolol must be adjusted to your individual needs by your doctor. Seniors may be more likely to suffer from cold hands and feet and reduced body temperature, chest pains, a general feeling of ill health, sudden difficulty breathing, sweating, or changes in heartbeat because of this medicine.

Possible Side Effects

Oxprenolol side effects are relatively uncommon, usually develop early in the course of treatment, are relatively mild, and are rarely a reason to stop taking the medication. Side effects increase with increasing dosage and include dizziness, tingling of the scalp, nausea, vomiting, upset stomach, taste distortion, fatigue, sweating, male impotence, urinary difficulty, diarrhea, bile duct blockage, breathing difficulty, bronchial spasms, muscle weakness, cramps, dry eyes, blurred vision, skin rash, hair loss, and facial swelling. Like other beta blockers, Oxprenolol can cause mental depression, confusion, disorientation, short-term memory loss, and emotional instability.

Rare side effects include aggravation of lupus erythematosus (a disease of the body's connective tissues), stuffy nose, chest pains, back or joint pains, colitis, drug allergy (fever, sore throat), and unusual bleeding or bruising.

Drug Interactions

Beta-blocking drugs may interact with surgical anesthetics to increase the risk of heart problems during surgery. Some

anesthesiologists recommend stopping your beta blocker
gradually 2 days before surgery.

Oxprenolol may interfere with the normal signs of low
blood sugar and can interfere with the action of oral antidiabetes medicines.

Taking Oxprenolol together with Aspirin-containing drugs,
Indomethacin, or Sulfinpyrazone can interfere with its blood-
pressure-lowering effect.

The effects of Oxprenolol may be increased by Molindone,
phenothiazine antipsychotic medicines with other antihypertensives like Clonidine, Diazoxide, Nifedipine, or Reserpine,
or with other drugs that can reduce blood pressure, like
Nitroglycerin.

Cimetidine increases the amount of Oxprenolol absorbed
into the bloodstream from oral tablets.

Oxprenolol may interfere with the effectiveness of some
anti-asthma drugs, especially Ephedrine and Isoproterenol,
and with Theophylline or Aminophylline.

The combination of Oxprenolol and Phenytoin or digitalis
drugs can result in excessive slowing of the heart and possible heart block.

Estrogen drugs can interfere with the blood-pressure-
lowering effect of Oxprenolol.

Food Interactions

Take this medicine with food if it upsets your stomach.

Usual Dose

Starting dose, 60 milligrams per day, taken all at once or in 3
divided doses. The daily dose may be gradually increased.
Maintenance dose, 60 to 480 milligrams per day.

Overdosage

Symptoms are changes in heartbeat (unusually slow, unusually fast, or irregular), severe dizziness or fainting, difficulty
breathing, bluish-colored fingernails or palms of the hands,
and seizures.

Special Information

Oxprenolol is meant to be taken on a continuing basis. Do
not stop taking it unless directed to do so by your doctor.
Possible side effects of abrupt withdrawal of Oxprenolol are:

chest pain, difficulty breathing, sweating, and unusually fast or irregular heartbeat.

Call your doctor at once if any of the following symptoms develop: back or joint pains, difficulty breathing, cold hands or feet, depression, skin rash, changes in heartbeat.

Call your doctor only if the following side effects persist or are bothersome: anxiety, diarrhea, constipation, sexual impotence, mild dizziness, headache, itching, nausea or vomiting, nightmares or vivid dreams, upset stomach, trouble sleeping, stuffed nose, frequent urination, unusual tiredness or weakness.

If you forget to take a dose of Oxprenolol, take it as soon as possible. However, if it is within 4 hours of your next dose (8 hours if you take the medicine once a day), skip the forgotten dose and go back to your regular schedule. Do not take a double dose.

Generic Name

Oxtriphylline

Brand Names

Choledyl
Choledyl SA

(Also available in generic form)

Type of Drug

Xanthine bronchodilator.

Prescribed for

Relief of bronchial asthma and spasms of bronchial muscles associated with emphysema, bronchitis, and other diseases.

General Information

Oxtriphylline is one of several drugs known as xanthine derivatives which are the mainstay of therapy for bronchial asthma and similar diseases. Other members of this group include Aminophylline, Dyphylline, and Theophylline. Although the dosage for each of these drugs is different, they all work by relaxing bronchial muscles and helping reverse spasms in these muscles.

Cautions and Warnings

Do not use this drug if you are allergic or sensitive to it or to any related drug, such as Aminophylline. If you have a stomach ulcer or heart disease, you should use this drug with caution.

Pregnancy/Breast-feeding

This drug passes into the circulation of the developing baby. It does not cause birth defects but may result in dangerous drug levels in the infant's bloodstream. Babies born of mothers taking this medication may be nervous, jittery, and irritable, and may gag and vomit when fed. Women who must use this medication to control asthma or other conditions should talk with their doctor about the relative risks of using this medication and the benefits it will produce for them.

This medication passes into breast milk and may cause a nursing infant to have difficulty sleeping and be nervous or irritable.

Seniors

Older adults may take longer to clear this drug from their bodies than younger adults. Older adults with heart failure or other cardiac conditions, chronic lung disease, a virus infection with fever, or reduced liver function may require a lower dosage of this medication to account for the clearance effect.

Possible Side Effects

Possible side effects from Oxtriphylline or other xanthine derivatives are nausea, vomiting, stomach pain, diarrhea, irritability, restlessness, difficulty sleeping, excitability, muscle twitching or spasms, heart palpitations, other unusual heart rates, low blood pressure, rapid breathing, and local irritation (particularly if a suppository is used).

Infrequent: vomiting blood, fever, headache, dehydration.

Drug Interactions

Taking Oxtriphylline at the same time as another xanthine

derivative may increase side effects. Don't do it except under the direct care of a doctor.

Oxtriphylline is often given in combination with a stimulant drug such as Ephedrine. Such combinations can cause excessive stimulation and should be used only as specifically directed by your doctor.

Some reports have indicated that combining Erythromycin and Oxtriphylline will give you higher blood levels of Oxtriphylline. Remember that higher blood levels mean the possibility of more side effects. Other drugs that may increase blood levels are: Cimetidine flu vaccine and Allopurinol. Cigarette smoking may decrease this drug's effectiveness.

Food Interactions

Take on an empty stomach, at least 1 hour before or 2 hours after meals; but occasional mild stomach upset can be minimized by taking the dose with some food (note if you do this, a reduced amount of drug will be absorbed into your bloodstream).

The way Oxtriphylline acts in your body may be influenced by your diet. Charcoal-broiled beef, for example, may cause a greater amount of Oxtriphylline to be eliminated in the urine. Therefore you may experience a decreased effect of the drug. This effect also occurs in people whose diet is low in carbohydrates and high in protein or in people who smoke. Caffeine (also a xanthine derivative) may add to the side effects of Oxtriphylline. It is recommended that you avoid large amounts of caffeine-containing foods such as coffee, tea, cocoa, cola, or chocolate.

Usual Dose

Adult: 200 milligrams 4 times per day. SA (sustained action): 400 to 600 milligrams every 12 hours.

Child (age 2 to 12): 100 milligrams for every 60 pounds of body weight taken four times a day.

Note: Each 100 milligrams of Oxtriphylline is equal to 64 milligrams of Theophylline in potency.

Overdosage

The first symptoms are loss of appetite, nausea, vomiting, difficulty sleeping, and restlessness, followed by unusual behavior patterns, frequent vomiting, and extreme thirst, with delirium, convulsions, very high temperature, and collapse. These serious toxic symptoms are rarely experienced after overdose by mouth, which produces loss of appetite, nausea, vomiting, and stimulation. The overdosed patient should be taken to a hospital emergency room where proper treatment can be given. ALWAYS bring the medicine bottle.

Special Information

Oxtriphylline and the other xanthine drugs are intended to be taken around the clock to maintain constant levels in your body. If you miss a dose, take it as soon as you can. If it is almost time for your next dose, skip the missed dose and go back to your usual dose schedule.

Generic Name

Oxybutinin

Brand Name

Ditropan

Type of Drug

Antispasmodic, anticholinergic.

Prescribed for

Excessive urination in people with bladder conditions.

General Information

Oxybutinin directly affects the smooth muscle that controls the opening and closing of the bladder. It is 4 to 10 times more potent an antispasmodic than Atropine, but has only one-fifth the anticholinergic effect of that drug. This is important because the anticholinergic properties are most responsible for the drug's side effects.

Cautions and Warnings

Do not take Oxybutinin if you are allergic to it or have developed itching or rash while taking it in the past, as these symptoms may be mild signs of drug allergy.

Oxybutinin should be used with caution if you have glau-coma, intestinal obstruction, poor intestinal function, mega-colon, severe or ulcerative colitis, myasthenia, or an unstable cardiovascular status.

Oxybutinin should be used with caution if you have liver or kidney disease. It may worsen symptoms of an overactive thyroid gland, coronary heart disease, abnormal heart rhythm, rapid heartbeat, high blood pressure, and prostate disease. Oxybutinin may worsen the symptoms of hiatus hernia.

Pregnancy/Breast-feeding

The safety of Oxybutinin in pregnant women is not known. It should only be used when the benefits outweigh the possi-ble damage the drug might do.

It is not known if Oxybutinin passes into breast milk. Nurs-ing mothers should use another feeding method if they must take this drug.

Seniors

Older adults may be more susceptible to the side effects of Oxybutinin and should take it with caution. Report anything unusual to your doctor at once.

Possible Side Effects

Most common: Dry mouth, decreased sweating, constipation.

Other side effects include difficulty urinating, blurred vision, widening of the pupils of your eyes, worsening of glaucoma, palpitations, drowsiness, sleeplessness, weakness, nausea, vomiting, constipation, a bloated feeling, male impotence, reduced production of breast milk (women), itching and rash.

Drug Interactions

Oxybutinin may interact with other anticholinergic drugs, including some antihistamines, to produce excessive dry mouth or blurred vision.

It may increase the effects of nervous system depressants such as tranquilizers, antihistamines, barbiturates, pain med-icines, or anticonvulsants.

Food Interactions

This drug is best taken on an empty stomach, but may be taken with food or milk if it upsets your stomach.

Usual Dose

10 to 20 milligrams per day in divided doses.

Overdosage

The result of Oxybutinin overdose is exaggerated side effects. Overdose victims should be taken to a hospital emergency room at once. ALWAYS remember to bring the prescription bottle with you.

Special Information

Avoid alcohol and other nervous system depressants while taking Oxybutinin, since the combination will add to the depressant effect.

Oxybutinin may interfere with your ability to concentrate. Take care while doing anything that requires a lot of concentration, including driving a car. Blurred vision, another effect of Oxybutinin, may also make it difficult for you to drive.

Your eyes may become more sensitive to bright light while taking Oxybutinin. You may compensate for this by wearing sunglasses or protective lenses.

Dry mouth may be treated with sugarless gum or candy or with ice chips. Excessive dryness of the mouth can lead to tooth decay and should be brought to your dentist's attention if it lasts for more than 2 weeks.

Generic Name

Oxiconazole

Brand Name

Oxistat

Type of Drug

Antifungal.

Prescribed for

Fungus infections of the skin.

General Information

Oxiconazole is a general purpose antifungal product. It works by interfering with the cell membrane of the fungal organism. Oxiconazole penetrates the skin after application, but little is absorbed into the bloodstream.

Cautions and Warnings

Do not take this product if you are allergic to Oxiconazole or any other ingredient in Oxistat Cream.

Large doses of Oxiconazole have caused reduced fertility in lab animals. This should be taken into account when considering the use of this product, although there is no evidence that Oxiconazole reduces fertility in women.

Pregnancy/Breast-feeding

Pregnant animals fed doses of approximately 1 milligram per pound of body weight per day showed no damage to the developing fetus. However, Oxiconazole has not been tested on pregnant women and should be used by pregnant women only if it is absolutely necessary.

Nursing mothers should avoid using this drug because significant amounts of Oxiconazole may pass into breast milk.

Seniors

Seniors may use Oxiconazole without special precautions.

Possible Side Effects

The most common side effect of Oxiconazole is itching and irritation of the skin after application.

Other side effects include burning, irritation, swelling, cracking, and redness of the skin.

Drug Interactions

None known.

Food Interactions

None known.

Usual Dose

Oxiconazole should be applied to affected areas every evening for 2 weeks to a month, depending on the type of fungus present.

Overdosage

Oxiconazole is not intended to be taken internally. People who swallow Oxiconazole should be taken to a hospital emergency room for evaluation and treatment.

Special Information

Oxiconazole is meant only for application to the skin. Do not put this product into the eyes or swallow it.

If redness or irritation develops, stop using the product at once and notify your doctor.

If you forget to apply a dose of Oxiconazole, apply it as soon as you remember. If it is almost time for your next dose, skip the forgotten dose and continue with your regular schedule.

Generic Name

Oxymetazoline Hydrochloride

Brand Names

Afrin (nose drops and spray)
Allerest 12 Hour Nasal (spray)
Coricidin Nasal Mist (spray)
Dristan Long Lasting (nose spray)
Duramist Plus (nose spray)
Duration (nose spray)
4 Way Long Acting (nose spray)

NASAL (nose drops and spray)
Neo-Synephrine 12 Hour (nose drops and spray)
Nostrilla (nose spray)
NTZ Long Acting
Sinarest 12-hour (nose spray)
Sinex Long-Acting (nose spray)

(Also available in generic form)

Type of Drug

Nasal decongestant.

Prescribed for

Relief of stuffy nose secondary to allergy, the common cold, or any other cause.

Cautions and Warnings

Do not use Oxymetazoline Hydrochloride if you are taking an MAO inhibitor or antidepressant, if you are allergic to Oxymetazoline or any similar preparations, or if you have glaucoma, high blood pressure, heart disease, chest pains, thyroid disease, or diabetes.

Pregnancy/Breast-feeding

This drug crosses into the blood circulation of a developing baby. It has not been found to cause birth defects. Pregnant women, or those who might become pregnant while taking this drug, should not take it without their doctor's approval. When the drug is considered essential by your doctor, the potential risk of taking the medicine must be carefully weighed against the benefit it might produce.

This drug passes into breast milk, but has caused no problems among breast-fed infants. You must consider the potential effect on the nursing infant if breast-feeding while taking this medicine.

Seniors

Older adults are more sensitive to the effects of this drug. Follow your doctor's directions and report any side effects at once.

Possible Side Effects

Common side effects are burning, stinging, dryness of the mucosa inside the nose, and sneezing.

Less commonly, Oxymetazoline Hydrochloride may produce abnormal heart rhythms, increase in blood pressure, headache, feeling of light-headedness, nervousness, difficulty in sleeping, blurred vision, and some drowsiness or lethargy.

Adverse effects are more likely to occur in the elderly.

Drug Interactions

Oxymetazoline Hydrochloride is a stimulant drug which will increase the effect of any other stimulant. It may block some of the effect of depressant drugs such as tranquilizers or sleeping medications, but this is unusual if recommended doses are observed.

Interaction with MAO inhibitor drugs may cause severe stimulation.

Food Interactions

Take this medicine with food if it upsets your stomach.

Usual Dose

Adult and child (age 6 and over): 2 to 3 drops or sprays of the (generally 0.05 percent) solution in each nostril no more than twice a day.

Child (age 2 to 5): 2 to 3 drops of half-strength (0.025 percent) solution in each nostril no more than twice a day.

Overdosage

Symptoms are sedation, desire to go to sleep, possible coma—or with extreme overdosage, high blood pressure, low heart rate, other effects on the heart, with even collapse of the cardiovascular system, and depressed breathing. The patient should be taken to a hospital emergency room immediately, where proper care can be provided. ALWAYS bring the medicine bottle.

Special Information

Use this drug exactly as directed—not more frequently. If Oxymetazoline Hydrochloride is used more than twice a day or in excessive quantities, "rebound congestion" will occur. The nose will produce excessive amounts of mucus in reaction to the medication, which may lead to overdosage and possible toxicity.

If you forget to take a dose of Oxymetazoline Hydrochloride, take it as soon as you remember. If it is almost time for your next regularly scheduled dose, skip the forgotten dose and continue with your regular schedule. Do not take a double dose.

Generic Name

Oxyphenbutazone

Brand Name

Oxalid

(Also available in generic form)

Type of Drug

Anti-inflammatory agent.

Prescribed for

Local inflammation related to gout, rheumatoid arthritis, osteoarthritis, painful shoulder such as bursitis or arthritis of a joint, or other inflammatory diseases which cause pain that cannot be controlled by Aspirin, and when severe disability, because of the inflammation, is not relieved by usual treatment.

General Information

This drug should never be taken without strict medical supervision. Oxyphenbutazone should be used only for the short-term relief of pain due to inflammation of muscles, tendons, and joint area.

Oxyphenbutazone and its sister drug Phenylbutazone are toxic and dangerous and should only be used when absolutely necessary. The list of potential side effects is long. Therefore, any change in habits or unusual effect which may be even remotely connected with the use of these drugs should be reported immediately to your doctor.

Cautions and Warnings

You should not take Oxyphenbutazone if you have a history of symptoms associated with gastrointestinal inflammation or ulcer, including severe, recurrent, or persistent upset stomach. This drug is not a simple pain reliever and should never be taken casually. It should not be prescribed before a careful and detailed history, plus physical and laboratory tests, have been completed by the doctor. If your problem can be treated by a less toxic drug such as Aspirin, use that first and try to stay away from Oxyphenbutazone. Never take more than the recommended dosage: this would lead to toxic effects. If you have blurred vision, fever, rash, sore throat, sores in the mouth, upset stomach or pain in the stomach, feeling of weakness, bloody, black, or tarry stool, water retention, or a significant or sudden weight gain, report this to the doctor immediately. In addition, stop taking the drug. If the drug is not effective after 1 week, stop taking it. Use Oxyphenbutazone with caution and in consultation with a doctor if you are a pregnant or lactating woman.

Pregnancy/Breast-feeding

This drug crosses into the blood circulation of a developing baby. It is not recommended for use late in pregnancy because of the possibility that the drug will affect your developing baby's heart. It may delay or prolong your labor. Studies in laboratory animals have shown that this medication produces birth defects. Pregnant women, or those who might become pregnant while taking this drug, should not take it without their doctor's approval. When the drug is considered essential by your doctor, the potential risk of taking the medicine must be carefully weighed against the benefit it might produce.

This drug passes into breast milk and should not be taken if you are nursing an infant. The drug can cause severe blood problems in a nursing infant. Use an alternate feeding method if you must take this medicine.

Seniors

Seniors are more likely to develop the blood, stomach, kidney, and liver side effects of this drug because of a general reduction in kidney function. People 60 years of age and older should be limited to short periods of treatment (no more than 1 week, if possible) because of the possibility of severe, possibly fatal reactions.

Some doctors recommend that drug dosage be reduced by ½ in people age 60 and older.

Possible Side Effects

Most common: stomach upset, drowsiness, water retention.
Infrequent: acute gastric or duodenal ulcer, ulceration or

perforation of the large bowel, bleeding from the stomach, anemia, stomach pain, vomiting, vomiting of blood, nausea, diarrhea, changes in the components of the blood, water retention, disruption of normal chemical balance of the body. This drug can cause fatal or nonfatal hepatitis, black-and-blue marks on the skin, serum sickness, drug allergy serious enough to cause shock, itching, serious rashes, fever, and signs of arthritis. It has been known to cause kidney effects including bleeding and kidney stones. Oxyphenbutazone may be a cause of heart disease, high blood pressure, blurred vision, bleeding in the back of the eye, detachment of a retina, hearing loss, high blood sugar, thyroid disease, agitation, confusion, or lethargy.

Drug Interactions

Oxyphenbutazone increases the effects of blood-thinning drugs, Phenytoin, Insulin, and oral antidiabetic agents. If you are taking any of these drugs, discuss this matter with your doctor immediately.

Food Interactions

Oxyphenbutazone causes stomach upset in many patients; take your dose with food or antacids, and if stomach pain continues, notify your doctor.

Usual Dose

Adult and child (age 14 years or over): depending upon the condition being treated, 300 to 600 milligrams per day in 3 to 4 equal doses for 7 days. If dose is effective it can then be reduced to 100 to 400 milligrams per day, depending on the condition being treated.

Senior: to be given for only 7 days because of high risk of severe reactions. Not to be given to senile patients.

Child (under age 14): not recommended.

Overdosage

Symptoms are upper stomach pain, nausea, vomiting, convulsions, euphoria, depression, headache, hallucinations, giddiness, dizziness, coma, rapid breathing rate, and insomnia or sleeplessness. Contact your doctor immediately. If you must go to a hospital emergency room, ALWAYS bring the medicine bottle.

Special Information

Oxyphenbutazone is a central nervous system depressant that can cause drowsiness and tiredness: be careful when driving or operating other equipment, and avoid large quantities of alcoholic beverages, which will aggravate the situation.

If you take Oxyphenbutazone once or twice a day and forget to take a dose, take it as soon as you remember. If it is almost time for your next regularly scheduled dose, skip the one you forgot and continue with your regular schedule. Do not take a double dose.

If you take Oxyphenbutazone 3 or 4 times a day and forget to take a dose, and you remember within about an hour of your regular time, take it right away. If you do not remember until later, skip the forgotten dose and go back to your regular schedule. Do not take a double dose.

Brand Name

Parafon Forte DSC

Ingredients

Acetaminophen
Chlorzoxazone

Other Brand Names

Blanex	Lobac
Chlorofon-F	Muslax
Chlorzone Forte	Paracet Forte
Flexaphen	Polyflex
Flexin	Zoxaphen

(Also available in generic form)

Type of Drug

Skeletal muscle relaxant.

Prescribed for

Relief of pain and spasm of muscular conditions, including lower back pain, strains, sprains, or muscle bruises.

General Information

Parafon Forte DSC is one of several drugs used to treat the aches and pains associated with muscle aches, strains, or a bad back. It gives only temporary relief and is not a substitute for other types of therapy such as rest, surgery, or physical therapy.

Chlorzoxazone acts primarily at the spinal cord level and on areas of the brain. It does not directly relax tense muscles.

A half-strength tablet is also available in generic form or the brand Paraflex.

Cautions and Warnings

Do not take Parafon Forte DSC if you are allergic to it. Do not take more than the exact amount of medication prescribed.

Pregnancy/Breast-feeding

This drug crosses into the blood circulation of a developing baby. It has not been found to cause birth defects. Pregnant women, or those who might become pregnant while taking this drug, should not take it without their doctor's approval. When the drug is considered essential by your doctor, the potential risk of taking the medicine must be carefully weighed against the benefit it might produce.

This drug passes into breast milk, but has caused no problems among breast-fed infants. You must consider the potential effect on the nursing infant if breast-feeding while taking this medicine.

Seniors

Older adults with severe liver disease are more sensitive to the effects of this drug. Follow your doctor's directions and report any side effects at once.

Possible Side Effects

The major side effects are stomach upset and other gastrointestinal problems. Parafon Forte DSC has been associated with bleeding from the stomach, drowsiness, dizziness, light-headedness, not feeling well, and overstimulation.

Less commonly, Parafon Forte DSC has been associated with liver disease.

Notify your physician if itching or skin rash occurs.

Food Interactions

Take this drug with food if it upsets your stomach. Parafon Forte DSC may be crushed and mixed with food.

Usual Dose

Adult: 250 to 750 milligrams 3 to 4 times per day.
Child: 125 to 500 milligrams 3 to 4 times per day.

Overdosage

Symptoms of massive overdosage are sleepiness, weakness, tiredness, turning blue of lips, fingertips, or other areas, and signs of liver damage such as nausea, vomiting, diarrhea, and severe abdominal pain. Contact your doctor immediately or go to a hospital emergency room where appropriate therapy can be provided. ALWAYS bring the medicine bottle.

Special Information

Parafon Forte DSC can make you sleepy, dull your senses, or disturb your concentration, so be extremely careful while driving or operating equipment or machinery. Drinking alcoholic beverages further complicates this problem and enhances the sedative effects of Parafon Forte DSC.

A breakdown product of the Chlorzoxazone ingredient in Parafon Forte DSC can turn your urine orange to purple-red: this is not dangerous.

If you forget to take a dose of Parafon Forte DSC, take it as soon as you remember. If it is almost time for your next regularly scheduled dose, skip the forgotten dose and continue with your regular schedule. Do not take a double dose.

Generic Name

Paregoric

Brand Name

Camphorated Tincture of Opium

(Also available in generic form)

Type of Drug

Antidiarrheal.

Prescribed for

Symptomatic treatment of diarrhea.

General Information

Paregoric is only a symptomatic treatment: It should be accompanied by fluids and other therapy prescribed by your doctor.

Paregoric and other antidiarrheal agents should only be used for short periods: They will relieve the diarrhea, but not its underlying causes. Sometimes these drugs should not be used even though there is diarrhea present: People with some kinds of bowel, stomach, or other disease may be harmed by taking antidiarrheal drugs. Obviously, the decision to use Paregoric must be made by your doctor. Do not use Paregoric without his advice.

Cautions and Warnings

Paregoric is a derivative of Morphine; the cautions and warnings that go with the use of narcotics also go with the use of Paregoric. When taken in the prescribed dose, however, there should be no serious problems.

Pregnancy/Breast-feeding

This drug crosses into the blood circulation of a developing baby. It has not been found to cause birth defects. If used continuously for long periods, however, both the mother and child may become addicted and undergo withdrawal when the drug is stopped. Pregnant women or those who might become pregnant while taking this drug should not take it without their doctor's approval. When the drug is considered essential by your doctor, the potential risk of taking the medicine must be carefully weighed against the benefit it might produce.

This drug passes into breast milk, but has caused no problems among breast-fed infants. Some physicians recommend waiting 4 to 6 hours after taking the drug before beginning a breast-feeding session. You must consider the potential effect on the nursing infant if breast-feeding while taking this medicine.

Seniors

Older adults are more sensitive to the effects of this drug, and may especially have difficulty breathing. Follow your doctor's directions and report any side effects at once.

Possible Side Effects

Most people do not experience side effects from Paregoric, but some may experience nausea, upset stomach, and other forms of gastrointestinal disturbance.

Rarely, prolonged use of Paregoric may produce some of the narcotic effects such as difficulty in breathing, lightheadedness, dizziness, sedation, nausea, and vomiting.

Drug Interactions

Paregoric, a depressant on the central nervous system, may cause tiredness or inability to concentrate, and may thus increase the effect of sleeping pills, tranquilizers, and alcohol. Avoid large amounts of alcoholic beverages.

Food Interactions

To help mask the taste, Paregoric can be mixed with a small amount of water or juice immediately before it is taken. The milky color of the mixture is of no consequence.

Usual Dose

Adult: for diarrhea, 1 to 2 teaspoons 4 times per day.
Infant: for diarrhea, 2 to 10 drops up to 4 times per day.

Overdosage

A patient with Paregoric overdose should be taken to a

hospital emergency room immediately. ALWAYS bring the medicine bottle.

Special Information

Take care while driving, or operating any appliance or machine.

If you forget to take a dose of Paregoric, take it as soon as you remember. If it is almost time for your next regularly scheduled dose, skip the forgotten dose and continue with your regular schedule. Do not take a double dose.

Brand Name

Pediazole

Ingredients

Erythromycin Ethylsuccinate
Sulfisoxazole Acetyl

Type of Drug

Antibiotic anti-infective.

Prescribed for

Middle-ear and sinus infections in children.

General Information

This combination of an antibiotic and a sulfa drug has been specifically formulated for its effect against Hemophilus influenza, an organism responsible for many cases of difficult-to-treat middle-ear infection in children. At present, Pediazole is approved by the Food and Drug Administration only for this specific use, although common sense would indicate that the combination might also be useful for other infections against which both drugs are effective.

Each teaspoonful of the medicine contains 200 milligrams of Erythromycin and 600 milligrams of Sulfisoxazole. The two drugs work by completely different mechanisms and complement each other by working against organisms that the other is unable to affect. Pediazole is especially valuable in cases of Hemophilus influenza middle-ear infection that do not respond to Ampicillin, a widely used and generally effective antibiotic.

Cautions and Warnings

This combination should not be given to infants under 2 months of age because their body systems are not yet sufficiently developed to break down sulfa drugs. Children who are allergic to any sulfa drug or to any form of Erythromycin should not be given this product.

Possible Side Effects

It is possible for children given this combination to develop any side effect known to be caused by either Erythromycin or Sulfisoxazole. However, the most common side effects are upset stomach, cramps, drug allergy, and rashes.

Less common side effects: nausea, vomiting, and diarrhea. Sulfa drugs may make your child more sensitive to sunlight, an effect that can last for many months after the medicine has been discontinued.

Drug Interactions

Pediazole may increase the effects of Digoxin (a heart medicine), Tolbutamide and Chlorpropamide (antidiabetes drugs), Methotrexate (an immune suppressant), Theophylline (for asthma), Warfarin (an anticoagulant), Phenylbutazone (a potent anti-inflammatory agent), Aspirin or other Salicylates, Carbamazepine and Phenytoin (for control of seizures), and Probenecid (for gout). The potential results of such an interaction are an increase in drug side effects and a possible need for dosage adjustment of the interacting drug.

Food Interactions

This combination is best taken on an empty stomach, at least 1 hour before or 2 hours after meals. However, if it causes upset stomach, take each dose with food or meals, and be sure to drink lots of water while using Pediazole.

Usual Dose

The dosage of Pediazole depends on your child's body weight and varies from ½ teaspoonful to 2 teaspoonsful every 6 hours, usually for 10 days.

Overdosage

The strawberry-banana flavoring of this product makes it a good candidate for accidental overdosage, so be sure it is stored in an area of your refrigerator that is least accessible to your child. Overdosage with Pediazole is most likely to result in blood in the urine, nausea, vomiting, stomach upset and cramps, dizziness, headache, and drowsiness. Sulfisoxazole overdosage is more dangerous than Erythromycin overdosage. Patients taking an overdose of this drug must be made to vomit with Syrup of Ipecac (available at any pharmacy) to remove any remaining drug from the stomach. Call your doctor or a poison control center before doing this. If you must go to a hospital emergency room, ALWAYS bring the medicine bottle.

Special Information

This product must be stored under refrigeration and discarded after 2 weeks.

Sulfa drugs may make your child more sensitive to the burning effects of the sun's rays. Avoid excessive exposure to the sun while giving your child Pediazole.

Each dose of Pediazole should be followed by a full glass of water. Do not stop giving your child this medicine when the symptoms disappear. It must be taken for the complete course of treatment prescribed by your doctor.

Call your doctor if nausea, vomiting, diarrhea, stomach cramps, discomfort, or other symptoms persist, especially after giving the dosage with meals or food. Your child may be unable to tolerate the antibiotic and will have to receive different therapy.

Severe or unusual side effects should be reported to your doctor at once. Especially important are yellow discoloration of the eyes or skin, darkening of the urine, pale stools, or unusual tiredness, which can be signs of liver irritation.

If your child misses a dose of Pediazole, he or she should take it as soon as possible. If it is almost time for the next dose, space the missed dose and the next dose by 2 to 4 hours and then continue with your child's regular schedule.

Generic Name

Pemoline

Brand Names

Cylert
Cylert Chewable

Type of Drug

Psychotherapeutic.

Prescribed for

Children with attention deficit syndrome who are also in a
program that includes social, psychological, and educational
counseling. Pemoline may also be prescribed to treat daytime sleepiness.

General Information

This drug stimulates the central nervous system, although
its mechanism of action is not known in children with attention deficit disorder (formerly called hyperactivity). It should
always be used as part of a total therapeutic program and
only when prescribed by a qualified pediatrician.

Cautions and Warnings

Do not use if the patient is allergic or sensitive to Pemoline.
Children under age 6 should not receive this medication.
Psychotic children may experience worsening of symptoms
while taking Pemoline. Patients taking this drug should have
periodic blood tests for the liver.

Pregnancy/Breast-feeding

This drug crosses into the blood circulation of a developing
baby. It has not been found to cause human birth defects,
but animal studies have shown that large doses can cause
stillbirths and decreased newborn survival. Pregnant women,
or those who might become pregnant while taking this drug,
should not take it without their doctor's approval. When the
drug is considered essential by your doctor, the potential
risk of taking the medicine must be carefully weighed against
the benefit it might produce.

This drug passes into breast milk, but has caused no problems among breast-fed infants. You must consider the potential effect on the nursing infant if breast-feeding while taking this medicine.

Possible Side Effects

Sleeplessness, appetite loss, stomachache, rash, irritability, depression, nausea, dizziness, headache, drowsiness, hallucination. Drug hypersensitivity may occur.

Uncontrolled movements of lips, face, tongue, and the extremities; wandering eye may also occur.

Food Interactions

This medicine is best taken on an empty stomach, but you may take it with food if it upsets your stomach.

Usual Dose

37.5 to 75 milligrams per day. Do not take more than 112.5 milligrams per day.

Overdosage

Symptoms are rapid heartbeat, hallucinations, agitation, uncontrolled muscle movements, and restlessness. Patients suspected of taking an overdose of Pemoline must be taken to a hospital. ALWAYS bring the medicine bottle with you.

Special Information

Take the daily dose at the same time each morning. If Pemoline is taken too late in the day, you may have trouble sleeping. Call your doctor if sleeplessness develops.

If you forget to take a dose of Pemoline, take it as soon as you remember. If it is almost time for your next regularly scheduled dose, skip the forgotten dose and continue with your regular schedule. Do not take a double dose.

Generic Name

Penbutolol

Brand Name

Levatol

Type of Drug

Beta blocker.

Prescribed for

High blood pressure.

General Information

Penbutolol is like other beta blockers that slow the heart, control abnormal heart rhythms, blood vessels, and cause "tightening" in the respiratory tract. It is thought that beta blockers lower blood pressure by affecting body hormone systems and the heart, but the exact mechanism is not known. Penbutolol causes fewer side effects than Propranolol does because of the specific nature of its effect on the heart.

Cautions and Warnings

You should be cautious about taking Penbutolol if you have asthma, severe heart failure, very slow heart rate, or heart block because the drug can aggravate these conditions.

People with angina who take Penbutolol for high blood pressure should have their drug dosage reduced gradually over 1 to 2 weeks rather than suddenly discontinued This will avoid possible aggravation of the angina.

Penbutolol should be used with caution if you have liver disease, which impairs your ability to eliminate the drug from your body.

Pregnancy/Breast-feeding

Animal studies in which pregnant rats were given 5 to 50 times the human dose of Penbutolol revealed toxic effects on the developing fetus. Penbutolol should be avoided by pregnant women or women who might become pregnant while taking it. When the drug is considered essential by

your doctor, the potential risk of taking the medicine must
be carefully weighed against the benefit it might produce.

It is not known if Penbutolol will pass into breast milk.
Nursing mothers taking this drug must observe their infants
for possible drug-related side effects.

Seniors

Older adults may be more or less sensitive to the effects of
this medication. Your dosage should be adjusted to your
individual needs by your doctor.

Seniors may be more likely to suffer from Penbutolol side
effects, including cold hands and feet, reduced body temperature, chest pains, a general feeling of ill health, sudden
difficulty breathing, sweating, or changes in heartbeat.

Possible Side Effects

Penbutolol side effects are relatively uncommon, usually develop early in the course of treatment, are relatively mild,
and are rarely a reason to stop taking the medication. Side
effects increase with increasing dosage and include dizziness,
tingling of the scalp, nausea, vomiting, upset stomach, taste
distortion, fatigue, sweating, male impotence, urinary difficulty, diarrhea, bile duct blockade, breathing difficulty, bronchial spasms, muscle weakness, cramps, dry eyes, blurred
vision, skin rash, hair loss, and facial swelling. Like other
beta blockers, Penbutolol can cause depression, disorientation, short-term memory loss, and emotional instability.

Rare side effects include aggravation of lupus erythematosus (a disease of the body's connective tissues), stuffy nose,
chest pains, colitis, drug allergy (fever, sore throat), and
unusual bleeding or bruising.

Drug Interactions

Beta blocking drugs, including Penbutolol, may interact with
anesthetics to increase the risk of heart problems during
surgery. Some anesthesiologists recommend that you gradually stop taking your beta blocker 2 days before surgery.

Penbutolol may interfere with the normal signs of low
blood sugar and can interfere with the action of Insulin or
oral antidiabetes medicines.

Taking Penbutolol with estrogen drugs, Aspirin-containing

drugs, Indomethacin, or Sulfinpyrazone can interfere with its blood-pressure-lowering effect.

The effects of Penbutolol may be increased by combining phenothiazine antipsychotic medicines with other antihypertensives, such as Clonidine, Diazoxide, Nifedipine, and Reserpine, or with other drugs that can reduce blood pressure, such as Nitroglycerin.

Penbutolol may interfere with the effectiveness of some anti-asthma drugs, especially Ephedrine and Isoproterenol, and with Theophylline and Aminophylline.

The combination of Penbutolol and Phenytoin or a digitalis drug can result in excessive slowing of the heart and possible heart block.

Food Interactions

Take this medicine with food if it upsets your stomach.

Usual Dose

20 milligrams once a day. Larger doses are well-tolerated but do not lower blood pressure any more effectively. Lower doses take 4 to 6 weeks to reduce blood pressure.

Overdosage

Symptoms are changes in heartbeat (either unusually slow, unusually fast, or irregular), severe dizziness or fainting, difficulty breathing, bluish-colored fingernails or palms, and seizures.

Special Information

Penbutolol is meant to be taken on a continuing basis. Do not stop taking it unless directed to do so by your doctor. Possible side effects of abrupt withdrawal of Penbutolol are chest pain, difficulty breathing, sweating, and unusually fast or irregular heartbeat.

Call your doctor at once if any of the following symptoms develop: back or joint pains, difficulty breathing, cold hands or feet, depression, skin rash, changes in heartbeat.

Call your doctor if the following side effects persist or are bothersome: anxiety, diarrhea, constipation, sexual impotence, mild dizziness, headache, itching, nausea or vomiting, nightmares or vivid dreams, upset stomach, trouble sleep-

ing, stuffed nose, frequent urination, unusual tiredness or
weakness.

If you forget to take a dose of Penbutolol, take it as soon
as you remember. If it is almost time for your next dose, skip
the forgotten dose and continue with your regular schedule.
Do not take a double dose of Penbutolol.

Generic Name

Penicillin G

Brand Names

Penicillin GK
Pentids

(Also available in generic form)

Type of Drug

Antibiotic.

Prescribed for

Bacterial infections susceptible to this drug.

General Information

Penicillin-type antibiotics fight infection by killing bacteria.
They do this by destroying the cell wall of invading bacteria.
Other antibiotics simply prevent bacteria from reproducing.
Many infections can be treated by almost any member of
this family, but some infections can only be treated by cer-
tain penicillin-type antibiotics.

Penicillins cannot treat against a cold, flu, or any virus
infection and should never be taken unless prescribed by a
doctor for a specific illness. Always take your antibiotic exactly according to your doctor's directions for use, including
the number of pills to take every day and the number of
days to take the medicine. If you do not follow directions,
you may not get the antibiotic's full benefit.

Cautions and Warnings

Serious and occasionally fatal hypersensitivity reaction has been reported to Penicillin G. Although this is more common following injection of the drug, it has occurred with oral use. It is more likely to occur in individuals with a history of sensitivity to this drug or sensitivity in general as indicated by multiple allergies.

Pregnancy/Breast-feeding

Penicillin has not caused birth defects. Make sure your doctor knows you are taking it.

Penicillin G is generally safe during breast-feeding; however, it is possible for the baby to receive enough of this drug to cause upset stomach and diarrhea.

Seniors

Seniors may take Penicillin without special precautions.

Possible Side Effects

The most important side effect seen with Penicillin G is sensitivity or allergic reaction.

Less common side effects: stomach upset, nausea, vomiting, diarrhea, coating of the tongue, rash, itching, various types of anemia, other effects on the blood system, oral or rectal infestation with fungal diseases.

Drug Interactions

Penicillin G should not be given at the same time as one of the bacteriostatic antibiotics such as Erythromycin, Tetracycline, or Neomycin, which may diminish the effectiveness of Penicillin G.

Aspirin or Phenylbutazone will increase the level of free Penicillin G in the blood by making more of it available from blood proteins.

Food Interactions

Do not take Penicillin G with fruit juice or carbonated beverages, because the acid in these beverages can destroy the Penicillin.

Penicillin G is best absorbed on an empty stomach. It can be taken 1 hour before or 2 hours after meals, or first thing in the morning and last thing at night with the other doses spaced evenly through the day.

Usual Dose

200,000 to 800,000 units (125 to 500 milligrams) every 6 to 8 hours for 10 days.

Overdosage

Penicillin overdose is unlikely but may result in diarrhea or upset stomach.

Special Information

Oral Penicillin G liquid should be stored in a refrigerator. The bottle should be labeled to that effect and must be discarded after 14 days.

It takes 7 to 10 days for Penicillin G to be effective against most susceptible organisms; be sure to take all the medicine prescribed for the full period prescribed.

If you miss a dose of Penicillin G, take it as soon as possible. If it is almost time for your next dose, space the missed dose and your next dose by 2 to 4 hours and then continue with your regular schedule.

Generic Name

Penicillin V (Phenoxymethyl Penicillin)

Brand Names

Beepen-VK	Pen-Vee K
Betapen-VK	Robicillin VK
Ledercillin VK	Suspen
Penapar VK	Uticillin VK
Penicillin VK	V-Cillin K
Pen-V	Veetids

(Also available in generic form)

Type of Drug

Antibiotic.

Prescribed for

Bacterial infections susceptible to this drug.

General Information

Penicillin-type antibiotics fight infection by killing bacteria. They do this by destroying the cell wall of invading bacteria. Other antibiotics simply prevent bacteria from reproducing. Many infections can be treated by almost any member of this family, but some infections can only be treated by certain penicillin-type antibiotics.

Penicillins cannot treat against a cold, flu, or any virus infection and should never be taken unless prescribed by a doctor for a specific illness. Always take your antibiotic exactly according to your doctor's directions for use, including the number of pills to take every day and the number of days to take the medicine. If you do not follow directions, you may not get the antibiotic's full benefit.

Cautions and Warnings

Serious and occasionally fatal hypersensitivity reaction has been reported to Penicillin V. Although it is more common following injection of the drug, it has occurred with oral use. It is more likely to occur in individuals with a history of sensitivity to this drug or sensitivity in general as indicated by multiple allergies.

Pregnancy/Breast-feeding

Penicillin V has not caused birth defects. Make sure your doctor knows you are taking it.

It is generally safe to take this drug during breast-feeding, but it is possible for the baby to be affected by the medicine.

Seniors

Seniors may take Penicillin without special precautions.

Possible Side Effects

The most important side effect seen with Penicillin V is sensitivity or allergic reaction.

Less common side effects: stomach upset, nausea, vomiting, diarrhea, coating of the tongue, rash, itching, various types of anemia, other effects on the blood system, oral or rectal infestation with fungal diseases.

Drug Interactions

Penicillin V should not be given at the same time as one of

the bacteriostatic antibiotics such as Erythromycin, Tetracycline, or Neomycin, which may diminish the effectiveness of Penicillin V.

Aspirin or Phenylbutazone will increase the level of free Penicillin V in the blood by making more of it available from blood proteins.

Food Interactions

Penicillin V is best absorbed on an empty stomach. It can be taken 1 hour before or 2 hours after meals, or first thing in the morning and last thing at night with the other doses spaced evenly through the day.

Usual Dose

125 to 500 milligrams every 6 to 8 hours for 10 days.

Overdosage

Penicillin V overdose is unlikely but can result in diarrhea or upset stomach.

Special Information

Oral Penicillin V liquid should be stored in a refrigerator. The bottle should be labeled to that effect and must be discarded after 14 days.

Do not take this medicine after the expiration date on the label. Be sure to take this medicine exactly according to your doctor's directions.

Stop taking the medicine and call your doctor if any of the following side effects develop; skin rash, hives, itching, wheezing. Other side effects that demand your doctor's attention are: blood in the urine, passage of large amounts of light-colored urine, swelling of the face or ankles, trouble breathing, unusual weakness or tiredness.

If you miss a dose of Penicillin V, take it as soon as possible. If it is almost time for your next dose, space the missed dose and your next dose by 2 to 4 hours and then continue with your regular schedule.

Generic Name

Pentazocine

Brand Names

Talacen (Pentazocine with Acetaminophen)
Talwin Compound (Pentazocine with Aspirin)
Talwin NX (Pentazocine with Naloxone)

Type of Drug

Nonnarcotic analgesic.

Prescribed for

Relief of moderate to severe pain.

General Information

Pentazocine is used for mild to moderate pain. Fifty to 100 milligrams of Pentazocine is approximately equal in pain-relieving effect to 2 Aspirin tablets (650 milligrams). Pentazocine may be less active than Aspirin for types of pain associated with inflammation, since Aspirin reduces inflammation but Pentazocine does not. Talwin NX was formulated to prevent drug abuse.

Cautions and Warnings

Do not use Pentazocine if you believe that you are allergic to it. It is possible to develop addiction to or dependence on Pentazocine but addiction is much more likely to occur with people who have a history of abusing narcotics or other drugs. Abrupt stoppage of Pentazocine after extended periods of therapy has produced withdrawal symptoms such as stomach cramps, fever, stuffy or runny nose, restlessness, anxiety, and tearing of the eyes. The drug may cause visual hallucinations or make you disoriented and confused; if this happens, stop taking the drug immediately and contact your physician. Never give this drug or any other potent painkillers to a patient with a head injury.

Pregnancy/Breast-feeding

No studies of this medication have been done in women and no reports of human birth defects exist, but animal studies show that high doses of the drug can cause problems in a developing fetus. Pregnant women, or women who might become pregnant while using this drug, should talk to their doctor about the risk of taking this medicine versus the benefits it can provide.

This drug passes into breast milk, but no problems in nursing infants have been seen. Breast-feeding women should consider the possibility of adverse effects on their nursing infant. Choose another feeding method if you must take this medicine.

Seniors

Seniors are more likely to be sensitive to the side effects of this drug and should be treated with smaller dosages than younger adults.

Possible Side Effects

Nausea, vomiting, constipation, cramps, stomach upset, loss of appetite, diarrhea, dry mouth, alteration of taste, dizziness, light-headedness, sedation, euphoria, headache, difficulty sleeping, disturbed dreams, hallucinations, muscle spasms, irritability, excitement, nervousness, apprehension and depression, feeling of being disoriented and detached from your body.

Less common side effects: blurred vision, difficulty in focusing the eyes, double vision, sweating, flushing chills, rash, itching, swelling of the face, flushing and reddening of the skin, changes in blood pressure, abnormal heart rate, difficulty in breathing, effects on components of the blood, difficult urination, tingling in the arms and legs.

Drug Interactions

Avoid interaction with drugs that have a sedative or depressive effect, such as alcohol, barbiturates, sleeping pills, and some pain-relieving medications. The combination will produce extreme sedation, sleepiness, and difficulty concentrating.

Pentazocine has the unusual effect of being a mild narcotic antagonist. If you must take narcotics for pain relief, do not take Pentazocine at the same time, because it will reverse the effect of the narcotic drug. This can be a special problem for patients in Methadone treatment programs. If one of these patients takes Pentazocine, he will experience narcotic withdrawal effects.

Food Interactions

This product is best taken on an empty stomach but can be taken with food.

Usual Dose

Adult: 50 milligrams every 3 to 4 hours. Maximum dose, 600 milligrams per day to control pain.
Child: not recommended.

Overdosage

Symptoms resemble those of narcotic overdose: decreased breathing, sleepiness, lassitude, low blood pressure, and even coma. The patient should be taken to a hospital emergency room immediately. ALWAYS bring the medicine bottle.

If you forget to take a dose of Pentazocine, take it as soon as you remember. If it is almost time for your next regularly scheduled dose, skip the forgotten dose and continue with your regular schedule. Do not take a double dose.

Generic Name

Pentobarbital

Brand Name

Nembutal

(Also available in generic form)

Type of Drug

Hypnotic; sedative.

Prescribed for

Daytime sedation; sleeping medication.

General Information

Pentobarbital, like the other barbiturates, appears to act by interfering with nerve impulses to the brain.

Cautions and Warnings

Pentobarbital may slow down your physical and mental reflexes, so you must be extremely careful when operating machinery, driving an automobile, or performing other potentially dangerous tasks. Pentobarbital is classified as a barbiturate; long-term or unsupervised use may cause addiction. Elderly people taking Pentobarbital may exhibit nervousness and confusion at times. Barbiturates are neutralized in the liver and eliminated from the body through the kidneys; consequently, people who have liver or kidney disorders—namely, difficulty in forming or excreting urine—should be carefully monitored by their doctor when taking Pentobarbital.

If you have known sensitivities or allergies to barbiturates, or if you have previously been addicted to sedatives or hypnotics, or if you have a disease affecting the respiratory system, you should not take Pentobarbital.

Pregnancy/Breast-feeding

Regular use of any barbiturate during the last 3 months of pregnancy can cause the baby to be born dependent on the medicine. Also, barbiturate use increases the chance of bleeding problems, brain tumors, and breathing difficulties in the newborn.

Barbiturates pass into breast milk and can cause drowsiness, slow heartbeat, and breathing difficulty in nursing infants.

Seniors

Older adults are more sensitive to the effects of barbiturates, especially nervousness and confusion, and often require a lower dose than a younger adult to do the same job. Follow your doctor's directions and report any side effects at once.

Possible Side Effects

Drowsiness, lethargy, dizziness, hangover, difficulty in breathing, rash, and general allergic reaction such as runny nose, watering eyes, and scratchy throat.

Less common side effects: nausea, vomiting, diarrhea. More severe adverse reactions may include anemia and yellowing of the skin and eyes.

Drug Interactions

Interaction with alcohol, tranquilizers, or other sedatives increases the effect of Pentobarbital.

Interaction with anticoagulants (blood-thinning agents) can reduce their effect. This is also true of muscle relaxants, pain-killers, anticonvulsants, Quinidine, Theophylline, Metronidazole, Phenmetrazine, birth control pills, and Acetaminophen.

Food Interactions

This medicine is best taken on an empty stomach, but may be taken with food if it upsets your stomach.

Usual Dose

Daytime sedative: 30 milligrams 3 to 4 times per day.
Hypnotic for sleep: 100 milligrams at bedtime; this may be repeated once if necessary (occasionally) to induce sleep.

Overdosage

Symptoms are difficulty in breathing, decrease in size of the pupils of the eyes, lowered body temperature progressing to fever as time passes, fluid in the lungs, and eventually coma.

Anyone suspected of having taken an overdose must be taken to the hospital for immediate care. ALWAYS bring the medicine bottle to the emergency room physician so he or she can quickly and correctly identify the medicine and start treatment. Severe overdosage of this medication can kill; the drug has been used many times in suicide attempts.

Special Information

Avoid alcohol and other drugs that depress the nervous system while taking this barbiturate. Be sure to take this medicine according to your doctor's direction. Do not change your dose without your doctor's approval. This drug causes drowsiness and poor concentration, and makes it more diffi-cult to drive a car, operate machinery, or perform compli-cated activities.

Call your doctor at once if you develop fever, sore throat, nosebleeds, mouth sores, unexplained black-and-blue marks, easy bruising or bleeding.

If you forget to take a dose of Pentobarbital, take it as soon as you remember. If it is almost time for your next regularly scheduled dose, skip the one you forgot and continue with your regular schedule. Do not take a double dose.

Generic Name

Pentoxifylline

Brand Name

Trental

Type of Drug

Blood viscosity reducer.

Prescribed for

Relief of intermittent claudication, or blood vessel spasms and painful leg cramps, caused by poor blood supply associated with arteriosclerotic disease. It has also been used to treat cases of inadequate blood flow to the brain.

General Information

This medicine, available in Europe since 1972, is the first true "blood thinner." It reduces the blood's viscosity, or thickness, and improves the ability of red blood cells to modify their shape. In doing so, this medication may help people who experience severe leg pains, when they walk, by improving blood flow to their leg muscles. Leg cramps occur when muscles are deprived of oxygen. When blood flow is improved, the cramps are less severe or do not occur at all. Studies of Pentoxifylline's effectiveness have yielded mixed results, but it may be helpful for people who do not respond to other treatments.

It should be noted that physical training is probably a more effective treatment for intermittent claudication than is Pentoxifylline. However, the medicine may be helpful for people who cannot follow a training program and who are not candidates for surgery, which is another treatment for this condition.

Cautions and Warnings

People who cannot tolerate Caffeine, Theophylline, or Theobromine should not use this medicine, since Pentoxifylline is chemically related to those products.

Pregnancy/Breast-feeding

This drug crosses into the blood circulation of a developing

baby. It has not been found to cause birth defects. Pregnant women, or those who might become pregnant while taking this drug, should not take it without their doctor's approval. When the drug is considered essential by your doctor, the potential risk of taking the medicine must be carefully weighed against the benefit it might produce.

This drug passes into breast milk, but has caused no problems among breast-fed infants. You must consider the potential effect on the nursing infant if breast-feeding while taking this medicine.

Seniors

Older adults are more sensitive to the effects of this drug because they absorb more and eliminate it more slowly than younger adults. Follow your doctor's directions and report any side effects at once.

Possible Side Effects

Most common: mild nausea, upset stomach, dizziness, and headache.

Less frequently encountered reactions to Pentoxifylline include chest pains, difficulty breathing, swelling of the arms or legs, low blood pressure, stomach gas, loss of appetite, constipation, dry mouth, excessive thirst, tremors, anxiety, confusion, stuffy nose, nosebleeds, flu symptoms, sore throat, laryngitis, swollen glands, itching, rash, brittle fingernails, blurred vision, conjunctivitis (red-eye), earache, a bad taste in the mouth, a general feeling of ill health, and changes in body weight.

The rarest side effects of Pentoxifylline are rapid or abnormal heart rhythms, hepatitis, yellow discoloration of the skin, reduction in white-blood-cell count, and small hemorrhages under the skin.

Drug Interactions

Pentoxifylline may add to the blood-pressure-lowering effects of other medicines. Your doctor may have to change the dosage of your blood-pressure medicines.

Food Interactions

It is preferable to take each dose of Pentoxifylline on an

empty stomach. However, if it causes stomach upset or gas, the medicine may be taken with food.

Usual Dose

400 milligrams 2 to 3 times per day.

Overdosage

The severity of symptoms is directly related to the amount of drug taken. Symptoms of overdosage usually appear 4 to 5 hours after the medicine was taken and can last for about 12 hours. Some of the reported effects of Pentoxifylline overdose are flushing, low blood pressure, fainting, depression of the nervous system, and convulsions. Patients taking an overdose of this drug must be made to vomit with Syrup of Ipecac (available at any pharmacy) to remove any remaining drug from the stomach. Call your doctor or a poison control center before doing this. If you must go to a hospital emergency room, ALWAYS bring the medicine bottle.

Special Information

Call your doctor if any side effects develop. Some people may have to stop using this medicine if side effects become intolerable. You may feel better within 2 weeks after starting to take Pentoxifylline, but the treatments should be continued for at least 2 months to gain maximum benefit.

If you forget to take a dose of Pentoxifylline, take it as soon as you remember. If it is almost time for your next regularly scheduled dose, skip the one you forgot and continue with your regular schedule. Do not take a double dose.

Brand Name

Percocet

Ingredients

Acetaminophen
Oxycodone Hydrochloride

Other Brand Names

Oxycet
Roxicet
Tylox

(Also available in generic form)

Type of Drug

Narcotic analgesic combination.

Prescribed for

Relief of mild to moderate pain.

General Information

Percocet is generally prescribed for the patient who is in pain but is allergic to Aspirin. Percocet is probably not effective for arthritis or other pain associated with inflammation because the Acetaminophen ingredient does not produce an anti-inflammatory effect.

Cautions and Warnings

Do not take Percocet if you know you are allergic or sensitive to any of its components. Use this drug with extreme caution if you suffer from asthma or other breathing problems. Long-term use of this drug may cause drug dependence or addiction. The Oxycodone Hydrochloride component of Percocet is a respiratory depressant, and affects the central nervous system, producing sleepiness, tiredness, and/or inability to concentrate. Be careful if you are driving, operating machinery, or performing other functions requiring concentration.

Pregnancy/Breast-feeding

Neither Acetaminophen nor Oxycodone has been associated with birth defects. But, taking too much Oxycodone, or any other narcotic, during pregnancy can lead to the birth of a drug-dependent infant and drug-withdrawal symptoms in the baby. All narcotics, including Oxycodone, can cause breathing problems in the newborn if taken just before delivery.

Percocet has not caused any problems among nursing mothers or their infants.

Seniors

The Oxycodone in this combination product may have more of a depressant effect on seniors than younger adults. Other effects that may be more prominent are dizziness, light-headedness, or fainting when rising suddenly from a sitting or lying position.

Possible Side Effects

Most frequent: light-headedness, dizziness, sleepiness, nausea, vomiting, loss of appetite, sweating. If these effects occur, consider calling your doctor and asking him about lowering your dose of Percocet. Usually the side effects disappear if you simply lie down.

More serious side effects of Percocet are shallow breathing or difficulty in breathing.

Less common side effects; euphoria (feeling high), weakness, sleepiness, headache, agitation, uncoordinated muscle movement, minor hallucinations, disorientation and visual disturbances, dry mouth, loss of appetite, constipation, flushing of the face, rapid heartbeat, palpitations, faintness, urinary difficulties or hesitancy, reduced sex drive and/or potency, itching, rashes, anemia, lowered blood sugar, and a yellowing of the skin and/or whites of the eyes. Narcotic analgesics may aggravate convulsions in those who have had convulsions in the past.

Drug Interactions

Because of its depressant effect and potential effect on breathing, Percocet should be taken with extreme care in combination with alcohol, sleeping medicine, tranquilizers, or other depressant drugs.

Food Interactions

Percocet is best taken with food or at least ½ glass of water to prevent stomach upset.

Usual Dose

Adult: 1 to 2 tablets every 4 hours.
Child: not recommended.

Overdosage

Symptoms are depression of respiration (breathing), extreme tiredness progressing to stupor and then coma, pinpointed pupils of the eyes, no response to stimulation such as a pin stick, cold and clammy skin, slowing down of the heart rate, lowering of blood pressure, yellowing of the skin and/or whites of the eyes, bluish color of skin of hands and feet, fever, excitement, delirium, convulsions, cardiac arrest, and liver toxicity (shown by nausea, vomiting, pain in the abdomen, and diarrhea). The patient should be taken to a hospital emergency room immediately. ALWAYS bring the medicine bottle.

Special Information

If you forget to take a dose of Percocet, take it as soon as you remember. If it is almost time for your next regularly scheduled dose, skip the one you forgot and continue with your regular schedule. Do not take a double dose.

Brand Name

Percodan

Ingredients

Aspirin
Oxycodone Hydrochloride
Oxycodone Terephthalate

Other Brand Names

Codoxy
Oxycodone with Aspirin
Percodan-Demi

(Also available in generic form)

Type of Drug

Narcotic analgesic combination.

Prescribed for

Relief of mild to moderate pain.

General Information

Percodan is one of many combination products containing narcotics and analgesics. These products often also contain barbiturates or tranquilizers, and Acetaminophen which may be substituted for Aspirin.

Cautions and Warnings

Do not take Percodan if you know you are allergic or sensitive to any of its components. Use this drug with extreme caution if you suffer from asthma or other breathing problems. Long-term use of this drug may cause drug dependence or addiction. The Oxycodone component of Percodan is a respiratory depressant and affects the central nervous system, producing sleepiness, tiredness, and/or inability to concentrate.

Pregnancy/Breast-feeding

Check with your doctor before taking any Aspirin-containing product during pregnancy. Aspirin can cause bleeding problems in the developing fetus during the last 2 weeks of a pregnancy. Taking Aspirin during the last 3 months of pregnancy may lead to a low-birth-weight infant, prolong labor, extend the length of pregnancy, and cause bleeding in the mother before, during, or after delivery.

Oxycodone has not been associated with birth defects. But, taking too much of it, or any other narcotic, during pregnancy can lead to the birth of a drug-dependent infant and drug-withdrawal symptoms in the baby. All narcotics, including Oxycodone, can cause breathing problems in the newborn if taken just before delivery.

Percodan has not caused any problems among nursing mothers or their infants.

Seniors

The Oxycodone in this combination product may have more of a depressant effect on seniors than younger adults. Other effects that may be more prominent are dizziness, lightheadedness, or fainting when rising suddenly from a sitting or lying position.

Possible Side Effects

Most frequent: light-headedness, dizziness, sleepiness, nausea, vomiting, loss of appetite, sweating. If these effects occur, consider calling your doctor and asking him about lowering the dose of Percodan you are taking. Usually the side effects disappear if you simply lie down.

More serious side effects of Percodan are shallow breathing or difficulty in breathing.

Less common side effects: euphoria (feeling high), weakness, sleepiness, headache, agitation, uncoordinated muscle movement, minor hallucinations, disorientation and visual disturbances, dry mouth, loss of appetite, constipation, flushing of the face, rapid heartbeat, palpitations, faintness, urinary difficulties or hesitancy, reduced sex drive and/or potency, itching, skin rashes, anemia, lowered blood sugar, yellowing of the skin and/or whites of the eyes. Narcotic analgesics may aggravate convulsions in those who have had convulsions in the past.

Drug Interactions

Interaction with alcohol, tranquilizers, barbiturates, or sleeping pills produces tiredness, sleepiness, or inability to concentrate, and seriously increases the depressive effect of Percodan.

The Aspirin component of Percodan can affect anticoagulant (blood-thinning) therapy. Be sure to discuss this with your doctor so that the proper dosage adjustment can be made.

Interaction with adrenal corticosteroids, Phenylbutazone, or alcohol can cause severe stomach irritation with possible bleeding.

Food Interactions

Take with food or ½ glass of water to prevent stomach upset.

Usual Dose

1 tablet every 6 hours as needed for relief of pain.

Overdosage

Symptoms are depression of respiration (breathing), extreme tiredness progressing to stupor and then coma, pinpointed pupils of the eyes, no response to stimulation such as a pin

stick, cold and clammy skin, slowing down of the heartbeat,
lowering of blood pressure, convulsions, and cardiac arrest.
The patient should be taken to a hospital emergency room
immediately. ALWAYS bring the medicine bottle.

Special Information

Drowsiness may occur: be careful when driving or operating
hazardous machinery.

If you forget to take a dose of Percodan, take it as soon as
you remember. If it is almost time for your next regularly
scheduled dose, skip the one you forgot and continue with
your regular schedule. Do not take a double dose.

Brand Name

Peri-Colace

Ingredients

Casanthranol
Docusate Sodium

Other Brand Names

Dialose Plus	Di-Sosul Forte
Diocto C	D-S-S Plus
Diocto-K Plus	Genasoft-Plus
Diolax	Peri-Dos
Diothron	Pro-Sof Plus
Disanthrol	Regulace

(Also available in generic form)

Type of Drug

Laxative and stool-softener combination.

Prescribed for

Treatment or prevention of constipation. Also used to clear
intestines before X-ray procedures.

General Information

This is one of many laxative combinations available without

a prescription. Composed of a stool-softener and a stimulant which makes the stool easier to pass by acting directly on the intestine to move the stool through it, such laxatives should be used for short periods only when necessary. Long-term use of a stimulant laxative can produce laxative dependency, where normal bowel function is lost and the stimulant is required to pass any stool.

Cautions and Warnings

Patients with abdominal pain, nausea, vomiting, or symptoms of appendicitis should not take a laxative.

Pregnancy/Breast-feeding

This drug is considered relatively safe for use during pregnancy. Consult your doctor before taking it or any other medication.

Casanthranol, an ingredient in this drug, may pass into breast milk and can affect your nursing infant. If you need a laxative, use a different one that will not affect your baby.

Seniors

Older adults can use this medication without special restriction. However, you must take caution to avoid becoming "laxative dependent," which can happen if you overuse any laxative product.

Possible Side Effects

Severely constipated patients may experience stomach cramps. Nausea, vomiting, and diarrhea may occur after excessive amounts have been taken.

Food Interactions

Take this drug on an empty stomach. You should drink 6 to 8 full glasses of water every day while taking a laxative product. This will help soften your stool.

Usual Dose

1 to 2 capsules at bedtime with an 8-ounce glass of water.

Special Information

If this laxative is not effective after 7 days, stop taking it and call your doctor.

Generic Name

Phenazopyridine Hydrochloride

Brand Names

Azo-Standard	Phenazodine
Baridium	Pyridiate
Di-Azo	Pyridium
Eridium	Urodine
Geridium	Urogesic

(Also available in generic form)

Type of Drug

Urinary analgesic.

Prescribed for

Relief of pain and discomfort associated with urinary tract infections.

General Information

Phenazopyridine Hydrochloride is used only to relieve the pain associated with urinary infections. It has little antibacterial action and cannot be used, therefore, to cure a urinary infection. It is usually used in combination with an antibacterial sulfa drug.

Cautions and Warnings

This drug should not be used if you have kidney disease or are experiencing decrease in urination.

Pregnancy/Breast-Feeding

Pregnant and breast-feeding women may use this product with no restriction.

Seniors

Older adults may use this product with no restriction.

Possible Side Effects

Occasional stomach upset.

Usual Dose

Adult: 200 milligrams 3 times per day after meals.
Child: 100 milligrams 3 times per day after meals.

Special Information

Phenazopyridine Hydrochloride may produce an orange-red color in the urine. This is normal, but the color change may interfere with urine tests to monitor diabetes.

If you forget to take a dose of Phenazopyridine Hydrochloride, take it as soon as you remember. If it is almost time for your next regularly scheduled dose, skip the one you forgot and continue with your regular schedule. Do not take a double dose.

Generic Name

Phendimetrazine Tartrate

Brand Names

Adphen	Phenzine
Anorex	Plegine
Bacarate	Sprx
Bontril PDM	Statobex
Di-Ap-Trol	Statobex G
Hyrex	Trimstat
Melfiat	Trimtabs
Metra	Weh-less
Obalan	Weightrol
Obeval	

Sustained-Release Products

Adipost	Prelu-2
Bontril Slow Release	Slyn-LL
Dyrexan-OD	Sprx-105
Hyrex 105	Trimcaps
Melfiat-105	Weh-less 105

(Also available in generic form)

Type of Drug

Nonamphetamine appetite suppressant.

Prescribed for

Suppression of appetite and treatment of obesity.

General Information

Although Phendimetrazine Tartrate is not an amphetamine, it can produce the same adverse effects as the amphetamine appetite suppressants. There are several other nonamphetamine appetite suppressants. One, Phenmetrazine Tartrate (Preludin), is closely related to Phendimetrazine Tartrate and has similar actions and effects.

Cautions and Warnings

Do not use Phendimetrazine Tartrate if you have heart disease, high blood pressure, thyroid disease, or glaucoma, or if you are sensitive or allergic to this or similar drugs. Prolonged use of this drug may be habit-forming.

Pregnancy/Breast-feeding

This drug may cause birth defects or interfere with your baby's development. Check with your doctor before taking it if you are, or might be, pregnant.

This drug may pass into breast milk and should be avoided if you are nursing.

Seniors

Older adults should not take this medicine unless it is prescribed by a doctor. It can aggravate diabetes and high blood pressure, conditions common to older adults.

Possible Side Effects

Common side effects are a false sense of well-being, nervousness, overstimulation, restlessness, and trouble sleeping. Other side effects are palpitations, high blood pressure, drowsiness, sedation, weakness, dizziness, tremor, headache, dry mouth, nausea, vomiting, diarrhea and other intestinal disturbances, rash, itching, changes in sex drive, hair loss, muscle pain, difficulty in passing urine, sweating, chills, blurred vision, fever.

Drug Interactions

Do not take Phendimetrazine Tartrate if you take other stimulants or antidepressants.

This drug may reduce the effectiveness of antihypertensive drugs.

Food Interactions

Take this drug before meals.

Usual Dose

Tablets: 35 milligram tablet 1 hour before meals 2 to 3 times per day.

Sustained-release capsules: 105 milligrams once per day in the morning.

Overdosage

Symptoms are restlessness, tremor, shallow breathing, confusion, hallucinations, and fever, followed by fatigue and depression, with additional symptoms such as high or possibly low blood pressure, cold and clammy skin, nausea, vomiting, diarrhea, and stomach cramps. The patient should be taken to a hospital emergency room immediately. ALWAYS bring the medicine bottle.

Special Information

Use for no more than 12 weeks as an adjunct to diet, under strict supervision of your doctor.

Medicine alone will not take off weight. You must limit and modify your food intake, preferably under medical supervision. This drug can cause dry mouth which may be relieved by sugarless gum, candy, or ice chips.

If you take Phendimetrazine Tartrate once a day and forget to take a dose, take it as soon as you remember. If it is almost time for your next regularly scheduled dose, skip the one you forgot and continue with your regular schedule. Do not take a double dose.

If you take it 2 to 3 times a day and forget to take a dose, and you remember within about an hour of your regular time, take it right away. If you do not remember until later, skip the forgotten dose and go back to your regular schedule. Do not take a double dose.

Brand Name

Phenergan with Dextromethorphan Syrup

Ingredients

Alcohol
Dextromethorphan Hydrobromide
Promethazine Hydrochloride

Other Brand Names

Pherazine DM
Promethazine with Dextromethorphan Syrup
Prometh with Dextromethorphan
Prothazine Pediatric Syrup

(Also available in generic form)

Type of Drug

Cough suppressant combination.

Prescribed for

Relief of coughs and symptoms associated with the common cold.

General Information

Phenergan with Dextromethorphan Syrup is one of many combination products marketed for the relief of coughs. The major active ingredient is an antihistamine, Promethazine. Therefore the drug is most effective in relieving the symptoms of excess histamine production, like the symptoms associated with allergies. Dextromethorphan treats coughing. It is just as effective as Codeine, but is not a narcotic drug and does not have the same side effects. It cannot help you recover more quickly, only more comfortably.

Cautions and Warnings

Drowsiness or sleepiness may occur. Do not use this product with similar products such as sedatives, tranquilizers, sleeping pills, antihistamines, or other drugs which can cause sleepiness or drowsiness.

Pregnancy/Breast-feeding

Phenergan with Dextromethorphan Syrup used by pregnant women has caused side effects in newborns such as jaundice (yellowing of skin and eyes) and twitching. These medications should be stopped 1 to 2 weeks before expected delivery to avoid this.

This combination product contains 7 percent alcohol (14 proof). Large amounts of alcohol have been associated with birth defects.

Antihistamines like Promethazine are not recommended during breast-feeding because of possible side effects.

Seniors

Seniors are more sensitive to some side effects of this product. Confusion, difficult or painful urination, dizziness, drowsiness, a faint feeling, dry mouth, nose, or throat, nightmares or excitement, nervousness, restlessness, or irritability are more likely to occur among older adults.

Possible Side Effects

Dryness of the mouth, blurred vision, occasional dizziness.

Drug Interactions

Avoid alcohol, which increases central nervous system depression and will increase drowsiness, sleepiness, or similar problems.

Food Interactions

Take with a full glass of water to help reduce any stomach upset caused by the drug.

Usual Dose

1 teaspoon every 4 to 6 hours.

Special Information

If you forget to take a dose of Phenergan with Dextromethorphan Syrup, take it as soon as you remember. If it is almost time for your next regularly scheduled dose, skip the one you forgot and continue with your regular schedule. Do not take a double dose.

Brand Name

Phenergan Syrup with Codeine

Ingredients

Alcohol
Codeine Phosphate
Promethazine Hydrochloride

Other Brand Names

Promethazine with Codeine Syrup
Prometh with Codeine Syrup
Prothazine DC Syrup

(Also available in generic form)

Type of Drug

Cough suppressant combination.

Prescribed for

Coughs, symptoms of the common cold.

General Information

Phenergan Syrup with Codeine is one of almost 100 products marketed to treat symptoms of the common cold or other upper respiratory problems. It is useful in helping to relieve symptoms but does not treat the basic problem.

Phenergan is an antihistamine used to relieve the symptoms associated with hay fever or allergies. Codeine is a narcotic and is the active anti-cough ingredient.

Cautions and Warnings

Do not take this medicine if you are allergic to any of its ingredients.

Pregnancy/Breast-feeding

Phenergan Syrup with Codeine when used by pregnant

women has caused side effects in newborns such as jaundice (yellowing of skin and eyes) and twitching. These medications should be stopped 1 to 2 weeks before expected delivery to avoid this. This drug has not been shown to cause problems during breast-feeding.

Codeine has not been associated with birth defects. But, taking too much codeine, or any other narcotic, during pregnancy can lead to the birth of a drug-dependent infant and can lead to drug-withdrawal symptoms in the baby. All narcotics, including Codeine, can cause breathing problems in the newborn if taken just before delivery.

Antihistamines can cause side effects in breast-fed newborns. They are not recommended during breast-feeding.

Seniors

Older adults are more sensitive to the effects of this drug. Follow your doctor's directions and report any side effects at once.

Possible Side Effects

Drowsiness, dry mouth, blurred vision, difficulty in urination, constipation.

Less common: palpitations—pounding of the heart.

Drug Interactions

Avoid alcohol, sedatives, tranquilizers, antihistamines, or other medication which can cause tiredness and/or drowsiness.

Taking Phenergan Syrup with Codeine with Isocarboxazid (Marplan), Tranylcypromine Sulfate (Parnate), Phenelzine Sulfate (Nardil), or other MAO inhibitor drugs can produce a severe interaction. Consult your doctor first.

Food Interactions

Take with a full glass of water to reduce stomach upset.

Usual Dose

Adult: 1 to 2 teaspoons 4 times per day.
Child (over age 1): ½ to 1 teaspoon 3 to 4 times per day.

Special Information

Be aware of the potential depressive effects of Phenergan Syrup with Codeine; be careful when driving, or operating heavy or dangerous machinery.

If you forget to take a dose of Phenergan Syrup with Codeine, take it as soon as you remember. If it is almost time for your next regularly scheduled dose, skip the one you forgot and continue with your regular schedule. Do not take a double dose.

Brand Name

Phenergan VC Syrup

Ingredients

Alcohol
Phenylephrine Hydrochloride
Promethazine Hydrochloride

Other Brand Names

Promethazine VC Syrup
Prometh VC Plain Liquid

(Also available in generic form)

Type of Drug

Cough suppressant and decongestant combination.

Prescribed for

Coughs.

General Information

Phenergan VC syrup is one of many combination products marketed to relieve the symptoms of the common cold or other upper respiratory infections, relieve runny nose, and unclog nasal and sinus passages.

Cautions and Warnings

Drowsiness, dry mouth, blurred vision, difficulty in urination, and/or constipation can occur.

Pregnancy/Breast-feeding

Phenergan VC Syrup, when used by pregnant women, has caused side effects in newborns such as jaundice (yellowing

of skin and eyes) and twitching. This medication should
be stopped 1 to 2 weeks before expected delivery.

Promethazine is an antihistamine and is not recommended
during breast-feeding.

Seniors

Older adults are more sensitive to the effects of this drug.
Follow your doctor's directions and report any side effects at
once.

Possible Side Effects

The drug may cause mild stimulation and you may experience nervousness, restlessness, or even inability to sleep.

Drug Interactions

Avoid alcohol, sedatives, tranquilizers, antihistamines, or other
medication which can cause tiredness and/or drowsiness.
Taking Phenergan VC Syrup with MAO inhibitor drugs can
produce severe interaction. Consult your doctor first.

Usual Dose

1 teaspoon every 4 to 6 hours as needed for the relief of
cough.

Special Information

Be aware of the potential depressive effects of this drug;
take care when driving, or operating heavy or dangerous
machinery.

If you forget to take a dose of Phenergan VC Syrup, take it
as soon as you remember. If it is almost time for your next
regularly scheduled dose, skip the one you forgot and continue with your regular schedule. Do not take a double dose.

Brand Name

Phenergan VC Syrup with Codeine

Ingredients

Alcohol   Phenylephrine Hydrochloride
Codeine Phosphate   Promethazine Hydrochloride

Other Brand Names

Mallergan VC with Codeine Syrup
Prometh VC with Codeine Syrup

(Also available in generic form)

Type of Drug

Cough suppressant and decongestant combination.

Prescribed for

Relief of cough, nasal congestion, runny nose, and other symptoms associated with the common cold, viruses, or other upper respiratory diseases. The drug may also be used to treat allergies, asthma, ear infections, or sinus infections.

General Information

Phenergan VC Syrup with Codeine is one of almost 100 products marketed to relieve the symptoms of the common cold and other respiratory infections. These products contain medicine to relieve congestion, act as an antihistamine, and relieve or suppress cough. They may contain medicine for each purpose, or may contain a combination of medicines. Some combinations leave out the antihistamine or the decongestant, or add an expectorant. You must realize while taking Phenergan VC Syrup with Codeine or similar products that these drugs only relieve symptoms and will not treat the underlying problem, such as a cold virus or other infections.

Cautions and Warnings

Drowsiness, dry mouth, blurred vision, urinary difficulty, and constipation may occur.

Pregnancy/Breast-feeding

Phenergan VC Syrup with Codeine, when taken by pregnant women, has caused side effects in newborns such as jaundice (yellowing of skin and eyes) and twitching. This medication should be stopped 1 to 2 weeks before expected delivery.

Codeine has not been associated with birth defects. But, taking too much Codeine, or any other narcotic, during pregnancy can lead to the birth of a drug-dependent infant and can lead to drug-withdrawal symptoms in the baby. All narcotics, including Codeine, can cause breathing problems in the newborn if taken just before delivery. This drug has not been shown to cause problems during breast-feeding.

Antihistamines can cause side effects in nursing infants. They are not recommended during breast-feeding.

Seniors

Older adults are more sensitive to the effects of this drug. Follow your doctor's directions and report any side effects at once.

Possible Side Effects

Dry mouth, blurred vision, difficulty passing urine, (possibly) constipation, nervousness, restlessness, or even inability to sleep. Can cause excessive tiredness or drowsiness.

Drug Interactions

Taking Phenergan VC Syrup with Codeine with MAO inhibitor drugs can produce severe interaction. Consult with your doctor first.

Food Interactions

Take with a full glass of water to reduce stomach upset.

Usual Dose

1 to 2 teaspoons 4 times per day.

Special Information

Drinking alcoholic beverages while taking Codeine may produce excessive drowsiness and/or sleepiness, or inability to concentrate.

Be aware of the depressive effects of this drug; take care while driving or operating complex equipment.

If you forget to take a dose of Phenergan VC Syrup with Codeine, take it as soon as you remember. If it is almost time for your next regularly scheduled dose, skip the one you forgot and continue with your regular schedule. Do not take a double dose.

Generic Name

Phenmetrazine

Brand Name

Preludin

Type of Drug

Nonamphetamine appetite suppressant.

Prescribed for

Short-term (2 to 3 months) appetite suppression, treating obesity.

General Information

Although this medicine is not an amphetamine, it has many of the same effects as amphetamine drugs and suppresses appetite by working on specific areas in the brain. The effects of a single dose of Phenmetrazine can last from 4 to 6 hours (non-sustained release).

Cautions and Warnings

Do not take Phenmetrazine if you have heart disease, high blood pressure, thyroid disease, or glaucoma, or if you are sensitive or allergic to this or other appetite suppressants. Do not use this medicine if you are prone to emotional agitation or drug abuse.

Pregnancy/Breast-feeding

Studies have shown that Phenmetrazine can affect an unborn baby. The use of this and other appetite suppressants should be avoided by women who are or could become pregnant, unless the potential benefit outweighs any possible drug hazard.

It is not known if Phenmetrazine passes into breast milk. Nursing mothers should not take this or any other appetite suppressant.

Seniors

Older adults should not take this medicine unless it is prescribed by a doctor. It can aggravate diabetes or high blood pressure, conditions common to older adults.

Possible Side Effects

Common side effects are a false sense of well-being, nervousness, overstimulation, restlessness, and trouble sleeping. Other, less common side effects are palpitations, high blood pressure, drowsiness, sedation, weakness, dizziness, tremor, headache, dry mouth, nausea, vomiting, diarrhea and other intestinal disturbances, rash, itching, changes in sex drive, hair loss, muscle pains, difficulty urinating, sweating, chills, blurred vision and fever.

Drug Interactions

Taking other stimulants together with Phenmetrazine may result in excessive stimulation. Taking this medicine within 14 days of any MAO inhibitor drug may result in severe high blood pressure.

Appetite suppressants may reduce the effects on some medicines used to treat high blood pressure.

Food Interactions

This medicine is best taken on an empty stomach; it should be taken 1 hour before meals.

Usual Dose

25 milligrams (1 tablet) 2 to 3 times per day, 1 hour before meals.

Sustained-release: 75 milligrams (1 capsule) once a day.

Overdosage

Symptoms of overdose are restlessness, tremor, shallow breathing, confusion, hallucinations, and fever, followed by fatigue and depression. Additional symptoms are changes in blood pressure, cold and clammy skin, nausea, vomiting, diarrhea, and stomach cramps. Take the victim to a hospital emergency room immediately. ALWAYS bring the medicine bottle.

Special Information

Do not take this medicine for more than 12 weeks as part of a weight control program, and take it only under a doctor's supervision. This medicine will not reduce body weight by itself. You must limit or modify your food intake.

This drug can cause dry mouth which can be relieved by
sugarless candy, gum, or ice chips.

If you forget to take a dose of Phenmetrazine, take it as
soon as you remember. If it is almost time for your next
regularly scheduled dose, skip the one you forgot and continue with your regular schedule. Do not take a double dose.

Generic Name

Phenobarbital

Brand Names

Barbita
Luminal
Solfoton

(Also available in generic form)

Type of Drug

Hypnotic; sedative, anticonvulsive.

Prescribed for

Epileptic seizures, convulsions, as an anticonvulsive or a
daytime sedative; as a mild hypnotic (sleeping medication);
for eclampsia (toxemia in pregnancy).

General Information

Phenobarbital, like the other barbiturates, appears to act by
interfering with nerve impulses to the brain. When used as an
anticonvulsive, Phenobarbital is not very effective by itself,
but when used with anticonvulsive agents such as Phenytoin,
the combined action of Phenobarbital and Phenytoin is dramatic. This combination has been used very successfully to
control epileptic seizures.

Cautions and Warnings

Phenobarbital may slow down your physical and mental
reflexes, so you must be extremely careful when operating
machinery, driving an automobile, or performing other potentially dangerous tasks. Phenobarbital is classified as a

barbiturate; long-term or unsupervised use may cause addiction. Barbiturates are neutralized in the liver and eliminated from the body through the kidneys: consequently, people who have liver or kidney disorders—namely, difficulty in forming or excreting urine—should be carefully monitored by their doctor when taking Phenobarbital.

If you have known sensitivities or allergies to barbiturates, or have previously been addicted to sedatives or hypnotics, or if you have a disease affecting the respiratory system, you should not take Phenobarbital.

Pregnancy/Breast-feeding

There is an increased chance of birth defects when women use Phenobarbital during pregnancy. Phenobarbital may be required to be used if a serious situation arises which threatens the mother's life.

Regular use of any barbiturate during the last 3 months of pregnancy can cause the baby to be born dependent on the medicine. Also, barbiturate use increases the chance of bleeding problems, brain tumors, and breathing difficulties in the newborn.

Barbiturates pass into breast milk and can cause drowsiness, slow heartbeat, and breathing difficulty in nursing infants.

Seniors

Older adults are more sensitive to the effects of barbiturates, especially nervousness and confusion, and often require a lower dose than a younger adult to do the same job. Follow your doctor's directions and report any side effects at once.

Possible Side Effects

Drowsiness, lethargy, dizziness, hangover, difficulty in breathing, skin rash, and general allergic reaction such as runny nose, watering eyes, and scratchy throat.

Less common side effects: nausea, vomiting, diarrhea. More severe adverse reactions may include anemia and yellowing of the skin and eyes.

Drug Interactions

Interaction with alcohol, tranquilizers, the antibiotic Chloramphenicol, or other sedatives increases the sedative effect of Phenobarbital.

Interaction with anticoagulants (blood-thinning agents) can reduce their effect. This is also true of muscle relaxants, other anticonvulsants, Quinidine, Theophylline, Metronidazole, Phenmetrazine, birth control pills, and Acetaminophen. Phenobarbital has been shown to reduce the potency of the antibiotic Doxycycline.

Food Interactions

This medicine is best taken on an empty stomach, but may be taken with food if it upsets your stomach.

Usual Dose

Anticonvulsant: 50 to 100 milligrams 2 to 3 times per day.
Hypnotic (for sleep): 100 to 320 milligrams at bedtime.
Sedative: 15 to 120 milligrams in 2 to 3 divided doses.
Specific dose is determined by patient's size, weight, and physical condition.

Overdosage

Symptoms are difficulty in breathing, decrease in size of the pupils of the eyes, lowered body temperature progressing to fever as time passes, fluid in the lungs, and eventually coma.

Anyone suspected of having taken an overdose must be taken to the hospital for immediate care. ALWAYS bring the medicine bottle to the emergency room physician so he can quickly and correctly identify the medicine and start treatment. Severe overdosage of this medication can kill; the drug has been used many times in suicide attempts.

Special Information

Avoid alcohol and other drugs that depress the nervous system while taking this barbiturate. Be sure to take this medicine according to your doctor's direction. Do not change your dose without your doctor's approval. This drug causes drowsiness and poor concentration, and makes it more difficult to drive a car, operate machinery, or perform complicated activities.

Call your doctor at once if you develop fever, sore throat, nosebleeds, mouth sores, unexplained black-and-blue marks, easy bruising or bleeding.

If you forget to take a dose of Phenobarbital, take it as soon as you remember. If it is almost time for your next regularly scheduled dose, skip the one you forgot and continue with your regular schedule. Do not take a double dose.

Generic Name

Phensuximide

Brand Name

Milontin

Type of Drug

Anticonvulsant.

Prescribed for

Control of petit mal seizures.

General Information

Phensuximide and the other succinimide-type anticonvulsants control petit mal seizures by slowing the transmission of impulses through certain areas of the brain. Generally, Ethosuximide is prescribed first for this type of seizure. Phensuximide may be prescribed if Ethosuximide does not work. If the succinimides are ineffective, the condition may then be treated with Clonazepam.

Cautions and Warnings

Phensuximide may be associated with severe reductions in white-blood-cell and platelet counts. Your doctor should perform periodic blood counts while you are taking this medicine.

In patients with grand mal and petit mal, succinimide-type anticonvulsants, when used alone, may increase the number of grand mal seizures and necessitate more medicine to control those seizures.

Abrupt withdrawal of any anticonvulsant may lead to severe seizures. It is important that your dosage be reduced gradually by your doctor.

Pregnancy/Breast-feeding

This drug should be avoided by women who may become
pregnant while using it and by pregnant and nursing mothers, since it will cross into the developing baby, and possible
adverse effects on the infant are not known. In those situations where it is deemed essential, the potential risk of the
drug must be carefully weighed against any benefit it might
produce.

Recent reports suggest a strong association between the
use of anticonvulsant drugs and birth defects. Although most
of the information pertains to Phenytoin and Phenobarbital,
not Phensuximide, other reports indicate a general association between all anticonvulsant drug treatments and birth
defects. It is possible that the epileptic condition itself or
genetic factors common to people with seizure disorders
may also figure in the higher incidence of birth defects.
Mothers taking Phensuximide should not breast-feed because of the possibility that the drug will pass into their
breast milk and affect the baby. Use an alternative feeding
method.

Seniors

Older adults may take this medication without special restriction. Follow your doctor's directions and report any side
effects at once.

Possible Side Effects

Nausea, vomiting, upset stomach, stomach cramps and pain,
loss of appetite, diarrhea, constipation, weight loss, drowsiness, dizziness, and poor muscle control.

Less common side effects: reductions in white-blood-cell
and platelet counts, nervousness, hyperactivity, sleeplessness,
irritability, headache, blurred vision, unusual sensitivity to
bright lights, hiccups, a euphoric feeling, a dreamlike state,
lack of energy, fatigue, confusion, mental instability, mental
slowness, depression, sleep disturbances, nightmares, loss
of the ability to concentrate, aggressiveness, constant concern with well-being and health, paranoid psychosis, suicidal
tendencies, increased sex drive, rash, itching, frequent urination, kidney damage, blood in the urine, swelling around the
eyes, hair loss, hairiness, muscle weakness, nearsighted-

ness, vaginal bleeding, and swelling of the tongue and/or gums.

Drug Interactions

The depressant effects of Phensuximide are increased by tranquilizers, sleeping pills, narcotic pain relievers, antihistamines, alcohol, MAO inhibitors, antidepressants, and other anticonvulsants.

Phensuximide may increase the action of Phenytoin by increasing the blood levels of that drug. Your doctor should be sure that your dosages of the two drugs are appropriate to your condition.

Carbamazepine, another medicine prescribed to treat seizure disorders, may interfere with Phensuximide action by increasing the rate at which it is removed from the body.

The action of Phensuximide may be increased by Isoniazid, prescribed for tuberculosis prevention, and by Valproic Acid, another anticonvulsant drug, possibly leading to an increase in drug side effects when both drugs are taken together.

Avoid alcoholic beverages, which increase the depressant effects of this medicine.

Food Interactions

Phensuximide is best taken on an empty stomach but may be taken with food if it upsets your stomach.

Usual Dose

500 to 1000 milligrams 2 or 3 times per day, with weekly adjustments to meet your individual needs.

Dosage adjustments may be required for people with reduced kidney or liver function.

Overdosage

Phensuximide overdose will cause exaggerated side effects. If the overdose is discovered immediately, it may be helpful to make the victim vomit. But all victims of Phensuximide overdose must be taken to a hospital emergency room for treatment. ALWAYS bring the prescription bottle with you.

Special Information

Phensuximide will color your urine pink or red-brown. This is harmless and should be ignored.

Call your doctor if side effects become intolerable. Especially important are sore throat, joint pains, unexplained fever, rashes, unusual bleeding or bruising, drowsiness, dizziness, and blurred vision. Be sure to tell your doctor if you become pregnant while taking this medicine.

Phensuximide may interfere with your ability to drive a car or perform other complex tasks because it can cause drowsiness and difficulty concentrating.

Your doctor should perform periodic blood counts while you are taking this drug to check for possible adverse drug effects.

Do not suddenly stop taking this medicine, since to do so can result in severe seizures. The dosage must be discontinued gradually by your doctor.

Carry identification or wear a bracelet indicating that you suffer from a seizure disorder for which you take Phensuximide.

If you forget to take a dose of Phensuximide, take it as soon as possible. However, if it is within 4 hours of your next dose, skip the forgotten dose and go back to your regular schedule. Do not take a double dose.

Generic Name

Phentermine Hydrochloride

Brand Names

Adipex-P	Parmine
Dapex 37.5	Phentamine
Fastin	Phentrol
Ionamin	Phentrol-2
Obe-Nix	Tora
Obephen	Unifast Unicelles
Obermine	Wilpowr
Obestin-30	

(Also available in generic form)

Type of Drug

Nonamphetamine appetite suppressant.

Prescribed for

Suppression of appetite and treatment of obesity.

General Information

Although Phentermine Hydrochloride is not an amphetamine, it can produce the same adverse effects as the amphetamine appetite suppressants.

The effects of a single dose of Phentermine Hydrochloride can last from 4 to 6 hours. The sustained-release lasts all day.

Cautions and Warnings

Do not use Phentermine Hydrochloride if you have heart disease, high blood pressure, thyroid disease, or glaucoma, or if you are sensitive or allergic to this or similar drugs. Prolonged use of this drug may be habit-forming.

Pregnancy/Breast-feeding

This drug may cause birth defects or interfere with your baby's development. Check with your doctor before taking it if you are, or might be, pregnant.

This drug may pass into breast milk and should be avoided if you are nursing.

Seniors

Older adults should not take this medicine unless it is prescribed by a doctor. It can aggravate diabetes and high blood pressure, conditions common to older adults.

Possible Side Effects

Common side effects are a false sense of well-being, nervousness, overstimulation, restlessness, and trouble sleeping. Other side effects are palpitations, high blood pressure, drowsiness, sedation, weakness, dizziness, tremor, headache, dry mouth, nausea, vomiting, diarrhea and other intestinal disturbances, rash, itching, changes in sex drive, hair loss, muscle pain, difficulty in passing urine, sweating, chills, blurred vision, and fever.

Drug Interactions

Do not take Phentermine Hydrochloride if you take other stimulants or antidepressants.

Phentermine Hydrochloride may reduce the effectiveness of antihypertensive drugs.

Food Interactions

Take this drug before meals.

Usual Dose

Adult: 8 milligrams ½ hour before meals, or 15 to 37.5 milligrams once a day before breakfast.

Child: not recommended.

Overdosage

Symptoms are restlessness, tremor, shallow breathing, confusion, hallucinations, and fever followed by fatigue and depression, with additional symptoms such as high or possibly low blood pressure, cold and clammy skin, nausea, vomiting, diarrhea, and stomach cramps. The patient should be taken to a hospital emergency room immediately. ALWAYS bring the medicine bottle.

Special Information

Use only for a few weeks as an adjunct to diet, under strict supervision of your doctor.

Medicine alone will not take off weight. You must limit and modify your food intake, preferably under medical supervision.

This drug can cause dry mouth which can be relieved by sugarless gum, candy, or ice chips.

If you forget to take a dose of Phentermine Hydrochloride, and you remember within about an hour of your regular time, take it right away. If you do not remember until later, skip the forgotten dose and go back to your regular schedule. Do not take a double dose.

Generic Name

Phenylbutazone

Brand Names

Azolid   Butazolidin
Butagen   Butazone

(Also available in generic form)

Type of Drug

Anti-inflammatory agent.

Prescribed for

Local inflammation of bone joints such as gout, rheumatoid arthritis, osteoarthritis, painful shoulder such as bursitis or arthritis of a joint, or other inflammatory diseases that cause pain which cannot be controlled by Aspirin; and when severe disability, because of the inflammation, is not relieved by usual treatment.

General Information

This drug should never be taken without strict medical supervision. Phenylbutazone should be used only for the short-term relief of pain due to inflammation of muscles, tendons, and joint area. It has anti-inflammatory, analgesic, and fever-reducing properties. This drug is quite useful but is limited by its side effects and adverse drug reactions.

Phenylbutazone and its sister drug Oxyphenbutazone are toxic and dangerous and should only be used when absolutely necessary. The list of potential side effects is long. Therefore, any change in habits or unusual effect which may be even remotely connected with the use of these drugs should be reported immediately to your doctor.

Cautions and Warnings

You should not take Phenylbutazone if you have a history of symptoms associated with gastrointestinal inflammation or ulcer, including severe, recurrent, or persistent upset stomach. This drug is not a simple pain reliever and should never be taken casually. It should not be prescribed before a careful and detailed history, plus physical and laboratory tests, have been completed by the doctor. Always discuss your state of health and medical history with your doctor completely before taking this medicine. If your problem can be treated by a less toxic drug such as Aspirin, use that first and try to avoid taking Phenylbutazone. Never take more than the recommended dosage: this would lead to toxic effects. If you have blurred vision, fever, rash, sore throat, sores in the mouth, upset stomach or pain in the stomach, feeling of weakness, bloody, black, or tarry stool, water retention, or a significant or sudden weight gain, report this to the doctor immediately. In addition, stop taking the drug. If the drug is not effective after 1 week, stop taking it.

Pregnancy/Breast-feeding

This drug crosses into the blood circulation of a developing baby. It is not recommended for use late in pregnancy because of the possibility that the drug will affect your developing baby's heart. It may delay or prolong your labor. Studies in laboratory animals have shown that this medication produces birth defects. Pregnant women, or those who might become pregnant while taking this drug, should not take it without their doctor's approval. When the drug is considered essential by your doctor, the potential risk of taking the medicine must be carefully weighed against the benefit it might produce.

This drug passes into breast milk and should not be taken if you are nursing an infant. The drug can cause severe blood problems in a nursing infant. Use an alternate feeding method if you must take this medicine.

Seniors

Seniors are more likely to develop the blood, stomach, kidney, and liver side effects of this drug because of a general reduction in kidney function. People 60 years of age and older should be limited to short periods of treatment (no more than 1 week, if possible) because of the possibility of severe, possibly fatal, reactions.

Some doctors recommend that drug dosage be reduced by ½ in people age 60 and older.

Possible Side Effects

Most common: stomach upset, drowsiness, water retention.

Less common side effects: gastric or duodenal ulcer, ulceration or perforation of the large bowel, bleeding from the stomach, anemia, stomach pain, vomiting, vomiting of blood, nausea, diarrhea, changes in the components of the blood, water retention, disruption of normal chemical balance of the body. This drug can cause fatal or nonfatal hepatitis, black-and-blue marks on the skin, serum sickness, drug allergy serious enough to cause shock, itching, serious rashes, fever, and signs of arthritis. It has been known to cause kidney effects including bleeding and kidney stones. Phenylbutazone may be a cause of heart disease, high blood pressure, blurred vision, bleeding in the back of the eye, detachment of a retina, hearing loss, high blood sugar, thyroid disease, agitation, confusion, or lethargy.

Drug Interactions

Phenylbutazone increases the effects of blood-thinning drugs, Phenytoin, Insulin, and oral antidiabetic agents. If you are taking any of these drugs, discuss this matter with your doctor immediately.

Food Interactions

Avoid alcoholic beverages. Phenylbutazone causes stomach upset in many patients; take your dose with food or antacids, and if stomach pain continues, notify your doctor.

Usual Dose

Adult and child (age 14 or over): 300 to 600 milligrams per day in 3 to 4 equal doses for 7 days. If dose is effective it can then be reduced to 100 to 400 milligrams per day, depending on the condition being treated.

Senior: to be given for 7 days because of high risk of severe reactions. Not to be given to senile patients.

Child (under age 14): not recommended.

Overdosage

If symptoms of nausea, vomiting, convulsions, euphoria, depression, headache, hallucinations, giddiness, dizziness, coma, rapid breathing rate, continued stomach pain, and insomnia or sleeplessness appear, contact your doctor immediately.

Special Information

This drug can make you drowsy and/or tired: be careful when driving or operating equipment.

If you take Phenylbutazone once or twice a day and forget to take a dose, take it as soon as you remember. If it is almost time for your next regularly scheduled dose, skip the one you forgot and continue with your regular schedule. Do not take a double dose.

If you take it 3 to 4 times a day and forget to take a dose, and you remember within about an hour of your regular time, take it right away. If you do not remember until later, skip the forgotten dose and go back to your regular schedule. Do not take a double dose.

Generic Name

Phenytoin

Brand Names

Extended-Action Products

Dilantin Kapseals
Phenytoin Sodium Extended

Prompt-Acting Products

Dilantin Infatab	Diphenylan Sodium
Dilantin-30 Pediatric	Phenytoin
Dilantin-125 Suspension	Phenytoin Sodium

(Also available in generic form)

Type of Drug

Anticonvulsant.

Prescribed for

Control of epileptic seizures.

General Information

Phenytoin is one of several drugs of the same chemical group used to control convulsions. All these drugs act by the same mechanism, although some patients may respond to some and not others.

There are 2 kinds of Phenytoin: prompt, which must be taken several times a day, and extended, which can be taken either once a day or several times a day. Many people find the extended action more convenient, but the shorter-acting product gives the doctor more flexibility in designing a daily dose schedule.

Phenytoin may or may not be used in combination with other anticonvulsants, like Phenobarbital.

Cautions and Warnings

If you have been taking Phenytoin for a long time and no longer need it, the dosage should be reduced gradually over a period of about a week. Stopping abruptly may bring on severe epileptic seizures.

Pregnancy/Breast-feeding

Phenytoin crosses into the blood circulation of a developing baby. Most mothers who take this medicine deliver healthy, normal babies, but some babies are born with cleft lip, cleft palate, and heart malformations. Also, there is a recognized group of deformities known as "fetal hydantoin syndrome" that affect children of mothers taking this medicine (although the medicine has not been definitely implicated as the cause of these deformities), which consists of abnormalities in the skull and face, small brain, growth deficiency, deformed fingernails, and mental deficiency.

Children born of mothers taking Phenytoin are more likely to have a Vitamin K deficiency, leading to serious, life-threatening hemorrhage during the first 24 hours of life. Also, the mother may be deficient in Vitamin K because of Phenytoin, leading to increased bleeding during delivery.

Phenytoin passes into breast milk and may affect a nursing infant. Use an alternate feeding method if you are taking this medication.

Seniors

Older adults break down this drug more slowly than younger adults and are more sensitive to the effects of this drug. Follow your doctor's directions and report any side effects at once.

Possible Side Effects

Most common: slurred speech, mental confusion, nystagmus (a rhythmic, uncontrolled movement of the eyeballs), dizziness, insomnia, nervousness, uncontrollable twitching, double vision, tiredness, irritability, depression, tremors, headaches. These side effects will generally disappear as therapy continues and the dosage is reduced.

Less common side effects: nausea, vomiting, diarrhea, constipation, fever, rashes, balding, weight gain, numbness of the hands and feet, chest pains, retention of water, sensitivity to bright lights, especially sunlight, conjunctivitis, changes of the blood system including anemia, swollen glands. Phenytoin can cause an abnormal growth of the gums surrounding the teeth, so good oral hygiene including gum massage, frequent brushing, and appropriate dental care is very important. Occasionally Phenytoin produces unusual hair growth over the body, and liver damage, including hepatitis.

Drug Interactions

A barbiturate taken with Phenytoin may increase the rate at which Phenytoin is excreted from the body; then if the barbiturate is discontinued the patient may show an increased response to Phenytoin, and the dose may have to be reduced slightly.

Warfarin, Isoniazid, Chloramphenicol, Disulfiram, Phenylbutazone, and Oxyphenbutazone can cause Phenytoin to remain in the body for a longer time, increasing the incidence of Phenytoin side effects. Folic acid or high doses of tricyclic antidepressant drugs may increase seizures. The dose of Phenytoin may have to be adjusted by your doctor.

Food Interactions

The amount of Phenytoin that is absorbed from the small intestine can be decreased if you eat foods high in calcium or take calcium supplements. This may result in less Phenytoin available for action in the body.

If you get upset stomach after taking Phenytoin, take the medicine with meals.

Usual Dose

Adult: initial dose, 300 milligrams per day. If this does not result in satisfactory control, gradually increase to 600 milligrams per day. (The most frequent maintenance dose is 300 to 400 milligrams per day.) Only Dilantin may be taken once daily. The other brands of Phenytoin must be taken throughout the day, as convenient.

Child: initial dose, 2.5 milligrams per pound of body weight per day in 2 to 3 equally divided doses; then adjust according to needs and response of child (normal maintenance dose, 2 to 4 milligrams per pound of body weight per day). Children over age 6 may require the same dose as an adult, but no child should be given more than 300 milligrams per day.

Overdosage

Symptoms are listed in "Possible Side Effects" above. The patient should be taken to a hospital emergency room immediately. ALWAYS bring the medicine bottle.

Special Information

If you develop a rash, sore throat, fever, unusual bleeding, or bruising, contact your doctor immediately. Phenytoin sometimes produces a pink-brown color in the urine; don't worry about it. Do not change brands of Phenytoin without notifying your doctor. Dosage adjustment may be required.

If you take Phenytoin once a day and forget to take a dose, take it as soon as you remember. If it is almost time for your next regularly scheduled dose, skip the one you forgot and continue with your regular schedule. Do not take a double dose.

If you take it several times a day and forget to take a dose, and you remember within 4 hours of your regular time, take it right away. If you do not remember until later, skip the forgotten dose and go back to your regular schedule. Do not take a double dose.

Generic Name

Pilocarpine Ophthalmic Solution

Brand Names

Adsorbocarpine	Ocusert Pilo
Akarpine	Pilocar
Almocarpine	Pilopine HS
Isopto Carpine	P.V. Carpine Liquifilm

(Also available in generic form)

Type of Drug

Miotic agent.

Prescribed for

Management of glaucoma (increased pressure in the eye).

General Information

Pilocarpine Ophthalmic Solution is the drug of choice in the treatment of open-angle glaucoma. It works on muscles in the eye to open passages so that fluid can normally flow out of the eye chamber, reducing fluid pressure inside the eye. Pilocarpine Ophthalmic Solution may also help reduce the amount of fluid produced within the eye.

Although used as eyedrops, the drug can affect other parts of the body, especially after long use. When this drug is prescribed, it is usually given for long periods of time, as long as eye pressure does not increase or eyesight does not worsen. The concentration of Pilocarpine Ophthalmic Solution is determined by the physician, and is based on the severity of the disease. The usual concentration of the eye drops is 0.5 to 4 percent. Concentrations above 4 percent are used less often. The most frequently used concentrations are 1 and 2 percent.

This drug is also marketed in a special form called Ocusert Pilo—a thin football-shaped wafer designed to continuously release the drug for 1 week. This eliminates the need for putting drops in your eyes 3 to 4 times a day. The wafer is placed under the eyelid similarly to the way contact lenses are placed. Pilopine HS is a gel rather than eye drops.

Pilocarpine is also available in many combination products. These may be useful in special circumstances.

If you use the conventional eye drops, be very careful not to touch the eyelids or surrounding area with the dropper tip; otherwise you will contaminate the dropper and cause the medicine to become unsterile. Be sure you recap the bottle tightly in order to preserve the sterility of the medicine.

Cautions and Warnings

Pilocarpine Ophthalmic Solution should only be used when prescribed by an eye specialist (ophthalmologist). This drug should not be used if you are allergic to it.

Pregnancy/Breast-feeding

This drug has been found to be safe for use during pregnancy and breast-feeding. Remember, you should check with your doctor before taking any drug if you are pregnant, since it may be absorbed into the bloodstream.

Seniors

Older adults may take this medication without special restriction. Follow your doctor's directions and report any side effects at once.

Possible Side Effects

This drug may produce spasms of the eye muscles resulting in an aching feeling over the brow. You may also find it hard to focus your eyes. These effects are seen in younger people and will disappear with continued use. Some people may complain of decreased vision in low light.

Less commonly, allergy or itching and tearing of the eye may develop after prolonged use.

Usual Dose

Initial dose, 1 to 2 drops in the affected eye up to 6 times per day. Maintenance dose is based on severity of disease.

Ocusert Pilo: insert into eye sac and replace weekly.

At first Pilocarpine Ophthalmic Solution is also placed in the healthy eye to keep it from becoming diseased.

Overdosage

After long-term use, small amounts of Pilocarpine Ophthalmic

Solution may be absorbed by the drainage systems of the eye. If symptoms of stomach upset, nausea, vomiting, diarrhea, and cramps appear, contact your doctor immediately.

Special Information

After placing drops in your eye you may feel a stinging sensation; this is normal in the Pilocarpine solutions. You should not close your eyes tightly or blink more than normally, which removes the drops from the eye.

If you forget to take a dose of Pilocarpine Ophthalmic Solution, take it as soon as you remember. If it is almost time for your next regularly scheduled dose, skip the one you forgot and continue with your regular schedule. Do not take a double dose.

Generic Name

Pindolol

Brand Name

Visken

Type of Drug

Beta-adrenergic blocking agent.

Prescribed for

High blood pressure.

General Information

Pindolol is a unique beta-adrenergic blocker. It is similar to Propanolol, Nadolol, and Timolol Maleate in that it works on both beta receptors in the heart and those in blood vessels. But it differs from those medications in its ability to increase the heart's activity. As a result, this drug causes less of a reduction in heart rate than the other beta blockers, making it useful for people with heart failure, who cannot take other beta blockers. Pindolol can be taken with a diuretic drug or by itself to treat high blood pressure.

Unlike other beta blockers, which can be used to treat a variety of heart conditions, migraine headaches, schizophrenia, tremors, panic, and other symptoms, Pindolol should not be taken for any purpose other than treating high blood pressure.

Cautions and Warnings

Heart failure, although far less likely with Pindolol than with the other beta blockers, is the most important caution for people taking this drug. Pindolol should not be discontinued abruptly because of the possibility of developing tremors, sweating, heart pain, palpitations, headache, and a feeling of ill health. The drug should be discontinued gradually over a period of several weeks.

Pindolol must be used with extreme caution by asthmatics and others with respiratory disease, since this and other beta blockers can worsen bronchial spasms. This effect is less prominent with Pindolol than some other drugs, but is still possible.

This drug should be stopped several days or weeks before major surgery to prevent the risk of its affecting the ability of your heart to respond during the surgical procedure.

All beta blockers can mask the signs or symptoms of diabetes and low blood sugar and an overactive thyroid. Be sure the doctor prescribing Pindolol knows your complete medical history.

This drug must be used with caution by people with severe liver disease.

Pregnancy/Breast-feeding

There are no adequate studies undertaken on the effects of Pindolol during pregnancy. This drug should be avoided by pregnant women or women who may become pregnant while using it. In those situations where it is deemed essential, the potential risk of the drug must be carefully weighed against any benefit it might produce. Nursing mothers who must take Pindolol should use an alternative method of feeding their infants since the drug definitely passes into breast milk.

Seniors

Senior citizens may be more or less sensitive to the effects of this medication. Your dosage of this drug must be adjusted to your individual needs by your doctor. Seniors may be more likely to suffer from cold hands and feet and reduced body temperature, chest pains, a general feeling of ill health, sudden difficulty breathing, sweating, or changes in heartbeat because of this medicine.

Possible Side Effects

Most side effects are mild and will pass on their own. The most common are anxiety, bizarre dreams, hallucinations, dizziness, fatigue or tiredness, lethargy, difficulty sleeping, nervousness, weakness, visual disturbances, tingling in the hands or feet, breathing difficulty, retention of fluid, heart failure, heart palpitations, weight gain (when the drug is taken alone), chest and joint pains, muscle cramps and pain, nausea, abdominal discomfort and pain, itching, and rash.

Less common side effects: sore throat, fever, slowing of the heart, coldness of the arms or legs, leg pains, stroke, fainting, low blood pressure, rapid heartbeat, abnormal heart rhythms, depression, loss of the ability to concentrate, sedation, odd behavior (especially in the elderly), memory loss, disorientation (especially in the elderly), emotional upset, slurred speech, ringing or buzzing in the ears, light-headedness, changes in blood-sugar level (up or down), stomach gas and pain, constipation, diarrhea, dry mouth, vomiting, loss of appetite, bloating, loss of sexual potency and/or drive, difficulty urinating, skin discoloration, sweating, hair loss, dry skin, eye irritation or discomfort, and dry or burning eyes.

Drug Interactions

Chlorpromazine, Cimetidine, Furosemide, Hydralazine Hydrochloride, oral contraceptive pills, and Reserpine increase Pindolol's effect on the body.

Indomethacin and Aspirin or Aspirin-containing drugs may counteract the blood-pressure-reducing effect of Pindolol.

Beta blockers, such as Pindolol, can antagonize the effects of Theophylline. They can increase the effects of Insulin and can worsen the body's reaction to the sudden discontinuation of Clonidine (taken for high blood pressure) and the usual "first dose" reaction to Prazosin Hydrochloride.

Food Interactions

Take this medicine with food if it upsets your stomach.

Usual Dose

Up to 60 milligrams per day has been used successfully.

Overdosage

The symptoms of Pindolol overdose can include a drastic reduction in heart rate, heart failure, very low blood pressure, breathing difficulty because of bronchial muscle spasm, seizures, delirium, coma, and possible loss of consciousness. Very large Pindolol overdoses can cause your heart to beat faster and blood pressure to increase. Patients taking an overdose of this drug must be made to vomit with Syrup of Ipecac (available at any pharmacy) to remove any remaining drug from the stomach. Call your doctor or a poison control center before doing this. If you must go to a hospital emergency room, ALWAYS bring the medicine bottle.

Special Information

Don't stop taking this medicine without your doctor's specific knowledge and approval. Sudden discontinuation could result in heart pains or other symptoms.

Call your doctor if it becomes gradually more difficult to breathe while you are taking Pindolol, especially when you are lying down, when you cough at night, or when you retain fluid in your legs. These may be signs of heart failure. Other symptoms to tell your doctor about are slow pulse, dizziness, light-headedness, depression, confusion, rash, fever, sore throat, and unusual bleeding or bruising.

Since Pindolol can cause loss of concentration and visual disturbances, be careful while driving or operating machinery.

If you forget to take a dose of Pindolol, take it as soon as possible. However, if it is within 8 hours of your next dose, skip the forgotten dose and go back to your regular schedule. Do not take a double dose.

Generic Name

Pirbuterol Acetate

Brand Name

Maxair

Type of Drug

Bronchodilator.

Prescribed for

Asthma and bronchospasm.

General Information

Pirbuterol is currently available only as an inhalation. It may be taken in combination with other medicines to control your asthma. The drug starts working 3 to 4 minutes after it is taken, and continues to work for 5 to 8 hours. It can be used only when necessary to treat an asthmatic attack or on a regular basis to prevent an attack.

Cautions and Warnings

Pirbuterol should be used with caution if you have had angina, heart disease, high blood pressure, a history of stroke or seizures, diabetes, prostate disease, or glaucoma.

Pregnancy/Breast-feeding

Pirbuterol should be used by a pregnant or breast-feeding woman only when it is absolutely necessary. The potential benefit of using this medicine must be weighed against the potential, but unknown, hazard it can pose to your baby.

Seniors

Older adults are more sensitive to the effects of this drug. They should closely follow their doctor's directions and report any side effects at once.

Possible Side Effects

Pirbuterol's side effects are similar to those associated with other bronchodilator drugs. The most common side effects are restlessness, weakness, anxiety, fear, tension, sleeplessness, tremors, convulsions, dizziness, headache, flushing, loss of appetite, pallor, sweating, nausea, vomiting, and muscle cramps.

Less common side effects include angina, abnormal heart rhythms, heart palpitations, high blood pressure, and urinary difficulty. Pirbuterol has been associated with abnormalities in blood tests for the liver and white blood cells and with tests for urine protein, but the true importance of this reaction is not known.

Drug Interactions

Pirbuterol's effects may be enhanced by MAO inhibitor drugs, antidepressants, thyroid drugs, other bronchodilators, and some antihistamines. It is antagonized by the beta-blocking drugs (Propranolol and others).

Pirbuterol may antagonize the effects of blood-pressure-lowering drugs, especially Reserpine, Methyldopa, and Guanethidine.

Food Interactions

Pirbuterol does not interact with food, since it is taken only by inhalation into the lungs.

Usual Dose

Adult and child (over age 12): 1 or 2 inhalations every 4 to 6 hours. Do not take more than 12 inhalations per day.

Overdosage

Pirbuterol overdosage can result in exaggerated side effects, including heart pains and high blood pressure, although the pressure can drop after a short period of elevation. People who inhale too much Pirbuterol should see a doctor, who may prescribe a beta-blocking drug like Atenolol or Metoprolol to counter the bronchodilator's effects.

Special Information

Be sure to follow your doctor's directions for using Pirbuterol, and do not take more than 12 inhalations of Pirbuterol each day. Using more than is prescribed can lead to drug tolerance and can actually cause your condition to worsen.

The drug should be inhaled during the second half of your

breath. This allows the medicine to reach more deeply into your lungs.

Call your doctor at once if you develop chest pains, rapid heartbeat or heart palpitations, muscle tremors, dizziness, headache, facial flushing, or urinary difficulty, or if you still have trouble breathing after using the medicine.

Generic Name

Piroxicam

Brand Name

Feldene

Type of Drug

Nonsteroidal anti-inflammatory.

Prescribed for

Arthritis and other forms of bone and joint inflammation.

General Information

This nonsteroidal anti-inflammatory drug (NSAID) represents an entirely different chemical class than any of its predecessors. It is long-acting and usually given only once a day, characteristics that have made Piroxicam one of the most widely prescribed NSAIDs in America. Like other nonsteroid anti-inflammatories, it is thought to work by preventing the body from manufacturing hormones called prostaglandins, thus reducing pain, inflammation, and fever.

Cautions and Warnings

Piroxicam should not be used by infants or children.

Do not take this drug if you are allergic to it, to Aspirin, or to other NSAIDs. It may cause stomach ulcers.

All patients taking this drug should have regular eye examinations since it may cause blurred vision or other problems.

Pregnancy/Breast-feeding

This drug may cause birth defects or interfere with your

baby's development. Check with your doctor before taking it if you are, or might be, pregnant.

Piroxicam has not been shown to cause problems during breast-feeding and may reduce the amount of milk you make.

Seniors

Older adults are more sensitive to the stomach, liver, and kidney side effects of this drug. Some doctors recommend that people age 70 and older take ½ the usual dose. Follow your doctor's directions and report any side effects at once.

Possible Side Effects

Most common: upset stomach, nausea, iron deficiency, and blood loss through the gastrointestinal tract.

Piroxicam may also cause loss of appetite, abdominal discomfort, constipation, diarrhea, stomach gas or pains, indigestion, adverse effects on the blood system, reduced kidney function, dizziness, sleepiness, ringing or buzzing in the ears, headache, a sickly feeling, fluid in the arms or legs, itching, and rash. The elderly are more likely to experience side effects.

Less common side effects: reduced liver function, vomiting with or without blood, blood in the urine or stool, bleeding from the stomach, dry mouth, sweating, unusual bruising, loss of patches of skin, swollen eyes, blurred vision, eye irritations, high blood pressure, lowered blood sugar, body weight changes (either up or down), depression, nervousness, sleeplessness, heart palpitations, difficulty breathing, and difficulty in urination.

Drug Interactions

Avoid alcohol, since this may increase upset stomach associated with Piroxicam or aggravate any problems with drowsiness or lack of alertness.

Piroxicam may interact with anticoagulant (blood-thinning) drugs. Although you will probably not experience a serious interaction, your doctor should monitor your anticoagulant therapy during the first few weeks of Piroxicam therapy in case any adjustment is needed.

Aspirin, in doses of 12 tablets per day or more, will reduce the effect of Piroxicam by reducing its level in the blood. These drugs should not be taken together since there is no special benefit from the combination and it may cause unwanted side effects.

Since Piroxicam may cause lowered blood-sugar levels, diabetics taking Piroxicam may need to have the dose of their antidiabetic drug reduced.

Usual Dose

10 to 20 milligrams per day.

Special Information

You will not feel the maximum effects of Piroxicam until you have taken the drug for 2 to 3 months, although you may begin to experience some relief as early as 2 weeks after beginning treatment.

If you get an upset stomach after taking Piroxicam, take the medicine with meals. If you develop swollen hands or feet, itching, rash, black tarry stools, vomiting, blurred vision or other visual disturbances, or unusual bruises, contact your doctor immediately.

If you forget to take a dose of Piroxicam, take it as soon as you remember. If it is almost time for your next regularly scheduled dose, skip the one you forgot and continue with your regular schedule. Do not take a double dose.

Brand Name

Poly-Vi-Flor Chewable Tablets

Ingredients

Folic Acid (Vitamin B_9)	Vitamin B_6 (Pyridoxine)
Sodium Fluoride	Vitamin B_{12} (Cyanocobalmin)
Vitamin A	Vitamin C
Vitamin B_1 (Thiamine)	Vitamin D
Vitamin B_2 (Riboflavin)	Vitamin E
Vitamin B_3 (Niacin)	

Other Brand Names

Florvite	Poly-Vitamins with Fluoride
Poly-Tabs-F	Vi-Daylin/F

(Also available in generic form)

Type of Drug

Multivitamin supplement with fluoride.

Prescribed for

Vitamin deficiencies and prevention of dental cavities in infants and children.

General Information

Fluorides taken in small daily doses have been effective in preventing cavities in children by strengthening their teeth and making them resistant to cavity formation. Multivitamins with fluoride are also available in preparations containing iron, if iron supplementation is required.

Too much fluoride can damage the teeth. Because of this, vitamins with a fluoride should not be used in areas where the water supply is fluoridated.

Cautions and Warnings

Poly-Vi-Flor Chewable Tablets should not be used in areas where the fluoride content exceeds 0.7 ppm (parts per million). Your pediatrician or local water company can tell you the fluoride content of the water you drink.

This drug has been found to be safe for use during pregnancy. Remember, you should check with your doctor before taking any drug if you are pregnant.

Possible Side Effects

Occasional skin rash, itching, stomach upset, headache, weakness.

Usual Dose

1 tablet chewed per day.

Special Information

If you forget to take a dose of Poly-Vi-Flor, take it as soon as you remember. If it is almost time for your next regularly scheduled dose, skip the one you forgot and continue with your regular schedule. Do not take a double dose.

Generic Name

Potassium Replacement Products

Brand Names

Potassium Chloride Liquids

Cena-K	Klor-Con
EM-K	Klorvess
Kaochlor	Potachlor
Kaochlor S-F	Potasalan
Kaon-Cl	Potassine
Kay Ciel	Rum-K
Klor	

Potassium Gluconate Liquids

Kaon	K-G Elixir
Kaylixir	My-K Elixir

Potassium Salt Liquid Combinations

Bi-K	Trikates
Duo-K	Twin-K
Kolyum	Twin-K-Cl
Tri-K	

Potassium Chloride Powders

Gen-K	Klor-Con
Kato	K-Lyte/Cl
Kay Ciel	Potage
K-Lor	

Potassium Salt Powder Combinations

Klorvess
Kolyum

Potassium Effervescent Tablets

Effer-K	K-Lyte
Kaochlor-Eff	K-Lyte/Cl
Klor-Con/EF	K-Lyte DS
Klorvess	

Potassium Chloride Controlled Release

Kaon-Cl	K-Tab
K-Dur	Micro-K
Klor-Con	Slow-K
Klotrix	Ten-K
K-Norm	

Potassium Gluconate Tablets

Kaon
Kao-Nor

Chewable Potassium Products

K-Forte
Osto-K

(Potassium Chloride and Gluconate also available in generic form)

Type of Drug

Potassium supplement.

Prescribed for

Replacement of potassium in the body.

General Information

Potassium is a very important component of the body and has a major effect in maintaining the proper tone of all body cells. Potassium is also important for the maintenance of normal kidney function; it is required for the passage of electrical impulses in the nervous system, and has a major effect on the heart and all other muscles of the body. Potassium also plays a role in the metabolism of proteins and carbohydrates.

Potassium supplements are available in a wide variety of dosage forms to meet your individual needs. Potassium chloride is most often used in these formulations because it contains the most potassium per unit weight. Potassium gluconate provides about ⅓ as much potassium as the chloride.

Foods rich in potassium can provide a natural potassium source; they include: apricots, avocados, bananas, beans, beef, broccoli, brussels sprouts, cantaloupes, chicken, dates, fish, ham, lentils, milk, potatoes, prunes, raisins, shellfish, spinach, turkey, veal, and watermelon.

Cautions and Warnings

Potassium replacement should always be monitored and controlled by your physician. Potassium tablets have produced ulceration in some patients with compression of the esophagus. Potassium supplements for these patients should be given in liquid form. Potassium tablets have been reported to cause ulcers of the small bowel, leading to hemorrhage, obstruction, and/or perforation.

Do not take Potassium supplements if you are dehydrated or experiencing muscle cramps due to excessive sun exposure. The drug should be used with caution in patients who have kidney and/or heart disease.

Pregnancy/Breast-feeding

This drug has been found to be safe for use during pregnancy. Remember, you should check with your doctor before taking any drug if you are pregnant. However, breast-feeding while taking Potassium may cause unwanted side effects in your infant. If you must take Potassium, you should temporarily stop nursing and discard pumped breast milk. Nursing can resume 1 to 2 days after stopping Potassium.

Seniors

Older adults may take this medication without special restriction. Follow your doctor's directions and report any side effects at once.

Possible Side Effects

Potassium toxicity, or overdose, is extremely rare. Toxicity can occur when high doses of Potassium supplements are taken in combination with foods high in Potassium. Common side effects are nausea, vomiting, diarrhea, and abdominal discomfort. Less common side effects are tingling of hands and feet, listlessness, mental confusion, weakness and heaviness of legs, decreased blood pressure, and/or heart rhythm changes.

Drug Interactions

Potassium supplements should not be taken with Spironolactone, Triamterene, or combinations of these drugs, as Potassium toxicity may occur.

Food Interactions

Salt substitutes may contain large amounts of Potassium. You should discuss their use with your doctor.

If stomach upset occurs, take after meals or with food.

Usual Dose

As regulated by physician; generally 20 to 60 milliequivalents per day.

Special Information

Directions for taking and using Potassium supplements should be followed closely. Effervescent tablets, powders, and liquids should be properly and completely dissolved or diluted in a glass of cold water or juice and drunk slowly. Oral tablets or capsules should not be chewed or crushed and are intended to be swallowed whole.

Notify your physician if you have continued abdominal pain or black stool.

If you forget to take a dose of Potassium, and you remember within about 2 hours of your regular time, take it right away. If you do not remember until later, skip the forgotten dose and go back to your regular schedule. Do not take a double dose.

Generic Name

Prazepam

Brand Name

Centrax

Type of Drug

Tranquilizer.

Prescribed for

Relief of symptoms of anxiety, tension, fatigue, or agitation.

General Information

Prazepam is a member of the group of drugs known as benzodiazepines. These drugs are used as either antianxiety agents, anticonvulsants, or sedatives (sleeping pills). They exert their effects by relaxing the large skeletal muscles and by a direct effect on the brain. In doing so, they can relax you and make you either more tranquil or sleepier, depending on the drug and how much you use. Many doctors prefer Prazepam and the other members of this class to other drugs that can be used for the same effect. Their reason is that the benzodiazepines tend to be safer, have fewer side effects, and are usually as, if not more, effective.

These drugs are generally used in any situation where they can be a useful adjunct.

Benzodiazepine tranquilizing drugs can be abused if taken for long periods of time and it is possible to develop withdrawal symptoms if you discontinue the therapy abruptly. Withdrawal symptoms include convulsions, tremor, muscle cramps, stomach cramps, vomiting, and sweating.

Cautions and Warnings

Do not take Prazepam if you know you are sensitive or allergic to this drug or other benzodiazepines such as Chlordiazepoxide, Oxazepam, Clorazepate, Diazepam, Lorazepam, Flurazepam, and Clonazepam.

Prazepam and other members of this drug group may aggravate narrow-angle glaucoma, but if you have open-angle glaucoma you may take the drugs. In any case, check this information with your doctor. Prazepam can cause tiredness, drowsiness, inability to concentrate, or similar symptoms. Be careful if you are driving, operating machinery, or performing other activities which require concentration.

Pregnancy/Breast-feeding

This drug, like all members of the benzodiazepine family, crosses into your developing baby's circulation and may cause birth defects if taken during the first 3 months of pregnancy. You should avoid taking this medication while pregnant.

Members of the benzodiazepine family pass into breast milk. Since infants break the drug down more slowly than adults, it is possible for the medicine to accumulate and have an undesired effect on the baby.

Seniors

Older adults are more sensitive to the effects of this drug, especially dizziness and drowsiness. Follow your doctor's directions and report any side effects at once.

Possible Side Effects

Most common: mild drowsiness during the first few days of therapy, especially in the elderly or debilitated. If drowsiness persists, contact your doctor.

Less common side effects: confusion, depression, lethargy, disorientation, headache, lack of activity, slurred speech, stupor, dizziness, tremor, constipation, dry mouth, nausea, inability to control urination, changes in sex drive, irregular menstrual cycle, changes in heart rhythm, lowered blood pressure, retention of fluids, blurred or double vision, itching, rash, hiccups, nervousness, inability to fall asleep, (occasional) liver dysfunction. If you experience any of these reactions stop taking the medicine and contact your doctor immediately.

Drug Interactions

Prazepam is a central nervous system depressant. Avoid alcohol, tranquilizers, narcotics, sleeping pills, barbiturates, MAO inhibitors, antihistamines, and other medicines used to relieve depression.

Food Interactions

Prazepam is best taken on an empty stomach but may be taken with food.

Usual Dose

Adult: 20 to 60 milligrams per day as individualized for maximum benefit, depending on symptoms and response to treatment, which may require a dose outside the range given. 20 milligrams may be taken at bedtime for sleep.

Senior: usually requires less of the drug to control anxiety and tension: about 10 to 15 milligrams per day.

Overdosage

Symptoms are confusion, sleep or sleepiness, lack of response to pain such as a pin stick, shallow breathing, lowered blood pressure, and coma. The patient should be taken to a hospital emergency room immediately. ALWAYS bring the medicine bottle.

Special Information

Avoid alcohol while taking Prazepam. Sleeping pills, narcotics, other tranquilizers, and drugs that depress the nervous system should be used with caution while taking Prazepam.

If you forget to take a dose of Prazepam, and you remember within about an hour of your regular time, take it right away. If you do not remember until later, skip the forgotten dose and go back to your regular schedule. Do not take a double dose.

Generic Name

Prazosin Hydrochloride

Brand Name

Minipress

Type of Drug

Antihypertensive.

Prescribed for

High blood pressure. Also prescribed for heart failure and for Raynaud's disease.

General Information

Prazosin Hydrochloride works by dilating and reducing pressure in blood vessels. It is quite effective when used in combination with a thiazide diuretic and/or beta-adrenergic blocker. It is much safer than the other drugs which work in the same way because it does not directly affect the heart.

Cautions and Warnings

This drug can cause dizziness and fainting, most often due to an effect called "postural hypotension" where blood supply to the brain is reduced when rising suddenly from a sitting or lying-down position. This often occurs after taking the first dose of 2 milligrams or more of Prazosin Hydrochloride.

Pregnancy/Breast-feeding

This drug has not been found to cause birth defects. Pregnant women, or those who might become pregnant while taking this drug, should not take it without their doctor's approval. When the drug is considered essential by your doctor, the potential risk of taking the medicine must be carefully weighed against the benefit it might produce.

This drug has caused no problems among breast-fed infants. You must consider the potential effect on the nursing infant if breast-feeding while taking this medicine.

Seniors

Older adults should use this product with caution because of greater sensitivity to the drug's effects and side effects. Older adults are more likely to develop Prazosin-caused low body temperature (hypothermia).

Possible Side Effects

The most common side effects of Prazosin Hydrochloride are dizziness, headache, drowsiness, lack of energy, weakness, heart palpitations, and nausea. Usually these side effects subside and people become more tolerant of the drug.

Less common side effects: vomiting, diarrhea, constipation, stomach upset or pain, unusual swelling in the arms or legs, shortness of breath, passing out, rapid heart rate, increased chest pain (angina), nervousness, depression, tingling in the hands or feet, rash, itching, frequent urination, poor urinary control, sexual impotence, blurred vision, redness of the eyes, ringing or buzzing in the ears, dry mouth, stuffy nose, sweating.

Drug Interactions

Prazosin Hydrochloride's effectiveness may be lessened when it is taken together with anti-inflammatory pain relievers, especially Indomethacin, with estrogen-containing drugs, or drugs with stimulant properties such as decongestants and diet pills.

Prazosin Hydrochloride's effectiveness is increased when combined with other antihypertensive medicines.

Food Interactions

Take this medicine with food if it upsets your stomach.

Usual Dose

1 milligram 2 to 3 times per day to start; the dose may be increased to 20 milligrams a day, and 40 milligrams has been used in some cases. The daily dose of Prazosin Hydrochloride must be tailored to patient's needs.

Overdosage

Overdosage may lead to very slow blood pressure. Call your doctor or poison control center for advice. If you go to a hospital emergency room, remember, ALWAYS bring the medicine bottle.

Special Information

Take this drug exactly as prescribed. Do not stop taking Prazosin Hydrochloride unless directed to do so by your doctor. Do not take over-the-counter medicines containing stimulants. If you are unsure which ones to avoid, ask your pharmacist.

Prazosin Hydrochloride can cause dizziness, drowsiness, or headache, especially when you begin taking the drug. Avoid driving or operating any equipment 4 hours after the first dose and take care for the first few days. You may want to take the first dose before you go to bed. If you experience severe dizziness, lie down and wait for the episode to pass.

If you forget to take a dose of Prazosin Hydrochloride, take it as soon as you remember. If it is almost time for your next regularly scheduled dose, skip the one you forgot and continue with your regular schedule. Do not take a double dose.

Generic Name

Prednisone

Brand Names

Deltasone	Prednicen-M
Liquid Pred	Prednisone Intensol
Meticorten	Concentrate
Orasone	Sterapred
Panasol-S	Sterapred DS

(Also available in generic form)

Type of Drug

Adrenal corticosteroid.

Prescribed for

The variety of disorders for which Prednisone is prescribed is almost endless, from skin rash to cancer. The drug may be used as a treatment for adrenal gland disease, since one of the hormones produced by the adrenal gland is very similar to Prednisone. If patients are not producing sufficient adrenal hormones, Prednisone may be used as replacement therapy. It may also be prescribed for the treatment of bursitis, arthritis, severe skin reactions such as psoriasis or other rashes, severe allergic conditions, asthma, drug or serum sickness, severe, acute, or chronic allergic inflammation of the eye and surrounding areas such as conjunctivitis, respiratory diseases including pneumonitis, blood disorders, gastrointestinal diseases including ulcerative colitis, and inflammation of the nerves, heart, or other organs.

General Information

Prednisone is one of many adrenal corticosteroids used in medical practice today. The major differences between Prednisone and other adrenal corticosteroids are potency of medication and variation in some secondary effects. Choice of an adrenal corticosteroid to be used for a specific disease is usually a matter of doctor preference and past experience. Other adrenal corticosteroids include Cortisone, Hydrocortisone, Prednisolone, Triamcinolone, Methylprednisolone,

Meprednisone, Paramethasone, Fluprednisolone, Dexamethasone, Betamethasone, and Fludrocortisone.

Cautions and Warnings

Because of the effect of Prednisone on your adrenal gland, it
is essential that the dose be tapered from a large dose down
to a small dose over a period of time. Do not stop taking this
medication suddenly or without the advice of your doctor. If
you do, you may cause a failure of the adrenal gland with
extremely serious consequences.

Prednisone has a strong anti-inflammatory effect, and may
mask some signs of infections. If new infections appear
during the use of Prednisone therapy, they may be difficult
to discover and may grow more rapidly due to your decreased resistance. If you think you are getting an infection
during the time that you are taking Prednisone, you should
contact your doctor, who will prescribe appropriate therapy.

If you are taking Prednisone, you should not be vaccinated
against any infectious diseases, because Prednisone interferes with the body's normal reaction to vaccination. Discuss
this with your doctor before he administers any vaccination.

Pregnancy/Breast-feeding

Studies have shown that corticosteroids taken in large amounts
or over long periods of time can be the cause of birth defects. Pregnant women or those who might become pregnant while using this medicine should not do so unless they
are under a doctor's care.

Corticosteroid drugs taken by mouth pass into breast milk
and large drug doses may interfere with the growth of a
nursing infant. Do not use the medicine unless under a
doctor's care.

Seniors

Older adults are more likely to develop high blood pressure
while taking this medicine (by mouth). Also, older women
have a greater chance of being susceptible to bone degeneration (osteoporosis) associated with large doses of this
class of medicines.

Possible Side Effects

Stomach upset is one of the more common side effects of

Prednisone, which may in some cases cause gastric or duodenal ulcers. Other side effects: retention of water, heart failure, potassium loss, muscle weakness, loss of muscle mass, loss of calcium which may result in bone fractures and a condition known as aseptic necrosis of the femoral and humoral heads (this means the ends of the large bones in the hip may degenerate from loss of calcium), slowing down of wound healing, black-and-blue marks on the skin, increased sweating, allergic skin rash, itching, convulsions, dizziness, headache.

Less common side effects: irregular menstrual cycles, slow growth in children, particularly after the medication has been taken for long periods of time, depression of the adrenal and/or pituitary glands, development of diabetes, increased pressure of the fluid inside the eye, hypersensitivity or allergic reactions, blood clots, insomnia, weight gain, increased appetite, nausea, and feeling of ill health. Psychic derangements may appear which range from euphoria to mood swings, personality changes, and severe depression. Prednisone may also aggravate existing emotional instability.

Drug Interactions

Prednisone and other adrenal corticosteroids may interact with Insulin and oral antidiabetic drugs, causing an increased requirement of the antidiabetic drugs.

Interaction with Phenobarbital, Ephedrine, and Phenytoin may reduce the effect of Prednisone by increasing its removal from the body.

If a doctor prescribes Prednisone you should discuss any oral anticoagulant (blood-thinning) drugs you are taking: the dose of them may have to be changed.

Interaction with diuretics such as Hydrochlorothiazide may cause you to lose blood potassium. Be aware of signs of lowered potassium level such as weakness, muscle cramps, and tiredness, and report them to your physician. Eat high-potassium foods such as bananas, citrus fruits, melons, and tomatoes.

Prednisone and other steroids can interfere with laboratory tests. You should notify your physician that you are taking these drugs so that the tests can be properly analyzed.

Food Interactions

If you notice a slight stomach upset when you take your dose of Prednisone, take this medication with food or a small amount of antacid. If stomach upset continues or bothers you, notify your doctor.

Usual Dose

Initial dose, 5 to 60 or more milligrams. Maintenance dose, 5 to 60 milligrams depending on patient's response.

Dose also varies according to disease being treated. The lowest effective dose is desirable. Stressful situations may cause a need for a temporary increase in your Prednisone dose.

This drug must be tapered off slowly, not stopped abruptly. Prednisone may be given in alternate day therapy; twice the usual daily dose is given every other day.

Overdosage

There is no specific treatment for overdosage of adrenal corticosteroids. Symptoms are anxiety, depression and/or stimulation, stomach bleeding, increased blood sugar, high blood pressure, and retention of fluid. The patient should be taken to a hospital emergency room immediately, where stomach pumping, oxygen, intravenous fluids, and other supportive treatments are available. ALWAYS bring the medicine bottle.

Special Information

Do not stop taking this medicine on your own. Suddenly stopping this or any other corticosteroid drug can have severe consequences; the dosage will be gradually reduced by your doctor.

If you miss a dose of Prednisone and you take several doses per day, take the missed dose as soon as you can. If it is almost time for your next dose, skip the missed dose and double the next dose.

If you take one dose per day, and you do not remember the missed dose until the next day, skip the missed dose and take your usual dose. Do not double up your dose.

If you take Prednisone every other day, take the missed dose if you remember it that morning. If it is much later in the day, skip the missed dose and take it the following morning, then go back to your usual dose schedule.

Generic Name

Primidone

Brand Names

Mysoline
Primoline

(Also available in generic form)

Type of Drug

Anticonvulsant.

Prescribed for

Control of epileptic and other seizures.

General Information

Although this drug is not a barbiturate, it is a close chemical cousin to the barbiturates and possesses many of their characteristics. It acts on a portion of the brain that inhibits the usual nerve transmissions that are present in seizure disorders.

Primidone may be used in combination with other anticonvulsant drugs to achieve the best results.

Cautions and Warnings

If you have been taking Primidone for a long time and no longer need it do not stop abruptly, but reduce the dosage gradually over a period of about a week. Stopping abruptly may bring on severe epileptic seizures.

Pregnancy/Breast-feeding

Primidone crosses into the blood circulation of a developing baby. Most mothers who take this medicine deliver healthy, normal babies, but some are born with cleft lip, cleft palate, and heart malformations. Also, there is a recognized group of deformities known as "fetal hydantoin syndrome" that affect children of mothers taking this medicine (although the medicine has not been definitely implicated as the cause of these deformities), which consists of abnormalities in the skull and face, small brain, growth deficiency, deformed fingernails, and mental deficiency.

Children born of mothers taking Primidone are more likely to have a Vitamin K deficiency, leading to serious, life-threatening hemorrhage during the first 24 hours of life. Also, the mother may be deficient in Vitamin K because of Primidone, leading to increased bleeding during delivery.

Primidone passes into breast milk and may affect a nursing infant. Use an alternate feeding method if you are taking this medication.

Seniors

Older adults sometimes become restless and excited while taking Primidone, just the opposite of what you might otherwise expect from this medicine.

Possible Side Effects

Dizziness and some loss of muscle coordination. Side effects tend to disappear with time.

Less common side effects include: fatigue, loss of appetite, nystagmus (a rhythmic, uncontrolled movement of the eyeballs), irritability, emotional upset, sexual impotence, double vision, rash. If side effects are persistent or severe, your doctor may have to discontinue treatment or use a different medication.

Drug Interactions

This drug, because of its relation to barbiturates, may affect oral anticoagulants, Doxycycline, corticosteroids, or Griseofulvin. Special care should be taken if you need any sedative, sleeping pill, antidepressant, or strong analgesic, because of the possibility of drug interaction. Consult your physician or pharmacist for more information. Avoid alcoholic beverages, which may enhance the side effects of fatigue and dizziness normally experienced with Primidone.

Food Interactions

If you get an upset stomach after taking Primidone, take the medicine with meals.

Usual Dose

Adult and child (age 8 and over): 250 milligrams per day to start. Dose may be increased in steps of 250 milligrams per day up to 1500 milligrams per day, according to patient's need.

Child (under age 8): 125 milligrams per day to start. Dose may be increased in steps of 125 milligrams per day up to 750 milligrams per day, according to patient's need. Doses may be divided 3 to 6 times per day.

Overdosage

Symptoms are listed in "Possible Side Effects" above. The patient should be taken to a hospital emergency room immediately. ALWAYS bring the medicine bottle.

Special Information

If you develop a rash, sore throat, fever, or unusual bleeding or bruising, contact your doctor immediately. Primidone sometimes produces a pink-brown color in the urine; this is normal, and not a cause for worry.

If you forget to take a dose of Primidone, take it as soon as you remember. If it is almost time for your next regularly scheduled dose, skip the one you forgot and continue with your regular schedule. Do not take a double dose.

Generic Name

Probucol

Brand Name

Lorelco

Type of Drug

Antihyperlipidemic (blood-fat reducer).

Prescribed for

People with excessively high levels of cholesterol.

General Information

Probucol consistently reduces blood-cholesterol levels, but is prescribed only for people who have not responded to diet changes or other therapies. Probucol has little effect on blood triglycerides.

Probucol increases the body's breakdown of cholesterol, reduces the amount of cholesterol manufactured by the liver, and reduces the amount of cholesterol absorbed from foods.

Cautions and Warnings

Probucol should not be taken by people who have had allergic reactions to the drug. Probucol users may have an increased chance of developing abnormal heart rhythms and should realize that this drug, like other blood-fat reducers, including Clofibrate and Gemfibrozil, have not been proven to reduce the chances of fatal heart attacks.

Pregnancy/Breast-feeding

Animal studies of this drug have revealed no harmful effects on the developing fetus. However, because there have been no controlled studies of pregnant women, Probucol should be avoided by pregnant women or women who may become pregnant while using it. Women who are trying to become pregnant should discontinue the drug and use birth control for at least 6 months before they want to conceive, because the drug remains in the body for extended periods. It is not known if Probucol passes into human breast milk, but this has been observed in animal studies. Nursing mothers should not breast-feed while taking this drug.

Seniors

Older adults may take this medication without special restriction. Follow your doctor's directions and report any side effects at once.

Possible Side Effects

Most side effects are mild and last for only short periods of time. The most common are diarrhea or loose stools, headaches, dizziness, and reduction in some white-blood-cell counts.

Less common side effects: abnormal heart rhythms, heart palpitations, chest pains, stomach and abdominal pains or gas, nausea, vomiting, anemia, itching, rash, male impotence, sleeplessness, conjunctivitis (red-eye), tearing, blurred vision, ringing or buzzing in the ears, loss of appetite, reduced senses of taste and/or smell, heartburn, indigestion, stomach or intestinal bleeding, easy bruising, goiter, night-time waking to urinate, and excessive and possibly malodorous sweat.

Food Interactions

Take each dose with food or a meal to ensure better drug absorption.

Usual Dose

500 milligrams twice per day with breakfast and evening meal.

Overdosage

There are no reports of Probucol overdosage, but victims might be expected to develop exaggerated versions of the drug's side effects. Less than 10 percent of each dose of Probucol is absorbed from the stomach and intestines. Because of this, the chances are that few symptoms other than those affecting the stomach and intestines will develop. Patients taking an overdose of this drug must be made to vomit with Syrup of Ipecac (available at any pharmacy) to remove any remaining drug from the stomach. Call your doctor or a poison control center before doing this. If you must go to a hospital emergency room, ALWAYS bring the medicine bottle.

Special Information

Follow your doctor's dietary guidelines.

Probucol occasionally causes dizziness and blurred vision. Use caution while driving or doing anything else that requires concentration and alertness.

Call your doctor if any drug side effects become severe or intolerable, especially diarrhea, nausea, vomiting, or stomach pains and/or gas. These may be resolved with a reduction in drug dose.

If you forget to take a dose of Probucol, take it as soon as you remember. If it is almost time for your next regularly scheduled dose, skip the one you forgot and continue with your regular schedule. Do not take a double dose.

Generic Name

Procainamide Hydrochloride

Brand Names

Promine
Pronestyl

Sustained-Release Products

Procamide SR	Pronestyl SR
Procan SR	Rhythmin

(Also available in generic form)

Type of Drug

Antiarrhythmic.

Prescribed for

Abnormal heart rhythms.

General Information

Procainamide Hydrochloride is frequently used as the primary treatment for arrhythmia (abnormal heart rhythms), which it controls by affecting the response of heart muscle to nervous system stimulation. It also slows the rate at which nervous system impulses are carried through the heart. It may be given to patients who do not respond to or cannot tolerate other antiarrhythmic drugs.

Cautions and Warnings

Tell your doctor if you have the disease myasthenia gravis. If you do, you should be taking a drug other than Procainamide Hydrochloride. Tell your doctor if you are allergic to Procainamide Hydrochloride or to the local anesthetic Procaine. Patients taking this drug should be under strict medical supervision.

This drug is eliminated from the body through the kidney and liver. Therefore, if you have either kidney or liver disease your dose of Procainamide Hydrochloride may have to be adjusted.

Pregnancy/Breast-feeding

This drug crosses into the blood circulation of a developing baby. It has not been found to cause birth defects. Pregnant women, or those who might become pregnant while taking this drug, should not take it without their doctor's approval. When the drug is considered essential by your doctor, the potential risk of taking the medicine must be carefully weighed against the benefit it might produce.

This drug passes into breast milk, but has caused no problems among breast-fed infants. You must consider the potential effect on the nursing infant if breast-feeding while taking this medicine.

Seniors

Older adults are more sensitive to the effects of this drug, especially low blood pressure and dizziness. Follow your doctor's directions and report any side effects at once.

Possible Side Effects

Large oral doses of Procainamide Hydrochloride may produce loss of appetite, nausea, or itching. A group of symptoms resembling the disease lupus erythematosus has been reported in patients taking the drug: fever and chills, nausea, vomiting, and abdominal pains. Your doctor may detect enlargement of your liver and changes in blood tests indicating a change in the liver. Soreness of the mouth or throat, unusual bleeding, rash, or fever may occur. If any of these symptoms occur while you are taking Procainamide Hydrochloride, tell your doctor immediately.

Less common: bitter taste in the mouth, diarrhea, weakness, mental depression, giddiness, hallucinations, drug allergy (such as rash and drug fever).

Drug Interactions

Avoid over-the-counter cough, cold, or allergy remedies containing drugs which have a direct stimulating effect on your heart. Ask your pharmacist to tell you about the ingredients in over-the-counter remedies.

Food Interactions

This medicine is best taken on an empty stomach, but you may take it with food if it upsets your stomach.

Usual Dose

Initial dose, 1000 milligrams. Maintenance dose, 25 milligrams per pound per day in divided doses every 3 hours, around the clock, adjusted according to individual needs.

The sustained-release products allow spacing doses 6 hours apart.

Special Information

If you forget to take a dose of Procainamide Hydrochloride, and remember within 2 hours (4 hours for long-acting Procainamide Hydrochloride), take it right away. If it is almost time for your next regularly scheduled dose, skip the one you forgot and continue with your regular schedule. Do not take a double dose.

Generic Name

Prochlorperazine

Brand Name

Compazine

(Also available in generic form)

Type of Drug

Phenothiazine antipsychotic, antinauseant.

Prescribed for

Severe nausea, vomiting, psychotic disorders, excessive anxiety, tension, and agitation.

General Information

Prochlorperazine and other members of the phenothiazine group act on a portion of the brain called the hypothalamus. They affect parts of the hypothalamus that control metabolism, body temperature, alertness, muscle tone, hormone balance, and vomiting, and may be used to treat problems related to any of these functions.

Cautions and Warnings

Sudden death has occurred in patients who have taken this drug, because of its effect on the cough reflex. In some cases the patients choked to death because of failure of the cough reflex to protect them. Prochlorperazine, because of its effect in reducing vomiting, can obscure signs of toxicity due to overdose of other drugs or symptoms of disease.

Prochlorperazine should not be taken if you are allergic to one of the drugs in the broad classification known as phenothiazine drugs. Do not take Prochlorperazine if you have any blood, liver, kidney, or heart disease, very low blood pressure, or Parkinson's disease. This medication is a tranquilizer and can have a depressive effect, especially during the first few days of therapy. Care should be taken when performing activities requiring a high degree of concentration, such as driving.

This drug should be used with caution and under strict supervision of your doctor if you have glaucoma, epilepsy, ulcers, or difficulty passing urine.

Avoid exposure to extreme heat, since this drug can affect your body's normal temperature mechanism.

Pregnancy/Breast-feeding

Infants born to women taking this medication have experienced drug side effects (liver jaundice, nervous system effects) immediately after birth. Check with your doctor about taking this medicine if you are, or might become, pregnant.

This drug may pass into breast milk and affect a nursing infant. Consider alternate feeding methods if you must take this medicine.

Seniors

Older adults are more sensitive to the effects of this medication than younger adults and usually require a lower dosage to achieve a desired effect. Also, older adults are more likely to develop drug side effects. Some experts feel that elderly people should be treated with ½ to ¼ the usual adult dose of Prochlorperazine.

Possible Side Effects

Most common: drowsiness, especially during the first or

second week of therapy. If the drowsiness becomes trouble-some, contact your doctor.

Prochlorperazine can cause jaundice (yellowing of the whites of the eyes or skin), usually in 2 to 4 weeks. The jaundice usually goes away when the drug is discontinued, but there have been cases when it did not. If you notice this effect or if you develop symptoms such as fever and generally not feeling well, contact your doctor immediately. Less frequent: changes in components of the blood including anemias, raised or lowered blood pressure, abnormal heart rates, heart attack, feeling faint or dizzy.

Phenothiazines can produce "extrapyramidal effects," such as spasm of the neck muscles, rolling back of the eyes, convulsions, difficulty in swallowing, and symptoms associated with Parkinson's disease. These effects look very serious but disappear after the drug has been withdrawn; however, symptoms of the face, tongue, and jaw may persist for as long as several years, especially in the elderly with a history of brain damage. If you experience extrapyramidal effects, contact your doctor immediately.

Prochlorperazine may cause an unusual increase in psychotic symptoms or may cause paranoid reactions, tiredness, lethargy, restlessness, hyperactivity, confusion at night, bizarre dreams, inability to sleep, depression, and euphoria. Other reactions are itching, swelling, unusual sensitivity to bright lights, red skin, and rash. There have been cases of breast enlargement, false positive pregnancy tests, changes in menstrual flow, impotence and changes in sex drive in males, as well as stuffy nose, headache, nausea, vomiting, loss of appetite, change in body temperature, pallor, excessive salivation, excessive perspiration, constipation, diarrhea, changes in urine and stool habits, worsening of glaucoma, blurred vision, weakening of eyelid muscles, and spasms in bronchial and other muscles, increased appetite, fatigue, excessive thirst, and changes in the coloration of skin, particularly in exposed areas.

Drug Interactions

Prochlorperazine should be taken with caution in combination with barbiturates, sleeping pills, narcotics, other tranquilizers, or any other medication which may produce a depressive effect.

Alcoholic beverages should be avoided. They can increase the depressant effects of Prochlorperazine.

Food Interactions

Antipsychotic effectiveness of Prochlorperazine or other members of the phenothiazine drug group may be counteracted by alcohol- or caffeine-containing food, such as coffee, tea, cola drinks, or chocolate.

Usual Dose

Adult: 15 to 150 milligrams per day, depending on disease and patient's response. For nausea and vomiting, 15 to 40 milligrams per day by mouth, 25 milligrams twice per day in rectal suppositories.

Child: 40 to 85 pounds, 10 to 15 milligrams per day; 30 to 40 pounds, 2.5 milligrams 2 to 3 times per day; 20 to 30 pounds, 2.5 milligrams 1 to 2 times per day; not recommended for children under age 2 or weight 20 pounds, except to save life. Usually only 1 to 2 days of therapy is needed for nausea and vomiting. For psychosis, doses of 25 milligrams or more per day may be required.

Overdosage

Symptoms are depression, extreme weakness, tiredness, desire to go to sleep, coma, lowered blood pressure, uncontrolled muscle spasms, agitation, restlessness, convulsions, fever, dry mouth, and abnormal heart rhythms. The patient should be taken to a hospital emergency room immediately. ALWAYS bring the medicine bottle.

Special Information

This medication may cause drowsiness. Use caution when driving or operating complex equipment and avoid alcoholic beverages while taking the medicine.

The drug may also cause unusual sensitivity to the sun and can turn your urine reddish-brown to pink.

If dizziness occurs, avoid sudden changes in posture and avoid climbing stairs.

Use caution in hot weather. This medicine may make you more prone to heat stroke.

The liquid form of Prochlorperazine can cause skin irritations or rashes. Do not get it on your skin.

If you miss a dose of Prochlorperazine, take it as soon as you can. If it is almost time for your next dose, skip the missed dose and go back to your usual dose schedule. Do not double any doses.

Generic Name

Propantheline Bromide

Brand Names

Norpanth
Pro-Banthine

(Also available in generic form)

Type of Drug

Gastrointestinal anticholinergic agent.

Prescribed for

Relief of stomach upset, spasms, and peptic ulcers. This medication is sometimes prescribed to treat morning sickness during the early months of pregnancy.

General Information

Propantheline Bromide works by reducing spasms in muscles of the stomach and other parts of the gastrointestinal tract. In doing so, it helps relieve some of the uncomfortable symptoms associated with peptic ulcer, irritable bowel and/or colon, spastic colon, and other gastrointestinal disorders. It only relieves symptoms, but does not cure the underlying disease.

Cautions and Warnings

Propantheline Bromide should not be used if you know you are sensitive or allergic to it. Do not use this medicine if you have glaucoma, asthma, obstructive disease of the gastrointestinal tract, or other serious gastrointestinal disease. Because this drug reduces your ability to sweat, its use in hot climates may cause heat exhaustion.

Pregnancy/Breast-feeding

This drug crosses into the blood circulation of a developing baby. It has not been found to cause birth defects. Pregnant women, or those who might become pregnant while taking this drug, should not take it without their doctor's approval. When the drug is considered essential by your doctor, the potential risk of taking the medicine must be carefully weighed against the benefit it might produce.

This drug passes into breast milk, but has caused no problems among breast-fed infants. You must consider the potential effect on the nursing infant if breast-feeding while taking this medicine.

Seniors

Older adults are more likely to become excited, agitated, confused, or drowsy while taking normal doses of this medicine. Continued use of Propantheline may lead to loss of memory. This medication blocks the hormone acetylcholine in the brain, which is responsible for many memory functions.

Possible Side Effects

Difficulty in urination, blurred vision, rapid heartbeat, skin rash, sensitivity to light, headache, flushing of the skin, nervousness, dizziness, weakness, drowsiness, nausea, vomiting, fever, nasal congestion, heartburn, constipation, loss of taste.

Drug Interactions

Interaction with antihistamines, phenothiazines, long-term use of corticosteroids, tranquilizers, antidepressants, and some narcotic painkillers may cause blurred vision, dry mouth, or drowsiness. Antacids should not be taken together with Propantheline Bromide, or they will reduce the absorption of the Propantheline Bromide; doses of antacids and Propantheline Bromide should be taken 2 hours apart.

Do not use with Tranylcypromine Sulfate (Parnate), Isocarboxazid (Marplan), Phenelzine Sulfate (Nardil), or other MAO inhibitor drugs, which will tend to prevent excretion of Propantheline Bromide from the body and thus potentiate it (increase its effect).

Food Interactions

This medicine is best taken on an empty stomach, but you may take it with food if it upsets your stomach.

Usual Dose

30 milligrams at bedtime or 7.5 to 15 milligrams 3 to 4 times per day, usually 30 minutes before meals.

Special Information

Dry mouth from Propantheline Bromide can be relieved by chewing gum or sucking hard candy; constipation can be treated by using a stool-softening laxative.

If you forget to take a dose of Propantheline Bromide, take it as soon as you remember. If it is almost time for your next regularly scheduled dose, skip the one you forgot and continue with your regular schedule. Do not take a double dose.

Generic Name

Propoxyphene

Brand Names

Propoxyphene Hydrochloride

Darvon	Doxaphene
Dolene	Prophene

Combination Products with Aspirin and Caffeine:

Bexophene	Dolene Compound
Darvon Compound	Doxaphene Compound

Combination Products with Acetaminophen:
Dolene AP-65
Wygesic

Propoxyphene Napsylate

Darvon N

Combination Product with Aspirin:
Darvon N with ASA

Combination Products with Acetaminophen:
Darvocet N 100   Lorcet
Doxapap N   Propacet
Genagesic   Prox/APAP

(Also available in generic form)

Type of Drug

Analgesic.

Prescribed for

Relief of pain.

General Information

Propoxyphene is a chemical derivative of Methadone, a narcotic used for pain relief. It is estimated that Propoxyphene is about ½ to ⅔ as strong a pain reliever as Codeine and about as effective as Aspirin. Propoxyphene is widely used for mild pain; it can produce drug dependence when used for extended periods of time.

Propoxyphene is more effective when used in combination products with Aspirin or Acetaminophen than when used alone. The Propoxyphene used in these combinations is either the Hydrochloride or Napsylate salt. The Hydrochloride salt is about 30 percent more potent.

Cautions and Warnings

Propoxyphene may interfere with your ability to concentrate. Therefore, be very careful when driving an automobile or operating complicated or dangerous machinery. Do not drink alcohol when taking this medicine. Never take more medicine than is prescribed by your doctor.

Do not take Propoxyphene if you are allergic to this or similar drugs. This drug can produce psychological or physical drug dependence (addiction). The major sign of dependence is anxiety when the drug is suddenly stopped. Propoxyphene can be abused to the same degree as Codeine.

Pregnancy/Breast-feeding

No studies of this medication have been done in women and no reports of human birth defects exist, but animal studies show that high doses of the drug can cause problems in a developing fetus. Pregnant women, or women who might become pregnant while using this drug, should talk to their doctor about the risk of taking this medicine versus the benefits it can provide.

This drug passes into breast milk, but no problems in nursing infants have been seen. Breast-feeding women should consider the possibility of adverse effects on their nursing infant. Choose another feeding method if you must take this medicine.

Seniors

Seniors are more likely to be sensitive to the side effects of this drug and should be treated with smaller dosages than younger adults.

Possible Side Effects

Dizziness, sedation, nausea, vomiting. These effects usually disappear if you lie down and relax for a few moments.

Infrequent: constipation, stomach pain, skin rashes, lightheadedness, headache, weakness, euphoria, minor visual disturbances. Taking Propoxyphene over long periods of time and in very high doses has caused psychotic reactions and convulsions.

Drug Interactions

Propoxyphene may cause drowsiness. Therefore, avoid other drugs which also cause drowsiness, such as tranquilizers, sedatives, hypnotics, narcotics, alcohol, and possibly antihistamines.

There may be an interaction between Propoxyphene and Orphenadrine. However, this reaction is only a probability and only for patients who have a tendency toward low-blood sugar.

Food Interactions

Take with a full glass of water or with food to reduce the possibility of stomach upset.

Usual Dose

Propoxyphene Hydrochloride: 65 milligrams every 4 hours as needed.

Propoxyphene Napsylate: 100 milligrams every 4 hours as needed.

Overdosage

Symptoms resemble those of a narcotic overdose: decrease in rate of breathing (in some people breathing rate is so low that the heart stops), changes in breathing pattern, extreme sleepiness leading to stupor or coma, pinpointed pupils, convulsions, abnormal heart rhythms, and development of fluid in the lungs. The patient should be taken to a hospital emergency room immediately. ALWAYS bring the medicine bottle.

Special Information

A "patient package insert" which provides detailed information about the drug is available from your pharmacist.

You should avoid alcohol or other depressant drugs. Use caution while performing any tasks that require you to be alert, such as driving or operating machinery.

If you forget to take a dose of Propoxyphene, take it as soon as you remember. If it is almost time for your next regularly scheduled dose, skip the one you forgot and continue with your regular schedule. Do not take a double dose.

Generic Name

Propranolol Hydrochloride

Brand Names

Inderal
Inderal LA
Propranolol Hydrochloride Intensol (liquid)

(Also available in generic form)

Type of Drug

Beta-adrenergic blocking agent.

Prescribed for

High blood pressure, angina pectoris (a specified type of chest pain), abnormal heart rhythm; to reduce the possibility

of a second heart attack; for thyroid disease, and pheochromocytoma, a tumor associated with hypertension. In addition,
Propranolol Hydrochloride has been studied for its effect on
migraine headaches, diarrhea, stagefright, and schizophrenia.

General Information

Propranolol Hydrochloride was the first beta-adrenergic blocking agent available in the United States. The drug acts to
block a major chemical reaction of the nervous system in
our bodies. For this reason, it can exert a broad range of
effects, as is evident from the wide variety of diseases in
which it can be used effectively. Because of this spectrum of
effects, it is impossible to say specifically what you will be
taking this drug for. Therefore, this information must be
discussed with your doctor. This drug has been used, for
example, in low (5 to 10 milligrams) doses by musicians and
others to treat nervousness and "butterflies" experienced
before going on stage.

Cautions and Warnings

Propranolol Hydrochloride should be used with care if you have
a history of asthma, upper respiratory disease, or seasonal
allergy, which may be made worse by the effects of this drug.

Pregnancy/Breast-feeding

This drug crosses into the blood circulation of a developing
baby. It has not been found to cause birth defects, but there
has been some association between Propranolol Hydrochloride and breathing problems or lower heart rates in newborns. Pregnant women, or those who might become pregnant
while taking this drug, should not take it without their doctor's approval. When the drug is considered essential by
your doctor, the potential risk of taking the medicine must
be carefully weighed against the benefit it might produce.

This drug passes into breast milk, but has caused no problems among breast-fed infants. You must consider the potential effect on the nursing infant if breast-feeding while
taking this medicine.

Seniors

Senior citizens may be more or less sensitive to the effects
of this medication. Your dosage of this drug must be ad-

justed to your individual needs by your doctor. Seniors may be more likely to suffer from cold hands and feet and reduced body temperature, chest pains, a general feeling of ill health, sudden difficulty breathing, sweating, or changes in heartbeat because of this medicine.

Possible Side Effects

Propranolol Hydrochloride may decrease the heart rate; may aggravate a condition of congestive heart failure; and may produce lowered blood pressure, tingling in the extremities, light-headedness, mental depression including inability to sleep, weakness, and tiredness. It may also produce a mental depression which is reversible when the drug is withdrawn, visual disturbances, hallucinations, disorientation, and short-term memory loss. Patients taking Propranolol Hydrochloride may experience nausea, vomiting, stomach upset, abdominal cramps and diarrhea, or constipation. If you are allergic to this drug, you may show typical reactions associated with drug allergies, including sore throat, fever, difficulty in breathing, and various effects on the blood system. Propranolol Hydrochloride may induce bronchospasms (spasms of muscles in the bronchi), which will aggravate any existing asthmatic condition or any severe upper respiratory disease.

Occasionally, patients taking Propranolol Hydrochloride may experience emotional instability, may appear to be somewhat detached or show other unusual personality changes, or the drug may produce unusual effects on the blood system.

Drug Interactions

This drug will interact with any psychotropic drug, including the MAO inhibitors, that stimulates one of the adrenergic segments of the nervous system. Since this information is not generally known, you should discuss the potential problem of using Propranolol Hydrochloride with your doctor if you are taking any psychotropic or psychiatric drug.

Propranolol Hydrochloride may cause increased effectiveness of Insulin or oral antidiabetic drugs. If you are diabetic, discuss the situation with your doctor, who will probably reduce the dose of antidiabetic medication.

Propranolol Hydrochloride may reduce the effectiveness of Digitalis on your heart. Any dose of Digitalis medication will have to be altered. If you are taking Digitalis for a purpose other than congestive heart failure, the effectiveness of the Digitalis may be increased by Propranolol Hydrochloride, and the dose of Digitalis may have to be reduced.

Propranolol Hydrochloride may interact with certain other drugs to produce lowering of blood pressure. This interaction often has positive results in the treatment of patients with high blood pressure.

Do not self-medicate with over-the-counter cold, cough, or allergy remedies which may contain stimulant drugs that will aggravate certain types of heart disease and high blood pressure, or other ingredients that may antagonize the effects of Propranolol Hydrochloride. Double-check with your doctor or pharmacist before taking any over-the-counter medication.

Food Interactions

Take Propranolol Hydrochloride before meals for maximum effectiveness.

Usual Dose

30 to 700 milligrams per day, depending on disease treated and patient's response. The drug is given in the smallest effective dose, that is, the smallest dose that will produce the desired therapeutic effect.

Overdosage

Symptoms are slowed heart rate, heart failure, lowered blood pressure, and spasms of the bronchial muscles which make it difficult to breathe. The patient should be taken to a hospital emergency room where proper therapy can be given. ALWAYS bring the medicine bottle with you.

Special Information

There have been reports of serious effects on the heart when this drug is stopped abruptly. Instead, the dose should be lowered gradually from what you are taking to nothing over a period of 2 weeks.

If you forget to take a dose of Propranolol Hydrochloride, take it as soon as possible. However, if it is within 4 hours of your next dose (8 hours if you take long-acting Propranolol Hydrochloride), skip the forgotten dose and go back to your regular schedule. Do not take a double dose.

Generic Name

Protriptyline Hydrochloride

Brand Name

Vivactil

Type of Drug

Antidepressant.

Prescribed for

Depression with or without symptoms of anxiety.

General Information

Protriptyline Hydrochloride and other members of this group are effective in treating symptoms of depression. They can elevate your mood, increase physical activity and mental alertness, improve appetite and sleep patterns. These drugs are mild sedatives and therefore useful in treating mild forms of depression associated with anxiety. You should not expect instant results with this medicine: benefits are usually seen after 1 to 4 weeks. If symptoms are not affected after 6 to 8 weeks, contact your doctor. Occasionally other members of this group of drugs have been used in treating nighttime bed-wetting in young children, but they do not produce long-lasting relief and therapy with one of them for nighttime bed-wetting is of questionable value.

Cautions and Warnings

Do not take Protriptyline Hydrochloride if you are allergic or sensitive to this or other members of this class of drug: Doxepin, Nortriptyline, Imipramine, Desipramine, and Amitriptyline. The drugs should not be used if you are recovering from a heart attack. Protriptyline Hydrochloride may be taken with caution if you have a history of epilepsy or other convulsive disorders, difficulty in urination, glaucoma, heart disease, or thyroid disease. Protriptyline Hydrochloride can interfere with your ability to perform tasks which require concentration, such as driving or operating machinery.

Pregnancy/Breast-feeding

This drug, like other tricyclic antidepressants, crosses into your developing baby's circulation and may cause birth defects if taken during the first 3 months of pregnancy. There have been reports of newborn infants suffering from heart, breathing, and urinary problems after their mothers had taken an antidepressant of this type immediately before delivery. You should avoid taking this medication while pregnant.

Antidepressants of this type are known to pass into breast milk and may affect a breast-feeding infant, although this has not been proven. Nursing mothers should consider alternate feeding methods if taking this medicine.

Seniors

Older adults are more sensitive to the effects of this drug and often require a lower dose than a younger adult to do the same job. Follow your doctor's directions and report any side effects at once.

Possible Side Effects

Changes in blood pressure (both high and low), abnormal heart rates, heart attack, confusion, especially in elderly patients, hallucinations, disorientation, delusions, anxiety, restlessness, excitement, numbness and tingling in the extremities, lack of coordination, muscle spasms or tremors, seizures and/or convulsions, dry mouth, blurred vision, constipation, inability to urinate, rash, itching, sensitivity to bright light or sunlight, retention of fluids, fever, allergy, changes in composition of blood, nausea, vomiting, loss of appetite, stomach upset, diarrhea, enlargement of the breasts in males and females, increased or decreased sex drive, increased or decreased blood sugar.

Infrequent: agitation, inability to sleep, nightmares, feeling of panic, a peculiar taste in the mouth, stomach cramps, black coloration of the tongue, yellowing eyes and/or skin, changes in liver function, increased or decreased weight, perspiration, flushing, frequent urination, drowsiness, dizziness, weakness, headache, loss of hair, nausea, not feeling well.

Drug Interactions

Interaction with monoamine oxidase (MAO) inhibitors can

cause high fevers, convulsions, and occasionally death. Don't take MAO inhibitors until at least 2 weeks after Protriptyline Hydrochloride has been discontinued.

Protriptyline Hydrochloride interacts with Guanethidine, a drug used to treat high blood pressure: if your doctor prescribes Protriptyline Hydrochloride and you are taking medicine for high blood pressure, be sure to discuss this with him.

Protriptyline Hydrochloride increases the effects of barbiturates, tranquilizers, other depressive drugs, and alcohol. Don't drink alcoholic beverages if you take this medicine.

Taking Protriptyline Hydrochloride and thyroid medicine will enhance the effects of the thyroid medicine. The combination can cause abnormal heart rhythms.

Large doses of Vitamin C (Ascorbic Acid) can reduce the effect of Protriptyline Hydrochloride. Drugs such as Bicarbonate of Soda or Acetazolamide will increase the effect of Protriptyline Hydrochloride.

Food Interactions

This drug is best taken on an empty stomach but you can take it with food if it upsets your stomach.

Usual Dose

Adult: 15 to 60 milligrams per day in 3 or 4 divided doses.

Adolescent and senior: lower doses are recommended, usually up to 20 milligrams per day. A senior taking more than 20 milligrams per day should have regular heart examinations.

The dose of this drug must be tailored to the patient's need.

Overdosage

Symptoms are confusion, inability to concentrate, hallucinations, drowsiness, lowered body temperature, abnormal heart rate, heart failure, large pupils of the eyes, convulsions, severely lowered blood pressure, stupor, and coma (as well as agitation, stiffening of body muscles, vomiting, and high fever). The patient should be taken to a hospital emergency room immediately. ALWAYS bring the medicine bottle.

Special Information

Avoid alcohol and other drugs that depress the nervous system while taking this antidepressant. Do not stop taking this medicine unless your doctor has specifically told you to do so. Abruptly stopping this medicine may cause nausea, headache, and a sickly feeling. This medicine can cause drowsiness, dizziness, and blurred vision. Be careful when driving or operating complicated machinery. Avoid exposure to the sun or sun lamps for long periods of time. Call your doctor if dry mouth, difficulty urinating, or excessive sedation develops.

If you take Protriptyline Hydrochloride several times a day and forget a dose, take it as soon as you remember. If it is almost time for your next regularly scheduled dose, skip the one you forgot and continue with your regular schedule. If you take it once a day at bedtime and forget, don't take it when you get up; go back to your regular schedule. Call your doctor if you skip 2 or more days of medication. Never take a double dose.

Generic Name

Pseudoephedrine

Brand Names

Cenafed	Historal Pediatric Drops
Children's Sudafed	NeoFed
Decofed	PediaCare Infants' Cold Relief
Dorcol Children's Formula	Pseudogest
Genafed	Sudafed
Halofed	Sudrin

Timed-release or repeat-action

Afrinol
Novafed
Sudafed 12 Hour

(Also available in generic form)

Type of Drug

Bronchodilator-decongestant.

Prescribed for

Symptomatic relief of stuffy nose, upper respiratory congestion, or bronchospasms associated with asthma, asthmatic
bronchitis, or a similar disorder.

General Information

There are almost 200 products available that contain Pseudoephedrine. These combinations range from pain relievers
to antihistamines to cough suppressants; some can be obtained only with a prescription while others are available
over the counter. These products provide symptomatic relief
of respiratory conditions, but do not treat the underlying
disease. If you are taking an over-the-counter (available without a prescription) Pseudoephedrine medication, you should
always inform your doctor.

Pseudoephedrine produces central nervous system stimulation, and it should not be taken by people with heart
disease or high blood pressure. Elderly people are more likely
to experience adverse effects from this and other stimulant
drugs; overdosage of stimulants in this age group may cause
hallucinations, convulsions, depression, and even death.

Cautions and Warnings

Do not take Pseudoephedrine if you are allergic or sensitive
to this or similar drugs or if you have severe high blood
pressure, coronary artery disease (angina pectoris), abnormal heart rhythms, or close-angle glaucoma.

This drug should be used with caution and only under
medical supervision if you have chest pain, stroke, diabetes,
overactive thyroid, or history of convulsions.

Pregnancy/Breast-feeding

This drug crosses into the blood circulation of a developing
baby. It has not been found to cause birth defects. Pregnant
women, or those who might become pregnant while taking
this drug, should not take it without their doctor's approval.
When the drug is considered essential by your doctor, the
potential risk of taking the medicine must be carefully weighed
against the benefit it might produce.

This drug passes into breast milk, but has caused no problems among breast-fed infants. You must consider the po-

tential effect on the nursing infant if breast-feeding while taking this medicine.

Seniors

Older adults with severe kidney problems may be more sensitive to the effects of this drug. Follow your doctor's directions and report any side effects at once.

Possible Side Effects

Excessive tiredness or drowsiness, restlessness, nervousness with an inability to sleep. Less frequent: tremor, headache, palpitations, elevation of blood pressure, sweating, sleeplessness, loss of appetite, nausea, vomiting, dizziness, constipation.

Drug Interactions

Pseudoephedrine may increase the effect of antidepressant drugs and antihistamines, and reduce the effect of some high blood pressure medicine like Reserpine or Guanethidine.

Do not self-medicate with additional over-the-counter drugs for the relief of cold symptoms: taking Pseudoephedrine with such drugs may result in aggravation of high blood pressure, heart disease, diabetes, or thyroid disease.

Do not take Pseudoephedrine if you are taking or suspect you may be taking a monoamine oxidase (MAO) inhibitor: severe elevation in blood pressure may result.

Interaction with alcoholic beverages may produce excessive drowsiness and/or sleepiness, and/or inability to concentrate.

Food Interactions

Take this medicine with food if it upsets your stomach.

Usual Dose

Adult: 60 milligrams every 6 hours.
Child (age 6 to 12): 30 milligrams every 6 hours.
Child (age 2 to 5): 15 milligrams every 6 hours.
Combination products provide a fixed amount of drug per dose and should be taken according to recommendations.

Special Information

If you forget to take a dose of Pseudoephedrine, take it as

soon as you remember. If it is almost time for your next regularly scheduled dose, skip the one you forgot and continue with your regular schedule. Do not take a double dose.

Brand Name

Quibron

Ingredients

Guaifenesin
Theophylline

Other Brand Names

Bronchial Capsules	Slo-Phyllin GG
Glyceryl T	Theocolate Liquid
Lanophyllin GG	Theolate Elixir
Quiagen	

The following products contain the same ingredients in different concentrations:

Asbron G	Synophylate-GG
Elixophyllin-GG	Theolair-Plus
Quibron-300	

(Also available in generic form)

Type of Drug

Antiasthmatic combination product.

Prescribed for

Relief of asthma symptoms or other upper respiratory disorders.

General Information

Quibron, a xanthine combination, is one of several antiasthmatic combination products prescribed for the relief of asthmatic symptoms and other breathing problems. These products contain drugs which help relax the bronchial muscles, drugs which increase the diameter of the breathing

passages, and a mild tranquilizer to help relax the patient.
Other products in this class may contain similar ingredients
along with other medicine to help eliminate mucus from the
breathing passages.

Cautions and Warnings

Do not use this drug if you are allergic or sensitive to it or to
any related drug, such as Aminophylline. If you have stomach ulcer or heart disease, you should use this drug with
caution.

This drug should not be taken if you have severe kidney or
liver disease.

Pregnancy/Breast-feeding

If you are pregnant or think that you may be pregnant you
should carefully discuss the use of this drug with your doctor.

Quibron may be required by a woman during pregnancy.
However, there is an increased chance of birth defects while
using Quibron during pregnancy. Regularly using Quibron
during the last 3 months of pregnancy may cause drug
dependency of the newborn. Labor may be prolonged and
delivery may be delayed, and there may be breathing problems in the newborn if Quibron is used.

Breast-feeding while using Quibron may cause increased
tiredness, shortness of breath, or a slow heartbeat in the
baby.

Theophylline, an ingredient in Quibron, may cause a fast
heartbeat, irritability, or breathing problems in the unborn or
nursing child if too much is used by the mother.

Seniors

Older adults may take longer to clear this drug from their
bodies than younger adults. Those with heart failure or other
cardiac conditions, chronic lung disease, a virus infection
with fever, or reduced liver function may require a lower
dosage of this medication to account for the clearance effect.

Possible Side Effects

Large doses of Quibron can produce excitation, shakiness,
sleeplessness, nervousness, rapid heartbeat, chest pains, or
irregular heartbeat. Occasionally people have been known to
develop hesitation or difficulty in urination.

Less common side effects: excessive urination, heart stimulation, drowsiness, muscle weakness, muscle twitching, unsteady walk. These effects can usually be controlled by having your doctor adjust the dose.

Drug Interactions

Quibron may cause sleeplessness and/or drowsiness.

Taking Quibron with an MAO inhibitor can produce severe interaction. Consult your doctor first.

Quibron or similar products taken together with Lithium Carbonate will increase the excretion of Lithium; they have neutralized the effect of Propranalol. Erythromycin and similar antibiotics cause the body to hold Theophylline, leading to possible side effects.

Do not take this drug with alcoholic beverages.

Food Interactions

The way Quibron acts in your body may be influenced by your diet. Charcoal-broiled beef, for example, may cause the amount of Quibron that is being eliminated in the urine to increase. Therefore you may experience a decreased effect of the drug. This is also true for people whose diet is low in carbohydrates and high in protein or for people who smoke.

Caffeine (also a xanthine derivative) may add to the side effects of Quibron. It is recommended that you avoid large amounts of caffeine-containing foods, such as coffee, tea, cocoa, colas, or chocolate.

Take this drug with food to avoid upset stomach.

Usual Dose

Capsules: 1 to 2 every 6 to 8 hours.
Liquid: 1 to 2 tablespoons every 6 to 8 hours.

Special Information

If you forget to take a dose of Quibron, take it as soon as you remember. If it is almost time for your next regularly scheduled dose, skip the one you forgot and continue with your regular schedule. Do not take a double dose.

Generic Name

Quinidine

Brand Names

Quinidine Sulfate

Cin-Quin
Quinora

Sustained-release product:
Quinidex Extentabs

Quinidine Gluconate

Sustained-release products:
Duraquin   Quinatime
Quinaglute Dura-Tabs   Quin-Release

Quinidine Polygalacturonate

Cardioquin

(Also available in generic forms)

Type of Drug

Antiarrhythmic.

Prescribed for

Abnormal heart rhythms.

General Information

Derived from the bark of the cinchona tree (which gives us Quinine), the drug works by affecting the flow of potassium into and out of cells of the heart muscle (myocardium). Its basic action is to slow down the pulse. Its action allows normal control mechanisms in the heart to take over and keep the heart beating at a normal rate of rhythm.

The 3 kinds of Quinidine provide different amounts of active drug. Quinidine Sulfate provides the most active drug.

Some of the different brands come in sustained-release form so that fewer pills are required throughout the day.

Cautions and Warnings

Do not take Quinidine Sulfate if you are allergic to it or a related drug.

Pregnancy/Breast-feeding

This drug may cause birth defects or interfere with your baby's development. Check with your doctor before taking it if you are, or might be, pregnant. Quinidine Sulfate does not cause problems while breast-feeding and may be used by nursing mothers.

Seniors

Older adults may take this medication without special restriction. Follow your doctor's directions and report any side effects at once.

Possible Side Effects

High doses of Quinidine Sulfate can give you rash, changes in hearing, dizziness, ringing in the ears, headache, nausea, or disturbed vision: this group of symptoms, called cinchonism, is due to ingestlon of large amounts of Quinidine Sulfate and is not necessarily a toxic reaction. However, report signs of cinchonism to your doctor immediately. Do not stop taking this drug unless instructed to do so by your doctor.

Less common side effects: Quinidine Sulfate may cause unusual heart rhythms, but such effects are generally found by your doctor during routine examination or electrocardiogram. It can cause nausea, vomiting, stomach pain, and diarrhea. It may affect components of the blood system and can cause headache, fever, dizziness, feeling of apprehension or excitement, confusion, delirium, disturbed hearing, blurred vision, changes in color perception, sensitivity to bright lights, double vision, difficulty seeing at night, flushing of the skin, itching, cramps, unusual urge to defecate or urinate, and cold sweat.

Drug Interactions

If you are taking an oral anticoagulant (blood-thinning medicine) and have been given a new prescription for Quinidine Sulfate, be sure your doctor knows about the blood-thinning medication, because Quinidine Sulfate may affect the ability of the anticoagulant to do its job. The anticoagulant dose may have to be adjusted for the effect of Quinidine Sulfate.

Either Phenobarbital or Phenytoin may reduce the time that Quinidine Sulfate is effective in your body, and may increase your need for it. Quinidine Sulfate in combination with Digoxin can increase the effects of the Digoxin causing possible Digoxin toxicity. This combination should be monitored closely by your doctor.

Avoid over-the-counter cough, cold, allergy, or diet preparations. These medications may contain drugs which will stimulate your heart; this can be dangerous while you are taking Quinidine Sulfate. Ask your pharmacist if you have any questions about the contents of a particular cough, cold, or allergy remedy.

Food Interactions

If Quinidine Sulfate gives you stomach upset, take it with food. Quinidine is also available in forms that are supposed to be less irritating to the stomach; contact your doctor if upset stomach persists.

Usual Dose

Extremely variable, depending on disease and patient's response. Most doses are 800 to 1200 milligrams per day.

Sustained-release: most doses are 600 to 1800 milligrams per day.

Overdosage

Produces abnormal effects on the heart and symptoms of cinchonism. Patient should be taken to a hospital emergency room where proper therapy can be given. ALWAYS bring the medicine bottle.

Special Information

Do not crush or chew the sustained-release products.

If you forget to take a dose of Quinidine Sulfate, and you remember within about 2 hours of your regular time, take it right away. If you do not remember until later, skip the forgotten dose and go back to your regular schedule. Do not take a double dose.

Generic Name

Ranitidine

Brand Name

Zantac

Type of Drug

Antiulcer, histamine H_2 antagonist.

Prescribed for

Short-term treatment of duodenal (intestinal) and gastric (stomach) ulcers. Also prescribed for other conditions characterized by the secretions of large amounts of gastric fluids. A surgeon may prescribe Ranitidine for a patient under anesthesia when it is desirable for the production of stomach acid to be stopped completely.

General Information

Ranitidine was the second histamine H_2 antagonist to be released in the United States. It is more potent than Cimetidine, the original histamine H_2 antagonist, and has less potential for causing drug interactions than Cimetidine.

Cautions and Warnings

Do not take Ranitidine if you have had an allergic reaction to it in the past.

Pregnancy/Breast-feeding

Although studies with laboratory animals have revealed no damage to a developing fetus, it is recommended that Ranitidine be avoided by pregnant women or women who might become pregnant while using it. In those situations where it is deemed essential, Ranitidine's potential risk must be carefully weighed against any benefit it might produce.

Ranitidine is known to pass into breast milk. No problems among nursing infants have been reported, but nursing mothers must consider the possibility of a drug effect while nursing their infants.

Seniors

Older adults respond well to Ranitidine but may need less medication than a younger adult to achieve the desired response, since the drug is eliminated through the kidneys and kidney function tends to decline with age. Older adults may be more susceptible to some side effects of this drug, especially confusion.

Possible Side Effects

Most common: headache, dizziness, constipation, abdominal discomfort, rash, and a feeling of ill health.

Ranitidine may rarely cause a reduction in the levels of either white blood cells or blood platelets. Hepatitis is another rare consequence of Ranitidine treatment.

Drug Interactions

The effects of Ranitidine may be reduced if it is taken together with antacids. This minor interaction may be avoided by separating doses of Ranitidine and antacid by about 3 hours.

Ranitidine may interfere with the absorption of Diazepam tablets into the blood. This interaction is considered of only minor importance and is unlikely to affect many people.

Ranitidine may decrease the effect of Theophylline, prescribed for asthma and other respiratory conditions, while the two drugs are being taken together and for several days after the Ranitidine has been discontinued. This interaction is far less severe than the Cimetidine-Theophylline interaction, which may require temporary dosage adjustments.

Food Interactions

You may take each dose with food or meals if Ranitidine upsets your stomach.

Usual Dose

150 to 300 milligrams per day. People with severe conditions may require more than the average dose.

Overdosage

Overdose victims may be expected to show exaggerated side-effect symptoms, but little else is known about Ranitidine overdose. Patients taking an overdose of this drug must be made to vomit with Syrup of Ipecac (available at any pharmacy) to remove any remaining drug from the stomach. Call your doctor or a poison control center before doing this. If you must go to a hospital emergency room, ALWAYS bring the medicine bottle.

Special Information

It may take several days for Ranitidine to begin to relieve stomach pains. You must take this medicine exactly as directed and follow your doctor's instructions for diet and other treatments in order to get the maximum benefit from it. Cigarettes are known to be associated with stomach ulcers and will reverse the effect of Ranitidine on stomach acid.

Call your doctor at once if any unusual side effects develop. Especially important are unusual bleeding or bruising, unusual tiredness, diarrhea, dizziness, rash, or hallucinations. Black, tarry stools or vomiting "coffee-ground" material may indicate your ulcer is bleeding.

If you forget to take a dose of Ranitidine, take it as soon as you remember. If it is almost time for your next regularly scheduled dose, skip the one you forgot and continue with your regular schedule. Do not take a double dose.

Brand Name

Regroton

Ingredients

Chlorthalidone
Reserpine

Other Brand Name

Demi-Regroton

Type of Drug

Antihypertensive combination.

Prescribed for

High blood pressure.

General Information

Regroton is a good example of a drug taking advantage of a drug interaction. Each of the drug ingredients works by different mechanisms to lower your blood pressure. The Chlorthalidone relaxes the muscles in your veins and arteries and also helps reduce the volume of blood flowing through those blood vessels. Reserpine works on the nervous system to reduce the efficiency of nerve transmissions which are contributing to the increased pressure. These drugs complement each other so that their combined effect is better than the effect of either one alone.

Cautions and Warnings

Do not take this drug if you are sensitive or allergic to either of its ingredients or if you have a history of mental depression, active peptic ulcer, or ulcerative colitis.

Pregnancy/Breast-feeding

Pregnant and nursing women should avoid this drug. The Reserpine in Regroton may cause unwanted effects (breathing problems, appetite loss, low temperature) in the baby if too much is taken during pregnancy or breast-feeding.

Seniors

Older adults are more sensitive to the effects of this drug, especially depressant effects and low blood pressure. Follow your doctor's directions and report any side effects at once.

Possible Side Effects

Loss of appetite, stomach irritation, nausea, vomiting, cramps, diarrhea, constipation, dizziness, headache, tingling in the arms and legs, restlessness, chest pains, abnormal heart rhythms, drowsiness, depression, nervousness, anxiety, nightmares, glaucoma, blood disorders, itching, fever, difficulty in breathing, muscle spasms, weakness, high blood sugar, sugar in the urine, blurred vision, stuffy nose, dryness of the mouth, rash. Occasional: impotence or decreased sex drive.

Drug Interactions

Interaction with Digitalis or Quinidine may cause abnormal heart rhythms.

Caution must be taken if this drug is given with other antihypertensive agents such as Guanethidine, Veratrum, Methyldopa, Chlorthalidone or Hydralazine: the dose of these drugs must be monitored carefully by your physician. It is strongly advised not to take MAO antidepressant drugs while taking Regroton.

Interaction with drugs containing Lithium may lead to toxic effects of Lithium.

Avoid over-the-counter cough, cold, or allergy remedies containing stimulant drugs which may raise your blood pressure.

Food Interactions

Take Regroton with food if it upsets your stomach.

Usual Dose

Must be individualized to patient's response. Regroton is usually taken in the morning with breakfast.

Special Information

It is essential that you take your medicine exactly as prescribed, for maximum benefit.

An ingredient in this drug may cause excessive loss of potassium, which may lead to a condition called hypokalemia. Warning signs are dryness of mouth, excessive thirst, weakness, drowsiness, restlessness, muscle pains or cramps, muscular fatigue, lack of urination, abnormal heart rhythms, and upset stomach. If warning signs occur, call your doctor. You may need potassium from some outside source. This may be done by taking a potassium supplement or by eating foods such as bananas, citrus fruits, melons, and tomatoes, which have high concentrations of potassium.

This drug should be stopped at the first sign of despondency, early morning insomnia, loss of appetite, or sexual impotence. Drug-induced depression may persist for several months after the drug has been discontinued; it has been known to be severe enough to result in suicide attempts.

If you forget to take a dose of Regroton, take it as soon you remember. If it is almost time for your next scheduled dose, skip the one you forgot and con your regular schedule. Do not take a double dose.

Generic Name

Rifampin

Brand Names

Rifadin
Rimactane

Type of Drug

Antitubercular.

Prescribed for

Tuberculosis. Also used to treat people who are carriers of certain infections rather than infected patients.

General Information

This is an important drug for the treatment of tuberculosis. It is always used together with Isoniazid or another antitubercular drug because it is not effective by itself. It also eradicates an organism which causes meningitis in people who are carriers: although they are not infected, they carry the organism and spread it to others.

Rifampin may also be prescribed for staff infections of the skin, bones, or prostate, for Legionnaires' disease (when Erythromycin doesn't work), for leprosy, and for the prevention of meningitis caused by H. Influenzae, especially common among children in day-care centers.

Cautions and Warnings

Do not take this drug if you are allergic to it. It may cause liver damage and should not be used by people with liver disease or those taking other drugs which may cause liver damage.

Pregnancy/Breast-feeding

This drug should only be used by pregnant women or nursing mothers if absolutely necessary. Animal studies indicate that Rifampin may cause backbone problems (spina bifida) in the fetus. Rifampin has not been shown to cause problems to the infant while the mother is breast-feeding.

Seniors

Older adults with severe liver disease may be more sensitive to the effects of this drug. Follow your doctor's directions and report any side effects at once.

Possible Side Effects

Flulike symptoms, heartburn, upset stomach, loss of appetite, nausea, vomiting, stomach gas cramps, diarrhea, headache, drowsiness, tiredness, menstrual disturbances, dizziness, fever, pains in the arms and legs, confusion, visual disturbances, numbness, hypersensitivity to the drug.

Less common: adverse effects on the blood, kidneys, or liver.

Drug Interactions

When this is taken with other drugs that cause liver toxicity, severe liver damage may develop.

Rifampin will increase patient requirements for oral anticoagulant drugs and may affect Methadone, oral antidiabetic drugs, digitalis drugs, or adrenal corticosteroids. Women taking oral contraceptives and Rifampin should supplement with other contraceptive methods while taking the two drugs together.

Food Interactions

Take this medicine 1 hour before or 2 hours after a meal, at the same time every day.

Usual Dose

Adult: 600 milligrams once daily.

Child: 4.5 to 9 milligrams per pound, or up to 600 milligrams per day.

Overdosage

Signs are nausea, vomiting, and tiredness. Unconsciousness may develop, with severe liver damage. A brown-red or orange discoloration of the skin may develop. Patients suspected of taking Rifampin overdose must be taken to the hospital at once. ALWAYS take the medicine bottle with you.

Special Information

This drug may cause a red-brown or orange coloration of the urine, stool, saliva, sweat, and tears.

Soft contact lenses may become permanently stained.

Call your doctor if you develop the flu, fever, chills, muscle pains, headache, tiredness or weakness, loss of appetite, nausea, vomiting, sore throat, unusual bleeding or bruising, or yellow discoloration of the skin or eyes, rash, or itching.

If you take daily doses of Rifampin and you miss a dose, consult your doctor. Reactions may occur if you start again.

If you forget to take a dose of Rifampin, take it as soon as you remember. If it is almost time for your next regularly scheduled dose, skip the one you forgot and continue with your regular schedule. Do not take a double dose.

Side effects may be more common and more severe if the drug is taken on an irregular basis.

Generic Name

Ritodrine Hydrochloride

Brand Name

Yutopar

Type of Drug

Uterine relaxant.

Prescribed for

Controlling preterm labor to prevent premature delivery.

General Information

This drug stimulates the beta nerve receptors in muscles in the uterus and prevents them from contracting. This drug must be used only under the direction of your doctor and only after the fifth month of pregnancy. It should be started with intravenous dosage and then continued as oral tablets.

Cautions and Warnings

This drug should not be used until after the twentieth week of pregnancy or if the mother has any complicating factors.

Possible Side Effects

Increased heart rate and blood pressure in both mother and child, palpitations, tremor, nausea, vomiting, headache, swelling of the extremities.

Less common side effects: nervousness, jitteriness, restlessness, emotional anxiety, upset, feeling of ill health, chest pains, abnormal heart rates, rash, heart murmur, upset stomach, bloating, constipation, diarrhea, sweating, chills, drowsiness, weakness, difficulty breathing, sugar in the urine.

Drug Interactions

Adrenal corticosteroids may lead to fluid in the lungs when given together with Ritodrine Hydrochloride.

All beta-adrenergic blocking drugs will directly inhibit the effect of Ritodrine Hydrochloride.

Usual Dose

30 minutes before intravenous therapy is to end, tablets are taken in a dose of 10 milligrams and every 2 hours for the first day; then 10 to 20 milligrams every 4 to 6 hours. The drug may be used as long as it is desirable to prolong the pregnancy.

Overdosage

Signs are rapid heart rate, palpitation, abnormal heartbeats, low blood pressure, nervousness, tremor, nausea, and vomiting. Take the patient to a hospital emergency room. ALWAYS bring the medicine bottle.

Special Information

Take only as directed by your doctor. Report any unusual effect immediately.

If you forget to take a dose of Ritodrine Hydrochloride, and you remember within about an hour of your regular time, take it right away. If you do not remember until later, skip the forgotten dose and go back to your regular schedule. Do not take a double dose.

Brand Name

Salutensin

Ingredients

Hydroflumethiazide
Reserpine

Other Brand Names

Hydropine H.P.
Salutensin-Demi

(Also available in generic form)

Type of Drug

Antihypertensive combination.

Prescribed for

High blood pressure.

General Information

Salutensin is a good example of a drug taking advantage of a drug interaction. Each of the drug ingredients works by different mechanisms to lower your blood pressure. The Hydroflumethiazide relaxes the muscles in your veins and arteries and also helps reduce the volume of blood flowing through those blood vessels. Reserpine works on the nervous system to reduce the efficiency of nerve transmissions which are contributing to the increased pressure. These drugs complement each other so that their combined effect is better than the effect of either one alone.

It is essential that you take your medicine exactly as prescribed, for maximum benefit.

Cautions and Warnings

Do not take this drug if you are sensitive or allergic to either of its ingredients or if you have a history of mental depression, active peptic ulcer, or ulcerative colitis.

Pregnancy/Breast-feeding

This drug crosses into the blood circulation of a developing

baby. Possible effects on infants born of mothers who have taken this drug during pregnancy are stuffed nose and respiratory congestion, a bluish coloration to the skin, poor appetite, and low body temperature. Pregnant women, or those who might become pregnant while taking this drug, should not take it without their doctor's approval. When the drug is considered essential by your doctor, the potential risk of taking the medicine must be carefully weighed against the benefit it might produce.

This drug passes into breast milk and may cause problems among nursing infants, including stuffed nose and respiratory congestion, a bluish coloration to the skin, poor appetite, and low body temperature. Consider using an alternative feeding method if you must take this medicine.

Seniors

Older adults are more sensitive to the depressant effects of this drug and the low blood pressure it can cause. Follow your doctor's directions and report any side effects at once.

Possible Side Effects

Loss of appetite, stomach irritation, nausea, vomiting, cramps, diarrhea, constipation, dizziness, headache, tingling in the arms and legs, restlessness, chest pains, abnormal heart rhythms, drowsiness, depression, nervousness, anxiety, nightmares, glaucoma, blood disorders, itching, fever, difficulty in breathing, muscle spasms, weakness, high blood sugar, sugar in the urine, blurred vision, stuffy nose, dryness of the mouth, rash. Occasional: impotence or decreased sex drive.

Drug Interactions

Interaction with Digitalis or Quinidine may cause abnormal heart rhythms.

Caution must be taken if this drug is given with other antihypertensive agents such as Guanethidine, Veratrum, Methyldopa, Chlorthalidone, or Hydralazine: the dose of these drugs must be monitored carefully by your physician. It is strongly advised not to take MAO antidepressant drugs while taking Salutensin.

Interaction with drugs containing Lithium may lead to toxic effects on Lithium.

Avoid over-the-counter cough, cold, or allergy remedies containing stimulant drugs which may raise your blood pressure.

Food Interactions

If Salutensin upsets your stomach, take it with food.

Usual Dose

Must be individualized to patient's response.

Special Information

You may need potassium from some outside source. This may be done by taking a potassium supplement or by eating foods such as bananas, citrus fruits, melons, and tomatoes, which have high concentrations of potassium.

An ingredient in this drug may cause excessive loss of potassium, which may lead to a condition called hypokalemia. Warning signs are dryness of mouth, excessive thirst, weakness, drowsiness, restlessness, muscle pains or cramps, muscular fatigue, lack of urination, abnormal heart rhythms, and upset stomach. If warning signs occur, call your doctor.

This drug should be stopped at the first sign of despondency, early morning insomnia, loss of appetite, or sexual impotence. Drug-induced depression may persist for several months after the drug has been discontinued; it has been known to be severe enough to result in suicide attempts.

If you forget to take a dose of Salutensin, take it as soon as you remember. If it is almost time for your next regularly scheduled dose, skip the one you forgot and continue with your regular schedule. Do not take a double dose.

Generic Name

Secobarbital

Brand Name

Seconal

(Also available in generic form)

Type of Drug

Hypnotic; sedative.

Prescribed for

Daytime sedation, sleeplessness, sedation before surgery.

General Information

Secobarbital, like the other barbiturates, works by interfering with the passage of certain nerve impulses to the brain. It is useful in any situation where a fast-acting sedative or hypnotic (sleep-producing) effect is needed. This drug can be addicting if taken for a period of time in large enough doses, especially if more than 400 milligrams a day is taken for 3 months. Larger doses will produce barbiturate addiction in a shorter time.

Cautions and Warnings

Secobarbital may slow down your physical and mental reflexes; be extremely careful when operating machinery, driving an automobile, or performing other potentially dangerous tasks. Secobarbital is classified as a barbiturate; long-term or unsupervised use may cause addiction. Barbiturates are neutralized in the liver and eliminated from the body through the kidneys; consequently, people who have liver or kidney disorders—namely, difficulty in forming or excreting urine—should be carefully monitored by their doctor when taking Secobarbital.

If you have known sensitivities or allergies to barbiturates, or if you have previously been addicted to sedatives or hypnotics, or if you have a disease affecting the respiratory system, you should not take Secobarbital.

Pregnancy/Breast-feeding

Regular use of any barbiturate during the last 3 months of pregnancy can cause the baby to be born dependent on the medicine. Also, barbiturate use increases the chance of bleeding problems, brain tumors, and breathing difficulties in the newborn.

Barbiturates pass into breast milk and can cause drowsiness, slow heartbeat, and breathing difficulty in nursing infants.

Seniors

Older adults are more sensitive to the effects of barbiturates, especially nervousness and confusion, and often require a lower dose than a younger adult to do the same job. Follow your doctor's directions and report any side effects at once.

Possible Side Effects

Drowsiness, lethargy, dizziness, hangover, difficulty in breathing, rash, and general allergic reaction such as runny nose, watery eyes, and scratchy throat.

Less common side effects: nausea, vomiting, diarrhea. More severe adverse reactions may include anemia and yellowing of the skin and eyes.

Drug Interactions

Interaction with alcohol, tranquilizers, or other sedatives increases the effect of Secobarbital.

Interaction with anticoagulants (blood-thinning agents) can reduce their effect. This is also true of muscle relaxants, painkillers, anticonvulsants, Quinidine, Theophylline, Metronidazole, Phenmetrazine, birth control pills, and Acetaminophen.

Food Interactions

This medicine is best taken on an empty stomach, but may be taken with food if it upsets your stomach.

Usual Dose

Daytime sedative: 30 to 50 milligrams.
Hypnotic for sleep: 100 to 200 milligrams.
Sedation before surgery: 200 to 500 milligrams 1 to 2 hours before surgery.
Child: sedative, 2.7 milligrams per pound per day; sedation before surgery, 50 to 100 milligrams.

Overdosage

Symptoms are difficulty in breathing, decrease in size of the pupils of the eyes, lowered body temperature progressing to fever as time passes, fluid in the lungs, and eventually coma.

Anyone suspected of having taken an overdose must be taken to the hospital for immediate care. ALWAYS bring the medicine bottle to the emergency room physician so he can quickly and correctly identify the medicine and start treatment. Severe overdosage of this medication can kill; the drug has been used many times in suicide attempts.

Special Information

Avoid alcohol and other drugs that depress the nervous system while taking this barbiturate. Be sure to take this medicine according to your doctor's direction. Do not change your dose without your doctor's approval. This drug causes drowsiness and poor concentration, and makes it more difficult to drive a car, operate machinery, or perform complicated activities.

Call your doctor at once if you develop fever, sore throat, nosebleeds, mouth sores, unexplained black-and-blue marks, easy bruising or bleeding.

If you forget to take a dose of Secobarbital, and you remember within about an hour of your regular time, take it right away. If you do not remember until later, skip the forgotten dose and go back to your regular schedule. Do not take a double dose.

Brand Name

Septra

Ingredients

Sulfamethoxazole
Trimethoprim

Other Brand Names

Bactrim/Bactrim DS	Co-trimoxazole
Bethaprim DS/Bethaprim SS	Septra DS
Comoxol	Sulfatrim/Sulfatrim DS
Cotrim/Cotrim DS/Cotrim	Sulmeprim
Pediatric	TMP-SMZ

(Also available in generic form)

Type of Drug

Anti-infective.

Prescribed for

Urinary tract infections. Septra can also be used to treat bronchitis or ear infections in children caused by susceptible organisms and as prevention against traveler's diarrhea and pneumocystis carinii infections in AIDS and leukemia patients.

General Information

Septra is one of many combination products used to treat infections. This is a unique combination because it attacks the infecting organism in two ways; it is effective in many situations where other drugs are not. Bacterial resistance to the effects of Septra develops more slowly than resistance to the effects of Sulfamethoxazole and Trimethoprim used alone.

Cautions and Warnings

Do not take this medication if you have a folic acid deficiency, are allergic or sensitive to either ingredient or to any sulfa drug.

Infants under age 2 months should not be given this combination product. Symptoms such as unusual bleeding or bruising, extreme tiredness, rash, sore throat, fever, pallor, or yellowing of the skin or whites of the eyes may be early indications of serious blood disorders. If any of these effects occur, contact your doctor immediately and stop taking the drug.

Pregnancy/Breast-feeding

This drug crosses into the blood circulation of a developing baby. Although it can affect the newborn infant, this rarely happens because of the mother's ability to protect her developing infant. Pregnant women, or those who might become pregnant while taking this drug, should not take it without their doctor's approval. When the drug is considered essential by your doctor, the potential risk of taking the medicine must be carefully weighed against the benefit it might produce.

Small amounts of this drug pass into breast milk, but it rarely causes problems among breast-fed infants. The notable exception to this are infants who are deficient in the enzyme known as G-6PD. Children deficient in this enzyme

can develop a severe form of anemia. Talk to your doctor
about the possible effect of this drug on your baby if you
take it while nursing.

Seniors

Older adults may take this medication without special restriction. Follow your doctor's directions and report any side
effects at once.

Possible Side Effects

Effects on components of the blood system, allergic reactions including itching, rash, drug fever, swelling around the
eyes, arthritislike pains. Septra can also cause nausea, stomach upset, vomiting, abdominal pain, diarrhea, coating on
the tongue, headache, tingling in the arms and/or legs, depression, convulsions, hallucinations, ringing in the ears,
dizziness, difficulty sleeping, feeling of apathy, tiredness,
weakness, and nervousness. Septra may affect your kidneys
and cause you to produce less urine.

Drug Interactions

This drug may prolong the effects of blood-thinning agents
(such as Warfarin) and antidiabetic oral drugs.
    Take each dose with a full glass of water and continue to
drink fluids throughout the day. This is to decrease the chances
of a stone forming in your kidneys.

Usual Dose

    Tablets: 1 to 2 tablets every 12 hours for 10 to 14 days.
    Oral suspension: 2 to 4 teaspoons every 12 hours for 10 to
14 days.
    Pneumocystis carinii: 4 double strength tablets every 6
hours.

Special Information

Take Septra in the exact dosage and for the exact period of
time prescribed. Do not stop taking it just because you are
beginning to feel better.
    You may develop unusual sensitivity to sun or bright light.
If you have a history of light sensitivity or if you have sensitive
skin, avoid prolonged exposure to sunlight while using Septra.

If you miss a dose of Septra, take it as soon as possible.

If it is almost time for your next dose and you take the medicine twice a day, space the next 2 doses 5 to 6 hours apart, then go back to your regular schedule.

If it is almost time for your next dose and you take the medicine 3 or more times a day, space the missed dose and your next dose by 2 to 4 hours, then continue with your regular schedule.

Brand Name

Ser-Ap-Es Tablets

Ingredients

Hydralazine
Hydrochlorothiazide
Reserpine

Other Brand Names

Cam-ap-es	Seralazide
Cherapas	Tri-Hydroserpine
H-H-R	Unipres
Ser-A-Gen	

(Also available in generic form)

Type of Drug

Antihypertensive combination.

Prescribed for

High blood pressure.

General Information

Ser-Ap-Es Tablets take advantage of three drugs working together to give enhanced action. The dosage of each ingredient is fixed and does not allow for flexible dosing. Flexibility can only be achieved by taking each ingredient as a separate tablet.

Cautions and Warnings

Do not take Ser-Ap-Es Tablets if you are sensitive or allergic to any of its ingredients or if you have a history of mental depression, active peptic ulcer, or ulcerative colitis. Long-term administration in large doses may produce symptoms similar to arthritis in a few patients. This usually resolves itself when you stop taking the drug. The recurrence of fever, chest pains, not feeling well, or other unexplained problems should be investigated further by your doctor.

An ingredient in this drug may cause you to lose an excessive amount of potassium, which may lead to a condition known as hypokalemia. Warning signs of hypokalemia are dryness of the mouth, excessive thirst, weakness, drowsiness, restlessness, muscle pain or cramps, muscular fatigue, lack of urination, abnormal heart rhythms, and upset stomach. If you notice these warning signs, call your doctor.

Pregnancy/Breast-feeding

This drug may cause birth defects or interfere with your baby's development. Check with your doctor before taking it if you are, or might be, pregnant. Problems have not been seen in breast-fed infants, even though Hydrochlorothiazide passes into breast milk.

Seniors

Older adults are more sensitive to the effects of this drug. Follow your doctor's directions and report any side effects at once.

Possible Side Effects

Common: headache, loss of appetite, vomiting, nausea, diarrhea, abnormal heart rate, chest pains, stomach upset, cramps, tingling in the arms and legs, restlessness, drowsiness, depression, nervousness, anxiety, nightmares, glaucoma, blood disorders, rash, itching, fever, difficulty in breathing, muscle spasms, weakness, high blood sugar, sugar in the urine, blurred vision, stuffy nose, dry mouth, rash. Impotence and decreased sex drive have also been reported.

Less common side effects: flushing of the skin, tearing of the eyes, conjunctivitis, disorientation, and anxiety. Rarely, long-term users have developed symptoms of hepatitis.

Drug Interactions

Ser-Ap-Es Tablets may interact with MAO inhibitor drugs, Digitalis, or Quinidine.

Ser-Ap-Es Tablets will interact with drugs containing Lithium, producing a higher incidence of adverse effects from the Lithium products.

Avoid over-the-counter cough, cold, or allergy remedies which contain stimulant drugs, as these can counteract the antihypertensive medication.

You may need to take extra potassium to replace the loss caused by the drug. You may do this either by taking a potassium supplement (liquid, powder, or tablet), or by increasing the amounts of foods in your diet which are high in potassium. Some of these foods are bananas, citrus fruits, melons, and tomatoes.

Food Interactions

Slight stomach upset from Ser-Ap-Es Tablets can be overcome by taking each dose with some food. If stomach pain continues or becomes severe, call your doctor.

Usual Dose

Must be individualized to patient's response.

Overdosage

Symptoms are extreme lowering of blood pressure, rapid heartbeat, headache, generalized skin flushing, chest pains, and poor heart rhythms. The patient should be treated in a hospital where proper facilities and procedures are available. ALWAYS bring the medicine bottle to the emergency room.

Special Information

It is important to eat a well-balanced diet or follow the special diet given to you by your doctor. You must take your medicine exactly as prescribed.

Be sure to take this medicine exactly as prescribed: if you don't, the medicine will not be able to work best for you.

One of the ingredients in Ser-Ap-Es Tablets, Reserpine, may cause mental depression. If you have a history of depressive problems, make sure your doctor knows, so that the appropriate changes can be made. Stop taking this drug at the first sign of despondency, early morning insomnia, loss of appetite, or sexual impotence. Drug-induced depression may persist for several months after the drug has been stopped; it has been known to be severe enough to result in suicide attempts.

If you forget to take a dose of Ser-Ap-Es, take it as soon as you remember. If it is almost time for your next regularly scheduled dose, skip the one you forgot and continue with your regular schedule. Do not take a double dose.

Brand Name

Sinemet

Ingredients

Carbidopa
Levodopa

Type of Drug

Anti-Parkinsonian.

Prescribed for

Parkinson's disease.

General Information

The two ingredients in Sinemet interact for a beneficial drug interaction. Levodopa is the active ingredient that aids treatment of Parkinson's disease. Vitamin B_6 (Pyridoxine) destroys Levodopa, but Carbidopa prevents this. This allows more Levodopa to get into the brain, where it works.

This combination is so effective that the amount of Levodopa can be reduced by about 75 percent, which results in fewer side effects and, generally, safer drug treatment.

Cautions and Warnings

Do not take this drug if you are allergic to either of the ingredients. Patients being switched from Levodopa to Sinemet should stop taking Levodopa 8 hours before their first dose of Sinemet. It can be increased gradually, as needed. Side effects with Sinemet can occur at much lower dosages than with Levodopa, because of the effect of Carbidopa.

Pregnancy/Breast-feeding

These drugs are known to cause birth defects in laboratory animals. The effect in humans is not known. However, women who are pregnant or breast-feeding should use this drug only if it is absolutely necessary.

Seniors

Older adults may require smaller doses of this drug than younger adults because they are less tolerant to the drug's effects. Also the body enzyme that breaks down Levodopa (and against which Carbidopa protects) decreases with age, reducing the overall dosage requirement. Seniors, especially those with heart disease, are more likely to develop abnormal heart rhythms and other cardiac side effects of this drug.

Seniors who respond to this treatment, especially those with osteoporosis, should resume activity gradually. Sudden increases in activity and mobility lead to a greater possibility of broken bones than a gradual return to physical activity.

Possible Side Effects

Uncontrolled muscle movements, loss of appetite, nausea, vomiting, stomach pain, dry mouth, difficulty swallowing, dribbling saliva from the side of the mouth, shaking of the hands, headache, dizziness, numbness, weakness, feeling faint, grinding of the teeth, confusion, sleeplessness, nightmares, hallucinations, anxiety, agitation, tiredness, feeling of ill health, feeling of euphoria (high).

Less common side effects of Sinemet are: heart palpitations, dizziness when rising quickly from a sitting or lying position, and sudden extreme slowness of movement (on-off phenomenon); mental changes including paranoia, psychosis and depression, and slowdown of mental functioning; also difficult urination, muscle twitching, spasms of the eyelids, lockjaw, burning sensation on the tongue, bitter taste, diarrhea, constipation, stomach gas, flushing of the skin, rash, sweating, unusual breathing, double or blurred vision, dilation of the pupils of the eyes, hot flashes, changes in body weight, darkening of the urine or sweat.

Occasionally Sinemet may cause bleeding of the stomach or development of an ulcer, high blood pressure, adverse

SINEMET   785

effects on components of the blood, irritation of blood vessels, convulsions, inability to control movements of the eye muscles, hiccups, feeling of being stimulated, retention of body fluid, hair loss, hoarseness of the voice, or persistent penile erection. The drug may affect blood tests for kidney and liver function.

Drug Interactions

The effectiveness of Sinemet may be increased by taking drugs with an anticholinergic effect, such as Trihexyphenidyl. Methyldopa, an antihypertensive drug, has the same effect on Levodopa as Carbidopa. It can increase the amount of Levodopa available in the central nervous system, and it may have a slight effect on Sinemet as well.

Patients taking Guanethidine or a diuretic to treat high blood pressure may find they need less medication to control their pressure.

Reserpine, benzodiazepine tranquilizers, major tranquilizers, Phenytoin, and Papaverine may interfere with the effects of Sinemet. Vitamin BF will interfere with Levodopa but not with Sinemet.

Diabetics who start taking Sinemet may need adjustments in their antidiabetic drugs.

Patients taking Sinemet together with an MAO inhibitor drug may experience a rapid increase in blood pressure. MAO inhibitors should be stopped 2 weeks before Sinemet.

Sinemet may increase the effects of Ephedrine, amphetamines, Epinephrine, and Isoproterenol. This interaction can result in adverse effects on the heart. This reaction may also occur with some of the antidepressants.

Food Interactions

This drug may be taken with food to reduce upset stomach.

Usual Dose

Dose must be tailored to individual need and based on previous drug treatment. Three different Sinemet strengths are available to allow for individual variation: Sinemet 10/100, 25/100, and 25/250. The first number represents the milligrams of Carbidopa and the second number the Levodopa content. Dosage adjustments are made by adding or omitting ½ to 1 tablet per day. Maximum dose is 8 of the 25/250 tablets per day.

Special Information

Take care while driving or operating machinery; Sinemet can cause tiredness or lack of concentration. Call your doctor if you experience dizziness, light-headedness, or fainting spells, uncontrollable movements of the face, eyelids, mouth, tongue, neck, arms, hands, or legs, mood changes, mental changes, abnormal heartbeats or heart palpitations, difficult urination, or persistent nausea or vomiting or other stomach complaints.

This drug may cause darkening of the urine or sweat. This effect is not harmful, but may interfere with urine tests for diabetes.

Call your doctor before making any adjustments in your treatment.

If you forget to take a dose of Sinemet, take it as soon as you remember. If it is within 2 hours of your next regularly scheduled dose, skip the one you forgot and continue with your regular schedule. Do not take a double dose.

Brand Name

Singlet Tablets

Ingredients

Acetaminophen
Chlorpheniramine Maleate
Pseudoephedrine Hydrochloride

Other Brand Names

The following products contain the same ingredients in different concentrations:

Children's Co-Tylenol Liquid	Sinutab Maximum Strength
Codimal	Sinutab Maximum Strength
Comtrex A/S	Sinus Nighttime Formula
Drixoral Plus	Sinutab Tablets
Sine-Off Extra Strength	Teldrin MultiSymptom

Type of Drug

Decongestant–antihistamine–analgesic combination.

Prescribed for

Relief of congestion, runny nose, and other general symptoms associated with the common cold, influenza, or other upper respiratory diseases.

General Information

Singlet Tablets is one of many products marketed to alleviate the symptoms of the common cold. These products contain medicine to relieve nasal congestion or to dry up runny noses or soothe scratchy throats; and several of them may contain ingredients to suppress cough, or to help eliminate unwanted mucus. All these products are only for the relief of symptoms and will not treat the underlying problem, such as a cold virus or other infections.

Cautions and Warnings

Can cause excessive tiredness or drowsiness.

People with glaucoma or difficulty in urinating should avoid this drug and other drugs containing antihistamines.

Pregnancy/Breast-feeding

This drug crosses into the blood circulation of a developing baby. It has not been found to cause birth defects. Pregnant women, or those who might become pregnant while taking this drug, should not take it without their doctor's approval. When the drug is considered essential by your doctor, the potential risk of taking the medicine must be carefully weighed against the benefit it might produce.

This drug passes into breast milk, but has caused no problems among breast-fed infants. You must consider the potential effect on the nursing infant if breast-feeding while taking this medicine.

Seniors

Older adults are more sensitive to the effects of this drug. Follow your doctor's directions and report any side effects at once.

Possible Side Effects

Excessive tiredness or drowsiness, restlessness, tension, nervousness, tremor, weakness, inability to sleep, headache, palpitations, elevation of blood pressure, sweating, sleeplessness, loss of appetite, nausea, vomiting, dizziness, constipation.

Drug Interactions

Interaction with alcoholic beverages may produce excessive drowsiness and/or sleepiness, or inability to concentrate. Also avoid sedatives, tranquilizers, antihistamines, and sleeping pills.

Do not self-medicate with additional over-the-counter drugs for the relief of cold symptoms; taking Singlet Tablets with such drugs may result in aggravation of high blood pressure, heart disease, diabetes, or thyroid disease.

Do not take Singlet Tablets if you are taking or suspect you may be taking a monoamine oxidase (MAO) inhibitor: severe elevation in blood pressure may result.

Food Interactions

Take this medicine with food it it upsets your stomach.

Usual Dose

1 tablet 3 times per day.

Special Information

Since drowsiness may occur during use of Singlet Tablets, be cautious while performing mechanical tasks requiring alertness.

If you forget to take a dose of Singlet Tablets, take it as soon as you remember. If it is almost time for your next regularly scheduled dose, skip the one you forgot and continue with your regular schedule. Do not take a double dose.

Brand Name

Sinubid

Ingredients

Acetaminophen
Phenyltoloxamine Citrate
Phenylpropanolamine Hydrochloride

Other Brand Names

The following products contain the same ingredients in different concentrations:

PhenAPAP
Sinus Relief

Type of Drug

Decongestant–antihistamine–analgesic combination.

Prescribed for

Relief of congestion, runny nose, and other general symptoms associated with the common cold, influenza, or other upper respiratory diseases.

General Information

Sinubid is one of many products marketed to relieve the symptoms of the common cold. These products contain medicine to relieve nasal congestion or dry up runny noses or relieve scratchy throats, and several of them may contain ingredients to suppress cough, or to help eliminate unwanted mucus. All these products are good only for the relief of symptoms and will not treat the underlying problem, such as cold virus, or other infections.

Cautions and Warnings

This drug can cause excessive tiredness or drowsiness. Sinubid should not be used for newborn infants. People with glaucoma or difficulty in urinating should avoid this drug and other drugs containing antihistamines.

Pregnancy/Breast-feeding

This drug crosses into the blood circulation of a developing

baby. It has not been found to cause birth defects. Pregnant women, or those who might become pregnant while taking this drug, should not take it without their doctor's approval. When the drug is considered essential by your doctor, the potential risk of taking the medicine must be carefully weighed against the benefit it might produce.

This drug passes into breast milk, but has caused no problems among breast-fed infants. You must consider the potential effect on the nursing infant if breast-feeding while taking this medicine.

Seniors

Older adults are more sensitive to the effects of this drug. Follow your doctor's directions and report any side effects at once.

Possible Side Effects

Excessive tiredness or drowsiness, restlessness, tension, nervousness, tremor, weakness, inability to sleep, headache, palpitations, elevation of blood pressure, sweating, loss of appetite, nausea, vomiting, dizziness, constipation.

Drug Interactions

Interaction with alcoholic beverages may produce excessive drowsiness and/or sleepiness, or inability to concentrate. Also avoid sedatives, tranquilizers, other antihistamines, and sleeping pills.

Do not self-medicate with over-the-counter drugs for the relief of cold symptoms; taking Sinubid with such drugs may result in aggravation of high blood pressure, heart disease, diabetes, or thyroid disease.

Do not take Sinubid if you are taking or suspect you may be taking a monoamine oxidase (MAO) inhibitor: severe elevation in blood pressure may result.

Food Interactions

Take this medicine with food if it upsets your stomach.

Usual Dose

1 tablet morning and night.

Special Information

Since drowsiness may occur during use of Sinubid, be cautious while performing mechanical tasks requiring alertness.

If you forget to take a dose of Sinubid, take it as soon as you remember. If it is almost time for your next regularly scheduled dose, skip the one you forgot and continue with your regular schedule. Do not take a double dose.

Generic Name

Spironolactone

Brand Names

Alatone
Aldactone

(Also available in generic form)

Type of Drug

Diuretic.

Prescribed for

High blood pressure; excess fluid in the body due to other diseases; cirrhosis of the liver; people who need a diuretic, but whose blood potassium level is already low.

General Information

Spironolactone is a specific physiologic antagonist of aldosterone. Therefore, it is extremely useful for the treatment of excess fluid in the body related to the presence of high levels of aldosterone (hyperaldosteronism) when used alone or in combination with other diuretics.

Spironolactone is a potassium-sparing diuretic. This means that, unlike the thiazide diuretics, it does not cause the body to lose potassium.

Cautions and Warnings

Do not use this drug if you know you have kidney failure or high blood levels of potassium. This drug has been shown to cause tumors when given in very high doses to experimental rats.

Pregnancy/Breast-feeding

This drug crosses into the blood circulation of a developing baby. It has not been found to cause birth defects. Pregnant women, or those who might become pregnant while taking this drug, should not take it without their doctor's approval. When the drug is considered essential by your doctor, the potential risk of taking the medicine must be carefully weighed against the benefit it might produce.

This drug passes into breast milk, but has caused no problems among breast-fed infants. You must consider the potential effect on the nursing infant if breast-feeding while taking this medicine.

Seniors

Older adults are more sensitive to the effects of this drug, especially high blood potassium levels. Follow your doctor's directions and report any side effects at once.

Possible Side Effects

Drowsiness, lethargy, headache, gastrointestinal upset, cramps and diarrhea, rash, mental confusion, fever, feeling of ill health, enlargement of the breasts, inability to achieve or maintain erection in males, irregular menstrual cycles or deepening of the voice in females. These side effects are generally reversible.

Drug Interactions

Spironolactone will potentiate (increase the action of) other antihypertensive drugs; frequently it is used for this effect. The dosage of other antihypertensive drugs may be reduced as much as 50 percent when Spironolactone is added to the regimen.

Patients taking Spironolactone for the treatment of high blood pressure should not self-medicate with over-the-counter cough, cold, or allergy remedies containing stimulant drugs which may counteract its effectiveness and have an adverse effect on their hearts.

Food Interactions

Patients taking Spironolactone need not take potassium or eat food rich in potassium.

Usual Dose

Adult: for high blood pressure, initial dose is 50 to 100 milligrams per day in divided doses; for excess fluids related to other diseases, 100 to 200 milligrams per day in divided doses.

Child: 1 to 1.5 milligrams per pound of body weight, if deemed necessary.

Special Information

Take the drug exactly as it has been prescribed for maximum therapeutic effect. High blood levels of potassium associated with the use of Spironolactone may cause weakness, lethargy, drowsiness, muscle pains or cramps, and muscular fatigue. Patients should be careful when driving or performing jobs that require alertness. Spironolactone does not cause the loss of potassium as do other diuretics. Therefore, potassium supplements are unnecessary.

If you forget to take a dose of Spironolactone, take it as soon as you remember. If it is almost time for your next regularly scheduled dose, skip the one you forgot and continue with your regular schedule. Do not take a double dose.

Generic Name

Sucralfate

Brand Name

Carafate

Type of Drug

Local antiulcer therapy.

Prescribed for

Duodenal ulcer.

General Information

Sucralfate is minimally absorbed into the body from the gastrointestinal (GI) tract, but instead works within the GI tract by exerting a soothing local effect. After the drug binds to proteins in the damaged mucous tissue within the ulcer, it forms a barrier to acids and enzymes normally found in the gastrointestinal tract, protecting the ulcerated tissue from further damage and allowing it to begin to heal naturally. Although Sucralfate does not have any pronounced acid neutralizing effects, and its mechanism of action is completely different from that of Cimetidine, Sucralfate is equally effective in treating duodenal ulcer disease.

Cautions and Warnings

The use of Sucralfate in children is not recommended because the drug has only been studied in adults.

Pregnancy/Breast-feeding

This drug has not been found to cause birth defects. Pregnant women, or those who might become pregnant while taking this drug, should not take it without their doctor's approval. When the drug is considered essential by your doctor, the potential risk of taking the medicine must be carefully weighed against the benefit it might produce.

This drug passes into breast milk, but has caused no problems among breast-fed infants. You must consider the potential effect on the nursing infant if breast-feeding while taking this medicine.

Seniors

Older adults may take this medication without special restriction. Follow your doctor's directions and report any side effects at once.

Possible Side Effects

Most frequent: constipation. Others are: diarrhea, nausea, upset stomach, indigestion, dry mouth, rash, itching, back pain, dizziness, sleepiness. The incidence of reported side effects of Sucralfate is only about 5 percent.

Drug Interactions

Sucralfate may decrease the action of Tetracycline, Phenytoin, or Cimetidine. To avoid this, separate doses by 2 hours.

Do not take antacids within a half hour of taking Sucralfate.

Usual Dose

One tablet 4 times per day on an empty stomach.

Overdosage

There have been no reports of human overdoses of Sucralfate. Animals given the equivalent of 5.5 grams per pound of body weight did not experience any unusual effects, and therefore the risk associated with Sucralfate overdose is thought to be minimal.

Special Information

Each dose may be taken 1 hour before meals or 2 hours after meals and before bedtime. Be sure to take the medicine for a full 6- to 8-week course of treatment. Notify your doctor if you develop constipation, diarrhea, or other gastrointestinal side effects. If you are taking antacids as part of your ulcer therapy, separate antacid doses from Sucralfate by at least 2 hours.

If you forget to take a dose of Sucralfate, take it as soon as you remember. If it is almost time for your next regularly scheduled dose, skip the one you forgot and continue with your regular schedule. Do not take a double dose.

Type of Drug

Sulfa Drugs

Brand Names

Generic Name: Sulfacytine

Renoquid

Generic Name: Sulfadiazine

Microsulfon
Renoquid

(Also available in generic form)

Generic Name: Sulfisoxazole

Gantrisin
Gulfasin

(Also available in generic form)

Generic Name: Sulfamethoxazole

Gamazole
Gantanol
Urobak

(Also available in generic form)

Generic Name: Sulfamethizole

Proklar
Thiosulfil

Generic Name: Sulfasalazine

Azaline   Azulfidine EN-Tabs
Azulfidine   SAS-500

(Also available in generic form)

Generic Name: Trisulfapyrimidines

Neotrizine   Terfonyl
Sulfaloid   Triple Sulfas

Prescribed for

Infections. Sulfasalazine may be prescribed for rheumatoid arthritis, colitis, or Crohn's Disease of the intestines. Sulfisoxazole has been used to prevent middle ear infection.

General Information

Sulfa drugs are prescribed for infections in various parts of the body. They are particularly helpful for urinary tract infections because they tend to be concentrated in the urine when they pass out of the body. They kill bacteria by interfering with the organism's metabolic process. Some organisms may become resistant to the effects of sulfa drugs. Your doctor will test infected urine, blood, or tissue, if possible, against the drug(s) that may be used to pick the best one. Sulfas are usually a part of this screening process.

Sulfasalazine is different from the other sulfa drugs in that only about ⅓ of the drug is absorbed into the blood stream. The rest of the dose stays in the intestines and has been found to be effective against colitis and other intestinal irritation.

Cautions and Warnings

Do not take any sulfa drug if you know you are allergic to any member of this group or to a drug chemically related to the sulfas (thiazide-type diuretic, oral antidiabetes medicines).

Sulfasalazine should not be used by people with Aspirin allergy or by children less than 2 years old.

Sulfas should not be taken by people with severe kidney or liver disease.

Sulfa drugs often cause unusual sensitivity to the sun. Be sure to use a sunscreen or wear protective clothing until you see how sulfas affect you.

Pregnancy/Breast-feeding

Sulfa drugs pass into the circulation of a developing fetus. Although this can affect the growing infant, this rarely happens because of the mother's ability to protect her unborn child. Nevertheless, pregnant women and those who might become pregnant should not take a sulfa drug unless directed to do so by their doctor. When the drug is considered essential, the potential benefit of the drug should be weighed against the possible harm it might cause.

Small amounts of sulfa drugs pass into breast milk, but this rarely causes problems. The notable exception are infants deficient in the enzyme known as G-6PD. Infants with this deficiency can develop a severe form of anemia. A nursing infant may also develop diarrhea, rashes, and other problems. Talk to your doctor about the possible effect of taking a sulfa drug while nursing.

Seniors

Seniors with kidney or liver problems should take these drugs with caution. Other seniors may take sulfa drugs without special precaution. Follow your doctor's directions and report any side effects at once.

Possible Side Effects

Headache, itching, rash, sensitivity to strong sunlight, nausea, vomiting, cramps or pains in the abdomen or stomach, a tired or sick feeling, hallucinations, dizziness, ringing or buzzing in the ears, or chills.

Less common: blood diseases or changes in blood composition, arthritic pain, itchy eyes, diarrhea, appetite loss, drowsiness, hearing loss, fever, hair loss, yellow eyes or skin. Sulfasalazine may cause a reduced sperm count.

Drug Interactions

Sulfa drugs may interact with oral antidiabetes drugs (Methotrexate, Warfarin, Phenylbutazone, nonsteroidal anti-inflammatory drugs, Thiazide diuretics, Aspirin drugs, Probenecid, and Phenytoin). In this interaction, amounts of either the sulfa or the other drug in the blood may increase. Contact your doctor or pharmacist for advice if you are taking a sulfa with one of these drugs.

Erythromycin increases the effect of sulfa drugs against infections caused by *H. Influenza*, a common cause of middle ear infections.

Sulfa drugs may reduce the effectiveness of oral contraceptives. Women taking this combination may experience breakthrough bleeding.

Sulfasalazine may decrease the effectiveness of Digoxin.

The effects of folic acid may be antagonized by Sulfasalazine.

Food Interactions

Sulfa drugs should be taken on an empty stomach with a full glass of water. Sulfasalazine may be taken with food if it upsets your stomach.

Usual Dose

Sulfacytine:
Adult: 500 to 1000 milligrams per day for 10 days.
Child (under 14 years of age): not recommended.

Sulfadiazine:
Adult: 2 to 6 grams per day.
Child (over 2 months of age): 34 to 68 milligrams per pound of body weight every day.

Sulfisoxazole:
Adult: 2 to 8 grams a day.
Child (over 2 months of age): 34 to 68 milligrams per pound of body weight every day.

Sulfamethoxazole:
Adult: 2 to 3 grams a day.
Child (over 2 months of age): 23 to 27 milligrams per pound of body weight every day.

Sulfamethizole:
Adult: 1.5 to 4 grams per day.
Child (over 2 months of age): 13 to 20 milligrams per pound of body weight every day.

Sulfasalazine:
Adult: 2 to 4 grams a day.
Child: 13 to 26 milligrams per pound of body weight every day.

Trisulfapyrimidines:
Adult: 2 to 4 grams a day.
Child (over 2 months of age): 34 to 68 milligrams per pound of body weight every day.

Overdosage

Overdose symptoms include appetite loss, nausea, vomiting and colic, dizziness, headache, drowsiness, unconsciousness, high fever. Individuals suspected of having taken a sulfa drug overdose should be taken to a hospital emergency room at once. ALWAYS remember to take the medicine bottle with you.

Special Information

Avoid prolonged exposure to the sun while taking a sulfa drug.

Sore throat, fever, chills, unusual bleeding or bruising, rash, and drowsiness are signs of serious blood disorders and should be reported to your doctor at once. Also call your doctor if you experience ringing in the ears, blood in the urine, difficulty breathing.

Be sure to take the full course of medicine your doctor has prescribed, even if you begin to feel a little better.

Sulfa drugs may interfere with the test for sugar in the urine.

If you forget to take a dose of sulfa medicine take it as soon as you remember. If it is almost time for your next dose and you take the medicine 2 times a day, space the missed dose and your next dose 5 to 6 hours apart, then go back to your regular schedule. If it is almost time for your next dose and you take the medicine 3 or more times a day, take the forgotten dose and the next dose 2 to 4 hours apart, then go back to your regular schedule.

Generic Name

Sulindac

Brand Name

Clinoril

Type of Drug

Nonsteroidal anti-inflammatory.

Prescribed for

Arthritis, bursitis, and other forms of inflammatory diseases.

General Information

Sulindac is one of ten drugs available in the United States for arthritis and joint pain. As with the other members of this group, patient response to Sulindac is individual. For some, this drug will work wonders; for others, it will do nothing.

Sulindac and several other nonsteroidal anti-inflammatory drugs (NSAIDs) reduce inflammation, relieve pain, or reduce fever. NSAIDs share the same side effects and may be used by patients who cannot tolerate Aspirin. Choice of one of these drugs over another depends on disease response, side effects seen in a particular patient, convenience of times to be taken, and cost. Different drugs or different doses of the same drug may be tried until the greatest effectiveness is achieved with the fewest side effects.

Treatment of some indications is required for only 7 to 14 days.

Cautions and Warnings

Use Sulindac with extra caution if you have a history of ulcers, bleeding diseases, or allergic reaction to Aspirin. Sulindac should be avoided by children under age 14 and those who have nasal polyps. It is not a simple pain reliever; it should be used only under the strict supervision of your doctor.

Pregnancy/Breast-feeding

Sulindac should be avoided by pregnant women and nursing mothers. When used by a pregnant woman, this drug may have unwanted effects on the heart and blood of the unborn child. If this drug is taken late in the pregnancy, the length of the pregnancy may be increased.

Seniors

Older adults are more sensitive to the effects of this drug. Follow your doctor's directions and report any side effects at once.

Possible Side Effects

Upset stomach, nausea, vomiting, constipation, loss of appetite, gas, stomach cramps and pain, itching and rash, dizziness, headache, nervousness, buzzing or ringing in the ears, swelling of the feet, legs, hands, or arms.

Less common side effects: stomach bleeding, irritation, and ulcer, as well as abnormal liver function, jaundice, and hepatitis. Heart failure in patients with already weak hearts, palpitations, blurred vision, and allergic reactions have occurred.

Drug Interactions

May increase the effect of anticoagulant (blood-thinning) drugs. Probenecid (Benemid) or Aspirin may increase the amount of Sulindac in your blood by reducing its elimination from the body. DMSO may reduce the effectiveness of

Sulindac. Sulindac may increase the effects of sulfa drugs, antidiabetes drugs, and Phenytoin or other drugs for severe disorders.

Food Interactions

Take this medicine with food if it upsets your stomach.

Usual Dose

Up to 200 milligrams twice per day.

Overdosage

Patients taking an overdose of Sulindac must be made to vomit to remove any remaining drug from the stomach. Call your doctor or poison control center before doing this. If you must go to a hospital emergency room, ALWAYS bring the medicine bottle.

Special Information

If you are allergic to Aspirin, you may be allergic to Sulindac. Since this drug can irritate the stomach, take each dose with food. While taking Sulindac, avoid taking Aspirin or alcoholic beverages. Sulindac may cause blurred vision or dizziness. Take care while driving or performing any task requiring alertness.

Call your doctor if you develop rash, itching, hives, yellowing of the skin or whites of the eyes, black or tarry stools, swelling of hands or feet, sore throat, mouth sores, unusual bleeding or bruising, or shortness of breath.

If you forget to take a dose of Sulindac, take it as soon as you remember. If it is almost time for your next regularly scheduled dose, skip the one you forgot and continue with your regular schedule. Do not take a double dose.

Brand Name

Synalgos-DC

Ingredients

Aspirin
Caffeine
Dihydrocodeine Bitartrate

(Also available in generic form)

Type of Drug

Narcotic analgesic combination.

Prescribed for

Relief of mild to moderate pain.

General Information

Synalgos-DC is one of many combination products containing narcotics and analgesics. These products often also contain barbiturates or tranquilizers, and Acetaminophen may be substituted for Aspirin, or Caffeine may be omitted.

Caffeine may be of benefit in treating vascular headaches.

Cautions and Warnings

Do not take Synalgos-DC if you know you are allergic or sensitive to it. Use this drug with extreme caution if you suffer from asthma or other breathing problems. Long-term use of Synalgos-DC may cause drug dependence or addiction. Synalgos-DC is a respiratory depressant and affects the central nervous system, producing sleepiness, tiredness, and/or inability to concentrate.

Pregnancy/Breast-feeding

Synalgos-DC may cause birth defects or interfere with your baby's development. Check with your doctor before taking it if you are, or might be, pregnant.

Aspirin used regularly may affect the heart of the newborn and if taken within the last 2 weeks of pregnancy may cause bleeding in the child. Problems may also be seen in the mother herself, such as bleeding or increasing the length of pregnancy or labor.

Caffeine can cause birth defects in animals but has not been shown to cause problems in humans.

Dihydrocodeine can cause addiction in the unborn child if used regularly during pregnancy. Dihydrocodeine may cause the unborn infant to become dependent on it and cause unwanted side effects. Dihydrocodeine, taken at the time of delivery, may cause breathing problems in the newborn.

Seniors

The Dihydrocodeine in this combination product may have more of a depressant effect on seniors than younger adults. Other effects that may be more prominent are dizziness, light-headedness, or fainting when rising suddenly from a sitting or lying position.

Possible Side Effects

Most frequent: light-headedness, dizziness, sleepiness, nausea, vomiting, loss of appetite, sweating. If these effects occur, consider asking your doctor about lowering your dose. Usually the side effects disappear if you simply lie down.

More serious side effects of Synalgos-DC are shallow breathing or difficulty in breathing.

Less common side effects: euphoria (feeling high), weakness, sleepiness, headache, agitation, uncoordinated muscle movement, minor hallucinations, disorientation and visual disturbances, dry mouth, loss of appetite, constipation, flushing of the face, rapid heartbeat, palpitations, faintness, urinary difficulties or hesitancy, reduced sex drive and/or potency, itching, rashes, anemia, lowered blood sugar, yellowing of the skin and/or whites of the eyes. Narcotic analgesics may aggravate convulsions in those who had convulsions in the past.

Drug Interactions

Interaction with alcohol, tranquilizers, barbiturates, or sleeping pills produces tiredness, sleepiness, or inability to concentrate and seriously increases the depressive effect of Synalgos-DC.

The Aspirin component of Synalgos-DC can affect anticoagulant (blood-thinning) therapy. Be sure to discuss this with your doctor so that the proper dosage adjustment can be made.

Interaction with adrenal corticosteroids, Phenylbutazone, or alcohol can cause severe stomach irritation with possible bleeding.

Food Interactions

Take with food or ½ glass of water to prevent stomach upset.

Usual Dose

2 capsules every 4 hours.

Overdosage

Symptoms are depression of respiration (breathing), extreme tiredness progressing to stupor and then coma, pinpointed pupils of the eyes, no response to stimulation such as a pin stick, cold and clammy skin, slowing down of heartbeat, lowering of blood pressure, convulsions, and cardiac arrest. The patient should be taken to a hospital emergency room immediately. ALWAYS bring the medicine bottle.

Special Information

Drowsiness may occur: be careful when driving or operating hazardous machinery.

If you forget to take a dose of Synalgos-DC, take it as soon as you remember. If it is almost time for your next regularly scheduled dose, skip the one you forgot and continue with your regular schedule. Do not take a double dose.

Generic Name

Tamoxifen Citrate

Brand Name

Nolvadex

Type of Drug

Antiestrogen.

Prescribed for

Breast cancer in women. When used together with chemo-therapy after mastectomy surgery, Tamoxifen is effective in delaying the recurrence of surgically curable cancers in postmenopausal women or women over age 50. Tamoxifen has also been prescribed to treat painful breasts and to decrease swollen painful breasts in men.

General Information

Tamoxifen is effective against breast cancer in women whose tumors are tested and found to be estrogen positive. It works by competing with the sites in tissues to which estrogens attach. Once Tamoxifen binds to an estrogen receptor, it disrupts the cell in the same way that an estrogen would and prevents the cancer cell from dividing. Of women whose breast cancer has spread to other parts of their bodies, 50 to 60 percent may benefit from taking Tamoxifen.

Cautions and Warnings

Eye side effects have occurred in patients taking Tamoxifen for a year or more in doses at least 4 times above the maximum recommended dosage. A few cases of decreased visual clarity and other eye side effects have been reported at normal doses.

Animal studies showed that very high doses of Tamoxifen (15 milligrams per pound of body weight) may cause liver cancer.

Pregnancy/Breast-feeding

Because of the antiestrogen effects of this drug, Tamoxifen may cause harm to a developing baby. Although there are no studies of the effects of Tamoxifen in pregnant women, this drug should be avoided by women who are or might become pregnant. Women who must take Tamoxifen should use an effective contraceptive method since Tamoxifen can actually make you more fertile than normal.

It is not known if Tamoxifen passes into breast milk. Nursing mothers should use an alternate feeding method if they must take Tamoxifen.

Seniors

Seniors may take Tamoxifen without special precaution.

Possible Side Effects

Most common: hot flashes, nausea, and vomiting.

Less common: vaginal bleeding or discharge, irregular periods, skin rash.

Infrequent: high blood calcium levels, swelling of the arms or legs, taste changes, vaginal itch, depression, dizziness, light-headedness, headache, visual difficulty, reduced white-blood-cell count or reduced platelet count. Increases in tumor pain and local disease sometimes follow a good response with Tamoxifen.

Drug Interactions

Tamoxifen may raise blood calcium.

Food Interactions

Tamoxifen is best taken on an empty stomach, but may be taken with food or milk if it upsets your stomach.

Usual Dose

10 to 20 milligrams twice a day (morning and evening).

Overdosage

Overdose may lead to difficulty breathing and convulsions.

Overdose victims should be taken to a hospital emergency room for treatment. ALWAYS remember to bring the prescription bottle with you.

Special Information

Be sure to tell your doctor if you become very weak or sleepy, or if you experience confusion, pain, or swelling of your legs, difficulty breathing, or blurred vision.

Tell your doctor if you experience bone pain, hot flashes, nausea, vomiting, weight gain, irregular periods, dizziness, headache, loss of appetite (all drug side effects) while taking Tamoxifen.

Tell your doctor if you vomit shortly after taking a dose of Tamoxifen. Your doctor may tell you to take another dose or wait until the next dose.

If you forget to take a dose of Tamoxifen, skip the forgotten dose, call your doctor, and continue your regular dosing schedule. Do not take a double dose of Tamoxifen.

Brand Name

Tedral

Ingredients

Ephedrine Hydrochloride
Phenobarbital
Theophylline

Other Brand Names

Azma Aid
Phedral C.T.

The following products contain the same ingredients in different concentrations:

Primatene "P" Formula	Theofedral
Tedral SA	Theophenyllin
T.E.P. Tablets	Theoral
Theodrine	

(Also available in generic form)

Type of Drug

Antiasthmatic combination product.

Prescribed for

Relief of asthma symptoms or other upper respiratory disorders. The actions of this drug should be considered "possibly effective." There is considerable doubt among medical experts that this drug produces the effects claimed for it.

General Information

Tedral is one of several antiasthmatic combination products prescribed for the relief of asthmatic symptoms and other breathing problems. These products contain drugs which help relax the bronchial muscles, drugs which increase the diameter of the breathing passages, and a mild tranquilizer to help relax the patient. Other products in this class may contain similar ingredients along with other medicine to help eliminate mucus from the breathing passages.

Cautions and Warnings

This drug should not be taken if you have severe kidney or liver disease.

Pregnancy/Breast-feeding

Tedral may be required for a woman during pregnancy or nursing. However, there is an increased chance of birth defects while using Tedral during pregnancy. Regularly using Tedral during the last 3 months of pregnancy may cause drug dependency of the newborn. Labor may be prolonged, delivery may be delayed, and there may be breathing problems in the newborn if Tedral is used. Breast-feeding while using Tedral may cause increased tiredness, shortness of breath, or a slow heartbeat in the baby.

Seniors

Older adults are more sensitive to the effects of this drug. Follow your doctor's directions and report any side effects at once.

Possible Side Effects

Large doses of Tedral can produce excitation, shakiness, sleeplessness, nervousness, rapid heartbeat, chest pains, irregular heartbeat, dizziness, dryness of the nose and throat, headache, and sweating. Occasionally people have been known to develop hesitation or difficulty in urination.

Less common side effects: excessive urination, heart stimulation, drowsiness, muscle weakness, muscle twitching, unsteady walk. These effects can usually be controlled by having your doctor adjust the dose.

Drug Interactions

Tedral may cause sleeplessness and/or drowsiness. Do not take this drug with alcoholic beverages.

Taking Tedral or similar medicines with an MAO inhibitor can produce severe interaction. Consult your doctor first.

Tedral or similar products taken together with Lithium Carbonate will increase the excretion of Lithium; they have neutralized the effect of Propranolol. Erythromycin and similar antibiotics cause the body to hold Theophylline, leading to possible side effects.

Food Interactions

Take the drug with food to help prevent stomach upset.

Usual Dose

1 to 2 tablets every 4 hours.
   Sustained-action tablet: 1 tablet every 12 hours.
   Elixir or suspension: 1 teaspoon per 60 pounds of body
weight every 4 hours.

Overdosage

Symptoms of overdose can include stimulation, nausea, vomiting, nervousness, loss of appetite, irritability, headache,
abnormal heart rhythms, convulsions, and seizures. Overdose victims should be taken to a hospital emergency room
at once. ALWAYS bring the medicine bottle with you.

Special Information

If you forget to take a dose of Tedral take it as soon as you
remember. If it is almost time for your next regularly scheduled dose, skip the one you forgot and continue with your
regular schedule. Do not take a double dose.

Generic Name

Temazepam

Brand Names

Razepam
Restoril

(Also available in generic form)

Type of Drug

Sedative; hypnotic.

Prescribed for

Insomnia or sleeplessness, frequent nighttime awakening, or
waking up too early in the morning.

General Information

Temazepam is a member of the group of drugs known as benzodiazepines. These drugs are used as antianxiety agents, anticonvulsants, or sedatives (sleeping pills). They exert their effects by relaxing the large skeletal muscles and by a direct effect on the brain. In doing so, they can relax you and make you either more tranquil or sleepier, depending on the drug and how much you use. Many doctors prefer Temazepam and the other members of this class to other drugs that can be used for the same effect. Their reason is that the benzodiazepines tend to be safer, have fewer side effects, and are usually as, if not more, effective.

These drugs are generally used in any situation where they can be a useful adjunct.

Benzodiazepine tranquilizing drugs can be abused if taken for long periods of time, and it is possible to develop withdrawal symptoms if you discontinue the therapy abruptly. Withdrawal symptoms include convulsions, tremor, muscle cramps, stomach cramps, insomnia, agitation, diarrhea, vomiting, sweating, and convulsions.

Cautions and Warnings

Do not take Temazepam if you know you are sensitive or allergic to this drug or other benzodiazepines such as Chlordiazepoxide, Oxazepam, Chlorazepate, Diazepam, Lorazepam, Prazepam, and Clonazepam.

Temazepam and other members of this drug group may aggravate narrow-angle glaucoma, but if you have open-angle glaucoma you may take the drugs. In any case, check this information with your doctor. Temazepam can cause tiredness, drowsiness, inability to concentrate, and similar symptoms. Be careful if you are driving, operating machinery, or performing other activities which require concentration.

Pregnancy/Breast-feeding

This drug may cause birth defects or interfere with your baby's development. Check with your doctor before taking it if you are, or might be, pregnant. Your baby may become dependent on Temazepam if it is used continually during pregnancy. If used during the last weeks of pregnancy or during breast-feeding, the baby may be overly tired, be short

of breath, or have a low heartbeat. Use during labor may
cause weakness in the newborn.

Seniors

Older adults are more sensitive to the effects of this drug,
especially daytime drowsiness. They should closely follow
their doctor's directions and report any side effects at once.

Possible Side Effects

Most common: mild drowsiness during the first few days of
therapy, especially in the elderly or debilitated. If drowsiness
persists, contact your doctor.

Less common side effects: confusion, depression, lethargy, disorientation, headache, tiredness, slurred speech, stupor, dizziness, tremor, constipation, dry mouth, nausea,
inability to control urination, changes in sex drive, irregular
menstrual cycle, changes in heart rhythm, lowered blood pressure, retention of fluids, blurred or double vision, itching,
rash, hiccups, nervousness, inability to fall asleep, liver dysfunction (occasional). If you experience any of these reactions, stop taking the medicine and contact your doctor
immediately.

Drug Interactions

Temazepam is a central nervous system depressant. Avoid
alcohol, tranquilizers, narcotics, sleeping pills, barbiturates,
MAO inhibitors, antihistamines, and other medicines used to
relieve depression.

Food Interactions

Temazepam is best taken on an empty stomach but may be
taken with food.

Usual Dose

15 to 30 milligrams at bedtime. Must be individualized for
maximum benefit.

Overdosage

Symptoms are confusion, sleepiness, lack of response to
pain such as a pin stick, shallow breathing, lowered blood
pressure, and coma. The patient should be taken to a hospi-

tal emergency room immediately. ALWAYS bring the medicine bottle.

Special Information

Avoid alcoholic beverages while taking Temazepam. Other sleeping pills, narcotics, tranquilizers, and other drugs that depress the nervous system should be used with caution while taking Temazepam.

If you forget to take a dose of Temazepam and you remember within about an hour of your regular time, take it right away. If you do not remember until later, skip the forgotten dose and go back to your regular schedule. Do not take a double dose.

Brand Name

Tenoretic

Ingredients

Atenolol
Chlorthalidone

Type of Drug

Antihypertensive.

Prescribed for

High blood pressure.

General Information

This combination drug product takes advantage of two different drug types that are effective in treating high blood pressure: Atenolol is a beta blocker and Chlorthalidone is a diuretic. It is thought that beta blockers lower blood pressure by affecting body hormone systems and the heart, but the exact mechanism is not known. Diuretics lower blood pressure by affecting the amount of potassium in the muscles of blood vessels, helping them to open wider, reducing blood pressure.

Cautions and Warnings

You should be cautious about taking this Atenolol-containing combination if you have asthma, severe heart failure, very slow heart rate, or heart block because the drug can aggravate these conditions. Compared with the other beta blockers, Atenolol has less of an effect on your pulse and bronchial muscles and less of a rebound effect when the drug is discontinued; it produces less tiredness, depression, and intolerance to exercise than other beta-blocking drugs.

People with angina who take Atenolol for high blood pressure should have their drug dosage reduced gradually over 1 to 2 weeks rather than suddenly discontinued. This will avoid possible aggravation of the angina.

Atenolol should be used with caution if you have liver disease because your ability to eliminate the drug from your body will be impaired.

Do not take Tenoretic if you are allergic or sensitive to it or any other thiazide drug or to any sulfa drug. If you have a history of allergy or bronchial asthma, you may also have a sensitivity or allergy to Tenoretic. It should be avoided if you have kidney or liver disease.

Pregnancy/Breast-feeding

Tenoretic should be avoided by pregnant women or women who might become pregnant while taking it. If the drug is considered essential by your doctor, the potential risk of taking the medicine must be carefully weighed against the benefit it might produce. Small amounts of Tenoretic may pass into your breast milk. Nursing mothers taking this drug should observe their infants for possible drug-related side effects.

Seniors

Senior citizens may be more sensitive to the effects of Tenoretic than young adults. Your dosage of this drug must be adjusted to your individual needs by your doctor. Seniors may be more likely to suffer from cold hands and feet and reduced body temperature, chest pains, a general feeling of ill health, sudden difficulty breathing, sweating, or changes in heartbeat because of this medicine.

Possible Side Effects

Atenolol's side effects are relatively uncommon, usually develop early in the course of treatment, are relatively mild, and are rarely a reason to stop taking the medication. Side effects increase with increasing dosage and include dizziness, tingling of the scalp, nausea, vomiting, upset stomach, taste distortion, fatigue, sweating, male impotence, urinary difficulty, diarrhea, bile duct blockage, breathing difficulty, bronchial spasms, muscle weakness, cramps, dry eyes, blurred vision, skin rash, hair loss, and facial swelling. Like other beta blockers, Atenolol can cause mental depression, disorientation, short-term memory loss, and emotional instability.

Common diuretic side effects are loss of body potassium, leading to dry mouth, thirst, weakness, drowsiness, restlessness, muscle pains, cramps, or tiredness, low blood pressure, decreased frequency of urination, abnormal heart rhythm, and upset stomach. Other side effects are loss of appetite, nausea, vomiting, stomach bloating or cramps, diarrhea, constipation, yellowing of the skin or whites of the eyes, pancreas inflammation, liver inflammation (hepatitis), frequent urination (especially at night), headache, dizziness, fatigue, loss of energy, tiredness, a feeling of ill health, numbness in the hands or feet, nervousness, tension, anxiety, irritability, and agitation.

Less common side effects are kidney inflammation, impotence, reduced sex drive, light-headedness, drowsiness, fainting, difficulty sleeping, depression, tingling in the hands or feet, blurred vision, reduced levels of white blood cells and platelets, dizziness when rising quickly from a sitting or lying position, heart palpitations, chest pain, gout attacks, chills, stuffed nose, facial flushing, weight loss, aggravation of lupus erythematosus (a disease of the body's connective tissues), colitis, drug allergy (fever, sore throat), and unusual bleeding or bruising.

Drug Interactions

Beta-blocking drugs may interact with surgical anesthetics to increase the risk of heart problems during surgery. Some anesthesiologists recommend stopping your beta blocker gradually 2 days before surgery.

Atenolol may interfere with the normal signs of low blood

sugar and can interfere with the action of insulin or oral antidiabetes medicines.

Taking Atenolol together with Aspirin-containing drugs, Indomethacin, or Sulfinpyrazone can interfere with its blood-pressure-lowering effect.

The effects of Atenolol may be increased by taking pheno-thiazine antipsychotic medicines with other antihypertensives like Clonidine, Diazoxide, Nifedipine, Reserpine, or with other drugs that can reduce blood pressure, like Nitroglycerin.

Atenolol may interfere with the effectiveness of some anti-asthma drugs, especially Ephedrine and Isoproterenol, and with Theophylline or Aminophylline.

The combination of Atenolol and Phenytoin or Atenolol and digitalis drugs can result in excessive slowing of the heart and possible heart block.

Estrogen drugs can interfere with the blood-pressure-lowering effect of Atenolol.

The chances of losing body potassium are increased if you take Chlorthalidone with Digoxin or with a corticosteroid anti-inflammatory drug. If you are taking medicine to treat diabetes and begin taking Chlorthalidone, the dose of your diabetes medicine may have to be adjusted.

Chlorthalidone will increase the effects of Lithium and the chances of developing Lithium toxicity by preventing it from passing out of your body.

People taking Chlorthalidone for high blood pressure or heart failure should take care to avoid nonprescription medi-cines that might aggravate your condition, such as decon-gestants, cold and allergy treatments, and diet pills, all of which can contain stimulants. If you are unsure about which medicine to choose, ask your pharmacist.

Dizziness when rising from a sitting or lying position may be worsened by taking Chlorthalidone with alcoholic beverages, barbiturate-type sleeping pills, or narcotic pain relievers.

The effects of Chlorthalidone may be counteracted by Indomethacin because of its effect on the kidneys. Taking Colestipol or Cholestyramine at the same time as Chlor-thalidone will reduce the drug's effect by preventing it from being absorbed into the bloodstream.

Taking Chlorthalidone and other thiazide-type diuretics with calcium or Vitamin D could result in excessive levels of calcium in the blood.

Sulfa drugs may increase the effects of Chlorthalidone by increasing the amount of diuretic drug in the bloodstream.

Chlorthalidone may increase the effect of Quinidine, prescribed for abnormal heart rhythms, by interfering with its release from the body via your kidneys.

Food Interactions

Take this medicine with food if it upsets your stomach. Chlorthalidone may cause loss of body potassium (hypokalemia), a complication that can be avoided by adding foods rich in potassium to your diet. Some potassium-rich foods are tomatoes, citrus fruits, melons, and bananas. It can also be prevented by taking a potassium supplement in pill, powder, or liquid form.

Usual Dose

Adult: 1 to 2 tablets a day.

Senior: older adults may respond to lower doses of this drug than younger adults, and should be treated more cautiously.

Overdosage

Symptoms are changes in heartbeat (either/or unusually slow, unusually fast, or irregular), severe dizziness or fainting, difficulty breathing, bluish-colored fingernails or palms of the hands and seizures, potassium deficiency and dehydration; confusion, dizziness, muscle weakness, upset stomach, excessive thirst, loss of appetite, lethargy (rare), drowsiness, restlessness (rare), tingling in the hands or feet, rapid heartbeat, nausea and vomiting. The drug may be successfully removed from the stomach by giving Syrup of Ipecac within an hour of the overdose. After an hour has passed, much of the drug will have been absorbed into the blood and symptoms can develop. Take the victim to a hospital emergency room for treatment, and ALWAYS remember to bring the prescription bottle with you.

Special Information

Tenoretic is meant to be taken on a continuous basis. Do not stop taking it unless directed do so by your doctor.

Possible side effects of abrupt withdrawal of Atenolol are: chest pain, difficulty breathing, sweating, and unusually fast or irregular heartbeat.

Call your doctor at once if any of the following symptoms develop: back or joint pains, difficulty breathing, cold hands or feet, depression, skin rash, changes in heartbeat.

Call your doctor only if the following side effects persist or are bothersome: anxiety, diarrhea, constipation, sexual impotence, mild dizziness, headache, itching, nausea or vomiting, nightmares or vivid dreams, upset stomach, trouble sleeping, stuffed nose, frequent urination, unusual tiredness or weakness.

Always take your daily dose of Tenoretic by 10:00 A.M. Taking it later in the day will increase your chances of being kept awake at night by the need to urinate frequently.

Call your doctor if muscle weakness, cramps, nausea, dizziness, or other severe side effects develop.

If you forget to take a dose of Tenoretic and remember later in the same day, take it as soon as you remember. If you don't remember until the next day, or if it is almost time for your next dose, skip the forgotten dose and continue with your regular schedule. Do not take a double dose of Tenoretic.

Generic Name
Terazosin

Brand Name
Hytrin

Type of Drug
Antihypertensive.

Prescribed for
High blood pressure.

General Information
Terazosin works by opening blood vessels and reducing pressure in them. The tendency of Terazosin to cause water retention limits the usefulness of Terazosin by itself. Thus,

Terazosin is generally used together with a diuretic and/or beta-blocking drug.

Cautions and Warnings

Terazosin can cause dizziness and fainting, especially after taking the first dose in Terazosin therapy. This effect is called "postural hypotension." This effect can be minimized by limiting the first dose of Terazosin to 1 milligram at bedtime. Postural hypotension occurs in about 1 percent of people taking Terazosin and can occur at any time while you are taking the drug; it is rarely severe.

Some people taking Terazosin experience a small but important increase in blood-cholesterol levels. Individuals with an already high blood-cholesterol level should discuss the potential of this problem with their doctor.

Pregnancy/Breast-feeding

There are no studies of Terazosin in pregnant women, and the safety of Terazosin use during pregnancy is not known. Terazosin should only be used when the drug's potential benefits outweigh its potential dangers.

It is not known if Terazosin passes into breast milk. Nursing mothers should use an alternate feeding method if they must take this medication.

Seniors

Older adults may be more sensitive to the effects of Terazosin. Report any unusual side effects to your doctor.

Possible Side Effects

Most common: dizziness, weakness, tiredness, headache.

Other common side effects are palpitations, nausea, stuffed nose, difficulty breathing, sinus irritation, pain in the arms or legs, back pain, nervousness, tingling in the hands or feet, sleepiness, bloating.

Less common side effects: dizziness when rising quickly from a sitting or lying position, rapid heartbeat, abnormal heart rhythms, chest pain, flushing, vomiting, dry mouth, diarrhea, constipation, abdominal pain or discomfort, weight gain, intestinal gas, symptoms of the common cold, flu, or bronchitis, nosebleeds, coughing, runny nose, sore throat,

neck or shoulder pains, arthritis or joint pains, symptoms of
gout, muscle aches, visual disturbances, reddened eyes, ringing or buzzing in the ears, anxiety and sleeplessness, urinary
tract infection, frequent urination, itching, rash, sweating,
swelling of the face, and fever.

Rare side effects include depression, reduced sex drive,
swelling of the arms or legs, and weight gain.

Drug Interactions

Terazosin may interact with Nitroglycerin or calcium-channel-
blocking drugs to increase the chances of dizziness and
fainting. The blood-pressure-lowering effect of Terazosin may
be reduced by Indomethacin.

Other blood-pressure-lowering drugs (diuretics, calcium
channel blockers, beta blockers, etc.) increase the blood-
pressure-lowering effect of Terazosin.

Food Interactions

Terazosin may be taken without regard to food or meals.

Usual Dose

The usual starting dose of Terazosin is 1 milligram at bedtime. The dosage may be increased to a total of 5 milligrams
a day. Terazosin may be taken once or twice a day.

Overdosage

Terazosin overdose may produce drowsiness, poor reflexes,
and reduced blood pressure. Overdose victims should be
taken to a hospital emergency room at once. ALWAYS remember to bring the prescription bottle with you.

Special Information

Take this drug exactly as prescribed. Do not stop taking
Terazosin unless directed to do so by your doctor. Avoid
nonprescription drugs that contain stimulants because they
can increase your blood pressure. Your pharmacist will be
able to tell what you can and cannot take.

Terazosin can cause dizziness, headache, and drowsiness,
especially after you take your drug dose. Before driving or
doing anything that requires intense concentration, wait sev-

eral hours after taking this medicine. Take your Terazosin at bedtime to avoid this problem.

Generic Name

Terbutaline Sulfate

Brand Names

Brethaire Aerosol
Brethine
Bricanyl

Type of Drug

Bronchodilator.

Prescribed for

Asthma and spasm of the bronchial muscles. This drug has been used experimentally to prevent or slow down premature labor in pregnant women.

General Information

Terbutaline has a more specific effect than some of the other bronchodilator drugs and can cause a somewhat lower incidence of side effects on the heart. Often Terbutaline Sulfate is used with other drugs to enhance beneficial effects. The tablet takes effect 30 minutes after it has been taken and continues working for 4 to 8 hours. Therefore it is not used for an acute asthma attack, but rather to prevent one. Terbutaline inhalation starts working within 5 to 30 minutes and lasts for 3 to 6 hours.

Cautions and Warnings

This drug should be used with caution by patients who have angina, heart disease, high blood pressure, a history of stroke or seizures, diabetes, thyroid disease, prostate disease, or glaucoma.

Pregnancy/Breast-feeding

This drug should be used by women who are pregnant or breast-feeding only when absolutely necessary. The poten-

tial hazard to the unborn child or nursing infant is not known
at this time.

Seniors

Older adults are more sensitive to the effects of this drug.
They should closely follow their doctor's directions and report any side effects at once.

Possible Side Effects

Restlessness, anxiety, fear, tension, sleeplessness, tremors,
convulsions, weakness, dizziness, headache, flushing, pallor,
sweating, nausea and vomiting, loss of appetite, muscle
cramps, urinary difficulties.

Less commonly, Terbutaline Sulfate can affect the heart
and cardiovascular system, causing high blood pressure,
abnormal heart rhythms, and angina. It is less likely to cause
these effects than some of the older drugs.

Drug Interactions

The effect of this drug may be increased by antidepressant
drugs, some antihistamines, and Levothyroxine. It may antagonize the effects of Reserpine or Guanethidine.

Food Interactions

If the drug causes upset stomach, each dose may be taken
with food.

Usual Dose

Adult: 5 milligrams 3 times per day, every 6 hours. No
more than 15 milligrams per day.

Child (age 12 to 15): 2.5 milligrams 3 times per day every 6
hours. No more than 7.5 milligrams per day.

Child (under age 12): not recommended.

Inhalation: two inhalations taken 1 minute apart every 4
to 6 hours.

Overdosage

Symptoms include palpitation, abnormal heart rhythms,
rapid heartbeat, slow heartbeat, chest pain, high blood
pressure, fever, chills, cold sweat, blanching of the skin,
nausea, vomiting, sleeplessness, delirium, tremor, pinpoint

pupils, convulsions, coma, and collapse. If you or someone you know has taken an overdose of this drug call your doctor or bring the patient to a hospital emergency room. ALWAYS remember to bring the prescription bottle with you.

Special Information

Be sure to follow your doctor's instructions for this drug. Using more of it than was prescribed can lead to drug tolerance and actually cause your condition to worsen.

Terbutaline inhalations should be used during the second half of your breath. This allows the medicine to reach more deeply into your lungs.

Call your doctor at once if you develop chest pains, palpitation, rapid heartbeat, muscle tremors, dizziness, headache, facial flushing, or urinary difficulty, or if you still have trouble breathing after using this medicine.

If you miss a dose of Terbutaline, take it as soon as possible. Take the rest of that day's doses at regularly spaced intervals. Go back to your regular schedule the next day.

Generic Name

Terconazole

Brand Name

Terazol 7

Type of Drug

Antifungal.

Prescribed for

Fungus infections of the skin or vaginal tract.

General Information

Terconazole is one of several antifungal products available in the United States. This drug may be effective against organisms that are not affected by other drugs. Up to 15 percent of the drug may be absorbed into the bloodstream after vaginal administration.

Cautions and Warnings

Do not use this product if you are allergic or sensitive to it. Stop using it if it causes irritation or itching.

Pregnancy/Breast-feeding

No problems have been reported among infants born of pregnant women who have used Terconazole, but the drug should be avoided during the first 3 months of pregnancy unless it is absolutely necessary. The use of a vaginal applicator may not be advised during pregnancy; another product that comes as a vaginal tablet may be preferred. Possible direct exposure of the fetus to Terconazole may occur if the drug is absorbed through an irritated vaginal tract. Pregnant women should not use this drug without their doctor's consent.

It is not known if Terconazole passes into breast milk, but nursing women should not use this drug because of the possibility of infant reaction.

Seniors

Seniors may use this drug without special precautions.

Possible Side Effects

About ¼ of all women who use Terconazole develop the side effect of headache. Other side effects are body pain, vaginal burning, itching, or irritation, and unusual sensitivity to the sun (after direct application to the skin).

Usual Dose

1 applicatorful at bedtime for 7 nights.

Special Information

The effectiveness of this drug is not affected by menstruation. Insert each dose of this medication high into the vagina. For maximum effect, you must complete the full course of treatment, even if you begin to feel better. Refrain from intercourse while using this drug or advise your partner to wear a condom to prevent reinfection. Use a sanitary napkin to prevent your clothes from being stained.

If you forget a dose of Terconazole, apply it as soon as you remember. If it is almost time for your next dose, skip the forgotten dose and continue with your regular schedule. Do not take a double dose.

Generic Name

Terfenadine

Brand Name

Seldane

Type of Drug

Antihistamine.

Prescribed for

Seasonal allergy, stuffy and runny nose, itching of the eyes, scratchy throat caused by allergies, and other allergic symptoms such as rash, itching, or hives.

General Information

Terfenadine causes less sedation than almost any other sedating antihistamine used in the United States. Available in Europe and Canada for several years, this drug has been widely used and accepted by people who find other antihistamines unacceptable because of the drowsiness and tiredness they cause. Terfenadine appears to work in exactly the same way as Chlorpheniramine and other widely used antihistamines.

Cautions and Warnings

Do not take Terfenadine if you have had an allergic reaction to it in the past. People with asthma or other deep-breathing problems, glaucoma (pressure in the eye), stomach ulcer or other stomach problems should avoid Terfenadine because its side effects may aggravate these problems.

Pregnancy/Breast-feeding

Antihistamines have not been proven to be a cause of birth

defects or other problems in pregnant women, although studies in animals have shown that some drugs (Meclizine and Cyclizine), used mainly against nausea and vomiting, may cause birth defects. Do not take any antihistamine without your doctor's knowledge. Animal studies of Terfenadine have shown that doses several times larger than the human dose lower the baby's weight and increase the risk of the baby's death.

Small amounts of antihistamine medicines pass into breast milk and may affect a nursing infant. Nursing mothers should avoid antihistamines or use alternate feeding methods while taking the medicine.

Seniors

Seniors are more sensitive to antihistamine side effects. Confusion, difficult or painful urination, dizziness, drowsiness, a faint feeling, dry mouth, nose, or throat, nightmares or excitement, nervousness, restlessness, or irritability are more likely to occur among older adults.

Possible Side Effects

Occasional: headache, nervousness, weakness, upset stomach, nausea, vomiting, dry mouth, nose or throat, sore throat, nosebleeds, cough, stuffy nose, change in bowel habits. In scientific studies, Terfenadine was found to cause the same amount of drowsiness as a placebo (inactive pill) and about half that caused by other antihistamines. It is considered safe for use by people who cannot tolerate the sedating effects of other antihistamine drugs.

Less common side effects: hair loss, allergic reactions, depression, sleeplessness, menstrual irregularities, muscle aches, sweating, tingling in the hands or feet, frequent urination, visual disturbances. A few people taking this drug have developed liver damage.

Drug Interactions

No interactions have been found between Terfenadine and other drugs. Unlike other antihistamines, Terfenadine does not interact with alcohol or other nervous system depressants to produce drowsiness or loss of coordination.

Food Interactions

Terfenadine should be taken on an empty stomach, 1 hour before or 2 hours after food or meals.

Usual Dose

Adult and child (over age 12): 60 milligrams twice a day.
Child (age 6 to 12): 30 to 60 milligrams twice a day.
Child (age 3 to 5): 15 milligrams twice a day.

Overdosage

Terfenadine overdose is likely to cause exaggerated side effects. Victims of Terfenadine overdose should be given Syrup of Ipecac to make them vomit and be taken to a hospital emergency room for treatment. ALWAYS bring the prescription bottle with you.

Special Information

Report any unusual side effects to your doctor. Terfenadine's only disadvantage is its cost. Equally effective antihistamines are sold over-the-counter without a prescription and can be purchased for relatively little money.

If you forget to take a dose of Terfenadine, take it as soon as you remember. If it is almost time for your next regularly scheduled dose, skip the one you forgot and continue with your regular schedule. Do not take a double dose.

Generic Name

Terpin Hydrate with Codeine

Type of Drug

Cough suppressant and expectorant combination.

Prescribed for

Relief of coughs due to colds or other respiratory infections.

General Information

Terpin Hydrate decreases the production of mucus and other bronchial secretions which can cause coughs. The cough suppressant effect of Terpin Hydrate with Codeine is primarily due to the Codeine.

Cautions and Warnings

Do not take Codeine if you know you are allergic or sensitive to this drug. Use this drug with extreme caution if you suffer from asthma or other breathing problems. Long-term use of Codeine may cause drug dependence or addiction. Codeine is a respiratory depressant and affects the central nervous system, producing sleepiness, tiredness, and/or inability to concentrate. Be careful if you are driving, operating machinery, or performing other functions requiring concentration.

Pregnancy/Breast-feeding

Terpin Hydrate with Codeine is 80 proof (40 percent alcohol). Too much alcohol taken by the mother during pregnancy and lactation may cause birth defects and unwanted problems during breast-feeding.

Terpin Hydrate has not been shown to cause birth defects. Too much (large amounts taken for a long time) narcotic used during pregnancy and breast-feeding may cause the baby to become dependent on the narcotic. Narcotics may also cause breathing problems in the infant during delivery.

Seniors

Older adults are more sensitive to the effects of this drug. Follow your doctor's directions and report any side effects at once.

Possible Side Effects

Most frequent: light-headedness, dizziness, sedation or sleepiness, nausea, vomiting, sweating. Terpin Hydrate with Codeine elixir contains 40 percent alcohol (80 proof), and it is an easily abused drug product.

Less common side effects: euphoria (feeling high), weakness, sleepiness, headache, agitation, uncoordinated muscle movement, minor hallucinations, disorientation and visual disturbances, dry mouth, loss of appetite, constipation, flushing of the face, rapid heartbeat, palpitations, faintness, urinary difficulties or hesitancy, reduced sex drive and/or potency, itching, rashes, anemia, lowered blood sugar, yellowing of the skin and/or whites of the eyes. Narcotic analgesics may aggravate convulsions in those who have had convulsions in the past.

Drug Interactions

Codeine has a depressant effect and a potential effect on breathing, and it should be taken with extreme care in combination with alcohol, sedatives, tranquilizers, antihistamines, or other depressant drugs.

Usual Dose

1 to 2 teaspoons every 3 or 4 hours as needed for relief of cough.

Special Information

To help reduce the cough, try to cough up as much mucus as possible while taking this medication.

If you forget to take a dose of Terpin Hydrate with Codeine, take it as soon as you remember. If it is almost time for your next regularly scheduled dose, skip the one you forgot and continue with your regular schedule. Do not take a double dose.

Generic Name

Tetracycline Hydrochloride

Brand Names

Achromycin V	Sumycin
Cyclinex	Tetra-C
Cyclopar	Tetracap
Nor-Tet	Tetracyn
Panmycin	Tetralan
Retet	Tetram
Robitet	

Products available in non-pill form:

Achromycin (eye ointment and drops)
Topicycline (topical solution)

(Also available in generic form)

Type of Drug

Broad-spectrum antibiotic effective against gram-positive and gram-negative organisms.

Prescribed for

Bacterial infections such as gonorrhea, infections of the mouth, gums and teeth, Rocky Mountain spotted fever and other fevers caused by ticks and lice from a variety of carriers, urinary tract infections, and respiratory system infections such as pneumonia and bronchitis.

These diseases are produced by gram-positive and gram-negative organisms such as diplococci, staphylococci, streptococci, gonococci, *E. coli,* and *Shigella.*

Tetracycline has also been successfully used to treat some skin infections, but it is not considered the first-choice antibiotic for the treatment of general skin infections or wounds. It may be applied to the skin to treat acne.

General Information

Tetracycline Hydrochloride works by interfering with the normal growth cycle of the invading bacteria, preventing them from reproducing and thus allowing the body's normal defenses to fight off the infection. This process is referred to as bacteriostatic action. Tetracycline Hydrochloride has also been used along with other medicines to treat amoebic infections of the intestinal tract, known as amoebic dysentery. It is also prescribed for diseases caused by ticks, fleas, and lice, such as Lyme disease.

Tetracycline Hydrochloride has been successfully used for the treatment of adolescent acne, in small doses over a long period of time. Adverse effects or toxicity in this type of therapy are almost unheard of.

Since the action of this antibiotic depends on its concentration within the invading bacteria, it is imperative that you completely follow the doctor's directions. Another form of Tetracycline Hydrochloride is Oxytetracycline (Terramycin) which is given in the same dose and has the same effects as Tetracycline Hydrochloride.

Cautions and Warnings

Tetracycline Hydrochloride should not be given to people

with known liver disease or kidney or urine excretion problems. You should avoid taking high doses of Tetracycline Hydrochloride or undergoing extended Tetracycline Hydrochloride therapy if you will be exposed to sunlight for a long period because this antibiotic can interfere with your body's normal sun-screening mechanism, possibly causing a severe sunburn. If you have a known history of allergy to Tetracycline Hydrochloride you should avoid taking this drug or other drugs within this category such as Aureomycin, Terramycin, Rondomycin, Doxycycline, Demeclocycline, and Minocycline.

Pregnancy/Breast-feeding

You should not use Tetracycline Hydrochloride if you are pregnant, especially during the last half of pregnancy or when breast-feeding, when the child's bones and teeth are being formed. Tetracycline Hydrochloride when used in children has been shown to interfere with the development of the long bones and may retard growth. Exceptions would be when Tetracycline Hydrochloride is the only effective antibiotic available and all risk factors have been made known to the patient.

Seniors

Older adults, especially those with poor kidney function, may be more susceptible to long-term side effects from Tetracycline.

Possible Side Effects

As with other antibiotics, the common side effects of Tetracycline Hydrochloride are stomach upset, nausea, vomiting, diarrhea, and rash. Less common side effects include hairy tongue and itching and irritation of the anal and/or vaginal region. If these symptoms appear, consult your physician immediately. Periodic physical examinations and laboratory tests should be given to patients who are on long-term Tetracycline Hydrochloride.

Less common side effects: loss of appetite, peeling of the skin, sensitivity to the sun, fever, chills, anemia, possible brown spotting of the skin, decrease in kidney function, damage to the liver.

Drug Interactions

Tetracycline Hydrochloride (a bacteriostatic drug) may interfere with the action of bactericidal agents such as Penicillin. It is not advisable to take both during the same course of therapy.

Don't take multivitamin products containing minerals at the same time as Tetracycline Hydrochloride, or you may reduce the antibiotic's effectiveness. Space the taking of these two medicines at least 2 hours apart.

People receiving anticoagulation therapy (blood-thinning agents) should consult their doctor, since Tetracycline Hydrochloride will interfere with this form of therapy. An adjustment in the anticoagulant dosage may be required.

Food Interactions

Take on an empty stomach 1 hour before or 2 hours after meals and with 8 ounces of water. The antibacterial effect of Tetracycline Hydrochloride may be neutralized when taken with food, some dairy products (such as milk or cheese), or antacids.

Usual Dose

Adult: 250 to 500 milligrams 4 times per day.

Child (age 9 and over): 50 to 100 milligrams 4 times per day.

Child (up to age of 8): should avoid Tetracycline Hydrochloride, as it has been shown to produce serious discoloration of the permanent teeth.

Special Information

Do not take after the expiration date on the label. The decomposition of Tetracycline Hydrochloride produces a highly toxic substance that can cause serious kidney damage.

If you miss a dose of Tetracycline Hydrochloride, take it as soon as possible. If it is almost time for your next dose and you take the medication once a day, space the missed dose and your next dose 10 to 12 hours apart, then go back to your regular schedule.

If it is almost time for your next dose and you take the medicine twice a day, space the missed dose and your next dose by 5 to 6 hours, then go back to your regular schedule.

If it is almost time for your next dose and you take the medicine 3 or more times a day, space the missed dose and your next dose by 2 to 4 hours, then go back to your regular schedule.

Generic Name

Theophylline

Brand Names

Accurbron	Lanophyllin
Aerolate	Lixolin
Aquaphyllin	Quibron-T
Asmalix	Slo-Phyllin
Bronkodyl	Somophyllin-T
Elixicon	Theoclear
Elixomin	Theolair
Elixophyllin	Theophyl

Timed-Release Products

Aerolate Capsules	Theobid Jr. Duracaps
Bronkodyl S-R	Theoclear L.A. Cenules
Constant-T	Theocron
Duraphyl	Theo-Dur
Elixophyllin SR	Theo-Dur Sprinkle
LāBID	Theolair-SR
Lodrane	Theophylline S.R.
Quibron-T/SR Dividose	Theophyl-SR
Respbid	Theospan-SR
Slo-Bid Gyrocaps	Theo-Time
Slo-Phyllin Gyrocaps	Theo-24
Somophyllin-CRT	Theovent Long-Acting
Sustaire	Uniphyl
Theobid Duracaps	

(Also available in generic form)

Type of Drug

Xanthine bronchodilator.

Prescribed for

Relief of bronchial asthma and spasms of bronchial muscles associated with emphysema, bronchitis, and other diseases.

General Information

Theophylline is one of several drugs known as xanthine derivatives which are the mainstay of therapy for bronchial asthma and similar diseases. Other members of this group are Aminophylline, Dyphylline, and Oxtriphylline. Although the dosage for each of these drugs is different, they all work by relaxing bronchial muscles and helping reverse spasms in these muscles.

Timed-release products allow Theophylline to act continually throughout the day. This usually allows you to decrease the total number of different doses to be taken during a 24-hour period.

Initial Theophylline treatment requires your doctor to take blood samples to assess how much Theophylline is in your blood. Usually a level of between 10 and 20 micrograms per milliliter (quantity per blood volume) is considered normal. Dosage adjustments may be required based on these blood tests and your response to the therapy.

Theophylline, or another xanthine, can be found combined in almost 100 prescription or nonprescription drugs.

Cautions and Warnings

Do not use this drug if you are allergic or sensitive to it or to any related drug, such as Aminophylline. If you have a stomach ulcer or heart disease, you should use this drug with caution.

Pregnancy/Breast-feeding

This drug passes into the circulation of the developing baby. It does not cause birth defects, but may result in dangerous drug levels in the infant's bloodstream. Babies born of mothers taking this medication may be nervous, jittery, and irritable, and may gag and vomit when fed. Women who must use this medication to control asthma or other conditions should talk with their doctor about the relative risks of using this medication and the benefits it will produce for them.

This medication passes into breast milk and may cause a nursing infant to have difficulty sleeping and be nervous or irritable.

Seniors

Older adults may take longer to clear this drug from their bodies than younger adults. Older adults with heart failure or other cardiac conditions, chronic lung disease, a virus infection with fever, or reduced liver function may require a lower dosage of this medication to account for the clearance effect.

Possible Side Effects

Possible side effects from Theophylline or other xanthine derivatives are nausea, vomiting, stomach pain, diarrhea, irritability, restlessness, difficulty sleeping, excitability, muscle twitching or spasms, heart palpitations, other unusual heart rates, low blood pressure, rapid breathing, and local irritation (particularly if a suppository is used).

Infrequent: vomiting blood, fever, headache, dehydration.

Drug Interactions

Taking Theophylline at the same time as another xanthine derivative may increase side effects. Don't do it except under the direct care of a doctor.

Theophylline is often given in combination with a stimulant drug such as Ephedrine. Such combinations can cause excessive stimulation and should be used only as specifically directed by your doctor.

Reports have indicated that combining Erythromycin, Flu vaccine, Allopurinol, or Cimetidine with Theophylline will give you higher blood levels of Theophylline. Remember that higher blood levels mean the possibility of more side effects. Smoking cigarettes or marijuana makes Theophylline less effective.

Food Interactions

Take on an empty stomach, at least 1 hour before or 2 hours after meals; but occasional mild stomach upset can be minimized by taking the dose with some food (note that if you do this, a reduced amount of drug will be absorbed into your bloodstream).

The way Theophylline acts in your body may be influenced by your diet. Charcoal-broiled beef, for example, may cause the amount of Theophylline that is being eliminated in the urine to increase. Therefore you may experience a decreased effect of the drug. This is also true for people with a diet low in carbohydrates and high in protein or for people who smoke.

Caffeine (also a xanthine derivative) may add to the side effects of Theophylline. It is recommended that you avoid large amounts of caffeine-containing foods such as coffee, tea, cocoa, cola, or chocolate.

Usual Dose

These dosage guidelines may seem backwards because children require more drug per pound of body weight than adults. This is because children metabolize (chemically change) Theophylline faster than adults do.

Adult: 6 to 7.5 milligrams per pound of body weight per day, up to 900 or 1,100 milligrams.

Adolescent (age 12 to 16): 8.1 to 10.4 milligrams per pound of body weight per day.

Child (age 9 to 11): 9 to 11.5 milligrams per pound of body weight per day.

Child (under age 9): 10.9 to 13.8 milligrams per pound of body weight per day.

Timed-released products are usually taken 1 to 3 times per day at the same doses, depending on your response.

The best dose of Theophylline is tailored to your needs and the severity of your disease: it is the lowest dose that will produce maximum control of your symptoms.

Overdosage

The first symptoms are loss of appetite, nausea, vomiting, difficulty sleeping, and restlessness, followed by unusual behavior patterns, frequent vomiting, and extreme thirst, with delirium, convulsions, very high temperature, and collapse. These serious toxic symptoms are rarely experienced after overdose by mouth, which produces loss of appetite, nausea, vomiting, and stimulation. The overdosed patient should be taken to a hospital emergency room where proper treatment can be given. ALWAYS bring the medicine bottle.

If you forget to take a dose of Theophylline, take it as soon as you remember. If it is almost time for your next regularly scheduled dose, skip the one you forgot and continue with your regular schedule. Do not take a double dose.

Generic Name

Thioguanine

Type of Drug

Antimetabolite, antineoplastic.

Prescribed for

Treatment of leukemias.

General Information

Thioguanine is a member of the antimetabolite group of drugs used to treat neoplastic diseases. These drugs work by interfering with the metabolism of the cancerous cells. In doing so, they disrupt the cell reproduction cycle of the disease and slow its progress.

Cautions and Warnings

Frequent blood counts should be taken while on Thioguanine to avoid excessive lowering of white-cell counts. It should be used with extreme care by patients with kidney or liver disease.

Pregnancy/Breast-feeding

This and other antineoplastic drugs should be used with extreme caution during any stage of pregnancy and avoided during the first three months because of the possibility that they will affect early fetal development. These drugs act on dividing cells and may cause serious defects or death. Both men and women need be concerned about their offspring after using this medication. There are two case reports of birth deformities that occurred after the fathers had been treated with a combination anticancer treatment program.

There is little information on the passage of this or other antineoplastic drugs into breast milk. Nursing mothers should use an alternate feeding method.

Seniors

Older adults may take this medication without special restriction. Follow your doctor's directions and report any side
effects at once.

Possible Side Effects

Nausea, vomiting, loss of appetite, stomach irritation or pains.

Food Interactions

This medication should be taken on an empty stomach,
about 1 hour before or 2 hours after a meal.

Usual Dose

1 to 1.5 milligrams per pound of body weight per day given
in a single dose; adjusted to patient's response.
   Doses should be calculated to the nearest 20 milligrams.
The tablets are only available in a 40-milligram size.

Overdosage

Overdosage with Thioguanine leads to an excessive drop in
white-blood-cell counts. In case of overdosage, bring the
patient to a hospital emergency room immediately. ALWAYS
bring the medicine bottle.

Special Information

Due to the nature of the disease treated with this drug, it is
absolutely essential that you remain in close contact with
the doctor providing your treatment, to obtain maximum
benefit with minimum side effect.
   Contact your doctor if you experience swelling of the feet,
joint or stomach pain, sore throat, fever, chills, unusual bleeding, bruising, or yellow discoloration of skin.
   If you forget to take a dose of Thioguanine, do not take
the forgotten dose. Skip the dose and go back to your regular schedule, and call your doctor. Do not take a double
dose.

Generic Name

Thioridazine Hydrochloride

Brand Names

Mellaril
Mellaril-S
Millazine

(Also available in generic form)

Type of Drug

Phenothiazine antipsychotic.

Prescribed for

Psychotic disorders, moderate to severe depression with anxiety, control of agitation or aggressiveness of disturbed children, alcohol withdrawal symptoms, intractable pain, and
senility.

General Information

Thioridazine Hydrochloride and other members of the phenothiazine group act on a portion of the brain called the
hypothalamus. They affect parts of the hypothalamus that
control metabolism, body temperature, alertness, muscle tone,
hormone balance, and vomiting, and may be used to treat
problems related to any of these functions.

Cautions and Warnings

Thioridazine Hydrochloride should not be taken if you are
allergic to one of the drugs in the broad classification known
as phenothiazine drugs. Do not take Thioridazine Hydrochloride if you have any blood, liver, kidney, or heart disease,
very low blood pressure, or Parkinson's disease. This medication is a tranquilizer and can have a depressive effect, especially during the first few days of therapy. Care should be
taken when performing activities requiring a high degree of
concentration, such as driving.

This drug should be used with caution and under strict
supervision of your doctor if you have glaucoma, epilepsy,
ulcer, or difficulty passing urine.

Avoid insecticides; also avoid exposure to extreme heat, as this drug can affect your body's temperature control center.

Pregnancy/Breast-feeding

Infants born to women taking this medication have experienced drug side effects (liver jaundice, nervous system effects) immediately after birth. Check with your doctor about taking this medication if you are, or might become, pregnant.

This drug may pass into breast milk and affect a nursing infant. Consider alternate feeding methods if you must take this medicine.

Seniors

Older adults are more sensitive to the effects of this medication than younger adults, and usually require a lower dosage to achieve a desired effect. Also, older adults are more likely to develop drug side effects. Some experts feel that elderly people should be treated with ½ to ¼ the usual adult dose.

Possible Side Effects

Most common: drowsiness, especially during the first or second week of therapy. If the drowsiness becomes troublesome, contact your doctor.

Thioridazine Hydrochloride can cause jaundice (yellowing of the whites of the eyes or skin), usually in 2 to 4 weeks. The jaundice usually goes away when the drug is discontinued, but there have been cases when it did not. If you notice this effect or if you develop symptoms such as fever and generally not feeling well, contact your doctor immediately. Less frequent: changes in components of the blood including anemias, raised or lowered blood pressure, abnormal heart rates, heart attack, feeling faint or dizzy.

Phenothiazines can produce "extrapyramidal effects," such as spasms of the neck muscles, rolling back of the eyes, convulsions, difficulty in swallowing, and symptoms associated with Parkinson's disease. These effects look very serious but disappear after the drug has been withdrawn; however, symptoms of the face, tongue, and jaw may persist for as long as several years, especially in the elderly with a history of brain damage. If you experience extrapyramidal effects contact your doctor immediately.

Thioridazine Hydrochloride may cause an unusual increase in psychotic symptoms or may cause paranoid reactions, tiredness, lethargy, restlessness, hyperactivity, confusion at night, bizarre dreams, inability to sleep, depression and euphoria. Other reactions are itching, swelling, unusual sensitivity to bright lights, red skin, and rash. There have been cases of breast enlargement, false positive pregnancy tests, changes in menstrual flow in females, and impotence and changes in sex drive in males, as well as stuffy nose, headache, nausea, vomiting, loss of appetite, change in body temperature, loss of facial color, excessive salivation, excessive perspiration, constipation, diarrhea, changes in urine and stool habits, worsening of glaucoma, blurred vision, weakening of eyelid muscles, spasms in bronchial and other muscles, increased appetite, fatigue, excessive thirst, and changes in the coloration of skin, particularly in exposed areas.

Drug Interactions

Thioridazine Hydrochloride should be taken with caution in combination with barbiturates, sleeping pills, narcotics, other tranquilizers, or any other medication which may produce a depressive effect. Avoid alcohol.

Food Interactions

Caffeine-containing foods such as coffee, tea, cola drinks, or chocolate may counteract the effects of Thioridazine Hydrochloride.

Usual Dose

Adult: for treatment of psychosis, 50 to 100 milligrams per day at first, then 50 to 800 milligrams per day as required to control symptoms effectively without overly sedating the patient.

Child: 20 to 75 milligrams per day.

Overdosage

Symptoms are depression, extreme weakness, tiredness, desire to go to sleep, coma, lowered blood pressure, uncontrolled muscle spasms, agitation, restlessness, convulsions, fever, dry mouth, and abnormal heart rhythms. The patient

should be taken to a hospital emergency room immediately.
ALWAYS bring the medicine bottle.

Special Information

This medication may cause drowsiness. Use caution when
driving or operating complex equipment and avoid alcoholic
beverages while taking the medicine.

The drug may also cause unusual sensitivity to the sun
and turn your urine reddish-brown to pink.

If dizziness occurs, avoid sudden changes in posture and
avoid climbing stairs.

Use caution in hot weather. This medicine may make you
more prone to heat stroke.

Liquid Thioridazine concentrate can cause local reactions;
avoid skin contact. You should dilute the concentrate just
before you take it by adding it to about 4 ounces of juice or
water.

If you take Thioridazine once a day and forget your dose,
take it as soon as possible. If you don't remember until the
next day, skip the forgotten dose and continue with your
regular schedule.

If you take the medicine more than once a day and forget
a dose, take the forgotten dose as soon as possible. If it is
almost time for your next dose, skip the forgotten dose and
go on with your regular schedule.

Generic Name

Thiothixene

Brand Name

Navane

(Also available in generic form)

Type of Drug

Thioxanthene antipsychotic.

Prescribed for

Psychotic disorders.

General Information

Thiothixene is one of many nonphenothiazine agents used in the treatment of psychosis. The drugs in this group are usually about equally effective when given in therapeutically equivalent doses. The major differences are in type and severity of side effects. Some patients may respond well to one and not at all to another: this variability is not easily explained and is thought to relate to inborn biochemical differences.

Cautions and Warnings

Thiothixene should not be used by patients who are allergic to it. Patients with blood, liver, kidney or heart disease, very low blood pressure, or Parkinson's disease should avoid this drug.

Pregnancy/Breast-feeding

Infants born to women taking this medication have experienced drug side effects (liver jaundice, nervous system effects) immediately after birth. Check with your doctor about taking this medicine if you are, or might become, pregnant.

This drug may pass into breast milk and affect a nursing infant. Consider alternate feeding methods if you must take this medicine.

Seniors

Older adults are more sensitive to the effects of this medication than younger adults, and usually require a lower dosage to achieve a desired effect. Also, older adults are more likely to develop drug side effects. Some experts feel that elderly people should be treated with ½ to ¼ the usual adult dose.

Possible Side Effects

Most common: drowsiness, especially during the first or second week of therapy. If the drowsiness becomes troublesome, contact your doctor.

Thiothixene can cause jaundice (yellowing of the whites of the eyes or skin), usually in 2 to 4 weeks. The jaundice usually goes away when the drug is discontinued, but there have been cases when it did not. If you notice this effect or if you develop symptoms such as fever and generally do not feel well, contact your doctor immediately. Less frequent: changes in components of the blood including anemias, raised or lowered blood pressure, abnormal heartbeat, heart attack, feeling faint or dizzy

Thioxanthene drugs can produce "extrapyramidal effects," such as spasms of the neck muscles, severe stiffness of the back muscles, rolling back of the eyes, convulsions, difficulty in swallowing, and symptoms associated with Parkinson's disease. These effects look very serious but disappear after the drug has been withdrawn; however, symptoms of the face, tongue, and jaw may persist for several years, especially in the elderly with a long history of brain damage. If you experience extrapyramidal effects contact your doctor immediately.

Thiothixene may cause an unusual increase in psychotic symptoms or may cause paranoid reactions, tiredness, lethargy, restlessness, hyperactivity, confusion at night, bizarre dreams, inability to sleep, depression, or euphoria. Other reactions are itching, swelling, unusual sensitivity to bright lights, red skin, and rash. There have been cases of breast enlargement, false positive pregnancy tests, changes in menstrual flow in females, and impotence and changes in sex drive in males.

Thiothixene may also cause dry mouth, stuffy nose, headache, nausea, vomiting, loss of appetite, change in body temperature, loss of facial color, excessive salivation, excessive perspiration, constipation, diarrhea, changes in urine and stool habits, worsening of glaucoma, blurred vision, weakening of eyelid muscles, and spasms in bronchial and other muscles, as well as increased appetite, fatigue, excessive thirst, and changes in the coloration of skin, particularly in exposed areas.

Drug Interactions

Thiothixene should be taken with caution in combination with barbiturates, sleeping pills, narcotics, other tranquilizers, or any other medication which produces a depressive effect. Avoid alcohol.

Usual Dose

Adult and child (age 12 and over): 2 milligrams 3 times per day, to start. Dose is increased according to patient's need and may go to 60 milligrams per day.

Child (under age 12): not recommended.

Overdosage

Symptoms are depression, extreme weakness, tiredness, desire to go to sleep, coma, lowered blood pressure, uncontrolled muscle spasms, agitation, restlessness, convulsions, fever, dry mouth, and abnormal heart rhythms. The patient should be taken to a hospital emergency room immediately. ALWAYS bring the medicine bottle.

Special Information

This medication may cause drowsiness. Use caution when driving or operating complex equipment and avoid alcoholic beverages while taking the medicine.

The drug may also cause unusual sensitivity to the sun and can turn your urine reddish-brown to pink.

If dizziness occurs, avoid sudden changes in posture and avoid climbing stairs.

Use caution in hot weather. This medicine may make you more prone to heat stroke.

Liquid Thiothixene concentrate can cause local reactions; avoid skin contact. You should dilute the concentrate just before you take it by adding it to about 4 ounces of juice or water.

If you forget to take a dose of Thiothixene, take it as soon as you remember. If it is within 2 hours of your next regularly scheduled dose, skip the one you forgot and continue with your regular schedule. Do not take a double dose.

Generic Name

Thyroglobulin

Brand Name

Proloid

Type of Drug

Thyroid replacement.

Prescribed for

Replacement of thyroid hormone or low output of hormone from the thyroid gland.

General Information

Thyroglobulin is used to replace the normal output of the thyroid gland when it is unusually low. The drug is obtained from purified extract of frozen hog thyroid and is chemically standardized according to its iodine content. Thyroglobulin, or other forms of thyroid therapy, may be used for short periods in some people or for long periods in others. Some people take a thyroid replacement drug for their entire lives. It is important for your doctor to check periodically that you are receiving the correct dose. Occasionally a person's need for thyroid replacement changes, in which case the dose should also be changed: your doctor can do this only by checking certain blood tests.

Thyroglobulin is one of several thyroid replacement products available. The major difference between these products is in effectiveness in treating certain phases of thyroid disease.

Cautions and Warnings

If you have hyperthyroid disease or high output of thyroid hormone you should not use Thyroglobulin. Symptoms of hyperthyroid disease include headache, nervousness, sweating, rapid heartbeat, chest pains, and other signs of central nervous system stimulation. If you have heart disease or high blood pressure, thyroid replacement therapy should not be used unless it is clearly indicated and supervised by your doctor. If you develop chest pains or other signs of heart disease while you are taking thyroid medication, contact your doctor immediately.

Pregnancy/Breast-feeding

The amount of thyroid replacement hormone you take may have to be adjusted during pregnancy. Small amounts of the thyroid hormones will find their way into the bloodstream of a developing fetus. However, they have not been associated with birth defects or other problems when used in the dosages required to maintain normal thyroid function in the mother.

Small amounts of the thyroid hormones pass into breast milk but have not been associated with problems in nursing infants.

Seniors

Older adults are more sensitive to the effects of the thyroid hormones. The usual dosage of thyroid hormones should be reduced by about 25 percent after age 60.

Possible Side Effects

Most common: palpitations of the heart, rapid heartbeat, abnormal heart rhythms, weight loss, chest pains, menstrual irregularity, shaking hands, headache, diarrhea, nervousness, inability to sleep, heat discomfort, and sweating. These symptoms may be controlled by adjusting the dose of the medication. If you are suffering from one or more side effects, you must contact your physician immediately so that the proper dose adjustment can be made.

Drug Interactions

Avoid over-the-counter products containing stimulant drugs, such as many drugs used to treat coughs, colds, or allergies, which will affect your heart and may cause symptoms of overdosage.

Thyroid replacement therapy may increase the effect of anticoagulant (blood-thinning) drugs such as Warfarin or Bishydroxycoumarin. Be sure you report this to your physician as it will be necessary to reduce the dose of your anticoagulant drug by approximately ⅓ at the beginning of thyroid therapy (to avoid hemorrhage). Further adjustments may be made later, after your doctor reviews your blood tests.

Diabetics may have to increase their dose of Insulin or oral antidiabetic drugs. Changes in dose must be made by a physician.

Taking a thyroid hormone together with Colestipol or Cholestyramine can reduce the effect of the thyroid product by preventing its passage into your bloodstream. Separate doses of these 2 medicines by 4 to 5 hours.

The combination of Maprotiline and a thyroid hormone may increase the chances for abnormal heart rhythms. Your doctor may have to adjust the dose of your thyroid hormone.

Aspirin and other salicylate products may increase the effectiveness of your thyroid hormone by releasing more drug into the blood from body storage sites.

Estrogen drugs may increase your need for thyroid hormones.

Food Interactions

This drug is best taken on an empty stomach, but may be taken with food.

Usual Dose

Initial dose, 16 milligrams (¼ grain) per day, then increase at intervals of 1 to 2 weeks until response is satisfactory. Maintenance dose, 32 to 190 milligrams per day or even higher.

Overdosage

Symptoms are headache, irritability, nervousness, sweating, rapid heartbeat with unusual stomach rumbling and with or without cramps, chest pains, heart failure, and shock. The patient should be taken to a hospital emergency room immediately. ALWAYS bring the medicine bottle.

Special Information

Thyroid replacement therapy is usually lifelong treatment. Be sure you have a fresh supply of your medication, and always remember to take it according to your doctor's directions. Don't stop taking the medicine unless instructed to do so by your doctor.

Call your doctor if you develop nervousness, diarrhea, excessive sweating, chest pains, increased pulse rate, heart palpitations, intolerance to heat, or any other unusual occurrence.

Children beginning on thyroid treatment may lose some hair during the first few months, but this is only temporary and the hair generally grows back.

If you forget to take a dose of Thyroglobulin, take it as soon as you remember. If it is almost time for your next regularly scheduled dose, skip the one you forgot and continue with your regular schedule. Do not take a double dose. Call your doctor if you forget 2 or more doses in a row.

Generic Name

Thyroid Hormone

Brand Names

Armour Thyroid	Thyrar
S-P-T	Thyroid Strong

(Also available in generic form)

Type of Drug

Thyroid replacement.

Prescribed for

Replacement of thyroid hormone or low output of hormone from the thyroid gland.

General Information

Thyroid hormone is one of several thyroid replacement products available. The major difference between them is in effectiveness in treating certain phases of thyroid disease.

Other drugs, such as Methimazole (Tapazole) and Propylthiouracil (PTU), are given to people whose thyroid gland is overactive. Their effect on the thyroid gland is exactly the opposite of thyroid hormones. Check with your doctor if you are uncertain about why you have been given drugs which affect the thyroid gland.

If thyroid replacement therapy is required for a child, sleeping pulse rates or morning temperatures may have to be taken. These are good guides to treatment.

Cautions and Warnings

If you have hyperthyroid disease or high output of thyroid hormone you should not use thyroid hormone. Symptoms of hyperthyroid disease include headache, nervousness, sweating, rapid heartbeat, chest pains, and other signs of central nervous system stimulation. If you have heart disease or high blood pressure, thyroid therapy should not be used unless it is clearly indicated and supervised by your physician. If you develop chest pains or other signs of heart disease while you are taking thyroid medication, contact your doctor immediately.

Pregnancy/Breast-feeding

The amount of thyroid replacement hormone you take may have to be adjusted during pregnancy. Small amounts of the thyroid hormones will find their way into the bloodstream of a developing fetus. However, they have not been associated with birth defects or other problems when used in the dosages required to maintain normal thyroid function in the mother.

Small amounts of the thyroid hormones pass into breast milk, but have not been associated with problems in nursing infants.

Seniors

Older adults are more sensitive to the effects of the thyroid hormones. The usual dosage of thyroid hormones should be reduced by about 25 percent after age 60.

Possible Side Effects

Most common: palpitations of the heart, rapid heartbeat, abnormal heart rhythms, weight loss, chest pains, shaking hands, headache, diarrhea, nervousness, menstrual irregularity, inability to sleep, sweating, inability to stand heat. These symptoms may be controlled by adjusting the dose of the medication. If you are suffering from one or more side effects, you must contact your doctor immediately so that the proper dose adjustment can be made.

Drug Interactions

Avoid over-the-counter products containing stimulant drugs, such as many drugs used to treat coughs, colds, or allergies, which will affect your heart and may cause symptoms of overdosage.

Thyroid replacement therapy may increase the effect of anticoagulant (blood-thinning) drugs such as Warfarin or Bishydroxycoumarin. Be sure you report this to your physician as it will be necessary to reduce the dose of your anticoagulant drug by approximately one-third at the beginning of thyroid therapy (to avoid hemorrhage). Further adjustments may be made later, after your doctor reviews your blood tests.

Diabetics may have to increase their dose of Insulin or oral antidiabetic drugs. Changes in dose must be made by a doctor.

Taking a thyroid hormone together with Colestipol or Cholestyramine can reduce the effect of the thyroid product by preventing its passage into your bloodstream. Separate doses of these 2 medicines by 4-5 hours.

The combination of Maprotiline and a thyroid hormone may increase the chances for abnormal heart rhythms. Your doctor may have to adjust the dose of your thyroid hormone.

Aspirin and other salicylate products may increase the effectiveness of your thyroid hormone by releasing more drug into the blood from body storage sites.

Estrogen drugs may increase your need for thyroid hormones.

Food Interactions

This drug is best taken on an empty stomach, but may be taken with food.

Usual Dose

The dose is tailored to the individual.

Adult: Initial dose, 15 to 30 milligrams per day, depending on severity of disease; may be increased gradually to 195 milligrams per day.

Child: Initial dose, same as adult; but children may require greater maintenance doses because they are growing.

Take in 1 dose before breakfast.

Overdosage

Symptoms are headache, irritability, nervousness, sweating, rapid heartbeat with unusual stomach rumbling with or without cramps, chest pains, heart failure, and shock. The patient should be taken to a hospital emergency room immediately. ALWAYS bring the medicine bottle.

Special Information

Thyroid replacement therapy is usually lifelong treatment. Be sure you have a fresh supply of your medication, and always remember to take it according to your doctor's directions. Don't stop taking the medicine unless instructed to do so by your doctor.

Call your doctor if you develop nervousness, diarrhea,

excessive sweating, chest pains, increased pulse rate, heart palpitations, intolerance to heat, or any other unusual occurrence.

Children beginning on thyroid treatment may lose some hair during the first few months, but this is only temporary and the hair generally grows back.

If you forget to take a dose of thyroid hormone, take it as soon as you remember. If it is almost time for your next regularly scheduled dose, skip the one you forgot and continue with your regular schedule. Do not take a double dose. Call your doctor if you forget to take 2 or more doses in a row.

Generic Name

Timolol Maleate

Brand Names

Blocadren Tablets
Timoptic Eye Drops

Type of Drug

Beta-adrenergic blocking agent.

Prescribed for

Tablets: high blood pressure; reducing the possibility of a second heart attack, migraine headaches. Eye drops: glaucoma (increased fluid pressure inside the eye).

General Information

When applied directly to the eye, Timolol Maleate reduces fluid pressure inside the eye by reducing the production of eye fluids and increasing slightly the rate at which eye fluids leave the eye. Studies have shown Timolol Maleate to produce a greater reduction in eye fluid pressure than either Pilocarpine or Epinephrine.

Timolol Maleate Eye Drops should not be used by people who cannot take oral beta-blocking drugs, such as Propranolol. Studies have shown Timolol Maleate tablets to be very effective for treating heart pain called angina. It has also been used to treat high blood pressure.

The most famous Timolol Maleate study was published in April 1981 in the prestigious *New England Journal of Medicine.* This study showed that people who had a heart attack and took 20 milligrams of Timolol Maleate per day by mouth had fewer additional heart attacks and fewer additional heart problems, and survived longer. The death rate in non-Timolol Maleate patients was 1.6 times that in the Timolol Maleate group. Other beta-adrenergic blockers currently available, Propranolol, Metoprolol, Atenolol, Nadolol, and Pindolol, also have this effect on heart attack patients.

Cautions and Warnings

Timolol Maleate should be used with care if you have a history of asthma, upper respiratory disease, or seasonal allergy, which may become worsened by the effects of this drug. Do not use Timolol Maleate if you are allergic to it.

Pregnancy/Breast-feeding

This drug crosses into the blood circulation of a developing baby. It has not been found to cause birth defects. Pregnant women, or those who might become pregnant while taking this drug, should not take it without their doctor's approval. When the drug is considered essential by your doctor, the potential risk of taking the medicine must be carefully weighed against the benefit it might produce.

This drug passes into breast milk, but has caused no problems among breast-fed infants. You must consider the potential effect on the nursing infant if breast-feeding while taking this medicine.

Seniors

Senior citizens may be more or less sensitive to the effects of this medication. Your dosage of this drug must be adjusted to your individual needs by your doctor. Seniors may be more likely to suffer from cold hands and feet and reduced body temperature, chest pains, a general feeling of ill health, sudden difficulty breathing, sweating, or changes in heartbeat because of this medicine.

Possible Side Effects

Timolol Maleate may decrease the heart rate, aggravate or worsen a condition of congestive heart failure, and may produce lowered blood pressure, tingling in the extremities, light-headedness, mental depression, inability to sleep, weakness, and tiredness. It can also produce visual disturbances, hallucinations, disorientation, and loss of short-term memory. People taking Timolol Maleate may experience nausea, vomiting, upset stomach, abdominal cramps and diarrhea, or constipation. If you are allergic to Timolol Maleate, you may show typical reactions associated with drug allergies including sore throat, fever, difficulty breathing, and various effects on the blood system. Timolol Maleate may induce spasm of muscles in the bronchi, which will aggravate any existing asthma or respiratory disease.

Occasionally, people taking Timolol Maleate may experience emotional instability, become detached, or show unusual personality change. Timolol Maleate may cause adverse effects on the blood system.

Drug Interactions

Timolol Maleate will interact with any psychotropic drug, including the MAO inhibitors, that stimulates one of the segments of the central nervous system. Since this information is not often available to doctors, you should discuss this potential problem with your doctor if you are taking any psychotropic or psychiatric drug.

Timolol Maleate may cause increased effectiveness of Insulin or oral antidiabetic drugs. If you are diabetic, discuss the situation with your doctor. A reduction in dosage of your antidiabetic drug may be required.

Timolol Maleate may reduce the effectiveness of Digitalis on your heart. Any dose of Digitalis will have to be altered if you are taking Timolol Maleate. If you are taking Digitalis for a purpose other than heart failure, the effectiveness of the Digitalis may be increased by Timolol Maleate, and the dose of Digitalis reduced.

Timolol Maleate may interact with other drugs to cause lowering of blood pressure. This interaction often has positive effects in the treatment of patients with high blood pressure.

Do not self-medicate with over-the-counter drugs for colds, coughs, or allergy which may contain stimulants that will aggravate certain types of heart disease and high blood pressure, or other ingredients that may antagonize the effects of Timolol Maleate. Check with your doctor or pharmacist before taking any over-the-counter medication.

Food Interactions

Take Timolol Maleate tablets before meals for maximum effect. The eye drops may be used at any time.

Usual Dose

Eyedrops: 1 drop twice a day.
Tablets: 10 to 60 milligrams per day divided into 2 doses.

Overdosage

Symptoms are slowed heart rate, heart failure, lowered blood pressure, and spasms of the bronchial muscles which make it difficult to breathe. The patient should be taken to a hospital emergency room where proper therapy can be given. ALWAYS bring the medicine bottle with you.

Special Information

There have been reports of serious effects when Timolol Maleate is stopped abruptly. The dose should be lowered gradually over a period of two weeks.

If you are using Timolol Maleate Eye Drops, press your finger lightly just below the eye for one minute following the instillation of the eyedrops.

If you forget to take a dose of Timolol Maleate Tablets, take it as soon as possible. However, if it is within 4 hours of your next dose, skip the forgotten dose and go back to your regular schedule. Do not take a double dose.

If you forget to take a dose of Timolol Maleate Eye Drops, take it as soon as you remember. If it is almost time for your next regularly scheduled dose, skip the one you forgot and continue with your regular schedule. Do not take a double dose.

Generic Name

Tiopronin

Brand Name

Thiola

Type of Drug

Kidney stone preventive.

Prescribed for

Preventing kidney stones.

General Information

Tiopronin prevents the formation of kidney stones by forming a chemical complex with cysteine, an amino acid that is a key component of kidney stones. People with kidney stones normally have very high levels of cysteine in their urine. Each dose of Tiopronin causes a long-lasting reduction in the patient's urine cysteine level; the reduction lasts until he or she stops taking the drug.

Cautions and Warnings

Do not take Tiopronin if you are allergic to the active ingredient or to any component of the tablet.

People with a history of severe drops in white blood cell levels (agranulocytosis or thrombocytopenia) caused by drug treatment should avoid Tiopronin. Agranulocytosis or thrombocytopenia caused by Triopronin has the potential to bring about severe illness or death, although this has never actually happened to someone taking the drug.

Tiopronin can cause the loss of excessive amounts of protein through the urine.

Pregnancy/Breast-feeding

This drug can be expected to cause birth defects in laboratory animals and should be avoided by women who are, or might become, pregnant.

Tiopronin may pass into breast milk and should be avoided by nursing mothers. Mothers who must use Tiopronin should use an alternative feeding method.

Seniors

Seniors may be more sensitive to the side effects of this drug and should report any changes to the doctor at once.

Possible Side Effects

Drug fever may develop, especially during the first month of Tiopronin treatment. The drug may be restarted once the fever has gone down and gradually increased to the usual dose.

Other side effects include loss of taste sensation, vitamin B_6 (pyridoxine) deficiency, skin rash, and itching (the itching can be controlled with antihistamines and clears up when the drug is stopped). Because of the drug's effect on the skin's connective tissue, skin becomes thin and wrinkled after long-term Tiopronin treatment.

Fever, joint pain and swelling, and swollen lymph glands may be signs of serious drug side effects.

Drug Interactions

None yet known. Do not take Penicillamine, another drug that reduces urine levels of cysteine, and Tiopronin at the same time.

Food Interactions

You may take this drug with food if it upsets your stomach. Initial treatment to prevent kidney stones is typically based around diet and fluid intake. Be sure to follow your doctor's advice about diet restriction.

Usual Dose

800 to 1000 milligrams per day. Some people may require less.

Overdosage

Tiopronin overdose results in exaggerated side effects. Victims of Tiopronin overdose should be taken to a hospital emergency room for treatment. ALWAYS remember to bring the medicine bottle with you.

Special Information

Stop taking Tiopronin and call your doctor at once if you develop fever, joint pain, swelling, swollen lymph glands, changes in urinary function, unusual skin reactions, or muscle weakness, or if you begin to vomit blood or have difficulty breathing. These can be signs of severe side effects.

Generic Name

Tocainide Hydrochloride

Brand Name

Tonocard

Type of Drug

Antiarrhythmic.

Prescribed for

Abnormal heart rhythms.

General Information

First available in late 1984, Tocainide Hydrochloride is the first chemical derivative of Lidocaine, one of the most widely used injectable antiarrhythmic drugs, that can be taken orally. It affects the speed with which nerve impulses are carried through the heart's ventricle. Tocainide Hydrochloride affects different areas of your heart than other widely used oral antiarrhythmic drugs like Quinidine Sulfate, Procainamide Hydrochloride, and Disopyramide. Unlike those drugs, it does not interact negatively with Digoxin. Tocainide Hydrochloride is usually prescribed for people who have been given Lidocaine in the hospital and who require some form of oral follow-up treatment.

Cautions and Warnings

This drug should not be used by people who are allergic to Tocainide Hydrochloride, Lidocaine, or to local anesthetics. Some people using Tocainide Hydrochloride may develop respiratory difficulties, including fluid buildup in the lungs, pneumonia, and irritation of the lungs. Report any cough or difficulty breathing to your doctor immediately. Tocainide Hydrochloride should not be used by people with heart failure, since the drug can actually worsen that condition.

Pregnancy/Breast-feeding

Animal studies employing doses 1 to 4 times larger than the human equivalent reveal no adverse effect on the developing fetus, but they did result in an unusually high rate of stillbirth and spontaneous abortion. This drug should be avoided by pregnant women or women who may become pregnant while using it. In those situations where its use is essential, the potential risks must be carefully weighed against any benefits.

Nursing mothers must be aware of any possible drug effect on their infants while taking this medicine, since it is not known if the active ingredients in it pass into breast milk. Consider an alternative infant feeding method if you must take Tocainide Hydrochloride to control an abnormal heart rhythm.

Seniors

Older adults are more sensitive to the side effects of this drug, especially dizziness and low blood pressure. Follow your doctor's directions and report any side effects at once.

Possible Side Effects

Nausea, vomiting, tingling in the hands or feet, lightheadedness, dizziness, fainting, giddiness, tremors, confusion, disorientation, hallucinations, restlessness, blurred or double vision, visual disturbances, poor muscle coordination, anxiety, low blood pressure, slowing of the heart rate, heart palpitations, chest pains, cold sweats, headache, drowsiness, and lethargy.

Less common side effects: ringing or buzzing in the ears, rolling the eyes, loss of appetite, diarrhea, rash, unusual feelings of heat or cold, joint inflammation and pain, and muscle aches. Other uncommon reactions may include seizures, depression, psychosis, mental changes, alterations of taste (including a metallic taste) and/or smell, agitation, difficulty concentrating, memory loss, slurred speech, difficulty sleeping, nightmares, unusual thirst, weakness, upset stomach or abdominal pains and discomfort, difficulty swallowing, breathing difficulty (see "Cautions and Warnings"), changes in white-blood-cell counts, anemia, urinary difficulty, hair loss, cold hands or feet, leg pains after minor exercise, dry mouth, earache, fever, hiccups, aching, a feeling of ill health, muscle twitches or spasms, neck or shoulder pains, facial flushing or pallor, and yawning.

Drug Interactions

The combination of Tocainide Hydrochloride and Metoprolol, prescribed for high blood pressure, can cause too rapid a drop in blood pressure and slowing of the heart.

Unlike other oral antiarrhythmic drugs, Tocainide Hydrochloride does not interact with Digoxin. However, it is likely that the wide usage this drug will receive over the next several years will disclose other, previously unknown, interactions.

Food Interactions

You may take Tocainide Hydrochloride with food or meals if it causes upset stomach, nausea, or vomiting when taken alone.

Usual Dose

Adult: 1,200 to 1,800 milligrams per day, in divided doses.
Senior and patient with kidney or liver disease: less than 1,200 milligrams per day.

Overdosage

There are no reports of overdosage. However, the symptoms can be expected to be exaggerated versions of Tocainide Hydrochloride side effects. Patients taking an overdose of this drug must be made to vomit with Syrup of Ipecac (available at any pharmacy) to remove any remaining drug from the stomach. Call your doctor or a poison control center before doing this. If you must go to a hospital emergency room, ALWAYS bring the medicine bottle.

Special Information

Be sure to report any side effects to your doctor. Most of them are minor or will respond to minor dosage adjustments. Especially important symptoms are difficulty breathing, coughing, unusual or easy bruising, and frequent infections.

Do not take more or less of this drug than prescribed.

If you forget to take a dose of Tocainide Hydrochloride and you remember within about 4 hours of your regular time, take it as soon as you remember. If you do not remember until later, skip the forgotten dose and go back to your regular schedule. Do not take a double dose.

Generic Name

Tolazamide

Brand Names

Ronase
Tolamide
Tolinase

(Also available in generic form)

Type of Drug

Oral antidiabetic.

Prescribed for

Diabetes mellitus (sugar in the urine).

General Information

Tolazamide is one of several oral antidiabetic drugs that work by stimulating the production and release of Insulin from the pancreas. The primary difference between the oral antidiabetic drugs lies in their duration of action. Because these drugs do not lower blood sugar directly, they require some working pancreas cells.

Cautions and Warnings

Mild stress such as infection, minor surgery, or emotional upset reduces the effectiveness of Tolazamide. Remember that while you are taking this drug you should be under your doctor's continuous care.

Tolazamide and similar drugs are not oral Insulin, nor are they a substitute for Insulin. They do not lower blood sugar by themselves.

The treatment of diabetes is your responsibility. You should follow all instructions about diet, body weight, exercise, personal hygiene, and all measures to avoid infection. If you are not feeling well, or if you have symptoms such as itching, rash, yellowing of the skin or eyes, abnormally light-colored stools, a low-grade fever, sore throat, or diarrhea, contact your doctor immediately.

This drug should not be used if you have serious liver, kidney, or endocrine disease.

Pregnancy/Breast-feeding

This drug may cause birth defects or interfere with your baby's development. Check with your doctor before taking it if you are, or might be, pregnant. Nursing mothers should use an alternative feeding method; your baby's sugar level may be adversely affected.

Seniors

Older adults with reduced kidney function may be more sensitive to drug side effects because of a reduced ability to eliminate it from the body. Low blood sugar, the major sign of drug overdose, may be more difficult to identify in older adults than in a younger adult. Also, low blood sugar is more likely to be a cause of nervous system side effects in older adults.

Older adults taking antidiabetes drugs must keep in close touch with their doctor and closely follow his/her directions.

Possible Side Effects

Common: loss of appetite, nausea, vomiting, stomach upset. At times you may experience weakness or tingling in the hands and feet. These effects can be eliminated by reducing the daily dose of Tolazamide or, if necessary, by switching to a different oral antidiabetic drug. This decision must be made by your doctor.

Less commonly, Tolazamide may produce abnormally low levels of blood sugar when too much is taken for your immediate requirements. (Other factors which may cause lowering of blood sugar are liver or kidney disease, malnutrition, age, drinking alcohol, and diseases of the glands.)

Tolazamide may cause a yellowing of the whites of the eyes or skin, itching, rash, or changes in the results of laboratory tests made by your doctor. Usually these reactions will disappear in time. If they persist, you should contact your doctor.

Drug Interactions

Thiazide diuretics may call for a higher dose of Tolazamide, while Insulin, sulfa drugs, Oxyphenbutazone, Phenylbutazone, Aspirin and other salicylates, Probenecid, Dicoumarol, Bishydroxycoumarin, Warfarin, Phenyramidol, and MAO inhibitor drugs prolong and enhance the action of Tolazamide, possibly requiring dose reduction.

Interaction with alcoholic beverages will cause flushing of the face and body, throbbing pain in the head and neck, difficult breathing, nausea, vomiting, sweating, thirst, chest pains, palpitations, lowered blood pressure, weakness, dizziness, blurred vision, and confusion. If you experience these reactions, contact your doctor immediately.

Because of the stimulant ingredients in many over-the-counter drug products for the relief of coughs, colds, and allergies, avoid them unless your doctor advises otherwise.

Food Interactions

This medicine is best taken on an empty stomach, but may be taken with food. Dietary management is an important part of the treatment of diabetes. Be sure to follow your doctor's directions about the foods you should avoid.

Usual Dose

Moderate diabetes: 100 to 250 milligrams daily.
Severe diabetes: 500 to 1,000 milligrams daily.

Overdosage

A mild overdose of Tolazamide lowers the blood sugar, which can be treated by consuming sugar in such forms as candy, orange juice, or glucose tablets. A patient with a more serious overdose should be taken to a hospital emergency room immediately. ALWAYS bring the medicine bottle.

Special Information

Diet remains of primary importance in the treatment of your diabetes. Follow the diet plan your doctor has prescribed for you.

If you forget to take a dose of Tolazamide, take it as soon as you remember. If it is almost time for your next regularly scheduled dose, skip the one you forgot and continue with your regular schedule. Do not take a double dose.

Generic Name

Tolbutamide

Brand Names

Oramide
Orinase

(Also available in generic form)

Type of Drug

Oral antidiabetic.

Prescribed for

Diabetes mellitus (sugar in the urine).

General Information

Tolbutamide is one of several oral antidiabetic drugs that work by stimulating the production and release of Insulin from the pancreas. The primary difference between the oral antidiabetic drugs lies in their duration of action. Because they do not lower blood sugar directly, they require some function of pancreas cells.

Cautions and Warnings

Mild stress such as infection, minor surgery, or emotional upset reduces the effectiveness of Tolbutamide. Remember that while taking this drug you should be under your doctor's continuous care.

Tolbutamide is an aid to, not a substitute for, a diet. Diet remains of primary importance in the treatment of your diabetes. Follow the diet plan your doctor has prescribed for you.

Tolbutamide and similar drugs are not oral Insulin, nor are

they a substitute for Insulin. They do not lower blood sugar by themselves.

The treatment of diabetes is your responsibility. You should follow all instructions about diet, body weight, exercise, personal hygiene, and all measures to avoid infection. If you are not feeling well, or if you have symptoms such as itching, rash, yellowing of the skin or eyes, abnormally light-colored stools, a low-grade fever, sore throat, or diarrhea, contact your doctor immediately.

This drug should be used with caution and under strict supervision of your doctor if you have glaucoma, epilepsy, ulcers, or difficulty passing urine. Avoid insecticides and extreme exposure to heat.

Pregnancy/Breast-feeding

This drug may cause birth defects or interfere with your baby's development. Check with your doctor before taking it if you are, or might be, pregnant. Nursing mothers should use an alternative feeding method; your baby's sugar level may be adversely affected.

Seniors

Older adults with reduced kidney function may be more sensitive to drug side effects because of a reduced ability to eliminate it from the body. Low blood sugar, the major sign of drug overdose, may be more difficult to identify in older adults than in a younger adult. Also, low blood sugar is more likely to be a cause of nervous system side effects in older adults.

Older adults taking antidiabetes drugs must keep in close touch with their doctor and closely follow his/her directions.

Possible Side Effects

Common: loss of appetite, nausea, vomiting, stomach upset. At times you may experience weakness or tingling in the hands and feet. These effects can be eliminated by reducing the daily dose of Tolbutamide or, if necessary, by switching to a different oral antidiabetic drug. This decision must be made by your doctor.

Less commonly, Tolbutamide may produce abnormally low levels of blood sugar when too much is taken for your immediate requirements. (Other factors which may cause lowering of blood sugar are liver or kidney disease, malnutrition, age, drinking alcohol, and diseases of the glands.)

Tolbutamide may cause a yellowing of the whites of the eyes or skin, itching, rash, or changes in the results of laboratory tests made by your doctor. Usually these reactions will disappear in time. If they persist you should contact your doctor.

Drug Interactions

Thiazide diuretics may call for a higher dose of Tolbutamide, while Insulin, sulfa drugs, Oxyphenbutazone, Phenylbutazone, Aspirin and other salicylates, Probenecid, Dicoumarol, Bis-hydroxycoumarin, Warfarin, Phenyramidol, and MAO inhibitor drugs prolong and enhance the action of Tolbutamide, possibly requiring dose reduction.

Interaction with alcoholic beverages will cause flushing of the face and body, throbbing pain in the head and neck, difficult breathing, nausea, vomiting, sweating, thirst, chest pains, palpitations, lowered blood pressure, weakness, dizziness, blurred vision, and confusion. If you experience these reactions contact your doctor immediately.

Because of the stimulant ingredients in many over-the-counter drug products for the relief of coughs, colds, and allergies, avoid them unless your doctor advises otherwise.

Food Interactions

This medicine is best taken on an empty stomach, but may be taken with food. Dietary management is an important part of the treatment of diabetes. Be sure to follow your doctor's directions about the foods you should avoid.

Usual Dose

Begin with 1 to 2 grams per day; then increase or decrease according to patient's response. Maintenance dose, 250 milligrams to 2 (or, rarely, 3) grams per day.

Overdosage

A mild overdose of Tolbutamide lowers the blood sugar, which can be treated by consuming sugar in such forms as candy, orange juice, or glucose tablets. A patient with a more serious overdose should be taken to a hospital emergency room immediately. ALWAYS bring the medicine bottle.

Special Information

If you forget to take a dose of Tolbutamide, take it as soon as you remember. If it is almost time for your next regularly scheduled dose, skip the one you forgot and continue with your regular schedule. Do not take a double dose.

Generic Name

Tolmetin Sodium

Brand Names

Tolectin
Tolectin DS

Type of Drug

Nonsteroidal anti-inflammatory.

Prescribed for

Relief of pain and inflammation of joints and muscles; arthritis.

General Information

Tolmetin Sodium is one of several new drugs used to treat various types of arthritis. These drugs reduce inflammation and share side effects, the most common of which is possible formation of ulcers and upset stomach. The drugs are roughly comparable to Aspirin in controlling the symptoms of arthritis, and are used by some people who cannot tolerate Aspirin.

Cautions and Warnings

Do not take Tolmetin Sodium if you are allergic or sensitive to this drug, Aspirin, or other nonsteroidal anti-inflammatory drugs (NSAIDs). Tolmetin Sodium may cause stomach ulcers.

Pregnancy/Breast-feeding

This drug crosses into the blood circulation of a developing baby. If taken regularly during the last few months of pregnancy, Tolmetin Sodium may cause unwanted effects on the baby's heart or blood flow. Also, labor or the pregnancy itself may be prolonged. Pregnant women, or those who might become pregnant while taking this drug, should not take it without their doctor's approval. When the drug is considered essential by your doctor, the potential risk of taking the medicine must be carefully weighed against the benefit it might produce.

This drug passes into breast milk, but has caused no problems among breast-fed infants. You must consider the potential effect on the nursing infant if breast-feeding while taking this medicine.

Seniors

Older adults are more sensitive to the stomach, kidney, and liver effects of this drug. Some doctors believe that persons age 70 or older should take ½ the usual dose of Tolmetin. Follow your doctor's directions and report any side effects at once.

Possible Side Effects

Most frequent: stomach upset, dizziness, headache, drowsiness, ringing in the ears. Others: heartburn, nausea, vomiting, bloating, gas in the stomach, stomach pain, diarrhea, constipation, dark stool, nervousness, insomnia, depression, confusion, tremor, lack of appetite, fatigue, itching, rash, double vision, abnormal heart rhythm, anemia or other changes in the composition of the blood, changes in liver function, loss of hair, tingling in the hands and feet, fever, breast enlargement, lowered blood sugar, occasional effects on the kidneys. If symptoms appear, stop taking the medicine and see your doctor immediately.

Drug Interactions

Tolmetin Sodium increases the action of Phenytoin, sulfa drugs, drugs used to control diabetes, and drugs used to thin the blood. If you are taking one of these drugs, be sure you discuss it with your doctor, who will probably change the dose of the drug whose action is increased.

Avoid taking Aspirin while taking Tolmetin Sodium.

Food Interactions

If upset stomach occurs, take with food or milk.

Usual Dose

Adult: 400 milligrams 3 times per day, to start. Dosage must then be adjusted to individual need. Do not take more than 2,000 milligrams per day.

Child (age 2 and over): 9 milligrams per pound of body weight given in divided doses 3 to 4 times per day, to start. Adjust dose to individual need. Do not give more than 13.5 milligrams per pound of body weight to a child.

Child (under age 2): not recommended.

Overdosage

Symptoms may include drowsiness, dizziness, confusion, disorientation, lethargy, tingling in the hands or feet, numbness, nausea, vomiting, upset stomach, stomach pains, headache, ringing or buzzing in the ears, sweating, and blurred vision. Take the victim to a hospital emergency room at once for treatment. ALWAYS bring the medicine bottle with you.

Special Information

Avoid Aspirin and alcoholic beverages while taking this medication. You may become dizzy or drowsy while taking this medicine. Be careful while driving or operating complex equipment. Call your doctor if you develop a skin rash, itching, swelling, visual disturbances, black stools, or a persistent headache while taking this medication.

If you forget to take a dose of Tolmetin Sodium, take it as soon as you remember. If it is almost time for your next regularly scheduled dose, skip the one you forgot and continue with your regular schedule. Do not take a double dose.

Generic Name

Trazodone

Brand Name

Desyrel

(Also available in generic form)

Type of Drug

Antidepressant.

Prescribed for

Depression with or without anxiety. It may also be used for treating cocaine withdrawal and aggressive behaviors.

General Information

Trazodone is as effective in treating the symptoms of depression as are other antidepressant tablets. However, it is chemically different from the other antidepressants and may be less likely to cause side effects.

For many people, symptoms will be relieved as early as 2 weeks after starting the medicine, but 4 weeks or more may be required to achieve maximum benefit.

Cautions and Warnings

Do not use Trazodone if you are allergic to it. It is not recommended during the initial stages of recovery from a heart attack. People with a previous history of heart disease should not use Trazodone because it may cause abnormal heart rhythms.

Pregnancy/Breast-feeding

This drug should not be taken by women who may become pregnant while using it or by pregnant or nursing mothers, since this drug may pass into breast milk. In situations where it is deemed essential, the potential risk of the drug must be carefully weighed against any benefit it might produce.

Seniors

Older adults are likely to be more sensitive to the effects and

side effects of usual doses of Trazodone than younger adults.
Medical experts recommend that older adults be started out
with lower doses and increased more carefully and slowly
by their doctors.

Possible Side Effects

Most common: upset stomach, constipation, abdominal pains,
a bad taste in your mouth, nausea, vomiting, diarrhea, palpitations, rapid heartbeat, rashes, swelling of the extremities,
elevated or depressed blood pressure, difficulty breathing,
dizziness, anger, hostility, nightmares and/or vivid dreams,
confusion, disorientation, loss of memory or concentration,
drowsiness, fatigue, light-headedness, difficulty sleeping, nervousness, excitement, headache, loss of coordination, tingling in the hands or feet, tremor of the hands or arms,
ringing or buzzing in the ears, blurred vision, red, tired, and
itchy eyes, stuffy nose or sinuses, loss of sex drive, muscle
aches and pains, loss of appetite, changes in body weight
(up or down), sweating, clamminess, a feeling of ill health.

   Less frequent reactions to Trazodone include drug allergy,
chest pain, heart attack, delusions, hallucinations, agitation,
difficulty speaking, restlessness, numbness, weakness, seizures, increased sex drive, a sustained and painful male
erection, reverse ejaculation, impotence, missed or early menstrual periods, stomach gas, increased salivation, anemia,
reduced levels of some white blood cells, muscle twitches,
blood in the urine, reduced urine flow, increased urinary
frequency, increased appetite. Trazodone may cause elevations in levels of body enzymes used to measure liver function.

   In rare instances, males taking Trazodone may notice prolonged or inappropriate erections. They should immediately
discontinue taking Trazodone and contact their physician.

Drug Interactions

Trazodone, when taken together with Digoxin or Phenytoin,
may increase the amount of those drugs in your blood,
leading to a greater possibility of drug side effects.

   Trazodone may make you more sensitive to drugs that
work by depressing the nervous system, including sedatives,
tranquilizers, and alcohol.

   This medicine may cause a slight reduction in blood pressure. If you are taking medicine for high blood pressure and

begin to take Trazodone, you may find that a minor reduction in the dosage of your blood-pressure medicine is required.
On the other hand, the action of Clonidine, a high-blood-
pressure medicine, can be inhibited by Trazodone. These
interactions must be evaluated by your doctor. Do not change
any blood-pressure medicines on your own.

Little is known about the potential interaction between
Trazodone and the MAO inhibitor drugs. With most antidepressants, it is suggested that one drug be discontinued for
2 weeks before the other is begun. If these drugs are used
together, they should be used cautiously.

Food Interactions

Take each dose of Trazodone with a meal or snack to increase the amount of drug absorbed into your bloodstream
and to minimize the possibility of upset stomach, dizziness,
or light-headedness.

Usual Dose

150 milligrams per day with food, to start. This dose may be
increased by 50 milligrams per day every 3 to 4 days, to a
maximum of 400 milligrams per day. Severely depressed
people may be given as much as 600 milligrams per day.

Overdosage

Drowsiness and vomiting are the most frequent signs of
Trazodone overdose. The other signs are simply more severe side-effects symptoms, especially those affecting the
heart and mood. Fever may develop at first, but body temperature will drop below normal as time passes. ALL victims
of antidepressant overdosage, especially children, must be
taken to a hospital for treatment as quickly as possible.
ALWAYS bring the medicine bottle with you.

Special Information

Use care while driving or doing anything else requiring concentration or alertness, and avoid alcohol or any other depressant while taking Trazodone.

Call your doctor if any side effects develop, especially
blood in the urine, dizziness, or light-headedness. Trazodone
may cause dry mouth, irregular heartbeat, nausea, vomiting,

or difficulty breathing. Call your doctor if these symptoms become severe.

If you forget to take a dose of Trazodone, take it as soon as possible. However, if it is within 4 hours of your next dose, skip the forgotten dose and go back to your regular schedule. Do not take a double dose.

Generic Name

Tretinoin Cream/Gel/Liquid

Other Names

Retinoic Acid
Vitamin A Acid

Brand Name

Retin-A

Type of Drug

Antiacne.

Prescribed for

The early stages of acne. This drug is usually not effective in treating severe acne. It may also be prescribed for wrinkling, psoriasis, cancer, or other skin conditions.

General Information

This drug works by decreasing the cohesiveness of skin cells, causing the skin to peel, which is helpful in acne treatment. Because it is an irritant, any other skin irritant, such as extreme weather or wind, cosmetics, and some soaps, can cause severe irritation. Excessive application of Tretinoin will cause more peeling and irritation but will not give better results.

Medical research published in the *Journal of the American Medical Association* during January 1988 revealed that regular application of Tretinoin cream to aging skin prevented wrinkling and suggested that it could even reverse the wrinkling process for some people! As you might expect, this treatment, promoted in the media as "the closest thing we have to the fountain of youth," became instantly popular among older people who want younger skin and younger people who are concerned about future wrinkling and aging. No one knows how Tretinoin produces this effect. Other studies will have to be done to prove that the drug really can produce this effect and to establish the best drug concentration to use.

Cautions and Warnings

Do not use this drug if you are allergic to it or any of its components. This drug may increase the skin-cancer-causing effects of ultraviolet light. Therefore, people using this drug must avoid exposure to the sun. If you can't avoid exposure to the sun, use sunscreen products and protective covering. Do not apply to areas around the eyes, corner of the mouth, or sides of the nose.

Pregnancy/Breast-feeding

Tretinoin has been shown to cause abnormal skull formation in animal fetuses. Birth defects in animals have also been caused by Tretinoin, but studies with humans have not been conducted. Pregnant women should avoid this drug. Tretinoin has not caused problems in breast-fed infants.

Seniors

Older adults may use this product with no restriction.

Possible Side Effects

Redness, swelling, blistering, or formation of crusts on the skin near the areas to which the drug has been applied. Overcoloration of the skin, greater sensitivity to the sun.

All side effects disappear after the drug has been stopped.

Drug Interactions

Other skin irritants will cause excessive sensitivity, irritation, and side effects. Among the substances that cause this interaction are medications that contain sulfur (topical), resorcinol, benzoyl peroxide, or salicylic acid; abrasive soaps or skin cleansers; cosmetics or other creams, ointments, etc., with a severe drying effect; and products with a high alcohol, astringent, spice, or lime content.

Usual Dose

Apply a small amount to the affected area when you go to bed, and after thoroughly cleansing the area.

Special Information

You may experience an increase in acne lesions during the first couple of weeks of treatment, because the drug is acting on deeper lesions which you had not seen before. This is beneficial and is not a reason to stop using the drug.

Results should be seen in 2 to 6 weeks.

Keep this drug away from your eyes, nose, mouth, and mucous membranes.

Avoid exposure to sunlight or sunlamp.

You may feel warmth and slight stinging when you apply Tretinoin. If you develop an excessive skin reaction or are uncomfortable, stop using this product for a short time.

If you forget a dose of Tretinoin, do not take the forgotten dose. Skip the dose and go back to your regular schedule. Do not take a double dose.

Generic Name

Triamcinolone Acetonide Ointment/Cream/Lotion/Aerosol

Brand Names

Aristocort	Kenalog-H
Aristocort A	Triacet
Flutex	Triderm
Kenac	Trymex
Kenalog	

(Also available in generic form)

Type of Drug

Topical corticosteroid.

Prescribed for

Relief of inflammation in a local area, itching, or other dermatological (skin) problems.

General Information

Triamcinolone Acetonide is used to relieve the symptom of any itching, rash, or inflammation of the skin. It does not treat the underlying cause of the skin problem, only the symptoms. It exerts this effect by interfering with natural body mechanisms that produce the rash, itching, etc., in the first place. If you use this drug without finding the cause of the problem, the condition may return after you stop using the drug. Triamcinolone Acetonide should not be used without your doctor's consent because it could cover an important reaction, one that may be valuable to him in treating you.

Cautions and Warnings

Triamcinolone Acetonide should not be used if you have viral diseases of the skin (herpes), fungal infections of the skin (athlete's foot), or tuberculosis of the skin, nor should it be used in the ear if the eardrum has been perforated. People with a history of allergies to any of the components of the ointment, cream, lotion, or aerosol should not use this drug.

Using Triamcinolone Acetonide for prolonged periods around the eyes can cause cataracts or glaucoma.

Pregnancy/Breast-feeding

Studies have shown that corticosteroids applied to the skin in large amounts, or over long periods of time, can be the cause of birth defects. Pregnant women or those who might become pregnant while using this medicine should not do so unless they are under a doctor's care.

Corticosteroid drugs taken by mouth pass into breast milk, and large drug doses may interfere with the growth of a nursing infant. Steroids applied to the skin are not likely to cause problems, but you should not use the medicine unless under a doctor's care.

Seniors

Older adults are more likely to develop high blood pressure while taking this medicine (by mouth). Also, older women have a greater chance of being susceptible to bone degeneration (osteoporosis) associated with large doses of this class of medicines.

Possible Side Effects

After topically applying this drug, some people may experience burning sensations, itching, irritation, dryness, and secondary infection.

Special Information

Clean the skin before applying Triamcinolone Acetonide, to prevent secondary infection. Apply in a very thin film (effectiveness is based on contact area and not on the thickness of the layer applied).

If you forget to take a dose of Triamcinolone Acetonide, take it as soon as you remember. If it is almost time for your next regularly scheduled dose, skip the one you forgot and continue with your regular schedule. Do not take a double dose.

Generic Name

Triamcinolone Inhaler

Brand Name

Azmacort Inhaler

Type of Drug

Adrenal corticosteroid.

Prescribed for

Chronic asthma or other respiratory condition.

General Information

The Triamcinolone used in this product is the same drug applied to the skin as an ointment or other topical preparation. It can also be taken by mouth as a tablet. The Triamcinolone inhaler relieves the symptoms of asthma for people who require regular steroid treatment by mouth. Using the aerosol generally allows a reduction in the oral dose or elimination of oral steroids all together. It works by reducing the inflammation of the mucosal lining within the bronchi, making it easier to breathe. This product should be used only as part of a preventive therapy program. It will not treat an asthma attack.

Cautions and Warnings

This drug should not be used if your asthma can be controlled by other nonsteroid medicines. It is meant only for people taking Prednisone or another steroid by mouth and other asthma medicines but who are still not under control. Do not use a Triamcinolone inhaler if you are allergic to it or to any other steroid drug. During stressful periods, you may have to go back to taking steroids by mouth if your asthma is not controlled.

Pregnancy/Breast-feeding

Large amounts of Triamcinolone used during pregnancy or breast-feeding may slow the growth of a developing baby. Steroids can cause birth defects or interfere with the developing fetus. Check with your doctor if you are, or might be, pregnant.

Triamcinolone may pass into breast milk and cause unwanted effects in a nursing infant.

Seniors

Older adults may use this medicine without special precaution. Be sure your doctor knows if you have any bone disease, colitis, diabetes, bowel disease, glaucoma, fungus infection, heart disease, herpes infection, high blood pressure, high blood cholesterol, kidney disease, or underactive thyroid.

Possible Side Effects

Most common: dry mouth, hoarseness. Less common: fungus infections of the mouth or throat.

Rare: Deaths due to failure of the adrenal gland have occurred during the process of switching from an oral product. Aerosol Triamcinolone is given in a much smaller dose than the oral tablets, reducing the chance for side effects. However, if the drug is used in very large amounts for a long period of time, you may develop a variety of other side effects. Information on those can be found in the entry for Prednisone.

Food Interactions

Do not use this product if you have any food in your mouth.

Usual Dose

Adult: 2 inhalations (0.2 milligrams) 3 or 4 times a day. Do not take more than 16 inhalations a day. Allow at least 1 minute between inhalations. People with more severe asthma may start out with a higher dose.

Child (age 6 to 12): 1 or 2 inhalations 3 or 4 times a day. Do not exceed 12 inhalations a day.

Child (under age 6): not recommended.

Special Information

Follow the instructions that come with your inhaler.

If you use a bronchodilator inhaler (Isoproterenol, Metaproterenol, etc.) at the same time as your Triamcinolone inhaler, use the bronchodilator first to open your bronchial tree and increase the amount of Triamcinolone that gets into your lungs.

If you forget to take a dose of Triamcinolone Inhaler, take it as soon as you remember. If it is almost time for your next regularly scheduled dose, skip the one you forgot and continue with your regular schedule. Do not take a double dose.

Brand Name

Triavil

Ingredients

Amitriptyline Hydrochloride
Perphenazine

Other Brand Name

Etrafon

(Also available in generic form)

Type of Drug

Antidepressant tranquilizer combination.

Prescribed for

Relief of symptoms of anxiety or agitation and/or depression associated with chronic physical or psychiatric disease.

General Information

Triavil and other psychotherapeutic agents are effective in treating various symptoms of psychological or psychiatric disorders, which may result from organic disease or may be signs of psychiatric illness. Triavil must be used only under the supervision of a doctor. It will take a minimum of 2 weeks to 1 month for this medication to show beneficial effect, so don't expect instant results. If you feel there has been no change in symptoms after 6 to 8 weeks, contact your doctor and discuss it with him. He may tell you to continue taking the medicine and give it more time, or he may give you another drug which he feels will be more effective.

Cautions and Warnings

Do not take Triavil if you are allergic to it or to any related compound. For more information on drugs related to the ingredients found in Triavil, consult the entries for Amitriptyline and Chlorpromazine. Do not take Triavil if you have glaucoma or difficulty passing urine, unless you are specifically directed to by your physician. This drug is usually not recommended for patients who are recovering from heart attacks. Triavil may make you sleepy or tired and it may also cause difficulty in concentration. Be extremely careful when driving a car or operating machinery while taking this drug, especially during the first couple of weeks of therapy.

Pregnancy/Breast-feeding

Both ingredients in this drug cross into your developing baby's circulation and may cause birth defects if taken during the first 3 months of pregnancy. Newborn infants may suffer from drug side effects or heart, breathing, and urinary problems after their mothers take drugs of this type immediately before delivery. You should avoid taking this medication while pregnant.

Both the antidepressant and tranquilizer in Triavil are known to pass into breast milk and may affect a breast-feeding infant. Nursing mothers should consider alternate feeding methods if taking this medicine.

Seniors

Older adults are more sensitive to the effects of this drug and often require a lower dose than a younger adult to do the same job. Also, older adults are more likely to develop drug side effects. Follow your doctor's directions and report any side effects at once.

Possible Side Effects

Most frequent: dry mouth, difficulty in urination, constipation, blurred vision, rapid heartbeat, numbness and tingling sensation in the arms and legs, yellowing of the skin and/or whites of the eyes, unusually low blood pressure, drowsiness, sleepiness.

Infrequent: dizziness, nausea, excitement, fainting, slight twitching of the muscles, jittery feeling, weakness, headache, heartburn, loss of appetite, stomach cramps, increased perspiration, loss of coordination, skin rash with unusual sensitivity to bright lights, itching, redness, peeling away of large sections of skin. You may experience an allergic reaction: difficulty in breathing, retention of fluids in arms and legs, drug fever, swelling of the face and tongue.

Also infrequent: effects on the hormone and blood system, convulsions, development of unusual skin colorations and spots, effect on sex drive and sexual performance.

Drug Interactions

Quinidine or Procainamide, drugs which are used to control heart rhythm, will strongly increase the effects of this drug. Avoid depressive drugs such as other tranquilizers, sleeping pills, antihistamines, barbiturates, or alcohol. Interaction will cause excessive drowsiness, inability to concentrate, and/or sleepiness. Some patients may experience changes in heart rhythm when taking this drug along with thyroid medication.

One of the ingredients in Triavil may increase your response to common stimulant drugs found in over-the-counter cough and cold preparations, causing stimulation, nervousness, and difficulty in sleeping.

Avoid large amounts of Vitamin C, which may cause you

to release larger than normal amounts of Triavil from your body.

Both of the ingredients in Triavil may neutralize drugs used to treat high blood pressure. If you have high blood pressure and are taking Triavil, discuss this potential difficulty with your doctor or pharmacist to be sure that you are taking adequate doses of blood-pressure medicine.

If you are taking a drug which is an MAO inhibitor, discuss this matter with your doctor, because there have been severe interactions.

Food Interactions

This medicine is best taken on an empty stomach, but you may take it with food if it upsets your stomach.

Usual Dose

1 or 2 tablets 3 to 4 times per day.

Overdosage

Symptoms are central nervous system depression to the point of possible coma, low blood pressure, agitation, restlessness, convulsions, fever, dry mouth, abnormal heart rhythms, confusion, hallucinations, drowsiness, unusually low body temperature, dilated eye pupils, and abnormally rigid muscles. The patient should be taken to a hospital emergency room immediately. ALWAYS bring the medicine bottle.

Special Information

If you forget to take a dose of Triavil take it as soon as possible. However, if it is within 2 hours of your next dose, skip the forgotten dose and go back to your regular schedule. Do not take a double dose.

Generic Name

Triazolam

Brand Name

Halcion

Type of Drug

Sedative.

Prescribed for

Short-term treatment of insomnia or sleeplessness, frequent nighttime awakening, waking too early in the morning.

General Information

Triazolam, used only as a sleep inducer, is a member of the group of drugs known as benzodiazepines. Characterized by Diazepam (Valium), other benzodiazepine drugs are used as antianxiety agents, anticonvulsants, and sedatives (sleeping pills). They exert their effects by relaxing large skeletal muscles and through a direct effect on the brain. In doing so, they can relax you and make you either more tranquil or sleepier, depending on the specific drug taken and how much of it has been prescribed. Many doctors prefer Triazolam and the other members of this class to other drugs that can be used for the same effect, because the benzodiazepines tend to be safer, have fewer side effects, and are usually as, if not more, effective.

Triazolam is distinguished from other benzodiazepines by the fact that it has a very short duration of action and produces less hangover than other sleeping pills. However, some people who use it on a regular basis find that, because of the drug's short duration of effect, they still get up early in the morning or become anxious during the day.

Benzodiazepines can be abused if taken for long periods of time and it's possible to develop drug-withdrawal symptoms if therapy is suddenly discontinued. Withdrawal symptoms include convulsions, tremors, muscle cramps, insomnia, agitation, diarrhea, vomiting, sweating, and convulsions.

Cautions and Warnings

Triazolam is not intended for children under age 18.

Triazolam may interfere with daily tasks by producing some daytime drowsiness, although this is less of a problem than with other sedatives. Clinical depression may be increased by Triazolam or any other drug that has an ability to depress the nervous system. Intentional overdosage is more common among depressed people who take sleeping pills.

Pregnancy/Breast-feeding

This drug should not be used by pregnant women or women who may become pregnant while using it. Animal studies have shown that it passes easily into the blood system of a developing baby.

Triazolam and the products of its metabolism pass into mother's milk and the drug is not recommended for nursing mothers.

Seniors

Older adults are more susceptible to drug side effects than are younger adults and should take the lowest possible dosage of Triazolam.

Possible Side Effects

Drowsiness, headache, dizziness, nervousness, poor muscle coordination, light-headedness, nausea, and vomiting.

Less common side effects: a "high" feeling, rapid heartbeat, tiredness, confusion, temporary memory loss, cramps and pain, depression, blurred or double vision. The least often experienced adverse effects of Triazolam are constipation, changes in taste perception, stuffy nose, diarrhea, dry mouth, allergic reactions, rash, nightmares or strange dreams, difficulty sleeping, tingling in the hands or feet, temporary loss of normal sensation, and ringing or buzzing in the ears.

Drug Interactions

As for all other benzodiazepines, the effects of Triazolam may be enhanced if it is taken together with alcoholic beverages, antihistamines, tranquilizers, barbiturates, anticonvulsant medicines, antidepressants, and MAO inhibitor drugs (most often prescribed for severe depression).

Oral contraceptives, Cimetidine (for ulcers), and Disulfiram (for alcoholism) may increase the effect of Triazolam by interfering with the drug's breakdown in the liver.

Cigarette smoking may reduce the effect of Triazolam on your body, as it does with the other benzodiazepines.

The effectiveness of Levodopa (for Parkinson's disease) may be increased by benzodiazepine drugs, including Triazolam.

Food Interactions

Triazolam may be taken with food if it upsets your stomach.

Usual Dose

Adult: 0.25 to 0.5 milligrams about 30 minutes before you want to go to sleep.

Senior: 0.125 milligrams to start, then increase in 0.125-milligram increments until the desired effect is achieved.

Overdosage

The most common symptoms of Triazolam overdose are confusion, sleepiness, depression, loss of muscle coordination, and slurred speech. Coma may develop if the overdose was particularly large. Overdose symptoms can develop if a single dose of 2 milligrams (4 times the maximum daily dose) is taken. Patients taking an overdose of this drug must be made to vomit with Syrup of Ipecac (available at any pharmacy) to remove any remaining drug from the stomach. Call your doctor or a poison control center before doing this. If 30 minutes have passed since the overdose was taken or symptoms have begun to develop, the victim must be immediately transported to a hospital emergency room for treatment. ALWAYS bring the medicine bottle.

Special Information

Never take more of this medication than your doctor has prescribed. If you have been taking Triazolam for several months and decide to stop using it, your daily dosage should be gradually reduced, rather than stopping it all at once, to avoid drug-withdrawal symptoms.

If you forget to take a dose of Triazolam and you remember within about an hour of your regular time, take it as soon as you remember. If you do not remember until later, skip the forgotten dose and go back to your regular schedule. Do not take a double dose.

Generic Name

Trifluoperazine

Brand Names

Stelazine
Suprazine

(Also available in generic form)

Type of Drug

Phenothiazine antipsychotic.

Prescribed for

Psychotic disorders, moderate to severe depression with anxiety, control of agitation or aggressiveness of disturbed children, alcohol withdrawal symptoms, intractable pain, and senility.

General Information

Trifluoperazine and other members of the phenothiazine group act on a portion of the brain called the hypothalamus. They affect parts of the hypothalamus that control metabolism, body temperature, alertness, muscle tone, hormone balance, and vomiting, and may be used to treat problems related to any of these functions.

Cautions and Warnings

Trifluoperazine should not be taken if you are allergic to one of the drugs in the broad classification known as phenothiazine drugs. Do not take Trifluoperazine if you have any blood, liver, kidney, or heart disease, very low blood pressure, or Parkinson's disease. This medication is a tranquilizer and can have a depressive effect, especially during the first few days of therapy. Care should be taken when performing activities requiring a high degree of concentration, such as driving.

This drug should be used with caution and under strict supervision of your doctor if you have glaucoma, epilepsy, ulcers, or difficulty passing urine.

Avoid insecticides and exposure to extreme heat.

Pregnancy/Breast-feeding

Infants born to women taking this medication have experienced drug side effects (liver jaundice, nervous system effects) immediately after birth. Check with your doctor about taking this medicine if you are, or might become, pregnant.

This drug may pass into breast milk and affect a nursing infant. Consider alternate feeding methods if you must take this medicine.

Seniors

Older adults are more sensitive to the effects of this medication than younger adults and usually require a lower dosage to achieve a desired effect. Also, older adults are more likely to develop drug side effects. Some experts feel that elderly people should be treated with ½ to ¼ the usual adult dose.

Possible Side Effects

Most common: drowsiness, especially during the first or second week of therapy. If the drowsiness becomes troublesome, contact your doctor.

Trifluoperazine can cause jaundice (yellowing of the whites of the eyes or skin), usually in 2 to 4 weeks. The jaundice usually goes away when the drug is discontinued, but there have been cases when it did not. If you notice this effect or if you develop symptoms such as fever and generally not feeling well, contact your doctor immediately. Less frequent: changes in components of the blood including anemias, raised or lowered blood pressure, abnormal heart rates, heart attack, feeling faint or dizzy.

Phenothiazines can produce "extrapyramidal effects," such as spasm of the neck muscles, rolling back of the eyes, convulsions, difficulty in swallowing, and symptoms associated with Parkinson's disease. These effects look very serious but disappear after the drug has been withdrawn; however, symptoms of the face, tongue, and jaw may persist for as long as several years, especially in the elderly with a history of brain damage. If you experience extrapyramidal effects contact your doctor immediately.

Trifluoperazine may cause an unusual increase in psychotic symptoms or may cause paranoid reactions, tiredness, lethargy, restlessness, hyperactivity, confusion at night, bizarre dreams, inability to sleep, depression, and euphoria. Other reactions are itching, swelling, unusual sensitivity to bright lights, red skin, and rash. There have been cases of breast enlargement, false positive pregnancy tests, changes in menstrual flow in females, and impotence and changes in sex drive in males, as well as stuffy nose, headache, nausea, vomiting, loss of appetite, change in body temperature, loss of facial color, excessive salivation, excessive perspiration, constipation, diarrhea, changes in urine and stool habits, worsening of glaucoma, blurred vision, weakening of eyelid muscles, spasms in bronchial and other muscles, increased appetite, fatigue, excessive thirst, and changes in the coloration of skin, particularly in exposed areas.

Drug Interactions

Trifluoperazine should be taken with caution in combination with barbiturates, sleeping pills, narcotics, other tranquilizers, or any other medication which may produce a depressive effect. Avoid alcohol.

Usual Dose

Adult: 2 to 40 milligrams per day (the lowest effective dose should be used). This long-acting drug will then be taken once or twice per day.

Senior: lower dose, because of greater sensitivity to phenothiazines.

Child (age 6 to 12): 1 to 15 milligrams per day, slowly increased until satisfactory control is achieved.

Overdosage

Symptoms are depression, extreme weakness, tiredness, desire to go to sleep, coma, lowered blood pressure, uncontrolled muscle spasms, agitation, restlessness, convulsions, fever, dry mouth, and abnormal heart rhythms. The patient should be taken to a hospital emergency room immediately. ALWAYS bring the medicine bottle.

Special Information

This medication may cause drowsiness. Use caution when driving or operating complex equipment and avoid alcoholic beverages while taking the medicine.

The drug may also cause unusual sensitivity to the sun and can turn your urine reddish-brown to pink.

If dizziness occurs, avoid sudden changes in posture and avoid climbing stairs.

Use caution in hot weather. This medicine may make you more prone to heat stroke.

If you take Trifluoperazine once a day and forget your dose, take it as soon as possible. If you don't remember until the next day, skip the forgotten dose and continue with your regular schedule.

If you take the medicine more than once a day and forget a dose, take the forgotten dose as soon as possible. If it is almost time for your next dose, skip the forgotten dose and go on with your regular schedule.

Generic Name

Trihexyphenidyl Hydrochloride

Brand Names

Aphen   Trihexane
Artane   Trihexidyl
Artane Sequels (Long Acting)   Trihexy
Tremin

(Also available in generic form)

Type of Drug

Anticholinergic.

Prescribed for

Treatment of Parkinson's disease or prevention or control of muscle spasms caused by other drugs, particularly the phenothiazine drugs.

General Information

The drug has an action on the body similar to that of Atropine Sulfate. As an anticholinergic it has the ability to reduce muscle spasm, which makes the drug useful in treating Par-

kinson's disease and other diseases associated with spasm
of skeletal muscles.

Cautions and Warnings

Trihexyphenidyl Hydrochloride should be used with caution
if you have narrow-angle glaucoma, heart disease, stomach
ulcers, obstructions in the gastrointestinal tract, prostatitis,
or myasthenia gravis.

Pregnancy/Breast-feeding

Drugs of this type have not been proven to be a cause of
birth defects or of other problems in pregnant women. However, women who are, or may become, pregnant while taking this medication should discuss the possibility of birth
defects with their doctor and other therapies that may be
substituted for this medicine.

This medication may reduce the amount of breast milk
produced by a nursing mother.

Seniors

Seniors taking this medication on a regular basis may be
more sensitive to drug side effects, including a predisposition to developing glaucoma, confusion, disorientation, agitation, and hallucinations with normal drug doses.

Possible Side Effects

Dry mouth, difficulty in urination, constipation, blurred vision, rapid or pounding heartbeat, possible mental confusion, and increased sensitivity to strong light. The effects
may increase if Trihexyphenidyl Hydrochloride is taken with
antihistamines, phenothiazines, antidepressants, or other anticholinergic drugs.

Side effects are less frequent and severe than those seen
with Atropine Sulfate, to which this drug is therapeutically
similar.

Drug Interactions

Interaction with other anticholinergic drugs, including tricyclic antidepressants, may cause severe stomach upset or
unusual abdominal pain. If this happens, contact your doctor.

Avoid over-the-counter remedies which contain Atropine

Sulfate or similar drugs. Your pharmacist can tell you the ingredients of over-the-counter drugs.

This drug should not be taken with alcohol.

Food Interactions

This medicine is best taken on an empty stomach, but may be taken with food if it upsets your stomach.

Usual Dose

1 to 15 milligrams per day, depending on disease and patient's response.

Overdosage

Signs of drug overdose include clumsiness or unsteadiness, severe drowsiness, severely dry mouth, nose, or throat, hallucinations, mood changes, difficulty breathing, rapid heartbeat, and unusually warm and dry skin. Overdose victims should be taken to a hospital emergency room at once. ALWAYS bring the medicine bottle.

Special Information

Side effects of dry mouth, constipation, and sensitivity to bright lights can be easily relieved with candy or gum, a stool softener like Docusate, and sunglasses.

This medicine will reduce your tolerance to hot weather because it makes you sweat less than normal. Be careful not to become overheated in hot weather because of the chance of developing heat stroke.

If you forget to take a dose of Trihexyphenidyl Hydrochloride, take it as soon as possible. However, if it is within 4 hours of your next dose, skip the forgotten dose and go back to your regular schedule. Do not take a double dose.

Generic Name

Trimethobenzamide Hydrochloride

Brand Names

Tebamide
T-Gen
Tigan

(Also available in generic form)

Type of Drug

Antiemetic.

Prescribed for

Control of nausea and vomiting.

General Information

Trimethobenzamide Hydrochloride works on the "chemoreceptor trigger zone" of the brain through which impulses are carried to the vomiting center. It can help control nausea and vomiting.

Cautions and Warnings

Do not use this drug if you are allergic or sensitive to it. Trimethobenzamide Hydrochloride rectal suppositories contain a local anesthetic and should not be used for newborn infants or patients who are allergic to local anesthetics. Some drugs, when taken by children with a viral illness that causes vomiting, may contribute to the development of Reye's syndrome, a potentially fatal, acute childhood disease. Although this relationship has not been confirmed, caution must be exercised. Reye's syndrome is characterized by a rapid onset of persistent severe vomiting, tiredness, and irrational behavior. It can progress to coma, convulsions, and death—usually following a nonspecific illness associated with a high fever. It has been suspected that Trimethobenzamide Hydrochloride and other drugs which can be toxic to the liver may unfavorably alter the course of Reye's syndrome; such drugs should be avoided in children exhibiting signs and symptoms associated with Reye's syndrome.

Trimethobenzamide Hydrochloride can obscure the signs of overdosage by other drugs or signs of disease because of its effect of controlling nausea and vomiting.

Pregnancy/Breast-feeding

Do not use this drug if you are pregnant because Trimethobenzamide Hydrochloride may decrease your chances to have a successful pregnancy. No breast-feeding problems have been seen.

Seniors

Older adults may take this medication without special restriction. Follow your doctor's directions and report any side effects at once.

Possible Side Effects

Muscle cramps and tremors, low blood pressure (especially after an injection of this medication), effects on components of the blood, blurred vision, drowsiness, headache, jaundice (yellowing of skin or whites of the eyes). If you experience one of these side effects report it to your doctor. If you develop a rash or other allergic effects from Trimethobenzamide Hydrochloride, stop taking the drug and tell your doctor. Usually these symptoms will disappear by themselves, but additional treatment may be necessary.

Drug Interactions

Trimethobenzamide Hydrochloride may make you sleepy or cause you to lose concentration; therefore, avoid alcoholic beverages, antihistamines, sleeping pills, tranquilizers, and other depressant drugs which may aggravate these effects.

Food Interactions

This medicine is best taken on an empty stomach, but you may take it with food if it upsets your stomach.

Usual Dose

Capsule:
Adult: 250-milligram capsule 3 to 4 times per day.
Child (30 to 90 pounds): 100 to 200 milligrams 3 to 4 times per day.

Rectal suppository:

Adult: 200 milligrams 3 to 4 times per day.

Child (30 to 90 pounds): 100 to 200 milligrams 3 to 4 times per day.

Child (under 30 pounds): 100 milligrams 3 to 4 times per day.

Dose must be adjusted according to disease severity and patient's response.

Special Information

Severe vomiting should not be treated with an antiemetic drug alone: the cause of vomiting should be established and treated. Overuse of antiemetic drugs may delay diagnosis of the underlying condition or problem and obscure the signs of toxic effects from other drugs. Primary emphasis in the treatment of vomiting is on reestablishment of body fluid and electrolyte balance, relief of fever if present, and treatment of the causative disease process.

If you have taken Trimethobenzamide Hydrochloride, use special care when driving.

If you forget to take a dose of Trimethobenzamide Hydrochloride, take it as soon as you remember. If it is almost time for your next regularly scheduled dose, skip the one you forgot and continue with your regular schedule. Do not take a double dose.

Generic Name

Trimethoprim

Brand Names

Proloprim
Trimpex

(Also available in generic form)

Type of Drug

Anti-infective.

Prescribed for

Urinary tract infections.

General Information

This drug works by blocking the effects of folic acid in microorganisms which may infect the urinary tract. It is often used in combination with a sulfa drug and was first made available in the United States only as a combination known as Septra or Bactrim. However, it is effective by itself.

Cautions and Warnings

Do not take Trimethoprim if you are allergic to it.

Patients with a possible folic acid deficiency should not take this drug.

Pregnancy/Breast-feeding

This drug crosses into the blood circulation of a developing baby. It has not been found to cause birth defects. Pregnant women, or those who might become pregnant while taking this drug, should not take it without their doctor's approval. When the drug is considered essential by your doctor, the potential risk of taking the medicine must be carefully weighed against the benefit it might produce.

This drug passes into breast milk, but has caused no problems among breast-fed infants. You must consider the potential effect on the nursing infant if breast-feeding while taking this medicine.

Seniors

Older adults with poor kidney function are more sensitive to the effects of this drug; your doctor will tailor your dose to your kidney function. Follow your doctor's directions and report any side effects at once.

Possible Side Effects

Itching, rash, peeling of the skin.

Less common side effects: stomach upset, nausea, vomiting, fever, adverse effects on the blood, elevation of blood enzymes.

Drug Interactions

The anticonvulsant Phenytoin may have increased effects if you take Trimethoprim.

Food Interactions

This medicine is best taken on an empty stomach, but you may take it with food if it upsets your stomach.

Usual Dose

200 milligrams every day for 10 days. Patients with kidney disease should take less medication.

Overdosage

Signs may appear after taking 10 or more tablets. They are nausea, vomiting, dizziness, headache, depression, confusion, and adverse effects on the blood system. People taking high doses of this drug or those taking it for long periods of time may develop adverse effects on the blood system.

Special Information

Take exactly as directed. Call your doctor if you develop sore throat, fever, blood clots, black-and-blue marks, or a very pale sickly skin coloration.

If you miss a dose of Trimethoprim, take it as soon as possible. If it is almost time for your next dose and you take the medication once a day, space the missed dose and your next dose 10 to 12 hours apart, then go back to your regular schedule.

If it is almost time for your next dose and you take the medicine twice a day, space the missed dose and your next dose by 5 to 6 hours, then go back to your regular schedule.

Generic Name

Trimipramine Maleate

Brand Name

Surmontil

Type of Drug

Antidepressant.

Prescribed for

Depression with or without symptoms of anxiety.

General Information

Trimipramine Maleate and other members of the group known as tricyclic antidepressants are effective in treating symptoms of depression. They can elevate your mood, increase physical activity and mental alertness, improve appetite and sleep patterns. These drugs are mild sedatives and therefore useful in treating mild forms of depression associated with anxiety. You should not expect instant results with this medicine: benefits are usually seen after 1 to 4 weeks. If symptoms are not affected after 6 to 8 weeks, contact your doctor. Occasionally other members of this group of drugs have been used in treating nighttime bed-wetting in the young child, but they do not produce long-lasting relief and therapy with one of them for nighttime bed-wetting is of questionable value.

Cautions and Warnings

Do not take Trimipramine Maleate if you are allergic or sensitive to this or other members of this class of drug: Doxepin, Nortriptyline, Imipramine, Desipramine, Protriptyline, and Amitriptyline. The drugs should not be used if you are recovering from a heart attack. Trimipramine Maleate may be taken with caution if you have a history of epilepsy or other convulsive disorders, difficulty in urination, glaucoma, heart disease, or thyroid disease. Trimipramine Maleate can interfere with your ability to perform tasks which require concentration, such as driving or operating machinery.

Pregnancy/Breast-feeding

This drug, like other antidepressants, crosses into your developing baby's circulation and may cause birth defects if taken during the first 3 months of pregnancy. There have been reports of newborn infants suffering from heart, breathing, and urinary problems after their mothers had taken an antidepressant of this type immediately before delivery. You should avoid taking this medication while pregnant.

Antidepressants of this type are known to pass into breast milk and may affect a breast-feeding infant, although this has not been proven. Nursing mothers should consider alternate feeding methods if taking this medicine.

Seniors

Older adults are more sensitive to the effects of this drug and often require a lower dose than a younger adult to do the same job. Follow your doctor's directions and report any side effects at once.

Possible Side Effects

Changes in blood pressure (both high and low), abnormal heart rates, heart attack, confusion, especially in elderly patients, hallucinations, disorientation, delusions, anxiety, restlessness, excitement, numbness and tingling in the extremities, lack of coordination, muscle spasms or tremors, seizures and/or convulsions, dry mouth, blurred vision, constipation, inability to urinate, rash, itching, sensitivity to bright light or sunlight, retention of fluids, fever, allergy, changes in composition of blood, nausea, vomiting, loss of appetite, stomach upset, diarrhea, enlargement of the breasts in males and females, increased or decreased sex drive, increased or decreased blood sugar.

Less common side effects: agitation, inability to sleep, nightmares, feeling of panic, peculiar taste in the mouth, stomach cramps, black coloration of the tongue, yellowing eyes and/or skin, changes in liver function, increased or decreased weight, perspiration, flushing, frequent urination, drowsiness, dizziness, weakness, headache, loss of hair, nausea, not feeling well.

Drug Interactions

Interaction with monoamine oxidase (MAO) inhibitors can cause high fevers, convulsions, and occasionally death. Don't take MAO inhibitors until at least 2 weeks after Trimipramine Maleate has been discontinued.

Trimipramine Maleate interacts with Guanethidine, a drug used to treat high blood pressure: if your doctor prescribes Trimipramine Maleate and you are taking medicine for high blood pressure, be sure to discuss this with him.

Trimipramine Maleate increases the effects of barbiturates, tranquilizers, other depressive drugs, and alcohol. Don't drink alcoholic beverages if you take this medicine.

Taking Trimipramine Maleate and thyroid medicine will enhance the effects of the thyroid medicine. The combination can cause abnormal heart rhythms.

Large doses of Vitamin C (Ascorbic Acid) can reduce the effect of Trimipramine Maleate. Drugs such as Bicarbonate of Soda or Acetazolamide will increase the effect of Trimipramine Maleate.

Food Interactions

This drug is best taken on an empty stomach, but you can take it with food if it upsets your stomach.

Usual Dose

Adult: 150 to 200 milligrams per day in divided doses or as a single bedtime dose. Hospitalized patients may need up to 300 milligrams per day. The dose of this drug must be tailored to patient's need.

Adolescent and senior: lower doses are recommended; for people over 60 years of age, usually 50 to 100 milligrams per day.

Overdosage

Symptoms are confusion, inability to concentrate, hallucinations, drowsiness, lowered body temperature, abnormal heart rate, heart failure, large pupils of the eyes, convulsions, severely lowered blood pressure, stupor, and coma (as well as agitation, stiffening of body muscles, vomiting, and high fever). The patient should be taken to a hospital emergency room immediately. ALWAYS bring the medicine bottle.

Special Information

Avoid alcohol and other drugs that depress the nervous system while taking this antidepressant. Do not stop taking this medicine unless your doctor has specifically told you to do so. Abruptly stopping this medicine may cause nausea, headache, and a sickly feeling. This medicine can cause drowsiness, dizziness, and blurred vision. Be careful when driving or operating complicated machinery. Avoid exposure to the sun or sun lamps for long periods of time. Call your doctor if dry mouth, difficulty urinating, or excessive sedation develops.

If you take Trimipramine Maleate several times a day and forget a dose, take it as soon as you remember. If it is almost time for your next regularly scheduled dose, skip the one you forgot and continue with your regular schedule.

If you take it once a day at bedtime and forget, don't take it when you get up. Go back to your regular schedule. Call your doctor if you skip 2 or more days of medication. Never take a double dose.

Generic Name

Tripelennamine Hydrochloride

Brand Names

PBZ
PBZ-SR
Pelamine

(Also available in generic form)

Type of Drug

Antihistamine.

Prescribed for

Seasonal allergy, stuffy and runny nose, itching of the eyes, scratching of the throat caused by allergy, and other allergic symptoms such as itching, rash, or hives.

General Information

Antihistamines, including Tripelennamine Hydrochloride, act by blocking the release of the chemical substance histamine from body cells. Antihistamines work by drying up the secretions of the nose, throat, and eyes.

Cautions and Warnings

Tripelennamine Hydrochloride should not be used if you are allergic to this drug. It should be avoided or used with extreme care if you have narrow-angle glaucoma (pressure in the eye), stomach ulcer or other stomach problems, enlarged prostate, or problems passing urine. It should not be used by people who have deep-breathing problems such as asthma.

Use with care if you have a history of thyroid disease, heart disease, high blood pressure, or diabetes.

Young children can show signs of nervousness, increased tension, and anxiety.

Pregnancy/Breast-feeding

Antihistamines have not been proven to be a cause of birth defects or other problems in pregnant women, although studies in animals have shown that some drugs (Meclizine and Cyclizine), used mainly against nausea and vomiting, may cause birth defects. Do not take any antihistamine without your doctor's knowledge.

Small amounts of antihistamine medicines pass into breast milk and may affect a nursing infant. Nursing mothers should avoid antihistamines or use alternate feeding methods while taking the medicine.

Seniors

Seniors are more sensitive to antihistamine side effects. Confusion, difficult or painful urination, dizziness, drowsiness, a faint feeling, dry mouth, nose, or throat, nightmares or excitement, nervousness, restlessness, or irritability are more likely to occur among older adults.

Possible Side Effects

Occasional: itching, rash, sensitivity to light, perspiration, chills, dryness of the mouth, nose, and throat, lowered blood pressure, headache, rapid heartbeat, sleeplessness, dizziness, disturbed coordination, confusion, restlessness, nervousness, irritability, euphoria (feeling high), tingling of the hands and feet, blurred vision, double vision, ringing in the ears, stomach upset, loss of appetite, nausea, vomiting, constipation, diarrhea, difficulty in urination, tightness of the chest, wheezing, nasal stuffiness.

Drug Interactions

Tripelennamine Hydrochloride should not be taken with MAO inhibitors.

Interaction with tranquilizers, sedatives, and sleeping medication will increase the effects of these drugs; it is extremely important that you discuss this with your doctor so that doses of these drugs can be properly adjusted.

Be extremely cautious when drinking while taking Tripelennamine Hydrochloride, which will enhance the intoxicating effect of alcohol. Alcohol also has a sedative effect.

Usual Dose

Adult: 25 to 50 milligrams every 4 to 6 hours. Up to 600 milligrams per day may be used. Adult patients may take up to 3 of the 100-milligram long-acting (PBZ-SR) tablets per day, although this much is not usually needed.

Infant and child: 2 milligrams per pound of body weight per day in divided doses. No more than 300 milligrams should be given per day. Older children may take up to 3 of the extended-release (long-acting) tablets per day, if needed.

Overdosage

Symptoms are depression or stimulation (especially in children), fixed or dilated pupils, flushing of the skin, and stomach upset. Patients taking an overdose of this drug must be made to vomit with Syrup of Ipecac (available at any pharmacy) to remove any remaining drug from the stomach. Call your doctor or a poison control center before doing this. If you must go to a hospital emergency room, ALWAYS bring the medicine bottle.

Special Information

Antihistamines produce a depressing effect: be extremely cautious when driving or operating heavy equipment.

If you forget to take a dose of Tripelennamine Hydrochloride, take it as soon as you remember. If it is almost time for your next regularly scheduled dose, skip the one you forgot and continue with your regular schedule. Do not take a double dose.

Brand Name

Tuinal

Ingredients

Amobarbital
Secobarbital

(Also available in generic form)

Type of Drug

Hypnotic combination.

Prescribed for

Daytime sedation, or sleeping medication.

General Information

This drug is a combination of a short- and intermediate-acting barbiturate. The combination takes advantage of the fast-acting nature of Secobarbital and the longer duration of action of Amobarbital (about 8 hours). Although the combination works well, it can be addicting if taken daily for 3 months in sufficient doses (about 100 milligrams). Larger doses will result in addiction in a shorter period of time.

Cautions and Warnings

Tuinal may slow down your physical and mental reflexes, so you must be extremely careful when operating machinery, driving an automobile, or performing other potentially dangerous tasks. Tuinal is classified as a barbiturate; long-term or unsupervised use may cause addiction.

Barbiturates are neutralized in the liver and eliminated from the body through the kidneys; consequently, people who have liver or kidney disorders—namely, difficulty in forming or excreting urine—should be carefully monitored by their doctor when taking Tuinal.

If you have known sensitivities or allergies to barbiturates, or if you have previously been addicted to sedatives or hypnotics, or if you have a disease affecting the respiratory system, you should not take Tuinal.

Pregnancy/Breast-feeding

Regular use of any barbiturate during the last 3 months of pregnancy can cause the baby to be born dependent on the medicine. Also, barbiturate use increases the chance of bleeding problems, brain tumors, and breathing difficulties in the newborn.

Barbiturates pass into breast milk and can cause drowsiness, slow heartbeat, and breathing difficulty in the newborn.

Seniors

Older adults are more sensitive to the effects of barbiturates, especially nervousness and confusion, and often require a lower dose than a younger adult to do the same job. Follow your doctor's directions and report any side effects at once.

Possible Side Effects

Drowsiness, lethargy, dizziness, hangover, difficulty in breathing, skin rash, and general allergic reaction such as runny nose, watery eyes, and scratchy throat.

Less common side effects: nausea, vomiting, diarrhea. More severe adverse reactions may include anemia and yellowing of the skin and eyes.

Drug Interactions

Interaction with alcohol, tranquilizers, or other sedatives increases the effect of Tuinal.

Interaction with anticoagulants (blood-thinning agents) can reduce their effect. This is also true of muscle relaxants, painkillers, anticonvulsants, Quinidine, Theophylline, Metronidazole, Phenmetrazine, birth control pills, and Acetaminophen.

Food Interactions

This medicine is best taken on an empty stomach, but may be taken with food if it upsets your stomach.

Usual Dose

Up to 200 milligrams.

Overdosage

Symptoms are difficulty in breathing, decrease in size of the pupils of the eyes, lowered body temperature progressing to fever as time passes, fluid in the lungs, and eventually coma.

Anyone suspected of having taken an overdose must be taken to the hospital for immediate care. ALWAYS bring the medicine bottle to the emergency room physician so he can quickly and correctly identify the medicine and start treatment. Severe overdosage of this medication can kill; the drug has been used many times in suicide attempts.

Special Information

Avoid alcohol and other drugs that depress the nervous system while taking this barbiturate. Be sure to take this medicine according to your doctor's direction. Do not change your dose without your doctor's approval. This drug causes drowsiness and poor concentration, and makes it more difficult to drive a car, operate machinery, or perform complicated activities.

Call your doctor at once if you develop fever, sore throat, nosebleeds, mouth sores, unexplained black-and-blue marks, easy bruising, or bleeding.

If you forget to take a dose of Tuinal and you remember within about an hour of your regular time, take it right away. If you do not remember until later, skip the forgotten dose and go back to your regular schedule. Do not take a double dose.

Brand Name

Tussionex

Ingredients

Hydrocodone
Phenyltoloxamine

Type of Drug

Cough suppressant–antihistamine combination.

Prescribed for

Relief of cough and other symptoms of a cold or other respiratory condition.

General Information

This drug may be prescribed to treat a cough or congestion that has not responded to other medication. The cough suppressant ingredient (Hydrocodone) in this combination is more potent than Codeine.

Cautions and Warnings

Do not use Tussionex if you are allergic to any of the ingredients. Patients allergic to Codeine may also be allergic to

Tussionex. Long-term use of this or any other narcotic-containing drug can lead to drug dependence or addiction. Both ingredients in Tussionex can cause drowsiness, tiredness, or loss of concentration. Use with caution if you have a history of convulsions, glaucoma, stomach ulcer, high blood pressure, thyroid disease, heart disease, or diabetes.

Pregnancy/Breast-feeding

Narcotics like Hydrocodone have not been associated with birth defects. But taking too much of it, or any other narcotic, during pregnancy can lead to the birth of a drug-dependent infant and drug-withdrawal symptoms in the baby. All narcotics, including Hydrocodone, can cause breathing problems in the newborn if taken just before delivery.

Antihistamines like Phenyltoloxamine may pass into your developing baby's circulation but have not been the source of birth defects.

Seniors

Seniors are more likely to be sensitive to both the Hydrocodone and Phenyltoloxamine in this combination. The Hydrocodone may have more of a depressant effect on seniors than younger adults. Other effects that may be more prominent are dizziness, light-headedness, or fainting when rising suddenly from a sitting or lying position.

Also, antihistamines may produce confusion, difficult or painful urination, a faint feeling, dry mouth, nose, or throat, nightmares or excitement, nervousness, restlessness, or irritability.

Possible Side Effects

Light-headedness, dizziness, sleepiness, nausea, vomiting, sweating, itching, rash, sensitivity to light, excessive perspiration, chills, dryness of the mouth, nose, and throat.

Less common: euphoria (feeling high), weakness, agitation, uncoordinated muscle movement, minor hallucinations, disorientation and visual disturbances, loss of appetite, constipation, flushing of the face, rapid heartbeat, palpitations, faintness, difficult urination, reduced sexual potency, low blood sugar, anemia, yellowing of the skin or whites of the eyes, blurred or double vision, ringing or buzzing in the ears, wheezing, nasal stuffiness.

Drug Interactions

Do not use alcohol or other depressant drugs because they will increase the depressant effect of the Tussionex. This drug should not be taken in combination with MAO inhibitor drugs.

Food Interactions

This medicine is best taken on an empty stomach, but you may take it with food if it upsets your stomach.

Usual Dose

Tablet or capsule: 1 every 8 to 12 hours.
Suspension: 1 teaspoon every 8 to 12 hours.

Overdosage

Signs of overdose are depression, slowed breathing, flushing of the skin, upset stomach. In case of overdose, bring the patient to a hospital emergency room. ALWAYS bring the medicine bottle.

Special Information

Be careful while driving or operating any equipment.
     The liquid form of Tussionex does not contain any sugar.
     If you forget to take a dose of Tussionex, take it as soon as you remember. If it is almost time for your next regularly scheduled dose, skip the one you forgot and continue with your regular schedule. Do not take a double dose.

Brand Name

Tuss-Ornade Spansules/Liquid

Ingredients

Caramiphen Edisylate
Phenylpropanolamine Hydrochloride

Other Brand Names

Detuss   Tuss Allergine Modified T.D.
Rescaps-D.S.R.   Tuss-Genade Modified
Tussadon   Tussogest

(Also available in generic form)

Type of Drug

Decongestant; expectorant.

Prescribed for

Relief of cough, nasal congestion, runny nose, and other symptoms associated with the common cold, viruses, or other upper respiratory diseases. The drug may also be used to treat allergies, asthma, ear infections, or sinus infections.

General Information

Tuss-Ornade is one of almost 100 products marketed to relieve the symptoms of the common cold and other respiratory infections. These products contain ingredients to relieve congestion, act as an antihistamine, relieve or suppress cough, and help you to cough up mucus. They may contain medicine for each purpose, or may contain a combination of medicines. Some combinations leave out the antihistamine, the decongestant, or the expectorant. You must realize while taking Tuss-Ornade or similar products that these drugs are good only for the relief of symptoms and do not treat the underlying problem such as a cold virus or other infections.

The liquid formulations contain 5 percent alcohol (10 proof).

Cautions and Warnings

This drug can cause you to become overly anxious and nervous and may interfere with your sleep. It should be avoided if you have diabetes, heart disease, high blood pressure, thyroid disease, glaucoma, or a prostate condition.

Pregnancy/Breast-feeding

This drug crosses into the blood circulation of a developing baby. It has not been found to cause birth defects. Pregnant women, or those who might become pregnant while taking this drug, should not take it without their doctor's approval. When the drug is considered essential by your doctor, the potential risk of taking the medicine must be carefully weighed against the benefit it might produce.

This drug passes into breast milk, but has caused no problems among breast-fed infants. You must consider the potential effect on the nursing infant if breast-feeding while taking this medicine.

Seniors

Older adults are more sensitive to the effects of this drug. Follow your doctor's directions and report any side effects at once.

Possible Side Effects

Dry mouth, blurred vision, difficulty passing urine, (possibly) constipation, nervousness, restlessness or even inability to sleep.

Drug Interactions

Taking Tuss-Ornade with an MAO inhibitor can produce severe interaction, so consult your doctor before combining them.

Do not take this drug with sedatives, tranquilizers, antihistamines, sleeping pills, thyroid medicine, or antihypertensive drugs such as Reserpine or Guanethidine.

Since Tuss-Ornade contains ingredients which may cause sleepiness or difficulty in concentration, do not drink alcoholic beverages while taking this drug. The combination can cause excessive drowsiness or sleepiness, and result in inability to concentrate and carry out activities requiring extra concentration and coordination.

Food Interactions

Take with a full glass of water to remove excessive mucus from the throat and reduce stomach upset.

Usual Dose

Spansule (capsule): 1 every 12 hours.

Liquid: 1 to 2 teaspoons every 4 hours as needed for relief of cough, nasal congestion, runny nose, or other symptoms associated with the common cold or other upper respiratory diseases.

Special Information

If you forget to take a dose of Tuss-Ornade, take it as soon as you remember. If it is almost time for your next regularly scheduled dose, skip the one you forgot and continue with your regular schedule. Do not take a double dose.

Generic Name

Valproic Acid

Brand Names

Depakene
Depakote
Myproic Acid

(Also available in generic form)

Type of Drug

Anticonvulsant.

Prescribed for

Various seizure disorders.

General Information

Valproic Acid is used to treat absence seizures, mixed seizures, myoclonic seizures, partial seizures, grand mal seizures. It can be used for the special kind of seizures called petit mal.

Cautions and Warnings

Do not take Valproic Acid if you are allergic to it. Take this drug with caution if you have a history of liver problems. Some cases of liver failure have occurred in people taking Valproic Acid, especially children under 2 years old.

Pregnancy/Breast-feeding

Valproic Acid crosses into the blood circulation of a developing baby and is reported to have caused birth defects after having been taken during the first 3 months of pregnancy. Most mothers, though, who take this medicine deliver healthy, normal babies. If you are pregnant, discuss the relative risk of taking this medicine with your doctor.

Valproic Acid passes into breast milk and may affect a nursing infant. No problems have been found among breast-fed infants of mothers taking this medication, but you should discuss the possibility of using an alternate feeding method with your doctor.

Seniors

Older adults with poor kidney function are more likely to develop side effects from Valproic Acid, since the drug passes out of your body through the kidneys.

Possible Side Effects

Nausea, vomiting and indigestion, sedation or sleepiness, weakness, skin rash, emotional upset, depression, psychosis, aggression, hyperactive behavior. Valproic Acid can cause adverse effects on the blood system. The frequency of side effects increases as your dose of Valproic Acid increases.

Less common side effects: diarrhea, stomach cramps, constipation, appetite changes (either increase or decrease), headache, loss of control of eye muscles, drooping eyelids, double vision, spots before the eyes, loss of muscle control and coordination, tremors.

Drug Interactions

Valproic Acid may increase the depressive effects of alcohol, sleeping pills, tranquilizers, or other depressant drugs.

If you begin taking Valproic Acid while taking Phenytoin, your Phenytoin dosage may have to be adjusted. Use of Valproic Acid together with Clonazepam may produce a certain kind of seizure. This combination should be used with extreme caution.

Valproic Acid may affect oral anticoagulant (blood-thinning) drugs. If you begin taking Valproic Acid and have been taking an anticoagulant, your anticoagulant dose may have to be changed.

Aspirin may increase the chances of toxicity due to Valproic Acid.

Valproic Acid may cause a false positive interpretation of the test for ketones in the urine (used by diabetics).

Food Interactions

This medicine is best taken on an empty stomach, because food prolongs the time it takes for the medicine to be absorbed into the bloodstream. Nevertheless, you may take it with food if it upsets your stomach.

Usual Dose

7 to 27 milligrams per pound per day; up to 250 milligrams
per day.

Overdosage

Call your doctor or take the patient to a hospital emergency
room immediately. ALWAYS bring the medicine bottle.

Special Information

This medicine may cause drowsiness; be careful while driving or operating machinery. Do not chew or crush Valproic
Acid capsules or tablets.

Valproic Acid can cause mouth and throat irritation. All
seizure patients should carry special identification indicating
their disease and the medicine being taken for it.

If you take Valproic Acid once a day and forget your dose,
take it as soon as possible. If you don't remember until the
next day, skip the forgotten dose and continue with your
regular schedule.

If you take the medicine 2 or more times a day and forget
a dose, and you remember within 6 hours of your regular
time, take it as soon as possible. Take the rest of that day's
doses at regularly spaced time intervals. Go back to your
regular schedule the next day.

Brand Name

Vaseretic

Ingredients

Enalapril
Hydrochlorothiazide

Type of Drug

Antihypertensive combination.

Prescribed for

High blood pressure.

General Information

This medicine is a combination of a thiazide diuretic and a member of a relatively new class of drugs, ACE inhibitors, which work by preventing the conversion of a potent hormone called Angiotensin I. This directly affects the production of other hormones and enzymes which participate in the regulation of blood pressure. The blood-pressure-lowering effects of the two drugs add to each other to produce a result greater than could be expected from either ingredient.

Cautions and Warnings

This drug can cause kidney problems, especially loss of protein in the urine. Patients taking Enalapril should have the amount of protein in the urine measured during the first month of treatment and monthly for the next few months. The drug can also cause a reduction on white-blood-cell count, leading to a potential for increased susceptibility to infection. Enalapril should be used with caution by people who have kidney disease or diseases of the immune/collagen system (particularly lupus erythematosus), or who have taken other drugs that affect the white-blood-cell count.

Do not take this combination if you are allergic to either ingredient or to sulfa drugs. You may be sensitive to Hydrochlorothiazide if you have a history of allergy or bronchial asthma.

Pregnancy/Breast-feeding

The effect of Enalapril on a developing fetus is not known. Hydrochlorothiazide crosses into the developing baby's blood system and can cause jaundice, blood problems, and low potassium. Women who are, or might become, pregnant while taking this drug should discuss the matter with their doctor.

It is not known if Enalapril passes into breast milk and if it will affect a nursing infant. Hydrochlorothiazide passes into breast milk but no problems have been reported in nursing infants.

Seniors

Older adults may be less sensitive to the blood-pressure-lowering effects of this drug combination than younger adults, but they may be more sensitive to its side effects. Dosage must be individualized to your needs.

Possible Side Effects

Dizziness, tiredness, headache, diarrhea, rash (usually mild), and cough are the most common side effects.

Less common drug side effects are itching, fever, temporary loss of taste perception, stomach irritation, chest pain, low blood pressure, heart palpitations, difficulty sleeping, tingling in the hands or feet, nausea, vomiting, jaundice and liver damage, excessive sweating, muscle cramps, (male) impotence, and muscle weakness. Some people experience unusual reactions after taking the first dose of the drug which can include facial flushing and swelling, swelling of the arms and legs, and closing of the throat.

The Hydrochlorothiazide ingredient can cause a loss of body potassium. Signs of low potassium are dry mouth, thirst, weakness, lethargy, drowsiness, restlessness, muscle pains or cramps, muscle tiredness, low blood pressure, low urine production, abnormal heart rate, and upset stomach. Your doctor may prescribe a potassium-rich diet or a potassium supplement to counteract this problem, although Enalapril can counteract the Hydrochlorothiazide (see "Drug Interactions," below).

Drug Interactions

The blood-pressure-lowering effect of Vaseretic is additive with diuretic drugs and the beta blockers. Other drugs that cause rapid drops in blood pressure should be used with extreme caution because of a possible severe drop when taken together with Enalapril.

Enalapril may increase potassium levels in your blood, especially when given with potassium-sparing diuretics and/or potassium supplements.

People taking oral antidiabetic drugs who start taking Vaseretic may have to have their antidiabetic dosage adjusted. The chance of Lithium toxicity may be increased by Hydrochlorothiazide.

Food Interactions

This drug is best taken on an empty stomach, usually 1 hour before or 2 hours after a meal.

Usual Dose

1 tablet a day. Some people may take their total daily dosage in 2 divided doses.

People with poor kidney function have to take less of the medicine to achieve reduced blood pressure.

Overdosage

The primary effect of Vaseretic overdosage is a rapid drop in blood pressure, as evidenced by dizziness or fainting. Take the overdose victim to a hospital emergency room immediately. ALWAYS remember to bring the medicine bottle.

Special Information

Call your doctor if you develop fever, sore throat, mouth sores, abnormal heartbeat, or chest pain, or if you have persistent rash or loss of taste perception.

Vaseretic may cause dizziness when quickly rising from a lying or sitting position.

Avoid strenuous exercise and/or very hot weather as heavy sweating and/or dehydration can cause a rapid drop in blood pressure.

Do not stop taking this medicine without your doctor's knowledge.

Avoid nonprescription medicines such as diet pills, decongestants, and stimulants that can raise your blood pressure.

If you forget to take a dose of Vaseretic, take it as soon as you remember. If it is almost time for your next regularly scheduled dose, skip the one you forgot and continue with your regular schedule. Do not take a double dose.

Generic Name

Verapamil

Brand Names

Calan/Calan SR
Isoptin/Isoptin SR

(Also available in generic form)

Type of Drug

Calcium channel blocker.

Prescribed for

Angina pectoris and Prinzmetals's angina, high blood pressure, asthma, or Raynaud's disease.

General Information

Verapamil was the first calcium channel blocker available in the United States. It works by blocking the passage of calcium into heart and smooth muscle. Since calcium is an essential ingredient in muscle contraction, blocking calcium reduces both muscle contraction and oxygen use by the muscle. This is why Verapamil is used in the treatment of angina, a kind of heart pain related to poor oxygen supply to the heart muscles. Verapamil also dilates the vessels that supply blood to the heart muscles and prevents spasm of these arteries. Verapamil only affects the movement of calcium into muscle cells. It does not have any effect on calcium in the blood. Verapamil brands with "SR" after their name are sustained-release formulas. They should be used only for high blood pressure.

Cautions and Warnings

Verapamil may cause lowered blood pressure in some patients. Patients taking a beta-blocking drug who begin taking Verapamil may develop heart failure or increased angina pain. Do not take this drug if you have had an allergic reaction to it.

Pregnancy/Breast-feeding

Pregnant women should only use this drug if absolutely necessary. This drug may cause birth defects or interfere with your baby's development. Check with your doctor before taking it if you are, or might be, pregnant.

Although taking Verapamil during nursing has not been shown to cause problems, nursing mothers should only use the drug if absolutely necessary.

Seniors

Older adults are more sensitive to the effects of this drug. Follow your doctor's directions and report any side effects at once.

Possible Side Effects

Low blood pressure, swelling of the arms or legs, heart failure, slowed heartbeat, dizziness, light-headedness, weakness, fatigue, headache, constipation, nausea, liver damage, especially in patients with previous liver damage.

Less common: confusion, tingling in the arms or legs, difficulty sleeping, blurred vision, muscle cramps, shakiness, leg pains, difficulty maintaining balance, hair loss, spotty menstruation. In addition, some patients taking Verapamil have experienced heart attack and abnormal heart rhythms, but the occurrence of these effects has not been directly linked to Verapamil.

Drug Interactions

Long-term Verapamil use will cause the blood levels of digitalis drugs to increase by 50 to 70 percent. The dose of digitalis drugs will have to be drastically lowered. Disopyramide should not be given within 48 hours of taking Verapamil because of possible interaction. Patients taking Verapamil together with Quinidine may experience very low blood pressure.

Verapamil's effectiveness may be decreased by taking calcium.

Food Interactions

Take this drug 1 hour before or 2 hours after meals.

Usual Dose

240 to 480 milligrams per day. The dose must be individualized to patient's need.

Overdosage

Overdosage of Verapamil can cause low blood pressure. Symptoms are dizziness, weakness, and (possibly) slowed heartbeat. If you have taken an overdose of Verapamil, call your doctor or go to a hospital emergency room. ALWAYS bring the medicine bottle.

Special Information

Call your doctor if you develop swelling in the arms or legs, difficulty breathing, increased heart pains, dizziness, light-headedness, or low blood pressure. Do not stop taking Verapamil abruptly.

If you forget to take a dose of Verapamil, take it as soon as you remember. If it is almost time for your next regularly scheduled dose, skip the one you forgot and continue with your regular schedule. Do not take a double dose.

Brand Name

Vicodin

Ingredients

Acetaminophen
Hydrocodone Bitartrate

Other Brand Names

Amacodone	Hydrogesic
Anodynos-DHC	Hyphen
Bancap HC	Lorcet HD
Cogesic	Lortab 5
Damacet-P	Lortab 7
Dolacet	Norcet
Duradyne DHC	Vapocet
Hydrocet	Zydone

Type of Drug

Narcotic analgesic combination.

Prescribed for

Relief of mild to moderate pain.

General Information

Vicodin may be prescribed for anyone who is allergic to, or cannot take, Aspirin or who requires a narcotic pain reliever more potent than Codeine. This combination will relieve virtually any kind of pain, but is probably not effective for pain caused by arthritis or other inflammation because the Acetaminophen ingredient does not produce an anti-inflammatory effect. A better choice would be a drug that contains Aspirin instead of Acetaminophen.

Cautions and Warnings

Do not take Vicodin if you are allergic to Acetaminophen or to Codeine or any other narcotic pain reliever. People with asthma or other breathing problems should use this combination with caution. The long-term use of Vicodin can lead to drug dependence or addiction. Hydrocodone Bitartrate is a respiratory depressant and affects the central nervous system, producing sleepiness, tiredness, and an inability to concentrate.

Pregnancy/Breast-feeding

Neither Acetaminophen nor Hydrocodone has been associated with birth defects. But taking too much Hydrocodone, or any other narcotic, during pregnancy can lead to the birth of a drug-dependent infant and drug-withdrawal symptoms in the baby. All narcotics, including Hydrocodone, can cause breathing problems in the newborn if taken just before delivery.

Vicodin has not caused any problems among nursing mothers or their infants.

Seniors

The Hydrocodone in this combination product may have more of a depressant effect on seniors than younger adults. Other effects that may be more prominent are dizziness, lightheadedness, or fainting when rising suddenly from a sitting or lying position.

Possible Side Effects

Light-headedness, dizziness, sleepiness, nausea, vomiting, loss of appetite, and sweating. These side effects usually can be controlled by taking a preparation with a lower narcotic dose.

Less common: feeling "high," weakness, headache, agitation, loss of coordinated muscle movements, minor hallucinations, disorientation, blurred vision, dry mouth, constipation, facial flushing, rapid heartbeat, faintness, urinary difficulty or hesitancy, reduced sex drive and/or potency, itching, rash, anemia, low blood sugar, and yellowing of the skin or whites of the eyes. Narcotic drugs may aggravate convulsions in those who have had them in the past.

Drug Interactions

Alcohol, tranquilizers, sleeping pills, antihistamines, and other medicines that can depress the central nervous system should be avoided if you are taking Vicodin, because of the possibility of severe difficulty breathing. This interaction can be severe enough to make you stop breathing or can result in death.

Food Interactions

This combination may be taken with food or meals if it upsets your stomach.

Usual Dose

1 tablet every 6 hours.

Overdosage

The major signs of Vicodin overdose are extreme tiredness progressing to stupor and coma, difficulty breathing, pinpoint pupils of the eyes, loss of response to simple stimulation such as the prick of a pin, cold clammy skin, and reduced heart rate. Massive Acetaminophen overdose or chronic use of the maximum daily dose of Acetaminophen can result in liver failure, indicated by yellowing of the skin or whites of the eyes, nausea, vomiting, abdominal pain, and diarrhea.

Victims of Vicodin overdose, if discovered within 1 hour of the incident, should be given Syrup of Ipecac to induce vomiting to remove any remaining drug from the stomach. Call your doctor or poison control center before doing this. DO NOT try to induce vomiting if the victim is unconscious or having convulsions. If Vicodin overdose is discovered later than 1 hour after the medicine is taken, the victim will have to be taken to the hospital for treatment of narcotic overdose. Acetaminophen poisoning takes 24 to 36 hours to develop and requires continuous monitoring by a doctor. ALWAYS bring the medicine bottle with you.

Special Information

Use care while driving or doing anything else that requires concentration or alertness. Avoid alcohol and other nervous system depressants while taking Vicodin.

Call your doctor if you have trouble breathing normally or

if this product causes nausea, vomiting, constipation, or any other side effect that becomes unusually severe.

If you forget to take a dose of Vicodin, take it as soon as you remember. If it is almost time for your next regularly scheduled dose, skip the one you forgot and continue with your regular schedule. Do not take a double dose.

Generic Name

Warfarin Sodium

Brand Names

Carfin   Panwarfin
Coumadin   Sofarin

(Also available in generic form)

Type of Drug

Oral anticoagulant.

Prescribed for

Anticoagulation (thinning of the blood). This is generally a secondary form of treatment for other diseases—such as blood clots in the arms and legs, pulmonary embolism, heart attack, or abnormal heart rhythms—in which the formation of blood clots may cause serious problems.

Under investigation is the use of Warfarin to reduce the risk of recurring heart attack or stroke. It may also be of benefit in the treatment of lung cancer.

General Information

Anticoagulants act by depressing the body's normal production of various factors which are known to take part in the coagulation mechanism. If you are taking Warfarin it is absolutely essential that you take the exact dose in the exact way prescribed by your doctor. Notify your doctor at the earliest sign of unusual bleeding or bruising (that is, the formation of black-and-blue marks), if you pass blood in your urine or stool, and/or if you pass a black tarry stool. The interactions of this class of drugs are extremely important and are discussed in detail below.

Warfarin can be extremely dangerous if not used properly. Periodic blood tests of the time it takes your blood or various factors in your blood to begin to coagulate are required for proper control of oral anticoagulant therapy.

Cautions and Warnings

Warfarin must be taken with care if you have a preexisting blood disease associated with coagulation or lack of coagulation. Other conditions in which the use of Warfarin should be discussed with your doctor are threatened abortion, Vitamin C deficiency, stomach ulcers or bleeding from the genital or urinary areas, severe high blood pressure, disease of the large bowel such as diverticulitis or ulcerative colitis, and subacute bacterial endocarditis.

People taking Warfarin should be extremely cautious about being exposed to cuts, bruises, or other types of injury which might cause bleeding.

Pregnancy/Breast-feeding

If you are pregnant or think that you may be pregnant, you must discuss this with your doctor immediately: Warfarin can cause problems with the mother and will also pass into the fetus. It can cause and has caused bleeding and death of the fetus. A nursing mother should be careful, since the Warfarin will appear in the mother's milk. There are situations where the potential benefits to be gained from the use of Warfarin or one of the other anticoagulants may outweigh possible negative effects of these drugs in the pregnant patient: The decision to use one of these drugs is an important one which should be made cooperatively by you and your doctor. Often pregnant women who need an anticoagulant are treated with Heparin because it does not cross into the developing baby's blood system.

Seniors

Older adults may be more sensitive to the effects of Warfarin and other anticoagulant drugs. The reasons for this are not clear but may have to do with a reduced ability to clear the drug from their bodies. Seniors generally require lower doses to achieve the same effect as younger adults who must take this medication.

Possible Side Effects

The principal side effect experienced by patients taking Warfarin or other oral anticoagulant drugs is bleeding, which may occur within therapeutic dosage ranges and even when blood tests normally used to monitor anticoagulant therapy are within normal limits. If you bleed abnormally while you are taking anticoagulants and have eliminated the possibility of drug interactions, you should discuss this matter immediately with your doctor: It may indicate the presence of an underlying problem.

Less commonly, people taking oral anticoagulant drugs have reported bleeding from peptic ulcers, nausea, vomiting, diarrhea, blood in the urine, anemia, adverse effects on components of the blood, hepatitis, jaundice or yellowing of the skin and whites of the eyes, itching, rash, loss of hair, sore throat and mouth, and fever.

Drug Interactions

Warfarin and other oral anticoagulant (blood-thinning) drugs are probably involved in more drug interactions than any other kind of drug. Contact your pharmacist or doctor to discuss any other medications which you may be taking, in order to avoid serious adverse interactions, which may increase the effectiveness of Warfarin to the point of causing severe bleeding or hemorrhage, or decrease its effectiveness to the point of causing formation of blood clots. Your doctor and your pharmacist should have records of all medications which you are taking.

Drugs that may increase the effect of Warfarin include broad-spectrum antibiotics such as Neomycin or others which will act on the normal bacterial contents of the stomach and intestines to eliminate Vitamin K, the body's natural antidote to Warfarin; mineral oil; Cholestyramine; Phenylbutazone; Oxyphenbutazone; Clofibrate; Indomethacin; sulfa drugs; Chloral Hydrate; Ethacrynic Acid; Mefanamic Acid; Nalidixic Acid; Aspirin; oral antidiabetic drugs (Tolbutamide, Chlorpropamide, Tolazamide); Chloramphenicol; Allopurinol; Nortriptyline; Methylphenidate; alcohol; Cimetidine; Disulfiram; Chlortetracycline; Quinidine; Haloperidol; Ascorbic Acid in large quantities; MAO inhibitors; Meperidine; and Thyroid Hormone and the antithyroid drugs such as Propylthiouracil and Methylthiouracil.

There are fewer drugs that will decrease the effect of Warfarin, but the potential interaction can be just as dangerous with barbiturates, Glutethimide, Ethchlorvynol, Meprobamate, Griseofulvin, estrogens, oral contraceptive drugs, Chlorthalidone, corticosteroids, Phenytoin (see p. 702 for interaction resulting in Phenytoin toxicity), Carbamazepine, Vitamin K, and Rifampin.

No matter what the interaction, it is essential that you discuss all medications you are taking with your doctor or pharmacist, including not only prescription drugs but over-the-counter drugs containing Aspirin or other ingredients which may interact with Warfarin. Consult your physician or pharmacist before buying any over-the-counter drugs.

Food Interactions

Vitamin K is the antidote for Warfarin. Therefore, you should refrain from eating large quantities of foods rich in Vitamin K, like green leafy vegetables.

It should also be noted that any change in dietary habits or alcohol intake can affect Warfarin's action in your body.

This medicine is best taken on an empty stomach because food slows the rate at which the drug is absorbed into your blood.

Usual Dose

2 to 15 or more milligrams daily; dose is extremely variable and must be individualized for maximum effect.

Overdosage

The primary sympton is bleeding. A laboratory test will show longer blood-clotting time, and bleeding can make itself known by appearance of blood in the urine or stool, an unusual number of black-and-blue marks, oozing of blood from small cuts made while shaving or from other trivial nicks or cuts, or bleeding from the gums after brushing the teeth. If bleeding does not stop within 10 to 15 minutes, your doctor should be called. He may tell you to skip a dose of anticoagulant and continue normal activities, or to go to a local hospital or doctor's office where blood evaluations can be made; or he may give you a prescription for Vitamin K, which antagonizes the effect of Warfarin. The latter has dangers because it can complicate subsequent anticoagulant therapy, but this is a decision that your doctor must make.

Special Information

Some people have had problems with changing brands of Warfarin. Do not change brands without your doctor's knowledge.

If you forget to take a dose of Warfarin, take it as soon as you remember, then go back to your regular schedule. If you don't remember until the next day, skip the dose you forgot and continue with your regular schedule. Do not take a double dose. Doubling the dose may cause bleeding. Tell your doctor if you miss any doses.

Generic Name

Zidovudine

Brand Name

Retrovir

(Also known as AZT, Azidothymidine, and Compound S)

Type of Drug

Antiviral.

Prescribed for

AIDS and AIDS-related-complex (ARC).

General Information

Zidovudine was the first drug approved for use in the United States under a special government program for drugs considered essential for the treatment of specific diseases. Drugs in this program are released to the public before they have been completely tested for safety and effectiveness because of the concern for the severity of the disease they are designed to treat. Several other drugs for AIDS and ARC are being evaluated for release under this program.

Zidovudine inhibits the production of some viruses, including the AIDS virus. It works by interfering with specific enzymes within the virus that are responsible for essential steps in the reproduction process. Zidovudine has not been proven to reverse the course of AIDS, but it has been able to slow the process of the disease and add several months to the life span of AIDS victims.

Cautions and Warnings

The true safety and effectiveness of this drug after prolonged use, and in people with less advanced disease, is not known. It should be taken with caution by people with bone marrow disease or those whose bone marrow has already been compromised by other treatments. Zidovudine can cause anemia and reduced white-blood-cell counts. Your doctor should take a blood count every 2 weeks, and the drug dosage should be reduced if problems develop.

Pregnancy/Breast-feeding

It is not known if Zidovudine can harm a developing fetus or whether the drug affects a woman's capacity to have a baby.

It is not known if Zidovudine passes into breast milk. Nursing mothers taking this medication should use an alternate feeding method.

Seniors

Older adults may be at a greater risk of Zidovudine side effects because of reduced kidney function.

Possible Side Effects

Most common: anemia, reduced white-blood-cell count, headache, nausea, sleeplessness, muscle aches.

Less common: body odor, chills, swelling of the lip, flu-like symptoms, greater susceptibility to feeling pain, back pains, chest pains, swelling of the lymph nodes, flushing and warmth, constipation, difficulty swallowing, swelling of the tongue, stomach gas, flatulence, bleeding gums, mouth sores, bleeding from the rectum, joint pains, muscle spasms, tremors, twitching, anxiety, confusion, depression, emotional flare-ups, dizziness, fainting, loss of mental "sharpness," cough, nosebleeds, runny nose, sinus inflammation, hoarseness, acne, itching, rash, double vision, sensitivity to bright lights, hearing loss, painful, difficult urination, frequent urination.

Drug Interactions

Combining Zidovudine with other drugs (Pentamidine, Dapsone, Amphotericin, Flucytosine, Vincristine, Vinblastine, Adriamycin, and Interferon) that can damage your kidneys will increase the chances of loss of some kidney function.

Probenecid may reduce the rate at which your body eliminates this drug, increasing the amount of drug in your blood and the chances for drug side effects. Other drugs that can reduce the liver's ability to break down Zidovudine are Acetaminophen, Aspirin, and Indomethacin. This can lead to increased drug toxicity.

Acyclovir, often used in combination with Zidovudine to combat opportunistic infections in AIDS victims, may cause lethargy or seizure when taken together with Zidovudine.

Food Interactions

This medicine is best taken on an empty stomach, but you may take it with food if it upsets your stomach.

Usual Dose

Starting dose, 200 milligrams every 4 hours around the clock, even if sleep is interrupted. Your dosage may be reduced if signs of drug toxicity develop.

Overdosage

The most serious effect of drug overdose is suppression of the bone marrow and its ability to make red and white blood cells. Overdose victims should be taken to a hospital emergency room at once. ALWAYS bring the medicine bottle with you.

Special Information

This drug does not cure AIDS. It does not decrease the chances of your transmitting the AIDS virus to another person.

Be sure to take this drug exactly as prescribed (every 4 hours around the clock) even though it will interfere with your sleep. Do not take more than your doctor has prescribed.

People taking Zidovudine may continue to develop illnesses associated with AIDS or ARC even though they are taking the medication.

See your doctor if any significant change in your health develops. Periodic blood counts are very important while taking Zidovudine to detect possibly serious side effects.

Avoid Acetaminophen, Aspirin, and other drugs that can increase Zidovudine toxicity.

If you miss a dose of Zidovudine take it as soon as possible. If it almost time for your next dose, space the missed dose and your next dose by 2 to 4 hours and then continue with your regular schedule.

Drugs and . . .

DRUGS AND FOOD

The increased interest of many Americans in diet and nutrition has focused attention on how diet affects drug therapy and the effect of drugs on diet and nutrition.

How Does Diet Affect Drug Therapy?

Foods can interfere with the ability of drugs to be absorbed into the blood through the gastrointestinal system. For this reason, most medications are best taken at least 1 hour before or 2 hours after meals, unless specific characteristics of the drug indicate that it is better taken with or immediately following meals. Each drug profile contains a section on "Food Interactions" that tells you the best time to take your medicine and foods, if any, to avoid while taking your medication. Check with your doctor or pharmacist if you are unsure about how to best take your medicine.

Some drugs which are taken with meals because the food reduces the amount of drug-related stomach irritation are Indomethacin, Phenylbutazone, and Oxyphenbutazone. Other drugs such as Amoxicillin may not be affected at all by food.

Some food effects interfere with a drug by reducing the amount of medication available to be absorbed. Juice or milk taken to help you swallow drugs can interfere with them. Many fruit juices, because of their acid content, break down Penicillin-G, Erythromycin, and other antibiotics. Milk or milk products (like ice cream) can interfere with the absorption of Tetracycline antibiotics through the gastrointestinal tract.

Investigators have questioned the seriousness of such effects, and it is generally difficult to prove that people who experience these food-drug interactions don't get well as fast as others who did not. There probably is some effect, but its extent is not known.

Some medications react with specific diets. People taking anticoagulant (blood-thinning) drugs should avoid fat-rich foods because they may reduce anticoagulant effectiveness. People taking Levodopa (L-dopa) should avoid high-protein diets rich in Vitamin B_6 (Pyridoxine), which can reduce the effectiveness of Levodopa.

Raw vegetables (cabbage, okra, and some others) contain Vitamin K, which interferes with oral anticoagulant drugs. This interaction can contribute to the development of potentially fatal blood clots.

An ingredient in licorice can cause you to retain sodium and lose potassium. This can be dangerous if you have high blood pressure (increased sodium = increased water = higher blood pressure) or if you are taking a digitalis drug for your heart (less potassium = more digitalis drug side effects).

Many foods interact with MAO inhibitors.

Foods containing potassium can be useful to people taking diuretics who need to add potassium to their diet:

Apricots (dried)	Peaches (dried)
Bananas	Prune juice
Cantaloupe	Raisins
Dates	Steak
Figs (dried)	Turkey
Milk	Watermelon
Orange juice	

How Do Drugs Affect Diet and Nutrition?

Drugs can affect your appetite. Some medicines that can stimulate your appetite include tricyclic antidepressants and phenothiazine tranquilizers.

Drugs that can cause you to lose your appetite include

antibiotics (especially Penicillin) and any medication with a possible side effect of nausea and vomiting.

Many drugs can interfere with the normal absorption of one or more body nutrients:

Antacids	Colchicine
Anticholinergics	Glutethimide
(Atropine, etc.)	Isoniazid
Anticonvulsants	Methotrexate
Barbiturates	Neomycin Sulfate
Cathartics (laxatives)	Oral contraceptives
Chloramphenicol	Sulfa drugs
Clofibrate	

Drug Interactions with Food

In general, food will either interfere with or prolong the time it takes for a drug to be absorbed into the bloodstream. This happens because food prevents the drug molecules from getting to the wall of the intestine, or stomach, where drug absorption takes place. In most cases, the absorption of drugs is only delayed, not prevented or decreased. You should try to take your medication on an empty stomach to avoid any interference caused by food. However, drugs that are irritating to the stomach and intestines should be taken with food, as this will reduce the irritating effect.

Some foods can directly interfere with the absorption of drugs from the gastrointestinal tract. The drugs most often involved are antibiotics. In the case of the tetracyclines, any food product that contains large amounts of calcium interferes with the drug's action, because a complex is formed between the antibiotic and the calcium. This interaction can be avoided by simply separating your dose of antibiotic from the time that you eat ice cream, milk, or other dairy products by about 2 hours. This will allow sufficient time for the drug to be absorbed. Other foods do not contain enough calcium to effectively interfere with the drug's action.

Another important drug-food interaction involves foods that contribute to the body's manufacture of chemicals that control central nervous system activity. Some drugs affect the enzyme system most responsible for breaking down these chemicals and removing them from the nerve endings. This enzyme is called *Mon*Amine *O*xidase (capitals added), and abbreviated MAO.

Warfarin, an anticoagulant or blood-thinning drug, works by interfering with chemical reactions in the blood coagulation mechanism that depend upon the presence of Vitamin K. The effect of Warfarin, and other oral anticoagulant drugs, can be completely reversed by taking Vitamin K. In fact, Vitamin K is given by injection as an antidote to an overdose of these anticoagulants. We get most of our Vitamin K from microorganisms in the gut that manufacture it. However, we can also get Vitamin K from some raw vegetables such as cabbage and okra. If you eat too much of these vegetables, the Vitamin K content can interfere with the anticoagulant effect of Warfarin.

DRUGS AND ALCOHOL

Drug interactions with alcohol, itself a potent drug, are a significant problem and can be experienced by anyone, even those who avoid drinking near the time that they take prescription pills. Many over-the-counter medicines are alcohol-based and have the potential to interact with prescription drugs: there are more than 500 pharmaceutical items that contain alcohol, some in concentrations up to 68 percent. Alcohol is used to dissolve drugs, as in vitamin tonics and antitussive-decongestant liquids, and also to enhance sedative effects. Alcohol is found in almost all decongestant cold-suppressing mixtures.

Alcohol's action in the body is simply that of a central nervous system depressant. It may either enhance or reduce the effect of a drug. In some drug interactions, the amount of alcohol consumed may not be as important as the chemical reaction it causes in your body. Small concentrations can cause excess stomach secretions, while larger amounts can inhibit stomach secretions, eroding the stomach's lining. Use of over-the-counter alcohol-based products by the elderly is especially dangerous, since their systems may be more sensitive to alcohol. People with stomach disorders such as peptic or gastric ulcer should be fully aware of the alcohol levels in products they use.

The effects of alcohol on certain classes of drugs are described below.

One drug, Disulfiram (Anatabuse), is used to treat alcoholism. Alcoholics using this medication will experience abdominal cramps, nausea, vomiting, headaches, and flushing if they drink any alcohol, including beer, wine, whiskey, or medication with alcohol base such as cough medications. These effects help alcoholics abstain from drinking. Some other drugs also produce this effect, but they are not used in primary treatment programs. They include the oral antidiabetics and Metronidazole.

Analgesics

Certain pain relievers such as Aspirin (Salicylates) have been linked with intestinal bleeding. Use of alcohol with these products can aggravate an already existing condition. Strong narcotic pain relievers have a sedative effect on the central nervous system. Adding alcohol can lead to serious central nervous system depression, respiratory arrest, and death.

Alcohol should never be used with narcotic drugs.

Anticoagulants

Alcohol may interact with blood-thinning drugs, extending coagulation time. This is especially true for heavy drinkers. Those taking anticoagulant drugs should avoid alcohol and alcohol-based products.

Antihistamines

Alcohol enhances the sedative effects of antihistamines, even in small doses. Be especially careful, when taking antihistamines, to avoid driving a car or operating machinery.

Antihypertensive Drugs

Some antihypertensive drugs will interact with alcohol to cause orthostatic hypotension (dizziness, fainting). Be sure that the effectiveness of antihypertensive combinations is not being counteracted by alcohol-based over-the-counter products and remember, take all antihypertensive medication exactly as prescribed by your doctor.

Antianxiety Drugs and Antidepressants

Phenothiazines and other antipsychotic medicines like Thorazine work by depressing the central nervous system. Alcohol will increase this effect, leading to severely impaired ability to drive or operate machinery. Judgment, alertness, and coordination will be diminished. When taken in excess amounts, phenothiazines and alcohol can depress the respiratory control center, leading to death. Since phenothiazines are metabolized in the liver, they may impair livers already damaged by alcohol abuse.

Tricyclic antidepressants (Elavil, for example) have similar interactions when combined with alcohol; the drugs' central nervous system depressant effect is enhanced. Psychomotor skills—driving, etc.—are affected by alcohol combined with antidepressants; such combinations have led to serious accidents or death. Antidepressant drugs are also metabolized in the liver; they can reach toxic levels if a damaged liver cannot fully metabolize them.

MAO Inhibitors

Chianti wines, vermouth, and unpasteurized beer can cause serious drug interactions with MAO inhibitors. These drugs, which block a naturally occurring enzyme system called monoamine oxidase, are sometimes used to treat severe depression or high blood pressure. Using alcohol-based products with MAO inhibitors can result in increased blood pressure, headache, and fever; such use should be avoided.

Sedatives/Hypnotics

This frequently prescribed group of drugs is one of the most dangerous to mix with alcohol. Drugs like Chloral Hydrate. Carbromal, Methprylon, Glutethimide, Ethclorvynol, Ethinamate, and Flurazepam, when taken with alcohol, can cause excessive sedation and potentiate central nervous system effects. Barbiturates, Diazepam (Valium), and other sedative drugs can cause impairment of motor abilities when taken in combination with alcohol. Some studies have shown that Diazepam and alcohol abuse can lead to addiction, even at prescribed doses.

Before you use alcohol and sedative/hypnotic drugs together, check with your doctor.

Stimulants/Amphetamines

Alcohol in combination with Amphetamine or stimulant drugs can lead to a sudden, dangerous rise in blood pressure. The combination should be avoided.

Antidiabetics

Use of alcohol with antidiabetic drugs such as Insulin or oral antidiabetic pills such as Diabenese or Tolbutamide can be dangerous. The combination can cause excessive hypoglycemia, a dangerous lowering of the glucose (sugar) level in the blood, which can lead to coma.

DRUGS AND SEXUAL ACTIVITY

Sexual activity is usually not limited by drugs; however, some drugs can have an effect on sex drive, and their side effects can lead to impotence. This is especially true in men taking some high-blood-pressure drugs or beta blockers, which affect the central nervous or circulatory system. It's important to discuss such effects with your doctor: a simple reduction in dosage or the change to another drug in the same class may solve the problem.

Many antihypertensives can impair potency and cause retrograde ejaculation in the male. Antidepressants, amphetamines, and sedatives have similar effects on sex drive and can reduce potency. Oral contraceptives have been linked to reduced sex drive in some women. Anticancer drugs don't affect sex drive but will reduce sperm count in many men.

Some drugs, such as Levodopa, have been reported to increase sex drive; note that this is age- and dose-related.

DRUGS AND PREGNANCY

Today we are acutely aware of the potential damage to a fetus from drugs of all kinds. In order for a drug to affect the fetus, it must cross the placental barrier from the mother's bloodstream to that of the fetus. Once in the baby's bloodstream, the drug may affect any of the normal growth and development processes. Because a fetus grows much more rapidly than a fully developed human, the effects of a drug on this process are exaggerated. Adverse results can range from physical disfigurement to severe mental and/or physical damage to death.

An illustration of the damage caused by drug use during pregnancy is the discovery of the latent effect of DES (Diethylstilbestrol). This hormone, given to many women during the 1940s and 1950s to prevent miscarriage, has been linked to vaginal cancer in the daughters of the women who used it. The Thalidomide scandal of the 1960s was caused by a drug which was intended to help pregnant women but which resulted in birth defects and deformities in children. This led to a complete reevaluation of the use of drugs during pregnancy.

Most obstetricians recommend that pregnant women avoid all unnecessary medication during pregnancy and after birth while lactating. This includes analgesics such as Aspirin. Unfortunately, potential damage to a fetus is greatest during the first three months of pregnancy, when a woman may not be aware that she is pregnant. If you are considering becoming pregnant, it is wise to curtail any drug use immediately and discuss it fully with your ob/gyn specialist.

Today, most doctors suggest that pregnant women use only vitamins or iron supplements and limit their alcohol, tobacco, and caffeine intake.

The Food and Drug Administration has classified all prescription drugs according to their safety for use during pregnancy. Every profile in *The Pill Book* contains specific information on drug safety for pregnant and breast-feeding women.

DRUGS AND CHILDREN

Medications for children should only be given on direct orders from a pediatrician or other doctor. Of course, children suffer from colds and runny noses and there are many over-the-counter medicines which parents use frequently. Parents should be aware of the ingredients of such products—for example, the alcohol content—and of possible side effects.

Children are at greater risk for drug side effects and interactions because their body systems are not fully developed. This is especially true of infants and young children. Some drugs like the tetracyclines have been linked to serious side effects in children and should be avoided. It's wise to ask your doctor whether side effects such as fever or rash are to be expected when he prescribes a drug for a child.

Some drugs have opposite effects on adults and children. Ritalin, which is given to children to calm hyperactivity, acts as a stimulant in adults.

Drug doses for children are usually lower and are often determined by body weight. Be sure you know all there is to know about a drug before you give it to your child. If you can, check with your doctor about over-the-counter products unless you've used them before and are sure they can't interact with other drugs the child is taking.

DRUGS AND THE ELDERLY

Changes in the body caused either by age or disease make older adults three times as likely to have adverse drug reactions—nausea, dizziness, blurred vision, and others—as younger people. Drug interactions are another potential source of great danger for the elderly. Since many elderly are on multiple drug regimens for more than one chronic condition, the potential for drug interaction is much greater.

Older adults often suffer from "asymptomatic drug reaction," silent undetected reactions caused by slowly building amounts of drugs that are not being properly metabolized by the older, less efficient systems.

Two-thirds of people over the age of 65 take prescription drugs regularly; in fact, 30 percent of all prescriptions are filled for elderly customers, who make up only 15 percent of the population. Many spend several hundred dollars a year to get an average of 13 prescriptions filled. The 1.5 million elderly in nursing homes are also at great risk for drug interactions: 54 percent of them take 6 or more pills per day, and some receive as many as 23.

Studies have shown that 70 to 90 percent of the elderly take pills and over-the-counter medicines with little knowledge of their dangerous effects. Often elderly people who have speech or hearing problems, are absentminded, or are experiencing other symptoms we attribute to aging, are really suffering from drug reactions. This condition is called reversible dementia.

The elderly are often victims of overdose, and not necessarily because of mistaken dosages. Often body weight fluctuations and normal changes in body composition lead to overdose unless the dosage of a drug is altered accordingly.

Antihistamines, phenothiazines, and tricyclic antidepressants are known to cause frequent adverse reactions in the elderly. Older people are sometimes unknowing victims of a drug reaction that causes another disease state. For example, gout can be precipitated by certain diuretics, and kidney disease can be caused by long overuse of anti-inflammatories like Aspirin.

It's important to make sure that elderly people understand their drugs completely. Follow the tips for safe drug use on pages 944 to 945 to assist an older person in managing drug intake properly. Install a drug control system which lists the pills prescribed, the sequence in which they should be taken, the time of day, how they should be taken, and a place to indicate what was taken. Every drug profile in *The Pill Book* contains specific information on drug use by older adults.

Some more specific suggestions, classified by type of drug:

Analgesics

Pain relievers can be especially dangerous to older adults who tend to increase the dosages in order to manage pain. This can lead to overdose, since the drugs are excreted more slowly by aging kidneys. The adverse effects vary with the pain reliever used.

Antiarthritics

Antiarthritics are widely used by the elderly and are generally effective to control pain caused by swollen or inflamed joints. Side effects are gastric upset, blurred vision, and nausea.

Mild anti-inflammatories used by the elderly to combat arthritis include Motrin, Nalfon, Indocin, Naprosyn, and Clinoril. Stronger anti-inflammatories include Oxalid, Tandearil, Azolid, and Butazolidin.

The mild analgesics most commonly used to combat the effects of arthritis are the salicylates, mainly Aspirin. There are hundreds of brand-name products which have been shown to be effective in reducing the pain of mild arthritic conditions. Main drawbacks are stomach irritation, Aspirin's link to blood thinning which may increase the effect of anticoagulants, and Aspirin's excretion through the kidneys.

Strong analgesics such as Codeine Sulfate, Talwin, and narcotics such as Demerol, are especially dangerous to the elderly and should be carefully monitored by a doctor. They can provoke serious drug interactions with glaucoma drugs, tranquilizers, antidepressants, and antihypertensives, and should only be used under a doctor's close supervision.

Oral Antidiabetics

Although most diabetic conditions in the elderly can be controlled by dietary supervision, oral antidiabetics like Diabinese, DiaBeta, Glucotrol, Micronase, Tolinase, Orinase, and Dymelor are also used. These drugs differ in their length of effect; often a doctor will tailor the dosage to the individual. Side effects include loss of appetite, nausea, and general gastric distress. Minor infections and emotional problems can affect the actions of these drugs. They should be used carefully when taken with thiazide diuretics, sulfa drugs, Aspirin, anticoagulants, or MAO inhibitors.

Antihypertensive Drugs

Hypertension (high blood pressure) is experienced by 40 to 50 percent of those over 65. This condition, often linked to heart problems, is treated by control of diet and proper, consistent use of medication.

Some side effects can be serious, including depression, light-headedness, and dizziness or feeling faint. Contact your doctor immediately if any of these occur.

Antihypertensives must be taken exactly as prescribed.

Heart Drugs

Heart disease is the leading cause of death in the United States. For many of the elderly, treatment programs for heart disease are the focus of their lives. They must use their drugs exactly as prescribed, often in combination with strict dietary restrictions and technical equipment like pacemakers.

Digitalis drugs are commonly prescribed for congestive heart failure in the elderly. Digitalis intoxication occurs when digitalis drugs are excreted too slowly from the body and is more likely in the elderly because of reduced kidney function. Early symptoms include loss of appetite, vomiting, and nausea. They are serious and a doctor should be contacted immediately.

Diuretics eliminate excess fluid from the body and are often called water pills. The elderly should take the lowest dose possible when using these drugs, and a doctor should carefully monitor their use. They often are used in combination with other drugs; check with a doctor about potential side effects. Diuretics can cause potassium depletion which often results in dry mouth, thirst, weakness, lethargy, drowsiness, restlessness, and muscle pains or cramps.

Other Drugs

Some drugs are more often prescribed for elderly people because certain conditions are found more frequently in this group. One example is Hydergine-LC, often used to treat the symptoms of Alzheimer-like diseases (see p. 316—Ergoloid Mesylates). Another example of this would be Methandrostenolone (Dianabol), an anabolic steroid, which has been shown to be somewhat effective as secondary therapy in treating senile and post-menopausal osteoporosis (bone disease). Conditions like osteoporosis are treated primarily with diet, calcium balance, and physiotherapy.

Twenty Questions to Ask Your Doctor and Pharmacist about Your Prescription

1. What is the name of this medicine?

2. What results can be expected from taking it?

3. How long should I wait before reporting if this medicine does not help me?

4. How does the medicine work?

5. What is the exact dose of the medicine?

6. What time of day should I take it?

7. Can I drink alcoholic beverages while taking this medicine?

8. Do I have to take special precautions with this medicine in combination with other prescription drugs I am taking?

9. Do I have to take special precautions with this medicine in combination with nonprescription (over-the-counter) drugs?

10. Can I take this medicine without regard to food or mealtimes?

11. Are there any special instructions I should have about how to use this medicine?

942

12. How long should I continue to take this medicine?

13. Is my prescription renewable?

14. For how long a period can my prescription be renewed?

15. Which side effects should I report and which can I disregard?

16. Can I save any unused portion of this medicine for future use?

17. How should I store this medicine?

18. How long can I keep this medicine without its losing strength?

19. What should I do if I forget to take a dose of this medicine?

20. Is this medicine available in a less expensive, generic form?

Other Points to Remember for Safe Drug Use

- Store your medicines in a sealed, light-resistant container to maintain maximum potency, and be sure to follow any special storage instructions listed on your medicine bottle, such as "refrigerate," "do not freeze," "protect from light," or "keep in a cool place." Protect all medicines from excessive humidity.
- Make sure you tell the doctor everything that is wrong. The more information he has, the more effectively he can treat you.
- Make sure each doctor you see knows all the medicines you use regularly, including prescription and nonprescription drugs.
- Keep a record of any bad reaction you have had to a medicine.
- Fill each prescription you are given. If you don't fill a prescription, make sure the doctor knows it.
- Don't take extra medicine without consulting your doctor or pharmacist.
- Follow the label instructions *exactly*. If you have any questions, call your doctor or pharmacist.
- Report any unusual symptoms that develop after taking medicine.
- Don't save unused medicine for future use unless you have consulted your doctor. Dispose of unused medicine by flushing it down the toilet.
- Never keep medicine where children can see or reach it.
- Always read the label before taking your medicine. Don't trust your memory.

- Consult your pharmacist for guidance on the use of over-the-counter (nonprescription) drugs.
- Don't share your medicine with anyone. Your prescription was written for you and only you.
- Be sure the label stays on the container until the medicine is used or destroyed.
- Keep the label facing up when pouring liquid medicine from the bottle.
- Don't use a prescription medicine unless it has been specifically prescribed for you.
- When you travel, take your prescription with you in its original container.
- If you move to another city, ask your pharmacist to forward your prescription records to your new pharmacy.
- Carry important medical facts about you in your wallet. Such things as drug allergies, chronic diseases (diabetes, etc.), and special requirements can be very useful.
- Don't hesitate to discuss the cost of medical care with your doctor or pharmacist.
- Exercise your right to make decisions about buying medicines:
  1. If you suffer from a chronic condition, you can probably save by buying in larger quantities.
  2. Choose your pharmacist as carefully as you choose your doctor.
  3. Remember, the cost of your prescription includes the professional services offered by your pharmacy. If you want more service you will have to pay for it.

1988
THE TOP 200
PRESCRIPTION DRUGS

DISPENSED IN U.S. COMMUNITY PHARMACIES
BRAND NAME AS DISPENSED
NEW AND REFILL PRESCRIPTIONS—ALL STRENGTHS

Rank 1988	Drug Product	Manufacturer
1	Amoxil	Beecham
2	Lanoxin	Burroughs
3	Xanax	Upjohn
4	Zantac	Glaxo
5	Premarin	Ayerst
6	Dyazide	SKF
7	Tagamet	SKF
8	Tenormin	ICI Pharma
9	Naprosyn	Syntex
10	Cardizem	Marion
11	Tylenol w/Codeine	McNeil
12	Seldane	Merrell Dow
13	Synthroid	Flint
14	Ceclor	Lilly
15	Inderal	Ayerst
16	Capoten	Squibb
17	Halcion	Upjohn
18	Vasotec	MSD
19	Ortho-Novum	Ortho
20	Proventil	Schering
21	Lasix	Hoechst
22	Darvocet-N	Lilly
23	Procardia	Pfizer
24	Theo-Dur	Key
25	Ortho-Novum 7/7/7	Ortho
26	Lopressor	Geigy
27	Motrin	Upjohn
28	Ventolin	Glaxo
29	Dilantin	Parke Davis
30	Monistat	Ortho

Rank 1988	Drug Product	Manufacturer
31	Feldene	Pfizer
32	Calan	Searle
33	Valium	Roche
34	Micro-K	Robins
35	Slow-K	CIBA
36	Augmentin	Beecham
37	Micronase	Upjohn
38	Alupent	Boehringer
39	Lo/Ovral	Wyeth
40	Maxzide	Lederle
41	E-Mycin	Upjohn
42	Provera	Upjohn
43	Flexeril	MSD
44	Clinoril	MSD
45	APAP w/Codeine	Rugby
46	Minipress	Pfizer
47	Hydrochlorothiazide	Rugby
48	Triphasil	Weyth
49	E.E.S.	Abbott
50	Retin-A	Ortho
51	EryC	Parke Davis
52	Carafate	Marion
53	Timoptic	MSD
54	Coumadin	Du Pont
55	Ativan	Wyeth
56	Hydroxyzine	Rugby
57	Vicodin	Knoll
58	Nitrostat	Parke Davis
59	Transderm-Nitro	CIBA
60	Furosemide	Rugby
61	DiaBeta	Hoechst
62	Glucotrol	Roerig
63	Amoxicillin	Warner Chilcott
64	Corgard	Princeton
65	Dipyridamole	Rugby
66	Ibuprofen	Rugby
67	Anaprox DS	Syntex
68	Persantine	Boehringer
69	Entex LA	Norwich
70	Mevacor	MSD

Rank 1988	Drug Product	Manufacturer
71	Keflex	Dista
72	Moduretic	MSD
73	Tranxene	Abbott
74	Lopid	Parke Davis
75	Tavist-D	Sandoz
76	Zovirax	Burroughs
77	Beepen VK	Beecham
78	Duricef	Mead Johnson
79	Pen Vee K	Wyeth
80	Trental	Hoechst
81	Thyroid	USV
82	Tegretol	Geigy
83	Isordil	Wyeth
84	Aldomet	MSD
85	Lotrisone	Schering
86	K-Tab	Abbott
87	Penicillin VK	Warner Chilcott
88	Demulen	Searle
89	Nicorette	Lakeside
90	PCE	Abbott
91	Norinyl	Syntex
92	Percocet-5	Du Pont
93	Phenergan	Wyeth
94	Omnipen	Wyeth
95	Prednisone	Rugby
96	Macrodantin	Norwich
97	Fiorinal w/Codeine	Sandoz
98	Estraderm	CIBA
99	Indocin	MSD
100	Restoril	Sandoz
101	Slo-Bid	Rorer
102	Catapres	Boehringer
103	Fiorinal	Sandoz
104	Amitriptyline	Rugby
105	Nordette	Wyeth
106	Pediazole	Ross
107	Ibuprofen	Boots
108	Dolobid	MSD
109	Triamterene w/HCTZ	Schein
110	Propoxyphene Nap w/APAP	Rugby

Rank 1988	Drug Product	Manufacturer
111	Erythrocin Stearate	Abbott
112	Dalmane	Roche
113	Triamterene w/HCTZ	Rugby
114	Erythromycin Base	Abbott
115	Donnatal	Robins
116	Achromycin V	Lederle
117	Pepcid	MSD
118	Cortisporin	Burroughs
119	Sinemet	MSD
120	Nalfon	Dista
121	Ovral	Wyeth
122	Isosorbide Dinitrate	Rugby
123	Desyrel	Mead Johnson
124	Reglan	Robins
125	Isoptin	Knoll
126	Minocin	Lederle
127	Cipro	Miles
128	Acetaminophen w/Codeine	URL
129	Diazepam	Rugby
130	Tenoretic/50	ICI Pharma
131	Elavil	MSD
132	Propranolol	Rugby
133	Orudis	Wyeth
134	SMZ-TMP	Rugby
135	Lotrimin	Schering
136	Nitro-Dur II	Key
137	Diabinese	Pfizer
138	Questran	Bristol
139	Phenobarbital	Lilly
140	Pamelor	Sandoz
141	Betapen-VK	Bristol
142	Poly-Vi-Flor	Mead Johnson
143	Lozol	USV
144	Naldecon	Bristol
145	Tavist	Sandoz
146	Prozac	Dista
147	Trinalin	Schering
148	Tolectin DS	McNeil
149	Brethine	Geigy
150	Percodan	Du Pont

Rank 1988	Drug Product	Manufacturer
151	Sinequan	Roerig
152	Acetaminophen w/Codeine	Lemmon
153	Amcill	Warner Chilcott
154	Tylox	McNeil
155	Tri-Norinyl	Syntex
156	Nasalide	Syntex
157	Hydrochlorothiazide	URL
158	Intal	Fisons
159	Ledercillin VK	Lederle
160	Imodium	Janssen
161	BuSpar	Mead Johnson
162	Bumex	Roche
163	Lorazepam	Rugby
164	Sumycin	Squibb
165	Compazine	SKF
166	Tussi-Organidin DM	Wallace
167	Lidex	Syntex
168	Bactrim DS	Roche
169	Ovcon	Mead Johnson
170	Cephalexin	Rugby
171	Normodyne	Schering
172	Zyloprim	Burroughs
173	Nasalcrom	Fisons
174	Meclizine	Rugby
175	Tussi-Organidin	Wallace
176	APAP w/Codeine	Goldline
177	Gyne-Lotrimin	Schering
178	Septra DS	Burroughs
179	Fioricet	Sandoz
180	Septra	Burroughs
181	Trimox	Squibb
182	Acetaminophen w/Codeine	Barr
183	Klotrix	Mead Johnson
184	Anusol HC	Parke Davis
185	Topicort	Hoechst
186	Norpramin	Merrell Dow
187	Antivert	Roerig
188	Medrol	Upjohn
189	Aldoril	MSD
190	Doxycycline Hyclate	Rugby

Rank 1988	Drug Product	Manufacturer
191	Propine	Allergan
192	Prednisone	URL
193	Atrovent	Boehringer
194	Lomotil	Searle
195	Haldol	McNeil
196	Triavil	MSD
197	Propoxyphene w/APAP	Barr
198	Veetids	Squibb
199	Betoptic	Alcon
200	L-Thyroxine Sodium	Rugby

Data supplied by Pharmaceutical Data Services, Inc., Scottsdale, Arizona.

Index of Generic and Brand Name Drugs

Note: Generic drug names are indicated by bold type.

Index of Drug Types

ABOUT THE MEDICAL WRITERS

GILBERT I. SIMON, SC.D., is Vice President of the Geritrex Corporation in Mount Vernon, New York. From 1961 to 1982 he was Director of the Department of Pharmacy at Lenox Hill Hospital, New York City. Dr. Simon received his B.S. from Fordham University; his M.S. from Long Island University; his Doctorate, Honoris Causa, from the College of Pharmacy Sciences, City of New York (Columbia University); and his MPA in Health from Pace University. He was an associate professor of pharmaceutical sciences at Columbia University from 1964 to 1976. Dr. Simon has served as president of both the New York State Council of Hospital Pharmacists and the New York City Society of Hospital Pharmacists. In 1973 he was honored with the Award of Merit from the latter group for his contribution to the practice of institutional pharmacy. He has been a member of the Pharmacy Advisory Committee of the Greater New York Hospital Association and the Governor's (NYS) Medical Advisory Committee and has served on committees of the Hospital Association of the State of New York. Dr. Simon has served as a consultant to the pharmaceutical industry, publishers, advertising agencies, and the government. He has been a principal speaker on contemporary hospital pharmacy practice throughout the United States and in Europe. In 1975, Drs. Simon and Silverman co-authored MED FILE, a book on common non-prescription drugs and their interactions. Dr. Simon lives in Westchester County, New York with his wife, Sheila.

Educated at Columbia University, DR. HAROLD SILVERMAN has been a hospital pharmacist, author, educator, and consultant to the pharmaceutical industry. He currently directs the health care practice for the Washington, D.C. office of Hill and Knowlton, an international public affairs consulting firm. As an author, his guiding principle is that health reference books should help people understand why medicines are prescribed and how they can get the most from them. In addition to THE PILL BOOK, Dr. Silverman is co-author of THE VITAMIN BOOK: A No-Nonsense Consumer Guide and The MED FILE Drug Interactions System. He is the author of THE PILL BOOK GUIDE TO SAFE DRUG USE, THE CONSUMER'S GUIDE TO POISON PROTECTION, THE WOMEN'S DRUG STORE, and TRAVEL HEALTHY. Dr. Silverman's contributions to the professional literature include many articles, research papers, and textbook chapters. He is a member of many professional organizations and has served as an officer of several, including the New York State Council of Hospital Pharmacists, of which he was president. He has taught pharmacology and clinical pharmacy at several universities and won numerous awards for his work. Dr. Silverman resides in a Washington suburb with his family.

We Deliver!
And So Do These Bestsellers.